Everett Raymond Kinstler

The Artist's Journey through Popular Culture—1942-1962

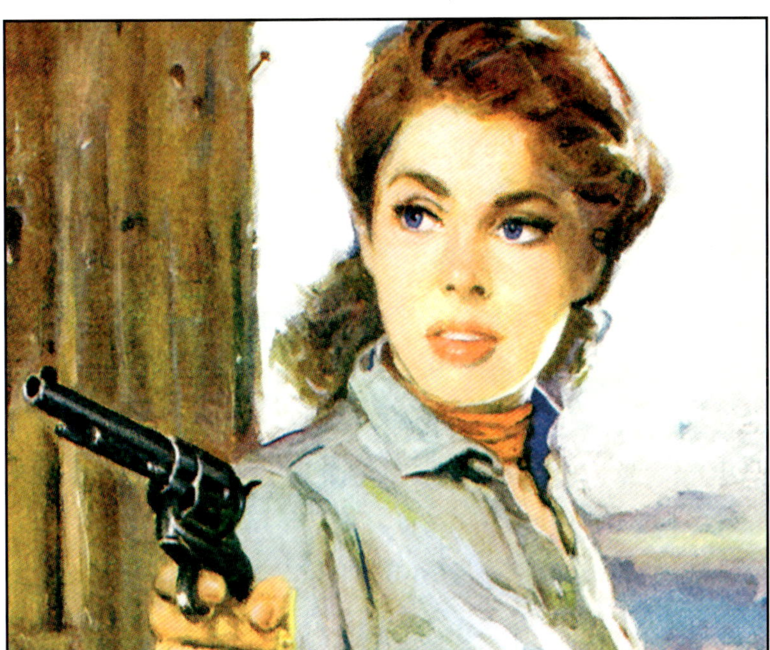

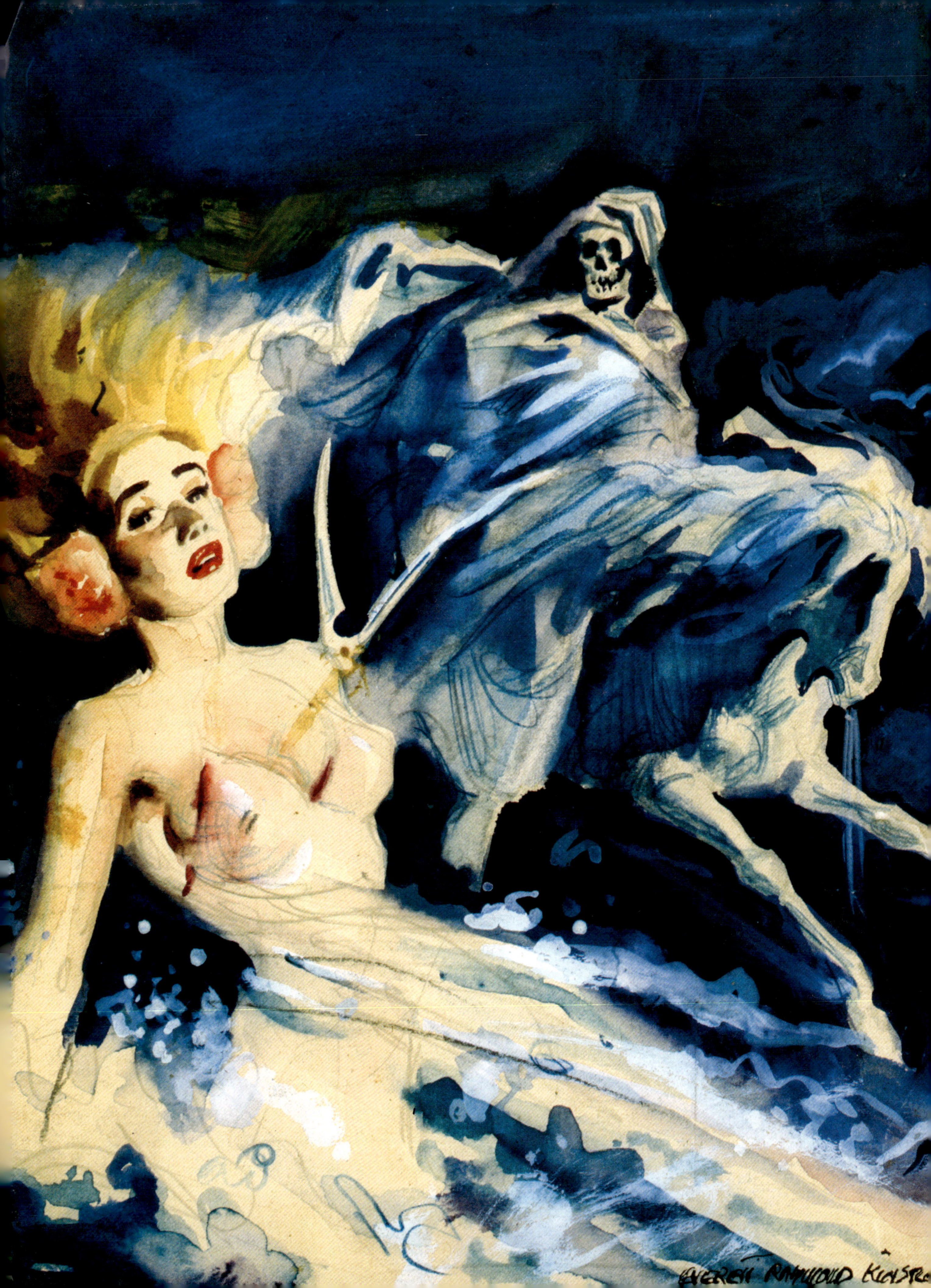

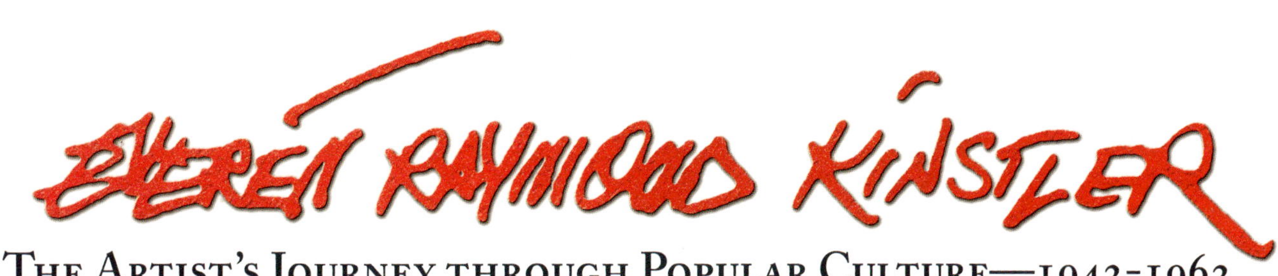

The Artist's Journey through Popular Culture—1942-1962

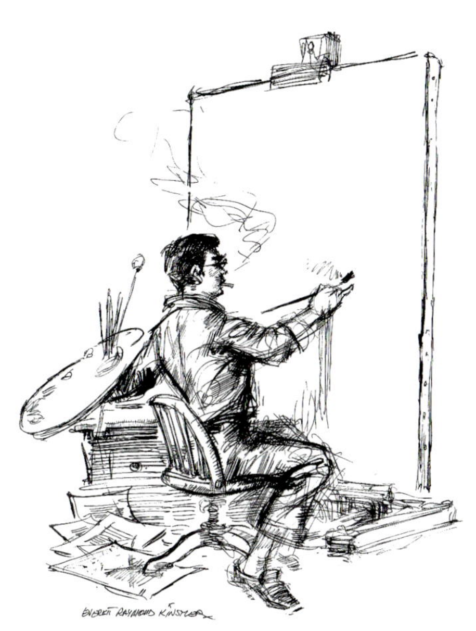

Jim Vadeboncoeur, Jr.

&

Everett Raymond Kinstler

UNDERWOOD BOOKS

Nevada City, California

2005

in cooperation with JVJ Publishing

The authors wish to extend very special acknowledgements and thanks to:
Peggy Kinstler, Karen Lane, Robert Brustein, Herb Rogoff, Noah Gordon, Greg Sadowski, Terry Brown, Bob Rickwell, John Fleskes, Bud Plant, Michelle Nolan, Robert Beerbohm, Steve Adamovich, Walter Lundin and Lee de Broff.

First soft cover edition — October, 2005. ISBN: 1-887424-93-8
10 9 8 7 6 5 4 3 2 1

Underwood Books
P.O. Box 1919
Nevada City, CA 95959
www.underwoodbooks.com

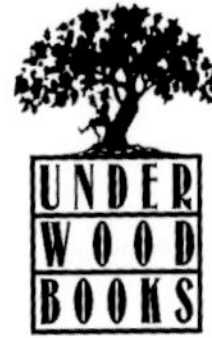

JVJ Publishing
3809 Laguna Ave
Palo Alto, CA 94306-2629
images@bpib.com
www.bpib.com/images.htm

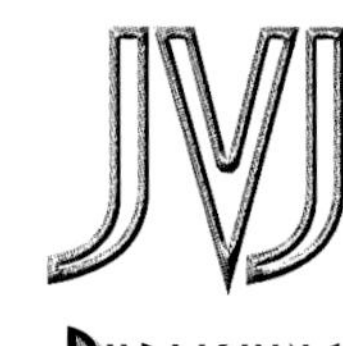

PUBLISHING

Printed in Hong Kong by Rainbow Graphics

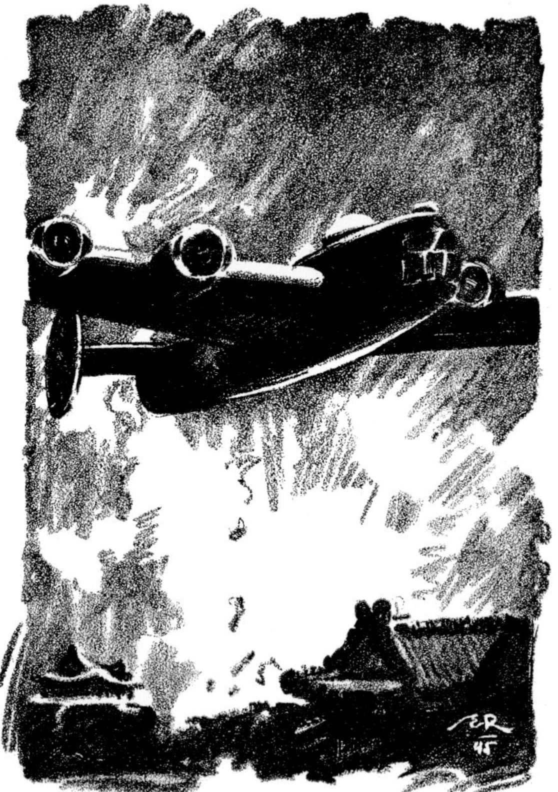

dedications

For Bob Brustein, my best and oldest friend, who has been there almost from the beginning.

And a deep bow to Jim Vadeboncoeur, Jr. who made this book a reality.

Everett Raymond Kinstler

For Peggy Kinstler, without whom this would have been a very different and a lesser book.

And to Karen Lane, who knows why and how much.

Jim Vadeboncoeur, Jr.

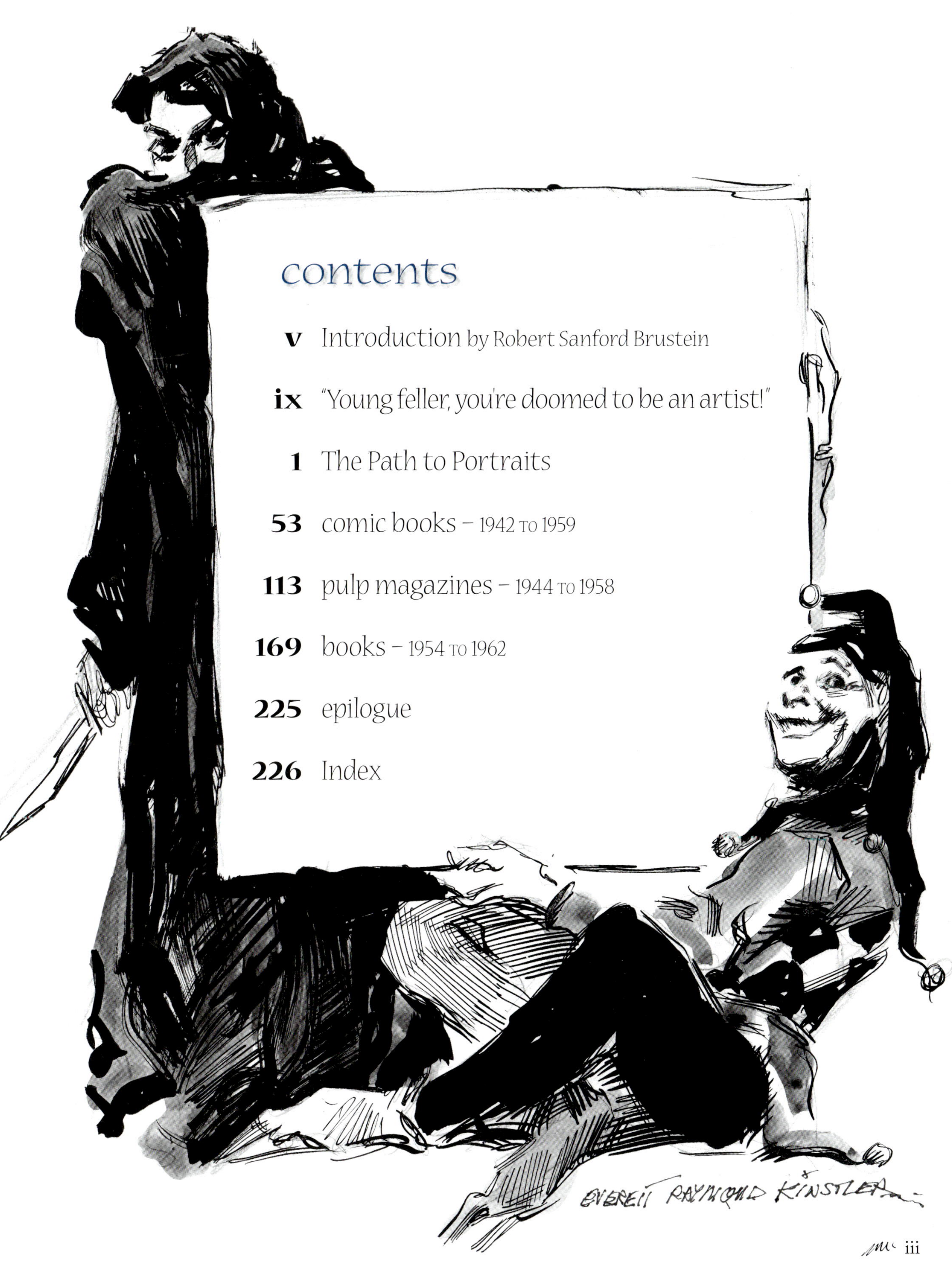

contents

EVERETT RAYMOND KINSTLER

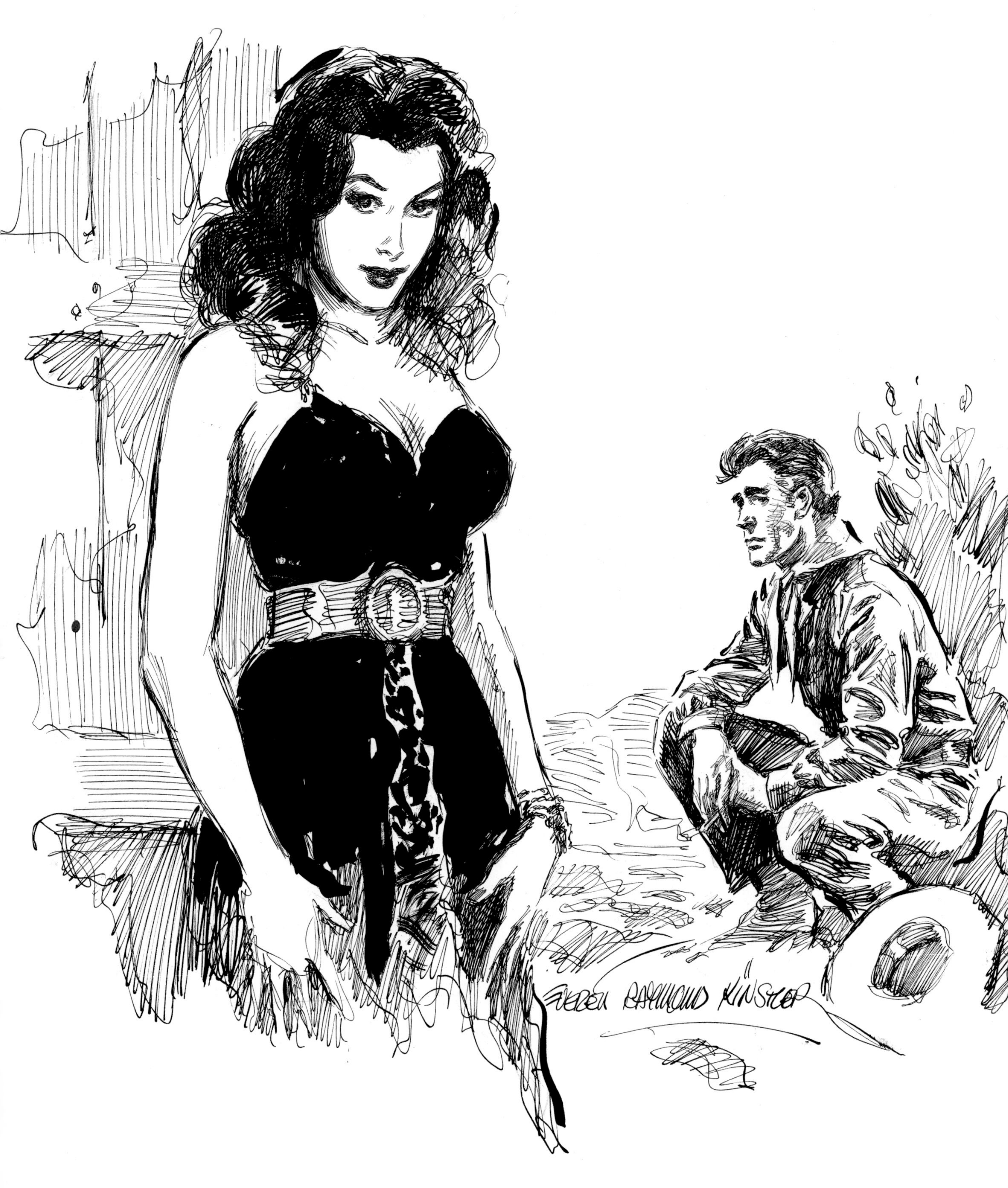

Introduction

by Robert Sanford Brustein

I first met Everett Raymond Kinstler in 1936 when we both were young boys in a West End Avenue grammar school known as Public School (P.S.) 9. He instantly became my oldest and closest friend. Ev or Everett, as he was known at the time (only decades later did people begin to call him "Ray"), was an incredibly handsome West Side kid, who, like me, attended upper West Side schools. But P.S. 9 only accepted boys through the fourth grade, so in the fifth grade we were both transferred from this silk stocking, largely middle-class sanctuary to a considerably more hazardous institution, known as P.S. 166, located on 89th Street and Columbus Avenue.

Since our mothers insisted on dressing us up like Little Lord Fauntleroys—coats, ties, and, in my case, green suede shoes—this made us prey to the tougher Irish and Italian kids in the neighborhood, so we both had to learn ingenious methods of survival. I avoided getting beaten up by finding a protector in a giant named "Fireman" Dan McNulty, who had been left back so many times he was almost as old as some of the teachers (he was certainly as big). Everett survived by circulating his drawings to appreciative young art collectors like Angelo Funari and Belford Vogelin.

The drawings were remarkable, especially for a ten-year-old. This was around the time of the comic book explosion, featuring such action heroes as *Superman* and *Batman* and *Submariner*, which we acquired with our allowance money at the luncheonette/candy store next to the school. (We also bought a few pornographic comic books, where *Popeye* demonstrated Herculean powers with other muscles than his biceps, and where *Dagwood* and *Blondie Bumstead* performed more strenuous domestic tasks than raiding the icebox and ironing sheets.) Everett's superheroes may have owed something to the comics draughtsmen, but to us they were dazzlingly original, and we all tried to copy his drawing style. No one could. He was obviously inimitable. But to this day, I still print out my name in imitation of his signature.

Another reason we became inseparable was because we were both interested in artistic expression, which in that day and age meant popular culture. Then, as now, there was little art appreciation taught in school. Each of us had to find his own creative path. Everett drew comic strips in imitation of Alex Raymond.

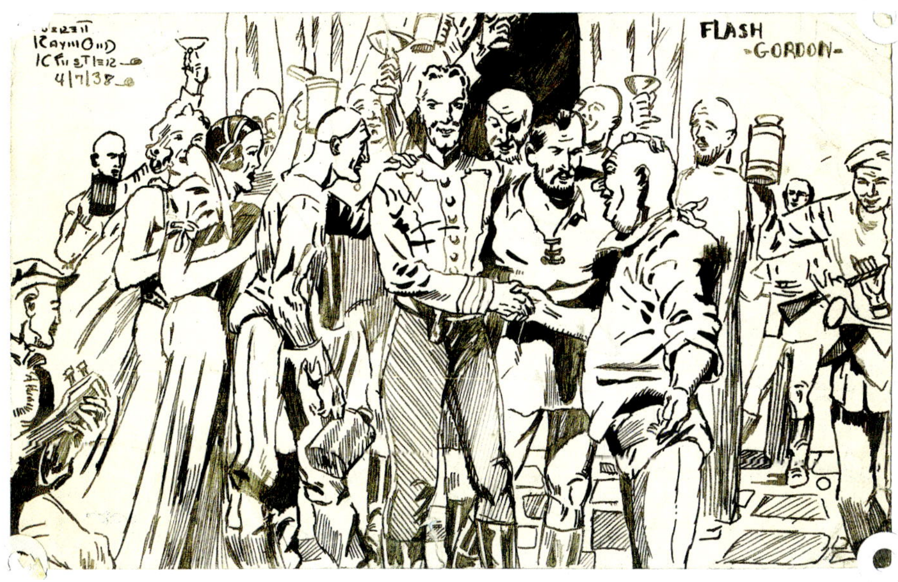

I played the clarinet in imitation of Artie Shaw. In School Assembly, I squeaked through "Ding dong the witch is dead" from *The Wizard of Oz* (Everett still kids me about that, and my green suede shoes), while he hung up his drawings on the school poster board to be admired by grateful kids. Those creative appetites led us both, after we managed to survive the perils of P.S. 166, to the High School of Music and Art. Neither of us stayed that rigorous course. I left in the middle of my Junior year. Everett cut out much earlier for the High School of Industrial Art.

Our real cultural education was essentially extracurricular. We shared a lot of reading in books like **Treasure Island** and **The Knights of the Round Table** which, in those days, were richly illustrated by such great artists as N.C. Wyeth. At night we listened to radio shows like "Bobby Benson and the H Bar O

Ranch," Fred Allen, and Jack Benny (and after bedtime to "The Witch's Tale"). On weekends, we went to 52nd St. jazz clubs, and in the afternoons watched double features at Loew's 83rd Street and RKO 81st, where we were hypnotized by such films as *Lost Horizon* with Ronald Colman, and *A Star is Born* with Fredric March, and Hitchcock's *Rebecca* with Laurence Olivier. Everett, who possesses incredible mimetic gifts, used to act out episodes from those movies, especially the great "I'm the expedition" drunk scene from *Gunga Din* in which he played Cutter (Cary Grant) and I did MacChesney (Victor McLaglen), and both of us alternated as Ballantine (Doug Fairbanks Jr.). After 1941, we also began to invent German-accented scenes from war movies with me cast as "Broitland" Brustein and Everett as "Knaidloch" Kinstler, a pair of incompetent Nazi submarine commanders. Everett's impersonation of Clark Gable, another actor whose every movie we saw at least three times, especially *Gone With the Wind*, was virtually perfect, as he tasted his lips and squinted his eyes, and slurped that famous verbal slap, "Frankly, Scarlett, I don't give a damn."

Some of those movie faces inevitably found their way into Everett's illustrations of the desperadoes, swashbucklers, and pirates on his pulp covers (isn't that Victor McLaglen brandishing his six-shooter on page 137?), just as such amply-endowed stars as Ava Gardner and Jane Russell eventually became the models for his voluptuous heroines (like that luscious beauty he painted for the uncensored version of his **Women in Love** cover). And surely that tense trio of gunslingers on page 39 owes something to Fred Zinneman's staging of the shootout in *High Noon*.

Of course, Ev also painted from life, and occasionally invited me to be one of his male subjects, in exchange for the chance to ogle one of his bare-breasted models. (That pretext explains how I came to appear as the painter Sir Thomas Lawrence on the Avon jacket of **Artist in Love**.) Everett and I both had a prediliction for the undraped female form, and much of our leisure time was spent in Minsky's enjoying the strippers, not to mention the great burlesque clowns who shared the stage with them.

It was not too long before our mutual love of movies (and of burlesque) led us to the theatre, where we delighted in such extravaganzas as Orson Welles' *Around the World in Eighty Days*, and despaired over such legendary one-night flops as *Grandma's Diary*. When I began reviewing for ***The New Republic***, Everett was my uncomplaining companion for hundreds of shows, even some he would gladly have missed. At one such event, I asked him not to prejudice me. After ten minutes, he promptly fell asleep. ("You're prejudicing me," I said as I elbowed him awake.)

Everett's wit is legendary, and it is accompanied by an uncanny memory. He will never forget something silly that you said or did, and he will never let you forget it either. But then I won't let him forget that moment when, smoking a cigar in my apartment when my father came in unexpectedly, he hid the lit stogie in his pocket and burned a hole in his pants. He is also an unstoppable talker. Phone conversations with him are pretty one-sided, even when you pay for the call. And when he does your portrait, he will conduct a monologue through the entire sitting. The novelist Tom Wolfe once remarked that if Everett couldn't talk, he wouldn't be able to paint. He once did a head-and-shoulders portrait of me in front of a group of students, and instructed them non-stop during the entire two hours he was painting.

Everett chiefly delights in people with imagination, taste, and feeling. A meticulous craftsman himself, he also values people willing to be adventurous in their choices, who have a sense of the theatrical. This may be why, in his early years, Everett was drawn to such extravagant figures as John Barrymore, and that whole line of noble profiles who followed him—Ian Keith, John Carradine, Fredric March. His voluminous record collection included Barrymore's readings of "To Be Or Not To Be" from *Hamlet* and "Now is the winter of our discontent" from *Richard III*, and he could render those soliloquies perfectly, down to the last snort and cackle. By this time, however, Barrymore had degenerated from a legendary Shakespearean actor into a movie stereotype usually cast as an alcoholic. Everett imitated that character perfectly, too, not to mention the chortling, braying persona of the drunken W.C. Fields in his most bibulous moments ("Who put this grapefruit juice in my grapefruit juice?").

Everett's heroes became my heroes, and I impersonated his impersonations. In our teens, we travelled through the city like hungry luckless predators, up and down Broadway, looking for girls to pick up (we never succeeded). Often, we would stop to have an instant photo taken in some Broadway photomart. One of those is reproduced in this book. Another was taken when we were both in the service during World War Two, when we were desperately trying to extract some female sympathy in return for our patriotic sacrifice. Alas, those were virginal times, and our efforts went unrewarded.

Despite Everett's considerable histrionic talent, it was I who became the actor. But whenever and wherever I performed, whether in college, community theatre, or professional repertory companies, he would invariably travel long distances to demonstrate his support. (Usually, I would be further rewarded with a terrific sketch of the character I had just played.) His instinct for the theatrical explains how he has caught so precisely the iconographic essence of Jimmy Cagney, Katharine Hepburn, John Wayne, Tennessee Williams, George Bernard Shaw, and so many other figures from the entertainment world. It also informs all those paintings of captains of industry, majors of show business, and generals of politics that have made him the leading portrait painter of our time.

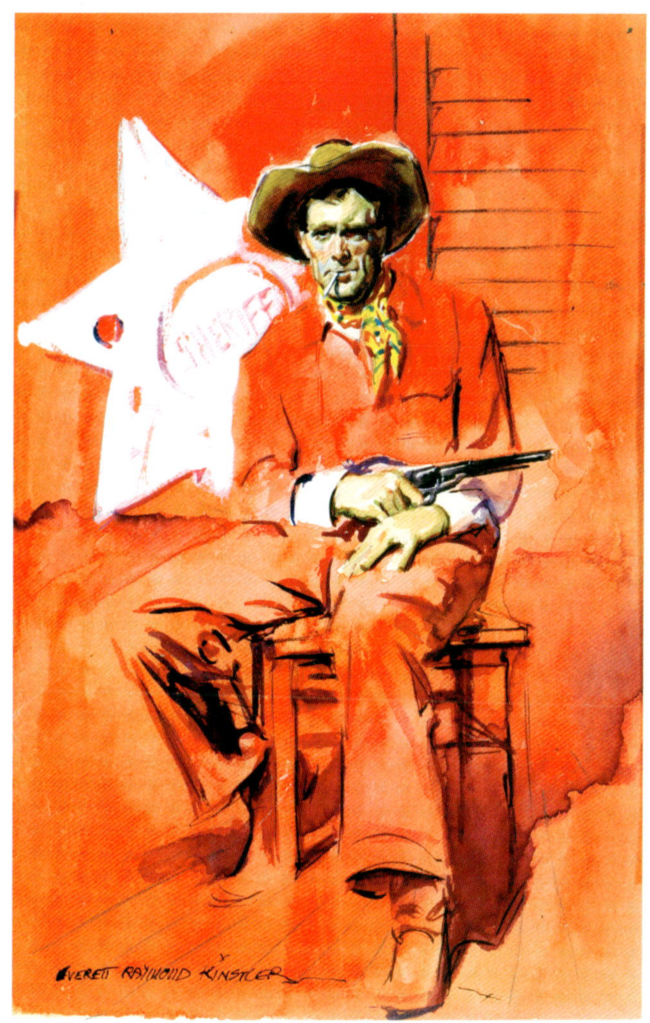

And his love of theatricality is, I suspect, what initially attracted him to that outsize figure James Montgomery Flagg, whom he worshipped as an exemplary American artist. Was it out of homage to Flagg (and his other favorites, Howard Chandler Christy, John Singer Sargent, George Bernard Shaw, Charles Dana Gibson and Frank Vincent DuMond) that he began to sign his drawings and paintings with his full name, Everett Raymond Kinstler? (In homage to Everett, whom I consider an exemplary American artist, I am uncharacteristically signing this preface with my middle name.) It is certainly no accident that, soon after he met Flagg, he began to cultivate his own bushy Mephistophelean eyebrows.

In the text of this book, one gets a sense that Everett regrets his lack of formal education. Aside from a few pieces of foolscap, what is there to regret? Everett is one of the best-read, best-educated, and most intellectually curious people I have ever known. His love of high art has always been as passionate as his feeling for popular culture. His reading has been omnivorous, not only in pulp magazines, but throughout the entire collected works of all the great authors. He introduced me to writers I had never heard of, who were to become lifelong companions. His love of opera resulted in another precious discovery I might never have made without him. He is an auto-didact who is, at the same time, a born teacher, whose classes at the Art Students League and elsewhere have become legendary.

I haven't said much about his distinguished later career as a Presidential portraitist and nature painter because this book is about his early years, and because, frankly, I still think of us as a couple of young kids, roving up and down Broadway, checking out the girls, going to movies. But I'd like to take this occasion to thank him publicly, not only for his lifelong friendship, but for the way he has taught me most of the valuable things I know. And for always keeping me laughing, throughout these seventy years.

Robert Brustein

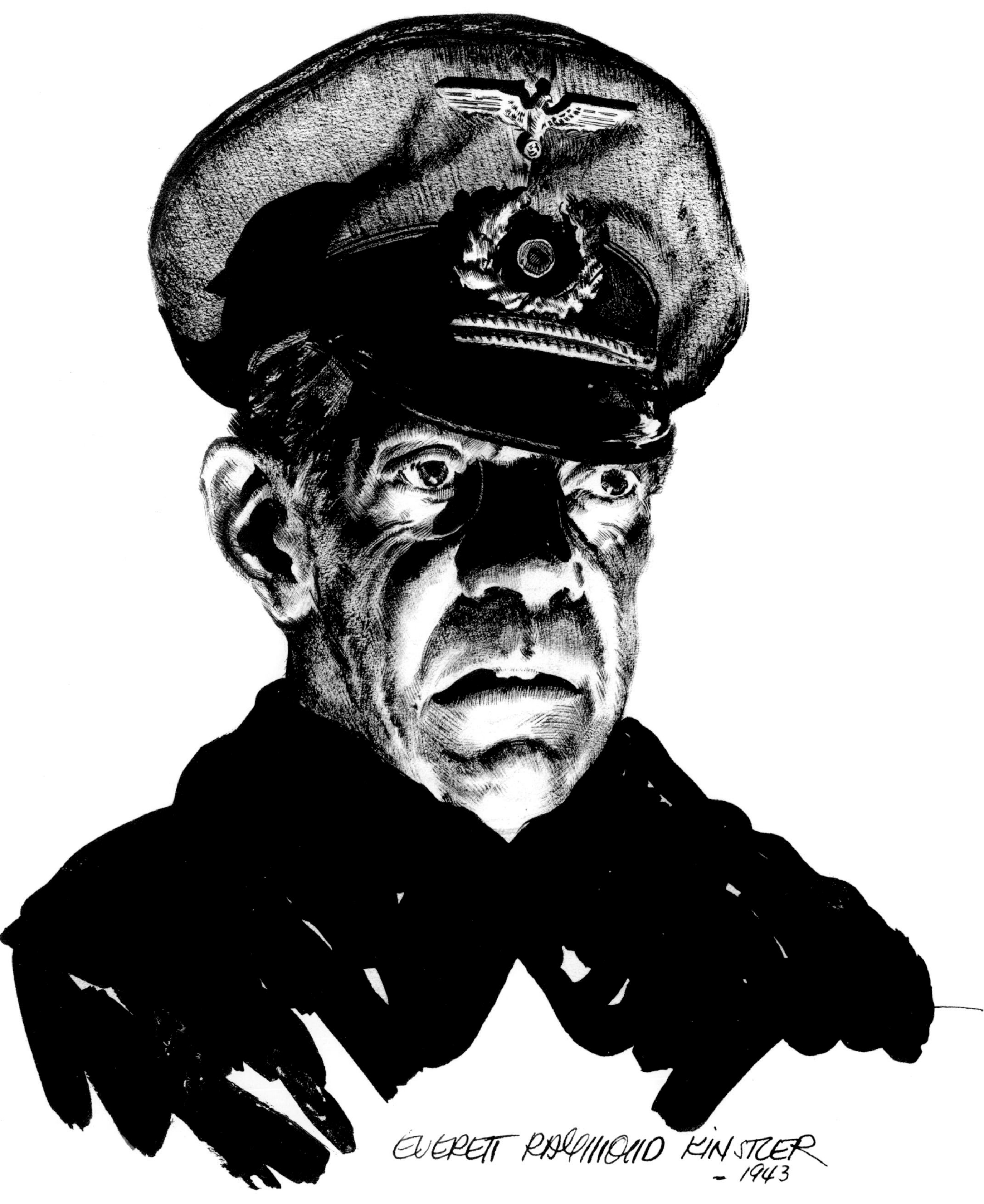

sample art work
1943

"Young feller, you're doomed to be an artist!"

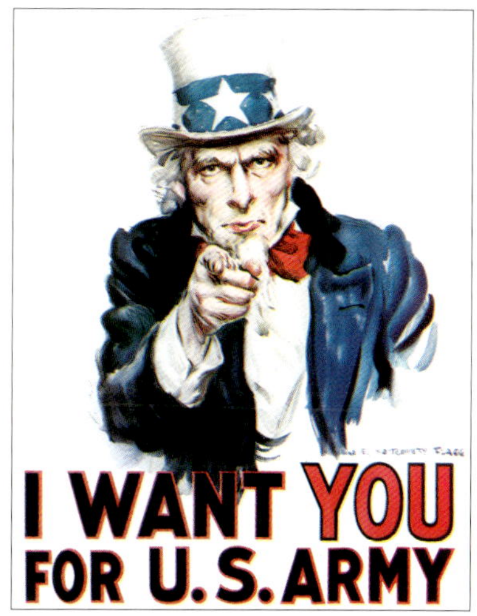

JM Flagg—1917

One day in 1944, the seventeen-year-old Everett Raymond Kinstler discovered that his artistic hero, James Montgomery Flagg, lived a few blocks from the Art Students League in Manhattan where Ray was studying under Frank V. DuMond, who had taught Flagg fifty years prior.

Anxious to meet a man whose work he admired and studied, Ray packed up samples of his own art and headed off to the 57th Street apartment building where Flagg lived.

Kinstler recalls that first encounter —

> Parc Vendome is a large, twenty-five-story building, and the 14th floor has double windows that go up two floors—you can see them from the street. It's the only floor in the building that extends that high. I walked over to the building with my samples and I said to the doorman, a feisty Irishman who knew Flagg well, "I would like to see Mr. Flagg."
>
> "Do ye have an appointment?"
>
> I said, "No, I don't have an appointment."
>
> "Well, he won't see ya, that old son of a bitch. He's as ornery as they come."
>
> "But I gotta see him!"
>
> I can't explain how it happened, but I finally got him to say, "I'll ring him up, but that S.O.B. won't see ya. He won't see anybody without an appointment."
>
> So he called up and Flagg got on the phone and I said, "Mr. Flagg, I want to see you. I'm an artist."
>
> Flagg said, "Well, I haven't got any time to look at work, and it's probably crap anyway."
>
> So I said, "Please, Mr. Flagg, I'm being drafted at any moment. I've got to show you my work." (I wasn't ready to be drafted because I was seventeen.)
>
> He said to me, in a very deep, theatrical voice, "OK. I'm upstairs in 14-B, as in Bastard."
>
> And I was up there in a flash. He opened the door wearing a blue short-sleeved shirt with red suspenders, looking very much like his Uncle Sam posters in World War One. I came into the studio and again he said, "I really don't have time for this and your work probably stinks anyway!"
>
> I said, "Well, can I show you what I'm doing?" And I showed him my comic book and pulp illustrations and several oil paintings I'd done in DuMond's class.
>
> He looked at my artwork, stuck his hand out to me and said, "Young feller, you're doomed to be an artist!"

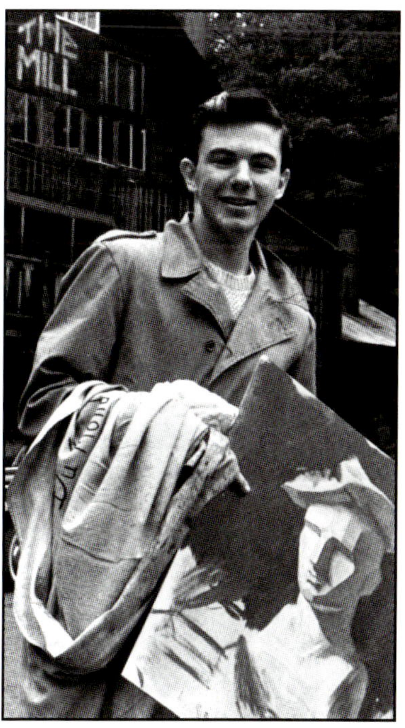

ERK in 1944

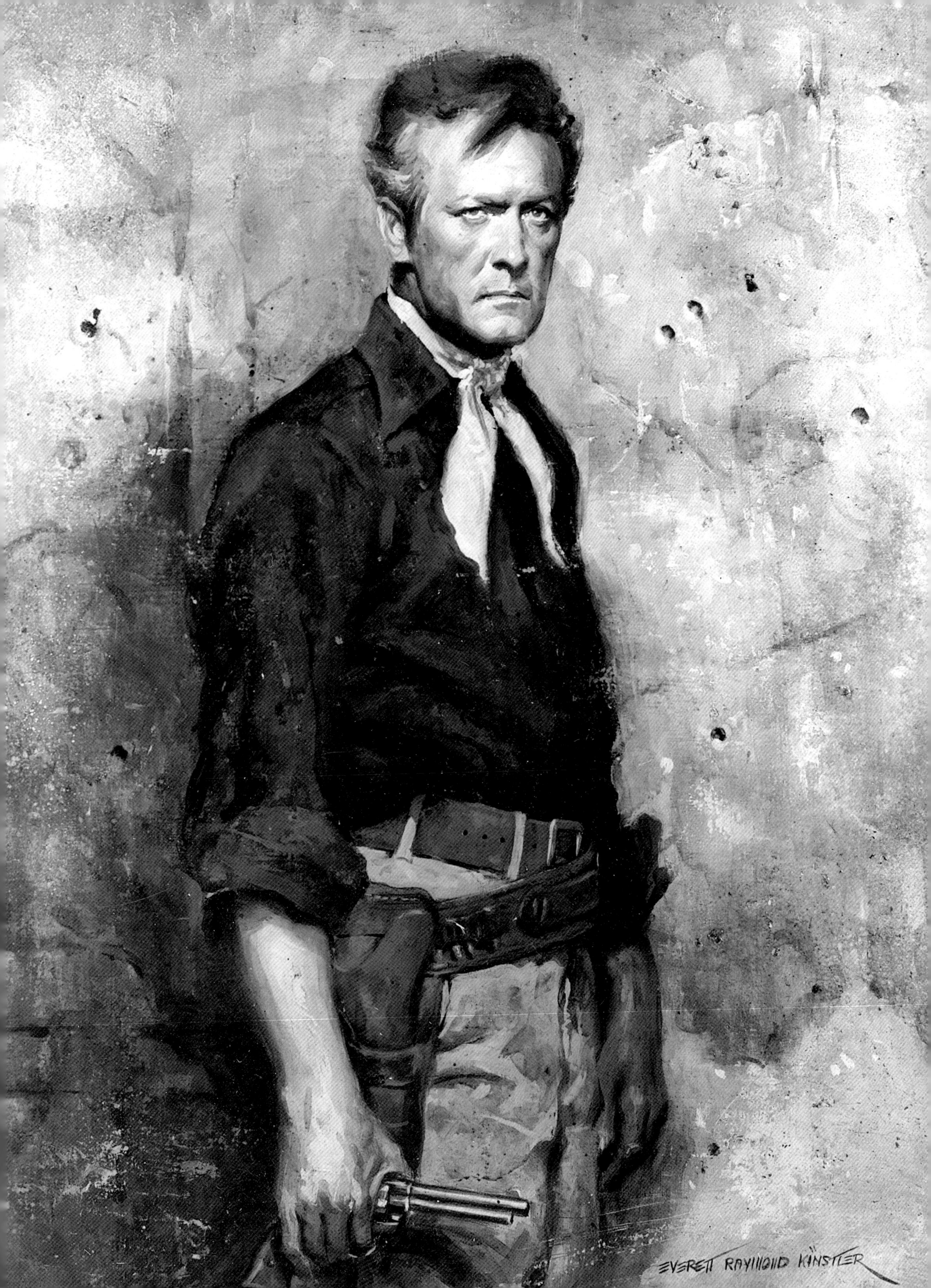
EVERETT RAYMOND KINSTLER

The Path to Portraits

Everett Raymond Kinstler paints portraits. His work hangs in museums, boardrooms, banks, private collections, The White House, and in the homes of his clients and friends. Before portraiture became his life's work, he spent two decades honing his craft on the pages of magazines and on the covers of books.

The structure and tone of his art were always founded on the face. He drew real people, using his friends or celebrity icons as models. A significant aspect of this early work is that the portrait was in service of a "type," rather than an attempt to capture a specific individual. Often these goals overlapped, but the "type" was more important than the likeness.

In popular culture, the character of the individual portrayed has to be immediately recognizable. Throughout the popular media, the good guy wore the white hat and rode the white horse. He was generally cleanshaven and good looking. A black hat or facial hair on anyone but a sidekick was shorthand for a dubious character. Artists, writers, and directors learned this iconic language early, and these simple shortcuts perpetuated themselves because they worked.

Ray Kinstler grew up during the Depression. It was also the heyday of American film and print culture. His goal was always a career as an artist, specifically as an illustrator. His major entertainments were newspaper comic strips and movies, both of which he devoured. These media would echo strongly throughout his life, providing raw material for drawings and paintings as he created images that connected with his newsstand audience. Telling stories and communicating through pictures were also lessons he soaked up from the magazines of the day and he reinvested these lessons into his art.

Ray remembers recreating, at age eleven, a panel from Alex Raymond's newspaper strip, *Flash Gordon*, and thinking that Flash was just Douglas Fairbanks without a mustache. At fifteen he drew a portrait of his high school friend, James Bama while they were on a rooftop sketching. He can't recall a time when he *wasn't* drawing.

For twenty years he worked, in a variety of capacities, in the realm of popular culture—always drawing, always growing, always learning. He entered the commercial art world as a sixteen-year-old apprentice comic book artist and left it as an accomplished and sophisticated portraitist. This is the story of that journey.

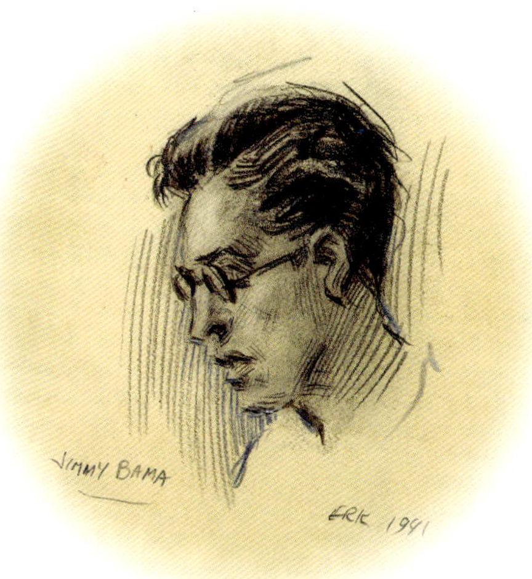

Portrait of James Bama, 1941

Gone to Texas
Avon paperback cover, 1954

The Young Artist

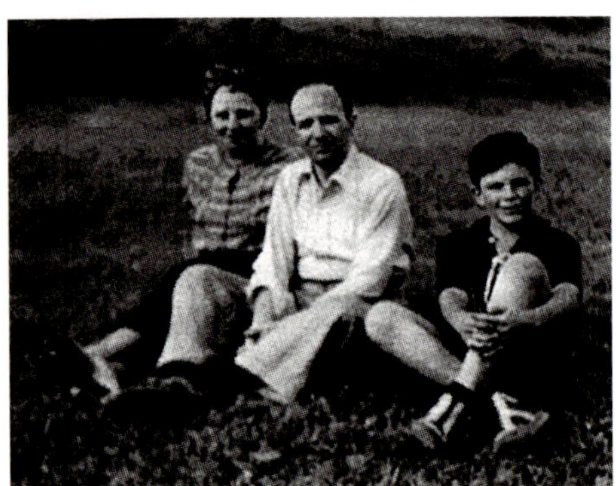

Essie, Joseph, and ERK
circa 1936

Born on 102nd Street in New York City in August of 1926, Everett Raymond Kinstler grew up on 90th Street, just a block from Broadway and the BMT Subway. Neither of his parents displayed any outward signs of artistic ability, although Ray's father, Joseph, was supposed to have had a cousin who was an artist and an illustrator. Many artists have related how their parents resisted their chosen career, but the Kinstlers were the opposite. As Ray's love for art became more evident, Joseph nurtured it, as did Essie Kinstler.

> My mother could have been played in the movies by a younger Bette Davis. She was an original, very much of the earth. Innately bright, but not an intellectual. She was very opinionated—no shades of gray. Hers was a very old-fashioned ethic. She would often dramatize things and I was never sure at any one time whether or not she was indulging in this.

Sunday, February 26, 1933 **SUNDAY MIRROR**

CROSBY IS TODAY'S RADIO SAMARITAN

Sang to Sickboy Over Telephone And Cured Him

By NICK KENNY
(Radio Editor, N. Y. Daily Mirror)

FOR A LONG time Bing Crosby's husky voice has made the great heart of American womanhood swell and throb. For years, under the spell of his airwave moaning, wives have kissed homely husbands fervently, yea, even passionately, the astonished husbands never realizing that their wives were closing their eyes and imagining hubby was Bing!!!

Lo and behold! Today we learn that the Crosby voice affects children as well. This incident gets Bing into the "Good Samaritans of the Air" Club.

It seems that the glamorous gargler was playing handball at the Friars' Club recently with a doctor who told him amusedly of a six-year-old patient, Everett Kinstler, who had the flu, but who wouldn't go to sleep before 9. p. m. because he wanted to hear Bing on the air.

Having a little brother of his own named Everett, over whom he watches like a protecting angel, Bing left the handball game, called up the boy, spoke to him, and then sang for him over the phone!!!

The kid wouldn't believe it was Bing at first, but when he heard the well-known Crosby burp he became so excited that he wept. He improved rapidly after that, and

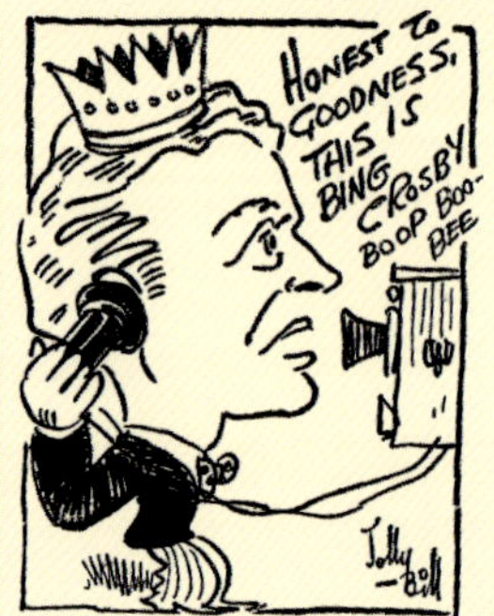

grand veteran of the outfit, Minnie Blauman!!! Friends of Paul Whiteman will present the "Dean of Modern Music" with a mammoth floral wreath at his farewell party in the Biltmore Tuesday night!!! Harold Stern has been signed for a year at the Biltmore with an NBC wire!!!

WILLIAM H. WOODIN, the next Secretary of the Treasury, has written a new composition, the "Fire Chief" March, for his friend, Ed Wynn. It will have its premiere on Wynn's program Tuesday night!!! Irving Mills plans a Carnegie Hall concert for Duke Ellington!!! Catch Baby Rose Marie on WJZ at noon today!!!

HOW MANY tuner-inners listening to Walter Winchell on WJZ at 9:30 tonight will be wishing he'd pull one of his old friendly slams at the expense of Ben Bernie???

I STILL think Al Jolson, whose

ISN'T IT THE TRUTH?

(These lines were written while Al Jolson was singing "April Showers," his last song of the present auto series on the NBC Friday night.

Have you ever sat in a hotel room
Alone with the dreadful blues
And heard a voice on the radio
That thrilled you right to your shoes?

Did the sympathy in that voice erase
The gloom from your lonely heart,
While tears went splattering down your face—
ach tear of your soul a part?

When the voice was gone did you sit and dream,
While back crept the bitter gloom?
Did you wish that the song would never end
And leave you a lonely room?

D. Roosevelt, on her cold cream hour, that's number one. Number two is the way Jolson sang Friday night, he had more feeling in anyone of his songs, than all the radio singers in the world could get in a thousand songs!!!

Lennie Hayton organized the Modern Music Society at dear old De Witt Clinton High School!! Henry Lloyd, the only New Yor member of the "Sizzlers" on NBC volunteered to play for t after their first broadcast. Reisman is raving about Ha Arlen's "Stormy Wea" !!!

IT'S A

As reported in a newspaper of the day, Ray's very first encounter with popular culture and celebrities, in the form of Bing Crosby's voice, happened at the precocious age of six. Many years later he met Bing in person and they shared a good chuckle, recalling the incident.

She told me often about my father's first cousin, Walter Kinstler, "who was a *very* brilliant cartoonist who died before you were born. He worked for ***The Saturday Evening Post*** and for Rube Goldberg." No one I knew had ever heard of this man.

Walter Kinstler "was a very brilliant cartoonist"

Throughout primary school, Ray was a happy, normal kid. Despite the Depression, both of his parents had jobs and they managed to support a lower middle class family lifestyle. His parents sought to encourage his interests. Essie once went out of her way (and outside of the family budget) to gift the seven-year-old Everett, as his family called him, with a set of illustrated books called **Journeys Through Bookland**. It strained the budget, but it also introduced him to pen and ink book illustration through the work of Donn P. Crane and others.

The weekly exposures to Lee Conrey in the Hearst Sunday supplement ***The American Weekly*** and to Hal Foster, Alex Raymond, and Milton Caniff in the Sunday funnies were additional inspiration and motivation to excel. He drew constantly, including murals for P.S. 166 on 89th Street, and he played baseball at school and stickball in the streets.

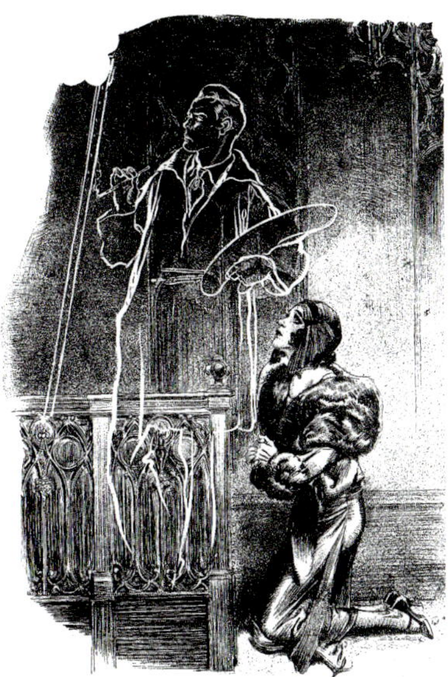

Lee Conrey in ***The American Weekly*** March 16, 1930

As he grew up, he had a goal. He set his sights on a career illustrating for the major magazines of the day like ***Collier's***, ***The Saturday Evening Post***, and ***The American Magazine*** where Flagg and Dean Cornwell, Norman Rockwell, Mead Schaeffer and other talented illustrators reigned. Before he reached his teens, Ray was certain that he would join them. To prepare, he focused on the artistic training he would need. He enrolled at Music and Art High School.

Two years later, at the age of fifteen, he quit school and chose another path. He had been a fine student in many subjects, but there was no doubt in his mind about his eventual career. Art and art instruction were moving towards Modern Art, but Ray saw no reason to blindly follow. Listen to him talk about those times and you detect an inevitability in his direction, a determination, almost a predestination to be an illustrator.

> I was a good student—an honor student. When I graduated middle school, I went to Music and Art High School which was for select students, both artistically *and* scholastically. Until that time my grades had been 'A's.
>
> When I entered Music and Art I was fourteen years old. There I was told that the work of the artists that I liked, Norman Rockwell and comic strip artists like Milton Caniff and Alex Raymond, was not art. That it was *just* commercial art, and that real artists paint what they *feel*. Well, as my friend Tony Bennett later said of me, "Kinstler was only fourteen, he was smart enough to know he didn't 'feel' anything, *yet*."
>
> It was that simple.

From a random issue of ***The American Magazine*** September, 1936 (left to right) Mead Schaeffer Matt Clark Pruett Carter John Alan Maxwell Saul Tepper

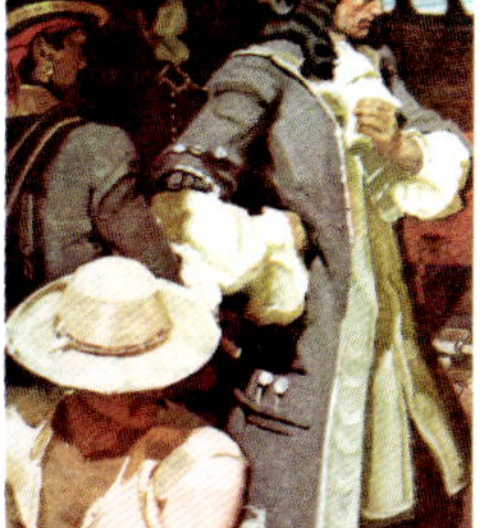

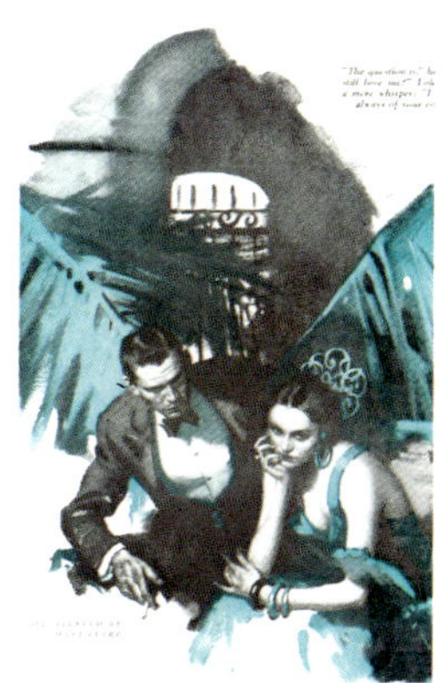

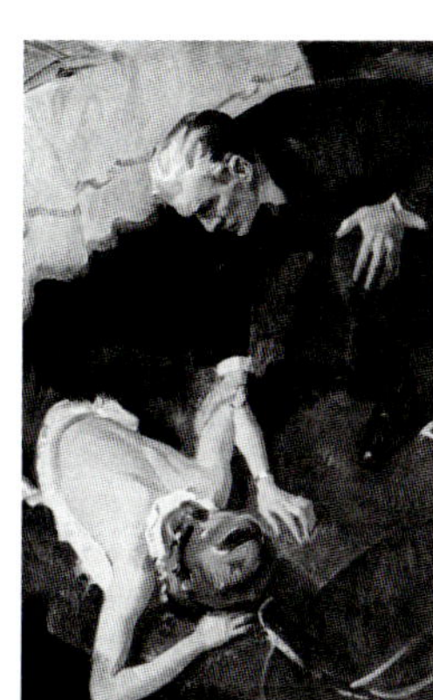

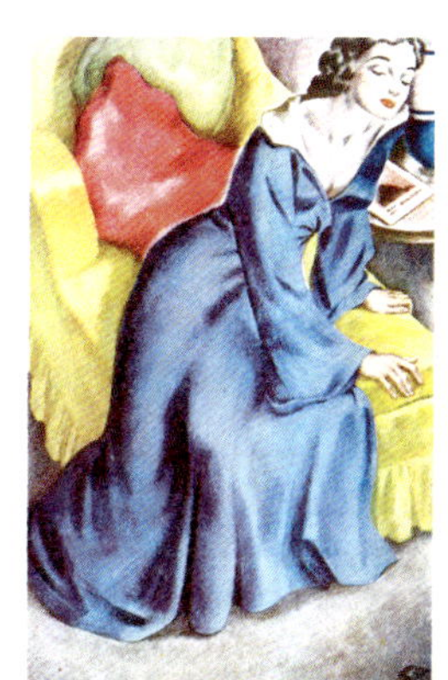

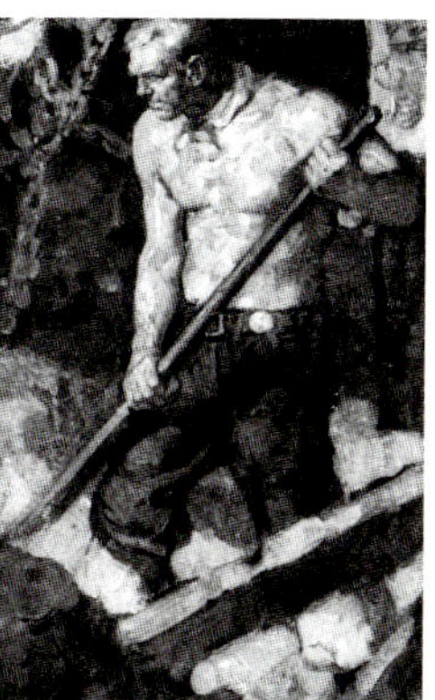

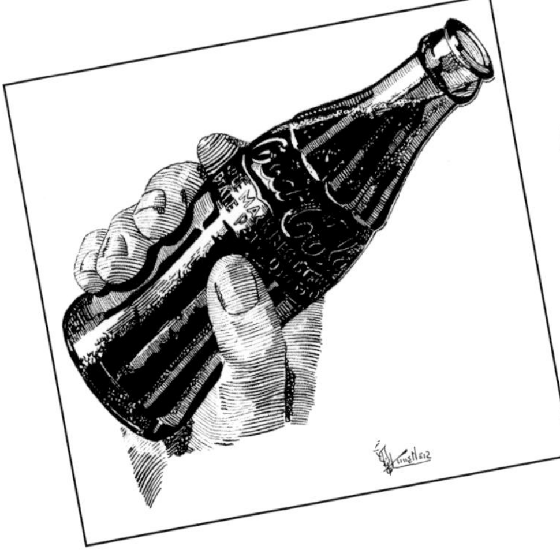

I was so unhappy with the art courses that I paid no attention to the mathematics and English courses, and my grades began to drop.

It's at this juncture that Kinstler's story departs from the norm. At fourteen he possessed a self-assuredness uncommon in young men half again that age. He recognized his problem, analyzed the probable causes and came up with what he considered a possible solution.

I thought maybe going to a trade school would be the answer. So for my sophomore year, I transferred to the High School of Industrial Arts. There were no scholastic expectations. There you were being trained to do rendering or scratchboard drawings of O-rings and automobile tires. You were learning a profession. It was a trade school for the kids who were going to do photoengraving, newspaper work.

But from the time I was a kid—I mean six or seven years old—I used to look at illustrations of movie actors in the ***New York Sun*** that were done with Crowquill pens. I loved the sports cartoonists. There was Willard Mullin and Paprocki who used to sign his work "PAP." I really loved looking at those images and anything else that showed imagination in the sense of illustration. Even at that age illustration was what I loved. I remember copying a James Montgomery Flagg drawing in pencil when I was eight years old, so I was aware of styles and techniques.

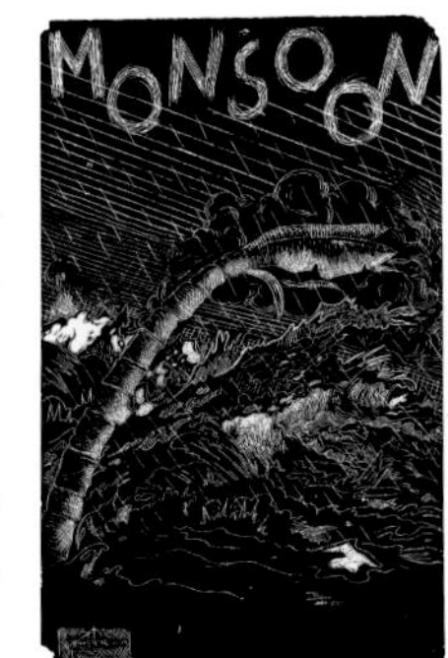

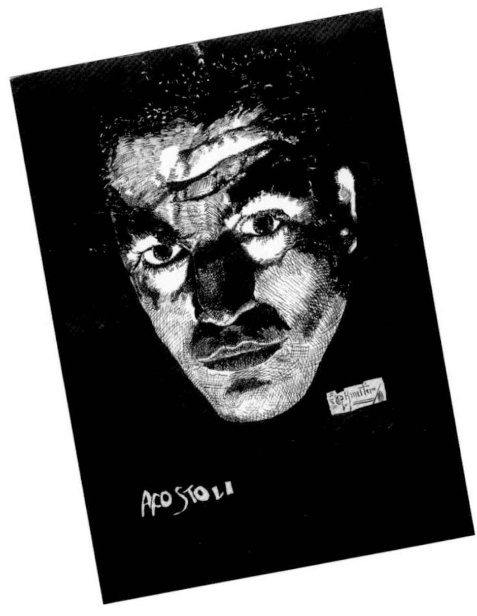

At the trade school, though, I was drawing a lot of scratchboard and pen and ink drawings of everything from wristwatches to automobile advertisements. I was not challenged.

The summer after that term at Industrial Arts, he still drew and still played ball with the guys, but he also searched the want ad sections of the newspapers to see what other options might be available. He had come to the conclusion that his path did not lead through the formal education system.

I was fifteen and I had tremendous energy, passion and unhappiness—in equal doses. It was a potent combination.

Fortunately, there was an out, and it didn't take Ray long to find it. In the fall of 1942 he took his first steps into the fledgling comic book field.

In 1942 comic books had been around for about nine years. However, it had only been six years since they started publishing new stories that were not reprinted from those wonderful newspaper strips on which Kinstler had cut his artistic teeth.

During World War II, the demand for comic books soared at the same time that the men who created them were being drafted in droves. So when Richard Hughes, who provided material to comic book publishers, ran an advertisement for an inker, it was not surprising that fifteen-year-old Ray Kinstler showed up and even less surprising that he was hired.

What was unusual was that in the summer after his sophomore year in high school he was scouring the want ads for job listings that would fit his goals. The passion to create illustrative art was being squelched by both of his educational options—one with its lofty aspirations and the other by its unchallenging pedestrian nature—and Ray wasn't going to tolerate either. The only other option left was the School of Hard Knocks, the real world.

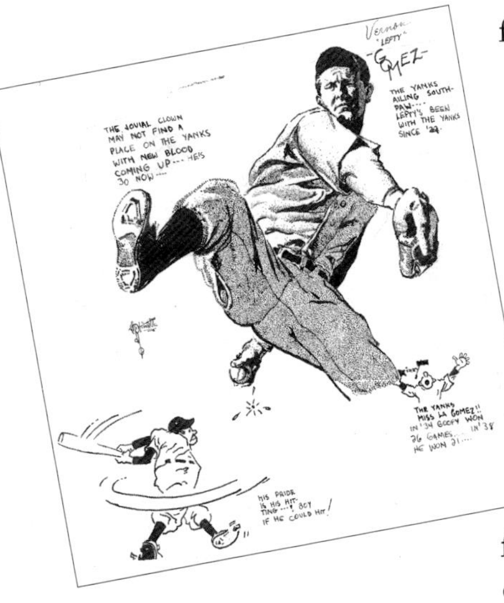

student works
1941–1942

The job at Cinema Comics offered Ray an escape from another bleak year at trade school and he would be working in an industry that was becoming famous for telling adventurous stories in pictures.

Just one last hurdle needed to be cleared before he could pursue his dream.

> Before I took the job, I talked to my parents. I told my father that I'd gone up to see this man at 45 W. 45th Street and that I'd been offered a job at, I think, fifteen dollars a week for six days a week to be a comic book inker. My mother was not very happy, but my father…

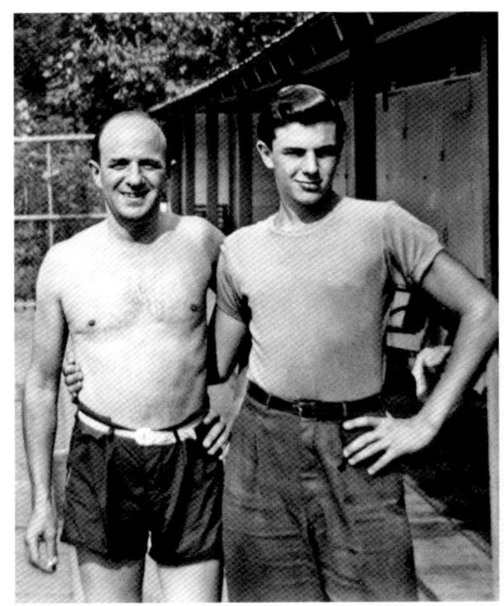

> All I can figure is that he saw in me someone with a passion. And my father knew what that was like. He loved music, particularly jazz piano. I think he would have sold his soul if he could have played the piano well. But instead he had worked at a job he hated for twenty-five years. So he went along with my taking the inking job and he said to me something I've never forgotten, "You're a very lucky young man because you're going to be able to earn your living doing something you love. Don't ever forget it."

> I don't think there's been a day in fifty years when I haven't thought of my father and I've often thought "How in the world could he have ever let me leave school at fifteen?" There's no question that I was his only son and that he loved me, but he had come out of World War One and gone into the family business. And he *hated* it. Part of the reason he allowed me to leave was my extreme unhappiness at Music and Art. He saw that Industrial Arts was just as unchallenging and I think he related to that.

Kinstler describes his father as an intelligent man, though not formally educated. It is obvious that he was perceptive and sensitive to his son's needs. He loved and trusted his son and knew that he had a drive and passion for his art and that Ray was basically a good kid. When he was happy, he got 'A's and was active in sports. It was clear that the art schools weren't making him happy and his father sensed that this new direction would.

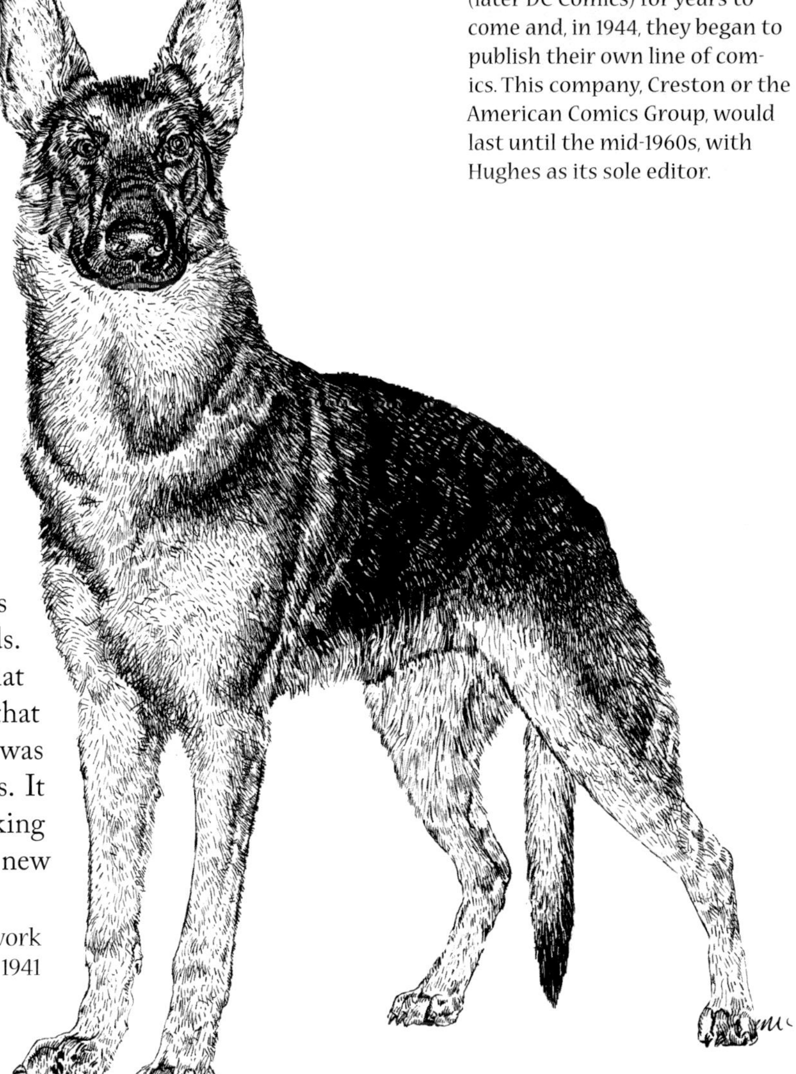

student work
1941

Cinema Comics

In 1941, Ben Sangor published ***Cinema Comics Herald***. It was a magazine for promoting the animated cartoons and films of the Max Fleischer Studios, creators of the famous *Superman*, *Popeye* and *Betty Boop* cartoons. It was distributed to theaters showing Fleischer features.

A year later, Fleischer animators were moonlighting for Sangor doing comic features. He brokered these finished stories to his father-in-law Ned Pines' new ***Coo Coo Comics*** title. Sangor hired Richard Hughes, a writer for Pines, to oversee the brokering organization. The company was called Cinema Comics and it quickly expanded to include the teen-age Everett Raymond Kinstler as one of its earliest staff members.

Sangor and Hughes would continue to provide stories and art in the "funny animal" vein to Pines and National Periodicals (later DC Comics) for years to come and, in 1944, they began to publish their own line of comics. This company, Creston or the American Comics Group, would last until the mid-1960s, with Hughes as its sole editor.

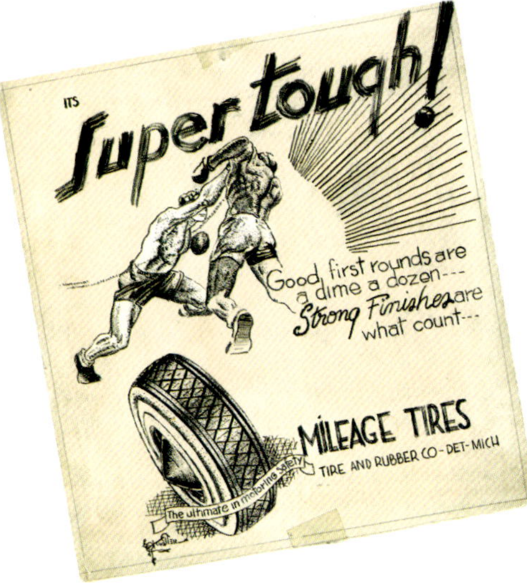

High School of Industrial Arts assignment, circa 1942

Since Ray was four or five years old, Joseph had watched him drawing incessantly. Unlike many children for whom drawing was a passing phase, with Ray it intensified over time. His father was quite aware of that intensity and was wise enough to step out of the way as Ray went rushing towards his goal. Leaving school was nothing compared to what his son was leaving it *for.*

From a perspective of sixty years, it's not easy to imagine how different the world was. It was a simpler age. Ray's father wasn't as concerned as a modern New York parent might be about crime and drugs and crazy people, and, as Ray says, "Forget about sex, I couldn't even spell it!" With his father's blessing, six days a week he would get on the subway and travel forty-five blocks from W. 90th Street to W. 45th Street to earn his living doing exactly what he loved—telling stories with pictures.

Ray doesn't see the unusual confidence he displayed in making this choice. To him it was the *natural* thing to do. Throughout his career he would display the same disregard for caution when faced with career-altering choices. The "rightness" of his decisions seemed obvious to him at all times, as if he had some secret guarantee that the path ahead of him, though unseen, was inevitable. Or, if that path didn't take him where he wanted to go, he was confident enough of himself and his skills that he would bend it, and the world, in the proper direction. Time has shown the validity of that confidence, but it is interesting to note that even now, looking back on it, that initial step out into the world at fifteen doesn't strike him as either brave or foolhardy. Just inevitable.

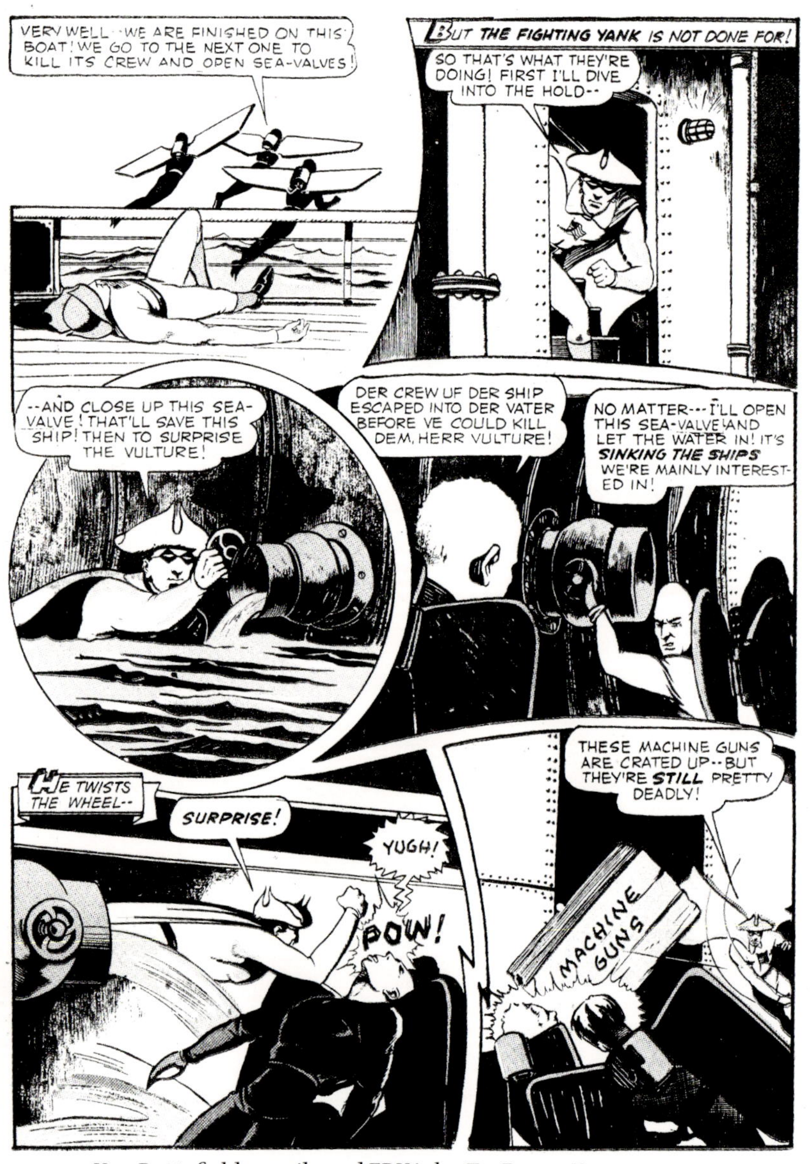

Ken Battefield pencils and ERK inks. *The Fighting Yank* in ***Startling Comics*** #30, November, 1944

Ray prepared for the job interview at Cinema Comics. Although the list of samples that he took with him has been lost to time, it must have consisted of wonderful drawings like those that he'd done while at Music and Art and earlier. It's no wonder that he was hired.

Despite his age, it seems that Ray knew what an "inker" did. It wasn't exactly common knowledge, as the occupation was obscure and a relatively recent invention of the new industry. An inker's job was to take a comic book page that another artist had drawn in pencil and render it in ink so that it was reproducible. By hiring a more experienced artist to draw the page first in pencil, the comic book editors were able to review the work while it was still easily modifiable. The word balloons could also be added at that time which eliminated a lot of unnecessary effort. The inker wouldn't have to waste time rendering parts of the story that would eventually be covered with text. Once the story was okayed and the text added, the pages were turned over to a lower-paid artist who "inked" the pencilled art.

The man who hired Kinstler, Richard E. Hughes, had been in the comic book business for several years as a writer supplying stories through Cinema Comics to Ned Pines at Standard Comics (also known as Nedor—for Ned and Dora, his wife). Pines had been publishing comics since 1939 and Hughes had created several of the super characters that were all the rage since the surprising success of *Superman* in 1938. Pines' stable included *Pyroman*, *The Fighting Yank*, *Captain Future*, and *The Black Terror*. Ray worked on them all from 1942 through 1945. But first he had to get started.

> I remember getting on the subway and going downtown. We lived forty-five blocks away. I went up to see Mr. Hughes. I remember him—he smoked a pipe—and he was really old. He must have been about forty!

Hughes, who was all of thirty-three, paired Kinstler with Ken Battefield, a young comics veteran who had been in the trenches for two years. Battefield was a prolific penciller whose forte was the telling of a story and who was 4F because of his flat feet—the perfect combination for a comic book production house in wartime. Ray's classical drawing style was a wonderful complement to Ken's "rough and tumble, get it down on the page" approach. Together they collaborated on adventure hero stories and true adventure stories, the latter for Pines' ***Real Life Comics***, which was then in its second year. At the time he was hired, Kinstler and Battefield were the only staff artists at Cinema. Everyone else worked on a freelance basis. It would be the first and only staff position Ray would ever hold.

The comic books of the day were produced primarily by very young men—although generally not quite as young as Kinstler—and by older artists who were finishing out their careers in the new medium. These latter had seen the existing markets for their pen work, like the humor magazines ***Judge*** and ***Life***, give way to the slicker, more colorful ***Collier's***, ***The Saturday Evening Post*** and ***The Ladies' Home Journal***. They had been professional freelance illustrators and now they labored for "shops" like Cinema Comics, producing stories aimed primarily at the servicemen of the war who were destined to eventually return and replace them.

Unlike today's multi-issue crossover comic book "epics," early titles contained multiple stories and often featured a variety of characters. It was also a time of experimentation and titles like ***Real Life Comics*** featured heroic tales of World War II mixed in with historic battle tales and stories of inventors and explorers. While the freelance staff generally remained the same from issue to issue, almost every story in each issue was drawn by a different artist. On this and the next page are a sampling of some of the dozen features of ***Real Life Comics*** #10 which was produced by the artists who were working for Ned Pines or Richard Hughes as freelancers. These stories were drawn just about the time that Ray reported for his first day of work at Cinema Comics.

> I was doing the inking for Ken (Battefield). We had drawing boards right across from each other. And the things you remember… I can still remember the smell of those artgum erasers that I used to erase the pencil lines when I was done inking.
>
> I went there six days a week on the subway from 91st to 42nd Street—there were only five stops. We're talking about an eighteen minute ride. I'd get there around nine o'clock.

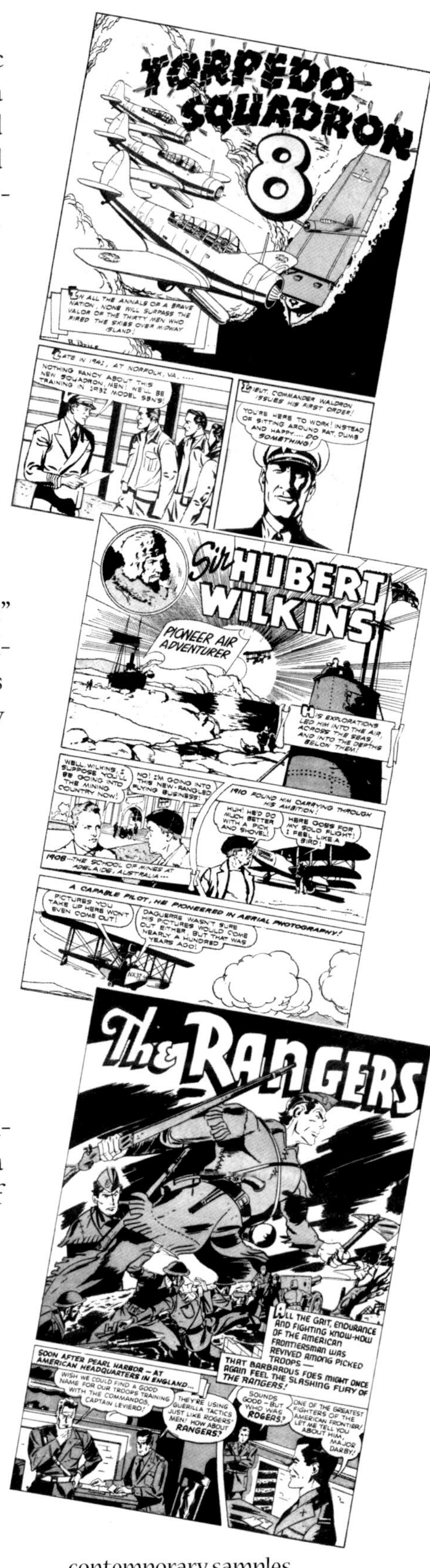

contemporary samples
from ***Real Life Comics*** #10
March, 1943
Robert Brice
August M. Froehlich
Bob Oksner

actual size

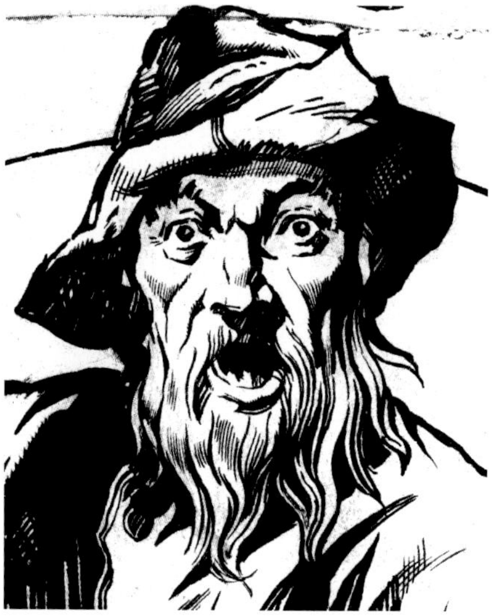

There was a lanky Barnard graduate there doing scripts for the comics. I had a terrific crush on her, but I was fifteen or sixteen so she must have been twenty-two or twenty-three, the 'older woman.' I must have driven her crazy with my offers of help. It was "Oh, can I do this for you, Miss Highsmith?" or "Can I get you a Coke, Miss Highsmith?" Once she gave in, probably out of frustration or exhaustion, and actually let me go down and get her a Coke. I brought back a Pepsi Cola instead.

I said, "Miss Highsmith, Coke and Pepsi were the same price, but the Pepsi was eight ounces and the Coca Cola was only six."

And she said to me, "When you get older, you'll go for quality not quantity." That's when I fell out of love with her. That was Patricia Highsmith, who wrote **Strangers on a Train** which was later made into a movie by Hitchcock.

Despite such office diversions, Ray dutifully fulfilled his assignments—for a while. Soon he couldn't suppress his ardent desire to tell the stories himself. Certain that he could manage the entire task, he set about planning his next move. First, he had to convince Richard Hughes that he could be trusted with the additional responsibility.

Like many of Ray's "promotions" in life, he took the most obvious way of proving himself: he just did the job. Working at night, he wrote and drew the title page for a hypothetical comic book story similar to those he saw in ***Real Life Comics***. We can chalk it up to youthful enthusiasm but, like many samples he prepared throughout his life, he left no doubt that he was capable of doing the work.

The result was "Ships and Men" and he still has that original page—albeit a little worse for wear after more than fifty years in his Gramercy Park studio. The original is fourteen inches by twenty inches, which is just about twice the size of a printed comic book page. This added size allowed the artist to include additional detail, despite the fact that reduction to fifty percent and cheap printing on pulpy paper would never have been able to reproduce it. But Ray was sixteen and trying to prove a point. And just maybe he was showing off a bit.

It worked. His first real comic book story appeared in ***Real Life Comics*** #11 which had a cover date of May, 1943.

A quick word about dates on comic books. The "cover date" was generally two to four months ahead of the calendar date. That is, a comic book dated "May, 1943" was probably put on the newsstands in February or March. The practice continues even today. Since it took a month or so to produce the material and perhaps several weeks to print and distribute it, work that appeared in such a comic was probably created in late 1942 or early 1943. Given the date of the "try-out" page, we can guess that Ray wasted no time in turning in his first solo work.

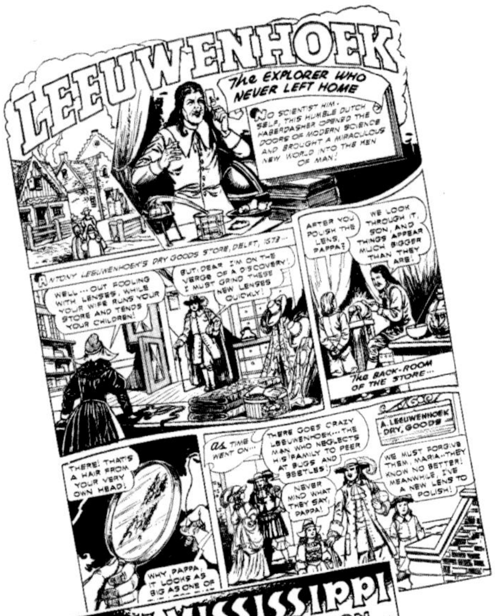

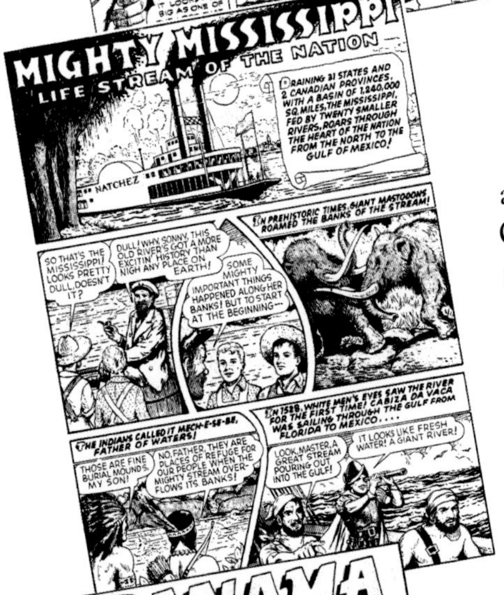

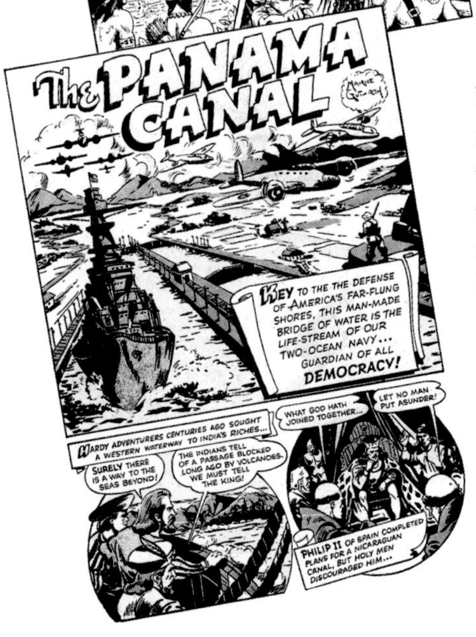

contemporary samples from ***Real Life Comics*** #10
March, 1943
Henry C. Kiefer
George Carl Wilhelms
Maurice Gutwirth

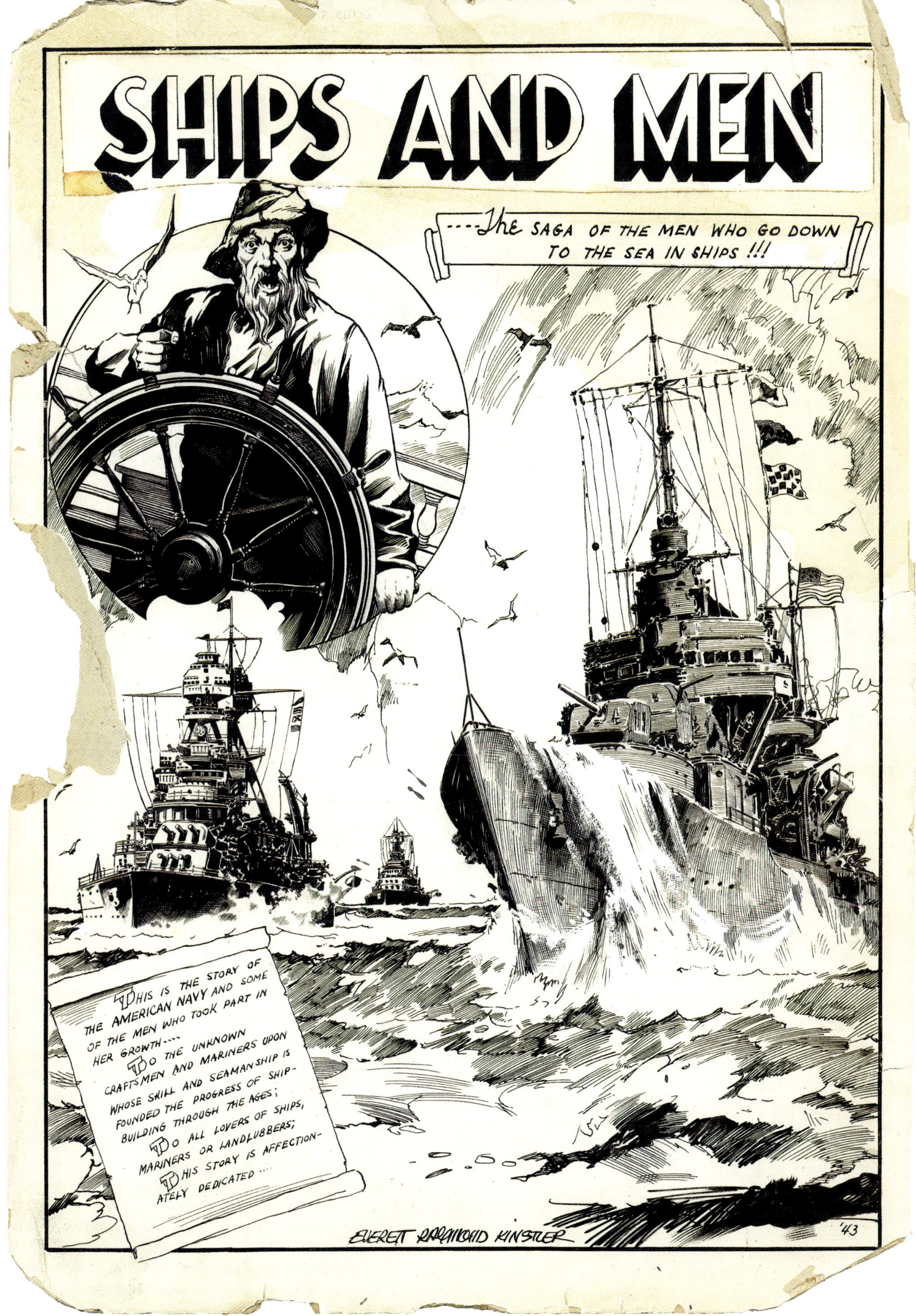

comic try-out sample page—1943

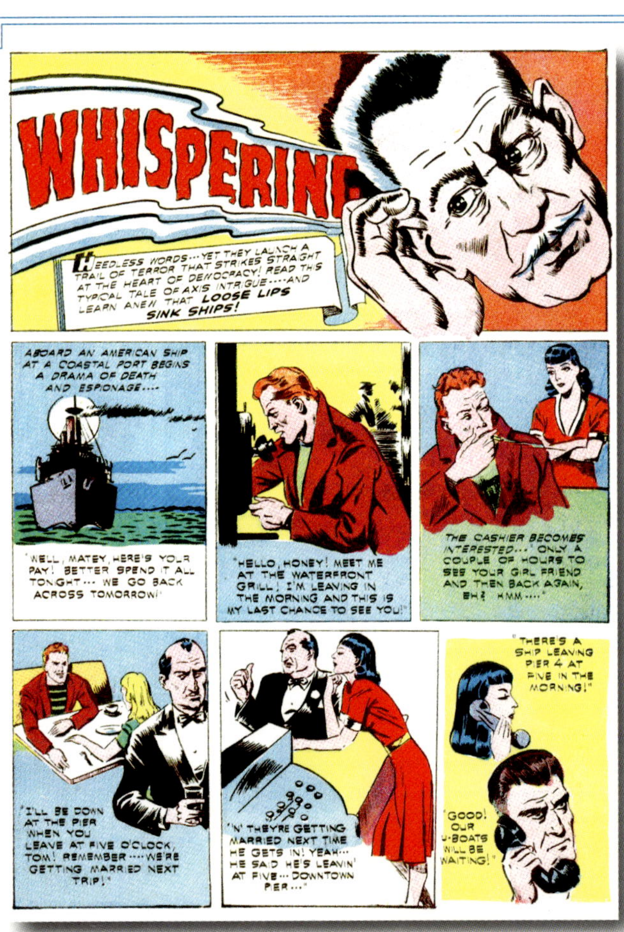

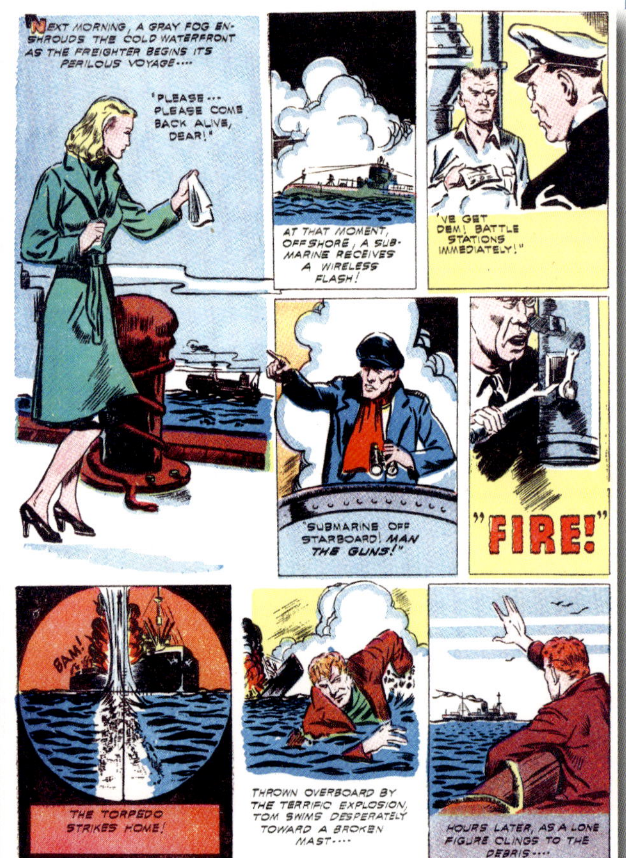

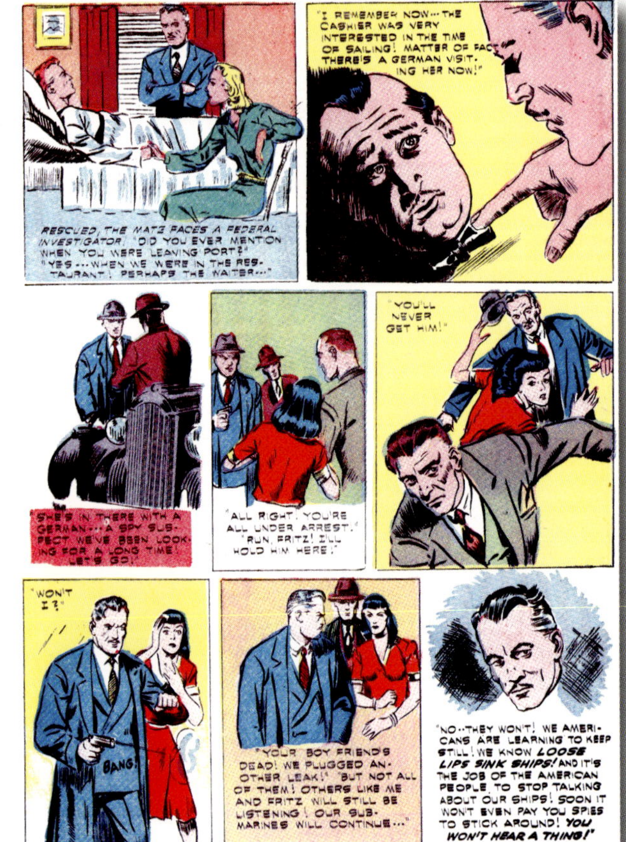

"Whispering"

This first solo story was a wartime warning to the readers that "Loose lips sink ships." Titled "Whispering," it was competent art, especially for a sixteen-year-old, but certainly not great literature. In the short three-page story, our hero Tom is lovestruck and needs to have his fiancée at the dock to wave goodbye as he sails. It's only after his ship is torpedoed by a German submarine that sole survivor Tom is "suddenly" suspicious of the German friend of the cashier at the diner where he and his girlfriend had their farewell date. And he also remembers how the cashier was very interested in the time he was sailing. Too soon old and too late smart it seems.

It is important to keep in mind that Ray was only responsible for the art—which owes a debt to the sophisticated drawings of Alex Raymond. At the time, this was not unusual as Raymond's *Flash Gordon* had redefined what could be done in the comics and most artists were paying close attention. Raymond-esque work was appearing everywhere.

Real Life Comics #11
May, 1943

Ken Battefield, who was destined to spend the next fifteen years laboring unheralded and virtually unknown in comic books, quickly saw Ray's raw talent and recommended that he return to school for more formal training. Ray wasn't immediately receptive to the idea.

"For an uneducated kid, I had really good taste!"

> But, I was getting this from several other people, too. There was an art school called the Grand Central School of Art on 43rd Street, right across from Grand Central Terminal. I found that they actually taught *illustration*, so I tried to get into the class of Harvey Dunn.
>
> For an uneducated kid, I had really good taste!
>
> By this time, artists like Harvey Dunn were becoming passé. They couldn't get work because a whole new style of illustration was developing.
>
> I couldn't get into Mr. Dunn's class, so I enrolled in the class of Cliff Young. He was a cartoonist who eventually finished his career in the 1960s and 70s assisting Allyn Cox on the restoration of murals in the U.S. Capitol Building. I could take his classes because they were in the evening.
>
> The classes provided me with some guidance and gave me the chance to draw more, but they didn't seem to be the answer. Then the school closed and I was forced to make a change.

Harvey Dunn
One of the great teachers of illustration, Dunn was a prize pupil of Howard Pyle and was instrumental in keeping Pyle's ideas and teaching techniques alive.

This was the last four months of 1942. Ray had just turned sixteen and he was operating on instinct and adrenalin. He couldn't define what he was after, but he was certain that he would know when it felt right to him. Going back to school was right, but he needed to find the right class and the right teacher. He wasn't thinking of practicality, only desire. Certain things made sense to him and others didn't. When The Grand Central School closed, Ray went looking for new answers.

His first stop was The Phoenix School of Design which was opposite the Grand Central Terminal on Lexington Avenue. One of the first lecturers to address his class was Franklin Booth, whose style brought comparisons to woodcuts and was somewhat antiquated. It wasn't what Ray wanted.

> I went to the Art Students League after The Phoenix School and I signed up with Robert Brackman. I was a rank amateur and Brackman came over to me early on and said "Kid, you're going to paint my way or you're going to get out of here." That made me *very* unhappy. And that same day I went down to the gallery/lunchroom on the second floor. There was an "Instructor Show" and I saw a painting on the wall which I can see now just as clearly as I can see my own hand. It was of a Boy Scout and it was everything I ever imagined my art could become. I thought, "That's how I'd like to work!"
>
> Up until this time I don't think I'd ever painted at all. Perhaps I used some gouache in art school, but everything else was pen and ink.

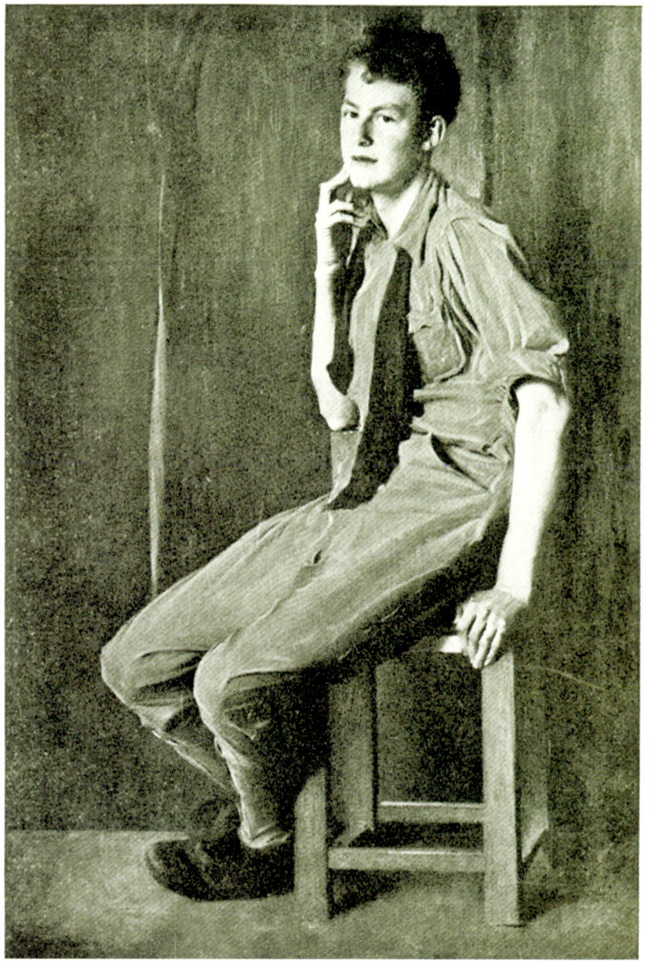

The painting by Frank Vincent DuMond that inspired Everett Raymond Kinstler in 1943

> The painting was by Frank Vincent DuMond and he actually taught *Life Drawing* and *Portrait Painting* at the Art Students League—but his classes were in the afternoon. I had a *job* in the afternoon and I'd just been raised to fifty-five dollars a week, from my starting salary of fifteen dollars a week, which was pretty damned good.

On the horns of a dilemma that might have stumped a less-determined youth, Kinstler simply approached Richard Hughes at Cinema Comics and asked to be given work on a freelance basis. Ray wanted to take the work home and do it in the evenings—freeing up his afternoons for class.

It's indicative of Ray's work ethic and of his character that Hughes said yes. After all, his business involved fixed deadlines and work of a minimum quality. He would be relying on a sixteen-year-old who was following a passion, which seems to be a classic formula for distraction. There was every likelihood that the young man would get caught up in his art lessons to the detriment of his comic book work, but both of them knew that wasn't going to happen. Ray has always been convincing and Hughes had obviously been convinced.

> One of the things I've realized for a long time is that I've been very fortunate in my life. A lot of people whom I've met over the years—I don't know how else to put this—*liked me*. I think Hughes knew I was a good kid. God knows that I was intense and passionate and honest. I guess that came through.

F.V. DuMond and the Art Students League gave Ray his first exposure to the techniques and skills demanded of a professional illustrator. DuMond had been a student at the League in the 1880s, trained in France, and had a career as a newspaper artist and magazine illustrator. He had been teaching at the League for fifty years when Kinstler enrolled in his class.

In marked contrast to his experience with Robert Brackman, Ray fondly recalls his first encounter with DuMond.

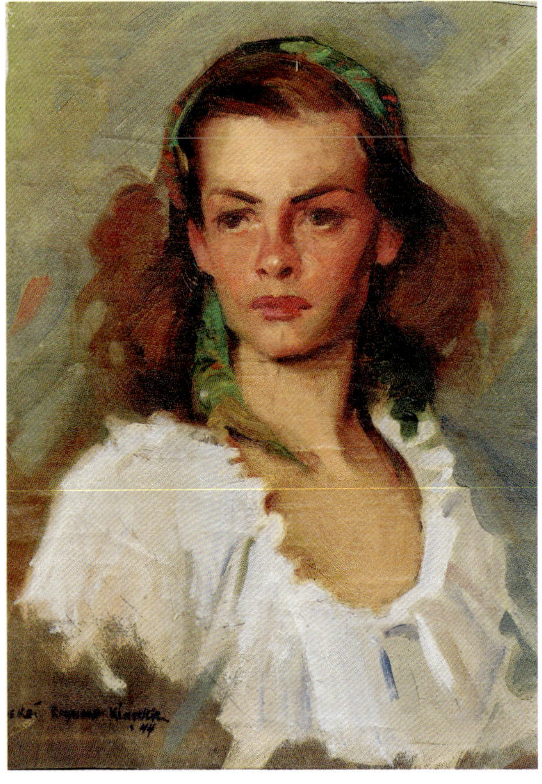

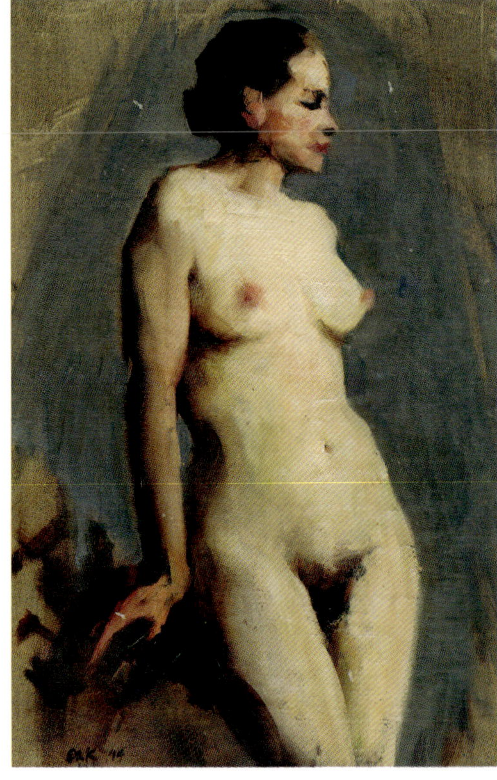

painting exercises
1944

It was early on in one of his painting classes. I was struggling with my very first painting and was using black paint for shadows and white paint for highlights. When I saw him approaching I put my hand out like a traffic cop signalling "Stop" and said "Before you say *anything*, this is the first painting I've ever done." He put his hand on my shoulder and said good-naturedly, "Really?"

"This is the first painting I've ever done."

Freelance

Ray found much to like in the new school/work arrangements. He lived at home where he had a small studio set up on the roof in what had been at one time the "maid's quarters" of the building. His strong work ethic quickly dealt with Hughes' piecemeal jobs and the payments allowed him the luxury of all the canvas, brushes and paint he could want.

He was immersed in this routine when he found out that James Montgomery Flagg lived just up the street from the League. Of the many artists that had influenced Ray up to this point, Flagg's bravura pen work had made one of the deepest impressions. To meet the man would have been special, but to share his own work as a fellow illustrator simply made the encounter irresistible. So, with some comic book pages and some recent exercises done in DuMond's classes, he probably ran the block and a half from school to Parc Vendome, the apartment building where Flagg lived and had his studio.

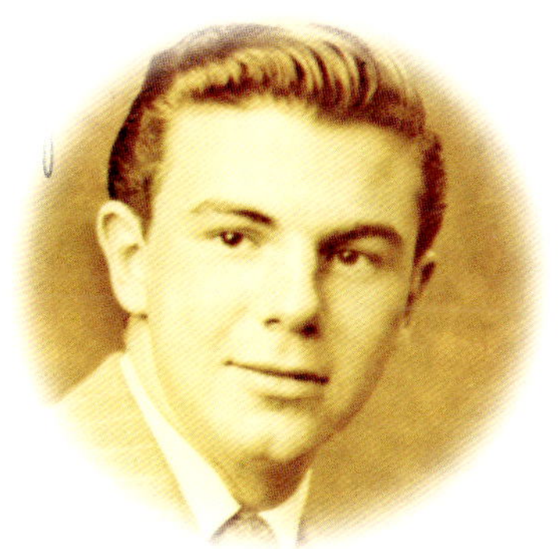

The Irish doorman, Kinstler quickly realized, did not like Flagg and made the entire encounter a test of wills—one where Ray prevailed. Or the Irishman simply saw Ray as one more way to get Flagg's goat. With Flagg, too, Ray had to overcome a natural antagonism and reluctance. He went so far as to bluff with the "getting drafted" card in order to gain admittance. He was eventually able to share his efforts and get some left-handed "encouragement" from Flagg. How else would you classify "you're doomed to be an artist"? It must have sounded like high praise to the young Kinstler, but Flagg surely meant it as a cautionary warning as well. One Ray didn't see.

When he showed Flagg the work he was doing under F.V. DuMond, Flagg's response was a cynical "Is that old bastard still alive?" Ray didn't learn the significance of the comment until a few days later when he told DuMond about the meeting. Then he got the perfect ending to his story.

"Oh yes," said DuMond, "Jimmy Flagg. He was one of my boys." Fifty years earlier, in one of his first years as a teacher at the Art Students League, DuMond had taught the seventeen-year-old James Montgomery Flagg. Similarities between Kinstler's painting style and that of Flagg are more attributable to both men studying with DuMond than to Flagg's influence on Kinstler. Flagg's penwork certainly impressed Ray early on, but by the time they were reintroduced a decade after that first meeting, Flagg had long since retired from illustrating and his failing eyesight left him in no position to instruct Ray—who by then was already painting pulp and paperback covers and had been drawing for the pulp and comic book markets for a dozen years.

An unanticipated advantage of these new arrangements was that Ray was able to fill any extra time he might have with assignments other than those from Cinema Comics.

So I went freelance for Richard Hughes and I worked for other companies, too. I started doing work directly with Pines at 20 W. 40th Street and I also went to Popular Publications at 205 E. 42nd Street. They published pulp magazines like ***Adventure***, ***Argosy*** and a whole string of other titles.

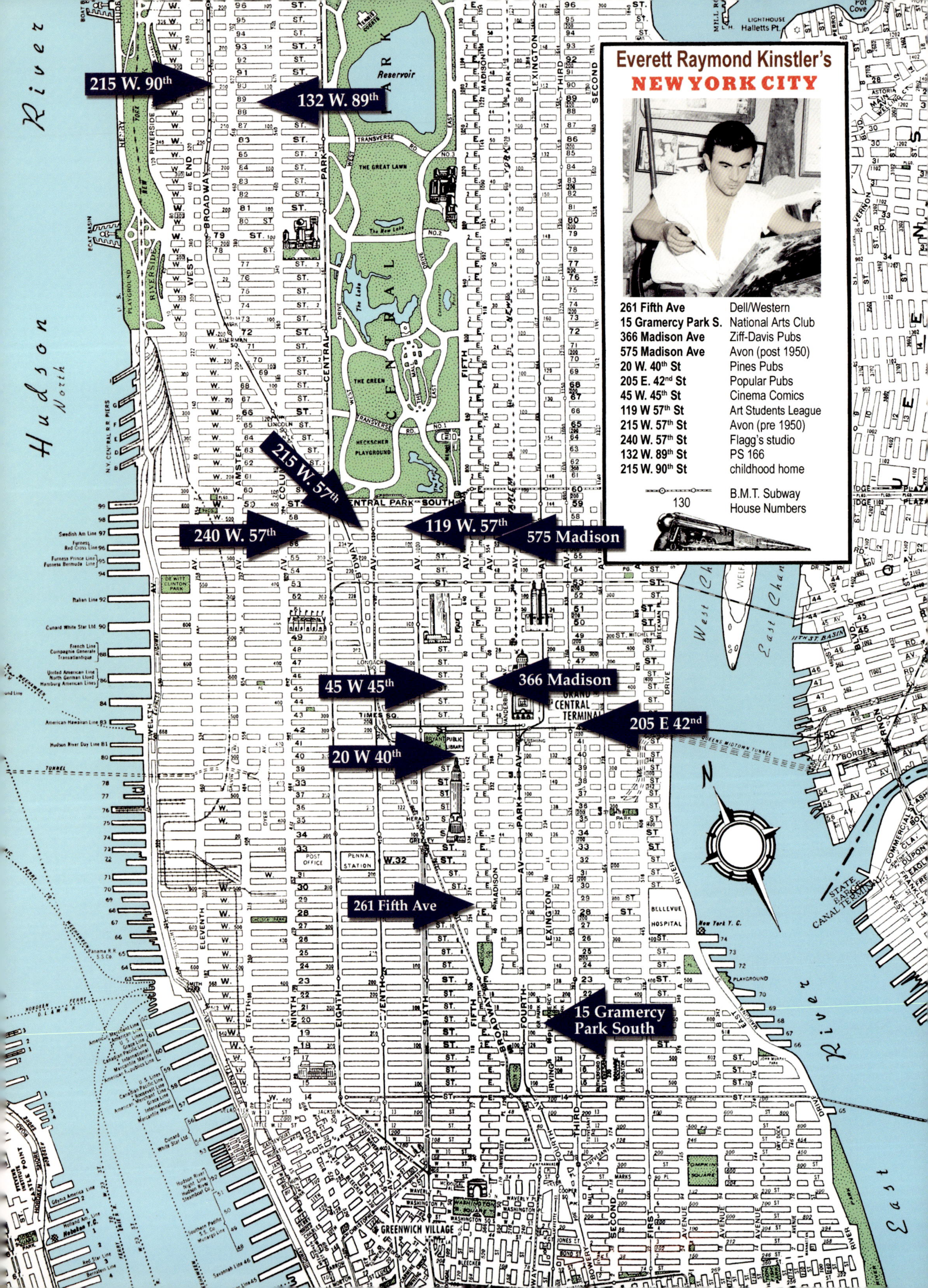

Everett Raymond Kinstler's
NEW YORK CITY
261 Fifth Ave — Dell/Western
15 Gramercy Park S. — National Arts Club
366 Madison Ave — Ziff-Davis Pubs
575 Madison Ave — Avon (post 1950)
20 W. 40th St — Pines Pubs
205 E. 42nd St — Popular Pubs
45 W. 45th St — Cinema Comics
119 W 57th St — Art Students League
215 W. 57th St — Avon (pre 1950)
240 W. 57th St — Flagg's studio
132 W. 89th St — PS 166
215 W. 90th St — childhood home
B.M.T. Subway
130 House Numbers
215 W. 90th
132 W. 89th
215 W. 57th
240 W. 57th
119 W. 57th
575 Madison
45 W 45th
366 Madison
205 E 42nd
20 W 40th
261 Fifth Ave
15 Gramercy Park South
Hudson River
East River
CENTRAL PARK
Reservoir
GREENWICH VILLAGE

> At Popular were people like Gerry McCann, Nick Eggenhofer, Ed deLavy—a whole gang of great illustrators—even the legendary Gordon Grant who was one of the greatest marine painters who ever lived.

It was at Popular and Street & Smith that Ray found his next path. The pulps were slowly being supplanted by paperback books and the comic books, but while they lasted they needed artwork for the interiors and paintings for the covers. While his comic book stories could serve as samples of his pen and ink abilities, he now approached class assignments with a consideration for his professional portfolio as well.

Street & Smith published a wide variety of pulps and his first illustrations for the company appeared in their prestigious ***The Shadow*** and ***Doc Savage*** magazines. Ray's only illustrations of *The Shadow* would later receive high praise from Tom Lovell, an earlier *Shadow* artist.

> When he told me how much he liked my *Shadow* illustrations I just nodded in agreement and said, "They *were* pretty good, weren't they?"
>
> My reaction surprised him and he repeated his praise. "No, I mean they were wonderfully composed and very dynamic." Again I agreed, "Weren't they, though?"
>
> I eventually had to explain to him that the only reason that they were so good was that I had referenced a couple of Tom Lovell *Shadow* drawings to make certain that I had the character right and to study Tom's approach. All the points that he found noteworthy in my drawings were because of Tom Lovell, not Everett Kinstler.

Pulp and comic book assignments continued throughout 1944 and most of 1945. His drawings were often signed "Everett Raymond" when they appeared in ***Detective Tales***, ***Star Western***, ***Doc Savage*** and other pulps. In comic books, the collaborations with Ken Battefield at Cinema Comics were a constant, but there were more stories that he completed on his own. Several of these were for new or secondary publishers who were trying to take advantage of the enormous demand for comic books during the war. For MLJ (later to become Archie Publishing) he did a few issues of ***The Black Hood*** and for the short-lived Four Star Comics he did one issue of ***Captain Flight***.

In August of 1944 he turned eighteen. One highlight of that summer was studying painting in upstate New York with Wayman Adams, who had been one of the instructors at the Grand Central School of Art. Adams was one of the preeminent portrait painters in America. It was just another of the many encounters Ray had with some of the major figures in American art. Like many others to whom he responded—Flagg, DuMond, and Dunn—Adams was a throwback to an earlier artistic sensibility that resonated with Kinstler.

Pulps

Imagine the cheapest paperback book that you can. Imagine the covers thinner and the paper even cruder. Now assemble it with bad glue and increase the dimensions by fifty percent. What you end up with is a Pulp.

Although no one realized it at the time, the heyday of the pulp magazine was over by the mid-1940s. Still, Popular Publications was churning out their thick magazines with titles like ***All-Story Love***, ***Argosy***, ***Big-Book Western***, ***Dare-Devil Aces***, ***Detective Stories***, ***Dime Detective***, ***Dime Mystery***, ***Dime Sports***, ***Dime Western***, ***Fifteen Western Tales***, ***G-8 and His Battle Aces***, and ***Love Book Magazine***.

The White Skull
The Shadow
November, 1945

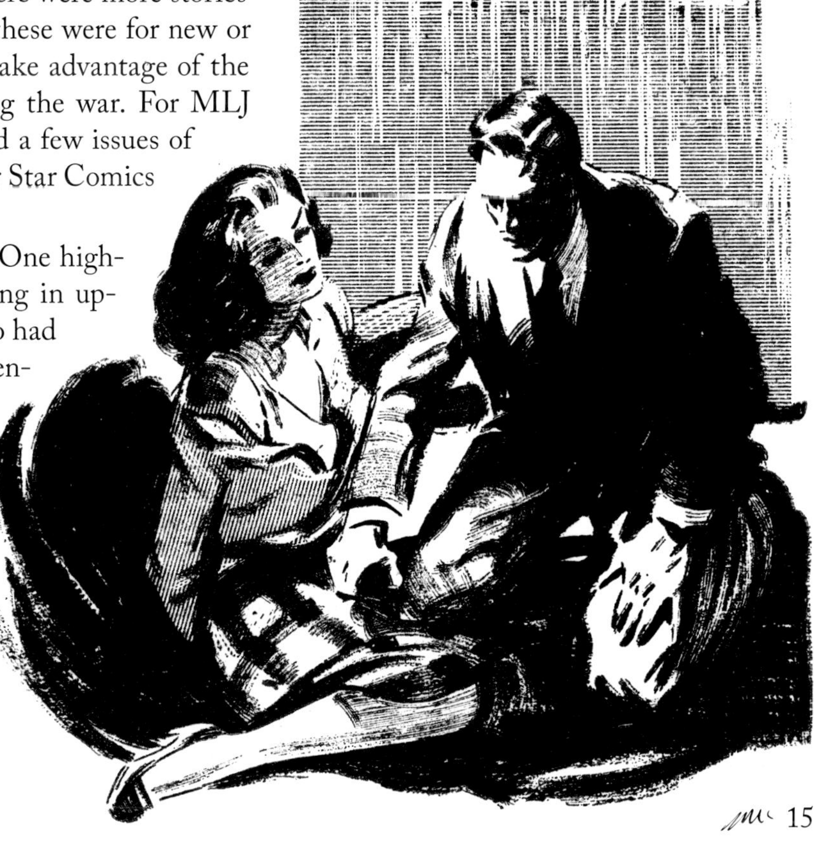

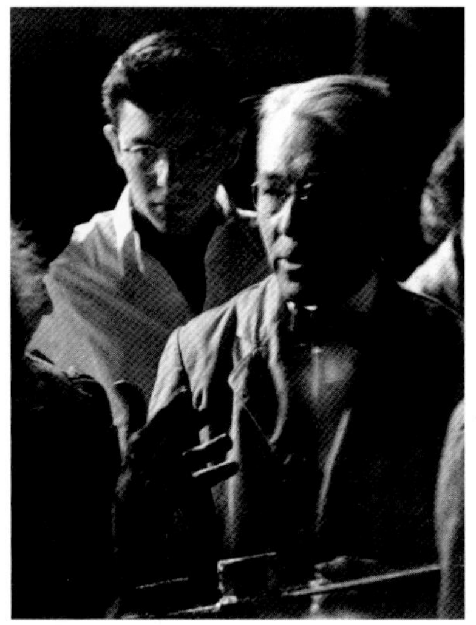
ERK and Wayman Adams, 1944

Having his days free allowed him to spend more time at some of the major galleries to study on his own. On one such visit to the National Academy he encountered one of his artistic heroes:

> I met Charles Dana Gibson in 1944 at a Red Cross Evening at the National Academy. I heard that Mr. Gibson was going to be there, so I went up to see him. The sculptor Jo Davidson was doing a bust of Gibson who was sitting on a high stool. I don't know how big he was but he looked awfully big to me, sitting there with his high stiff collar. He had a great bald dome and a very strong chin. I did a little pencil drawing at that moment of a bearded Jo Davidson sculpting Charles Dana Gibson right there while I was watching. It's now in the National Portrait Gallery collection.

In the early summer of 1945, he spent several weeks studying with Sidney Dickinson, a teacher at the Art Students League and portraitist. Later Ray painted landscapes with DuMond in Vermont. At the end of the summer, he was drafted, but he didn't have to report for active duty until December.

The Army

By then the war was officially over. The European war had ended in May and the Pacific war in August. Private Ray Kinstler was stationed at Fort Dix, New Jersey, and spent his entire stint in the Army processing the return and discharge of the fighting troops.

"Kid, you're it!"

It didn't take him long to make an impact. He volunteered at the base newspaper and was soon drawing a strip called *Strictly GI* on a regular basis. He eventually produced about forty episodes. And when one of the sergeants in charge of the mustering out was himself discharged, he turned to Ray and said, "Kid, you're it!" With that, he became Sergeant Everett Raymond Kinstler and took over the day-to-day organizational responsibilities.

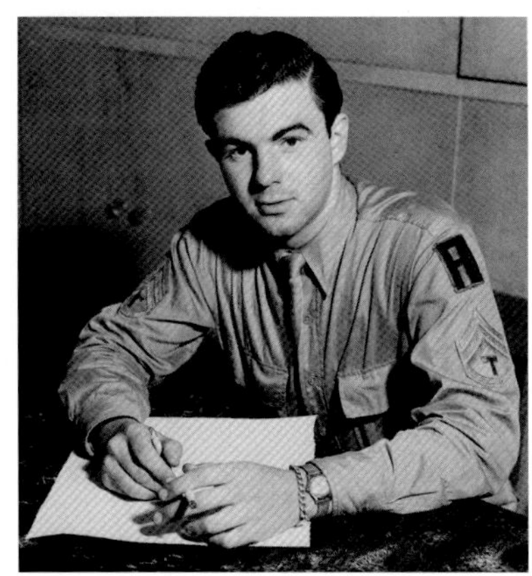
1946

Ray still recalls the name of that diabolical sergeant, Bernie Ginsberg, just as clearly he recalls the loss of individuality he felt while he was in the Army. One of the distractions he maintained that helped to sustain him was a constant stream of pulp illustration assignments.

Stationed just seventy-five miles south of New York City, it was easy for him to make the rounds delivering art and picking up new jobs on a day trip. In fact, since the "weekend pass" was the most desired, Ray was often able to negotiate advantageous trades. He would gladly give one weekend pass in exchange for a couple of two-day week*day* passes, when the publishers' offices were open. On the weekend he could stay in camp and actually earn some money drawing.

His drawings continued to appear throughout the year in many pulp titles for Popular Publications, for Street & Smith's ***Doc Savage*** and even in a few issues of ***Astounding Science Fiction*** where he was credited as simply *Raymond.* In December of 1946, he went home for good.

Post-War

The service experience had changed him. Throughout his time in the service, Ray maintained a relationship with Popular Publications and they continued to provide him with as much work as he wanted. But, he didn't want much. He was getting paid ten to fifteen dollars per illustration and could easily net one hundred dollars a week. Living at home with few ex-

Strictly GI, 1946

"Danger — Man At Work"

By Sgt. Everett Raymond

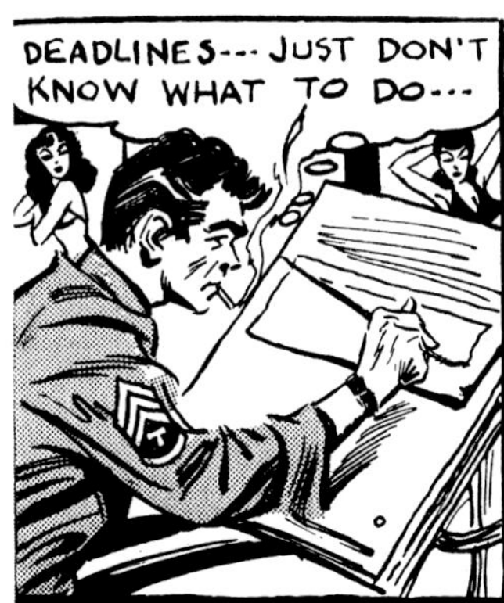

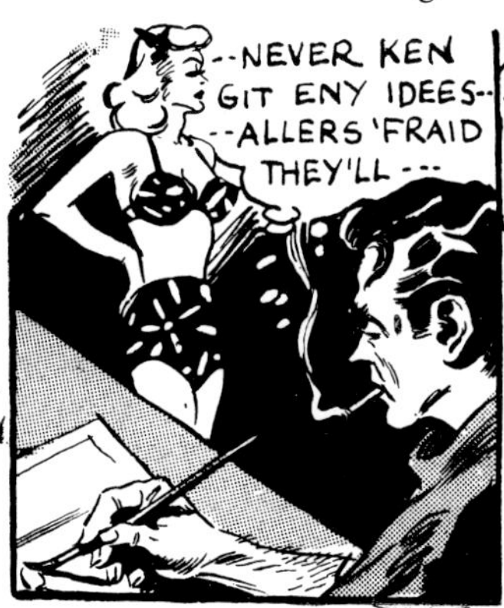

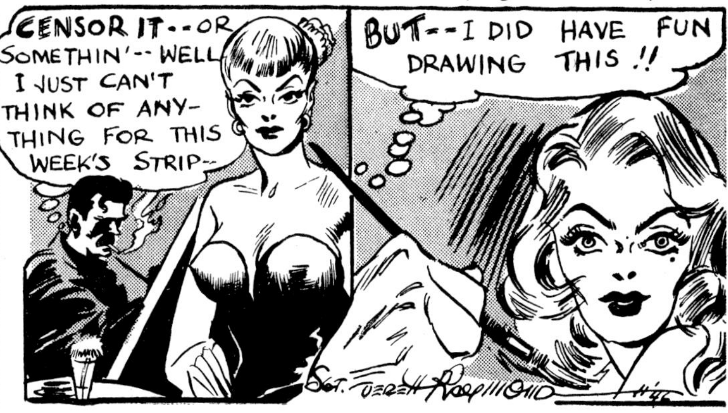

"This Dream's On Me . . . "

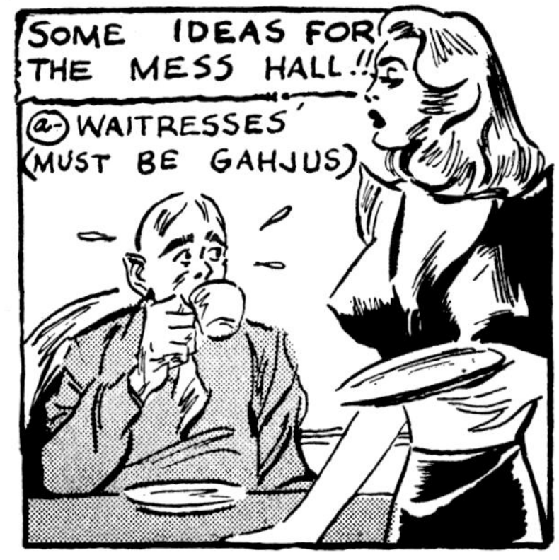

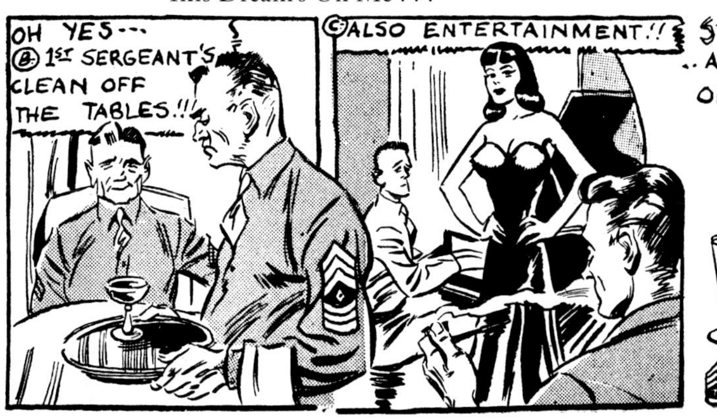

"Dog Face Data"

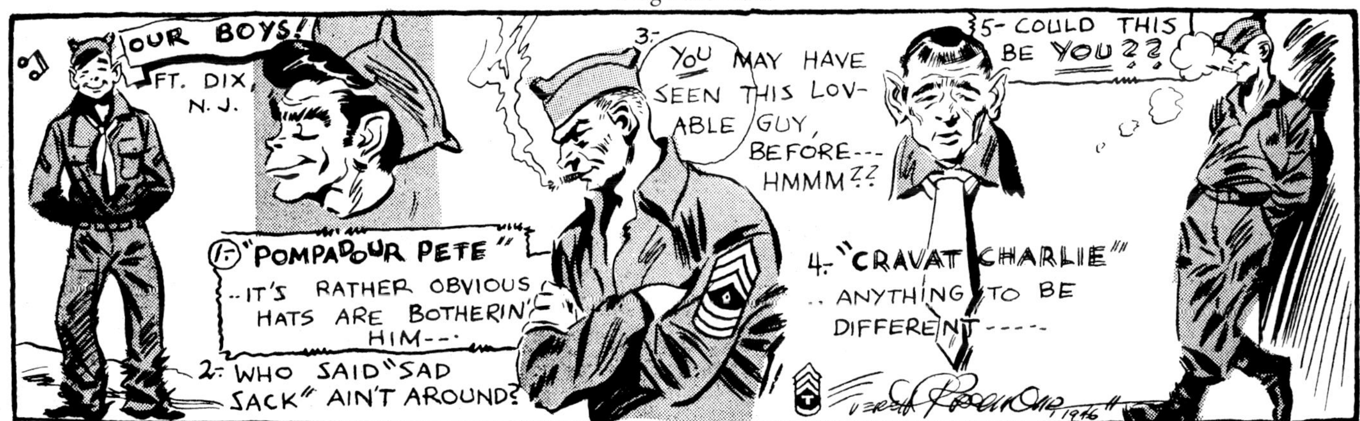

"What's Up, Doc ? ?"

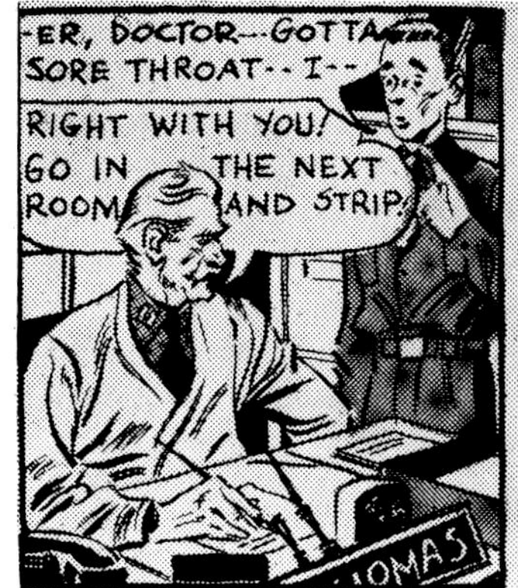

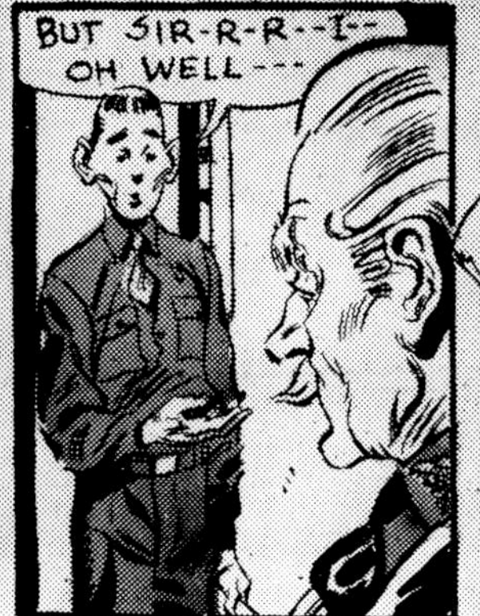

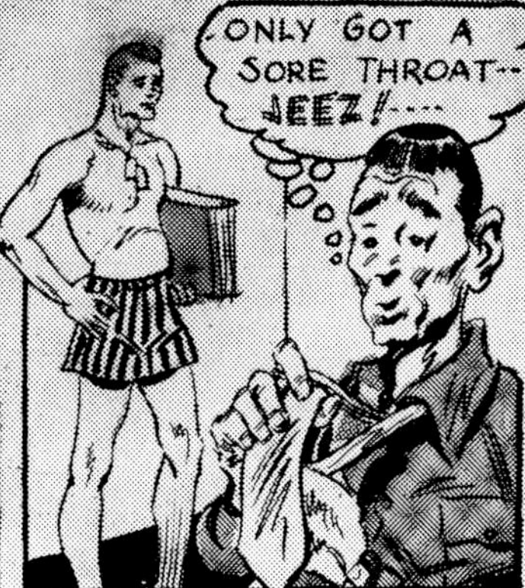

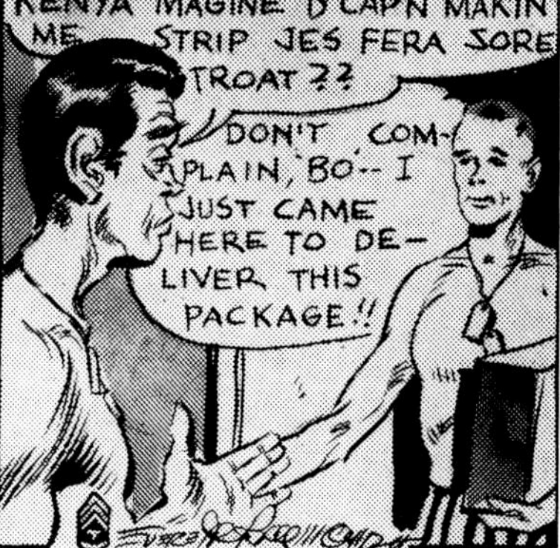

"It was time for me to get to work."

penses, he was free to devote much of his time to painting. His goal was still a career illustrating for ***Collier's*** and ***The Saturday Evening Post***. To achieve it he knew that he had to have a first rate professional portfolio. He knew that meant as much time devoted to painting as to earning a living.

> When I came home, I went back to living on E. 90th Street with my parents and using that little "maid's room" on the roof of their building as my studio. My father had paid the rent on it all during my stint in the Army.
>
> I wanted to go back to school, so I went to see Mr. DuMond at The Art Students League. I just walked in—and walked out. I guess you really can't go home again. It wasn't different, but I was. I knew it was time for me to get to work.

In addition to his pulp work, Ray turned again to the comic books, this time aiming for the top echelon—National Periodicals, the home of *Superman*. He drew four stories for them in early 1947, including two in ***Flash Comics*** featuring the winged hero *Hawkman*, but the people and the assignments didn't resonate with him, so he began to focus more on painting and the pulps. It would be almost two years before he would return to the comics medium.

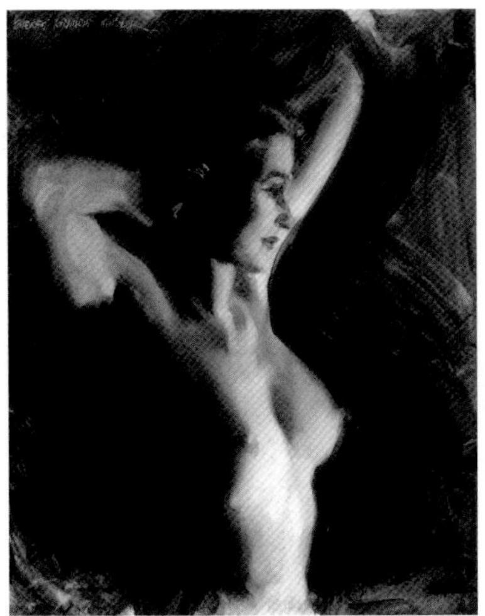

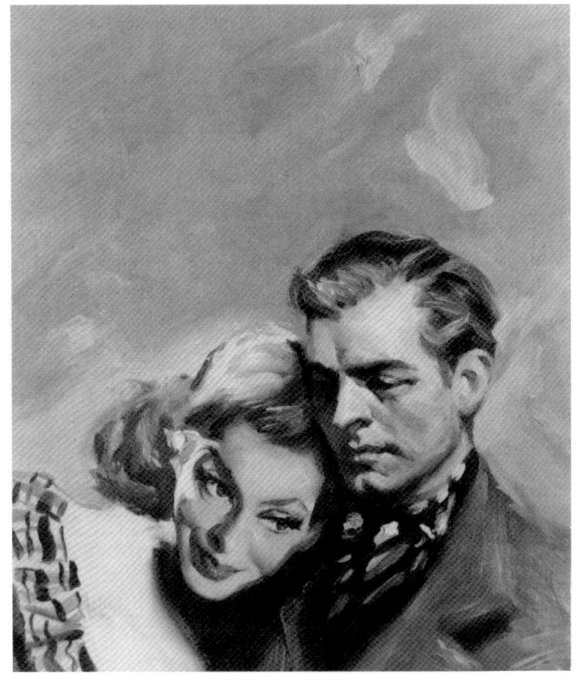

personal works
1947

Working at home led to the acquaintance of a neighbor in the same building who had just returned from the war. Bernie was five years older than Ray and had seen action in the Battle of the Bulge and was with troops that liberated some of the concentration camps. In early 1947, he planned a peacetime return visit to Europe and invited Ray to accompany him. Ray had a cousin who worked for the Holland-American line and got discount tickets for them. It was a ten-day sea voyage and it included a stop in Nova Scotia to pick up Canadian war brides.

This was the first time Ray had ever been out of the country. When they landed in France, they rented a car and drove through Alsace-Lorraine, a section of northern France bordering Germany which was bitterly contested by the two countries in both of the World Wars. Bernie was revisiting places he'd seen in the war and Ray was absorbing a whole new world. He had an old Windsor-Newton watercolor set that fit in his jacket pocket. Everywhere they went, Ray sketched. They drove through France and then into Italy where they toured Florence and Rome.

Six weeks in Europe went by too fast, though some of the memories are still fresh in his mind.

GBS & ERK

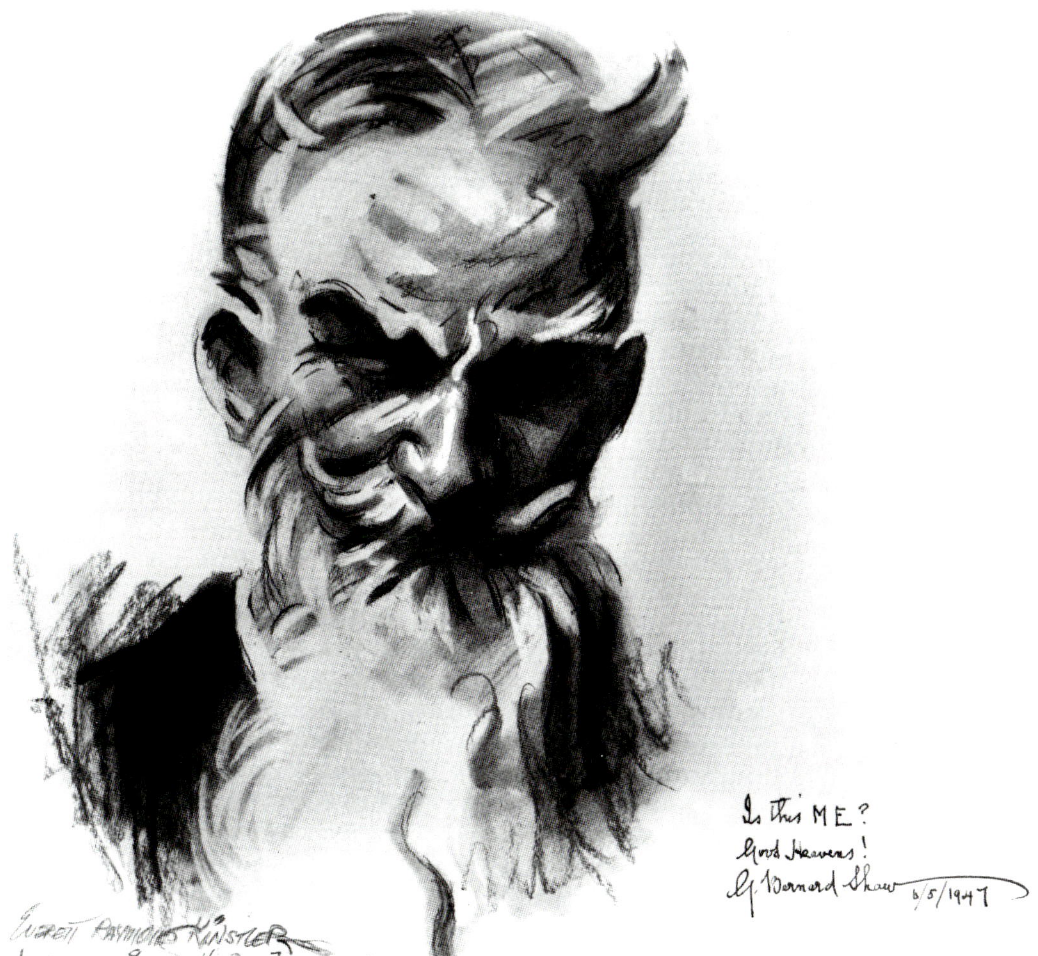

On July 26, 1947, George Bernard Shaw was to be ninety-two years old. ***The New York Times*** was preparing a retrospective of the life and work of the aging playwright. Letters were sent to Mr. Shaw requesting an interview or, barring that, some sage comments on the upcoming event.

What the prestigious Newspaper of Record received was a postcard from Mr. Shaw with a preprinted statement on the message side something like the following:

Bernard Shaw is unavailable for:

☐ Autographs	☑ Comments
☑ Interviews	☐ Photographs

The Times was relegated to printing a reproduction of the card, with the check marks as the great man's only contribution to the celebration.

While he was in the Army, Kinstler read whenever he wasn't drawing or soldiering. He discovered a favorite in the works of G.B. Shaw.

Ray has always felt the need to "connect" with those he admired. Throughout his life he reached out to people with the enthusiasm of a fan. He was twenty years old when he crafted this portrait, obtained Shaw's address in England, and mailed it off to him with a letter expressing his appreciation and admiration for Mr. Shaw and his writings.

Ray recalls reading the ***Times*** newspaper article and thinking "I guess I'm never going to see that drawing again!" He was wrong.

A month later, Kinstler's enthusiasm, talent and energy obtained that which the venerable ***Times*** could not: George Bernard Shaw's autograph and a personal comment as well.

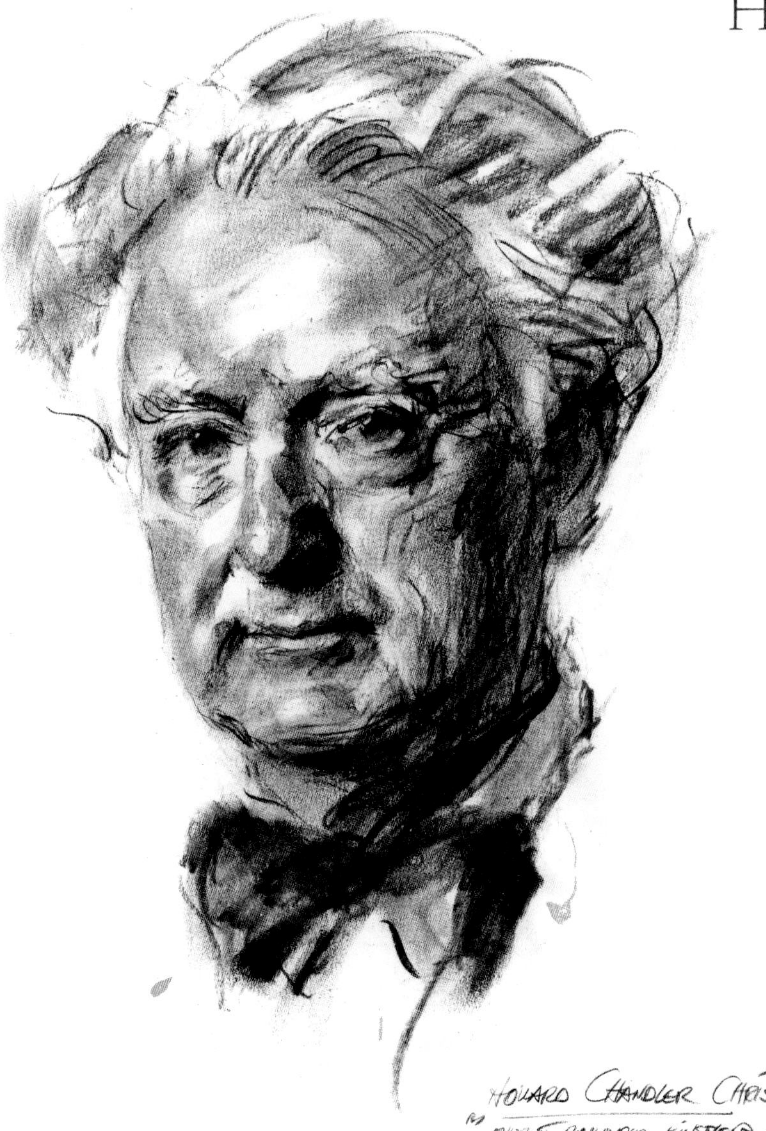

In 1948, Kinstler 'took a summer' near Provincetown with Jerry Farnsworth, a member of The National Academy and a regional painter who also painted portraits. Ray, who was always looking to improve himself, had seen some of Farnsworth's paintings and he thought it might be good to study with him.

He bought his first used car for the trip up to North Truro, Massachusetts, where he would spend the summer.

Also taking the same painting class with Mr. Farnsworth was a woman named Elsie Crowell. Over the course of the summer they compared their work. When Ray showed her some of his illustration work, Miss Crowell recognized Ray's influences, and told him that her cousin was Elise Ford.

Miss Ford was a model for, and some say mistress of, Howard Chandler Christy. She had posed for him for his NRA posters and for many of the nudes in the Hotel Des Artistes.

Christy was another of Ray's 'giants' and his enthusiasm bubbled to the surface. "I'd love to meet Mr. Christy," he told her. Eventually, in the autumn of 1949, Elsie Crowell took Ray to meet Mr. Christy at his studio at #1 W. 67th Street, which was upstairs from the Des Artistes Café.

The meeting went well. They arranged to meet again and Ray began a portrait which he finished in his studio. Later, Christy inscribed it: "With appreciation for a fine and truthful portrait, with admiration, Howard Chandler Christy." The drawing is now in the National Portrait Gallery.

I remember staying in Paris at the Rue Du Colisée Hotel off the Champs Elysées. It was probably about fifteen bucks a night. I used to buy a bottle of champagne for a dollar and some pâté de foie gras and French bread. I remember taking a bath once and looking out over the rooftops as I ate the foie gras and bread and drank the champagne. And I don't think that in the nearly sixty years since that I've ever enjoyed a meal more.

"It was heaven. I was twenty-two."

The pulp assignments continued to be steady and the money was sufficient for his needs, but Ray wasn't satisfied. Though he wasn't taking classes at the Art Students League, he still visited Frank V. DuMond at his studio at The National Arts Club on Gramercy Park. There they talked art and illustration and DuMond would critique the paintings Ray was doing for his portfolio. A strong friendship developed.

Mister DuMond got *me* a studio at the National Arts Club in 1949. I moved out of my little "maid's house" studio and worked (and sometimes *lived)* there in one room on the sixth floor overlooking Gramercy Park. It was all of twelve feet by eighteen feet with a single bed, a hotplate, chest of drawers, etc. It was heaven. I was twenty-two.

DuMond had a "duplex" studio a couple floors above me. I'd see him every day.

Every day at The National Arts Club brought new challenges and opportunities. Ray was a high school dropout in the midst of a "colony" of educated, in-

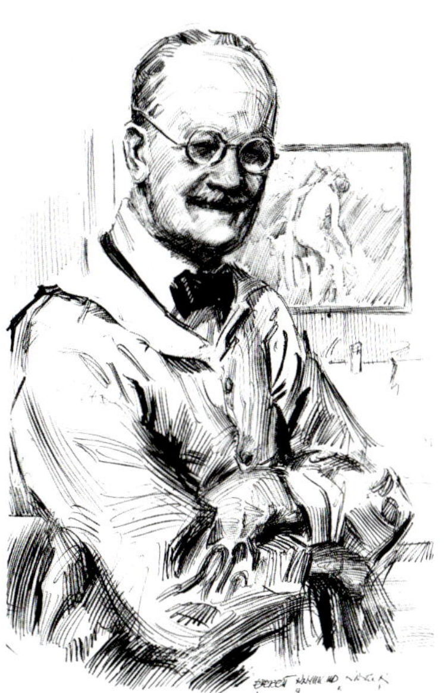

Frank Vincent DuMond
1951

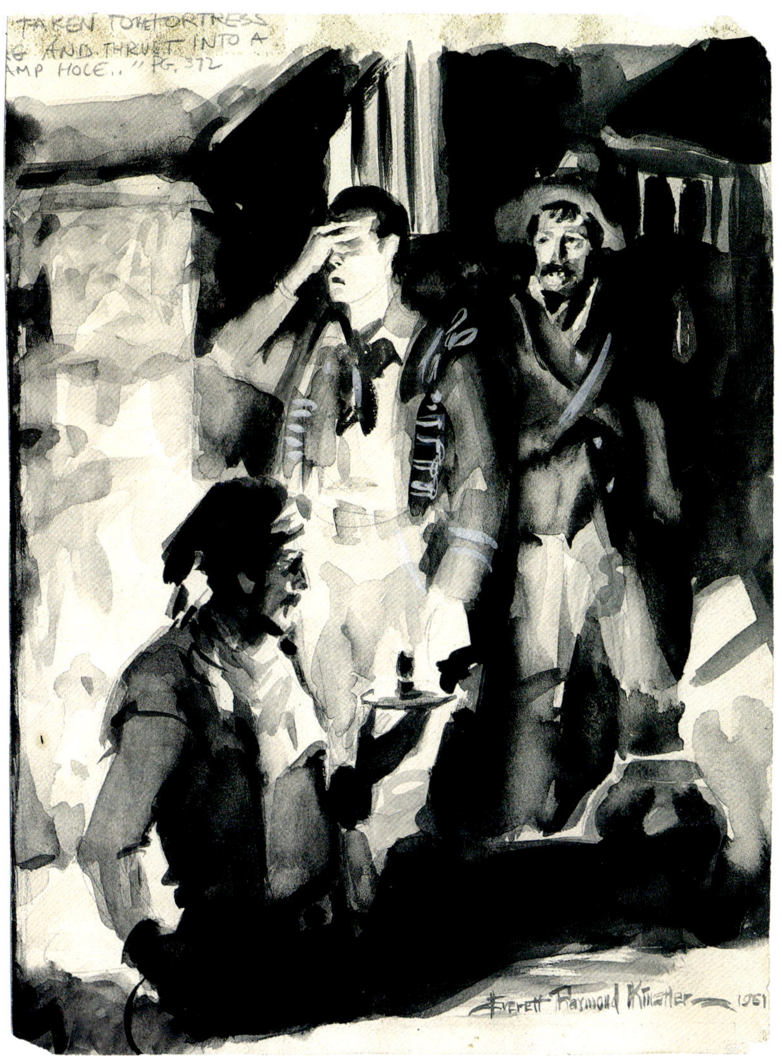

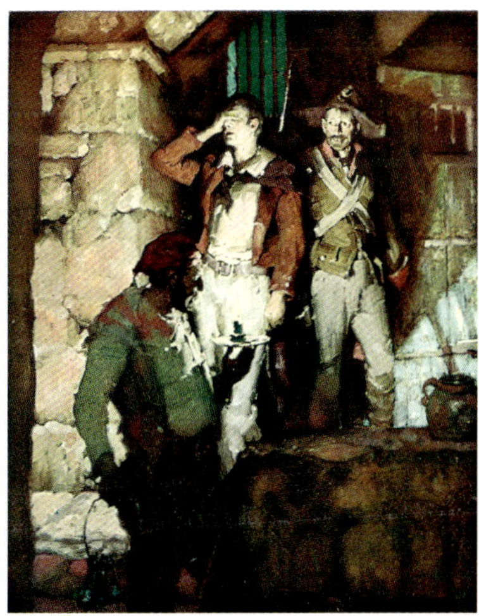

tonal study
November, 1951
and inspiration by
Mead Schaeffer from
The Count of Monte Cristo circa 1927

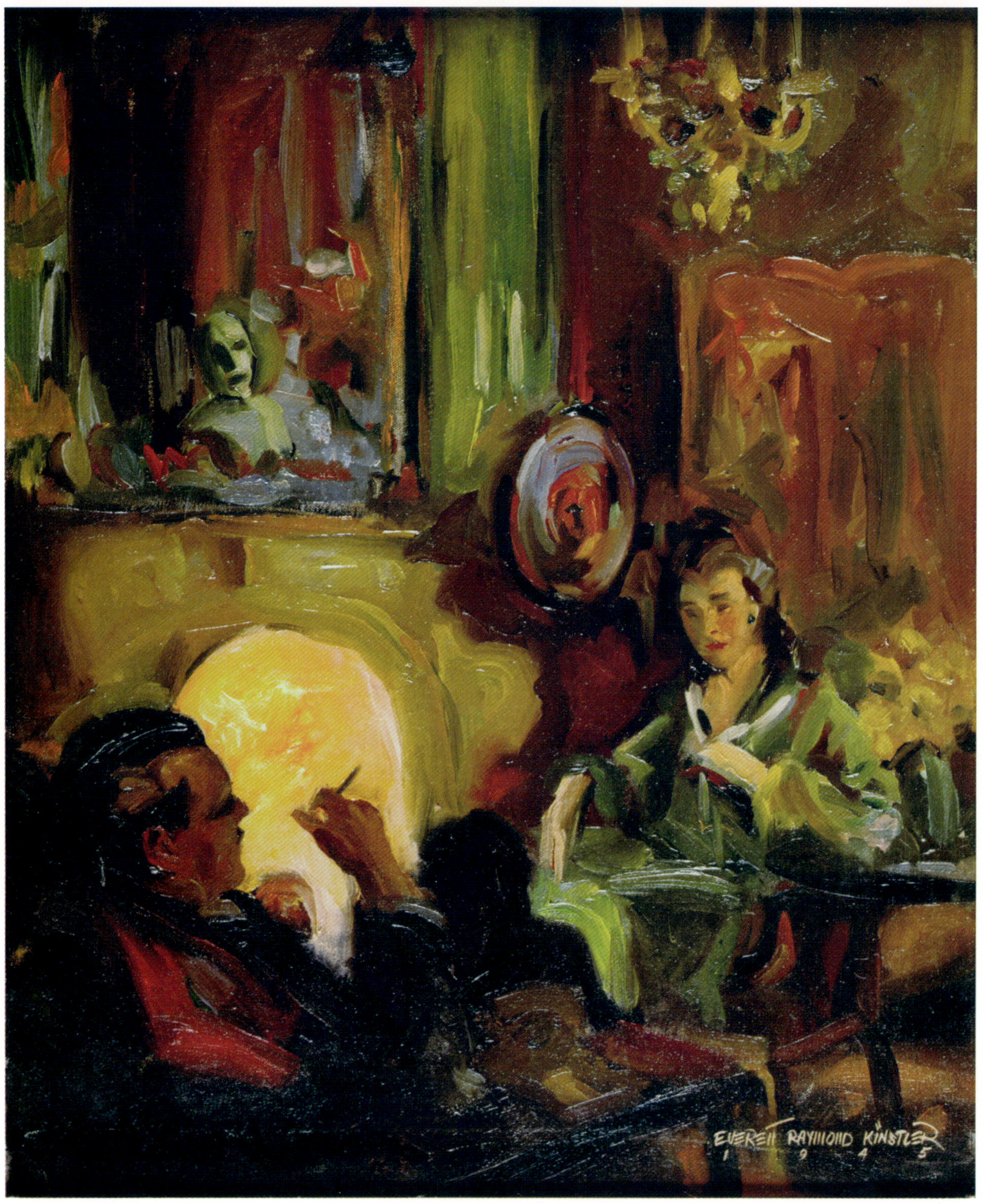

painting exercise, 1945

formed and sophisticated people. Despite some initial trepidations, he fit right in, partly because he never stopped educating himself. Learning had become a way of life for him—but at his pace and with his curriculum.

If he wanted to study Joaquin Sorolla, he would visit the Museum of the Hispanic Society of America and view the work of this great Spanish impressionist. If the next week he felt like reading Bernard Shaw, he did that. He went regularly to the opera with his friend Bernie, who was a member of the claque—a group given passes to operas in return for their applause to stimulate the reactions of the full audience. There he developed a life-long love of opera. This familiarity with the art form would eventually be a deciding factor in his being selected to illustrate two books. His life became part of his art.

Ray's art was filled with interpretations of the works of many of his illustrative idols. Over time, the lessons of these studies were incorporated into his own style or else they gave way to the next influence and the next examination and the next study.

"He was so into art that it just rubbed off on you."

By 1948, Ray had a few of his paintings reproduced as covers for some Fawcett Publications western comic books. It was a beginning. It wasn't ***Collier's***, but any cover painting had greater prestige than interior work. He never did any additional paintings for comic books, though he would eventually create many covers in pen and ink for Avon and he would soon be painting covers for pulps like ***Short Stories***.

While at Fawcett he remade the acquaintance of Bob Rickwell who became a life-long friend. He still remembers the young Kinstler:

"Ray Kinstler would come in with his portfolio under one arm and assignments under the other. We'd known each other from the High School of Industrial Arts. He quickly got a reputation for his drawings, but he was bucking the stylistic trends of the market even then. Still he was always a sincere and straight kind of person with lots of energy and drive—and he was *so* into art that it just rubbed off on you."

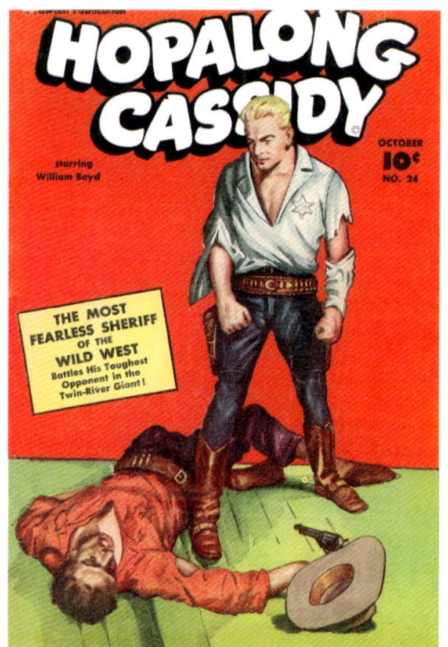

Hopalong Cassidy #24
Fawcett Publications
October, 1948

Rickwell was the Fawcett art director for a line of magazines that straddled the gap between the pulps and the more prestigious slicks—at least with the type of artwork they utilized. It could easily be said that the content of magazines like ***True Police Cases***, ***Startling Detective Adventures*** and ***Daring Detective*** was just as sensational as the pulps, but they were in magazine format and printed on slicker paper. The illustrations they used were in line and wash, with much better reproduction. It's no wonder Ray tried to get his work in them. He didn't.

The Rickwell connection got him those few assignments with the Fawcett comics arm. Ray only did one ***Hopalong Cassidy*** and two ***Tom Mix*** covers then went back to the pulps.

Ray spent the remainder of the 1940s working for ***Short Stories Magazine***, ***Adventure Magazine***, ***Ranch Romances***, and others. He dipped his hand back into the comic books, again with top-ranked National Periodicals, when the romance genre became popular.

Still, paramount in his mind was the goal of selling illustrations to the "quality" magazines. His personal paintings emulated the styles of popular illustrators of the day, like his John Gannam study at right. His intent was to show art directors that he could do the same work that they were used to getting from their current pool of artists. He never tried to convince them that he was as good as John Gannam or Mead Schaeffer or Howard Chandler Christy, any more than he was trying to fool DuMond when he was painting reproductions of John Singer Sargent and Anders Zorn as class exercises.

The various portfolio pieces were meant to convey versatility and the ability to capture an emotional level that was required to break into the market. After all, if he wanted to join these masters, he needed to work at their level.

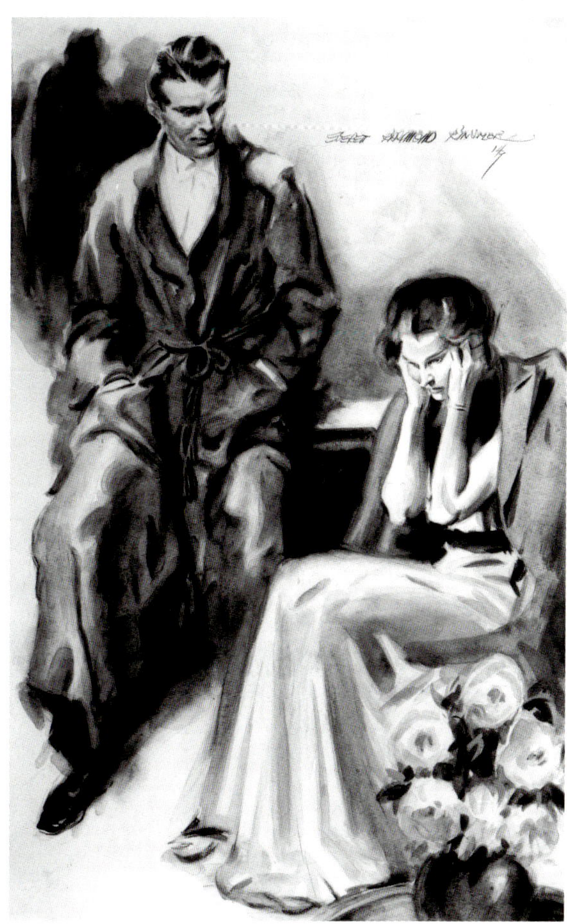

personal work
1949

The National Arts Club

Outside of the comics field, his world was changing. Kinstler's first two years at the National Arts Club at Gramercy Park had broadened his horizons and sharpened his skills immensely. While he still resided on 90th Street, he was no longer isolated in his rooftop studio. Prior to the new studio, he had only interacted with fellow artists during classes, which he was no longer taking, or during chance encounters at the offices of publishers and the occasional social interactions that followed. Such get-togethers for lunch or drinks focused more on marketing skills than artistic ones.

In order to succeed, Ray knew he needed both.

The National Arts Club was founded in 1898 as a society for the promotion of the arts. In 1906, the club purchased the mansion of Samuel Tilden at 15 Gramercy Park. It is a five-story building facing 20th Street and is currently a National Historic Landmark. A fourteen-story residential building was erected in the gardens and mews behind the mansion with an entrance on 19th Street. There are two floors of club and gallery space on the ground floors that connect to the mansion and twelve floors of studios above them.

By 1950, membership in the once-prestigious club had dwindled and the property had deteriorated to a point where a young Ray Kinstler could afford to rent a studio there. Some prominent members remained, but few of them lived at the club. Still they became a part of his life.

Ray in his first National Arts Club studio circa 1950

> The National Arts Club furnished me with a home and an atmosphere where people like DuMond were part of my daily life. Artist membership at the time included Dean Cornwell, Gordon Grant, John Johansen, and Ogden Pleissner—who also studied under Frank DuMond. I joined the club in 1947 and moved into the building in 1949. I was exhibiting in the Gallery as soon as I joined, so I would exhibit with these people regularly and would socialize with them there and in the building.
>
> There is only one elevator for fourteen floors in the "Annex," so I got to know most of the residents quite well.
>
> I never took any more art classes after 1947, but I had feedback from Mr. DuMond and John Johansen on a daily basis. Mr. Johansen would give me advice over the years, like: "Raymond, you must change the arm on that portrait. You mustn't let that painting go out like that." I saw him regularly; once or twice a day, but sometimes once a week. He was like a father to me. Well, a grandfather. These men also had another great quality. They knew that I was a serious, albeit young, artist; that I was honest; and they respected me to the point of allowing me to critique *their* work.
>
> And I would pose for John in his studio. There's a portrait of General Hap Arnold up at West Point that depicts *my* body. Once I posed as Bishop Fulton Sheen's arm and hand wearing his robes.

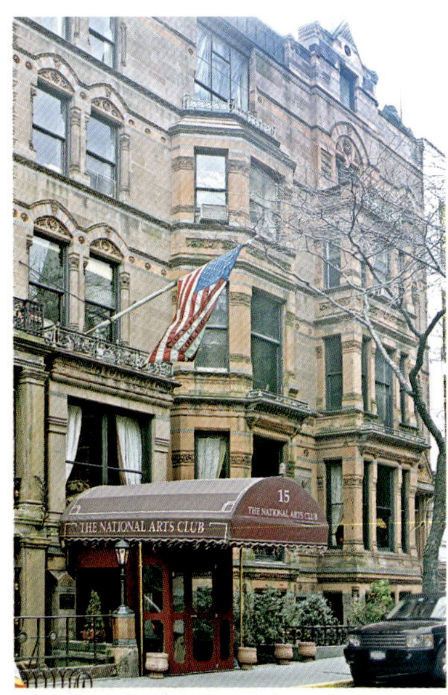

The National Arts Club today.

At Gramercy Park, artistic interactions became a part of his daily life. DuMond was just upstairs and could be approached for feedback and advice at a moment's notice. John Johansen, especially, became a close friend and mentor, immersing the young Kinstler in a live-in private art school with a class size of one. Class was always in session.

> When I moved into the National Arts Club building, it was very rundown—"on its uppers" as Flagg would say, referring to a pair of shoes so worn that the soles had holes in them and the upper soles were all that separated your foot from the pavement. We had fabulous paintings hung on the walls with the canvas coming

"Are you started?" I said, "I'm finished!"

obviously enjoyed the effort that Ray was expending on his behalf. Ray settled in for the long haul.

> My instincts carried me to places and people I enjoyed. So much of my life was based on instincts and a handshake and a twinkle of the eye. For Sol Cohen, I was soon drawing comic book stories that were fun and exciting—like ***Geronimo***, ***Jesse James*** and an entire issue of Western stories told by an early TV personality who called himself ***Sheriff Bob Dixon***. It was great fun.

The cover assignments were plentiful and Ray's facility led to his sharing the art chores on the ***Jesse James*** title. He alternated issues irregularly with the team of Joe Kubert and Carmine Infantino—a couple of youngsters his own age who were also making names for themselves in the industry.

Jesse James and ***Zorro*** are the titles most associated with Kinstler in comics. Both featured the outlaw as hero, a type exemplified in the movies by Douglas Fairbanks in such classics as *The Thief of Bagdad*, *Robin Hood*, *The Black Pirate* and two *Zorro* films. Kinstler had previously drawn a story for DC Comics titled "The Black Pirate" for which he took inspiration from the Fairbanks film. Now he was staging his own Westerns with cast and camera angles of his own devising. It was a lot more fun than rendering flying superheroes and text-heavy romance stories.

The first ***Jesse James*** by Kinstler was issue three. He drew the cover and two stories of eight and six pages, but there was also a one-page story on the inside of the front cover, printed in black and white, entitled "Jesse James and the Escape From Death!" As unremarkable as that may sound, it was a major turning point for Avon and for Ray Kinstler in that the page location became a setting for his most expressive pen and ink drawings.

The single-page story immediately gave way to an illustrated "preview of coming attractions" page where a collage of illustrations would serve as an invitation to and an opening look at the contents of the issue. As the covers were printed on better paper, the reproduction there was equivalent to that of the "slick" magazines to which Ray aspired. Quickly, an unspoken competition ensued among the artists doing these inside covers.

Ray and other artists like Wally Wood, Sid Check, Rafael Astarita, Philip "Tex" Blaisdell, Mort Lawrence, and Syd Shores would compete on a monthly basis to outdo themselves and each other. Some of these men seemed habitually wedded to the standard comic book approach, but others, like Kinstler, reveled in the advantages. Ray was always challenging himself with ever more complex compositions and more elaborate and innovative pen techniques.

> It was the most fun I ever had in comics.

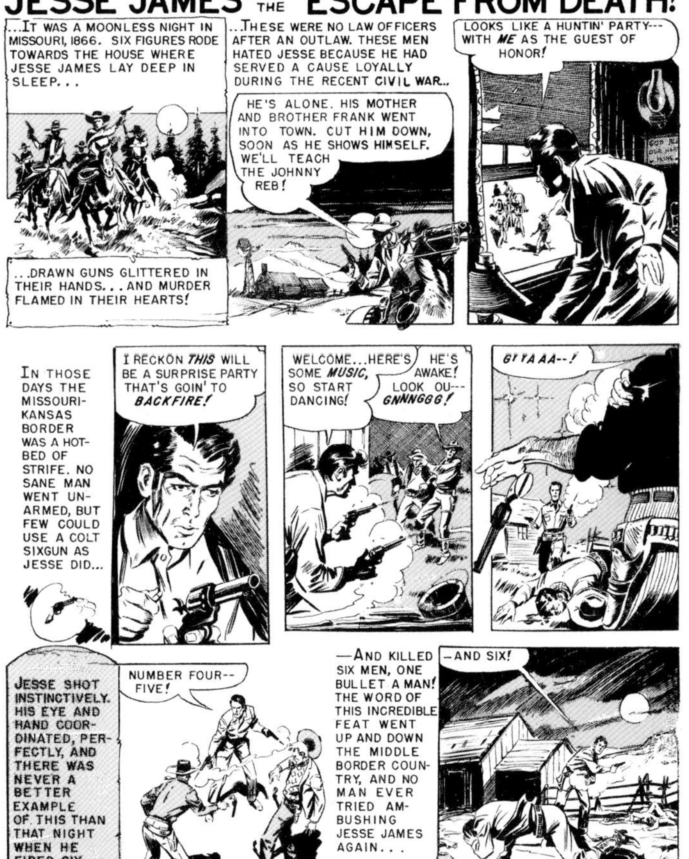

Jesse James #3
May, 1951

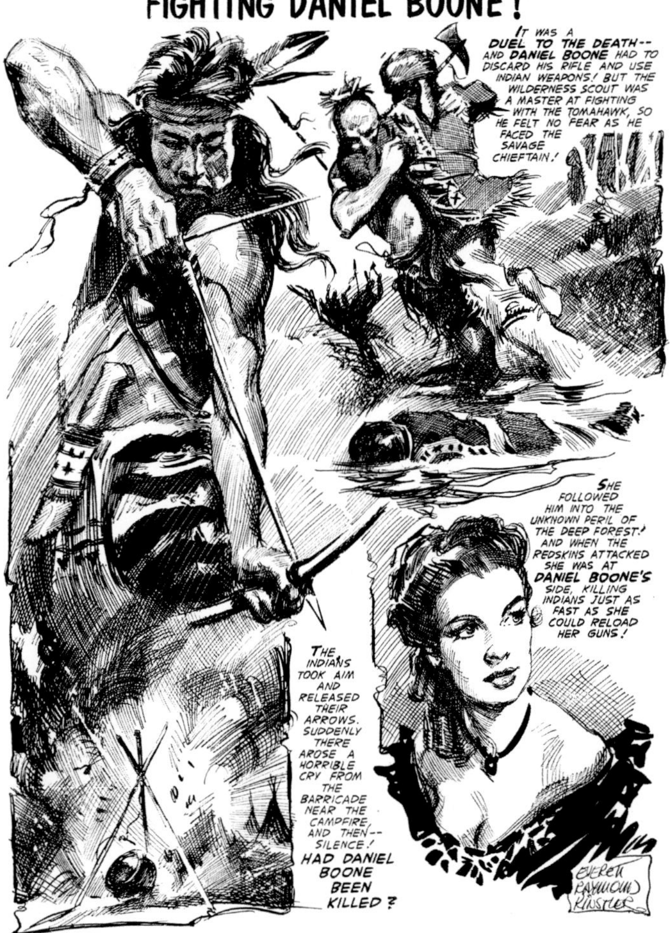

Daniel Boone?
In 1953, Ray drew twenty pages of what seems to be an adaptation of a George Montgomery "Daniel Boone" movie co-starring Helena Carter and Jay Silverheels, as the likenesses show.

He remembers getting stills to work from, little suspecting that they were from an adaptation of James Fenimore Cooper's **The Pathfinder**, and had no connection with Daniel Boone.

An Avon writer had simply restructured the story to star the famous Kentuckian, assuming that his name would be more familiar to comic book readers than Cooper's "Pathfinder" despite the recent 1953 George Montgomery film.

Armed with movie stills, a vivid imagination and equal amounts of ink and inspiration, Ray threw himself headlong into this new venue—producing some of the most intricate, complex and exciting published pen drawings of his career. Although many of his pulp illustrations compare quite favorably with these Avon drawings, none of them was ever reproduced in a pulp magazine even remotely close to the detail of the original. With these Avon inside covers, there was an impetus to experiment and stretch himself as an artist, with the results clearly evident on the printed page a month later. This was the first time he ever received such immediate and accurate feedback. He drew over seventy of them in less than two years. And Avon's entire ten year output of comic books only totaled about four hundred and ten issues.

He was quite aware of the value of his efforts as he carefully retrieved the original drawings for many of these. There's no evidence that Ray ever asked for any of his comic book interior pages to be returned. He has none of them.

In mid-1953, Avon dropped the practice, returning advertisements to the inside covers, and his experimentation took a different turn. Accepting the fact that his pen work would never accurately reproduce on the pulpish paper inside of a comic book, Kinstler adopted the more traditional comics rendering tool of the brush. He could draw faster with the brush and the way he told the stories began to take precedence over the way he rendered them.

1952 was very profitable for Ray, It would be eight years before he again reached the income level of that year, but the success came with a price. He had to deliver two hundred jobs, including one hundred and twenty-five to Avon alone. Each job required him to make at least one unique trip to the publisher. The time he spent picking up and delivering jobs was eating into the time he could devote to actually working and to his personal paintings. Often he could combine visits to more than one company, but the outings were occurring three or four times a week.

Some of his 1952 work was for the Ziff-Davis Publishing Company, where the rates were half again as high as at Avon. It was there that he first met long time friend Herb Rogoff. Rogoff was one of the editors who replaced Jerry Siegel, the man who had been hired to launch the Z-D comic book line.

Rogoff, a comics veteran of five years, had been a sports cartoonist, a writer for Hillman Publications, and an assistant editor under Siegel. At the time Herb was promoted to the editor position, Ray Kinstler had only done one or two single-page 'fillers' for Siegel. "I had seen Ray's Ziff-Davis work," says Rogoff, "I thought he was ninety years old! This was James Montgomery Flagg in the flesh. When he came up to deliver a job and I saw him for the first time, I said, 'You can't be! You can't be Ray Kinstler. You're too young!' But he was, and he continued to produce the most marvelous pen and ink work I'd seen."

Rogoff also attended Music and Art High School but started a year after Ray. They were essentially the same age, which lends an informed air to his recollections of the young Kinstler.

“Ray was a good looking guy and he didn’t sound like he was from New York City. He dressed quite nattily and he liked baseball. The first job I gave him was to draw cover portraits of the hosts for our three sports comics. We had ***Bill Stern’s Sports Book***, ***Red Grange’s Football Thrills*** and ***Bob Feller’s Baseball Thrills***.

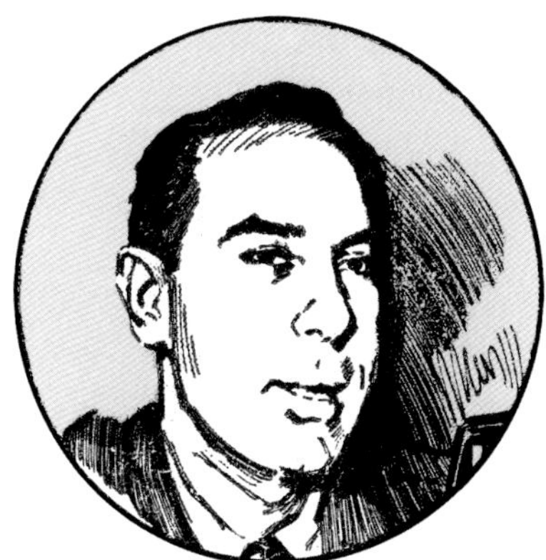

Bill Stern

“The only time I ever saw Ray disheveled was the time he painted a ***Wildboy*** cover for us overnight. It was a passable job, quite remarkable, actually, for an oil painting done start-to-finish in less than twenty hours. We paid him for it, but it was eventually replaced with a line drawing pen and ink cover. It was following a series of covers by famed pulp cover artist Norman Saunders and the discrepancy was just too great.”

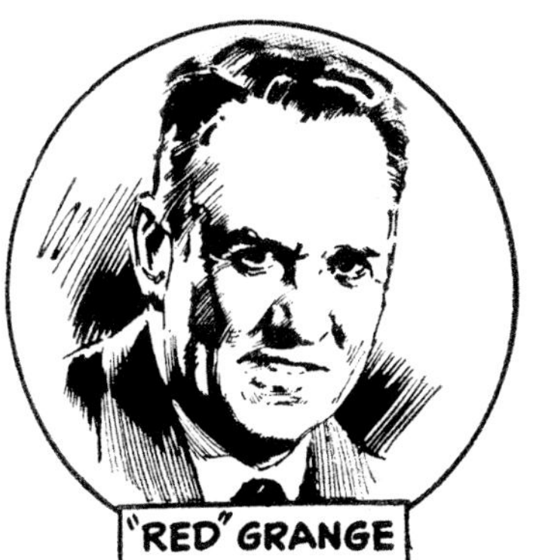

By 1953 the Ziff-Davis comic book line had folded. The inventory of stories and the reprint rights were sold to Archer St. John, who paid the same rates as everyone else. Ray did not pursue work at St. John but looked elsewhere in an effort to find assignments that would allow him to spend more time in the studio and less time on the streets of New York delivering jobs.

The difficulty lay in the nature of the pulp and comic book markets. The pulps required one or two illustrations per story. The comic book format was four to six stories per issue. The editors of both wanted variety, so an artist was seldom commissioned to illustrate more than a portion of an issue.

Dell/Western

There was one company bucking the trend of comics with multiple stories. That was Western Printing/Dell. Matt Murphy was the editor and his implementation of the anthology approach was to publish an ongoing series of comics with each issue devoted to a different character. If one particular character sold well, Murphy would devote another issue in the series to him. If it continued to sell, a new title would be introduced and the space in the ***Four Color Series***, as it was called, would be given over to a new character.

Ray walked into the Western offices in January of 1953 and was immediately assigned a thirty-four-page adaptation of a Max Brand western titled ***Silvertip***. The impact this made on his work schedule was immediate and enormous. Whereas in the first quarter of 1952 Ray worked on forty-four different jobs, in the same period of 1953 with the extended Western assignment, he did only nineteen and produced the same number of comic book pages. And when he delivered the finished ***Silvertip*** job in March, he picked up the script for ***The Sword of Zorro***.

Max Brand was the pseudonym of Frederick Faust, a prolific author who was killed in World War II. In addition to a half dozen *Silvertip* novels, he wrote over 250 books using a variety of pen names. Other famous Faust creations include *Destry* and *Doctor Kildare*.

That year, he pencilled and inked six thirty-four-page comic books for Matt Murphy. The only other comics work that Ray did was a five-page story for Stan Lee at Timely/Atlas and four covers and two inside covers for Avon. The Ziff-Davis assignments had tapered off as the company was winding down its comic book division. The black and white drawings on the inside of the Avon covers had been dropped in January. He still had the pulp assignments, including a new magazine from Avon, on which to maintain his facility with pen and ink. It was the long stories for Western and the continued pulp work for Popular Publications that kept him busy in 1953.

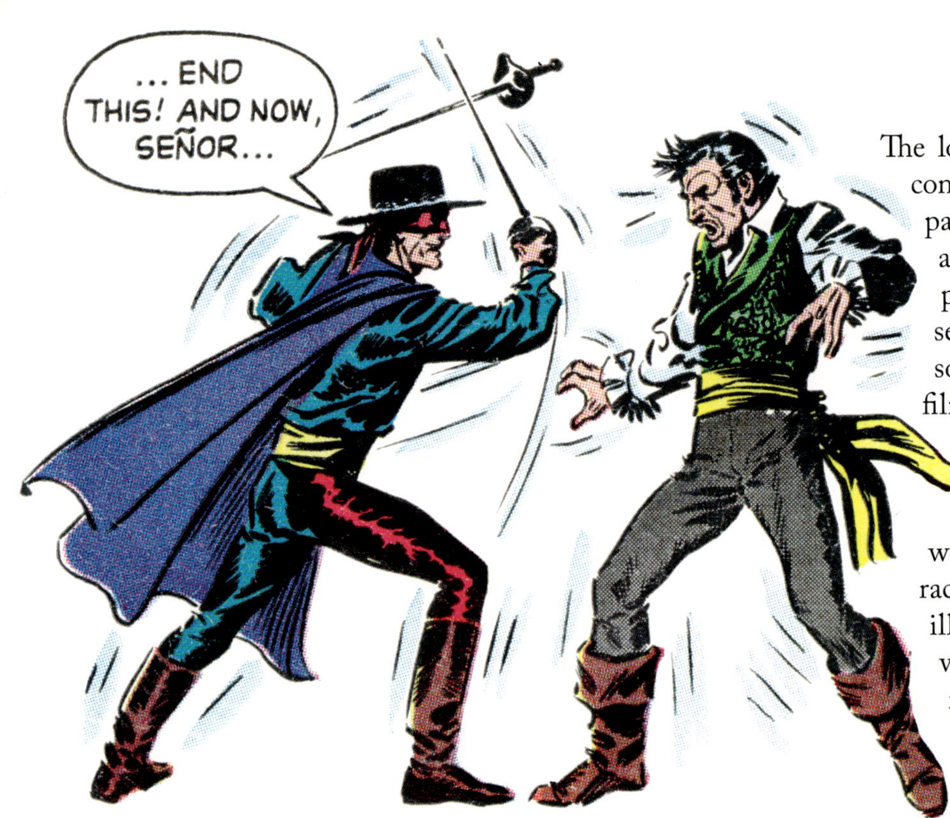

The longer stories brought out an aspect of comic books to which Ray had only been paying peripheral attention. That was the art of storytelling. Certainly he had applied to his earlier stories the lessons of sequential narration which he had absorbed from the newspaper strips and films of his youth, but these extended stories increased his awareness of the possibilities inherent in the medium. In shorter stories, clarity and brevity were the prime virtues as the narration raced along in the few pages allocated. The illustrator seldom had to be concerned with the more creative aspects of storytelling. There simply wasn't enough story being told, or if there was, it was as much in the text and dialog as in the pictures.

Ray was challenged with novel-length stories that allowed for, in fact required, character development, pacing and a certain amount of creative panel design in order to maintain reader interest over a prolonged story. His ability to depict types of characters and to maintain a consistent likeness from page to page stood him in good stead as he dealt with larger casts and more "screen time" for each cast member.

The other Kinstler-drawn 1953 titles in the ***Four Color Series*** were also westerns: ***Outlaw Trail*** (a Zane Grey adaptation), ***Western Marshall*** (Ernest Haycox), a second *Zorro* adaptation—***The Mask of Zorro***, and a second ***Silvertip***. It's obvious, from the fact that Ray was called upon to reprise two characters, that those introductory issues with his art must have sold well. There would be three additional Kinstler ***Western Marshall*** issues over the next few years, along with a third ***Zorro*** and probably five more ***Silvertips***.

With less time devoted to traipsing around Manhattan, Ray began to spend the extra time painting. He was preparing to take the first steps in a new career direction.

covers for some of the ***Dell Four Color Comics*** for which Kinstler did the interior drawings in 1953 and 1954

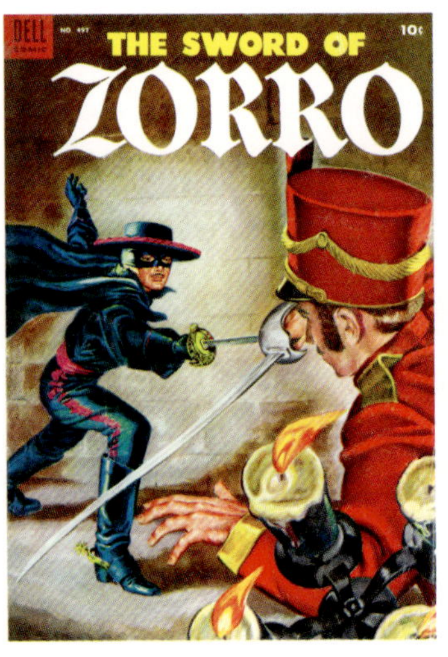

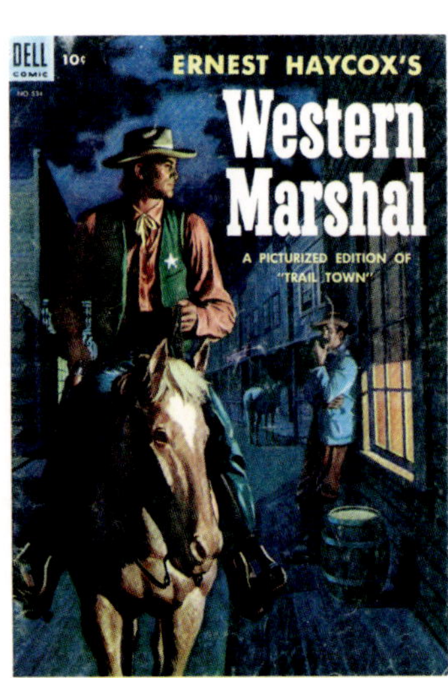

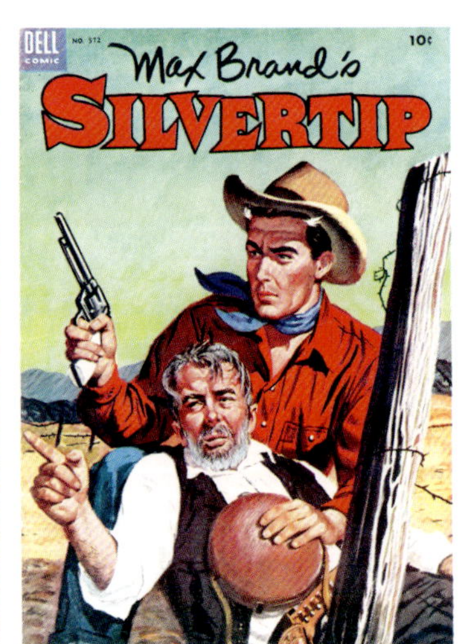

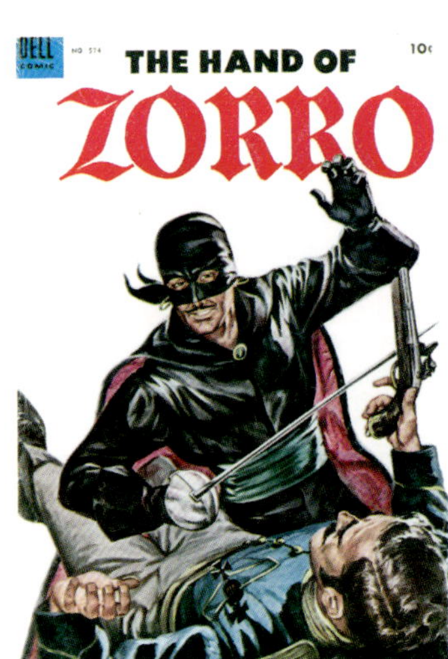

Europe 1954

But first there was a second excursion to Europe with his friend Bernie, and this time it was focused on music. In the summer of 1954, their destination was Germany for the Wagner festival in Bayreuth.

Ray's appreciation for music began with his love of singers like Bing Crosby whom he admired at the age of six. His tastes evolved into a love for the big band sounds of Artie Shaw and Benny Goodman, whom he and Bob Brustein, who played the clarinet, were able to see and hear on records and at the movies. He recalls going to see Art Tatum, the great jazz pianist, with his father just prior to Ray's induction into the Army. It took another leap forward when he began to accompany his friend Bernie to the opera.

> The nights I was free, I started going to the opera with Bernie, and I developed quite a love for it. That's what led to my doing the illustrations for **The Opera Companion** and **Verdi** for George Martin in 1961-63.
>
> They wanted someone who was really familiar with opera and I had been attending and enjoying opera since 1947 when Bernie introduced me to it via the claque.

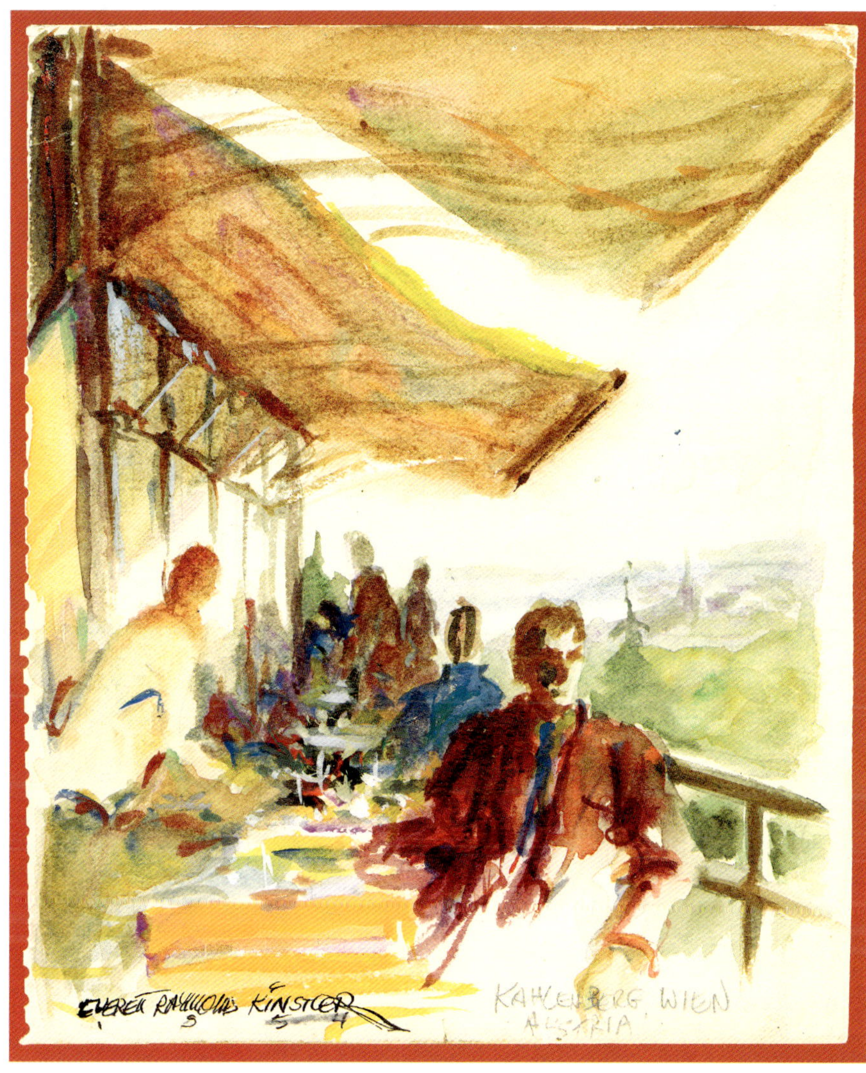

The second European trip deepened their appreciation for Wagner and Strauss. Their agenda took them to Bayreuth, where many of Wagner's operas were first staged and a festival is put on each year to commemorate his work. They also went to Vienna.

As with his first trip in 1947, Ray recorded the people and the towns in watercolors. It's our good fortune that several of these sketches have survived the ensuing half-century. Created using his pocket watercolor set and a spiral-bound pad of paper, the spontaneity and verve of these sketches demonstrates the discerning eye for color and composition that became a hallmark of his paintings and portraits.

They also reinforced his ongoing quest for personal expression and his ever growing need to create for himself rather than at the behest of an art director. These goals were constantly nurtured by his friends at the National Arts Club who urged him never to lose sight of that self-expressive aspect of his art and by the nature of many of the exhibitions that he would help to stage at the Club. His art began to take precedence over his occupation.

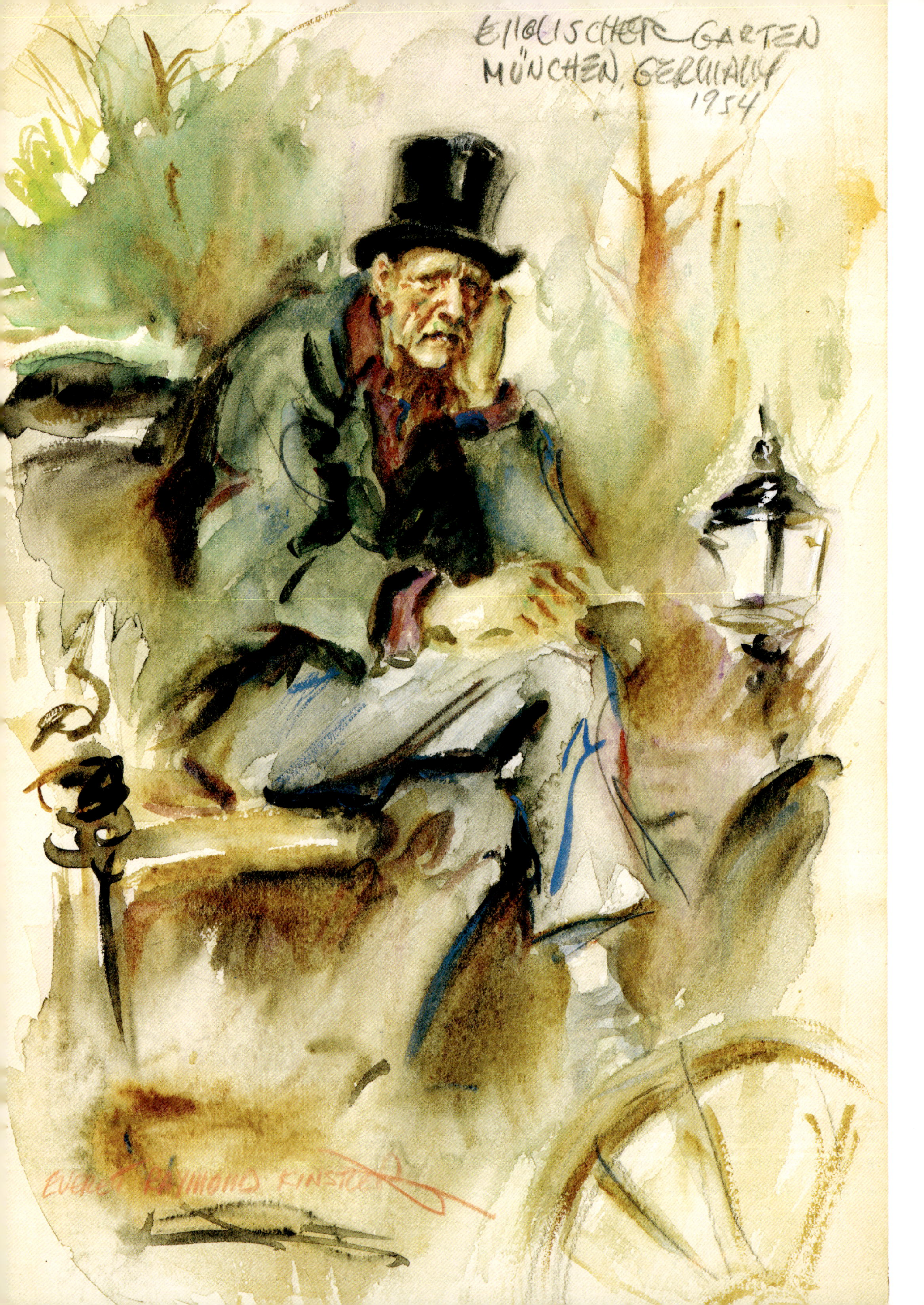
ENGLISCHER GARTEN
MÜNCHEN, GERMANY
1954

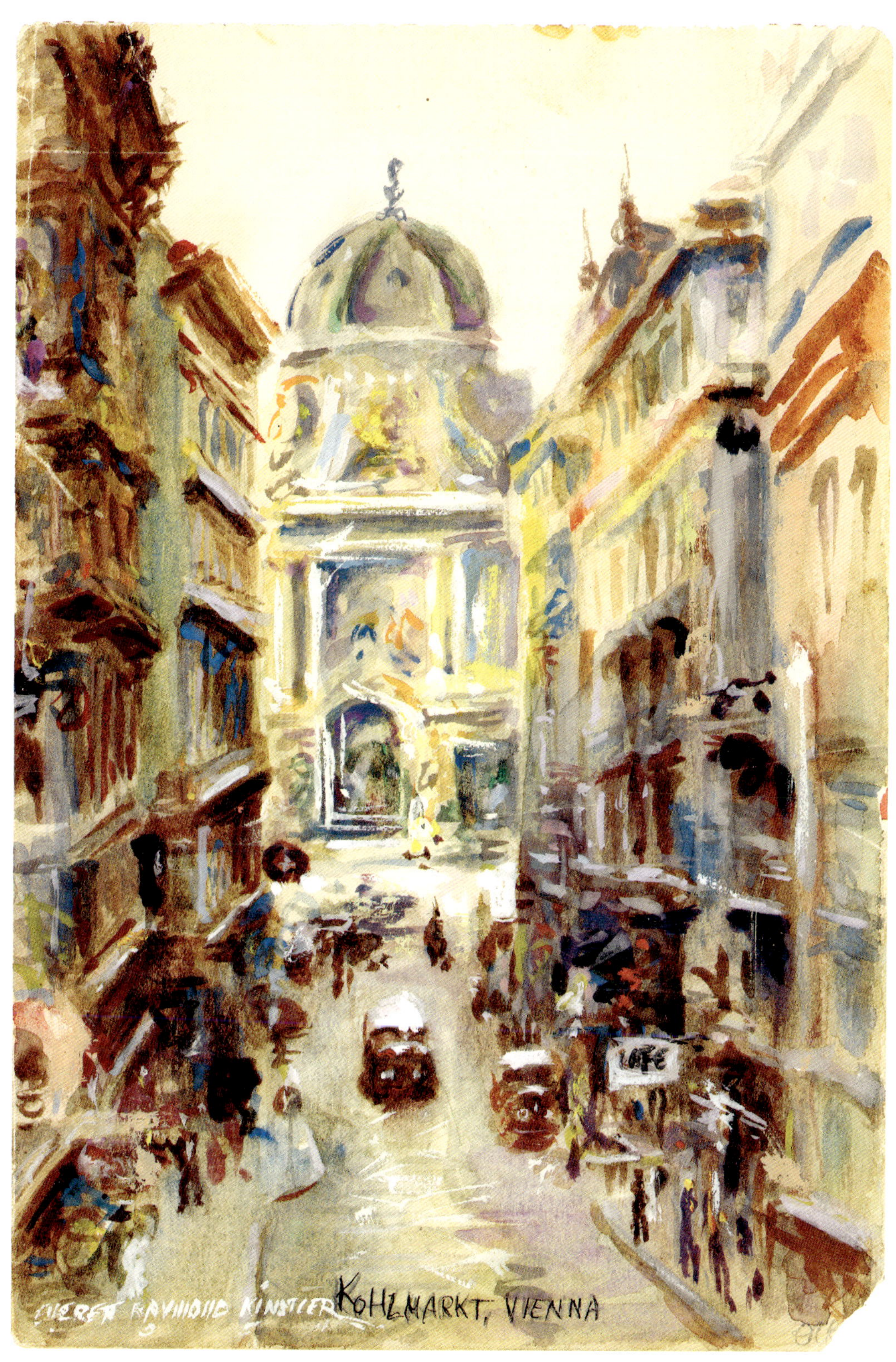

Watercolor sketches recording scenes from the 1954 European trip.

Flagg

"CIrcle 5-3153, I think it was."

The frenetic pace of servicing many small assignments and travelling between his home and his National Arts Club studio gave way to a more measured existence when he moved into the big duplex studio. Living there helped to develop Kinstler's social tendencies, too.

Elisabeth Gordon Chandler is a sculptor who went on to found the Lyme Academy College of Fine Arts in Old Lyme, Connecticut. She and her husband Robert moved into one of the duplex studios a few floors below Ray around 1952. The club membership was only about four hundred and the residential building was sparsely occupied, somewhat rundown, having seen better days. There was only one elevator and all of the residents got to know each other, intimately, from that elevator.

> Elisabeth and I were showing in the same exhibitions at the National Arts Club. Once, when visiting her studio, I saw a very fine bronze she'd done of James Montgomery Flagg. I told the Chandlers that I had met him in 1944 at the Parc Vendome. Elisabeth told me that she used to have a studio there, "right next to Monty. I got to know him well and saw him going up and down the elevator. He had a beautiful head and I wanted to do a bronze of him."
>
> Flagg took her into his studio and showed her a bust done of him by Wheeler Williams and asked her, "Can you do one as good as that?"
>
> "It was very intimidating but he was sweet and posed for me. We lived next to him for a couple of years and we keep in touch with him." I said I'd love to meet him again. She told me "We're going to get him down for dinner on Sunday night and we'll invite you."
>
> He came with his secretary, Florence Fair. Elisabeth had cautioned me that he didn't look like he did in 1944, but he looked *great* to me. He didn't remember our earlier meeting, but later in the evening, the secretary said to me, "Monty would really like to have you call him. Here's his number." CIrcle 5-3153, I think it was.
>
> So I called, and he invited me to have dinner with him and that was the beginning of our friendship. It was that simple. I went up to his studio one night a week; had dinner with him at Sardi's every Wednesday night for many years—until I met my wife Lea around 1957. I saw him once a week for five years.

When Ray first met him, Flagg was still a practicing illustrator, although very much in the twilight of his career. That career began in 1893 when he was fifteen with drawings in the old humor magazine, ***Life***, and was winding down at the Hearst Sunday Supplement, ***The American Weekly***—the same publication that gave J.C. Leyendecker an outlet when even ***The Saturday Evening Post*** would not give work to their most prolific cover artist.

Flagg's autobiography, **Roses and Buckshot**, was published in 1946. His eyesight and popularity faded over the ensuing years so that by 1953, he was relegated by all but a few friends to the painful status of a has-been. For a proud man who had experienced the most dizzying heights of fame that society could bestow, this was a bitter pill to swallow. It was one thing to skirt around the edges of polite society, a role that Flagg had played to the hilt, but he did not take gracefully to simply being ignored.

It was this démodé James Montgomery Flagg who asked Ray Kinstler to call on him at his 57th Street studio. And it was into a dwindling circle of friends that Ray was welcomed. Other than the Chandlers there were only Dean Cornwell, Arthur William Brown and Rube Goldberg.

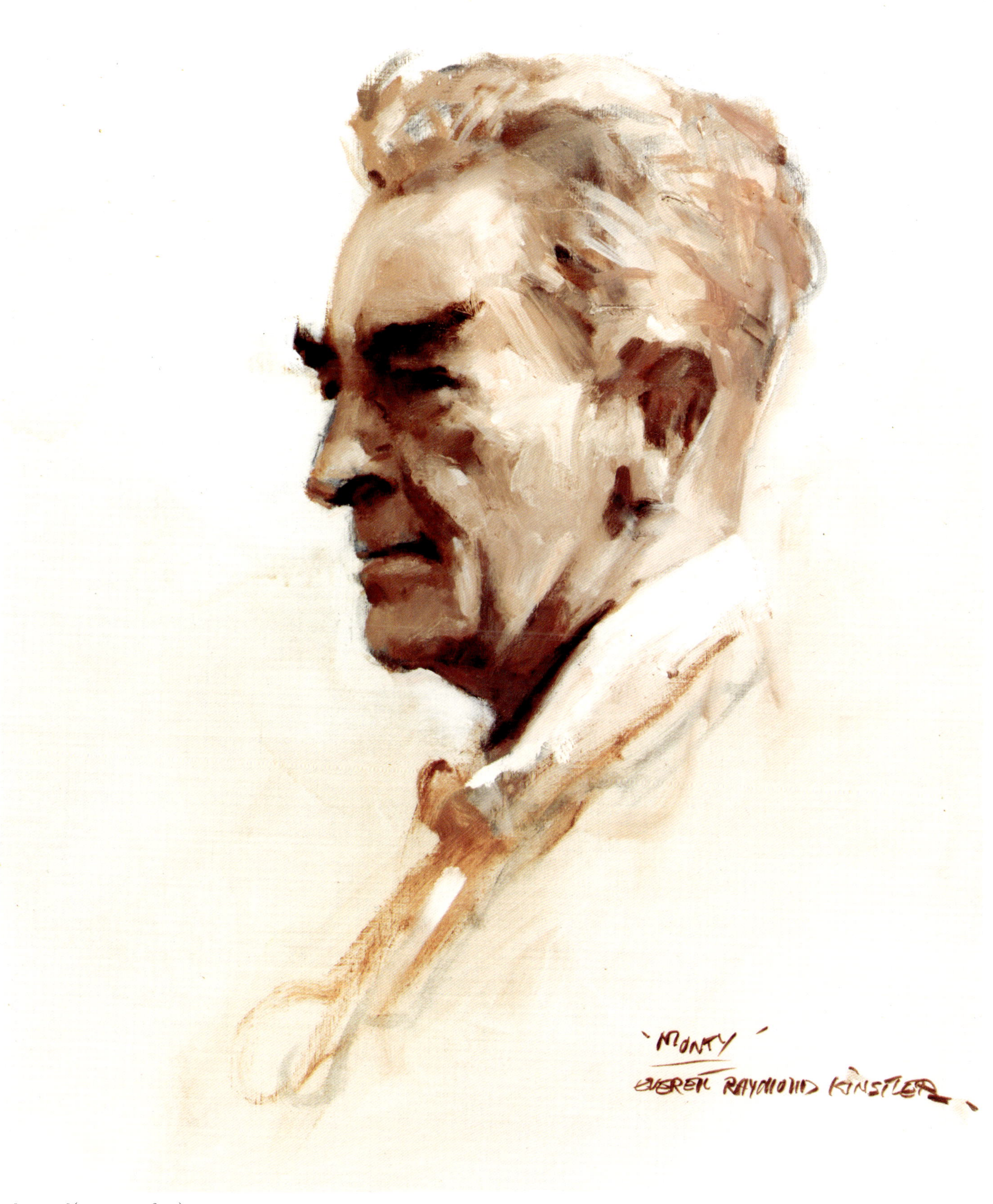

"Monty" (50 years after), 2003

"They don't make 'em like that any more."

And they were getting to the point where they couldn't take it anymore. He was difficult… embarrassing to be with because he was very rude. That didn't bother me. He *was* very difficult, but it was because he was very unhappy.

I would visit him on Wednesdays and go to dinner with him at Sardi's. We'd take a taxi. It was only twelve blocks, but it was too much for Monty. I'd always have to tell him, "Monty, let me pay for the cab." Every time. It wasn't much, but to me it was a lot. I'd have to take the subway home because it only cost a nickel and that was all I could afford after getting the two taxi bills. He would pay for the dinner, but I always paid for the cab.

Once when walking to the cab stand after dinner at Sardi's, we passed two young "packers" who were bundling newspapers to deliver to the newsstands in the morning. They were used to seeing Flagg walk past on his way to get a cab. They greeted him with a warm, "Good evening, sir." and Flagg said "Howdy young fellers." As we walked on, I heard one of them say to the other, "Boy, they don't make 'em like that any more."

That was a major part of the appeal for Ray. Flagg's generation of artists was passing and so many of its contributions to art, history and society were being overlooked, ignored or simply dismissed by the then-current art world. Being around Flagg, even just one night a week, was a reconfirmation of Kinstler's artistic predilections. He learned much from Flagg on those Wednesday nights. It was more than dinner at Sardi's. There were hours spent studying drawings and paintings—of Flagg and his contemporaries—and just talking about art. He especially enjoyed hearing Flagg's reminiscences of an era and a commercial art community that was becoming increasingly distant and unimaginable to Kinstler. There was also the joy of that shared appreciation of art, illustration, and the comfort of just being friends.

James Montgomery Flagg and Everett Raymond Kinstler, taken just two months before Flagg's death. 1960.

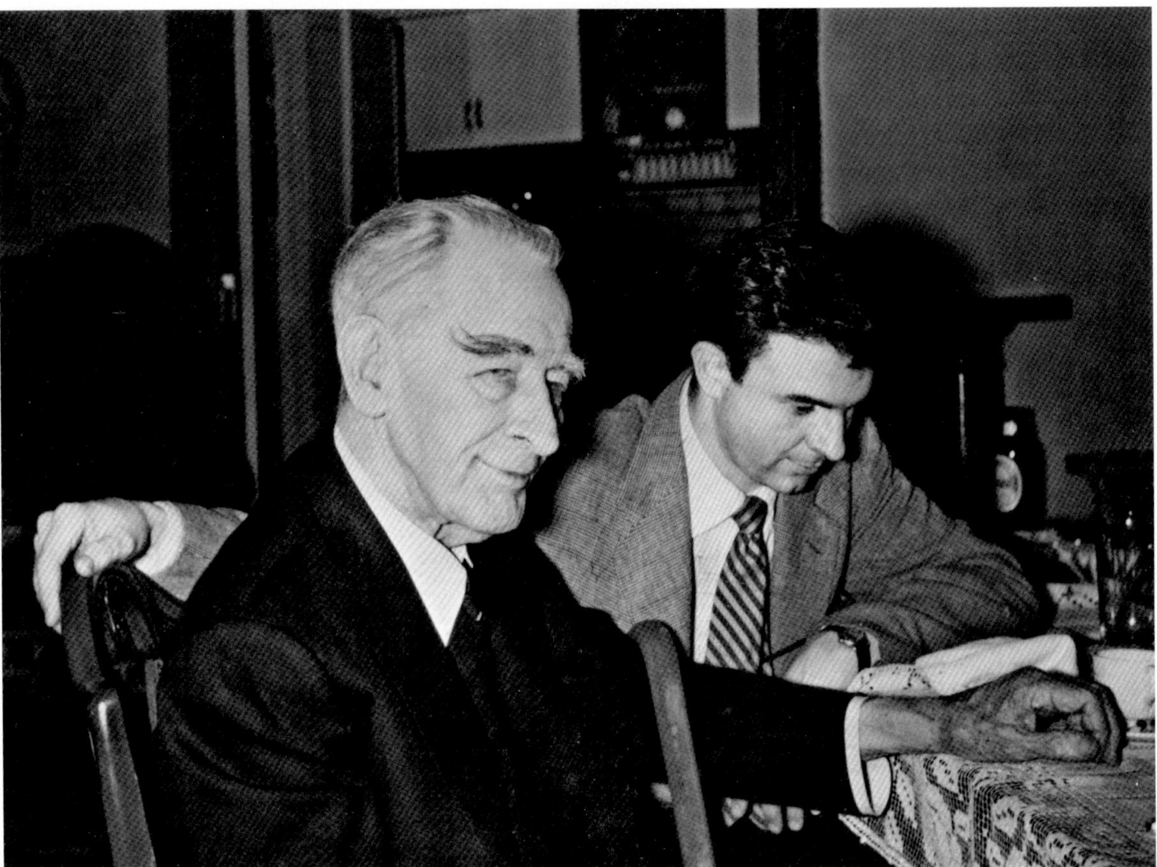

But before going to dinner, we'd visit in his studio. We talked about painting, art, Sargent, contemporary art, people he had known who had been part of his life through six decades, including John Barrymore, Charles Dana Gibson, both Teddy and Franklin D. Roosevelt.

Monty loved words and limericks—he nourished my love of limericks—so there was a great deal of laughter and healthy banter. It was all persiflage, what I used to call James Montgomery-Flage. We would have Cutty Sark scotch "neat" and smoke Lucky Strikes and he would usually doze off.

On the large studio walls were drawings, paintings, portraits, watercolors—and I never tired of looking at them. He had a large closet that contained hundreds of his original magazine illustrations and I would pore over them. I was among a few close friends, including Dean Cornwell, who delivered eulogies at his funeral.

The year they were reintroduced, Kinstler drew this portrait of Flagg. When Ray finished the drawing, Flagg looked at it, scrawled "It's me" across the bottom, and signed it.

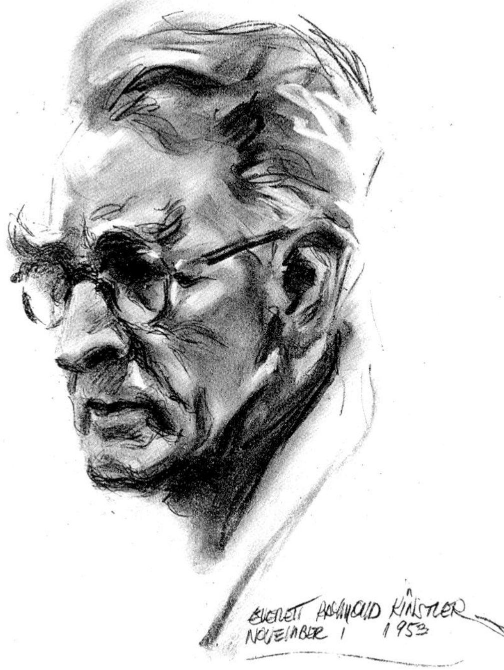

It was a great fulfillment to me. I could tell, even with his limited vision, that he was pleased with the style, with the statement. He could see that it was solid draftsmanship and had flair. I felt then, and I still feel, that I nailed his likeness.

For Ray, the drawing was an emotional connection as well as an artistic one relating to a man whom he had admired most of his life.

I remember years ago when Flagg first came down to my studio, and I showed him a drawing I did when I was about eight years old. The caption was **Everett Raymond Kinstler copied this from JMF**. Flagg, in his inimitable way, said, "It's a little bit better than you do today." Which really warmed us up. He had a *lovely* way of getting to your heart. But you had to look past that.

Ray is a person who easily looked beyond the surface gruffness and found the man who was still worthy of his admiration and friendship.

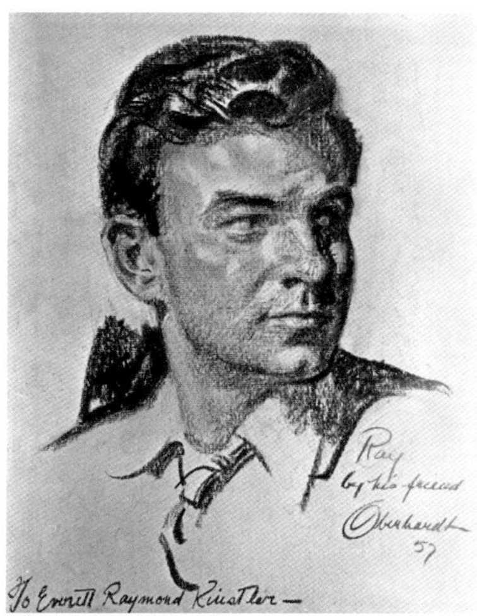

Everett Raymond Kinstler, by William Oberhardt. 1957

As the decade wore on, the old-guard of the illustration world was fading—into obscurity and death. His friend William Oberhardt, who had done this bright portrait of Kinstler in 1957, died in 1958. And as much as Ray admired the popular illustrators of his day, Rockwell and Lovell, Schaeffer and Gannam, Harold von Schmidt and Coby Whitmore, he revered those of the previous generation—Flagg, Cornwell, Oberhardt, etc. Some of these older men rallied around Flagg in the Fifties and kept their friend company during those twilight years, both figuratively and literally as a series of strokes steadily decreased Flagg's eyesight and increased his isolation.

"Any name after mine is sheer impertinence."

Dean was Sunday night, Brownie would come another evening, and a companion would be with him the other days. Monty couldn't see any more and he couldn't draw. His whole world was visual and that loss made him irascible.

It was a difficult time in Flagg's life. He was burned out and a very frustrated and bitter man. And he knew it. Occasionally he'd turn to me and say, "I wasn't always like this. I used to be a lot of fun."

I'd remember that when something he did would ruffle some feathers. When I joined the Society of Illustrators, I needed a member to propose me and another to second the nomination. In 1956, Flagg was my proposer and after he signed the letter he wrote under his signature: "Any name after mine is sheer impertinence." When I took the nomination letter to Arthur William Brown for his seconding signature, Brownie said "What's he trying to do, keep you *out*?"

Ray Kinstler, at thirty, was two generations removed from these men, but seemed to easily share their companionship and interests. He gave the eulogy at Flagg's funeral in 1960 and was one of the pallbearers at Dean Cornwell's that same year. At a time when the rest of the world had consigned these men to the status of historical footnotes, Kinstler became the repository of at least a portion of their knowledge and techniques. He did this by befriending them and believing in his own assessment of the worth of the men and their work.

He also acted as a conservator of Flagg's collection of art and memories, without which Susan E. Meyers' 1974 book on him would never have been written. Many treasured examples of Flagg's drawings in The National Portrait Gallery were preserved and donated by Ray. To this day in his studio he still paints on Flagg's easel and imparts to *his* students some of the precepts he learned from discussions on those Wednesday nights so long ago.

Books

The comic book industry was facing harsh public and social criticism for its supposed contributions to the growing juvenile deliquency problems of the 1950s. Ziff-Davis sold its fledgling comic book line to Archer St. John in 1953, eliminating one of Ray's markets. Avon cut back on the number of titles it published and in 1954 began to fill some of the existing ones with reprinted material. Ray executed over a dozen Avon covers in 1954, but not a single new interior page. He took on a new facet of the cover designs, however, with the addition of "coloring" to his responsibilities. It was an artistic decision, since the extra $3.50 per cover certainly wasn't sufficient incentive.

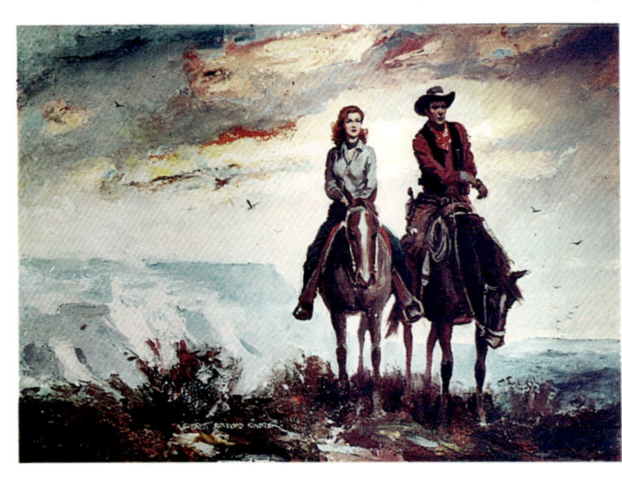

That year Ray created two covers for comic publisher Lev Gleason, but that company soon joined Avon in retrenching to fewer, and more innocuous, titles in the face of the anti-comics pressure. He did one illustration for ***Bluebook*** in 1954 and two Columbia Records album sleeve paintings. There were also a stream of titles for Matt Murphy at Western/Dell and a regular output of pulp drawings for ***Ranch Romances***.

An important breakthrough that year was his first dustwrapper painting for a hardcover book. Grosset and Dunlap was well-known for its inexpensive reprints of popular fiction and the early Fifties edition of Zane Grey's 1912 classic, **Riders of the Purple Sage** was enhanced by this Kinstler jacket painting.

As the comic book and pulp markets shrank, his painting skills began to earn him assignments in the growing paperback book industry, especially at Avon Books.

> Charlie Byrnes was the editor for paperbacks at Avon. He later went to Ballantine Books. I showed him some of my painting samples and in 1954 he began to give me cover assignments. My first was a western, but I quickly "graduated" to other types. It became convenient for me to combine a delivery to Sol Cohen of a comic book cover and a delivery to Charlie of a paperback cover painting.

Avon releases were often new, retitled editions. Ray was frequently required to compose a cover painting that reflected a salacious new title. **Here Comes the King**, by Philip Lindsay, is an historical novel about Catharine Howard, the fifth wife of Henry VIII. Its Avon incarnation was retitled **Royal Scandal** and featured a suggestive, though chastely-draped, Catharine in bed while a generic nobleman admires the view.

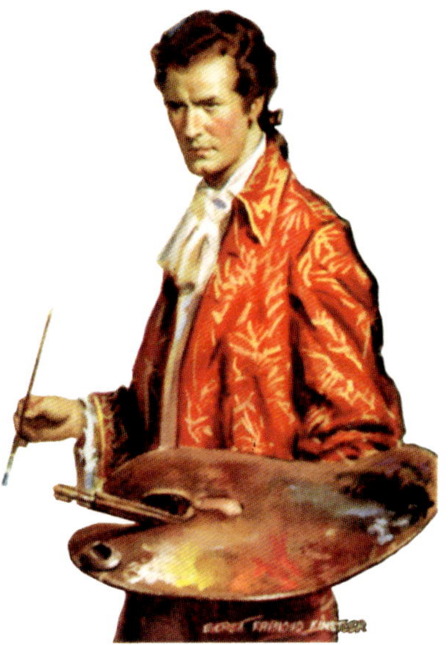

Bob Brustein was the model for this 1954 paperback cover, painted for **Artist in Love**.

From their prior experience with the pulp magazines, paperback publishers knew that sex and westerns sold books. The term *paperback rights* became a publishing staple. Though initially looked down upon by "serious" book publishers and underappreciated and undervalued, such rights gave many new novels an extended life as a retitled paperback.

Likeness and type began to blend as Ray began to rely more heavily on models to pose for the covers. Steve Holland, who would later pose for James Bama in the 1960s on a series of covers as the quintessential *Doc Savage*, was a hero type. Ray photographed him in costume for several paperback covers and he appeared in many guises in the illustrations Ray did for the men's magazines of the 1950s. Steve sometimes modeled for all of the figures in a painting and Ray worked hard to alter his body language, attitude and facial features, as in the black and white oil painting below.

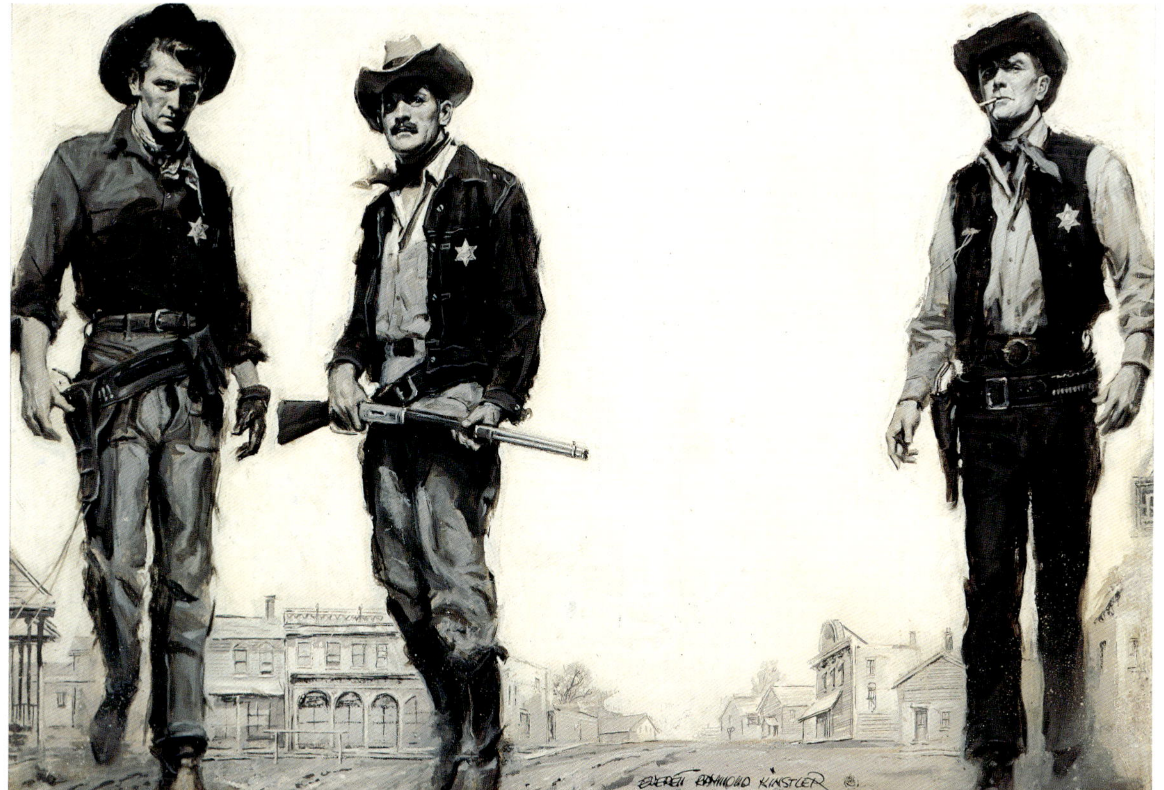

Steve Holland was a professional model whom Ray used frequently; here in a painting done for a Martin Goodman men's magazine, circa 1957.

Kinstler's records indicate several commissions for illustrations in Martin Goodman's adventure magazines circa 1957.

A phenomenon of the decade, such magazines were inspired by Fawcett's success with ***True Magazine***. With such "sweaty" titles as ***Male***, ***Men***, ***Man's Adventures***, and ***Man to Man***, they flourished in the vacuum left by the disappearance of the adventure pulps.

Other pulp genre staples like science fiction and mystery also translated easily into the paperback format. Kinstler's facility with faces and figures transitioned smoothly into the new medium, but it was a newly revitalized market that kept him busy through the second half of the decade.

As the post-World War II Baby Boomers reached reading age, publishers rushed to create material for their parents to purchase. The *historic biography* was a tiny niche market a decade earlier, but in the mid-Fifties, it became a growth industry. Bobbs-Merrill, Dodd, Mead, E.P. Dutton, Julian Messner, Random House, and even the venerable reprint house of Grosset and Dunlap initiated series of books aimed at the burgeoning young reader market. The common theme among them was the biography of an historic figure. Hire a writer to do a reasonable job of researching and an illustrator to make the information more palatable to the youngsters and the possibilities were endless—as were the plethora of titles that sought to satisfy a seemingly insatiable market.

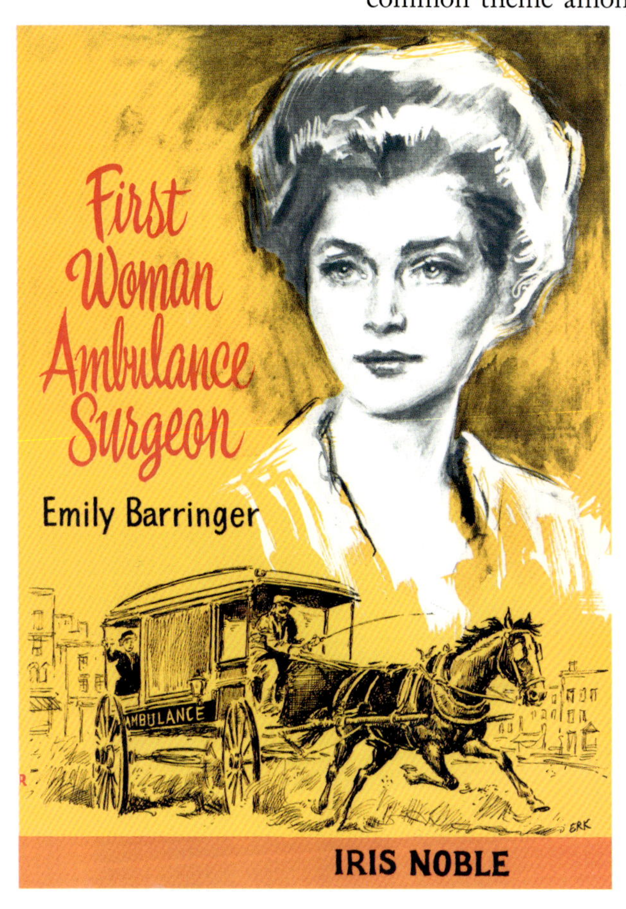

Subjects as diverse as Copernicus, William Shakespeare, Andrew Jackson, Doctor Edward L. Trudeau, Emily Barringer, Dag Hammarskjöld, Carl Ben Eielson, and Barney Ross were grist for the biographical mill. Kinstler painted or drew covers for all of these and more. His experience as an illustrator brought a dynamic sensibility to the designs which surely appealed to the young audience and his confidence with likenesses must have been a boon to the publishers vying for acceptance and respectability in the new market.

With his flair for accurate, consistent caricatures, Kinstler found these tailor-made for his talents. His comic book experience gave him the skills to quickly create rough compositions to suggest possible design solutions. His proximity to the publishers and his speed in executing the final painting made him the ideal freelancer. This is obvious from the number of covers and dustwrappers that he created in the short span of five years, and their consistent quality.

For many of these books he only painted a dustwrapper, but for **The Story of Dan Beard** he did dozens of interior illustrations, including many double-page spreads. These were classics of the genre and featured renditions of such familiar faces as Teddy Roosevelt and Mark Twain. Ray's Twain bears an eerie resemblance to Flagg, which could only be deliberate.

As the Baby Boomers aged, the publishers expanded their lines to include young adult titles. New authors built careers on stories of teenage girls and boys, their romances and their adventures. The permutations of these two themes were endless and just as he was called upon in the pulps to maintain interest while depicting countless variations upon a theme, Ray proved just as capable of rendering them in oil for dustwrappers as he had in pen and ink for ***Ranch Romances*** illustrations.

As these new markets matured and became saturated, a growing backlog of titles lessened the demand for new ones, prompting Kinstler to again look beyond his current outlets to find other options. At Dodd, Mead he moved into another niche in the non-fiction market with covers and illustrations for books like **Our Federal Government: How It Works**, **The Book of Negro Folklore** and **Life Was Simpler Then**.

One of his most rewarding experiences producing art for books was his collaboration with author George Martin on two books relating to opera. The first was the 1961 opus, **The Opera Companion: A Guide for the Casual Operagoer**. Martin wanted an illustrator who was familiar with his subject and Kinstler had a love for the opera that dated back to his experience in the claque in the late 1940s with Bernie, his friend, fellow music lover and European travel companion.

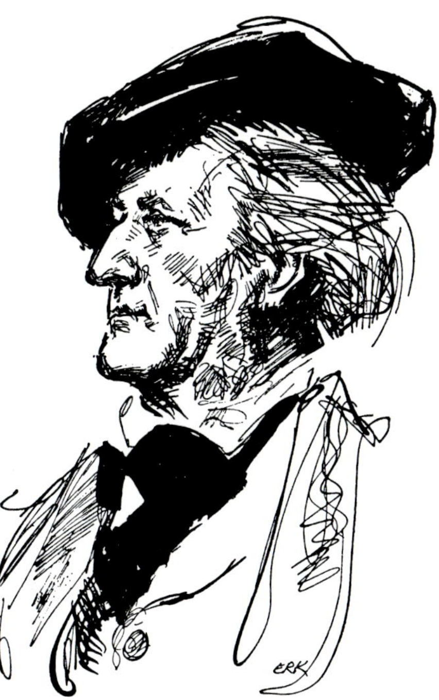

Richard Wagner from **Verdi: His Music, Life and Times**.

The success of this collaboration led to another. It was one of Ray's final efforts in the book field, **Verdi: His Music, Life and Times**. Published in 1963, the dustwrapper featured an impressive image of Verdi.

> When I turned in the rough sketches for the jacket, they chose the one that I preferred and then told me to do a finished version, "but keep the freshness" of the sketch. I politely told them that it was nearly impossible that a tighter version could be as "fresh" and that they could only get what they wanted by using the sketch as is. They did and I still think it's one of my best covers.

In those days, book publishers were on what is now Park Avenue South. Then it was 4th Avenue. They were all within walking distance of Kinstler's studio, which allowed him the luxury of picking up an assignment, producing several different suggested covers in his studio and presenting these the next day to allow the art director to choose the design he preferred. Samples of these rough color sketches for covers are some of the most striking examples of Kinstler's art. They amount to thoughts in paint and he would often do a half-dozen of these "roughs" in preparation for a job. In some cases, he would do designs "on spec" in hopes of getting an assignment that eventually might go to another artist. Here Broderick Crawford, then starring in the television hit, *Highway Patrol*, stands in for the bad guy.

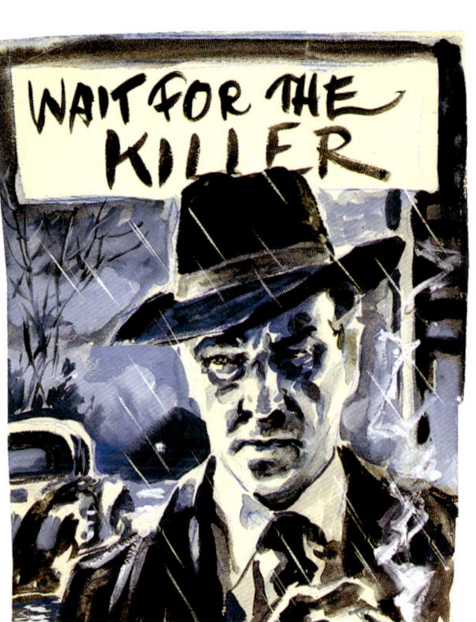

As portraiture loomed larger in his future in 1958, he began to take more and more commercial assignments that stressed those skills. ***Mediascope*** was a monthly trade magazine for the advertising industry and for two years Kinstler had a standing assignment to create a likeness of each issue's interview subject. The same repetitive challenges he had faced with the pulp drawings and with the young adult book jackets, he solved in this series of nearly two dozen cover portraits done in monochromatic oils or watercolors.

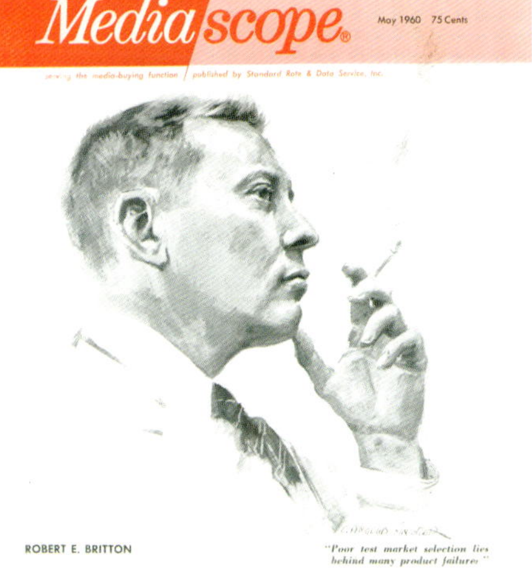

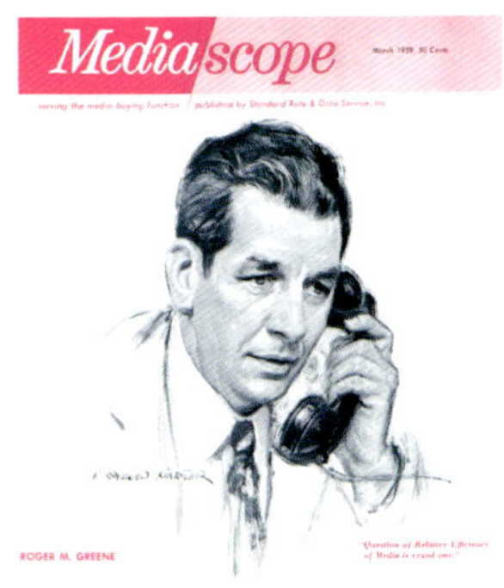

Everett Raymond Kinstler

The National Arts Club

(part two)

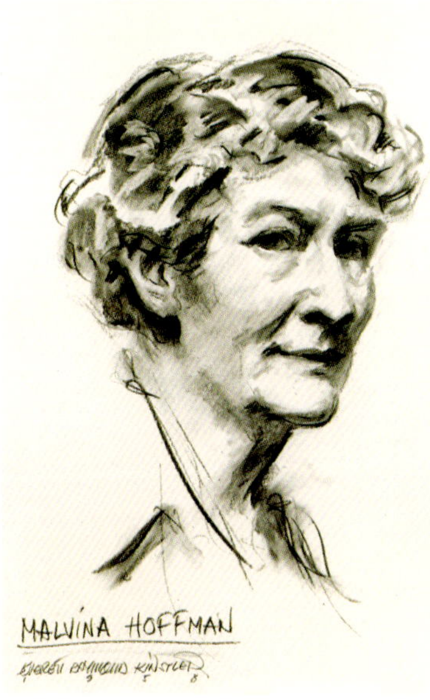

The club was responsible for other important friendships in Kinstler's life. During the mid-Fifties, two sculptors, Paul Manship and Malvina Hoffman, became members and Manship took a studio in the Annex.

> At this time Manship was past his prime and you couldn't give his sculptures away. Yet he looked like a giant to me as I was not caught up in the fashions of the day. I would sometimes see him five nights in a row for dinner.

Malvina Hoffman's work was known and admired by Kinstler. He was especially impressed by her Hall of Man at the Chicago Museum of Natural History where she had faithfully depicted one hundred and fifty separate ethnic types. She was a protégé of Auguste Rodin.

> She was my friend to the point that a researcher writing a biography of her after she died in 1966 asked me rather sheepishly if I had been her lover. I said—only of her art. I was just a personable young man, certainly intense and passionate and I loved her work. I would often serve as an escort for her. She was a formidable figure, artistically and socially—she was invited to extraordinary parties. I was in my twenties, single, and we were friends. She would call me and say "Raymond, I've been invited to a nice party at the Astors and would you come with me?" And I did. In the process, through Miss Hoffman, I met a lot of extraordinary people.

It's interesting that at the time Ray knew many of these artists, their work was out of vogue and the vagaries of the art world had passed them by. Manship had been a celebrity sculptor whose work had won medals in the first quarter of the century and who had contributed essays on sculpture to **The Encyclopedia Britannica**. Cornwell and Flagg had known enormous success and respect. Malvina Hoffman had been a popular phenomenon in sculpture twenty-five years earlier. Yet these people couldn't get work at the time Kinstler knew them. On one visit to Miss Hoffman she told Ray, "I've just seen Paul (Manship). He had a show at The Century Club and nobody came."

The respect and friendship of the younger artist must have meant a lot to them. It validated their worth to the extent that they still had appreciators in the current generation. John Johansen, who was eighty in 1956, was another who felt and enjoyed Ray's enthusiasm and friendship over the years.

"...all granddaddy would talk about was his friend Raymond."

> To the point that at his funeral in 1964 I met his grandchildren who told me "we were so jealous of you because all granddaddy would talk about was his friend Raymond." I was deeply touched by that.

As one of the younger members of the venerable Club, which has always been run by volunteers, more and more responsibilities devolved to Kinstler. In 1956, he won a medal in one of the exhibitions and they put him on the art committee. When the existing chairman stepped down shortly thereafter, he was given the job.

> Their attitude was, "He's here and he's been a member a couple of years, so why not?" Thus, I became Chairman of Exhibitions at the National Arts Club and was responsible for putting on the exhibitions in the Gallery and for arranging the Artists' Dinners. In those days, if we could get fifty people to show up it was deemed a great achievement. My challenge was always "who are we going to get as a speaker?" The older members would suggest people such as the Curator of the Smithsonian Institution—who may have been an excellent human being but who wasn't going to help sell out the dinner.

I had street smarts and I was always looking for a *name*. Once we had that, we could fill out the program with people like the Curator and other fascinating speakers with lesser name recognition.

For instance, for the first 1957 dinner, I asked Stuart Cloete to help me find a speaker. Stuart was a South African writer who lived below me and he had told me that he knew Victor Hammer of the Hammer Galleries (and brother of Armand). Victor had a great many contacts in the art world and Stuart offered to ask him about possible speakers. He called later and asked, "How about Salvador Dali?"

Now that was a *name*! I said *"Terrific!"* We got Dali.

As I was responsible for the arrangements, I invited him to come early so he could visit my studio and pose for a drawing. Later, I was the Master of Ceremonies at that memorable evening.

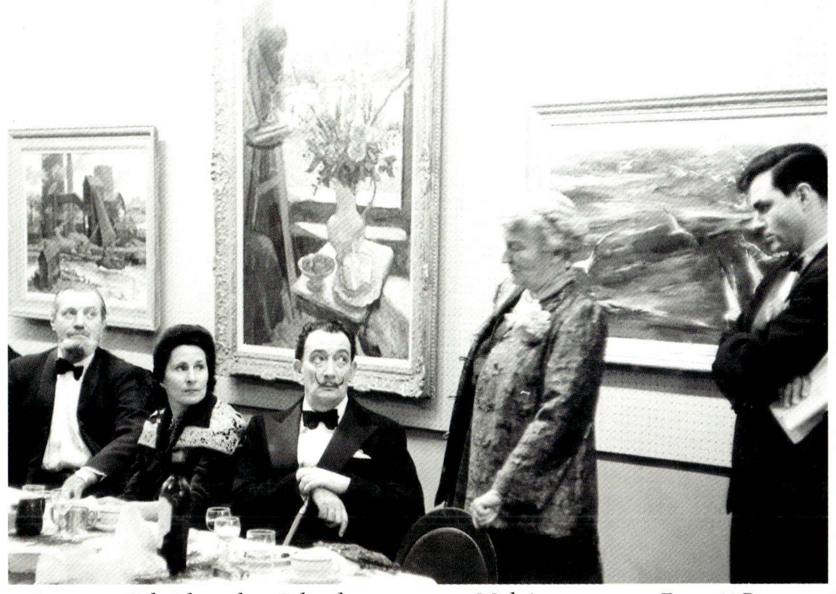

Stuart Cloete — Gala Eluard (Dali) — Salvador Dali — Malvina Hoffman — Everett Raymond Kinstler

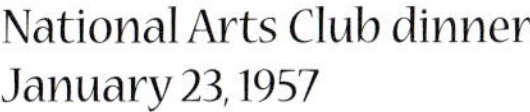

National Arts Club dinner
January 23, 1957

Today the National Arts Club boasts a splendid collection of portraits—many of which are of these speakers. Much of that collection exists simply because Ray Kinstler helped arrange their appearances at Club dinners and then took it upon himself to draw them for his own enjoyment. In 1957, his fascination with faces and his innate passion for depicting them were combining in his paperback covers, his book illustrations and his Club sketches to show him his future profession.

Other factors pushing him toward portraiture were the economic realities of the media in which he'd been earning a living. The comic book and pulp markets were shrinking and were never again likely to provide the income he had been earning there. He drew only one comic book in 1957 and just a handful of pulp illustrations. The paperback market kept the wolf from the door and he broke into the book and men's magazine markets that year, but his income had been decreasing for the last few years and that year it was half of what it had been in 1955.

His taste in art was being stimulated by his own curiosity and by his friends John Johansen, Paul Manship, and others with whom he exhibited in the Gallery at the Club. The commercial world of ***Collier's*** and ***The Saturday Evening***

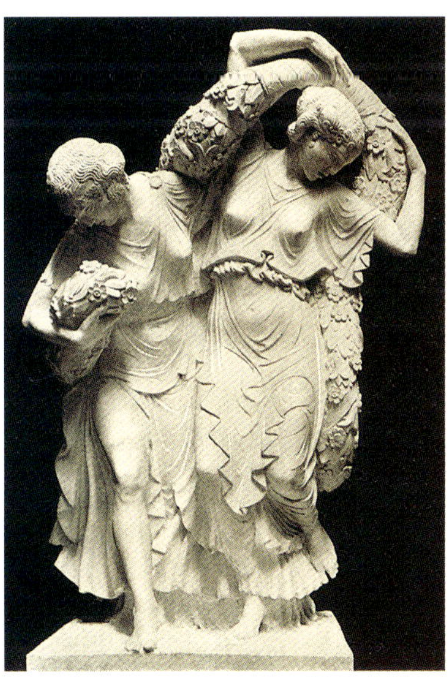

Paul Manship
The Harvest
Panama-Pacific Exposition, 1915

"There was a personal yen to express myself and to have that expression be valued."

Post was even conspiring to thwart his long-held goals by changing the type of art they used and often dropping the credit lines for the illustrators. He began to envision a future as something other than an Illustrator. And it was a future that for the first time encompassed more than just himself, as he met a young lady named Lea Nation who worked in the Secretary's office at the National Arts Club. They began seeing each other socially and were married in 1958.

As Events Chairman, Ray was also responsible for socializing with members and guests before, during and after the dinners. It was a heady responsibility for the self-educated young man, but one that he carried off with aplomb.

> Social skills were being forced upon me, both in my interactions at the Club and through the portraits I was painting. I learned a lot about people as I began to paint them and was learning how to move among them naturally.
>
> I was thrust among people, but a part of me was very private, a little self-conscious. I saw friends like Bob Brustein with their PhDs and I was still a little skittish about my leaving high school after a year and a half—thinking that perhaps I'd missed something in my life by not being more educated. I don't think I had any complexes, but I also didn't have a great sense of self. I was just working from day to day and trying to get better. Always in the back of my mind was the need to improve. There was also the drive to go beyond just having my work reproduced. There was a personal yen to express myself and to have that expression be valued.

In the process of arranging Dali's speaking engagement, Ray got to know Victor Hammer personally and soon he was making the arrangements for the speakers directly with Hammer, leveraging off Hammer's extensive social contacts. The network Kinstler was developing was solidly grounded in friendship, skills, and professional and personal respect. He may have had misgivings about the limits of his formal education, but he never had any second thoughts about his abilities.

The social skills he was honing seemed to dovetail neatly with what he calls his "street smarts" to form a well-rounded individual who could move easily from the halls of pulp fiction editors to the elite galleries of Victor Hammer. The exhibitions and dinners that Kinstler coordinated and staged at the Club showed him to be more capable than he might have imagined.

Certainly, by 1957, he was a functioning officer of a prestigious club and tasked with the responsibilities of dealing with a spectrum of personalities and sophisticates. He felt comfortable with his level of knowledge and with the thought processes he used to form his opinions. While he could mix easily with the famous people whom he brought to speak at the club, he wasn't overawed by their fame, nor was he afraid to present his own contrary opinions during conversations with them. Ayn Rand is a good example.

> Shortly after Dali's dinner, I began to feel more assured in contacting well-known people and I used to send out letters to those whom I felt might make interesting speakers. In 1958, I had just read **The Fountainhead** and **Atlas Shrugged** by Ayn Rand and sent her one such letter inviting her to speak at our next dinner. There was no reply.
>
> As I got to know Victor Hammer better, I would often approach him for suggestions. This time he said, "How about Eleanor Roosevelt?" But then he had second thoughts because "she doesn't know anything about art. " I told him not to worry. If he could arrange for Eleanor Roosevelt to speak, she could just talk

> about culture and her travels and I would make certain that we worked "art" into it. My contribution was that I arranged to get actor Vincent Price to speak also. It was shaping up to what I thought would be an interesting evening.
>
> The morning of the dinner, my phone rang. "Mr. Kinstler?" said a very masculine, humorless voice with a slight Russian accent. "This is Ayn Rand. I have your letter here." (which I'd written about a month before) "What is all this about?"
>
> I said, Miss Rand, there's an Artists' Dinner, tonight actually, and I had thought that since you'd written about the arts so passionately in **The Fountainhead**...
>
> "How do you know about this?"
>
> Because I read the book, I told her. Then she asked me a great deal about myself. During my response, I again said that the dinner is tonight.
>
> "Well, I will be there."
>
> I was a bit flustered. My reaction was, wait a minute—we won't even be able list you on the program. We're honoring Eleanor Roosevelt.
>
> "Oh, *THAT* woman, but I will come anyway, but ONLY if I can sit next to YOU."
>
> I told her that it was a black tie dinner and that I would meet her downstairs.
>
> "How will I know you?"
>
> I said, I will know YOU, Miss Rand. She appeared that night wearing a black dress with a diamond clip in the shape of a dollar sign and I did sit next to her during dinner. There must have been two or three hundred people there and when Mrs. Roosevelt was introduced everybody stood up except for Miss Rand, who was seated at the end of the dais.
>
> After the dinner, she came upstairs to my studio with my wife and me. I did a small charcoal head of her and she signed my copy of **Atlas Shrugged**.

"Oh, THAT woman."

To Everett Raymond Kinstler —
— with sincere appreciation of
your marks in this book – and with
admiration for the spirit behind
your work —
Ayn Rand

January 21, 1959

Ray didn't really take to Ayn Rand. There was a cult forming around her and her work that put him off. He liked to think for himself and the notion of a large group of people swearing fealty to one individual seemed to be a sort of groupthink that he could neither understand nor relate to. Ray also found out that her philosophy and his regarding art were diametrically opposed.

> We differed on many points. Her husband Frank O'Connor had been a silent film actor in Cecil B. DeMille movies and he was currently taking art courses at the Art Students League. She told me once, "Frank will be a great artist."
>
> My reaction was, "Miss Rand, what about *TALENT*?"
>
> She felt that "Anything can be done with the mind." I told her I didn't believe that and she simply repeated, "Everything can be done with the mind!"
>
> I think there is a god-given gift that some people have that they must nourish and nurture. Just thinking about it is not going to make anyone a "great artist."
>
> "No!" She said, "The mind is everything."

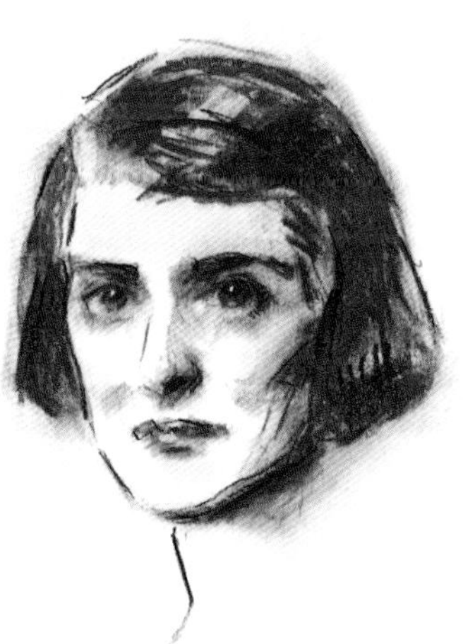

Ayn Rand

No matter how important, popular or sophisticated Ayn Rand might have been, Kinstler's beliefs were swayed by neither her fame nor her arguments.

Another instance of this involved actor Vincent Price.

> Price and I got into an argument over modern art at that dinner. He was very deep on modern art and I remember telling him about a modern art piece that had hung upside down for two weeks and no one noticed it. He said he

"I couldn't count on the next job being there."

didn't think that was very funny. I said, "No, but it's very revealing." I was a little peppery in those days and I kind of locked horns with him.

He did not require a college degree in Art to shore up his opinions and felt confident enough in them to voice them with conviction. Without being aware of it, Ray was developing a patina of sophistication himself.

It was during those years that the National Arts Club was rebuilding itself. Ray was a part of that renewal. He tried to raise the quality of the exhibitions, often making a personal effort to request and, if need be, to transport exhibition pieces from the more well-known Club members such as Dean Cornwell. He became adept at predicting the relative influence of having such a "name" in a show. As with the Dinners, where it was easier to convince a Vincent Price to attend if you already had a commitment from Eleanor Roosevelt, so, too, if he had Cornwell amongst his exhibitors, he was more likely able to secure work from others. And while the public may have forgotten James Montgomery Flagg and Dean Cornwell, the artistic community had a slightly more tenacious memory and their presence in one of the Gallery Exhibitions was sufficient to elicit contributions from reticent members.

The response from the members and the public to the speakers Ray lined up for the Artists' Dinners is easily calculated from his statement that when he took over that responsibility an audience of fifty was considered a success. Three years later, at the Eleanor Roosevelt dinner, that had been increased to two hundred plus. As nothing succeeds like success, each improvement in the Club's activities built up some momentum for the next.

But it wasn't just the Club functions that needed help. The buildings were suffering from a long period of neglect. Declining membership during the 1940s and 1950s led to fewer volunteers to maintain the facilities and fewer funds with which to do it. Kinstler became a Vice President of the Club, but he also functioned occasionally as the janitor and plumber.

He was married by this time, and the building was his home.

> I wasn't so much trying to improve things as to just preserve what we had. It was the place where I lived, the place where I worked—a place that I loved.
>
> It wasn't easy. My rent was about $250 a month which was about half of my monthly income, but I never focused on the money. I was working and I enjoyed it. I was caught up in the business of trying to better myself as an artist and I was stimulated by it. I remember those years when I first went out with Lea and the comic and pulp markets were drying up. I was really troubled as to where I would get the means. I didn't eat at fancy restaurants and didn't indulge particularly, but I always had that sense that I had to watch my spending. I knew I had to go out and look for work next week and I couldn't count on the next job being there. It was never life or death, but I didn't have much pocket money.

While his friends outside the Club continued to question the wisdom of his choice of residence, Ray set out to help make improvements. At first it might have been just re-stretching the canvas or fixing the frame on one of the Club's many pieces of artwork, but it escalated to repairing floors and stairways.

The Tilden Mansion, which houses the Club facilities on 20th Street, had been renovated so many times over the years that many of its most impressive features were buried behind plasterboard walls, drop ceilings and under linoleum floor coverings. As the old membership slowly ebbed, so too did the memory of how the original 19th Century Victorian brownstone had looked in its heyday. As they progressed, the repairs were an ongoing experience in rediscovery.

> As we went along the renovation attracted more money to the club and more young people. We started looking behind the fluorescent lights and discovered a glass ceiling that was fifty feet square. We wanted to restore some of the wood and when we took panels off the ceiling, we found skylights. We found marble underneath plasterboard. A lot of people were instrumental in this effort. One was my friend Hunter Jones.

The residential annex where Ray lived wasn't quite so plush, but it was a solidly crafted building with all the style and amenities one would expect from a classy New York City Club—albeit one that was built in 1906. In a club financed by dues and run by volunteers from a falling membership, it was difficult to find the means to increase the maintenance levels. One of the most effective was the one Ray believed in most strongly. He would actively proselytize the merits of the Club and encourage other artists to take up residence in the building. Whenever a studio was vacant, which in those days was all the time, he would call friends and fellow artists and let them know about it.

Today the Annex is fully populated, with a waiting list of a thousand members who want to live there. As portraiture became his major occupation, Ray eventually took his own advice and, in 1961, he rented a second large studio for himself and his family.

> I now have the two duplexes on the tenth floor. We were living in the one duplex when Kate was born in 1960, but I eventually needed a designated space to do portraits. It was the arrival of our second child, Dana, in 1962 that sort of forced me to expand.

Portraits, Inc.

In 1958, things were getting a bit tough** financially. The prior year had been his least successful as an illustrator since 1950. While the book covers and illustrations paid a bit better than the comics and the pulps had, he still was facing a new life and getting ready to start a family. It was time once again to reinvent himself.

He made one abortive attempt at teaching. Back in 1943 he had attended onc class taught by Franklin Booth at The Phoenix School of Design. It hadn't impressed him then, but the school was still in existence and Ray was hired to teach a class in "Rendering." He wanted to teach painting, but that was reserved for Mr. Phoenix, the founder. The Rendering curriculum was outdated back when Ray experienced it in the Forties and it hadn't taken the additional age gracefully. He only managed to devote himself to the task for six or seven months. As with the stories he drew for Classics Illustrated about a year later, this was one of the very few occasions where he took a job solely for the income it would provide. In both cases, he regretted that decision deeply. It would never happen again.

In 1957, Kinstler had taken some of his work to a local gallery called Portraits, Incorporated. This company represented artists and brokered portrait commissions for them. To be listed in their catalog, one had to paint at least one portrait through them. They agreed to show potential customers his work, but he wouldn't become an official Portraits, Incorporated artist until someone chose Ray for a job and he created a portrait with which they were satisfied.

> At the time I signed with Portraits, Incorporated they probably represented fewer than thirty artists. The company was essentially a portrait agent. Customers would come into their showroom, and choose an artist based on the samples they were shown and the rates a particular artist was charging.
>
> My first job through them was to paint Forrest E. Mars, Jr. (of the Mars Candy fortune). His parents had given him the present of a portrait for his 25th birthday. When he visited Portraits, Incorporated, they had just taken me on for the trial period and they described me to him as "a new young artist who we think has talent and is going to be a comer."

In Kinstler's ledger for 1957, that singular April event is recorded with one line: "30—1 portrait Inc. - $800." That entry sits between "25 - 3 singles - $45" and another for the beginning of May: "1 single, Ra(nch)Ro(mances) - $15."

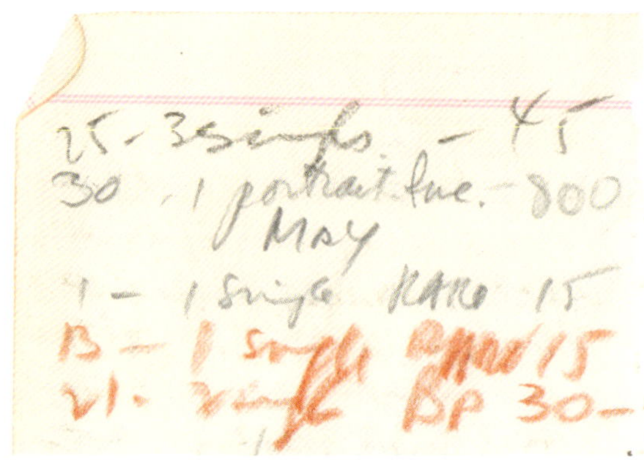

There is a certain charm to those few lines. He obviously wasn't about to give up his "day job" at the pulps just because he landed one portrait commission, but they also reflect his loyalty to a long-time customer *and* his continued joy at drawing illustrations in pen and ink. He liked Florence Hazard at ***Ranch Romances***. She was one of those special people in his life who allowed him a great deal of freedom. And he really enjoyed the work. It wasn't like him to quit just because he could earn more money by painting. However, the pulps were fading into oblivion and he eventually had to stop. As Ray puts it:

Forrest E. Mars, Jr.
1957
Mars, Incorporated Collection

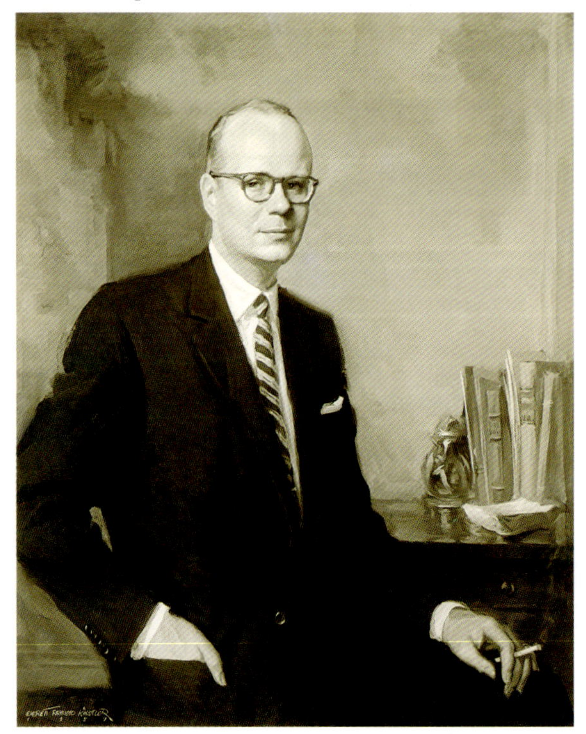

> I basically killed pulps all by myself. There was no one else left to do it.

Ray's goal of becoming an illustrator for the slick magazines was becoming less realistic. In January of 1957, ***Collier's Magazine*** stopped publishing. He also realized that in the other important magazines, the direction and style of the art was moving away from the classic illustration approach that he loved. He began to think that perhaps he needed to reassess his goals. The pulps were dying. Comic books had been fun but they were no longer satisfying. The other magazine markets were not clamoring for his work. And 1957 and 1958 had been two of his least rewarding financial years yet.

His book illustrations seemed to be the closest he was going to come to illustration in the current marketplace and that was satisfactory in the short term, but not really acceptable as a long-term career. All of these factors were present in his decision to approach Portraits, Incorporated in early 1957—possibly just after ***Collier's*** folded.

The next portrait he painted was not even commissioned through Portraits, Incorporated. As he was expanding his markets in search of additional work, a friend recommended Ray to a Mrs. Sedam, who had lost her son in World War II. The son had been a U.S. Marine pilot and Kinstler was commissioned to paint his portrait from a photograph. The painting was delivered late December of 1958.

The timing shows that Ray obviously wasn't immediately setting the portrait world on fire, though the Forrest E. Mars, Jr. portrait would certainly pay off over the long term.

> That initial portrait of Forrest Mars, Jr. led to my painting his wife, his father, Forrest E. Mars, Sr., his children, etc. over a thirty-five year period. Now he's retired and currently the twenty-seventh richest man in the world.

Still, in the two years he had been involved with Portraits, Incorporated, he painted just three portraits, with one commission coming from a friend. Portraiture was an appealing artistic goal, but it was only one possibility. He tried teaching and quickly abandoned the idea—more because of the venue than the concept. He secured the regular ***Mediascope*** covers commission. The young adult books were paying the bills, but they were artistically limiting. For the first time in his life, Kinstler's path was becoming indistinct.

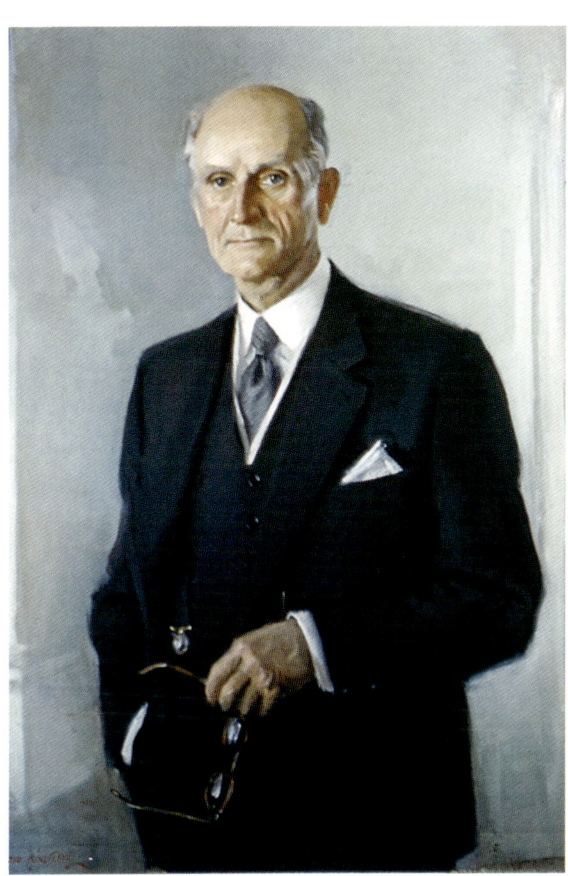

Forrest E Mars, Sr.
1960

All the while, he was exhibiting regularly at the National Arts Club gallery and his friends there were urging him to branch out into the social art world. There were many artistic societies centered in New York City and John Johansen and Paul Manship at the Club encouraged him to join them, if only for the practical aspects of getting his name and work known.

> I remember the first time I was proposed for the National Academy. I was turned down and I didn't really give a damn. I didn't actually *WANT* to be a member of the Academy. The second time I was turned down I got miffed. What was the matter with my work? They said something to the effect of "You're just a mere Illustrator" which really made me angry.
>
> But then I got a letter from a lovely painter named Everett Warner. He was a member of the impressionist school, an old timer. I had never met him, but he wrote me to encourage me to keep trying to join.
>
> "My dear Mr. Kinstler, I hope you're not too disappointed in not being elected to The Academy. The Academy needs young painters like you. Don't be discouraged. You're a fine young painter and one day you'll be a member and the Academy will be the richer for it."
>
> Things like that stuck with me and were indicative of what would happen. People like Warner or Johansen or Manship, who thought they saw something worthwhile in me, would give me advice: "We want you to be a member of this." Or "we want you to be a member of The Century Club." I had no real interest. I was just trying to earn a living, but these contacts made my life richer. I began to experience a lot more.
>
> And these people were quietly encouraging my work: "Raymond, you should be doing more landscapes." "Don't get too involved with your portraits. Make sure you do some personal work." These were things I needed to hear.

> I was not, however, affected by the whims of fashion, by what was popular, nor was I one to categorize art. When I had my first show at the Grand Central Gallery in 1959, Erwin Barrie, the director of the gallery, did *NOT* want me to mention that I had drawn comic books. I told him, "That's where I come from."
>
> It was not a badge of honor nor a badge of disgrace. It was just my background and I took pride in it.

There was that confidence again. Wherever he was going was a continuation of the road he had traveled. Becoming a member of the National Academy or having a gallery exhibition shouldn't require that he distance himself from his past. He never thought of himself as "just" an anything!

He eventually joined The Allied Artists, The Audubon Artists, The Artists Fellowship, The National Academy, and, in certain cases, he became an officer of the club. These societies expanded further his contacts. As with his later brushes with historic and popular personalities, some relationships clicked and others didn't.

> I've made lots of connections over the years—some of which developed into friendships. Others went nowhere, partly because I wasn't starstruck. That is, I didn't pursue relationships unless I felt a kinship and a spark.
>
> For instance, Katharine Hepburn. I visited her countless times and she came to my studio to pose on several occasions. When the portrait project was completed, however, though we kept in touch, I didn't pursue a friendship. Another example is Paul Newman. I was asked to work on a portrait collaboration to benefit his Hole in the Wall Gang charity. I admired him and found him likeable, but was not comfortable with the concept. Had I been startstruck, I'm sure that I would have stuck with the project.
>
> Whereas with someone like Jimmy Cagney, I felt like I was talking to a pal. We'd get on the phone and just talk. We became good friends.
>
> The art societies were like that. I would become very active in some and others I would eventually abandon as not a good fit for my needs.

Ray's 1959 exhibition at the Grand Central Gallery was an important event. He didn't sell all of the pieces in the show, but his work was well-received. He fulfilled two more commissions from Portraits, Incorporated that year, but he also returned to comic books with some short assignments from the non-fiction branch of Classics Illustrated. The portraits he enjoyed, the comic books he did not. He quit comics for a second and final time and continued to pursue book illustration as his primary source of income.

Perhaps it was the exhibition that turned things around. Perhaps it was painting the portrait of Forrest E. Mars, Sr., an important and influential man, or perhaps someone at Portraits, Incorporated began to really promote him as not just a "comer" but one who had arrived. Or perhaps it was a combination of all of these and other factors that can't be isolated so many decades later. Whatever the impetus, 1960 was the year that Everett Raymond Kinstler found the path to portraiture. The previous year, fifteen percent of his income came from two Portraits, Incorporated paintings. In 1960 his income doubled and sixty-one percent of it came from fifteen portraits.

There was no doubt as to what direction he would go with his life. He enjoyed the challenge and the people, and everything he had done over the past decades had prepared him for this. He had the people skills, the painting skills, and the discipline and sophistication to be a success.

Beginnings

Like so many other improvements in his life, he didn't study sophistication, he simply became sophisticated. He didn't get an Art History degree from a college, but he immersed himself in art and became an Art Historian. He never went to school to learn how to ink a comic book, he just did it. He applied the same method to drawing full comic book stories, to pulp illustration, and to cover painting.

No one taught him to paint portraits, but his entire life was in preparation for them. Go back and look at the portrait of "Jimmy Bama" done when he was fifteen. Linger a while on the faces in the following galleries and watch the progression and development of a skilled and sensitive renderer of people.

Certainly Kinstler has worked hard to achieve these skills, but he chose the teachers and developed his own curricula. And he bestowed the diplomas himself, grading, not on "the curve," but on an absolute scale that only he acknowledged and with a self-assurance that only comes with being able to honestly appraise his own efforts.

Forty-plus years later, he's still growing and loving every minute of it.

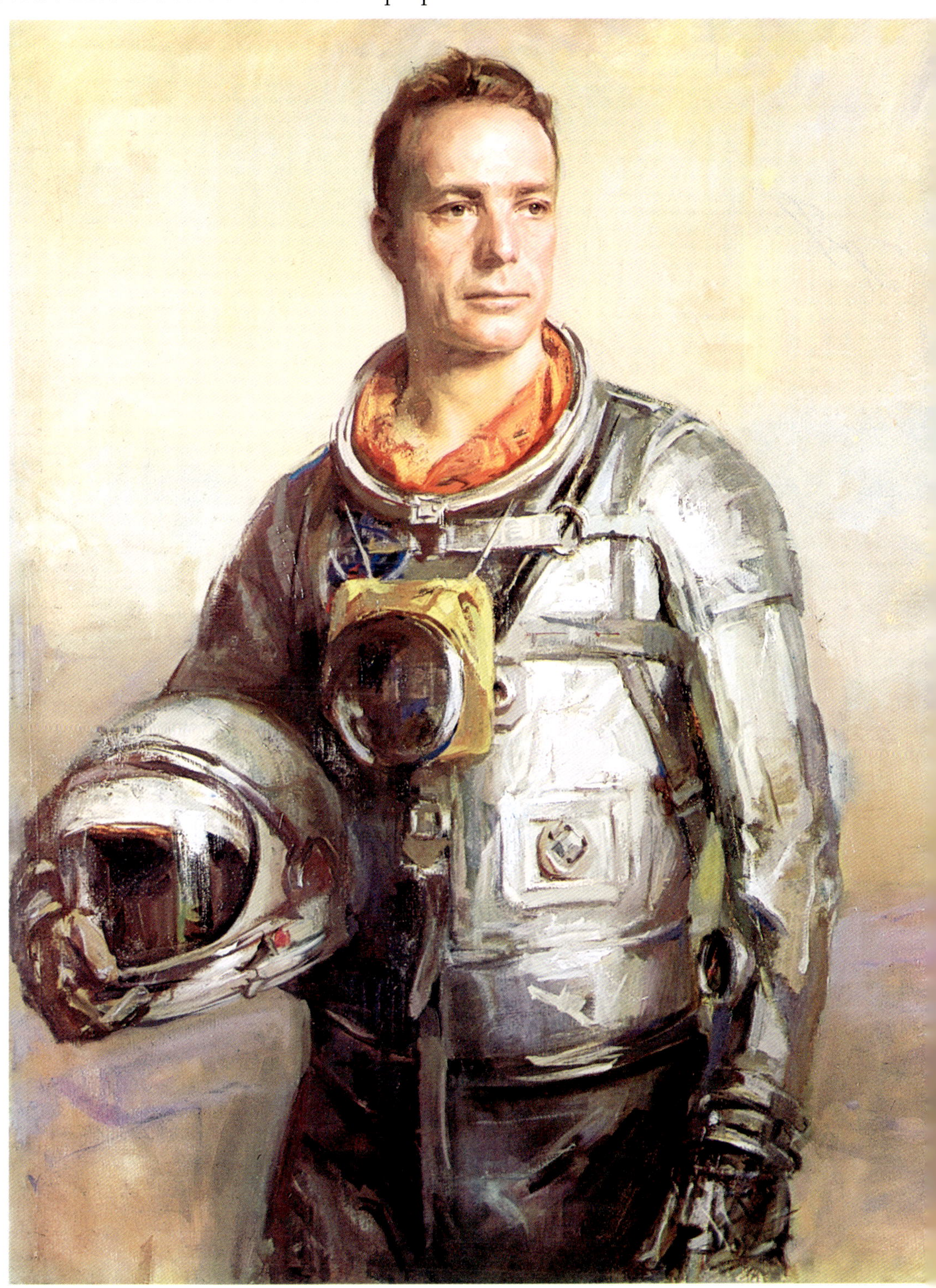

Scott Carpenter
1962
U.S. Navy Art Collection

comic books 1942 TO 1959

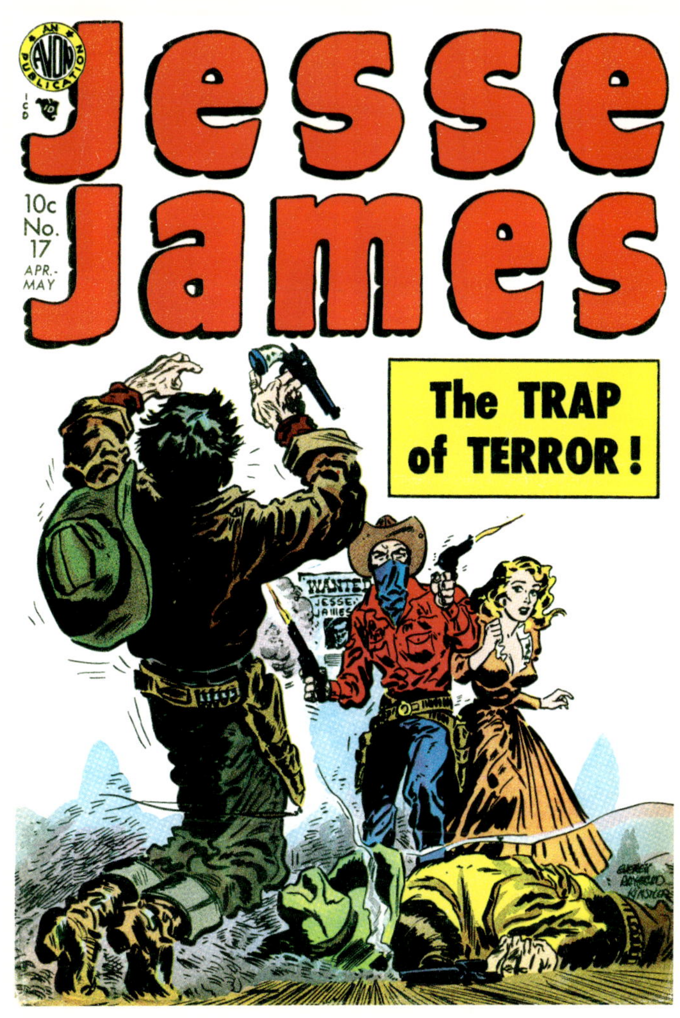

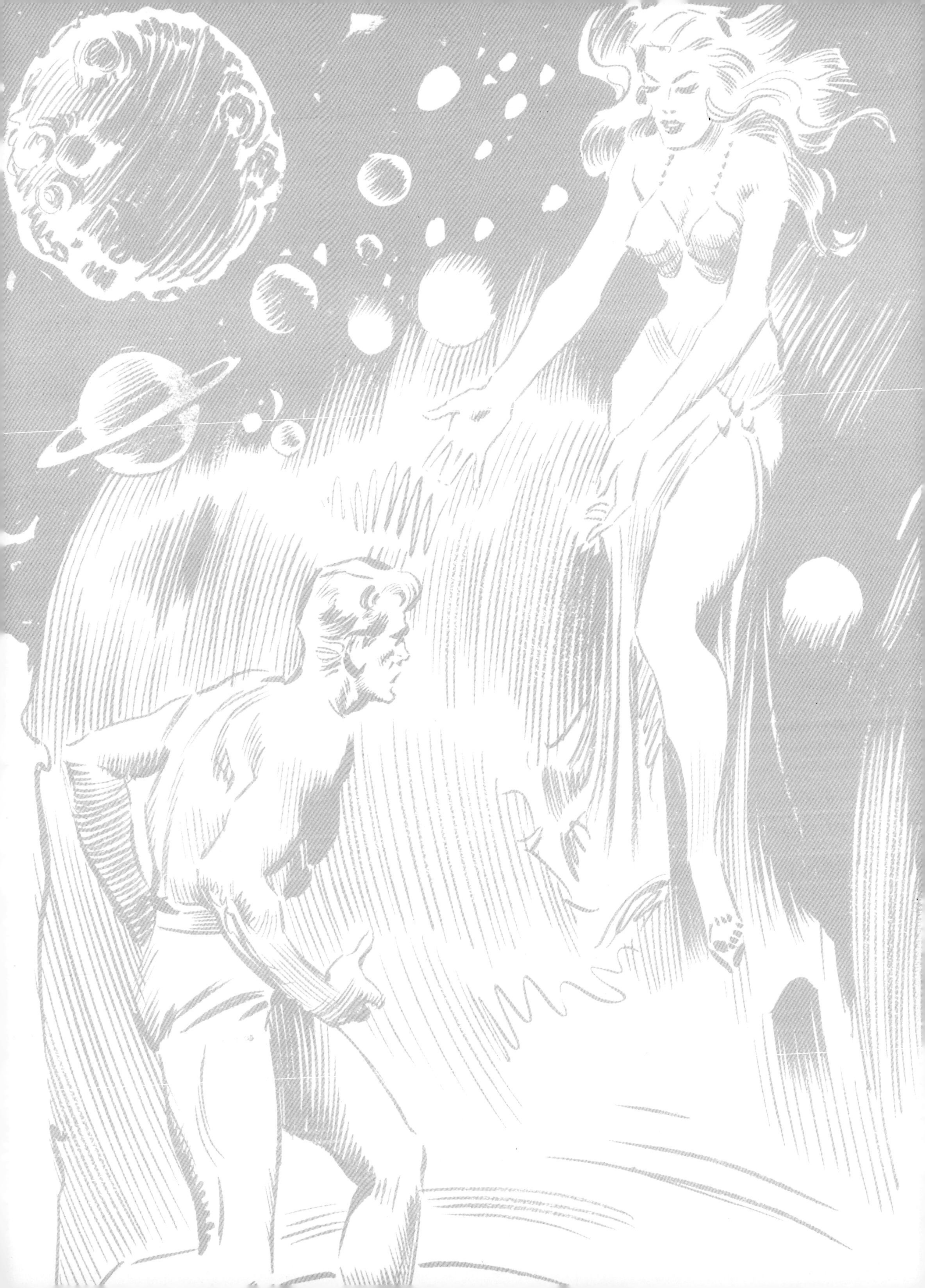

Not even the pulps offered him this freedom.

Kinstler's comic book career began in 1942 when at age sixteen he started working as an inker for Cinema Comics. His earliest work appeared in titles like ***Thrilling***, ***Startling*** and ***Real Life***.

After little more than a year, he left the staff position at Cinema and began freelancing, producing finished artwork primarily for his old boss Richard Hughes at Cinema while attending art school during the day.

A stint in the Army in 1946, a focus on illustrations for the pulps, and a trip to Europe precluded any further comic work until mid-1947. He returned to dabble in the medium with four stories and a cover for National/DC.

1948 was devoted to painting and pulp illustration. Comics work consisted of a few painted covers for Fawcett western titles like ***Hopalong Cassidy*** and ***Tom Mix***.

The romance comic genre was flourishing in mid-1949 when Kinstler returned to National/DC to try his hand at their new titles: ***Romance Trail***, ***Girls' Love Stories*** and ***Secret Hearts***. He used a more refined, illustrative style—often depicting a sophisticated world far beyond his personal experiences. Some stories were unsigned, hinting that perhaps Ray only did the pencilling, with someone else providing the finishing inks.

Avon Comics provided a total comics experience. Ray began there in mid-1950, starting with adaptations of historic adventure like ***Pancho Villa***, ***Teddy Roosevelt and His Rough Riders***, and ***Kit Carson***. He soon advanced into a position tailor-made for his style and temperament.

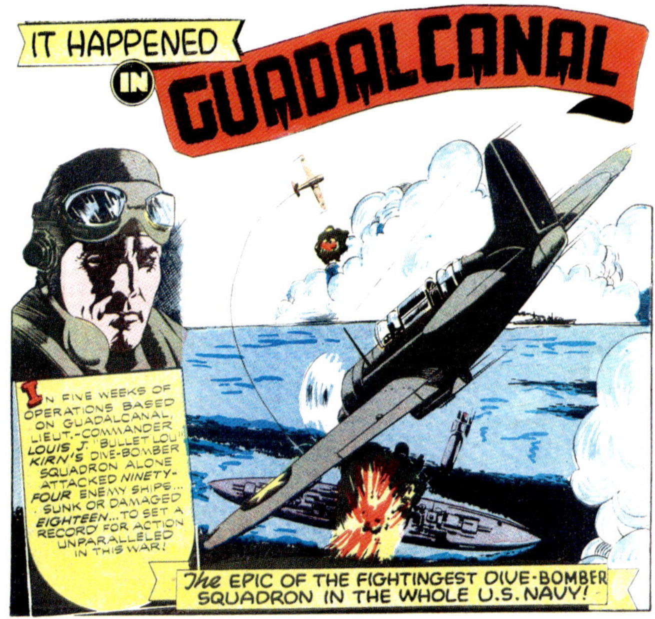

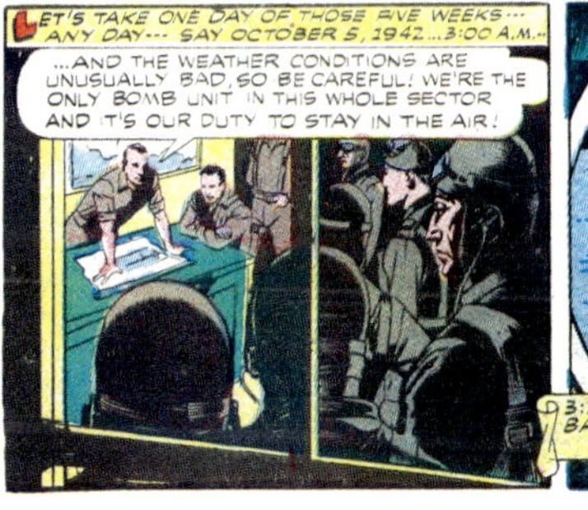

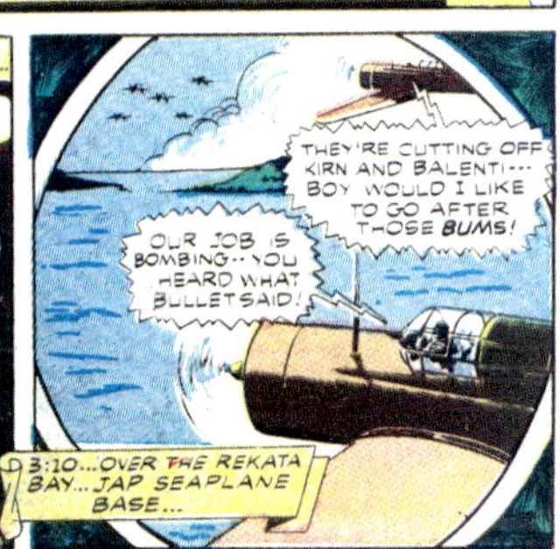

Real Life #14
Nedor Comics
November, 1943

On the inside of the front cover, many Avon comics featured a black and white montage/preview of the main stories inside. The better paper stock used for covers and the interpretive nature of the page allowed Kinstler to indulge his passion for pen and ink. Not even the pulps offered him this freedom. The Avon editors trusted him and turned him loose to create some of the most intricate and expressive pages ever to appear in comic books.

While indulging himself in these Avon pen and ink extravaganzas, he drew many covers and stories. He was also getting work in 1952 at the new comics division of Ziff-Davis. This noble experiment involved paying the highest rates in the industry and attracted some of the highest caliber talent.

This combination of Avon dream job and lavish Ziff-Davis paychecks ended in early 1953 when the Avon space was given over to advertisements and Ziff-Davis left the comic book field.

A looser, quicker style was evident at Western Publishing/Dell where in 1953 he drew a thirty-four-page adaptation of ***The Sword of Zorro***. A productive relationship resulted that lasted until mid-1956, when Ray felt his adaptation of the John Wayne film ***The Conqueror*** was desecrated by a perfunctory ink job by another artist. Ray finished a few books he had in the works and then quit.

The 1940s

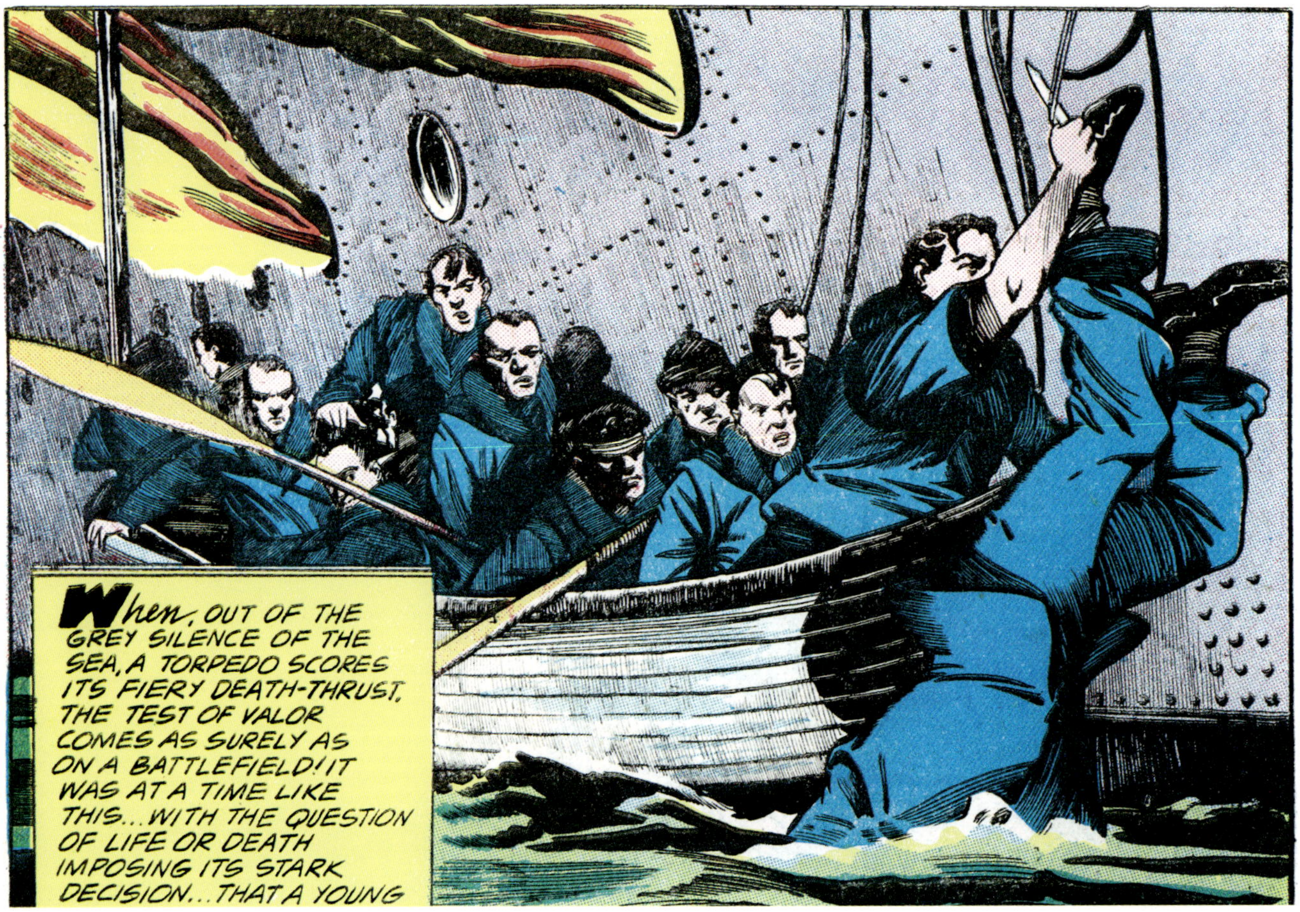

WHEN, OUT OF THE GREY SILENCE OF THE SEA, A TORPEDO SCORES ITS FIERY DEATH-THRUST, THE TEST OF VALOR COMES AS SURELY AS ON A BATTLEFIELD! IT WAS AT A TIME LIKE THIS... WITH THE QUESTION OF LIFE OR DEATH IMPOSING ITS STARK DECISION... THAT A YOUNG

ERK inks over Ken Battefield pencils
Real Life #20
Nedor Comics, November, 1944

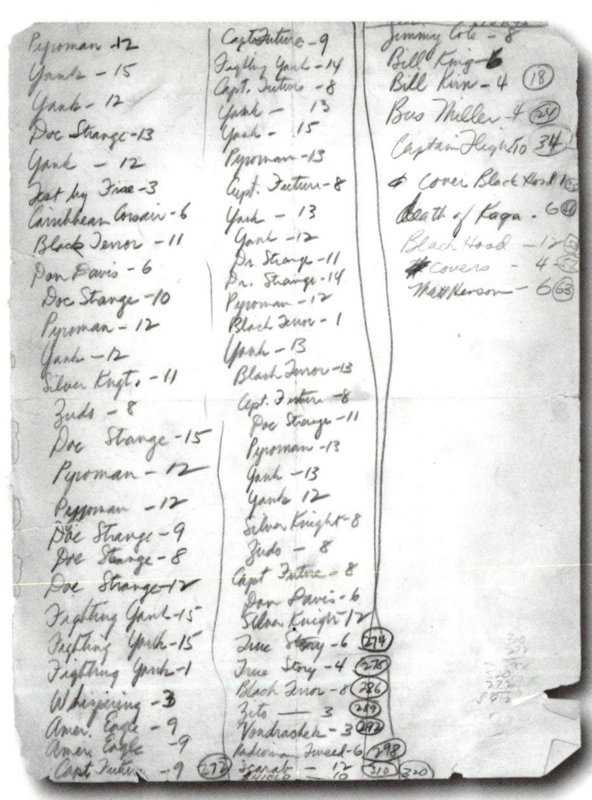

Pyroman - 12
Yank - 15
Yank - 12
Doc Strange - 13
Yank - 12
Test by Fire - 3
Caribbean Corsair - 6
Black Terror - 11
Don Davis - 6
Doc Strange - 10
Pyroman - 12
Yank - 12
Silver Knight - 11
Judo - 8
Doc Strange - 15
Pyroman - 12
Pyroman - 12
Doc Strange - 9
Doc Strange - 8
Doc Strange - 12
Fighting Yank - 15
Fighting Yank - 15
Fighting Yank - 1
Whispering - 3
Amer. Eagle - 9
Amer. Eagle - 9
Capt. Future - 9 (272)

Capt. Future - 9
Fighting Yank - 14
Capt. Future - 8
Yank - 13
Yank - 15
Pyroman - 13
Capt. Future - 8
Yank - 13
Yank - 12
Dr. Strange - 11
Dr. Strange - 14
Pyroman - 12
Black Terror - 1
Yank - 13
Black Terror - 13
Capt. Future - 8
Doc Strange - 11
Pyroman - 13
Yank - 13
Yank 12
Silver Knight - 8
Judo - 8
Capt Future - 8
Don Davis - 6
Silver Knight - 12
True Story - 6 (274)
True Story - 4 (278)
Black Terror - 8 (286)
Zito — 3 (289)
Vondracek - 3 (292)
Radio Tweed - 6 (298)
Scarab - 12 (310) (320)

Jimmy Cole - 8
Bill King - 6
Bill King - 4 (18)
Bus Miller - 4 (24)
Captain Flight 10 (34)
Cover Black Hood
Death of Kaga - 6
Black Hood - 12
Covers - 4
MacHenson - 6 (63)

For the first few years of his comics career, Kinstler kept a log of the jobs he did. The first two columns are primarily Cinema Comics work that appeared in Ned Pines' Nedor Comics. The third column is solo work for other companies.

His first solo story, "Whispering" (see page 10) appears fourth from the last in column one. Halfway down column two is the *Black Terror* story with the splash page shown at right and fifth from the bottom in that column is a notation for "Zito," a panel from which is shown above.

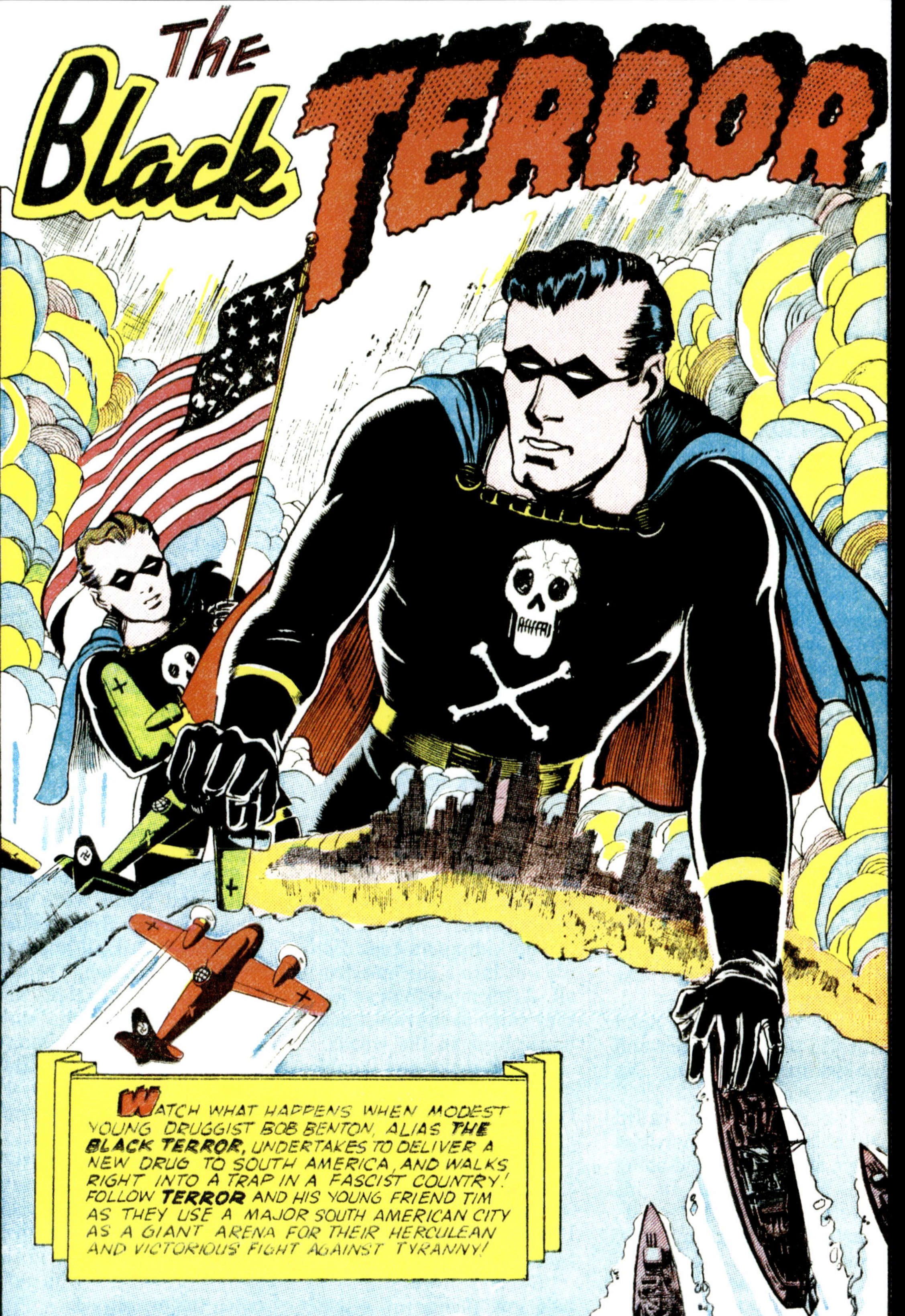

ERK inks over Ken Battefield penc
The Black Terror #7
Nedor Comics, August, 1944

Secret Identities: Unfortunately, by the time Richard Hughes and Ned Pines got around to creating *their* superheroes, all of the really good secret identities and chest emblems had been snatched up.

So ***The Black Terror*** got to be a "modest young druggist" which might explain why he has the international symbol for poison on his costume.

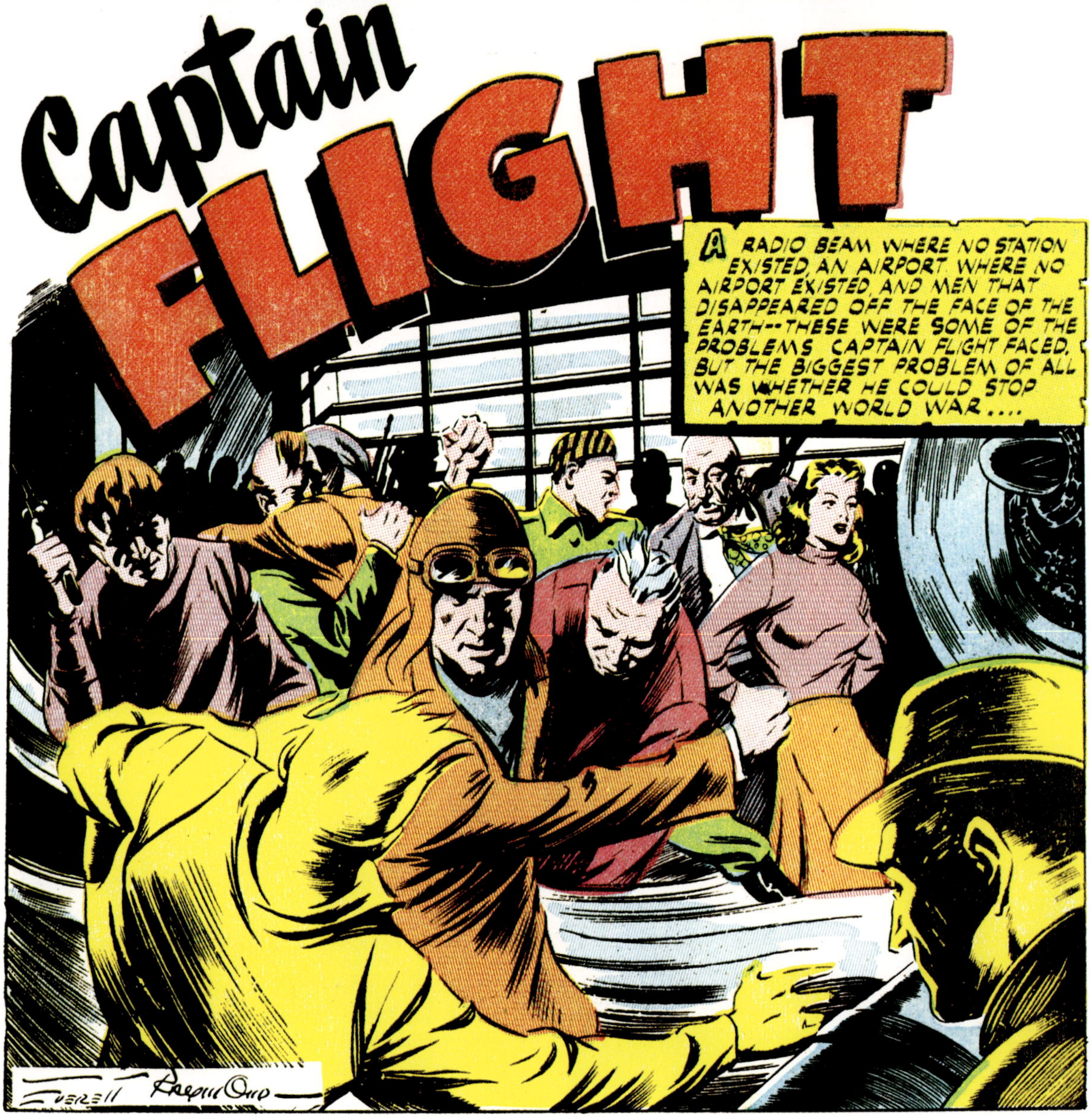

Captain Flight #9
Four Star Comics, September, 1945

During WWII, freelance work was plentiful for young artists. Cinema Comics kept Ray occupied with inking and full stories, but that wasn't enough. He took on work from smaller companies like Four Star, MLJ and Parents to stay busy.

Most of the work published in 1945 was produced very early in the year or late in 1944.

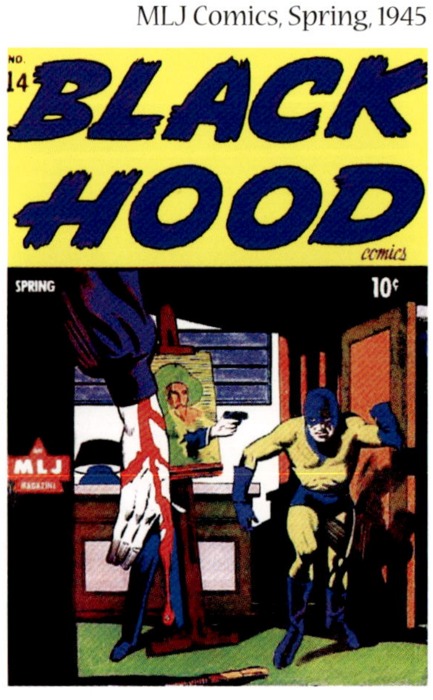

Black Hood #14
MLJ Comics, Spring, 1945

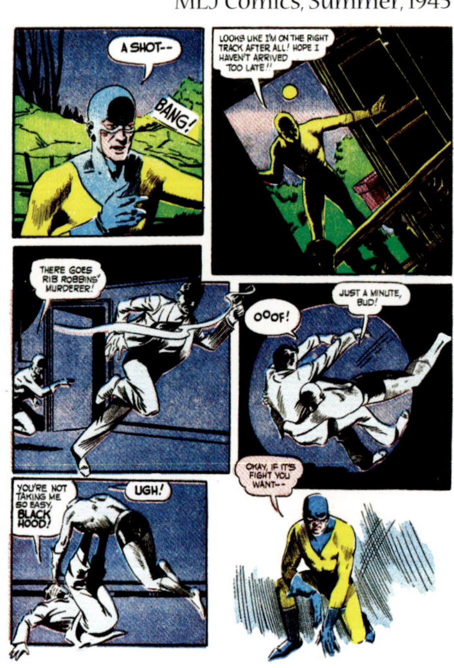

Black Hood #15
MLJ Comics, Summer, 1945

Comic book coloring: If you ever wondered why comic colorists couldn't seem to stay within the lines, it was all done in a very low-tech, mechanical fashion that was prone to error.

"Colorists" were employed by the printers to cut screens of various patterns to be photographed for each color. A 20% red pattern combined with 20% yellow would make a flesh tone. The two shapes may have been cut at separate times by two different people and it was piece work, so speed mattered and, the product being comics, quality didn't.

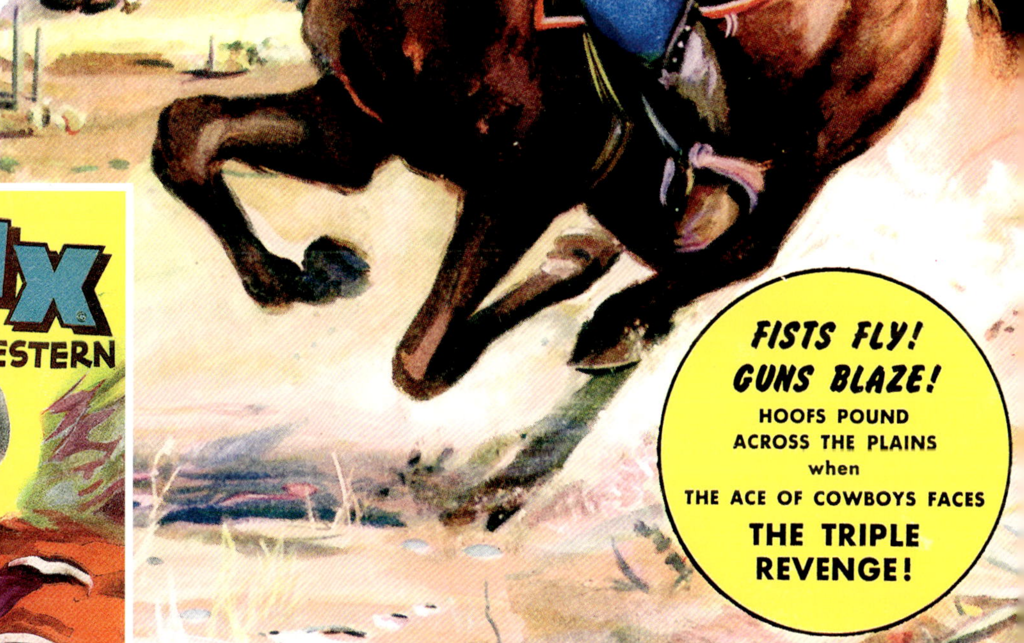

Fawcett Comics
November, 1948

Some of Kinstler's first published paintings appeared on Fawcett's western titles ***Tom Mix*** and ***Hopalong Cassidy***. Ray's "fascination with faces" is evident here as he maintains a continuity of characterization over several issues. If Tom Mix always wears the same shirt and hat, it seems that Ray insisted that he at least change his bandana.

Fawcett Comics
August, 1948

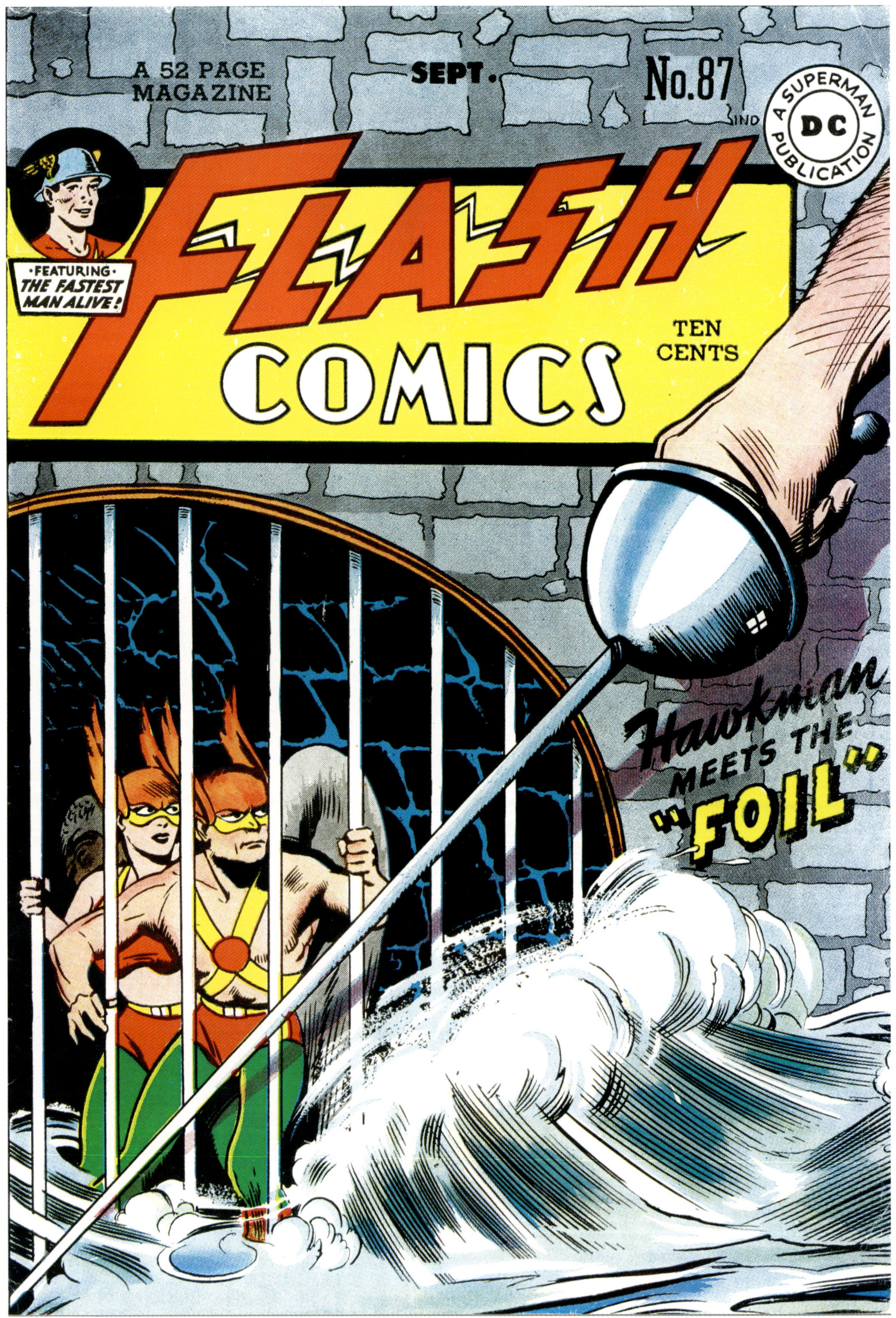
A 52 PAGE MAGAZINE
SEPT.
No.87
A SUPERMAN PUBLICATION
DC
FEATURING
THE FASTEST MAN ALIVE!
FLASH
COMICS
TEN CENTS
Hawkman
MEETS THE
"FOIL"

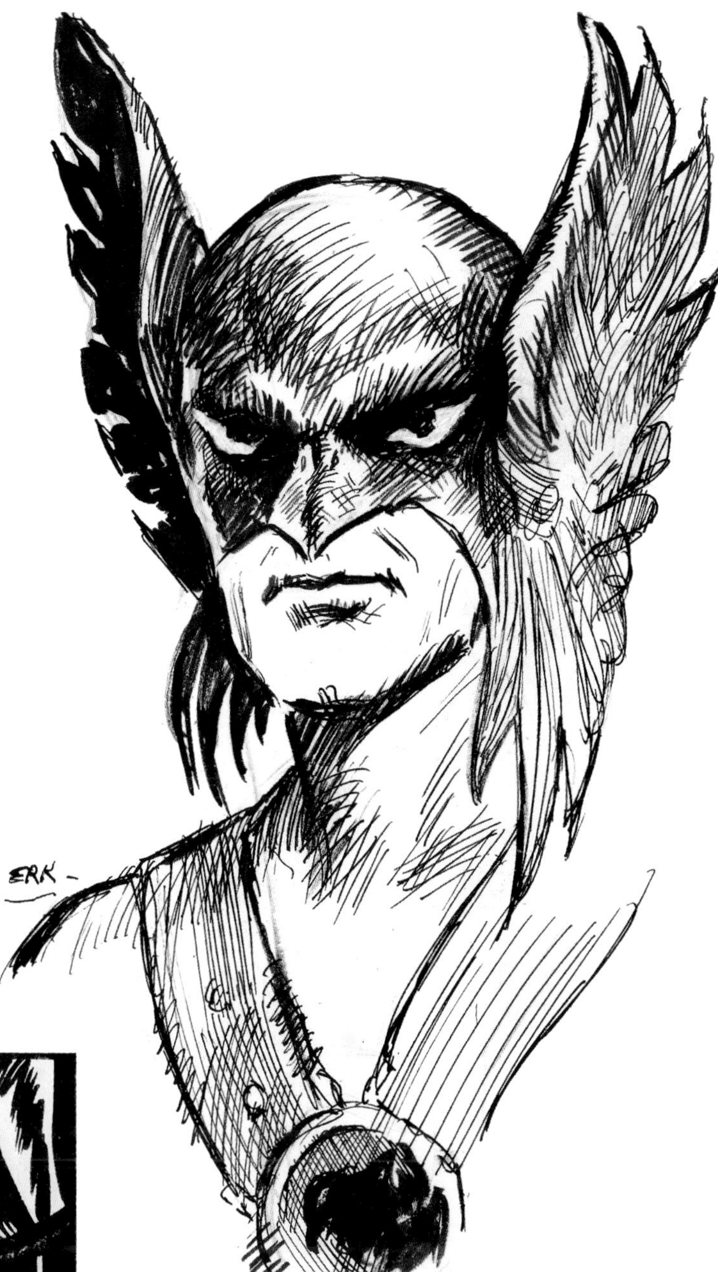

HAWKMAN™ DC COMICS

It was probably just coincidence that the first two stories that Ray did for DC Comics involved swordplay. *The Black Pirate* tale was more to his liking as he paid homage to the swashbuckling heroes of the cinema in nearly every panel.

The *Hawkman* stories in ***Flash Comics*** #87 and 89 were a change of pace and two of the very few costumed hero types he was to render over the years.

He still has the knack over fifty years later as the recent sketch above shows.

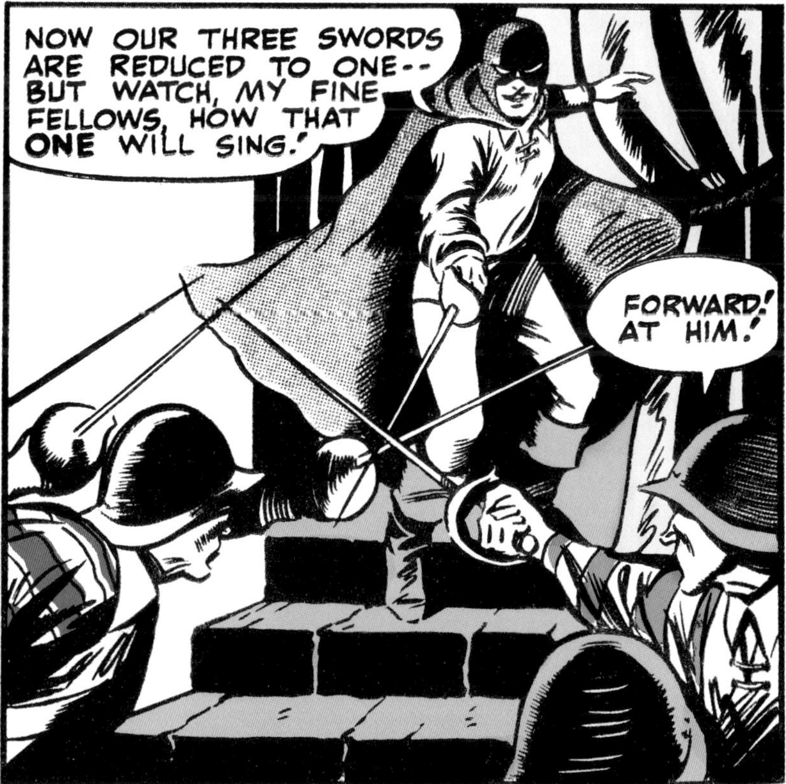

BLACK PIRATE - THE ADVENTURE IN CASTLE VILLON
All-American Comics #89
DC Comics, September, 1947

Flash Comics #87
DC Comics, September, 1947

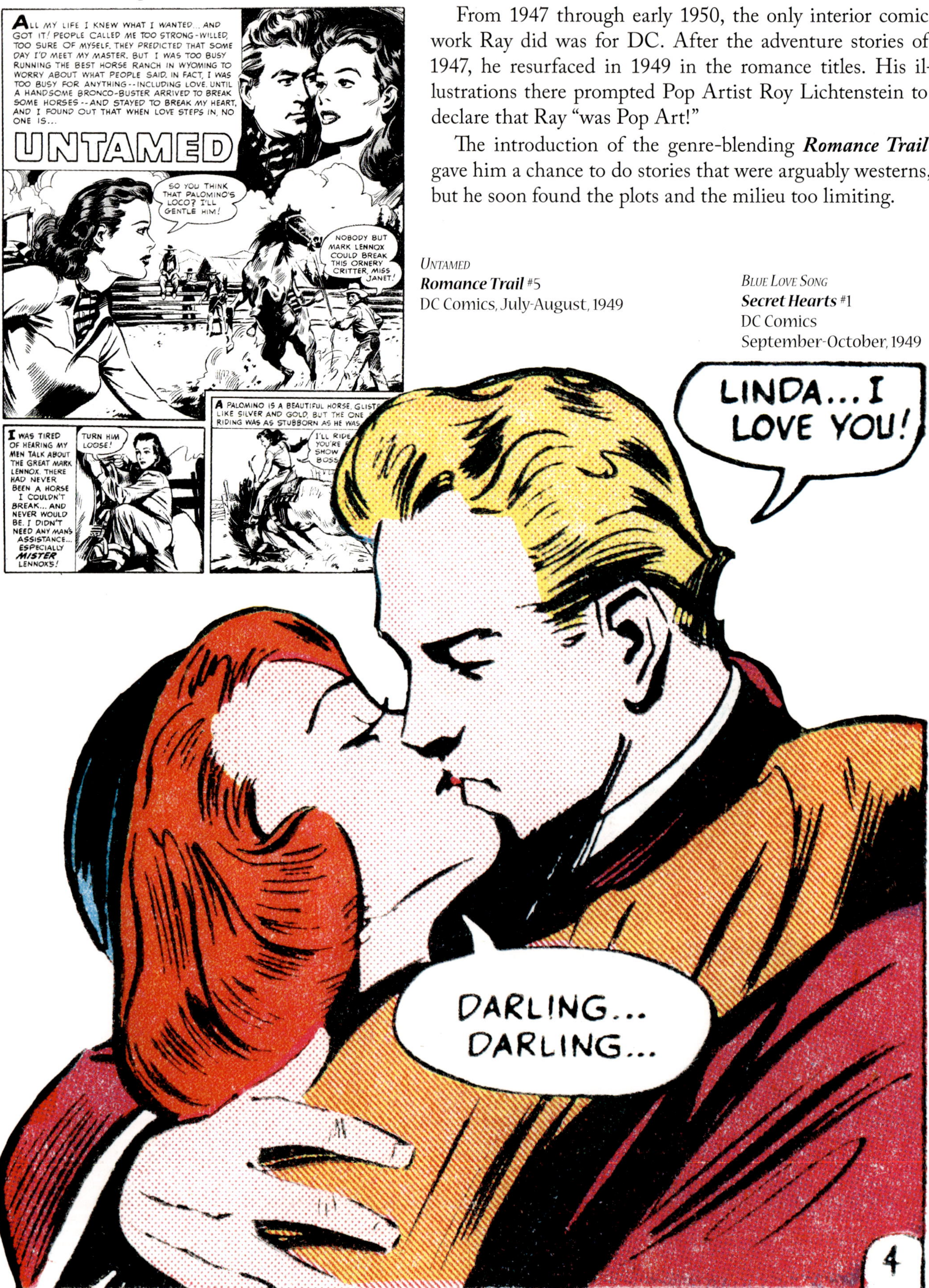

From 1947 through early 1950, the only interior comic work Ray did was for DC. After the adventure stories of 1947, he resurfaced in 1949 in the romance titles. His illustrations there prompted Pop Artist Roy Lichtenstein to declare that Ray "was Pop Art!"

The introduction of the genre-blending ***Romance Trail*** gave him a chance to do stories that were arguably westerns, but he soon found the plots and the milieu too limiting.

Untamed
Romance Trail #5
DC Comics, July-August, 1949

Blue Love Song
Secret Hearts #1
DC Comics
September-October, 1949

The 1950s

In 1950, Ray began a six-year association with Avon Comics where he produced covers, stories and some marvelous collage-like pen and ink drawings for the inside front covers of many of its comics. It was on these latter that he honed his skills and allowed his love affair with the pen to flourish and develop. Many of these are presented on the following pages reproduced directly from the original drawings that Ray has carefully retained for over fifty years.

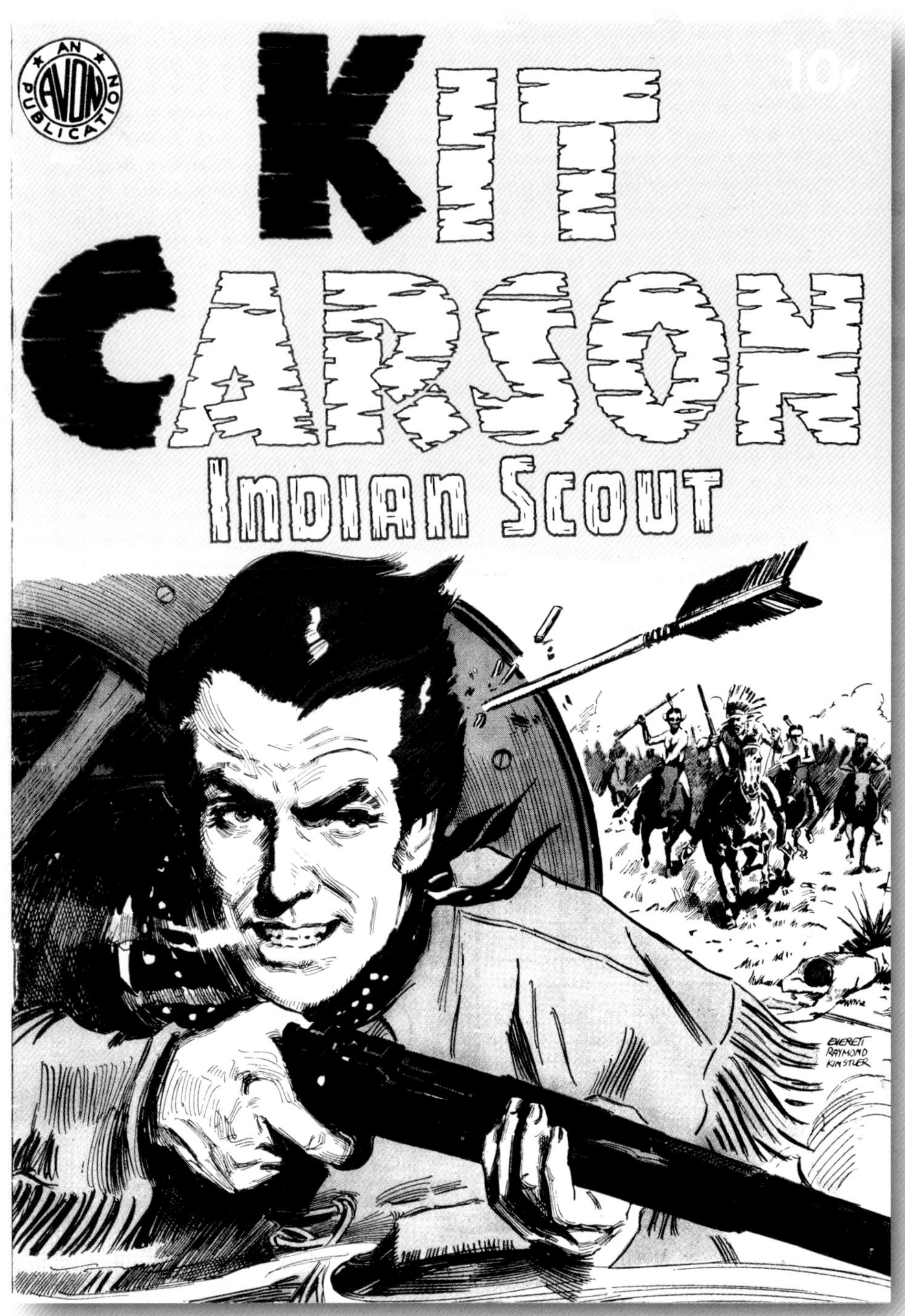

Kit Carson Indian Scout
Avon, 1950

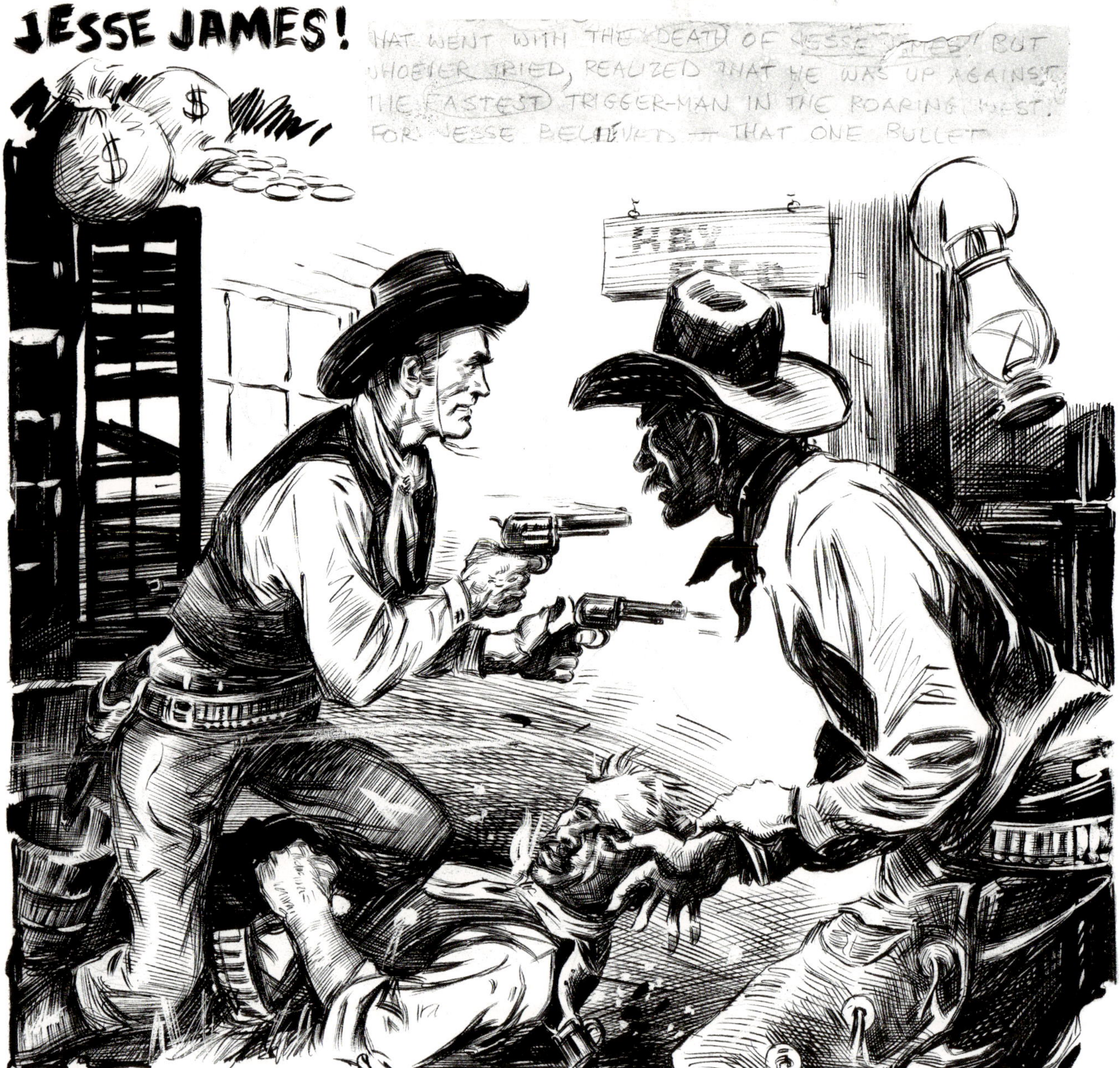

JESSE JAMES!
HAT WENT WITH THE DEATH OF JESSE JAMES! BUT
WHOEVER TRIED, REALIZED THAT HE WAS UP AGAINST
THE FASTEST TRIGGER-MAN IN THE ROARING WEST!
FOR JESSE BELIEVED — THAT ONE BULLET

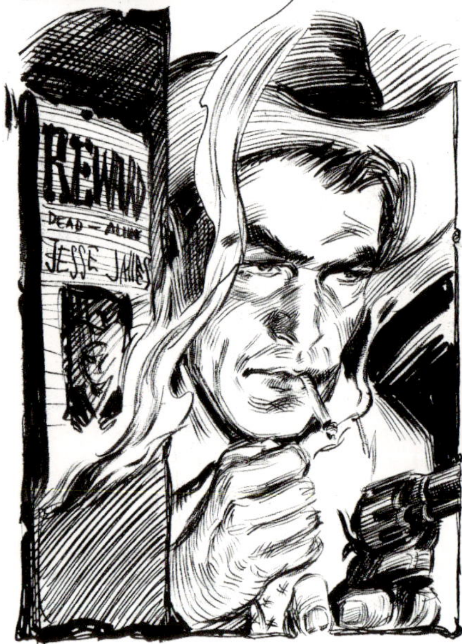

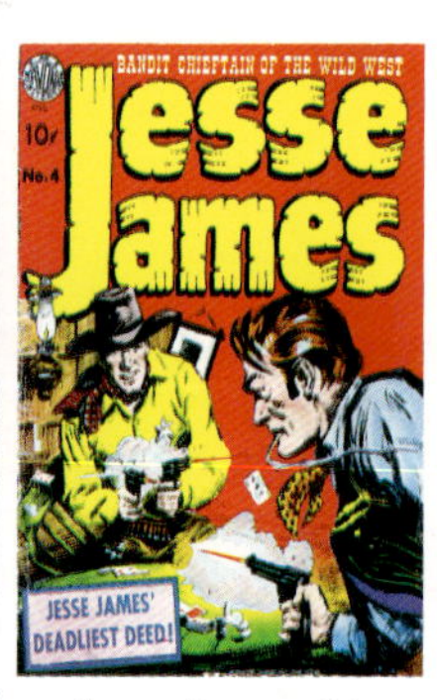

***Jesse James* #4**
Avon, July, 1951
original: 13"x18½"

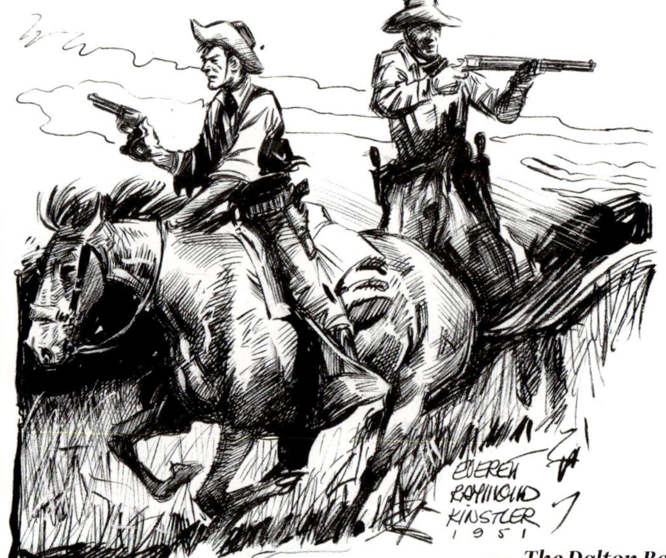

The Dalton Boys
Avon, 1951
original: 13"x18¼"

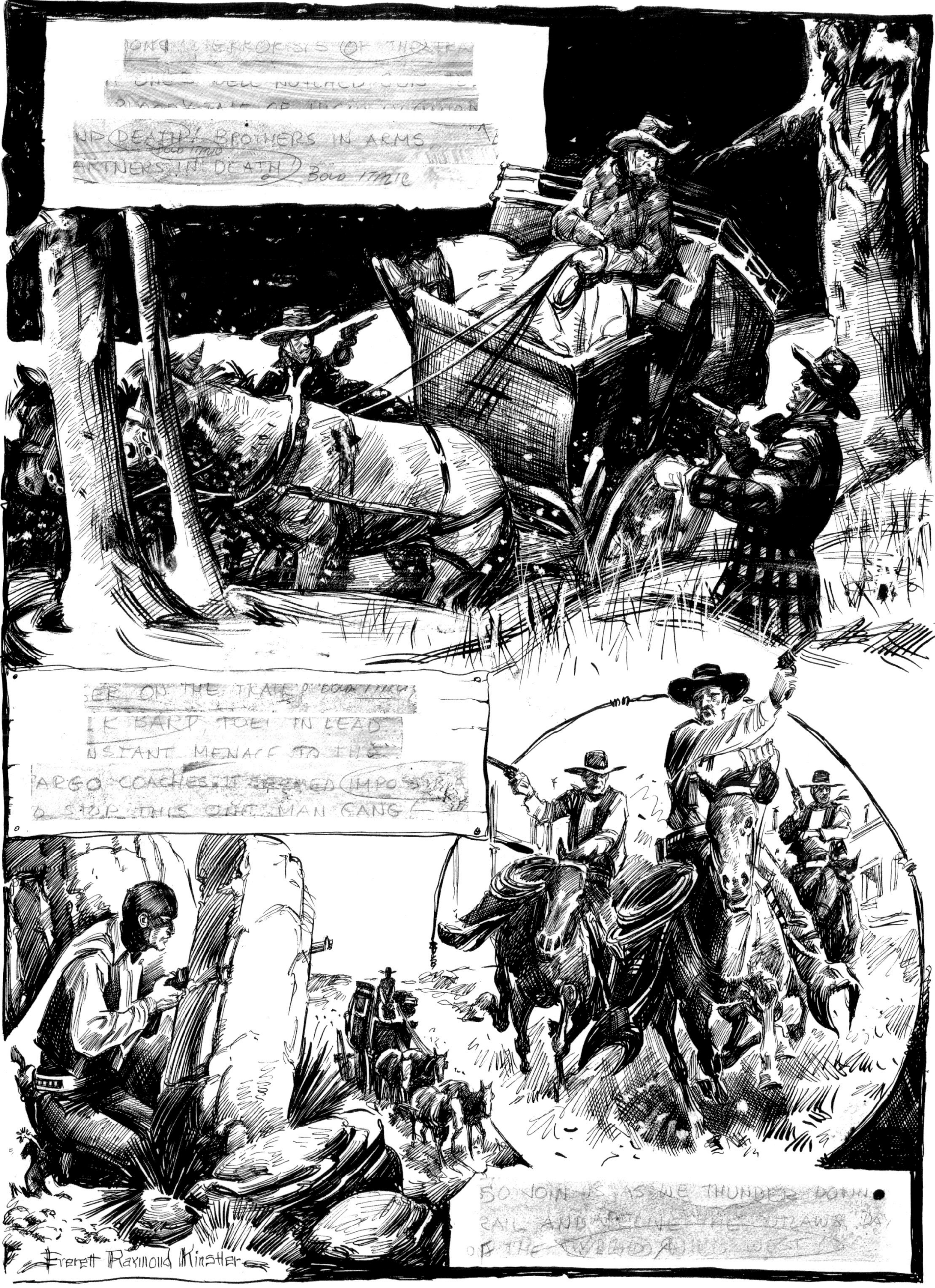
NOTCHED
DEATH! BROTHERS IN ARMS
ARTNERS IN DEATH!
BOLD ITALIC
BOLD ITALIC
ER ON THE TRAIL
K BART, TOEI IN LEAD
NSTANT MENACE TO THE
ARGO COACHES. IT
O STOP THIS
MAN GANG!
SO JOIN US AS WE THUNDER
AIL AND
OF THE
Everett Raymond Kinstler

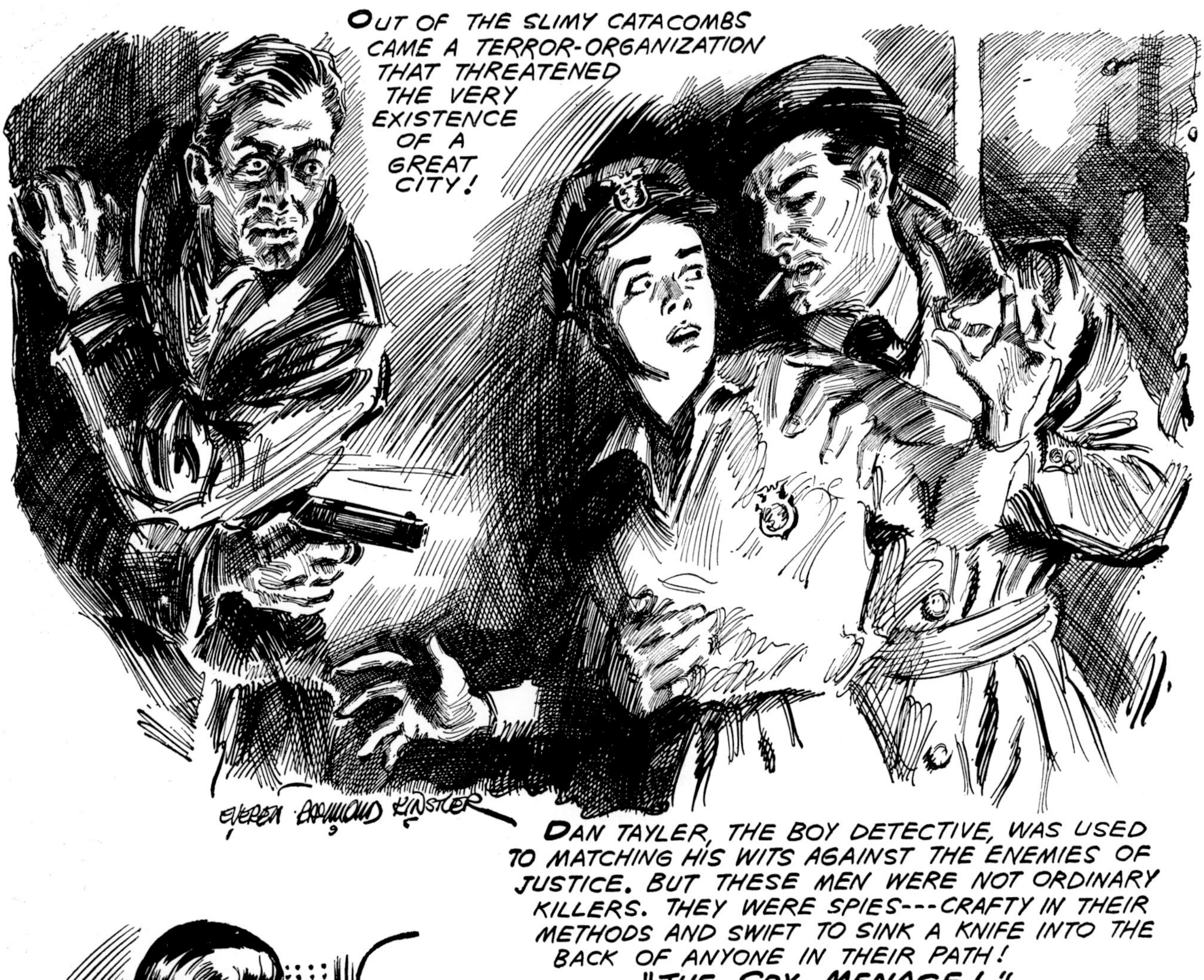

OUT OF THE SLIMY CATACOMBS CAME A TERROR-ORGANIZATION THAT THREATENED THE VERY EXISTENCE OF A GREAT CITY!

EVERETT RAYMOND KINSTLER

DAN TAYLER, THE BOY DETECTIVE, WAS USED TO MATCHING HIS WITS AGAINST THE ENEMIES OF JUSTICE. BUT THESE MEN WERE NOT ORDINARY KILLERS. THEY WERE SPIES---CRAFTY IN THEIR METHODS AND SWIFT TO SINK A KNIFE INTO THE BACK OF ANYONE IN THEIR PATH!

"THE SPY MENACE!"

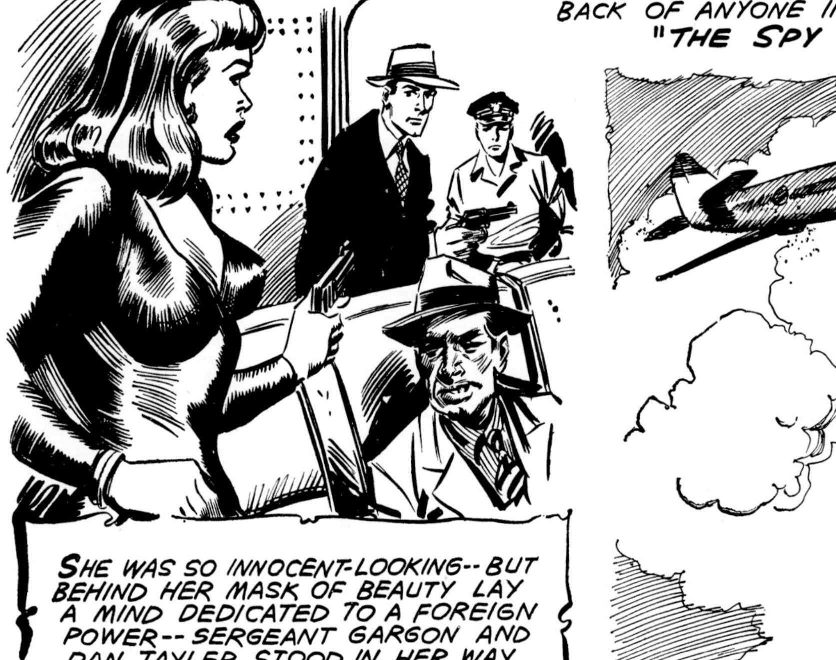

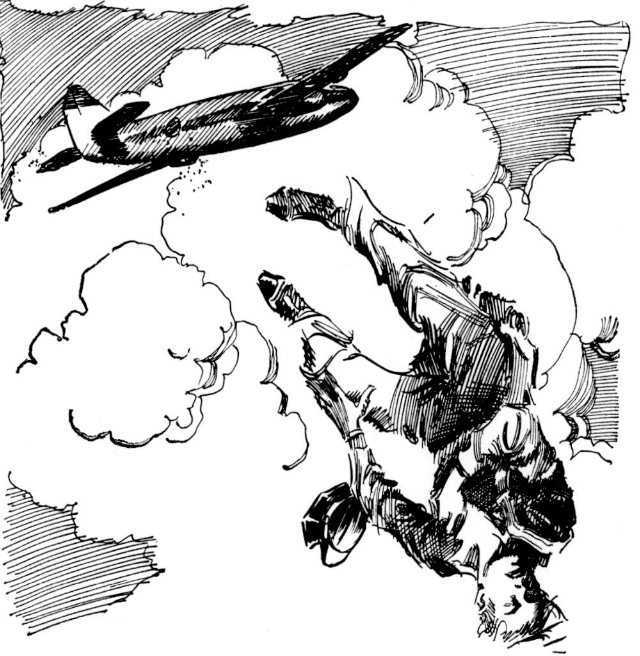

Dan Tayler Boy Detective Fights the Spy Menace
Boy Detective #3
Avon, February, 1952

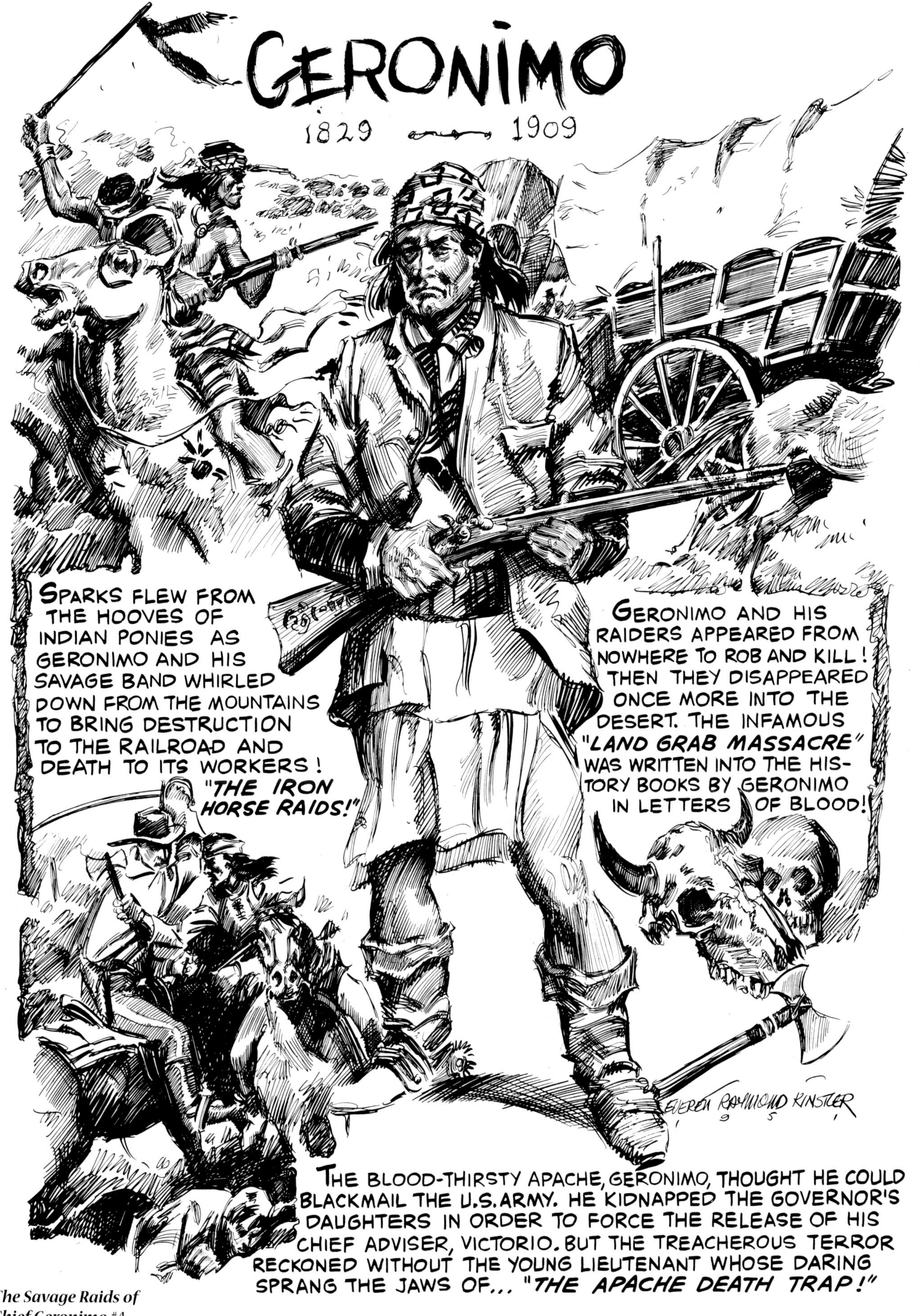

The Savage Raids of Chief Geronimo #4
Avon, February, 1952

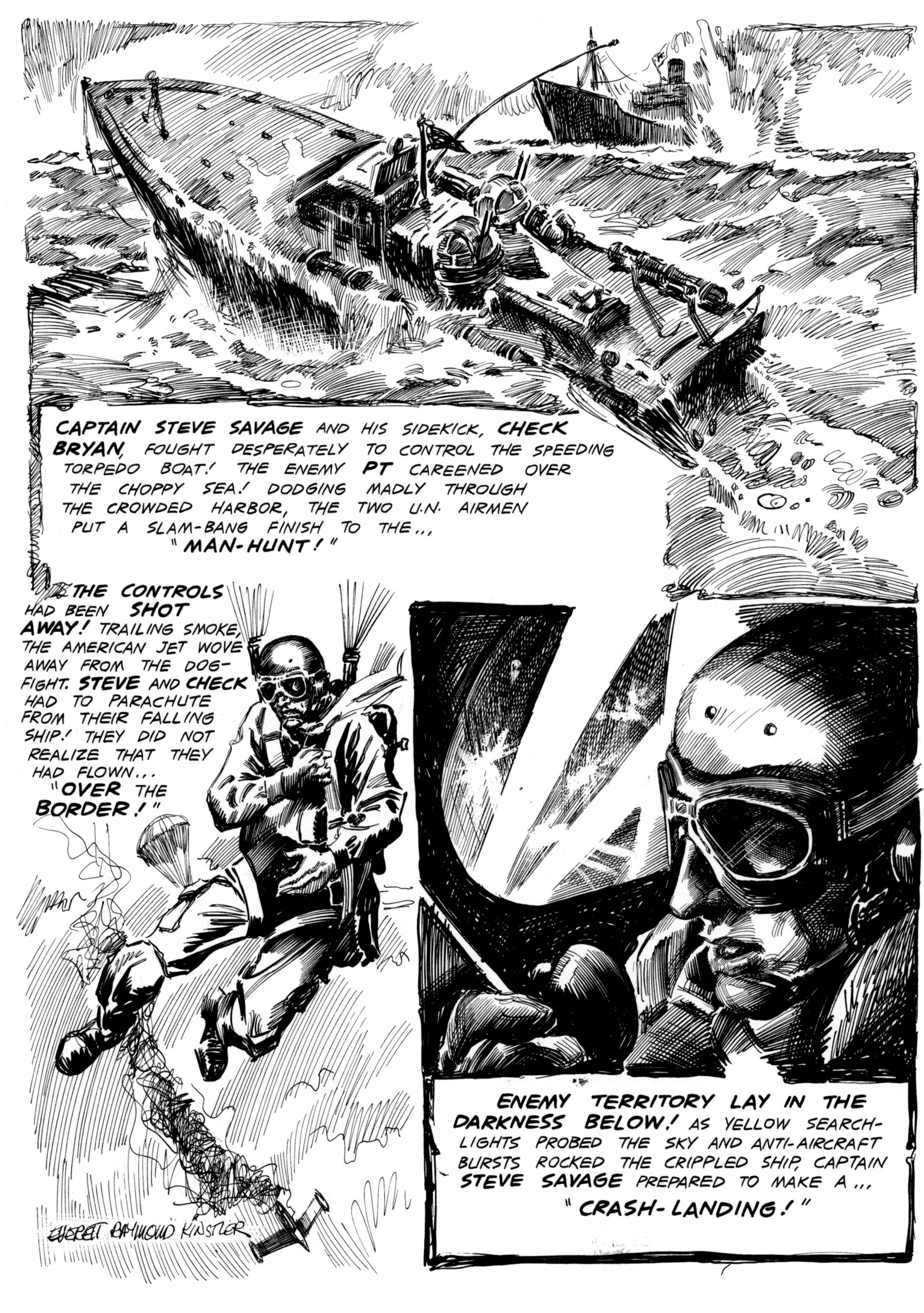
CAPTAIN STEVE SAVAGE AND HIS SIDEKICK, CHECK BRYAN, FOUGHT DESPERATELY TO CONTROL THE SPEEDING TORPEDO BOAT! THE ENEMY PT CAREENED OVER THE CHOPPY SEA! DODGING MADLY THROUGH THE CROWDED HARBOR, THE TWO U.N. AIRMEN PUT A SLAM-BANG FINISH TO THE... "MAN-HUNT!"
THE CONTROLS HAD BEEN SHOT AWAY! TRAILING SMOKE, THE AMERICAN JET WOVE AWAY FROM THE DOG-FIGHT. STEVE AND CHECK HAD TO PARACHUTE FROM THEIR FALLING SHIP! THEY DID NOT REALIZE THAT THEY HAD FLOWN... "OVER THE BORDER!"
ENEMY TERRITORY LAY IN THE DARKNESS BELOW! AS YELLOW SEARCH-LIGHTS PROBED THE SKY AND ANTI-AIRCRAFT BURSTS ROCKED THE CRIPPLED SHIP, CAPTAIN STEVE SAVAGE PREPARED TO MAKE A... "CRASH-LANDING!"
EVERETT RAYMOND KINSTLER

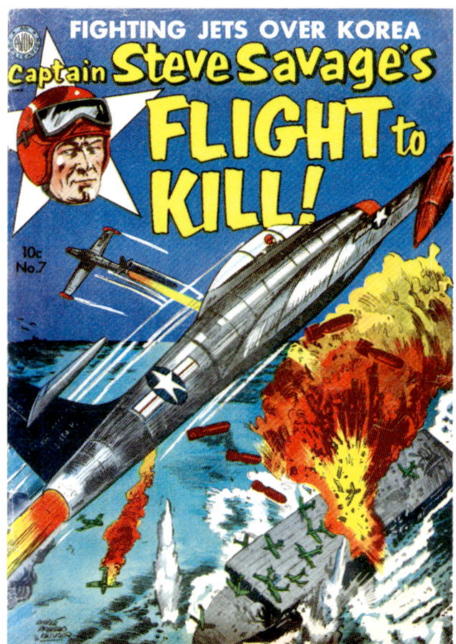

***Captain Steve Savage's Flight to Kill* #7**
Avon, October, 1952
original: 13"x17½"

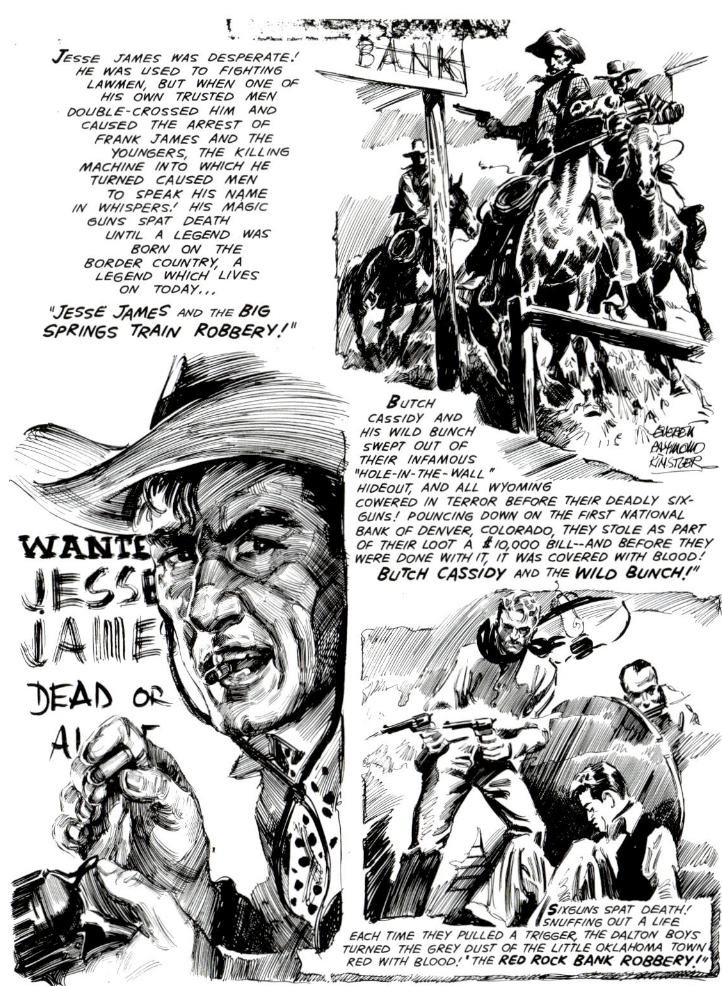

Western Bandits
Avon, 1952

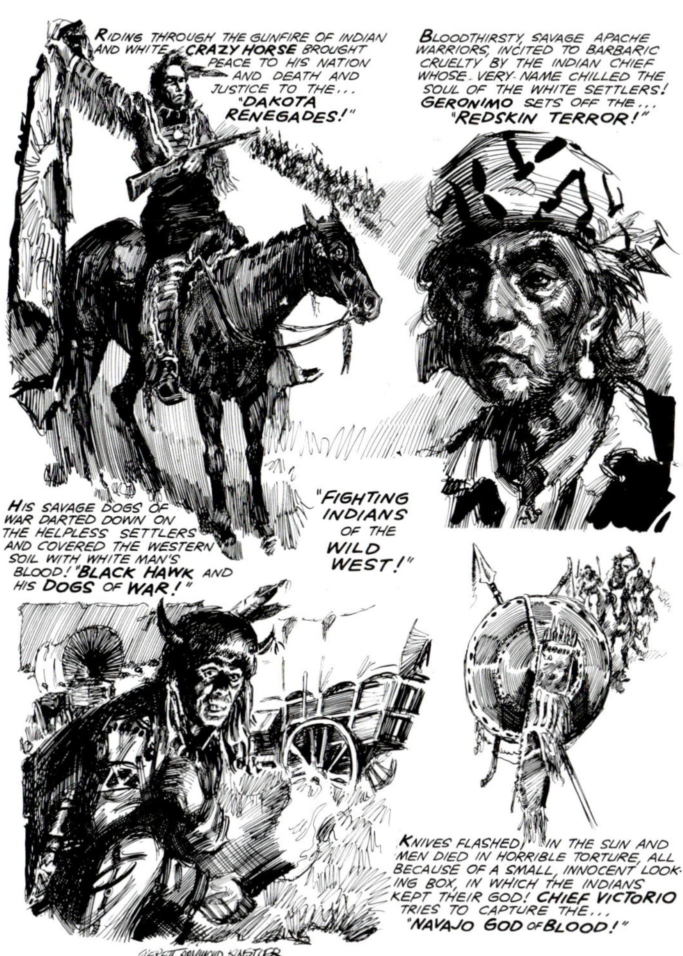

Fighting Indians of the Wild West
Avon, March, 1952

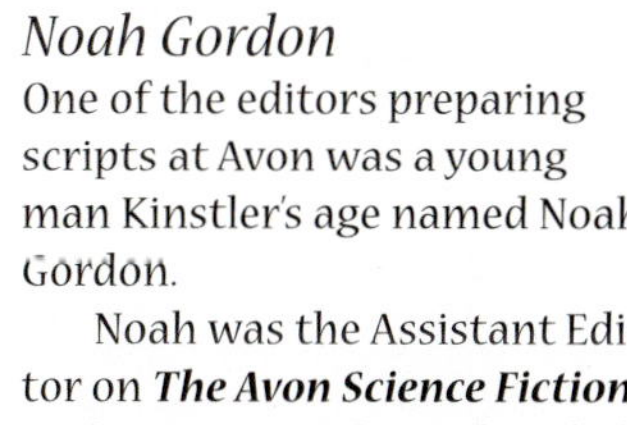

Noah Gordon

One of the editors preparing scripts at Avon was a young man Kinstler's age named Noah Gordon.

Noah was the Assistant Editor on ***The Avon Science Fiction and Fantasy Reader*** and probably played a role in getting illustrations into that digest pulp.

Ray used Noah as the model for the cover painting of Avon's **Out of the Silent Planet** in 1954 and for **Shadows of Shame** in 1956. Gordon was destined for greater achievements than comic books, pulps, or cover guy. He wrote the 1965 ***New York Times*** bestseller, **The Rabbi**, and has enjoyed a stellar career as a novelist of international renown.

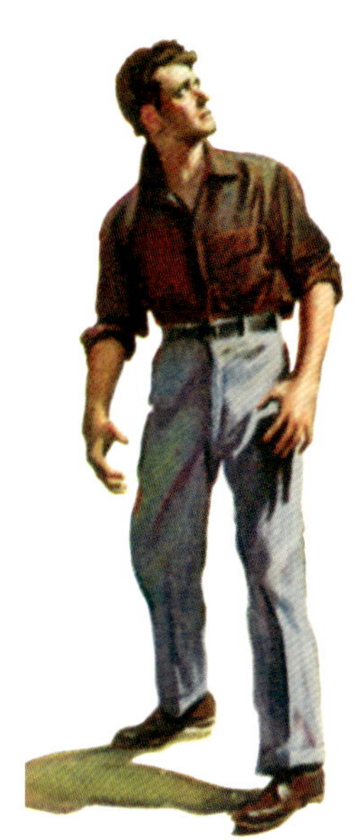

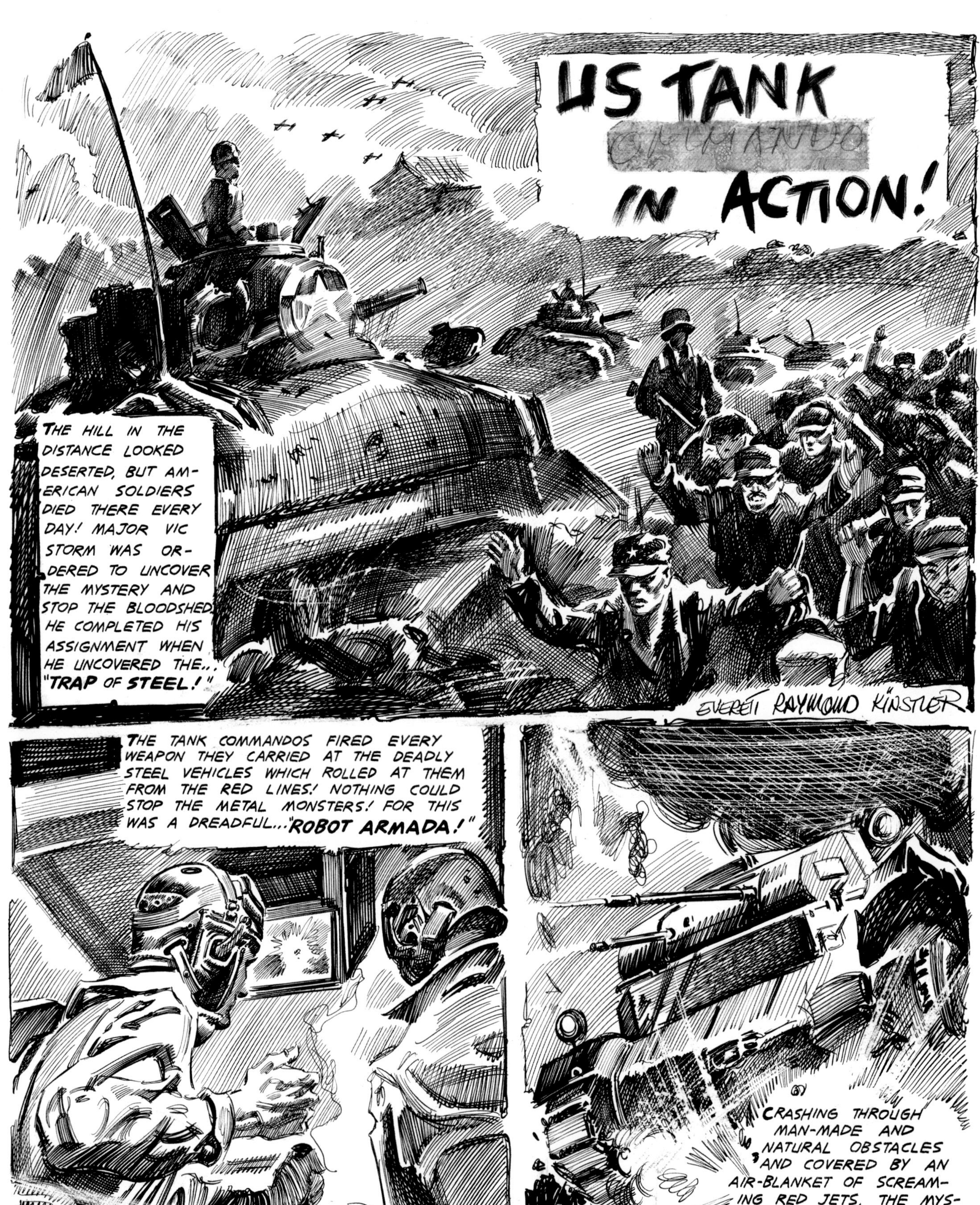
US TANK
IN ACTION!
THE HILL IN THE DISTANCE LOOKED DESERTED, BUT AMERICAN SOLDIERS DIED THERE EVERY DAY! MAJOR VIC STORM WAS ORDERED TO UNCOVER THE MYSTERY AND STOP THE BLOODSHED. HE COMPLETED HIS ASSIGNMENT WHEN HE UNCOVERED THE... "TRAP OF STEEL!"
EVERETT RAYMOND KINSTLER
THE TANK COMMANDOS FIRED EVERY WEAPON THEY CARRIED AT THE DEADLY STEEL VEHICLES WHICH ROLLED AT THEM FROM THE RED LINES! NOTHING COULD STOP THE METAL MONSTERS! FOR THIS WAS A DREADFUL... "ROBOT ARMADA!"
CRASHING THROUGH MAN-MADE AND NATURAL OBSTACLES AND COVERED BY AN AIR-BLANKET OF SCREAMING RED JETS, THE MYSTERY TANK TOOK A HORRIBLE TOLL IN AMERICAN LIVES. MAJOR VIC STORM AND HIS TANK COMMANDOS SPED TO INTERCEPT THE... "KILLER TANK!"

Kinstler was expected to create believable and accurate depictions of any situation that the writer could dream up. Like every other dedicated commercial artist of the day, he maintained a "scrap" file of photographs and illustrations on which he could rely for realistic renditions.

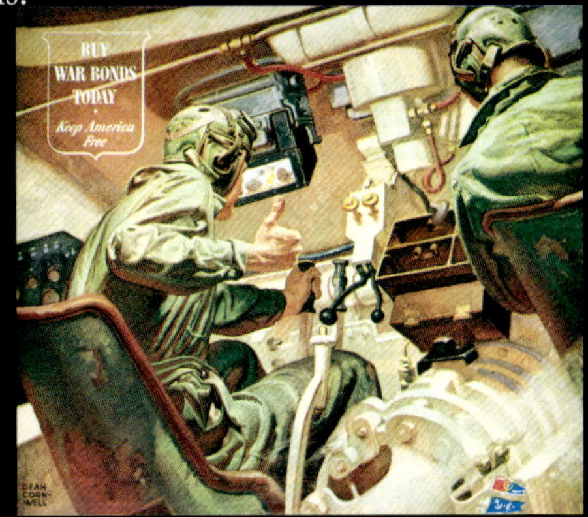

The two soldiers inside the tank were researched and painted from models by Dean Cornwell during World War II. Cornwell had the time and the resources to get everything just perfect for his inspirational illustrations for Fisher Body corporation that appeared in all of the major magazines.

Kinstler had neither the time nor the money, but he was just as determined to get it right. It's just that his reference material was secondhand.

The other illustrations were referenced from a series of paintings in ***Life Magazine*** by the artist Ogden Pleissner, who, a generation before Kinstler, had also studied at The Art Students League under Frank Vincent DuMond. Though never as famous as Cornwell, Pleissner also spent the years of World War II as a working artist—for the Air Force and as a reporting artist for ***Life***.

The skillful combination of these diverse source images and their transition from paint to the unifying medium of ink resulted in just the type of action-packed drawings upon which Avon editor Sol Cohen relied.

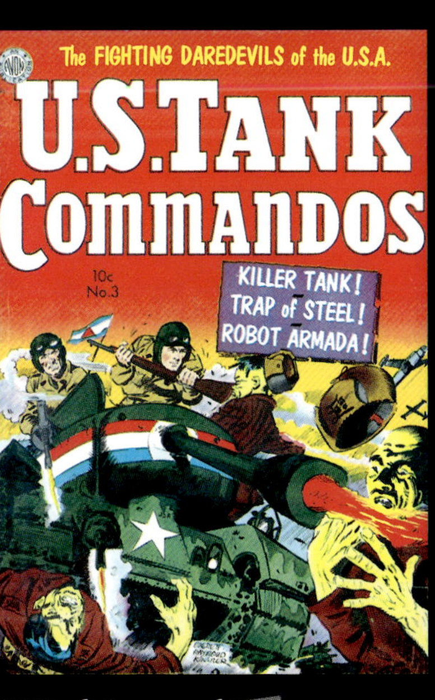

U.S. Tank Commandos #3
Avon, November, 1952
original: 12½"x17½"

ERK on Avon

I've always gravitated towards people I liked and could relate to. Those editors who respected my work brought out the best in me. Money was never my motivation. I was gaining experience, I enjoyed the work and I needed to survive.

I showed my portfolio to Avon editor Sol Cohen and we hit it off immediately, in that he gave me great freedom to experiment. His attitude and confidence were instrumental to my introduction of those "contents pages" on the inside covers. I enjoyed seeing my black and white drawings reproduced sharply on coated stock without color overlays to dull them.

These pages reflected a personal side of my comics, and I tried to get the originals returned to me. All too often, though, the art was given to friends of the art director. My originals have turned up in curious places… most recently in the possession of the niece of Avon publisher Joe Meyers.

When they started the ***Jesse James*** comic, Joe Kubert and I drew most of the stories. I admired Joe's layouts and strong brush work, and I was certainly influenced by his style. While I preferred pen and ink for my inside covers, I found the brush provided simpler and more vivid images, and retained the strength and character of my panels when color was added.

I have always been influenced by and learned from those artists that I admired. Kubert and Wally Wood were my contemporaries. Occasionally we'd meet at Avon, sometimes share lunch or coffee and exchange thoughts about the comics field, trends, who was hiring, etc. We were three very different people.

I worked at Dell and Ziff-Davis at the same time I was with Avon. I had the most fun at Avon. Sol Cohen offered me creative flexibility which enabled me to grow artistically.

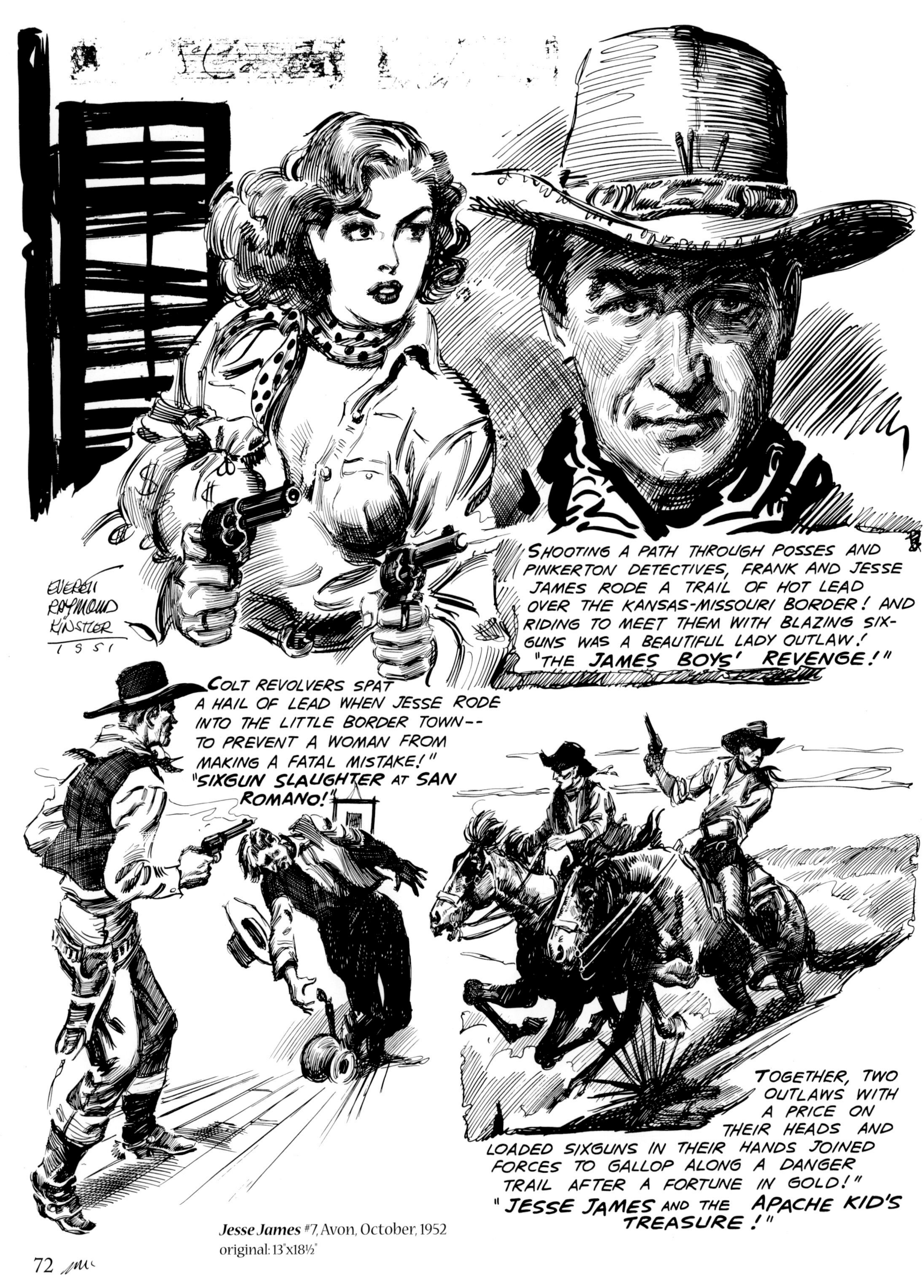

Jesse James #7, Avon, October, 1952
original: 13"x18½"

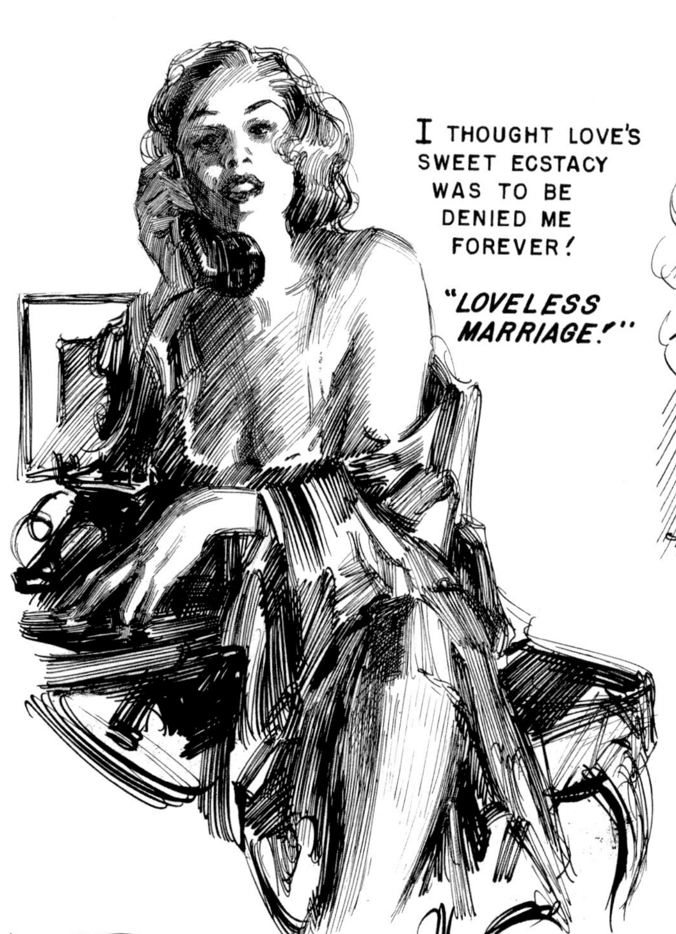

JOE CASSIDY WAS INVINCIBLE IN THE RING, BUT HELP-LESS BEFORE THE WITHERING GLANCE OF THE WOMAN WHO THOUGHT HE HAD WRONGED HER. WHEN HE FOUND THE TRUE LOVE WHICH BARBARA OFFERED HIM WITH OPEN ARMS, HE THOUGHT THAT HE HAD AT LAST FOUND REAL HAPPINESS. BUT HE SHOULD HAVE KNOWN THAT... *"LOVE IS LIKE HATE!"*

ANN HOLIDAY WAS BORED BY HER SMALL-TOWN EXISTENCE. SO WHEN SUAVE, SLEEK, RALPH BROOK WAS TRANSFERRED TO HER COMPANY FROM NEW YORK, ANN MADE UP HER MIND THAT SHE WAS GOING TO SNARE HER-SELF A MAN. READ HOW HER SCHEME BACKFIRED, WHEN SHE VOWED... *"I'LL MAKE HIM MINE!"*

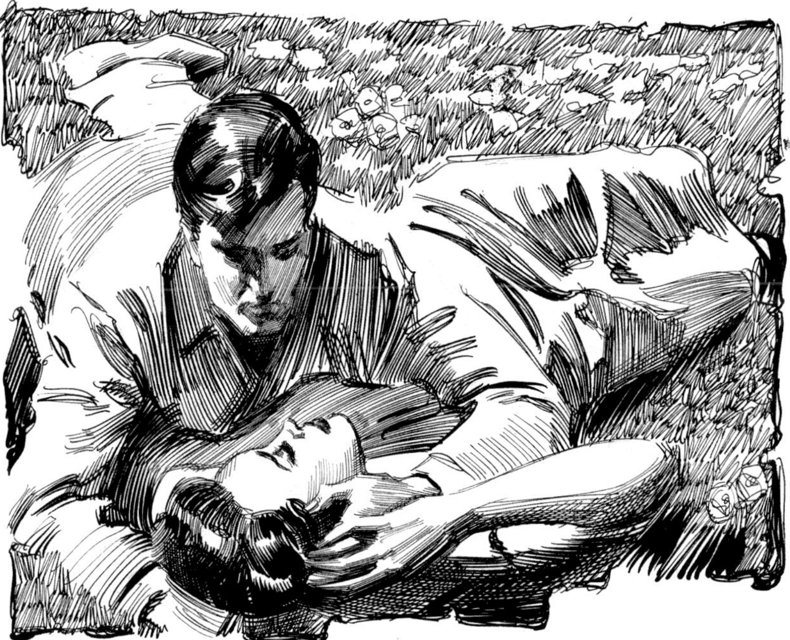

SHE WAS STILL THE COMBINATION OF INNOCENCE AND BEAUTY WHICH HAD DRIVEN ME WILD WHEN WE WERE BOTH YOUNGER AND LESS EXPERIENCED. BUT IT WAS HER SISTER MARY THAT I DREAMED ABOUT. I WAS BITTER EACH TIME I ENTERED MY HOME TO FIND CYNTHIA'S ARMS OPEN FOR MY EMBRACE, HER LIPS POSED TO RECEIVE MY KISS. I THOUGHT THAT... *"I WAS TRAPPED INTO MARRIAGE!"*

EVERETT RAYMOND KINSTLER 1951

Source unknown, Avon, 1951
original: 13"x17¼"

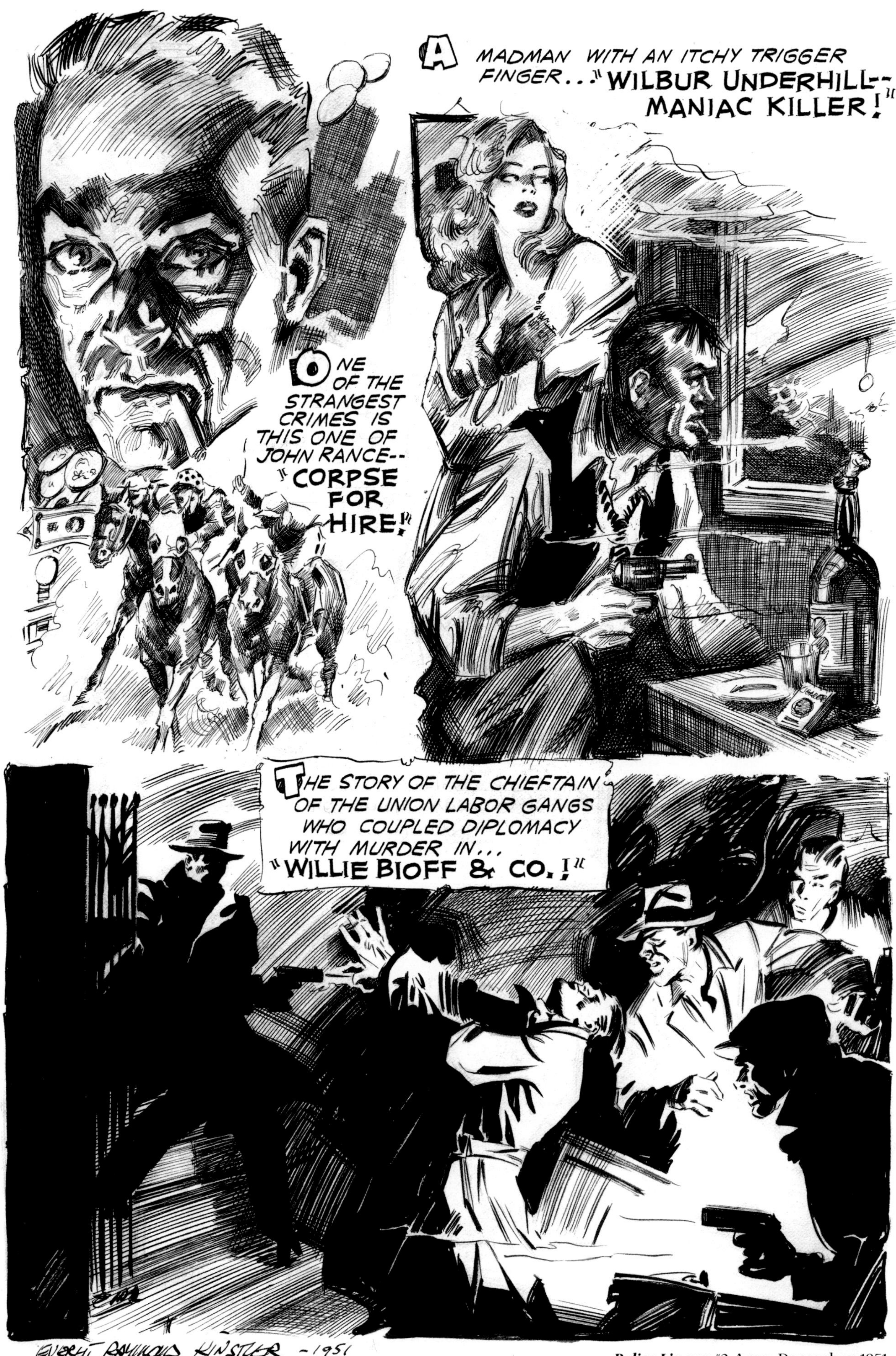

Police Lineup #2, Avon, December, 1951
original: 12½"x18"

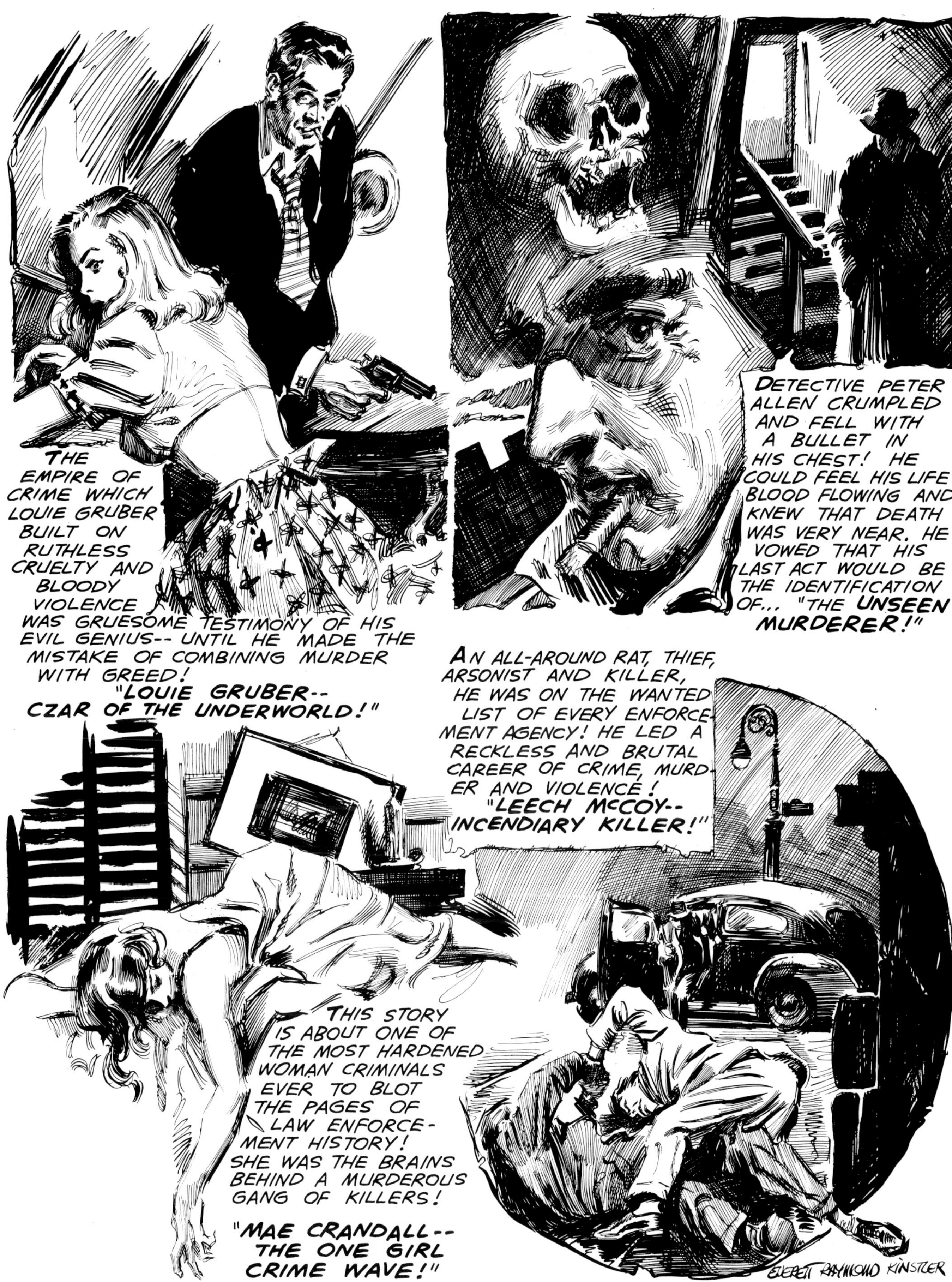

Police Lineup #3
Avon, April, 1952

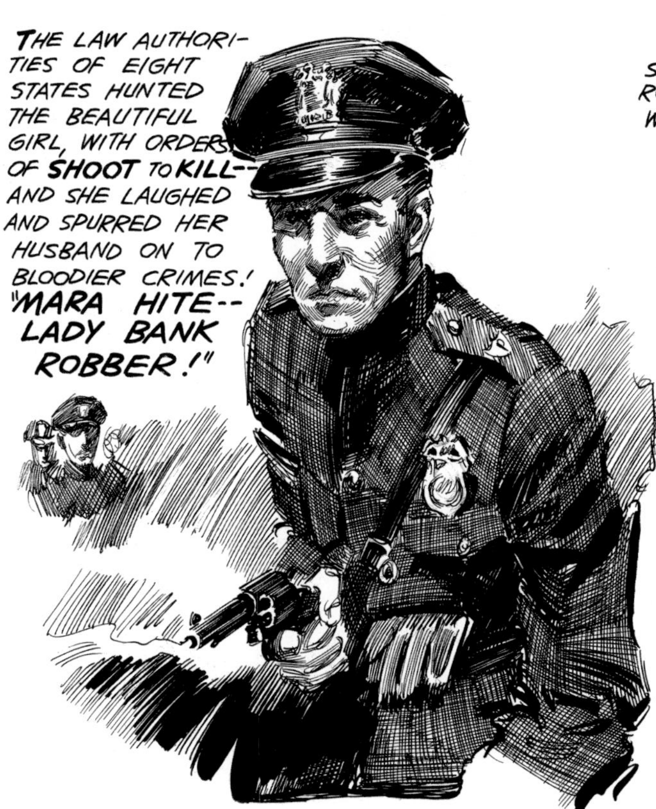

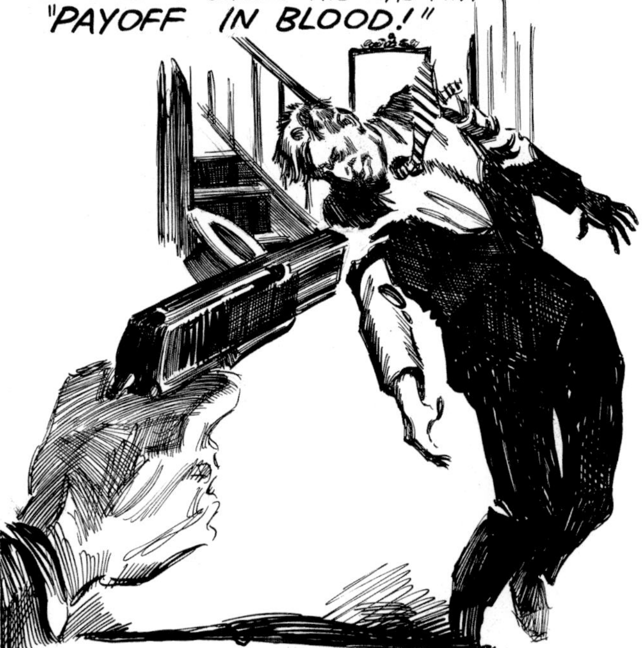

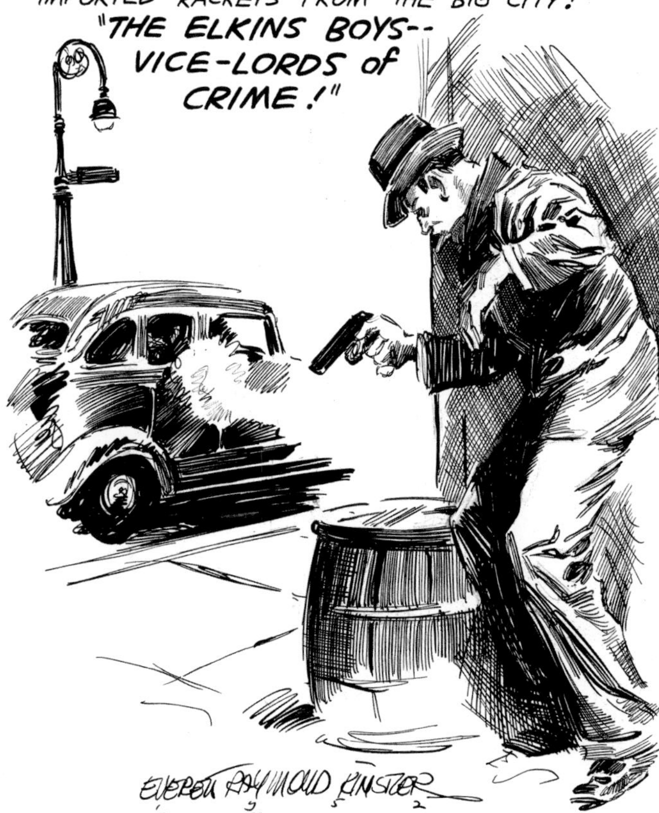

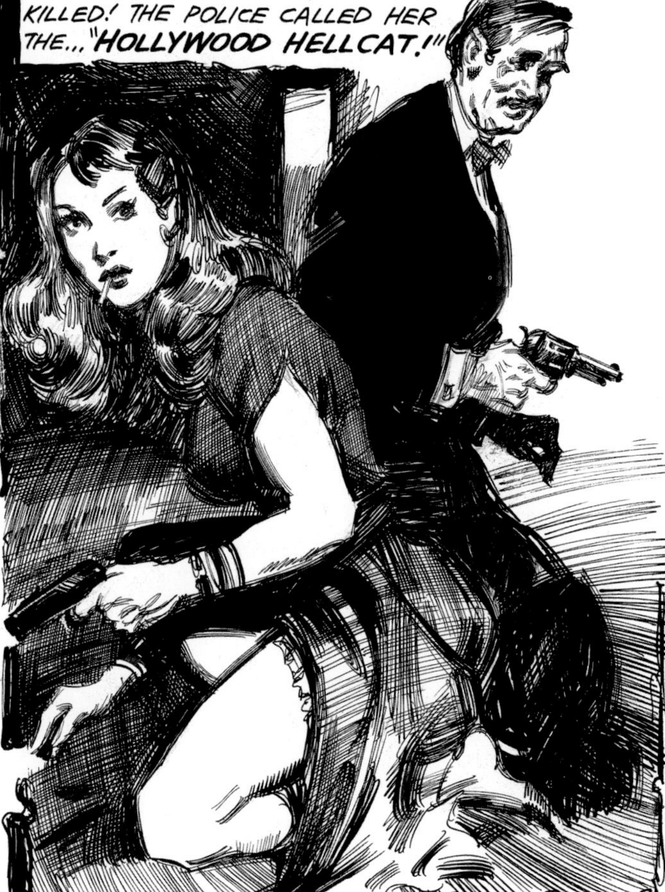

Gangsters and Gun Molls #4
Avon, June, 1952
original: 14¼"x18¼"

Avon, 1951

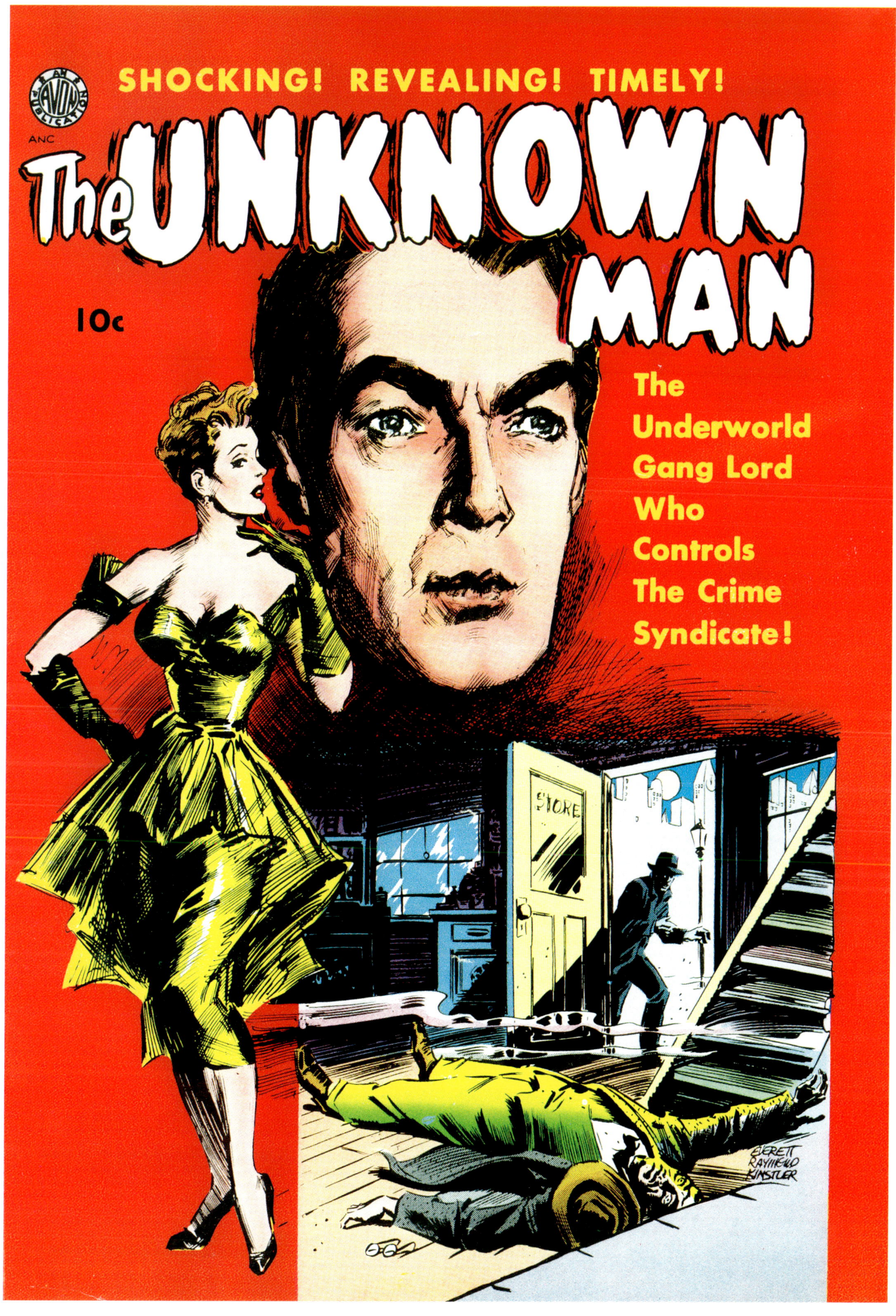

SHOCKING! REVEALING! TIMELY!
AVON PUBLICATION
ANC
The UNKNOWN MAN
10c
The Underworld Gang Lord Who Controls The Crime Syndicate!
STORE
EVERETT RAYMOND KINSTLER

The Steve Savage drawing on "Perilous Mission" below was based on a wonderful portrait of Captain Eddie Rickenbacker done by Howard Chandler Christy. It was a striking pose and fit the image of relaxed competence that Captain Savage was supposed to project.

When it came time to sign the page, Ray felt compelled to give a nod to the source material and so he signed his name in a manner similar to the one Christy used.

This signatory homage to Christy inspired Ray to consider adopting the new form as his standard signature and one can see several instances of its use during 1951. Later that year he resumed the old way of signing his work.

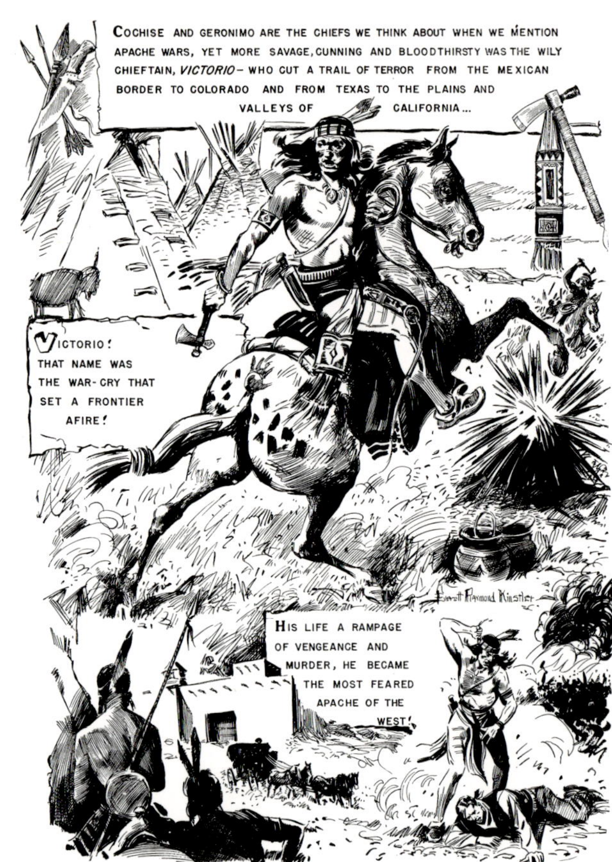

Chief Victorio's Apache Massacre
Avon, 1951

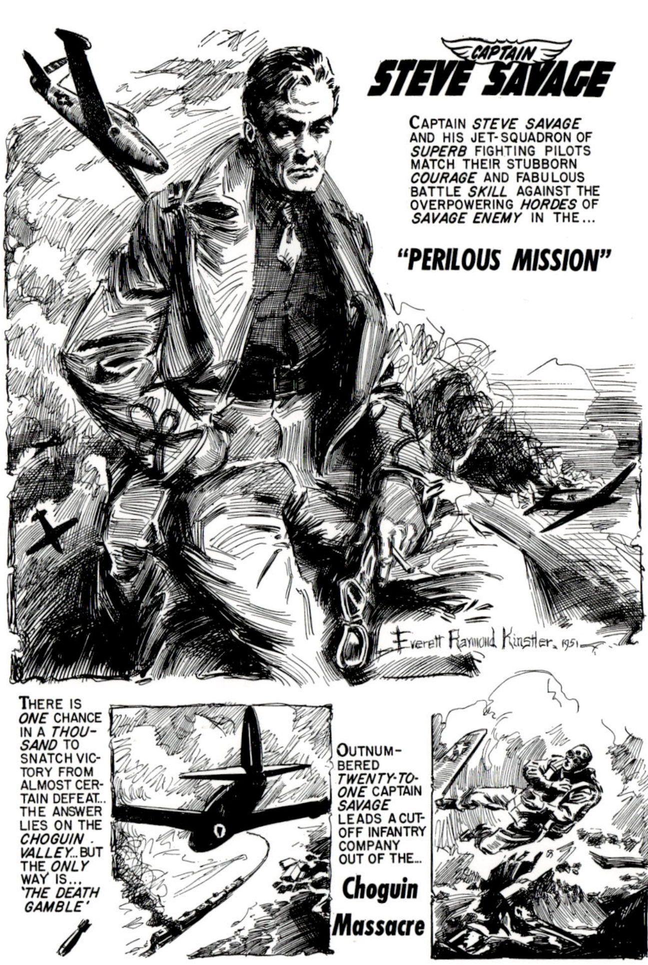

Captain Steve Savage and his Jet Fighters #2
Avon, September, 1951

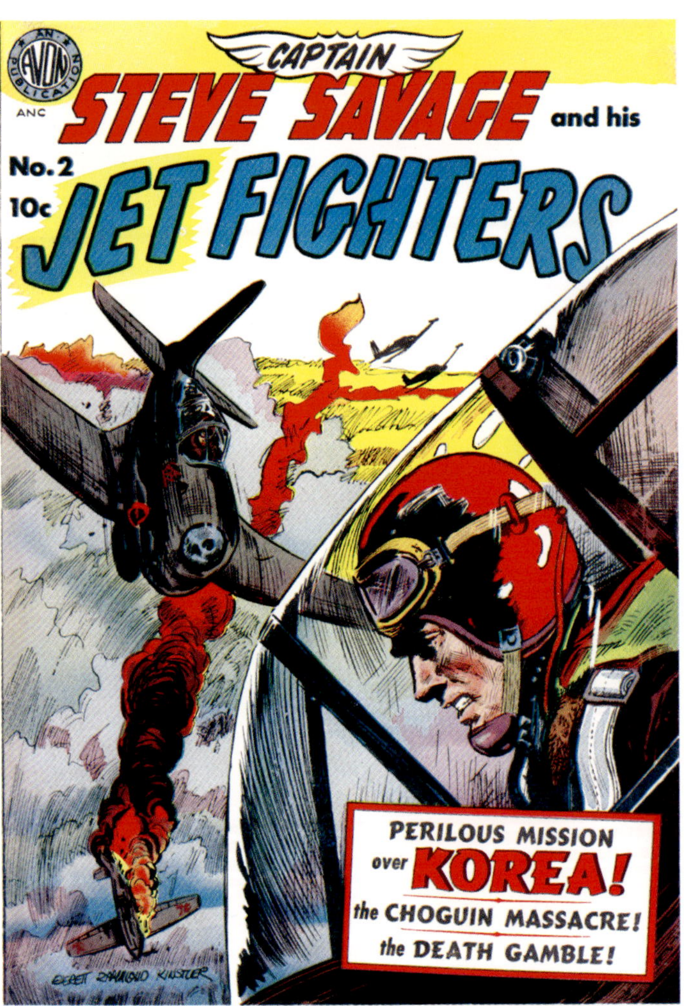

Avon, 1951

As with the cowboy characters, Avon relied upon historical Native American figures to give its books the appearance of a firm basis in fact.

Kinstler recalls researching material for some of the titles, trying to find actual photographs or artistic renditions of these men in order to do justice to his depictions of them.

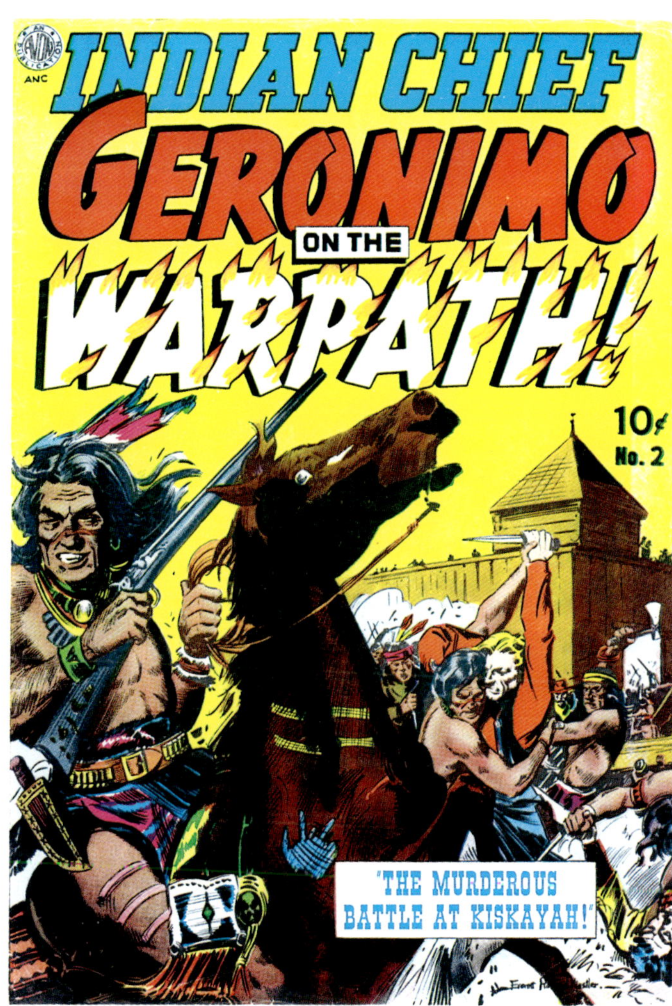

Avon, 1951

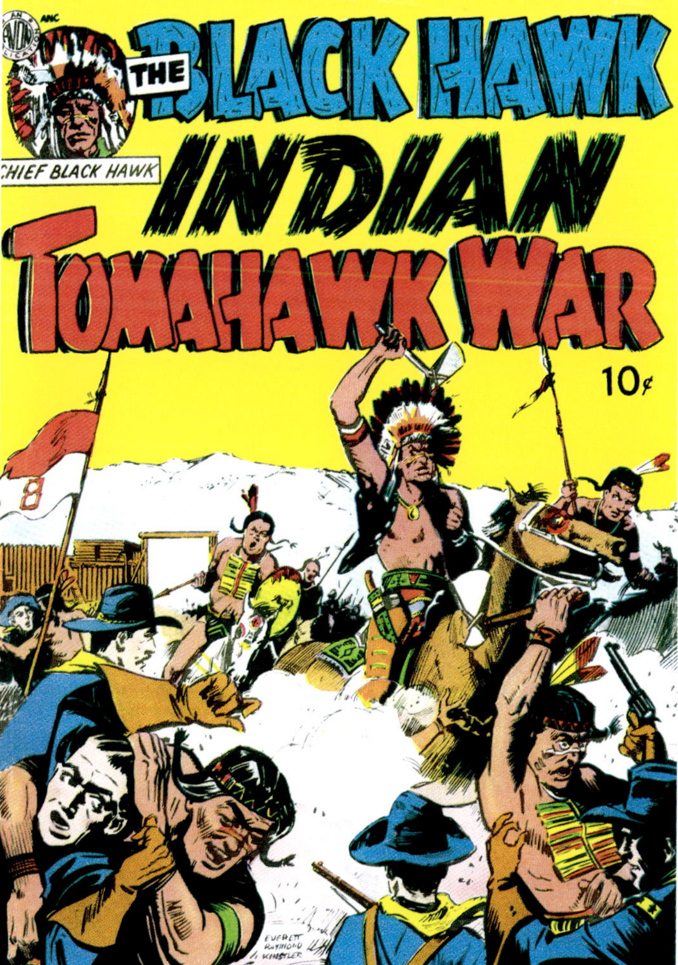

Avon, 1951

Though he had stills of George Montgomery, Helena Carter and Jay Silverheels from which to work when drawing the ***Fighting Daniel Boone*** comic, those stills were from a film called *The Pathfinder* which was not about Daniel Boone.

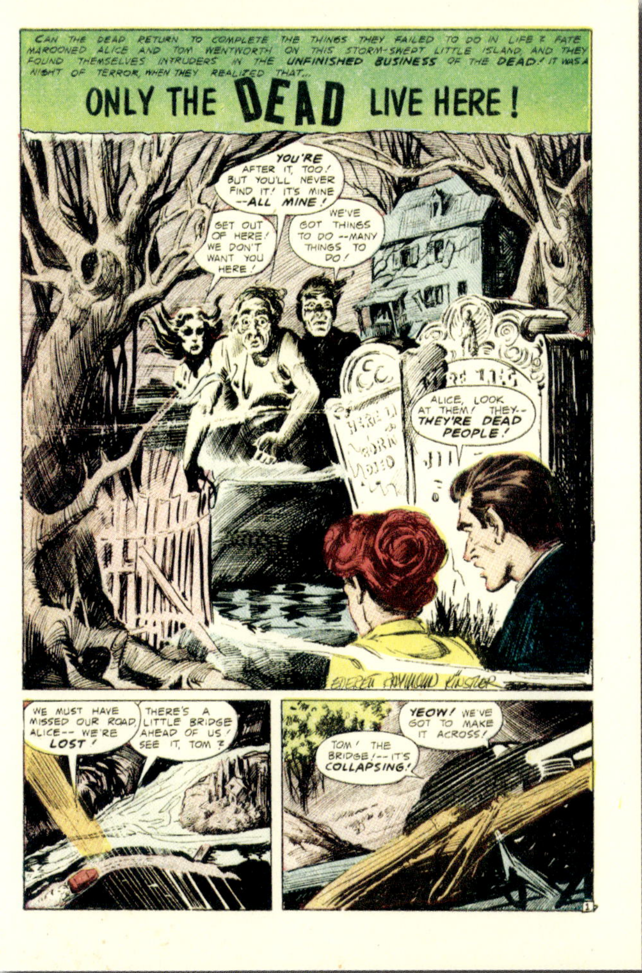

Eerie #10
Avon, December, 1952/
January, 1953

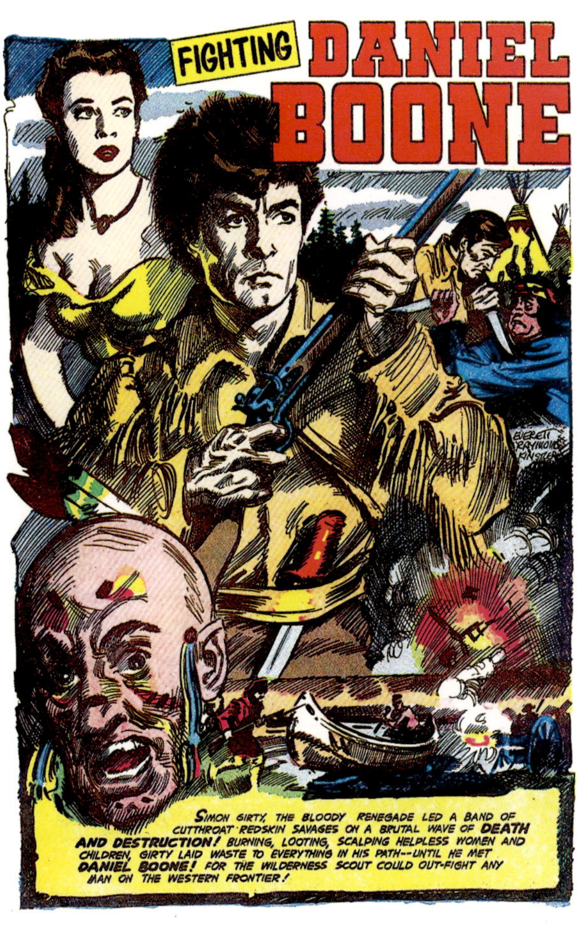

Fighting Daniel Boone, Avon, 1953

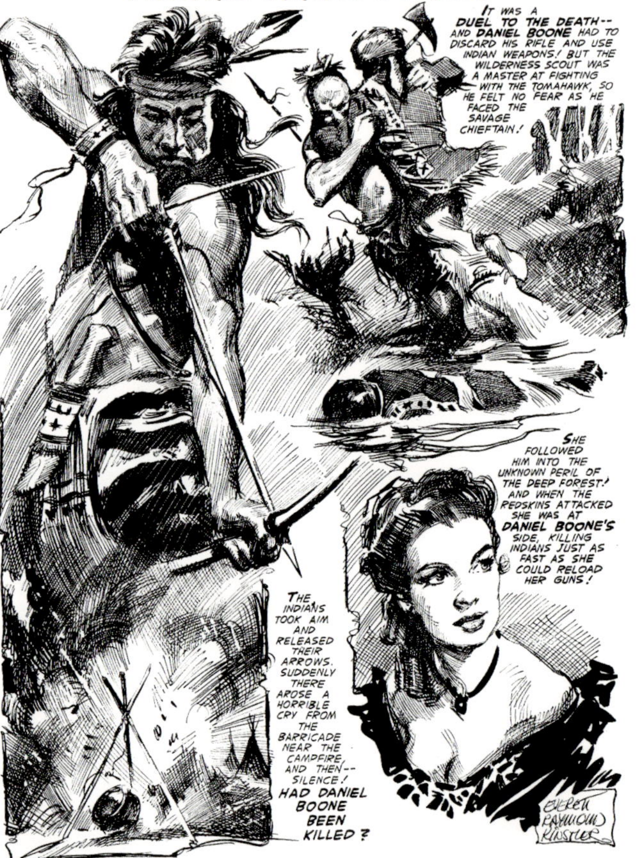

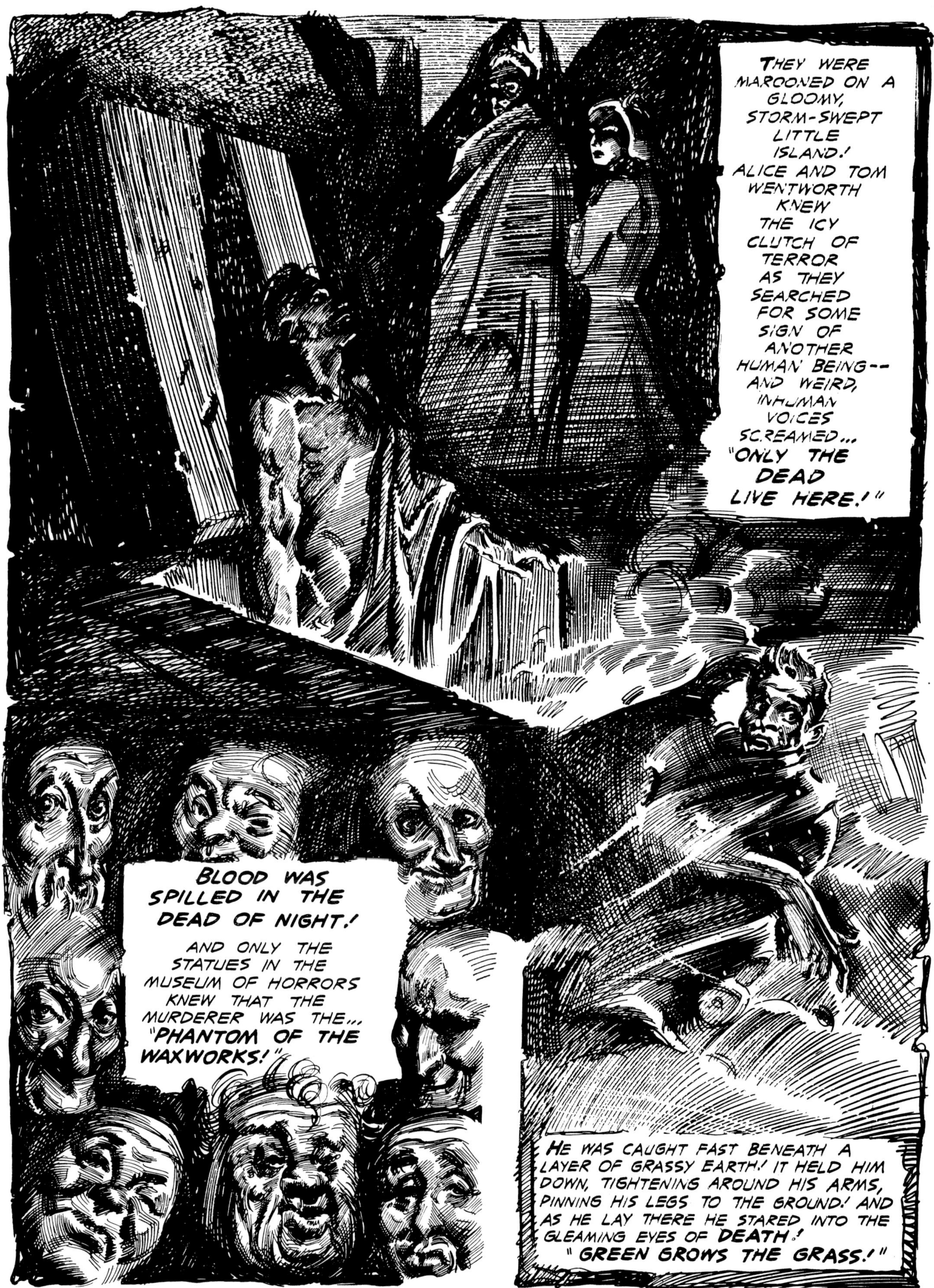
THEY WERE MAROONED ON A GLOOMY, STORM-SWEPT LITTLE ISLAND! ALICE AND TOM WENTWORTH KNEW THE ICY CLUTCH OF TERROR AS THEY SEARCHED FOR SOME SIGN OF ANOTHER HUMAN BEING-- AND WEIRD, INHUMAN VOICES SCREAMED... "ONLY THE DEAD LIVE HERE!"
BLOOD WAS SPILLED IN THE DEAD OF NIGHT!
AND ONLY THE STATUES IN THE MUSEUM OF HORRORS KNEW THAT THE MURDERER WAS THE... "PHANTOM OF THE WAXWORKS!"
HE WAS CAUGHT FAST BENEATH A LAYER OF GRASSY EARTH! IT HELD HIM DOWN, TIGHTENING AROUND HIS ARMS, PINNING HIS LEGS TO THE GROUND! AND AS HE LAY THERE HE STARED INTO THE GLEAMING EYES OF DEATH!
"GREEN GROWS THE GRASS!"

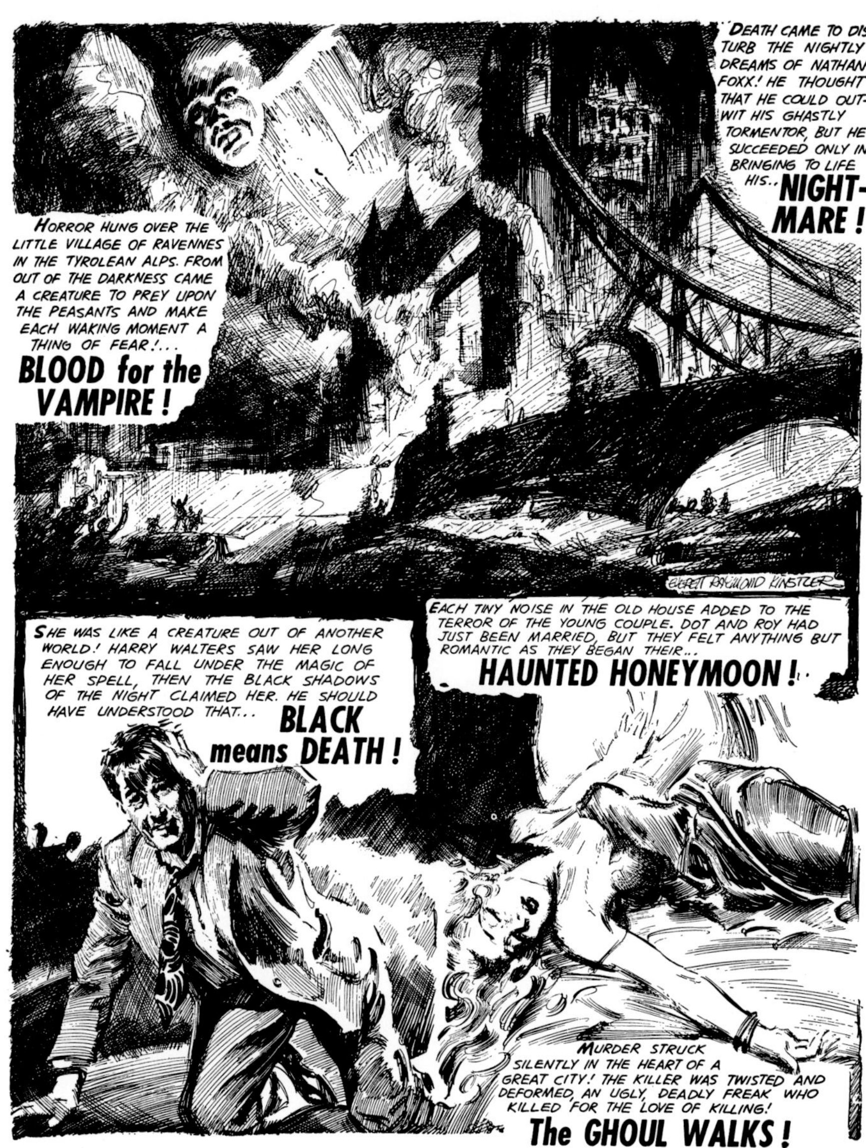

Avon published comics in many different genres. When the Horror craze hit in the early 1950's, it entered the fray with ***Eerie Comics*** #1 in May of 1951.

However, one of the very first comic books Avon published, in January of 1947, had the same title and issue number. In fact, that first ***Eerie*** #1 has a legitimate claim to being the very first Horror comic.

Eerie #8
Avon, August, 1952

Eerie #7, Avon, June-July, 1952

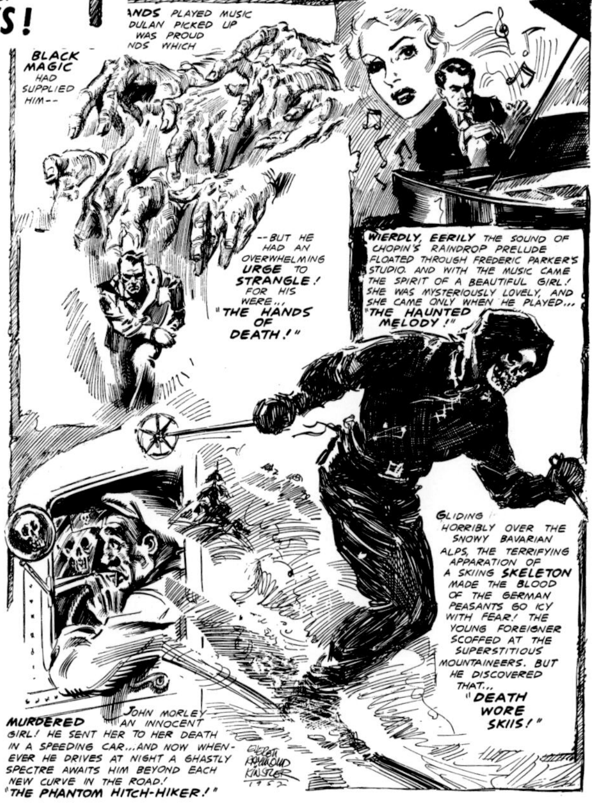

Eerie #9,
Avon, October-November, 1952

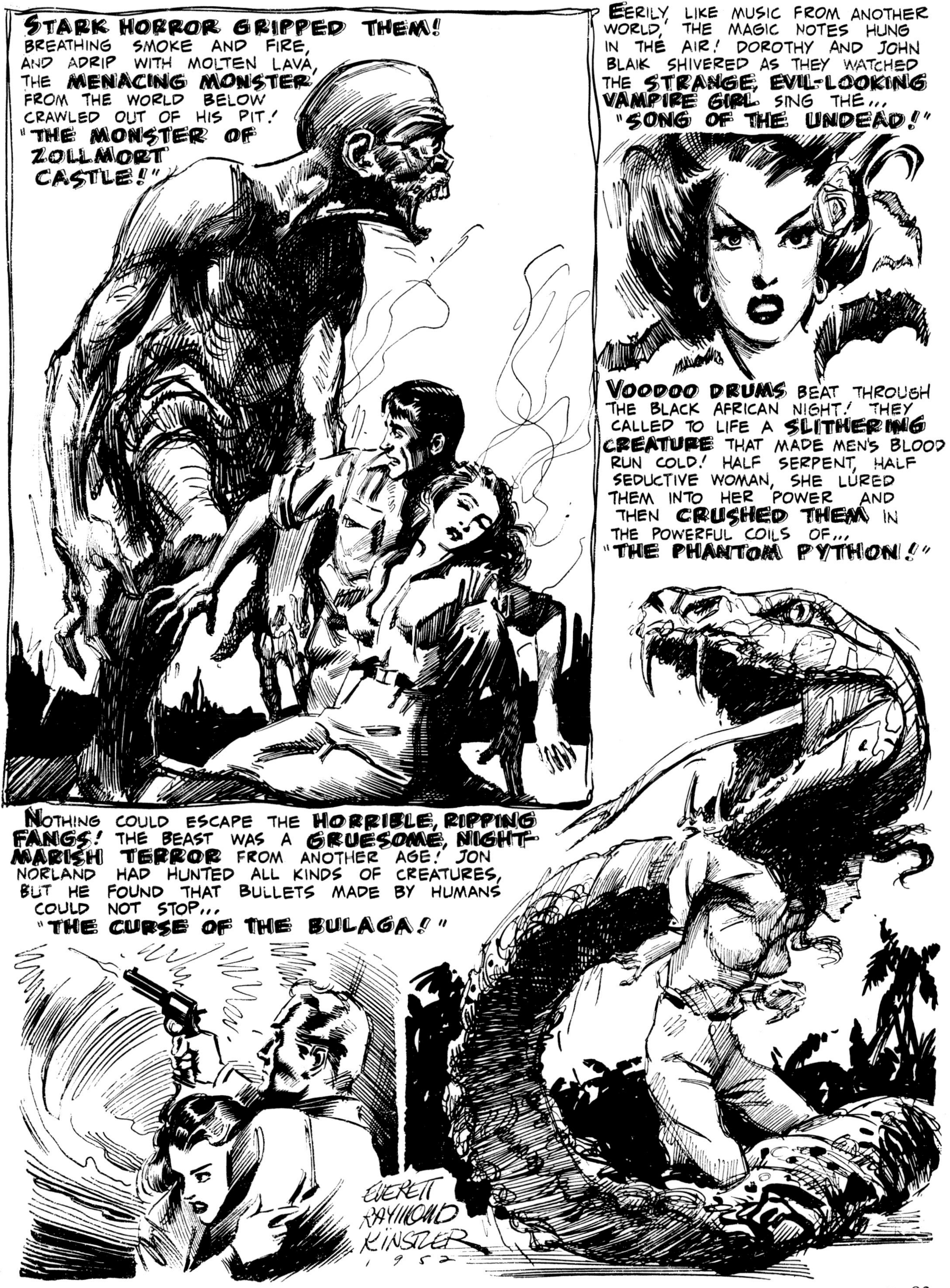
STARK HORROR GRIPPED THEM! BREATHING SMOKE AND FIRE, AND ADRIP WITH MOLTEN LAVA, THE MENACING MONSTER FROM THE WORLD BELOW CRAWLED OUT OF HIS PIT! "THE MONSTER OF ZOLLMORT CASTLE!"
EERILY, LIKE MUSIC FROM ANOTHER WORLD, THE MAGIC NOTES HUNG IN THE AIR! DOROTHY AND JOHN BLAIK SHIVERED AS THEY WATCHED THE STRANGE, EVIL-LOOKING VAMPIRE GIRL SING THE... "SONG OF THE UNDEAD!"
VOODOO DRUMS BEAT THROUGH THE BLACK AFRICAN NIGHT! THEY CALLED TO LIFE A SLITHERING CREATURE THAT MADE MEN'S BLOOD RUN COLD! HALF SERPENT, HALF SEDUCTIVE WOMAN, SHE LURED THEM INTO HER POWER AND THEN CRUSHED THEM IN THE POWERFUL COILS OF... "THE PHANTOM PYTHON!"
NOTHING COULD ESCAPE THE HORRIBLE, RIPPING FANGS! THE BEAST WAS A GRUESOME, NIGHT-MARISH TERROR FROM ANOTHER AGE! JON NORLAND HAD HUNTED ALL KINDS OF CREATURES, BUT HE FOUND THAT BULLETS MADE BY HUMANS COULD NOT STOP... "THE CURSE OF THE BULAGA!"
EVERETT RAYMOND KINSTLER 1952

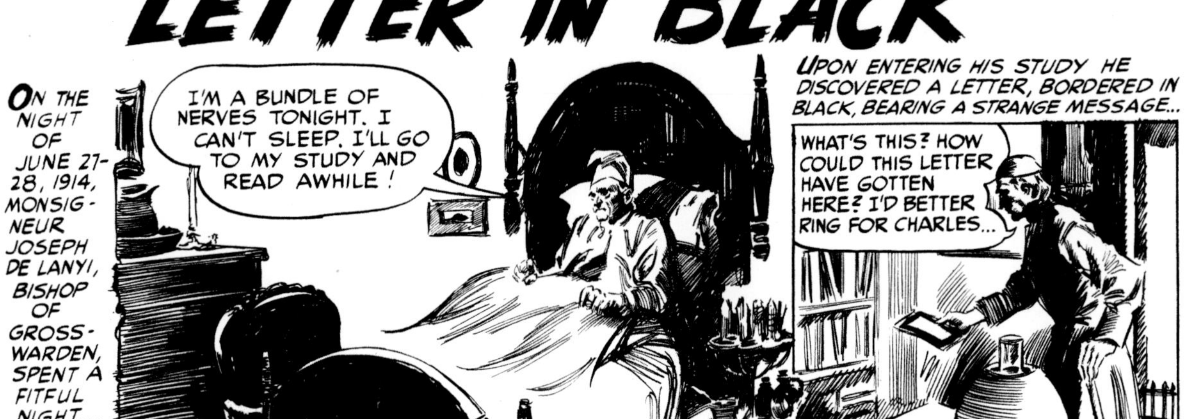

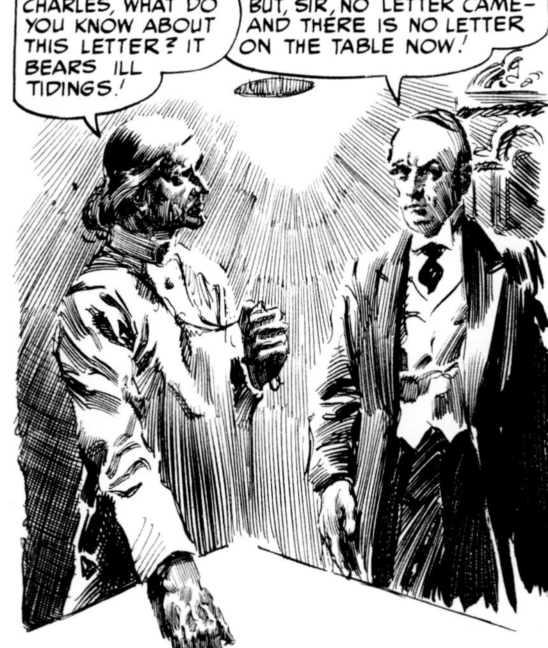

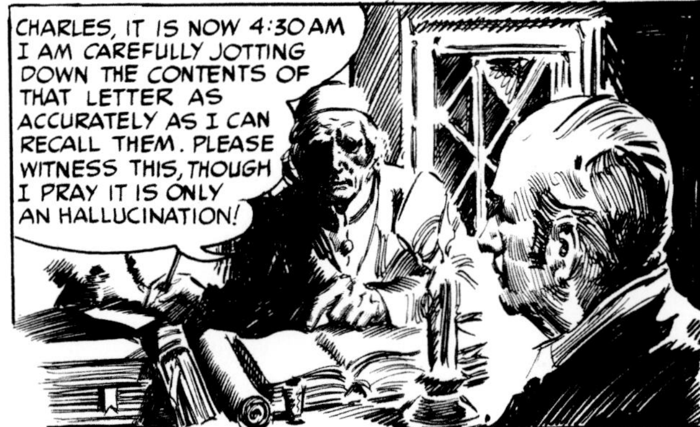

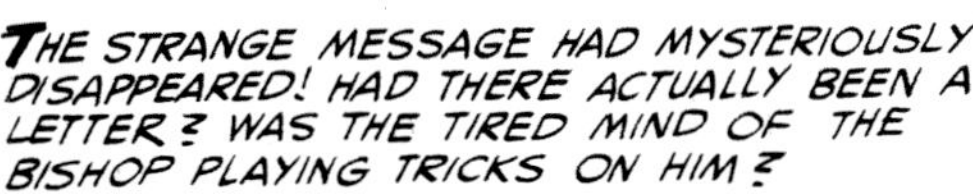

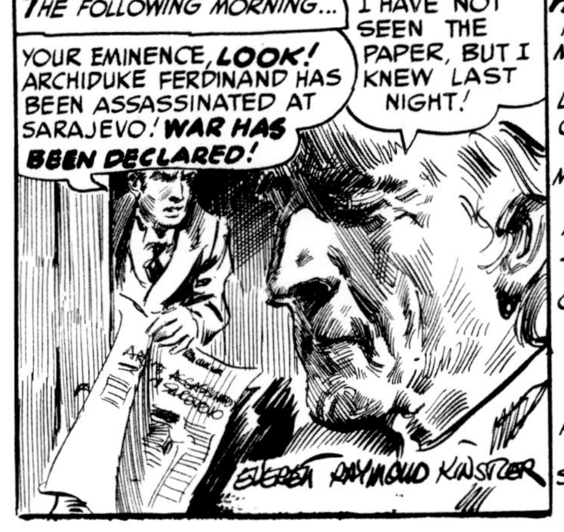

Ziff-Davis

As Avon was ramping up its comics line, publisher Ziff-Davis decided to enter the comic book market. It launched a full line of books in late 1950. These were edited by Jerry Siegel, who co-created *Superman* with Joe Shuster, and the page rates were half-again as much as most other companies.

Ray landed his first Z-D assignment in 1952 and split his time between Avon and Ziff that year. While the pay was better at Ziff-Davis, their editors' policy was to review the pencilled pages before allowing the artist to finish the inks. This meant an extra trip to the offices for every job that he accepted. And the competition was stiffer as the premium page rates attracted some of the best artists in the business.

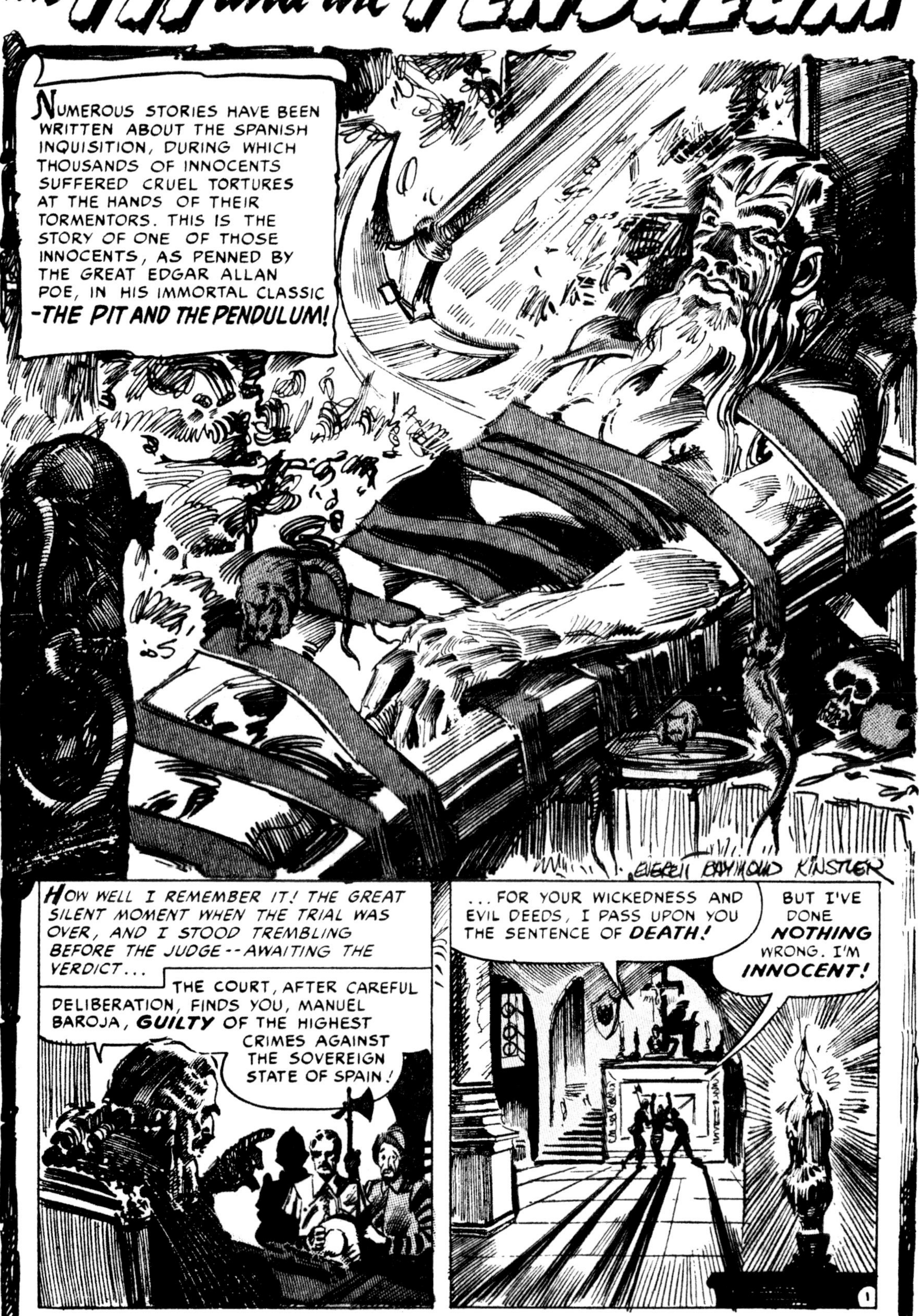

Letter in Black
Weird Thrillers #3
Ziff-Davis, Spring, 1952

The Pit and the Pendulum
Nightmare #2
Ziff-Davis, Fall, 1952

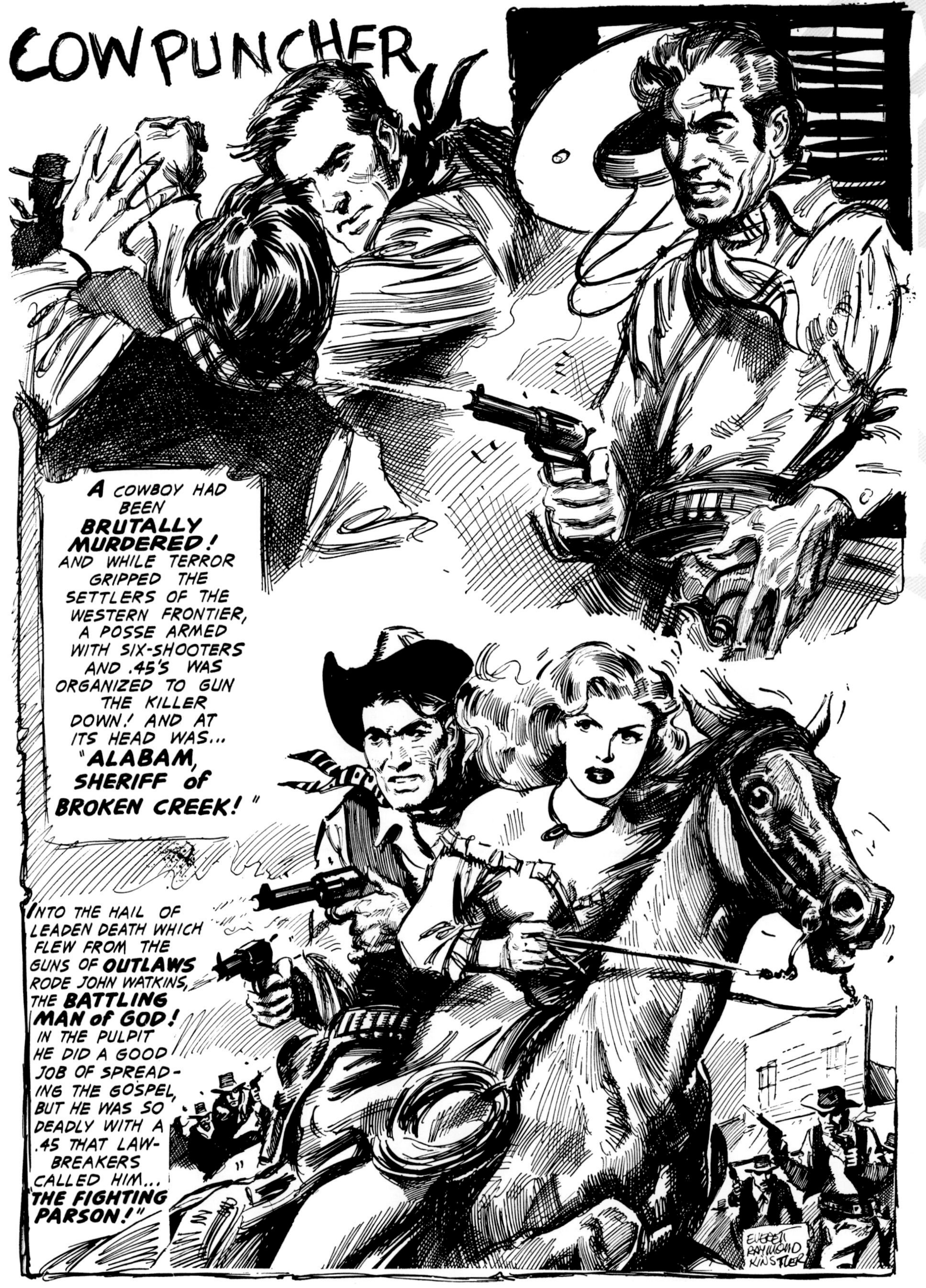

Cowpuncher
Avon (Realistic), 1953

Cowpuncher Comics: Avon released a second title in 1947. Unlike ***Eerie***, ***Cowpuncher Comics*** lasted more than one issue—stopping with issue seven in 1949. However, in 1953 issue two was reprinted by Realistic Comics, Avon's "B" label, with a new montage by Kinstler on the inside cover.

FIGHTING INDIANS of the WILD WEST!

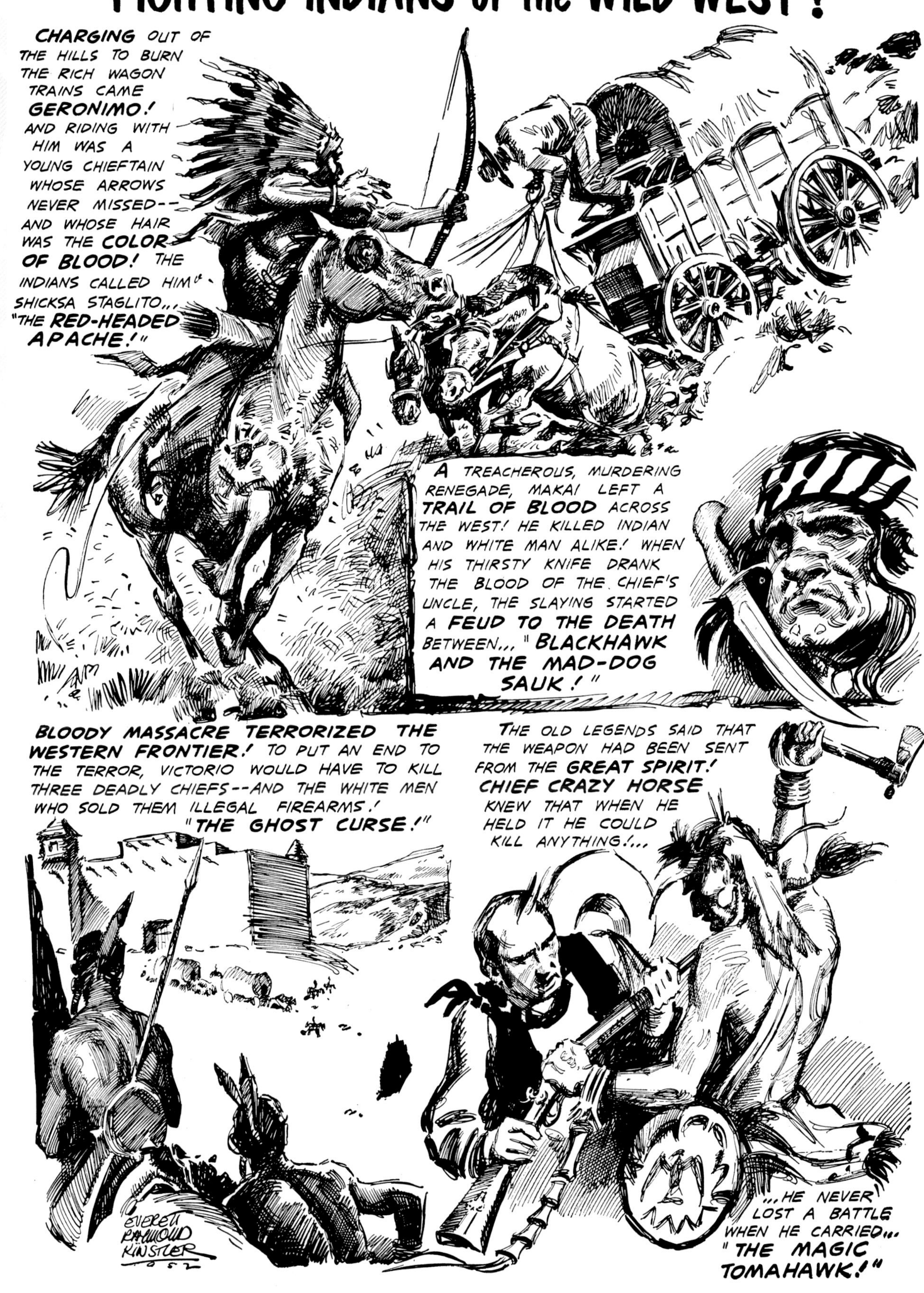

Fighting Indians of the Wild West #2
Avon, November, 1952

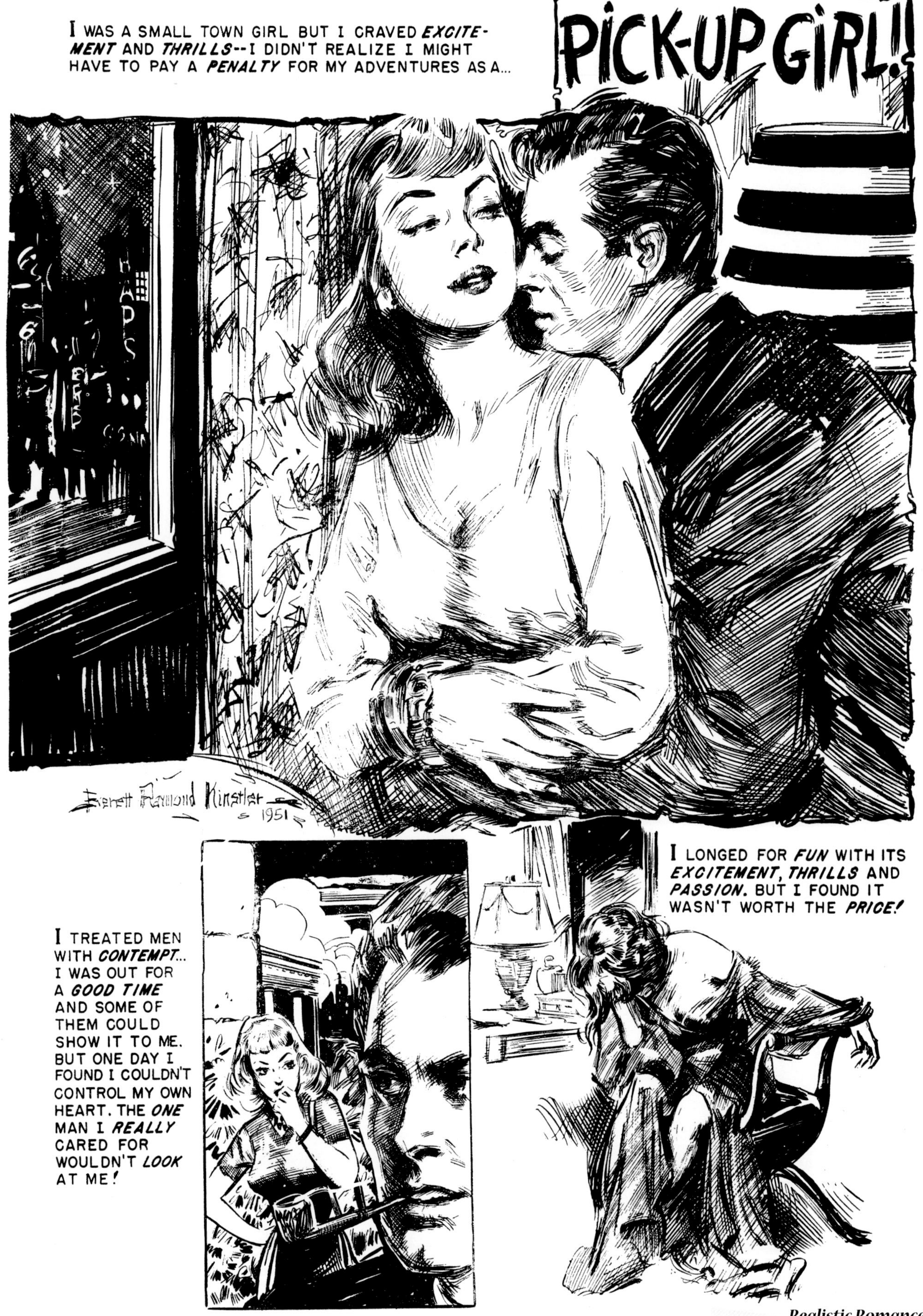

Intimate Confessions #1
Avon, July-August, 1951

Realistic Romances #3
Avon, November-December, 1951
original: 13¼"x17½"

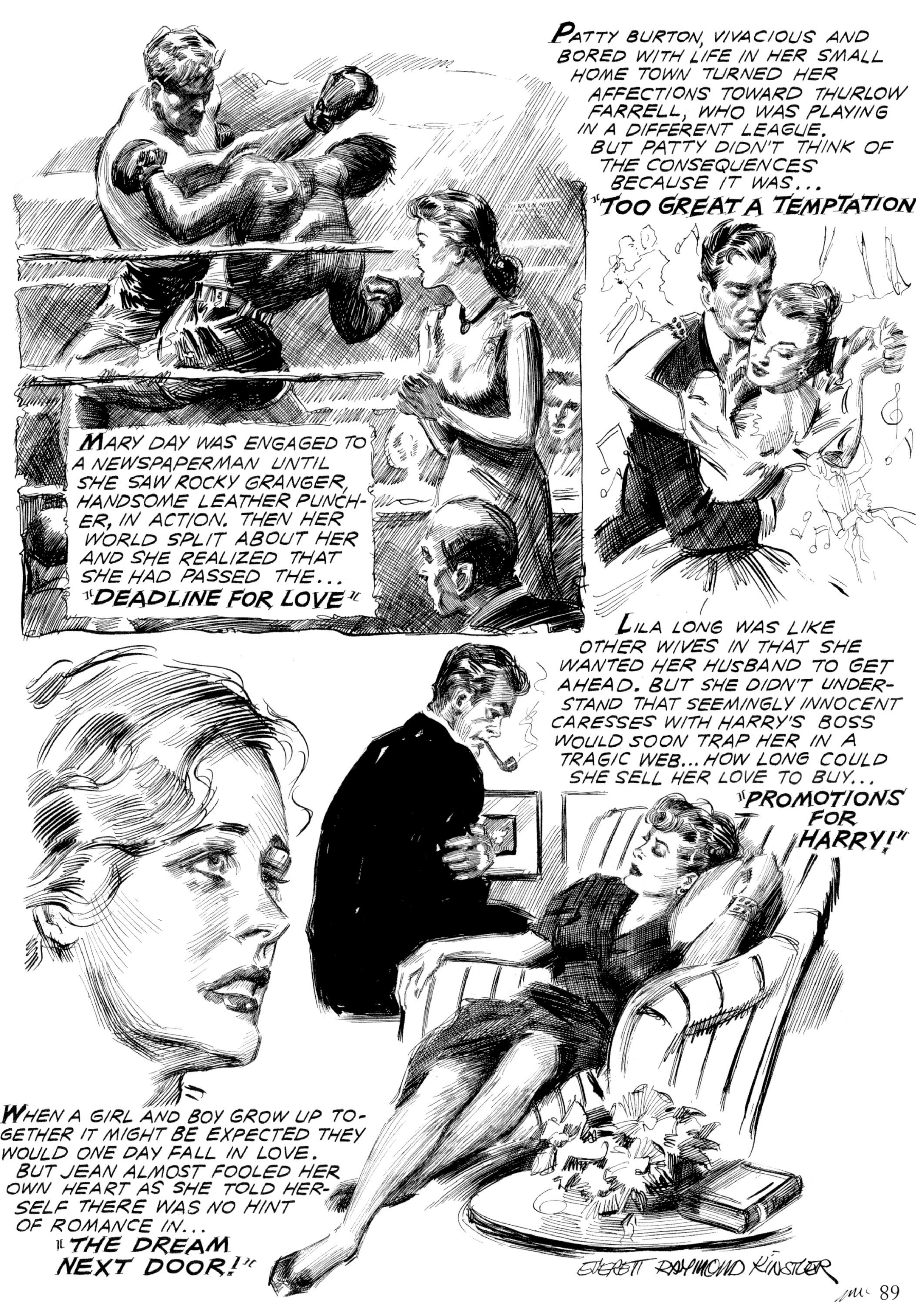
PATTY BURTON, VIVACIOUS AND BORED WITH LIFE IN HER SMALL HOME TOWN TURNED HER AFFECTIONS TOWARD THURLOW FARRELL, WHO WAS PLAYING IN A DIFFERENT LEAGUE. BUT PATTY DIDN'T THINK OF THE CONSEQUENCES BECAUSE IT WAS... "TOO GREAT A TEMPTATION"
MARY DAY WAS ENGAGED TO A NEWSPAPERMAN UNTIL SHE SAW ROCKY GRANGER, HANDSOME LEATHER PUNCHER, IN ACTION. THEN HER WORLD SPLIT ABOUT HER AND SHE REALIZED THAT SHE HAD PASSED THE... "DEADLINE FOR LOVE"
LILA LONG WAS LIKE OTHER WIVES IN THAT SHE WANTED HER HUSBAND TO GET AHEAD. BUT SHE DIDN'T UNDERSTAND THAT SEEMINGLY INNOCENT CARESSES WITH HARRY'S BOSS WOULD SOON TRAP HER IN A TRAGIC WEB... HOW LONG COULD SHE SELL HER LOVE TO BUY... "PROMOTIONS FOR HARRY!"
WHEN A GIRL AND BOY GROW UP TOGETHER IT MIGHT BE EXPECTED THEY WOULD ONE DAY FALL IN LOVE. BUT JEAN ALMOST FOOLED HER OWN HEART AS SHE TOLD HERSELF THERE WAS NO HINT OF ROMANCE IN... "THE DREAM NEXT DOOR!"
EVERETT RAYMOND KINSTLER

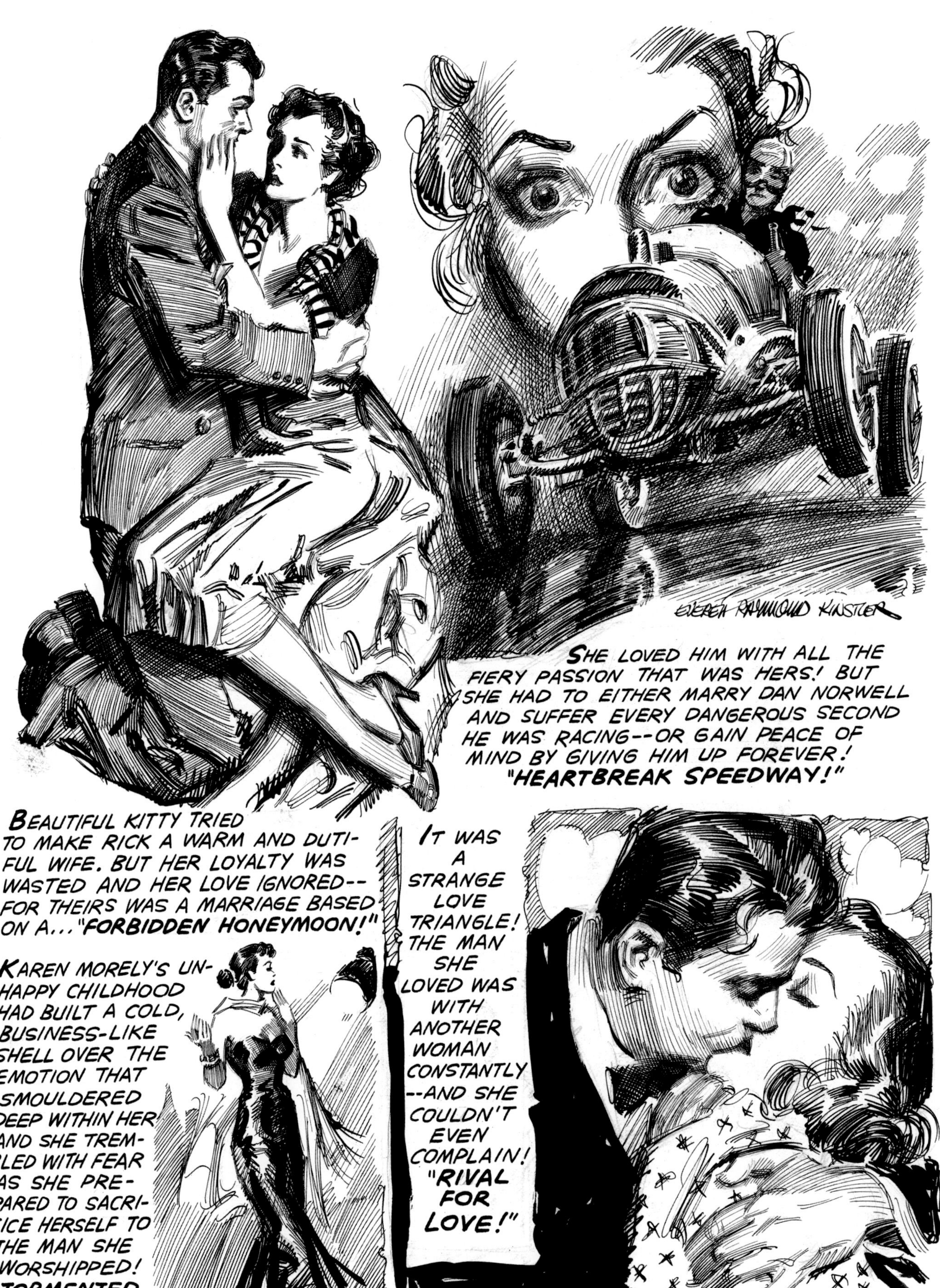

Intimate Confessions #4
Avon, February, 1952
original: 13¼"x17½"

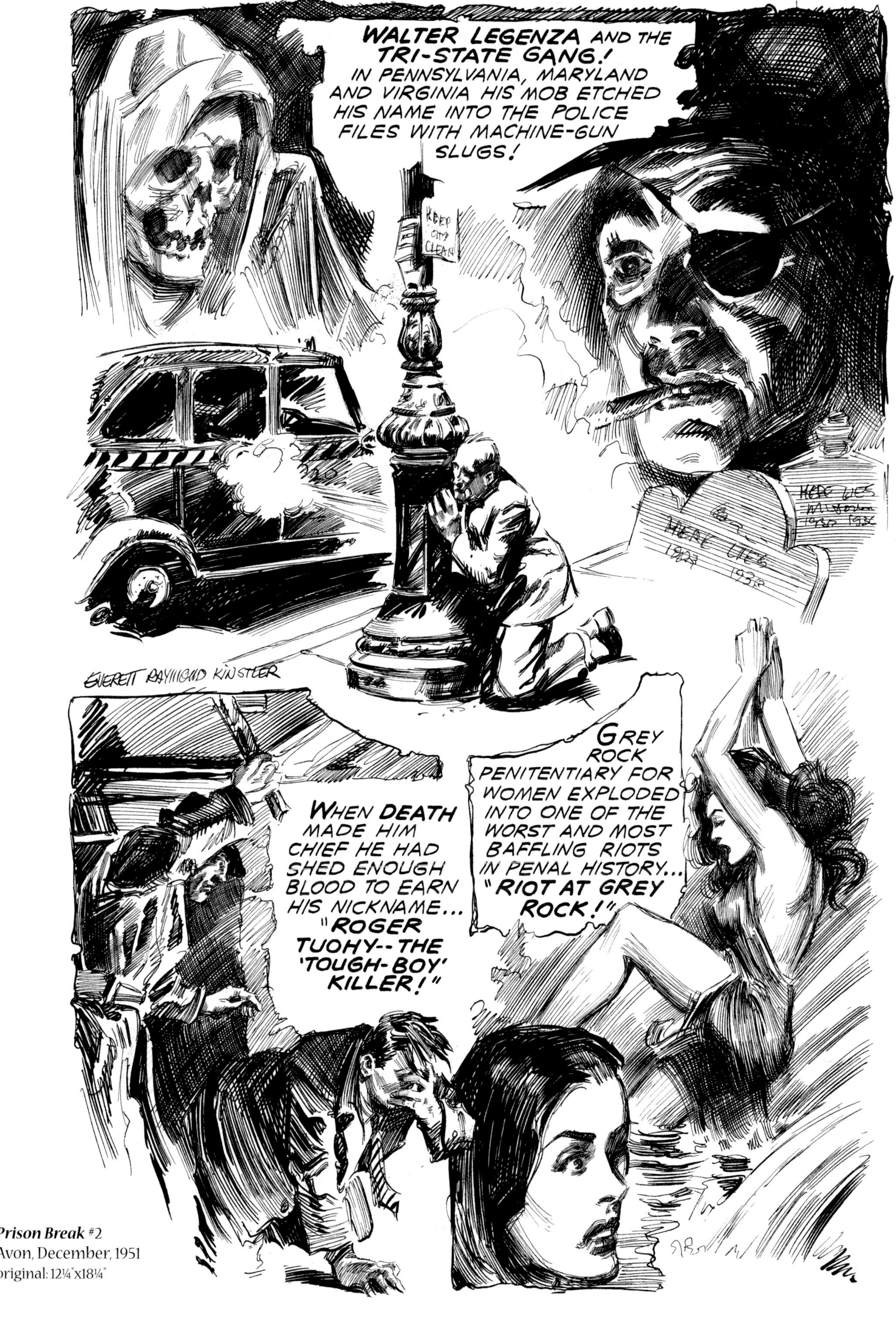

Prison Break #2
Avon, December, 1951
original: 12¼"x18¼"

WILD BILL HICKOK

A WHITE GIRL KNEW THE **SECRET** OF THE **AZTEC TREASURE**-- AND A WAR PARTY OF BLOODTHIRSTY OGLALLA SIOUX MASSACRED A WHOLE WAGON TRAIN TO CAPTURE HER! BUT **WILD BILL HICKOK** THUNDERED DOWN FROM THE HILLS TO RESCUE THE ONLY SURVIVOR OF...

"THE BLOODY CANYON MASSACRE!"

HE WAS PHYSICALLY HANDICAPPED, BUT HIS LAME FOOT DIDN'T STOP HIM FROM BECOMING THE MOST FEARED KILLER OF THE WESTERN FRONTIER! HE RODE HARD AND HE SHOT FAST! NO LAWMAN COULD STOP...

"CLAY ALLISON-- THE QUICK COLT KILLER!"

EVERETT RAYMOND KINSTLER

HE DIED ON THE GALLOWS! SUDDEN JIM DORN DIED A CRIMINAL'S DEATH-- BUT ONE MONTH AFTER THEY PLANTED HIS BODY ON BOOT HILL HE WAS TRAVELLING THE OUTLAW TRAIL, ROBBING AND MURDERING AS HE RODE! **WILD BILL HICKOK** SWORE EITHER TO KILL A VERY CLEVER IMPOSTER OR TO COME FACE-TO-FACE WITH...

"THE GHOST OF SUDDEN JIM!"

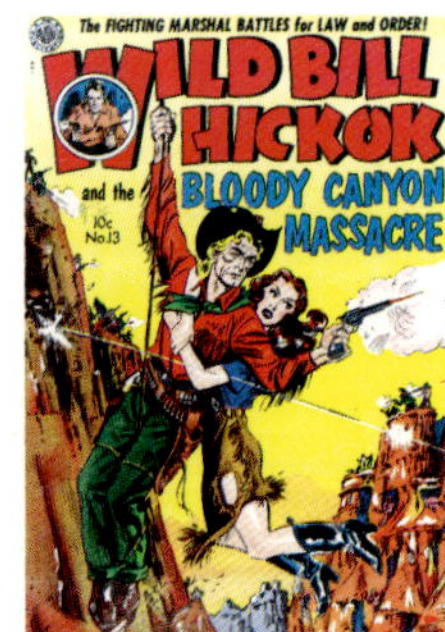

Wild Bill Hickok #13
Avon, November, 1952

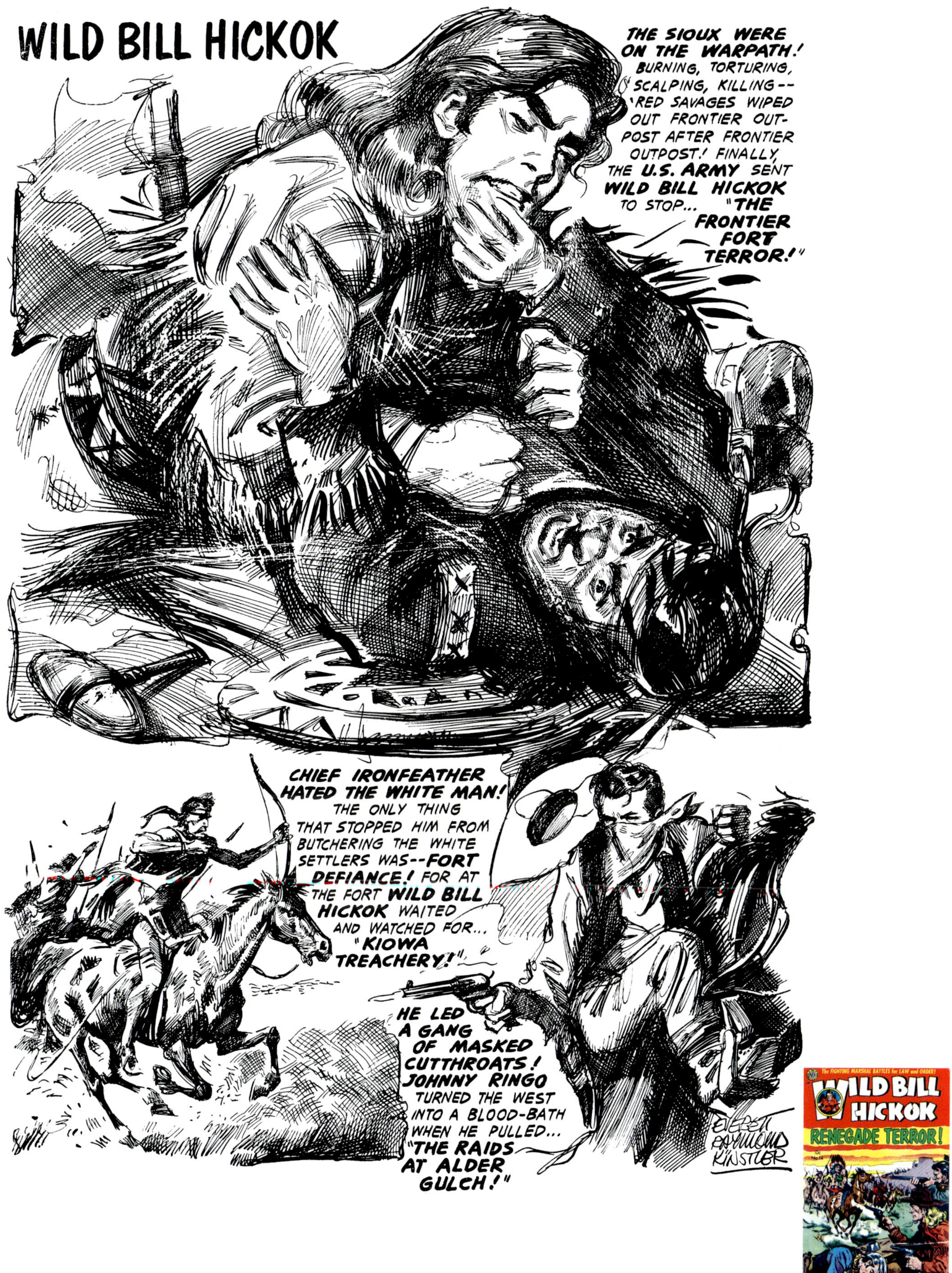

Wild Bill Hickok #14
Avon, March, 1953

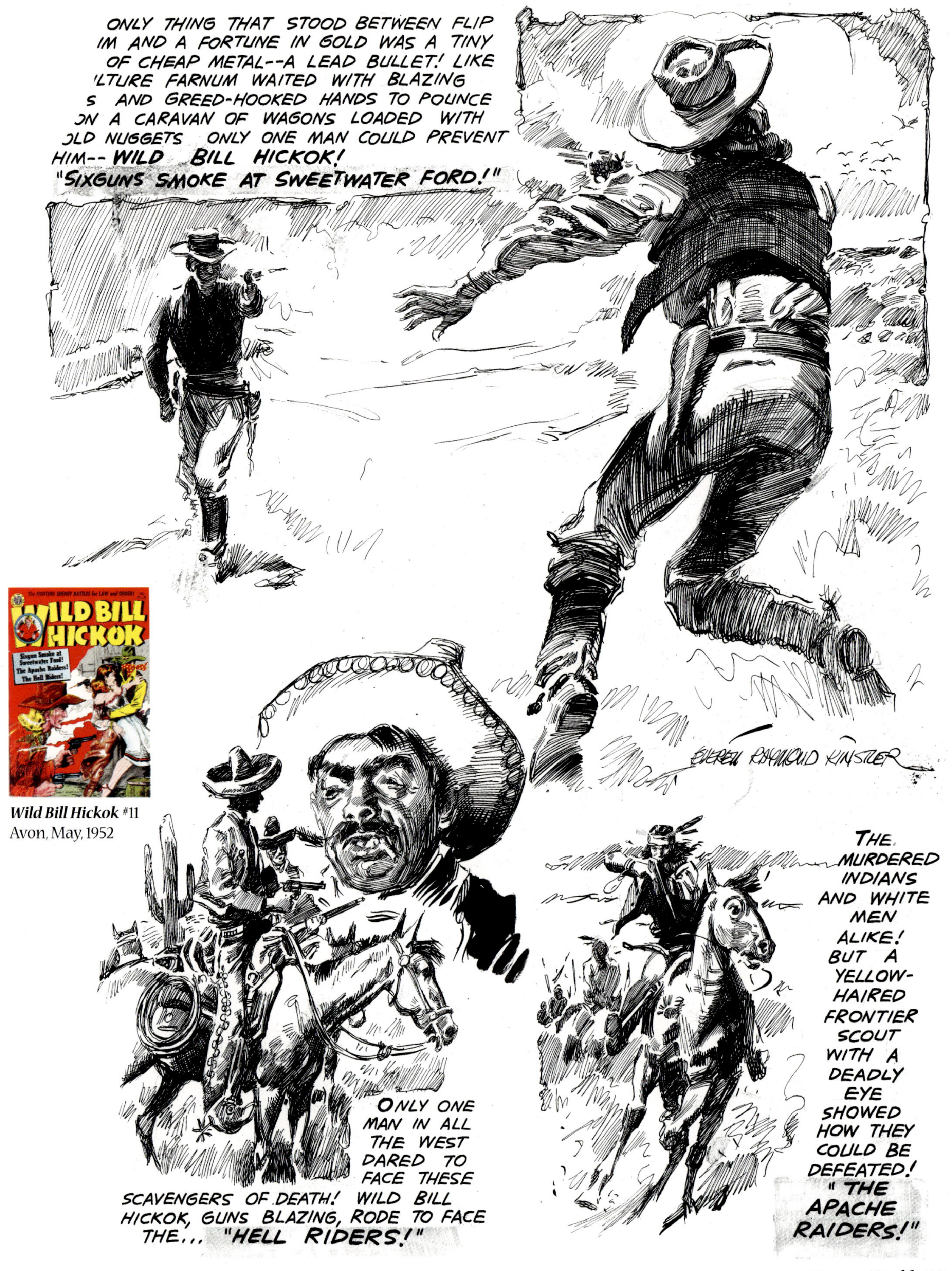

Wild Bill Hickok #11
Avon, May, 1952

Strange Worlds #22
Avon, September-October, 1955
A sample of Kinstler's coloring.

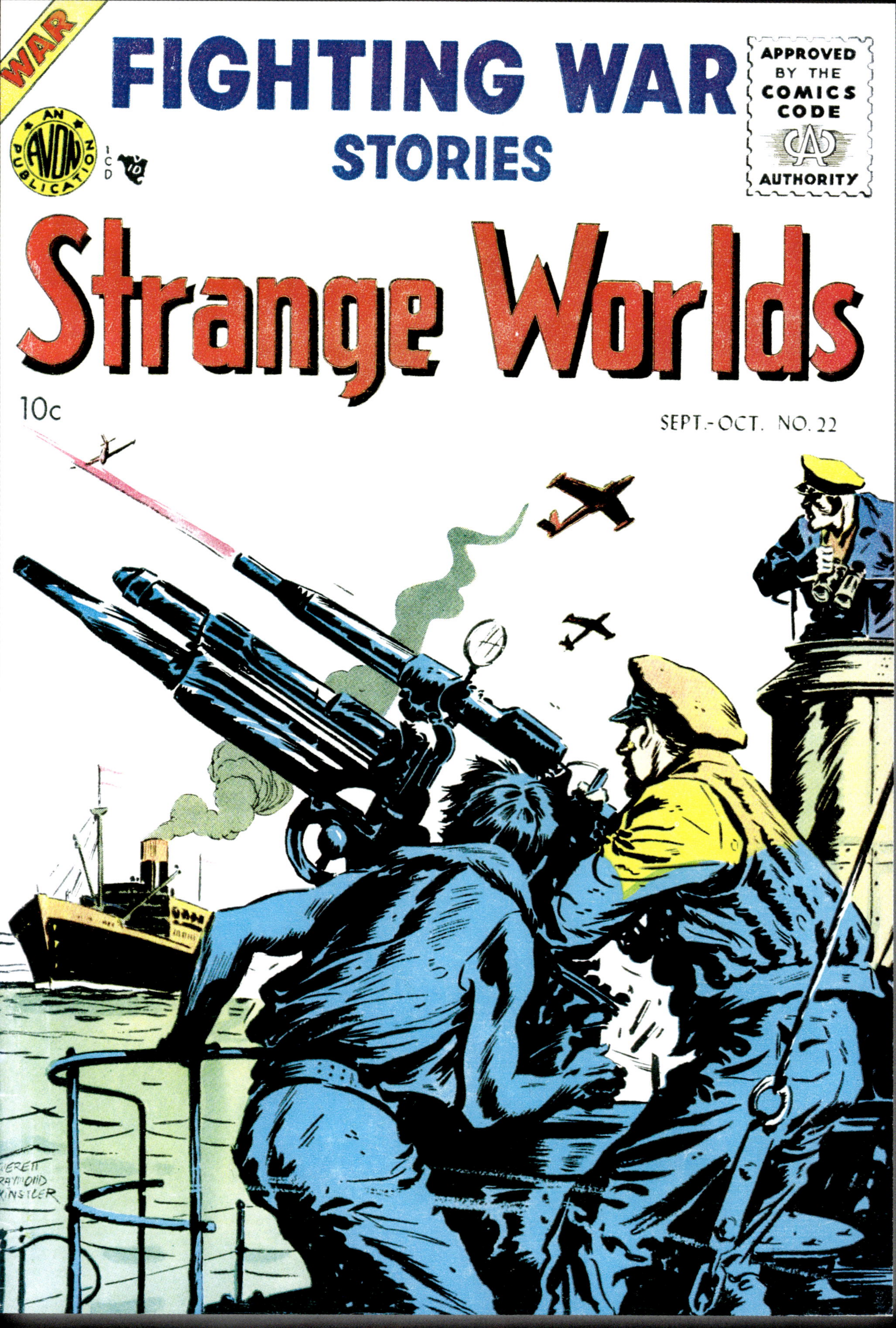

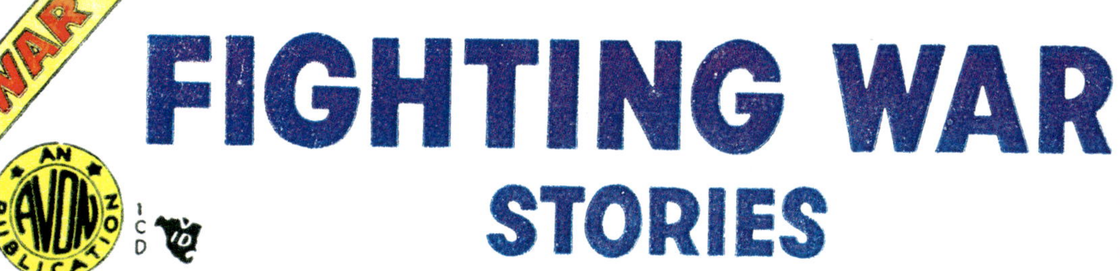

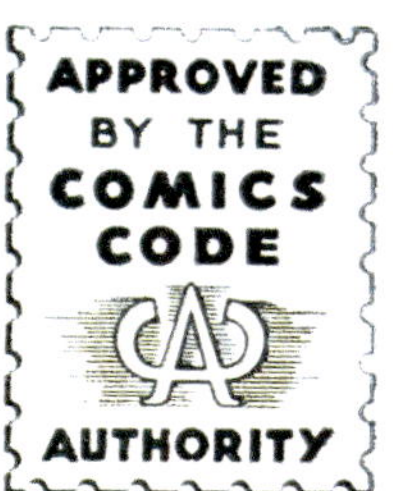

Strange Worlds

10c

SEPT.-OCT. NO. 22

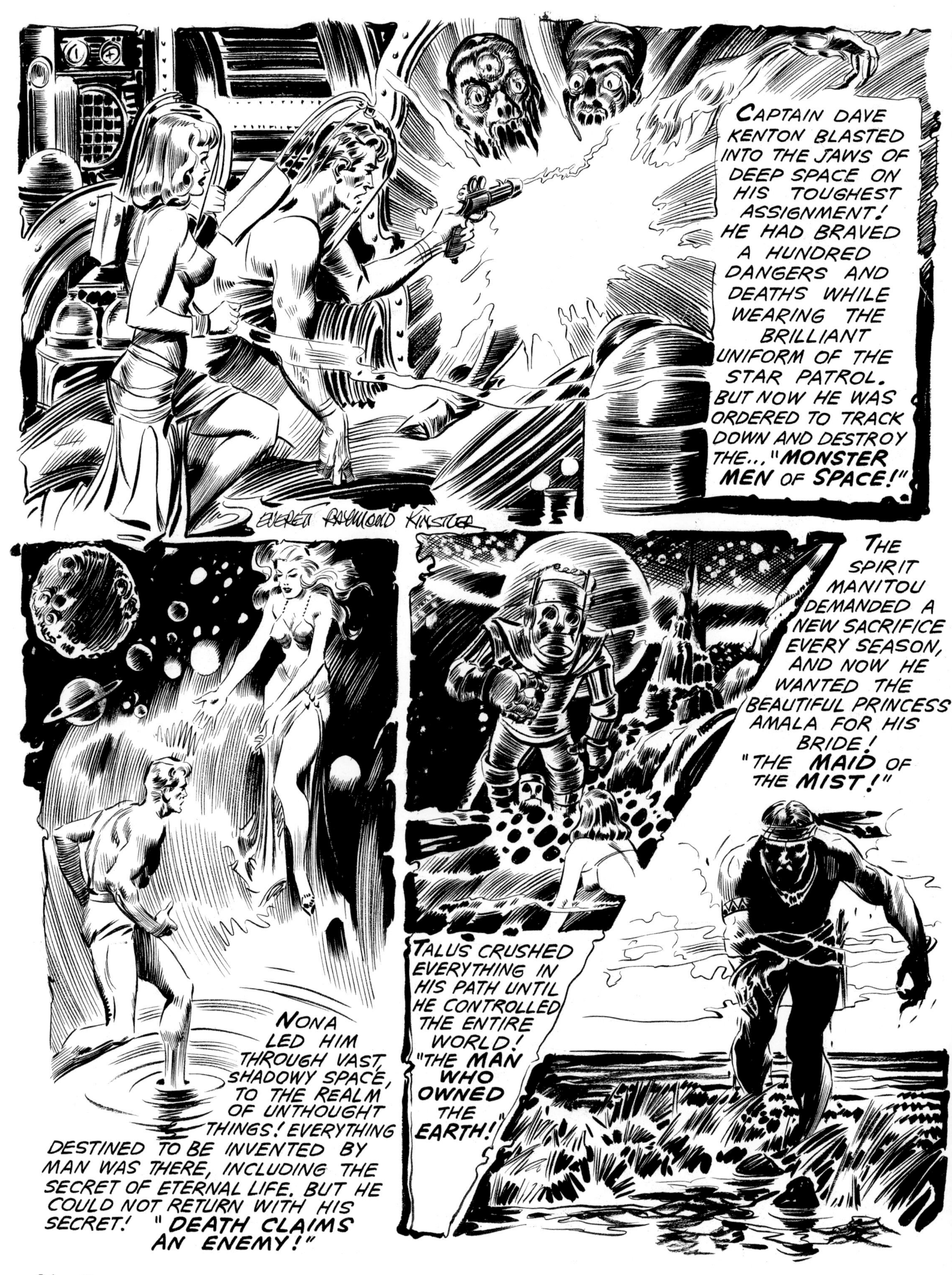
CAPTAIN DAVE KENTON BLASTED INTO THE JAWS OF DEEP SPACE ON HIS TOUGHEST ASSIGNMENT! HE HAD BRAVED A HUNDRED DANGERS AND DEATHS WHILE WEARING THE BRILLIANT UNIFORM OF THE STAR PATROL. BUT NOW HE WAS ORDERED TO TRACK DOWN AND DESTROY THE..."MONSTER MEN OF SPACE!"
EVERETT RAYMOND KINSTLER
NONA LED HIM THROUGH VAST, SHADOWY SPACE, TO THE REALM OF UNTHOUGHT THINGS! EVERYTHING DESTINED TO BE INVENTED BY MAN WAS THERE, INCLUDING THE SECRET OF ETERNAL LIFE. BUT HE COULD NOT RETURN WITH HIS SECRET! "DEATH CLAIMS AN ENEMY!"
TALUS CRUSHED EVERYTHING IN HIS PATH UNTIL HE CONTROLLED THE ENTIRE WORLD! "THE MAN WHO OWNED THE EARTH!"
THE SPIRIT MANITOU DEMANDED A NEW SACRIFICE EVERY SEASON, AND NOW HE WANTED THE BEAUTIFUL PRINCESS AMALA FOR HIS BRIDE! "THE MAID OF THE MIST!"

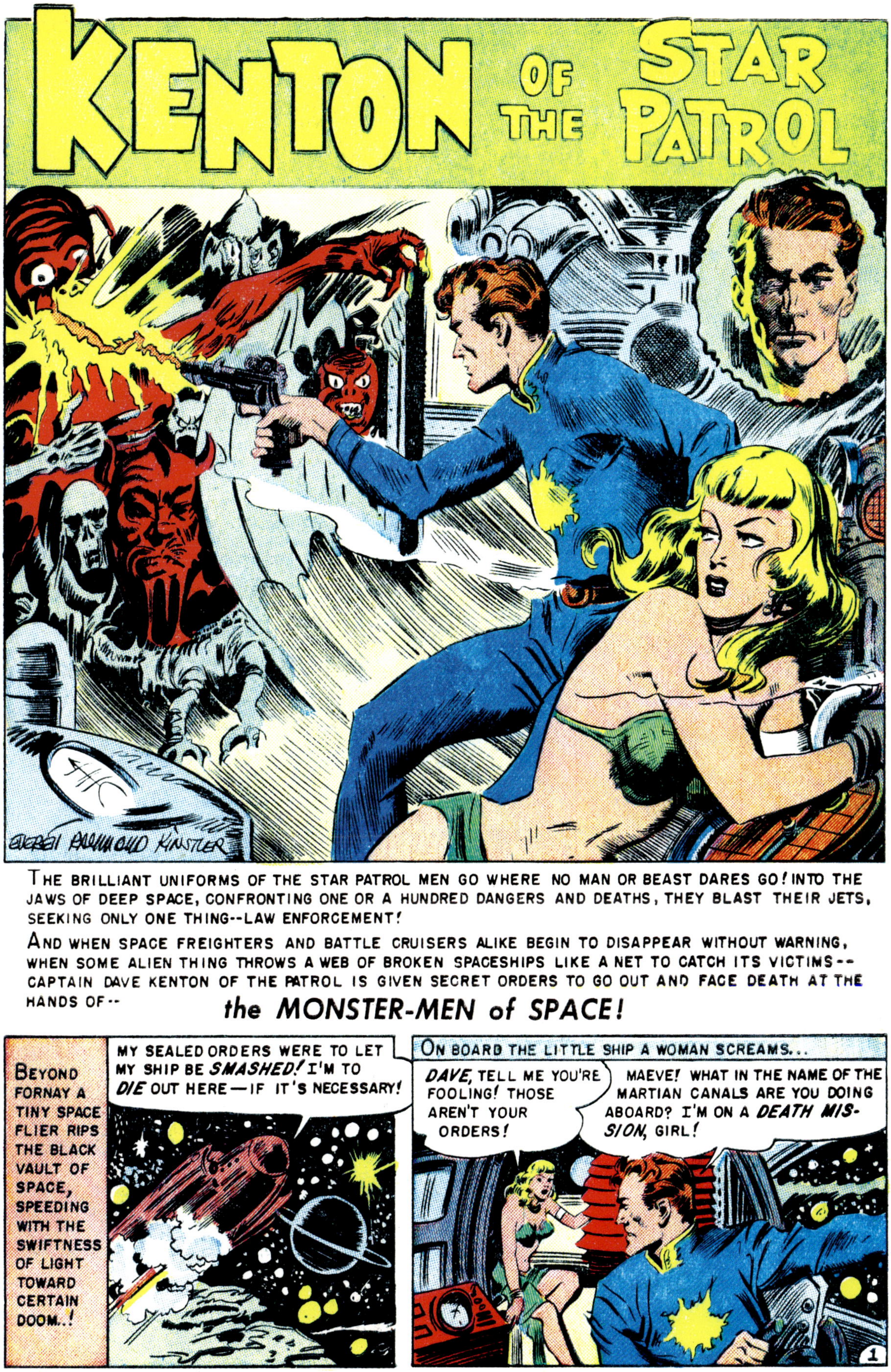

KENTON OF THE STAR PATROL

THE BRILLIANT UNIFORMS OF THE STAR PATROL MEN GO WHERE NO MAN OR BEAST DARES GO! INTO THE JAWS OF DEEP SPACE, CONFRONTING ONE OR A HUNDRED DANGERS AND DEATHS, THEY BLAST THEIR JETS, SEEKING ONLY ONE THING--LAW ENFORCEMENT!

AND WHEN SPACE FREIGHTERS AND BATTLE CRUISERS ALIKE BEGIN TO DISAPPEAR WITHOUT WARNING, WHEN SOME ALIEN THING THROWS A WEB OF BROKEN SPACESHIPS LIKE A NET TO CATCH ITS VICTIMS-- CAPTAIN DAVE KENTON OF THE PATROL IS GIVEN SECRET ORDERS TO GO OUT AND FACE DEATH AT THE HANDS OF--

the MONSTER-MEN of SPACE!

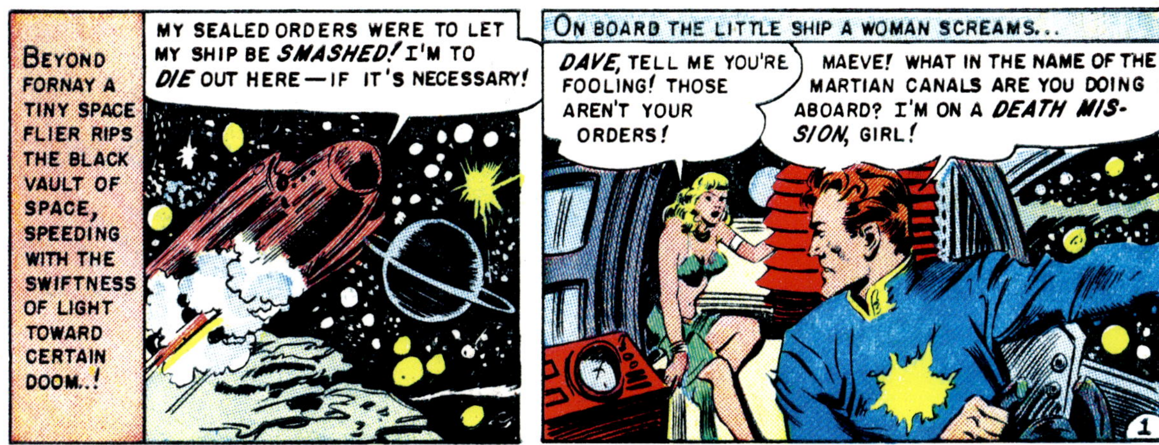

Strange Worlds #6
Avon, February, 1952
original: 13½"x17½"

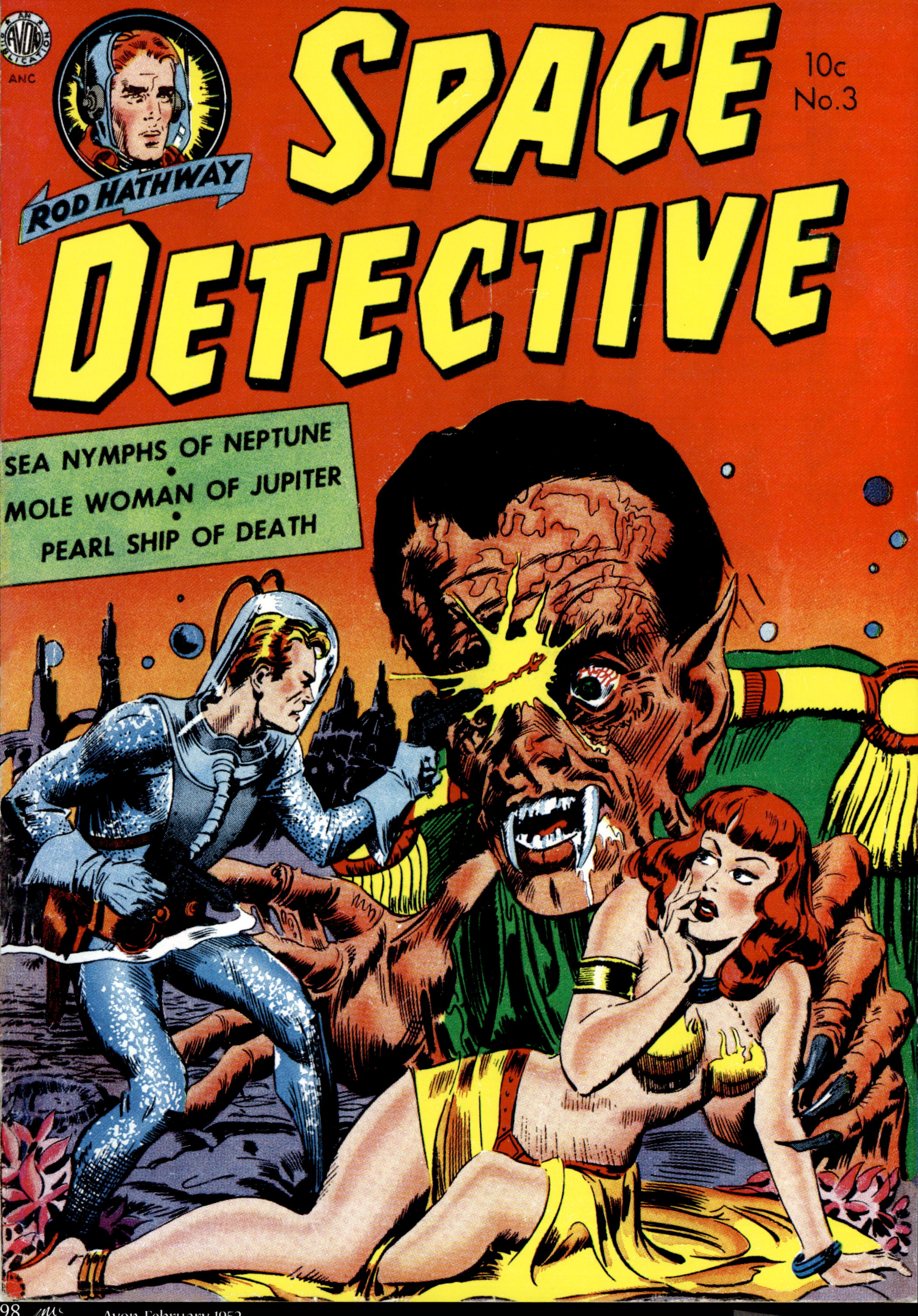

Avon, February, 1952

Avon, April-May, 1954

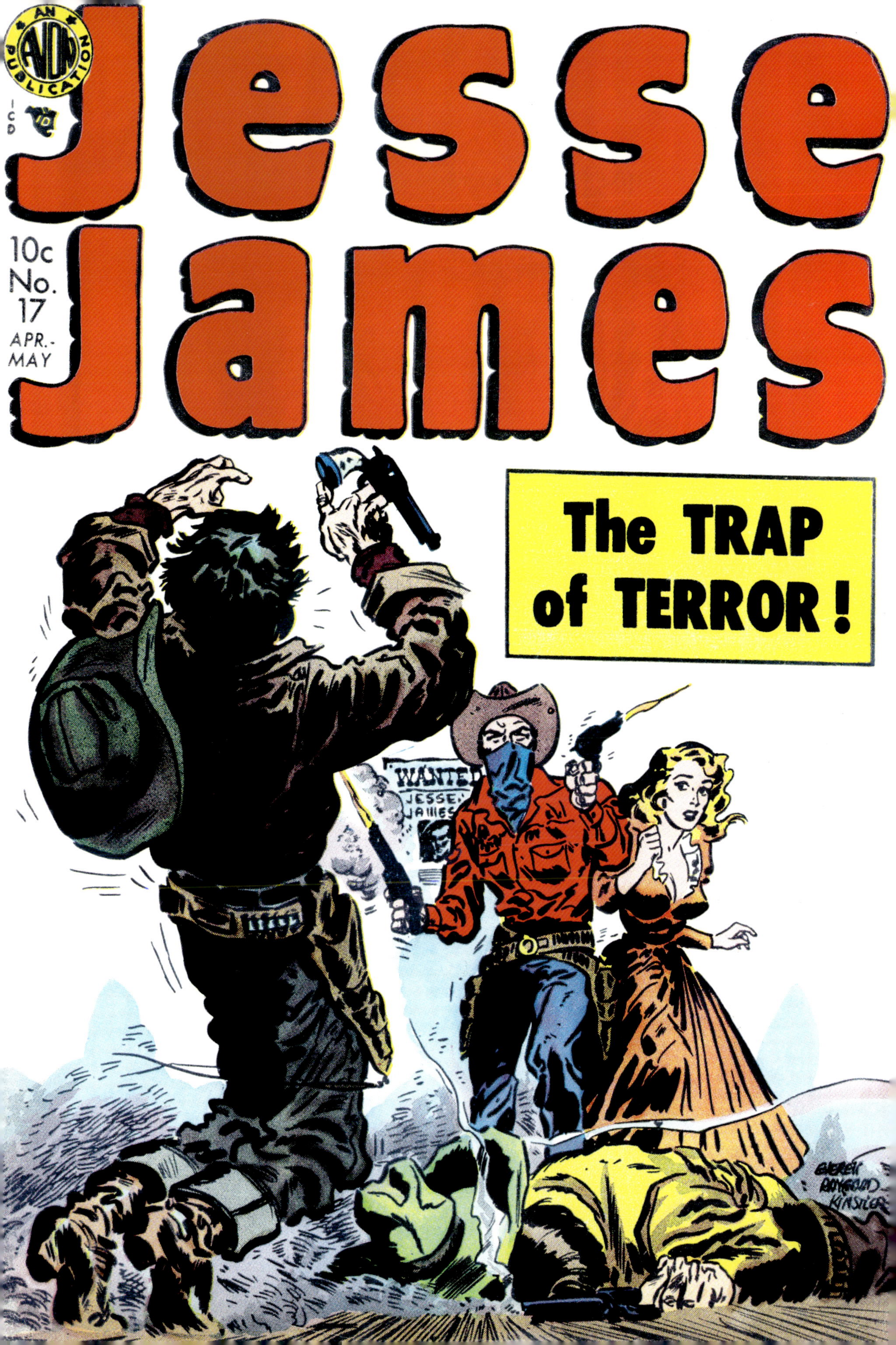
AN AVON PUBLICATION
Jesse James
10c
No.
17
APR.-
MAY
The TRAP of TERROR!
WANTED
JESSE
JAMES

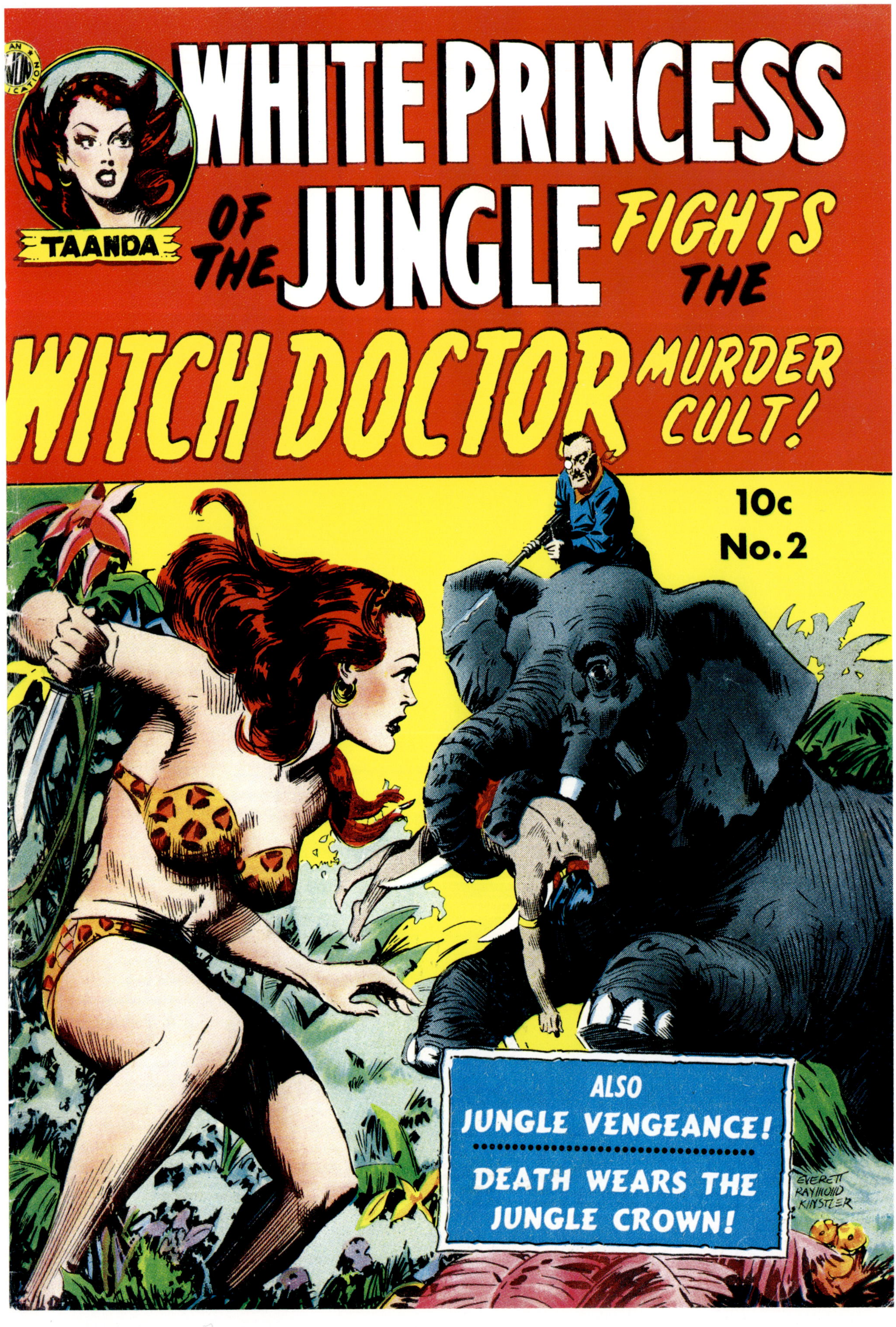

TAANDA
WHITE PRINCESS OF THE JUNGLE
FIGHTS THE
WITCH DOCTOR MURDER CULT!
10c
No.2
ALSO
JUNGLE VENGEANCE!
DEATH WEARS THE JUNGLE CROWN!
EVERETT RAYMOND KINSTLER

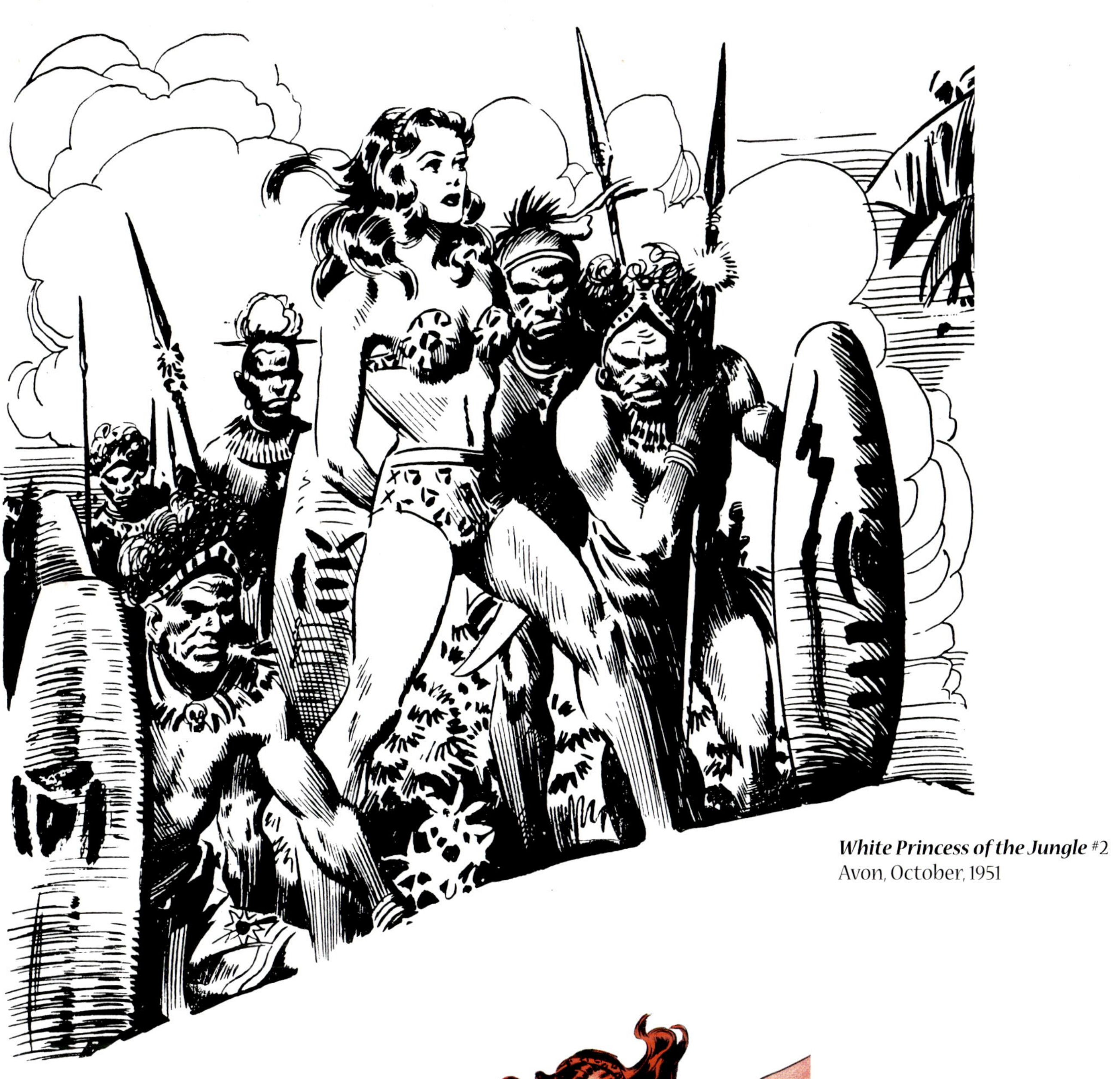

White Princess of the Jungle #2
Avon, October, 1951

When I turned in the first ***White Princess of the Jungle*** comic book cover, Sol Cohen took one look at it and told me that I should remove the smile from the face of the crocodile

I told him, "If you had the view that the crocodile has, you'd be smiling, too."

The smile stayed.

TERROR-FANGS AT TAURUTI KRAAL!

The smiling crocodile.
White Princess of the Jungle #1
Avon, July, 1951

THE SWORD OF ZORRO

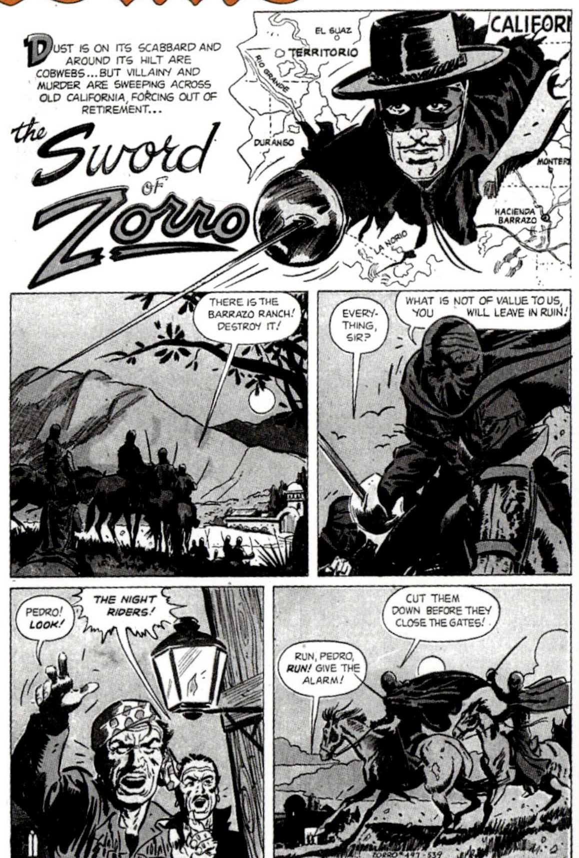

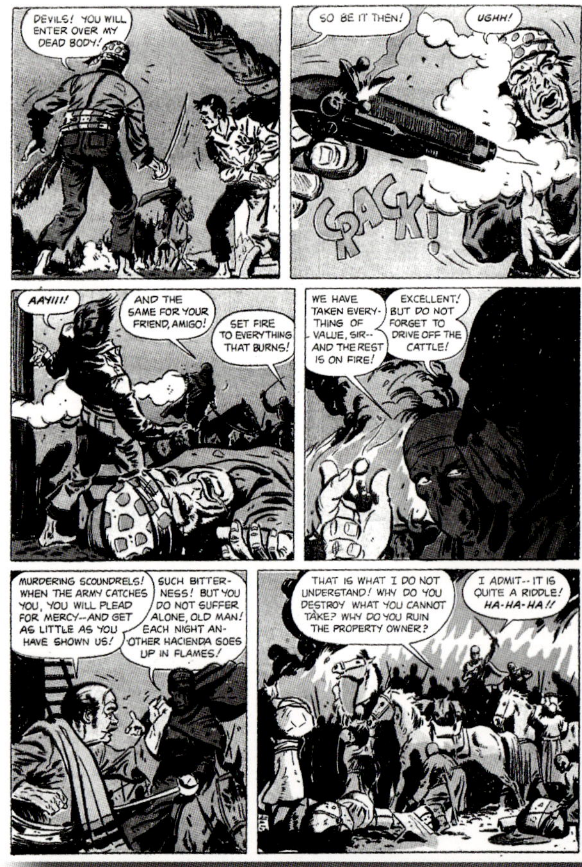

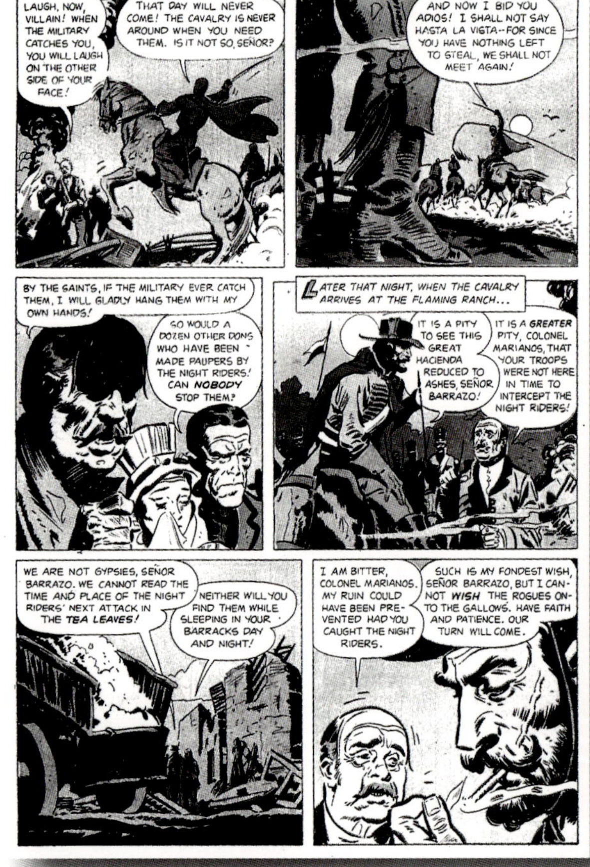

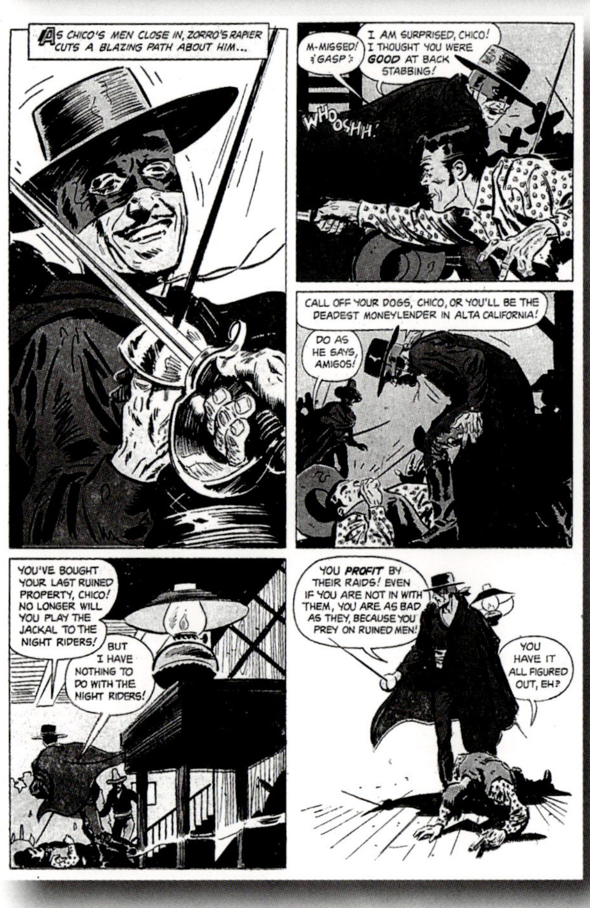

By 1953, Ray had abandoned the fine pen lines in his comic book work for the more evocative strokes of a brush. Now he was devoting as much time to the telling of the story as to the rendering of the panels.

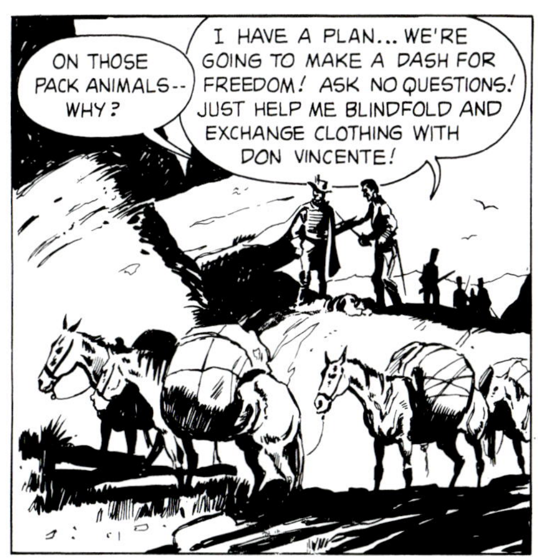

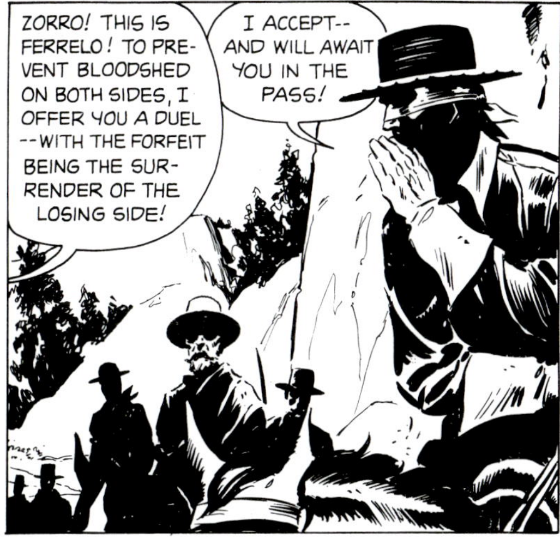

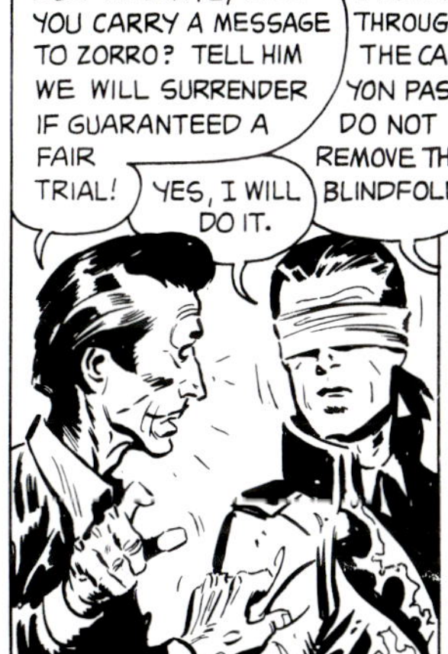

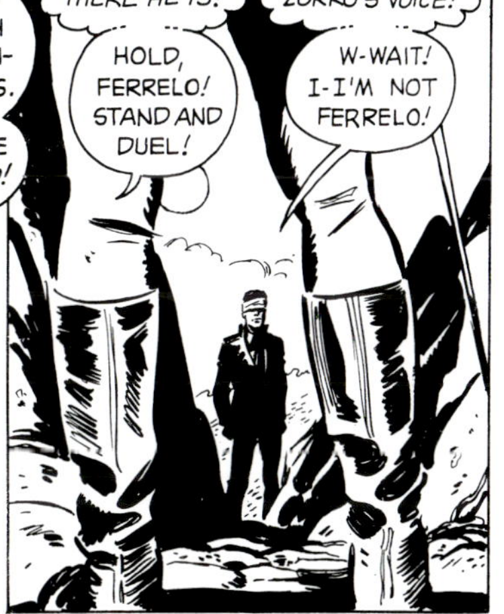

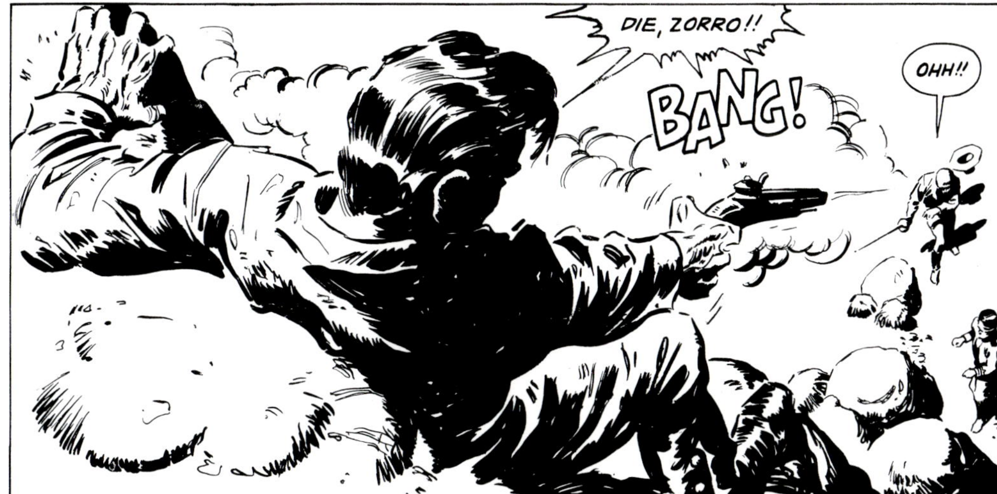

At Dell, art director Matt Murphy gave me two things I really appreciated: longer stories—that let me cut back on the time I spent searching for work—and a degree of freedom to tell the story my way.

With these thirty-four-page stories, I was the casting director, the stage manager, the prop man and the director with plenty of space to play around with staging shots in interesting ways—like framing a character through the legs of another [*immediate left*] or using more challenging viewpoints like the one in the last panel.

The instructions I actually received from the scriptwriters were more staid, but Matt trusted me and allowed me to reinterpret the story if I thought I could make it more exciting.

The Sword of Zorro
Dell Four Color #497
Dell, September, 1953

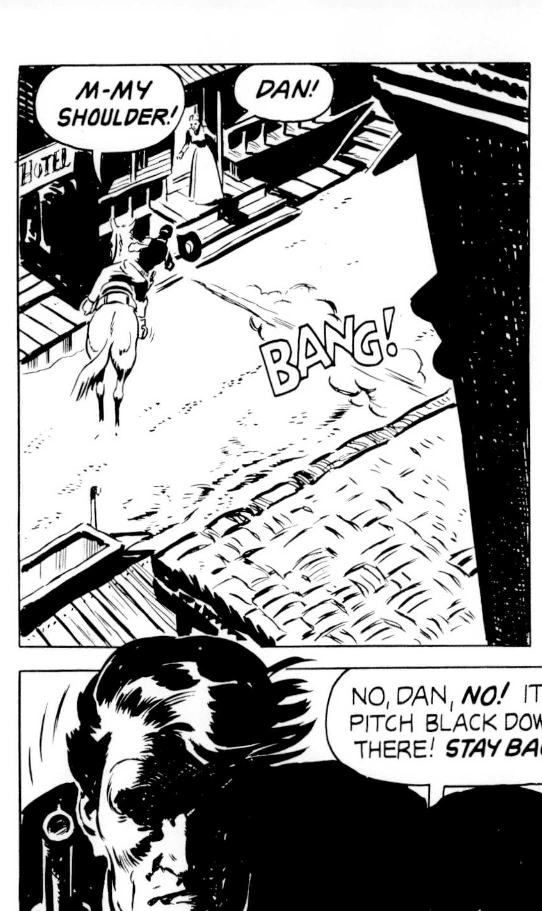

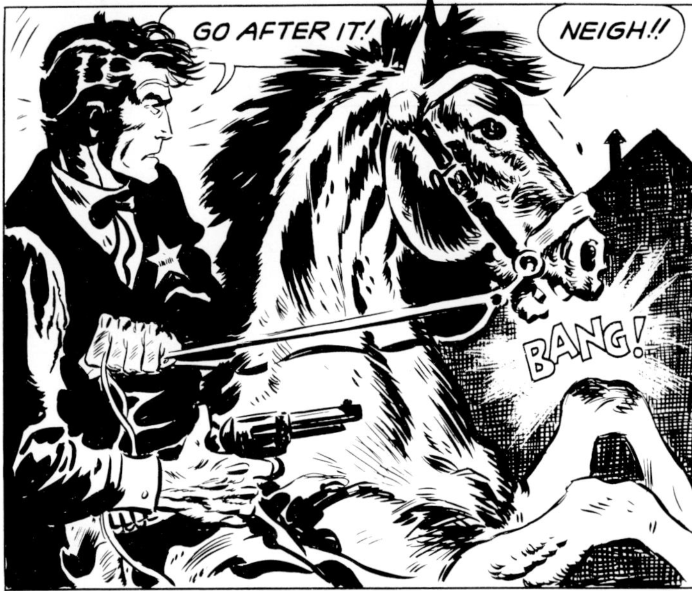

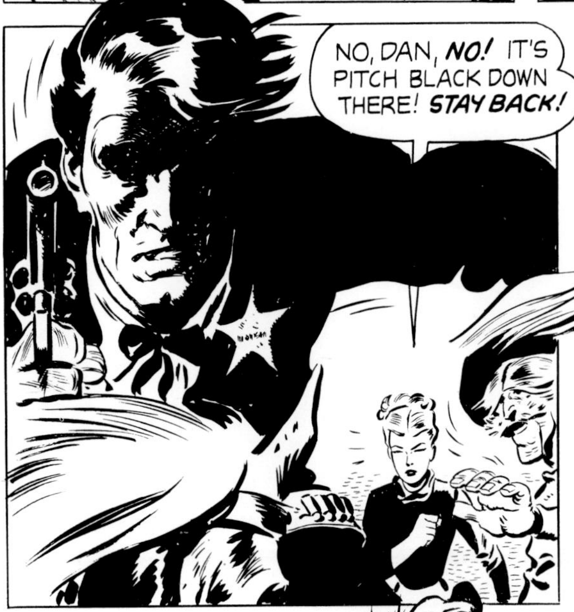

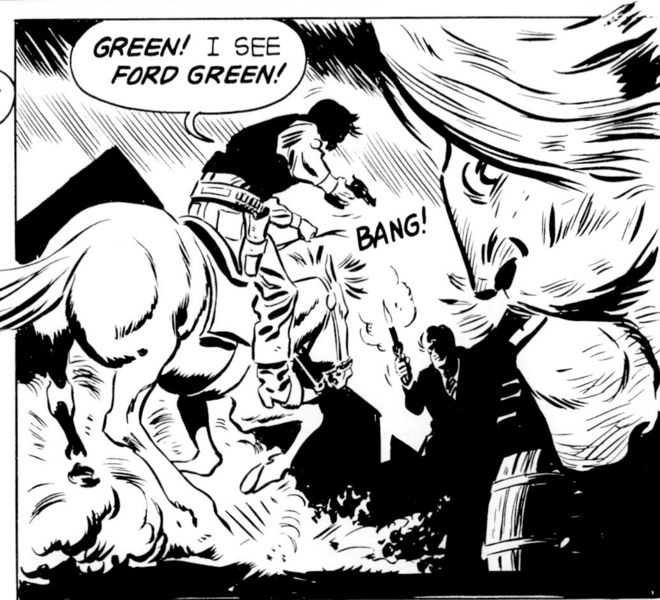

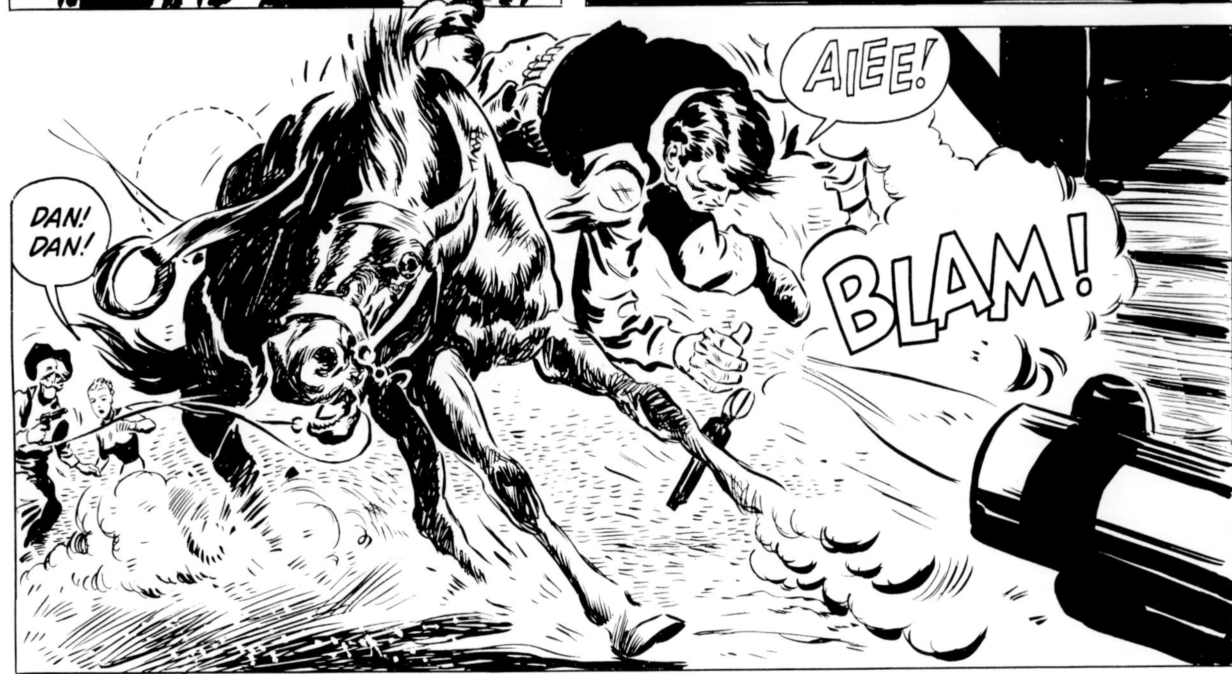

Western Marshall, ***Dell Four Color*** #534
Dell, February, 1954

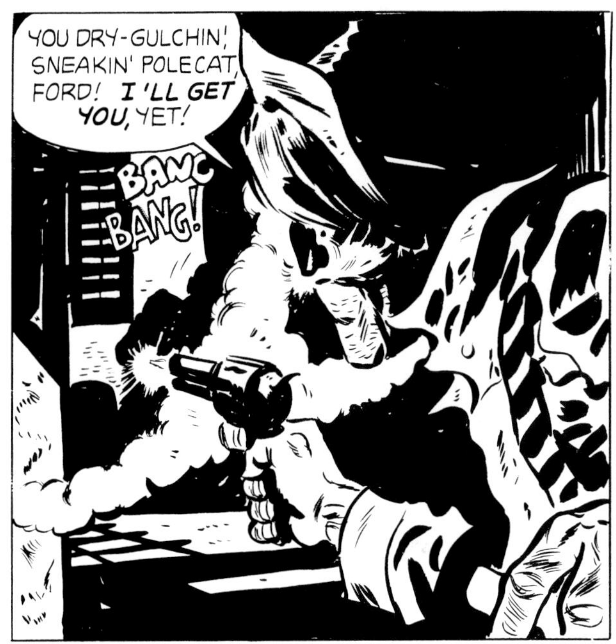

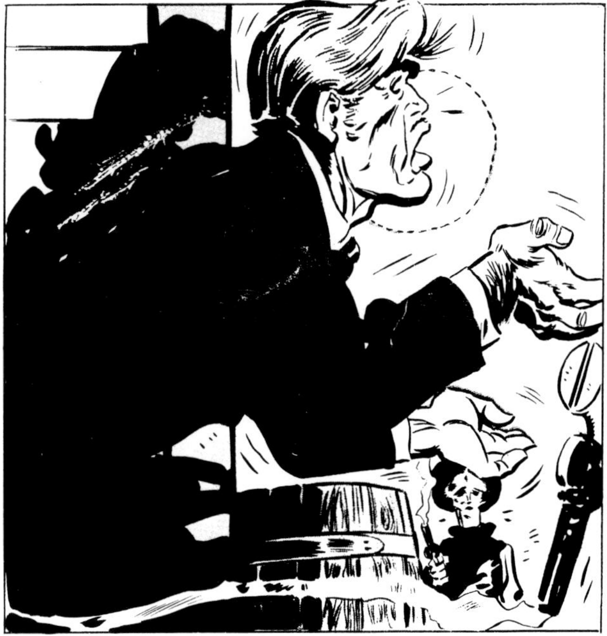

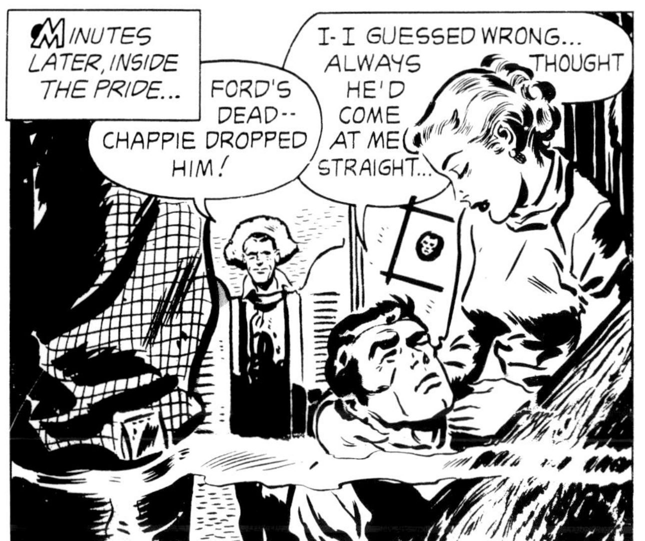

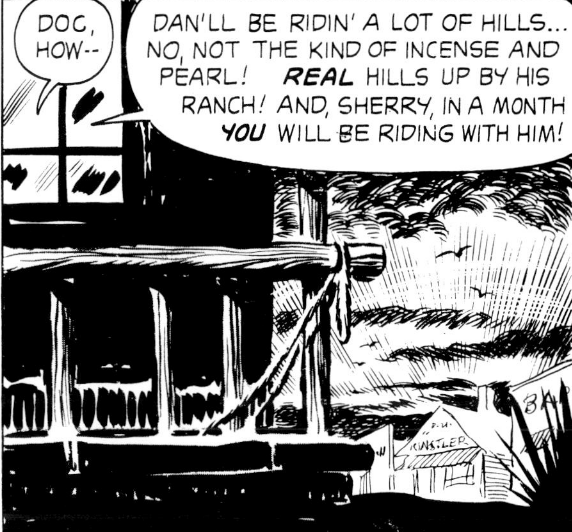

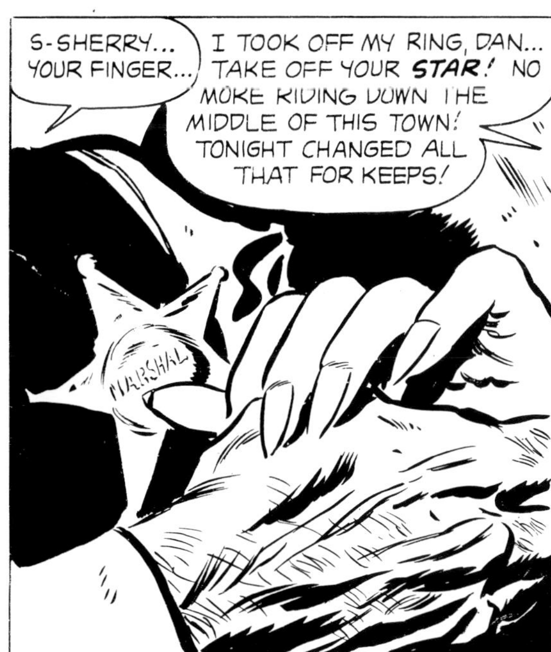

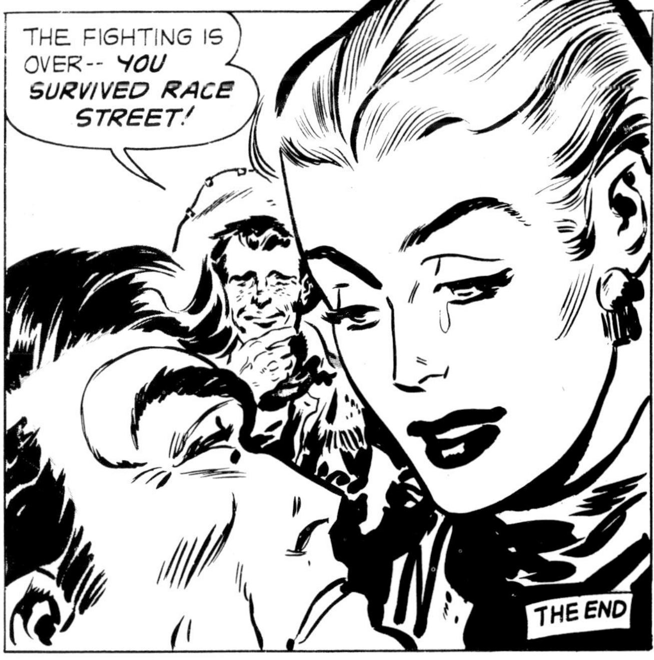

Kinstler was allowed to sign all of the covers and stories he did for Avon and Ziff-Davis. He even signed his stories at DC, which was unheard of. Only Dell restricted him, but he found a way around the ban. Look in the background on panel four, above.

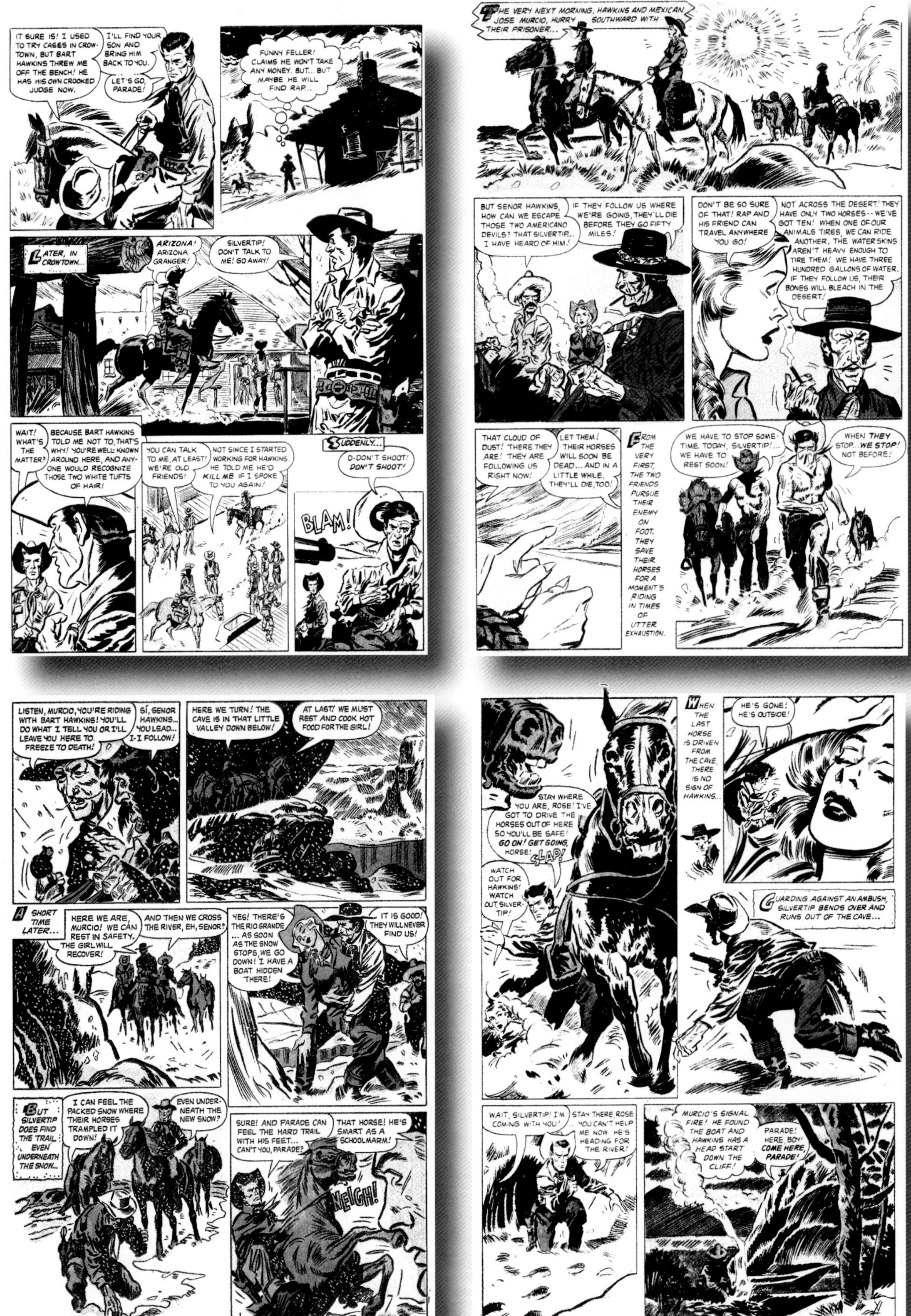

IT SURE IS! I USED TO TRY CASES IN CROWTOWN, BUT BART HAWKINS THREW ME OFF THE BENCH! HE HAS HIS OWN CROOKED JUDGE NOW.
I'LL FIND YOUR SON AND BRING HIM BACK TO YOU.
LET'S GO, PARADE!
FUNNY FELLER! CLAIMS HE WON'T TAKE ANY MONEY. BUT.. BUT MAYBE HE WILL FIND RAP...
LATER, IN CROWTOWN...
ARIZONA! ARIZONA GRANGER!
SILVERTIP! DON'T TALK TO ME! GO AWAY!
WAIT! WHAT'S THE MATTER?
BECAUSE BART HAWKINS TOLD ME NOT TO, THAT'S WHY! YOU'RE WELL-KNOWN AROUND HERE, AND ANYONE WOULD RECOGNIZE THOSE TWO WHITE TUFTS OF HAIR!
YOU CAN TALK TO ME, AT LEAST! WE'RE OLD FRIENDS!
NOT SINCE I STARTED WORKING FOR HAWKINS. HE TOLD ME HE'D KILL ME IF I SPOKE TO YOU AGAIN!
SUDDENLY...
D-DON'T SHOOT! DON'T SHOOT!
BLAM!
THE VERY NEXT MORNING, HAWKINS AND MEXICAN JOSE MURCIO, HURRY SOUTHWARD WITH THEIR PRISONER...
BUT SENOR HAWKINS, HOW CAN WE ESCAPE THOSE TWO AMERICANO DEVILS? THAT SILVERTIP.. I HAVE HEARD OF HIM!
IF THEY FOLLOW US WHERE WE'RE GOING, THEY'LL DIE BEFORE THEY GO FIFTY MILES!
DON'T BE SO SURE OF THAT! RAP AND HIS FRIEND CAN TRAVEL ANYWHERE YOU GO!
NOT ACROSS THE DESERT! THEY HAVE ONLY TWO HORSES -- WE'VE GOT TEN! WHEN ONE OF OUR ANIMALS TIRES, WE CAN RIDE ANOTHER. THE WATER SKINS AREN'T HEAVY ENOUGH TO TIRE THEM! WE HAVE THREE HUNDRED GALLONS OF WATER. IF THEY FOLLOW US, THEIR BONES WILL BLEACH IN THE DESERT!
THAT CLOUD OF DUST! THERE THEY ARE! THEY ARE FOLLOWING US RIGHT NOW!
LET THEM! THEIR HORSES WILL SOON BE DEAD... AND IN A LITTLE WHILE, THEY'LL DIE, TOO!
FROM THE VERY FIRST, THE TWO FRIENDS PURSUE THEIR ENEMY ON FOOT. THEY SAVE THEIR HORSES FOR A MOMENT'S RIDING IN TIMES OF UTTER EXHAUSTION.
WE HAVE TO STOP SOMETIME. TODAY, SILVERTIP!... WE HAVE TO REST SOON!
WHEN THEY STOP... WE STOP! NOT BEFORE!
LISTEN, MURCIO, YOU'RE RIDING WITH BART HAWKINS! YOU'LL DO WHAT I TELL YOU OR I'LL LEAVE YOU HERE TO. FREEZE TO DEATH!
SÍ, SENOR HAWKINS... YOU LEAD... I-I FOLLOW!
HERE WE TURN! THE CAVE IS IN THAT LITTLE VALLEY DOWN BELOW!
AT LAST! WE MUST REST AND COOK HOT FOOD FOR THE GIRL!
A SHORT TIME LATER...
HERE WE ARE, MURCIO! WE CAN REST IN SAFETY. THE GIRL WILL RECOVER!
AND THEN WE CROSS THE RIVER, EH, SENOR?
YES! THERE'S THE RIO GRANDE... AS SOON AS THE SNOW STOPS, WE GO DOWN! I HAVE A BOAT HIDDEN THERE!
IT IS GOOD! THEY WILL NEVER FIND US!
BUT SILVERTIP DOES FIND THE TRAIL EVEN UNDERNEATH THE SNOW...
I CAN FEEL THE PACKED SNOW WHERE THEIR HORSES TRAMPLED IT DOWN!
EVEN UNDERNEATH THE NEW SNOW?
SURE! AND PARADE CAN FEEL THE HARD TRAIL WITH HIS FEET... CAN'T YOU, PARADE?
THAT HORSE! HE'S SMART AS A SCHOOLMARM!
NEIGH!
STAY WHERE YOU ARE, ROSE! I'VE GOT TO DRIVE THE HORSES OUT OF HERE SO YOU'LL BE SAFE! GO ON! GET GOING, HORSE!
SLAP!
WATCH OUT FOR HAWKINS! WATCH OUT, SILVERTIP!
WHEN THE LAST HORSE IS DRIVEN FROM THE CAVE, THERE IS NO SIGN OF HAWKINS...
HE'S GONE! HE'S OUTSIDE!
GUARDING AGAINST AN AMBUSH, SILVERTIP BENDS OVER AND RUNS OUT OF THE CAVE...
WAIT, SILVERTIP! I'M COMING WITH YOU!
STAY THERE ROSE. YOU CAN'T HELP ME NOW. HE'S HEADING FOR THE RIVER!
MURCIO'S SIGNAL FIRE! HE FOUND THE BOAT AND HAWKINS HAS A HEAD START DOWN THE CLIFF!
PARADE! HERE, BOY! COME HERE, PARADE!

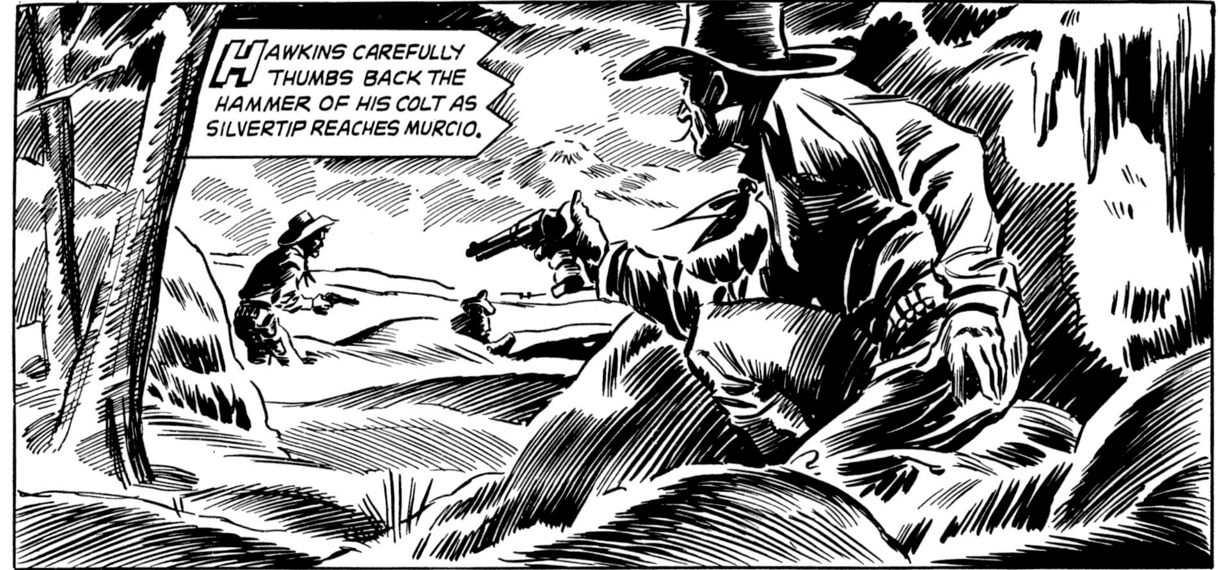

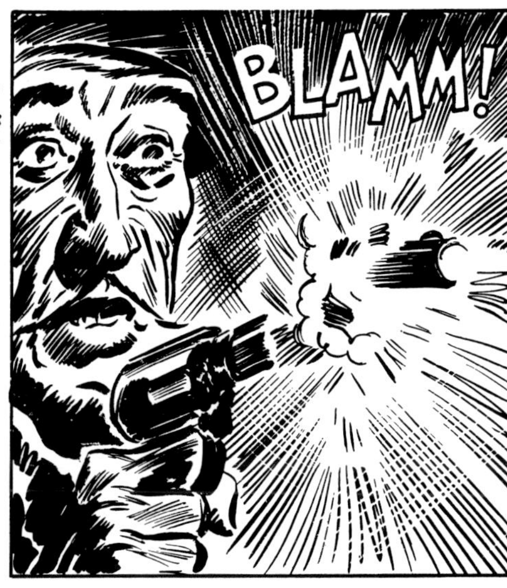

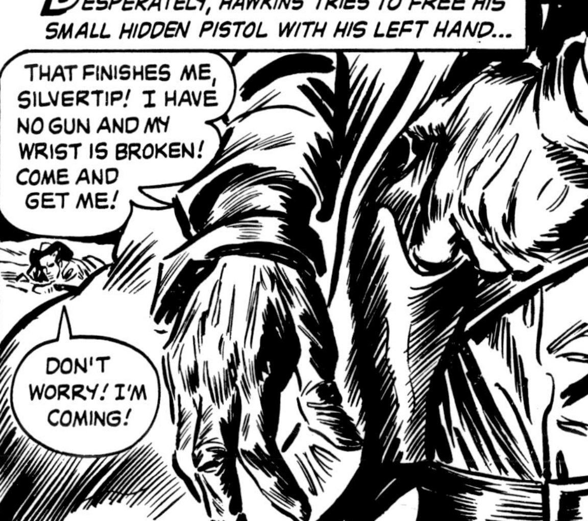

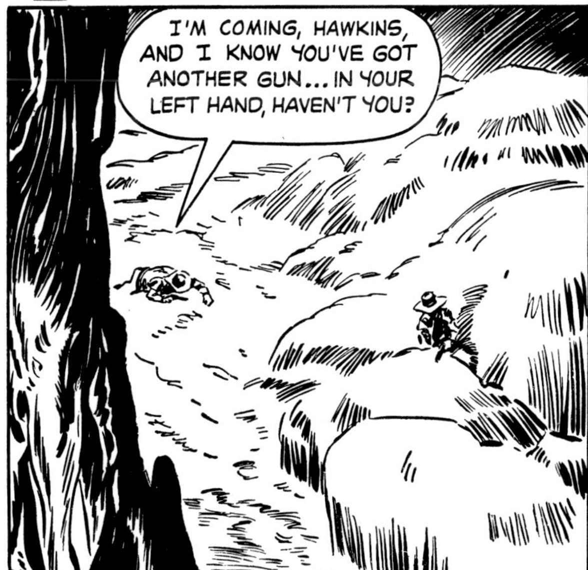

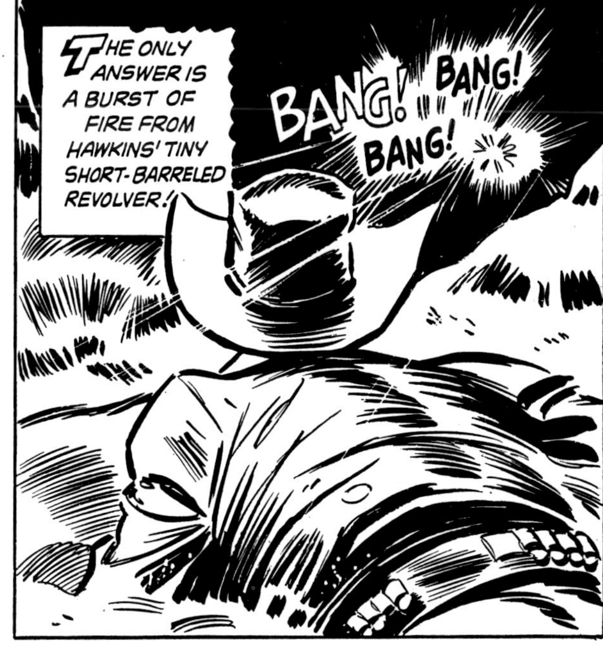

Max Brand's Silvertip's Search
Dell Four Color #572
Dell, July, 1954

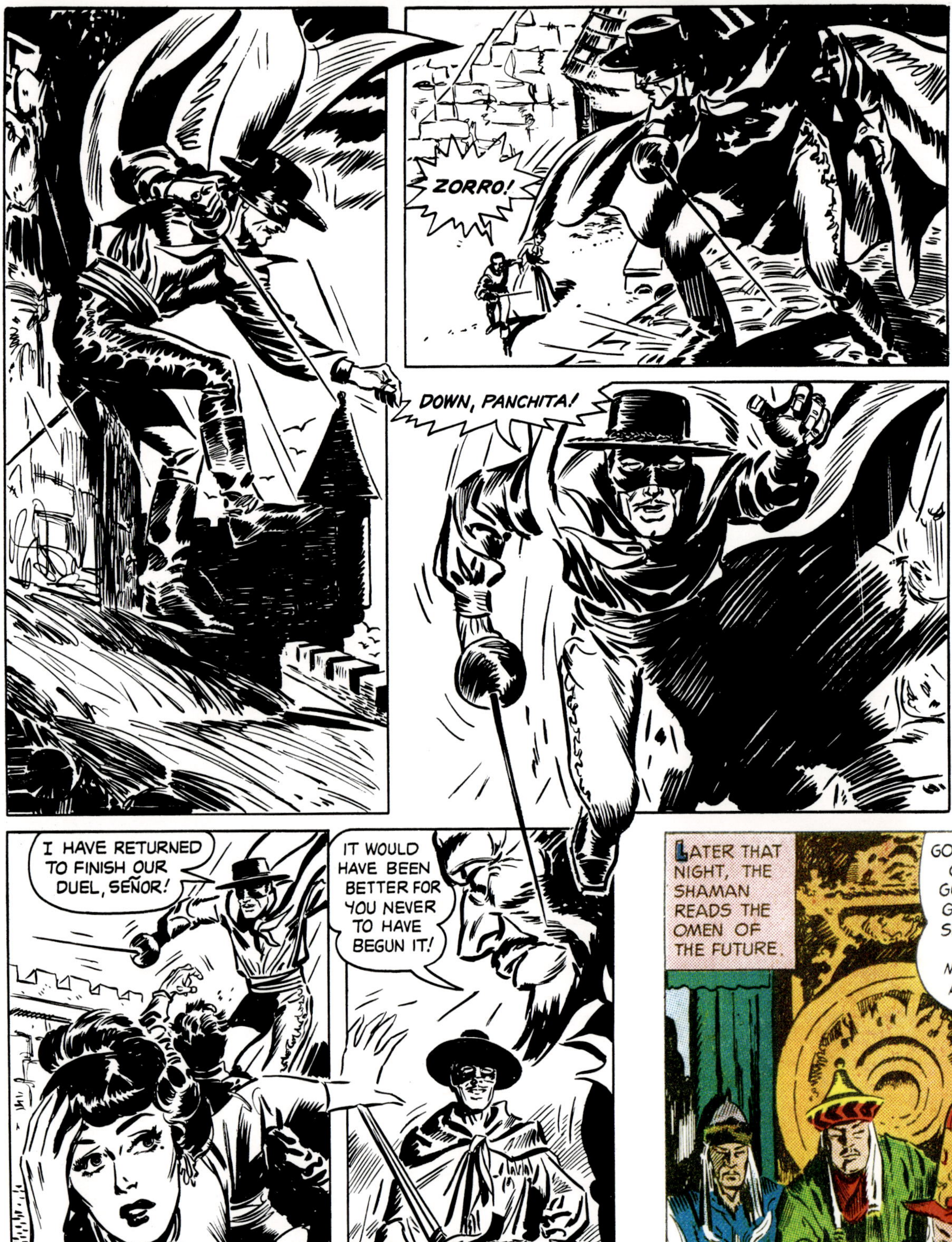

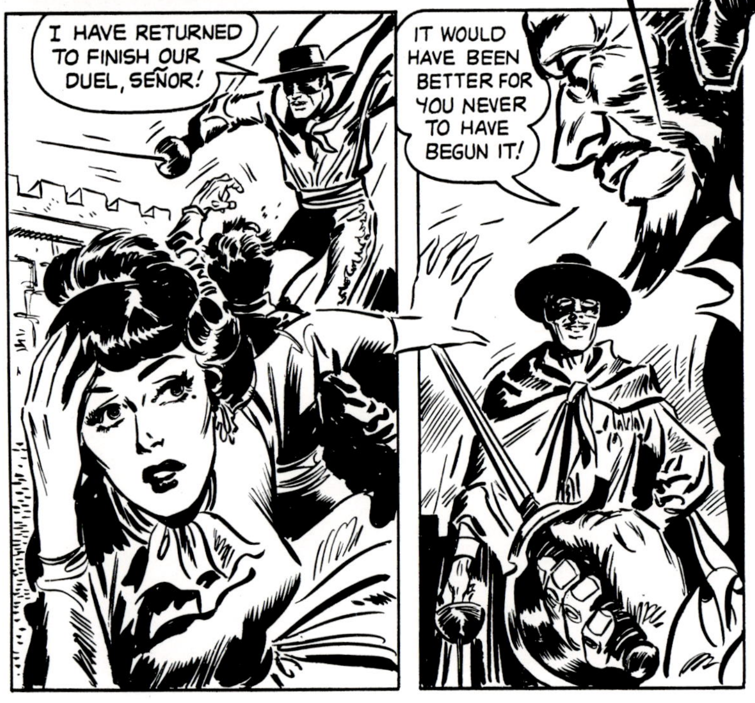

The Hand of Zorro
Dell Four Color #574
Dell, September, 1954

This is a sample of the pedestrian inking job afforded *The Conqueror* by another artist which caused Ray to rethink his relationship with Dell/Western.

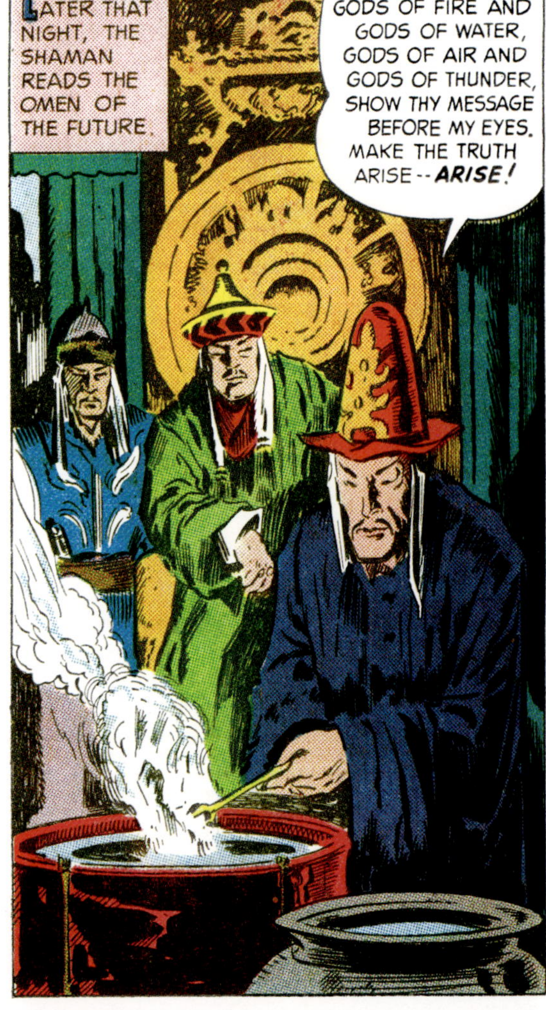

The Conqueror, ***Dell Four Color*** #690
Dell, April, 1956

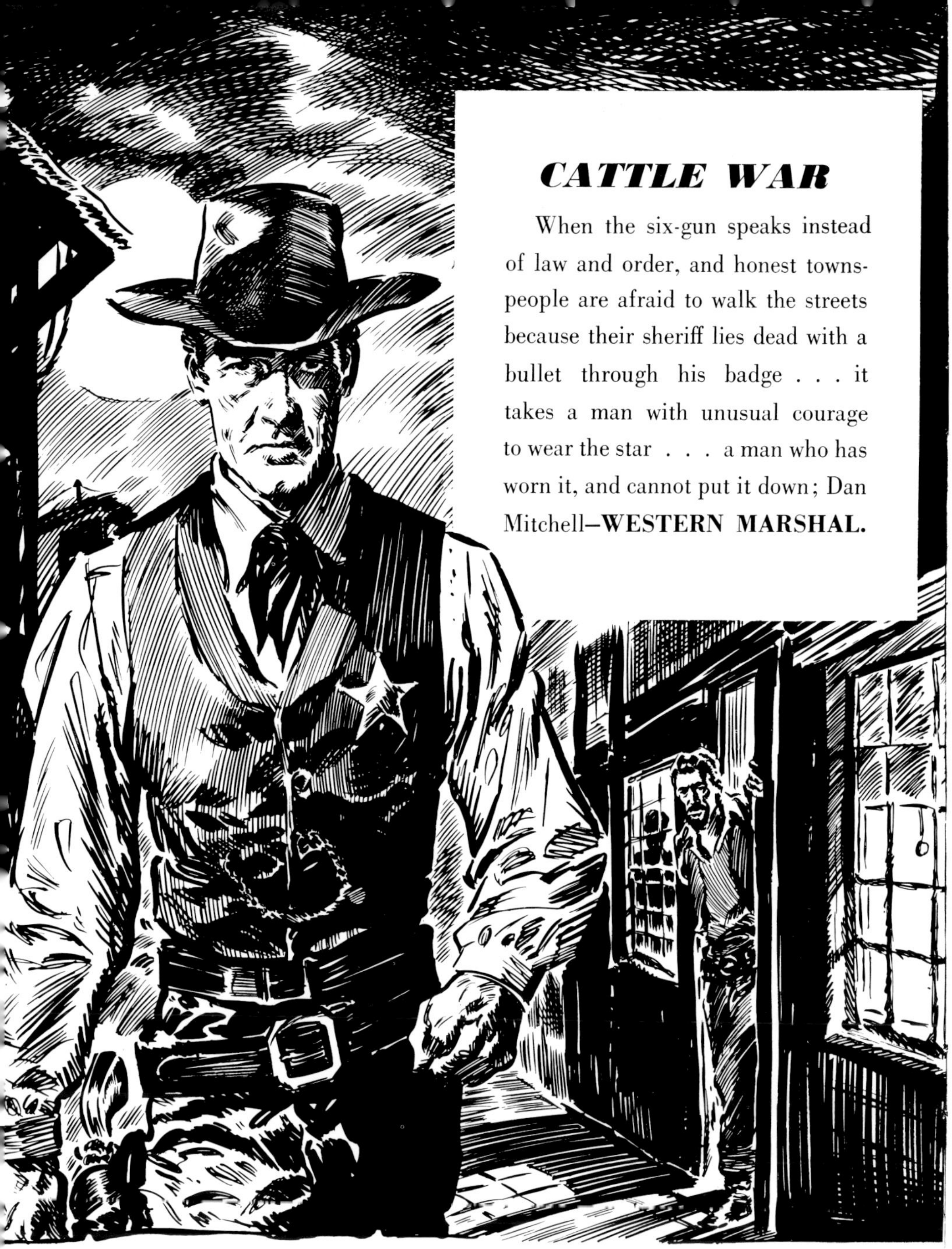

CATTLE WAR

When the six-gun speaks instead of law and order, and honest towns-people are afraid to walk the streets because their sheriff lies dead with a bullet through his badge . . . it takes a man with unusual courage to wear the star . . . a man who has worn it, and cannot put it down; Dan Mitchell—**WESTERN MARSHAL.**

Western Marshall
Dell Four Color #613
Dell, February, 1955

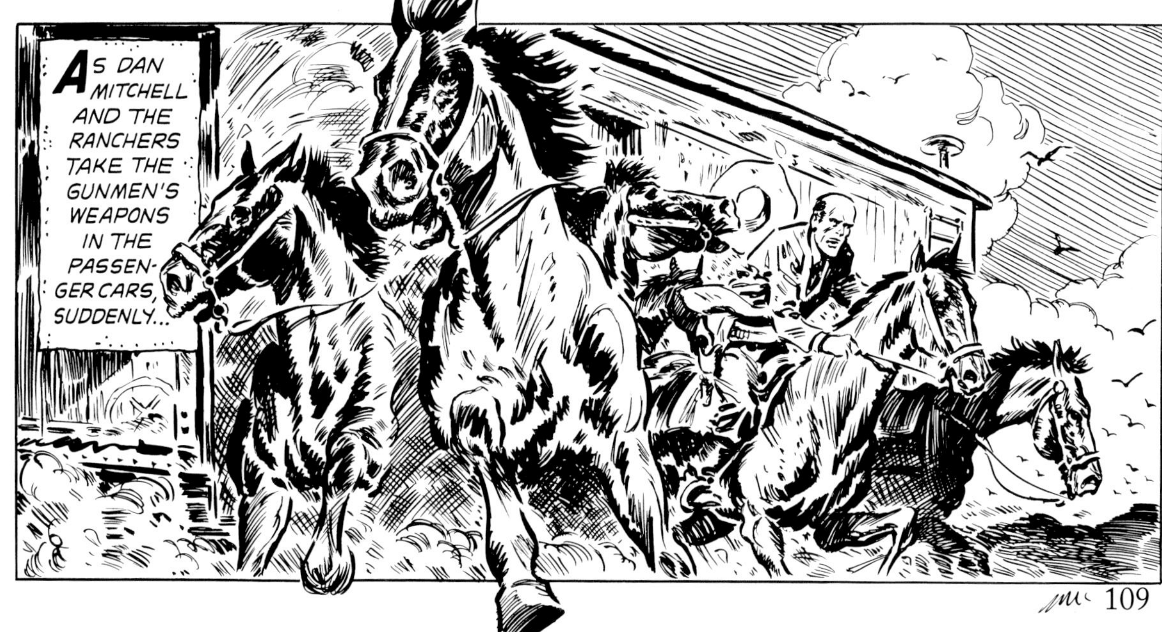

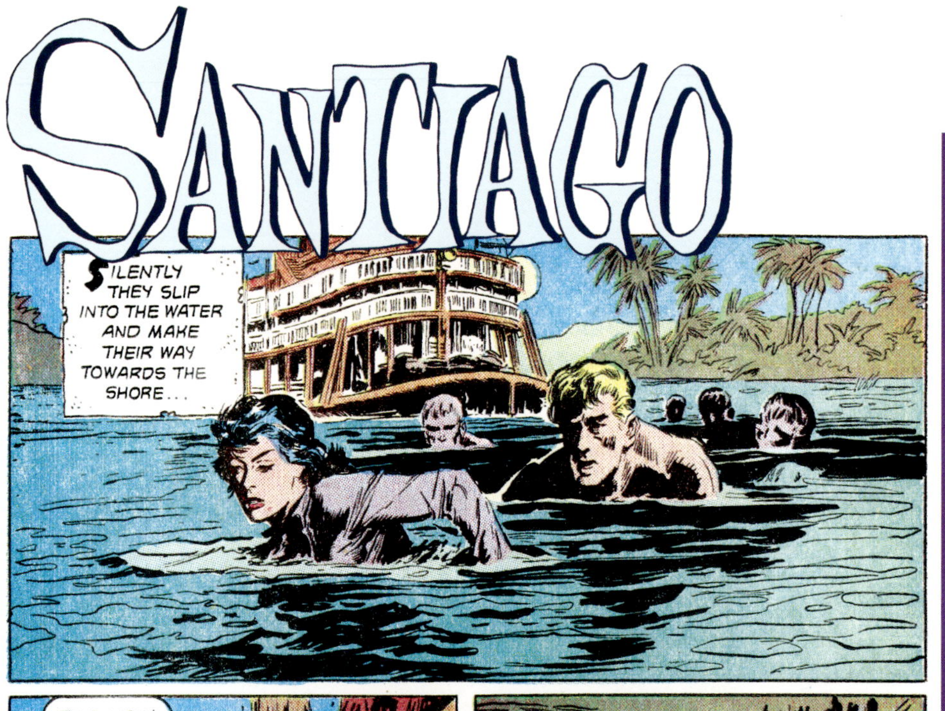

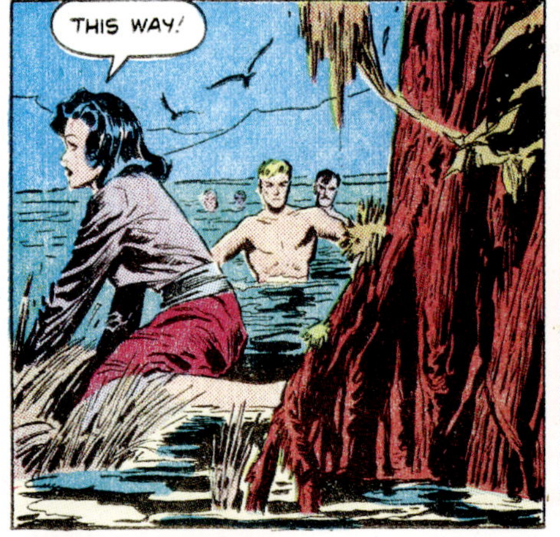

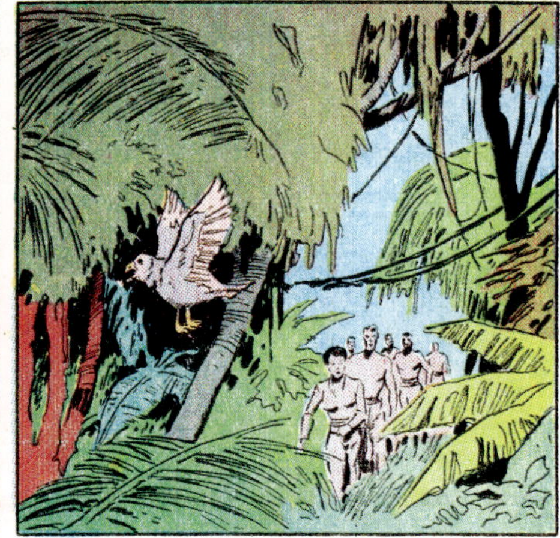

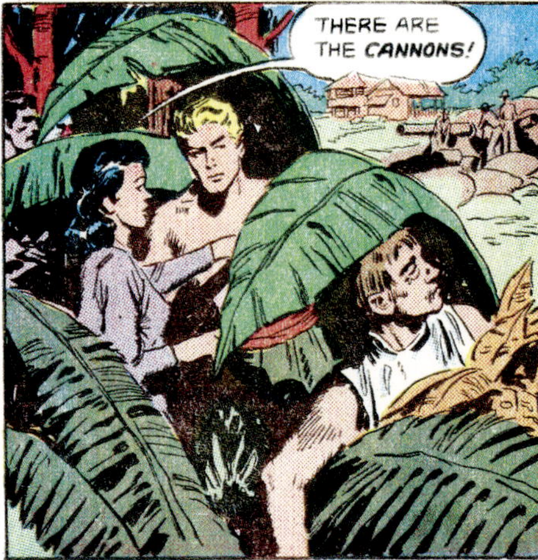

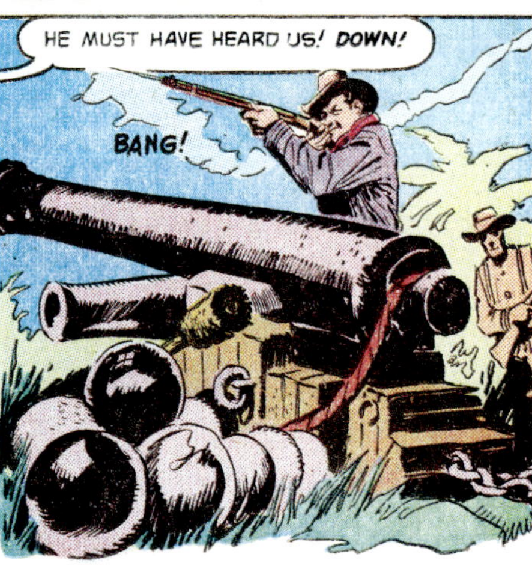

SANTIAGO
Dell Four Color #723
Dell, September, 1956

Atlas

Martin Goodman's Atlas Comics was one of the largest comic book companies of the 1950s.

Goodman sold paper - Atlas comic books, men's magazines like ***Men***, ***Male*** and ***Bachelor***, Lion paperbacks and even the occasional pulp magazine.

Stan Lee, the editor of the comic books, oversaw the creation of dozens of issues each week. There was always work to be had at 655 Madison Avenue.

So it is somewhat surprising that with all of those markets open to him, Ray Kinstler only did one comic story for Atlas and perhaps three illustrations for the men's magazines.

Another of Ray's later books for Dell was the adaptation of the 1956 Alan Ladd film, *Santiago*. It was his opportunity to make up for the debacle with *The Conqueror*. He inked all thirty-two pages himself and it shows in the character likenesses.

But the comic book market was shifting and opportunities continued to open up in book and magazine illustration. His future was elsewhere.

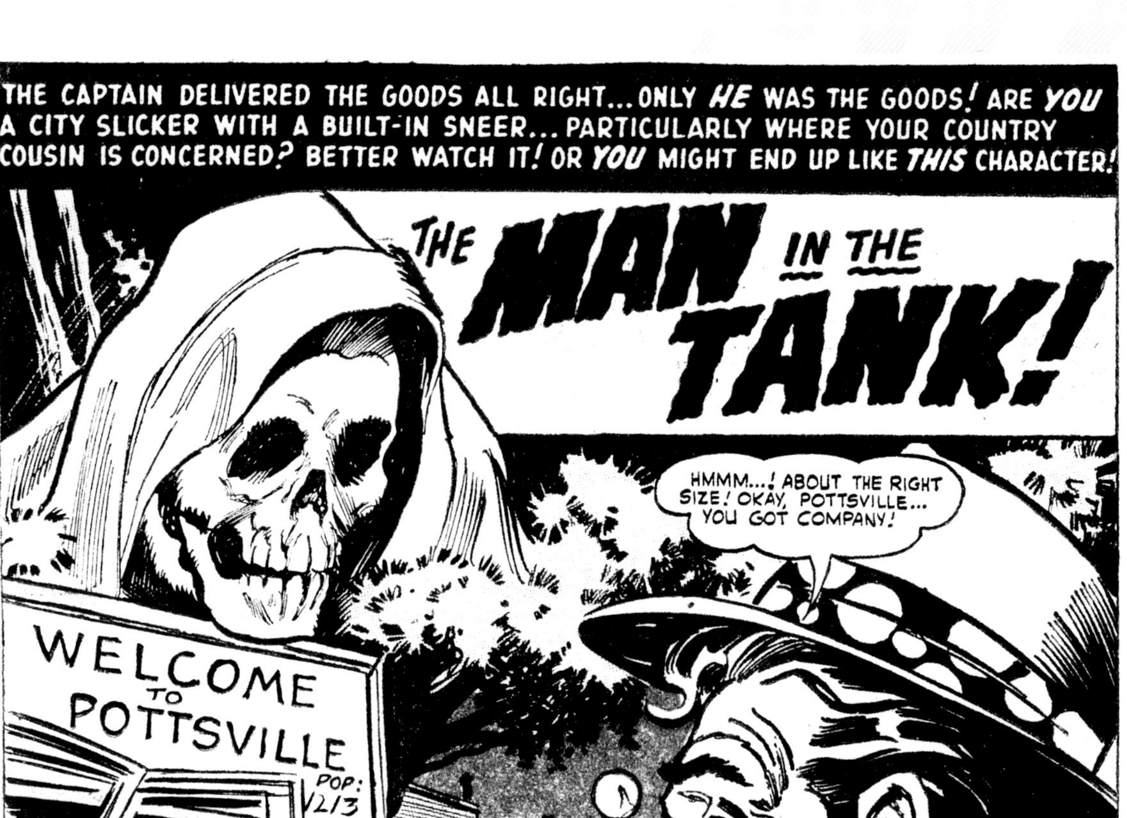

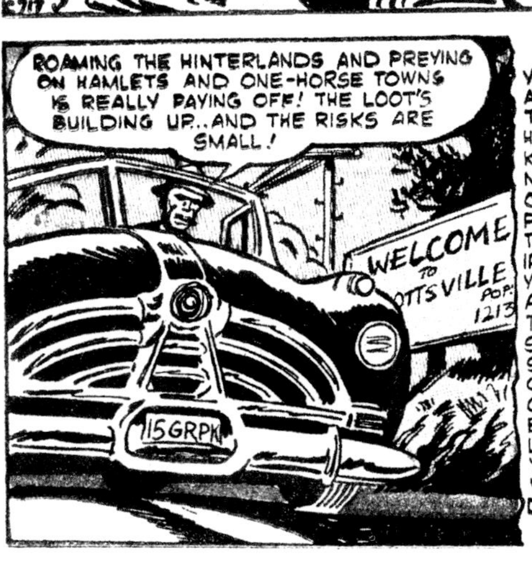

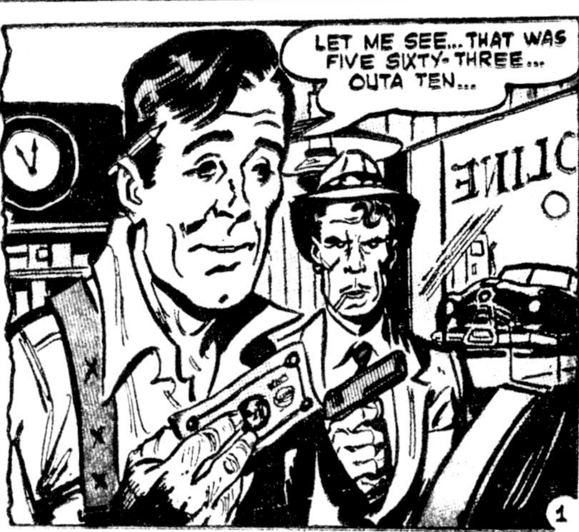

The Man in the Tank
Mystery Tales #15
Atlas
September, 1953

Classics

This panel is from one of the very last comic books on which Ray worked. Some of the best artists in the business resorted to Classics' standardized approach to comic art as other publishers trimmed their output or went out of business altogether. It was not a great time for comic books or for comic book artists. Kinstler was happy to leave the field.

actual size

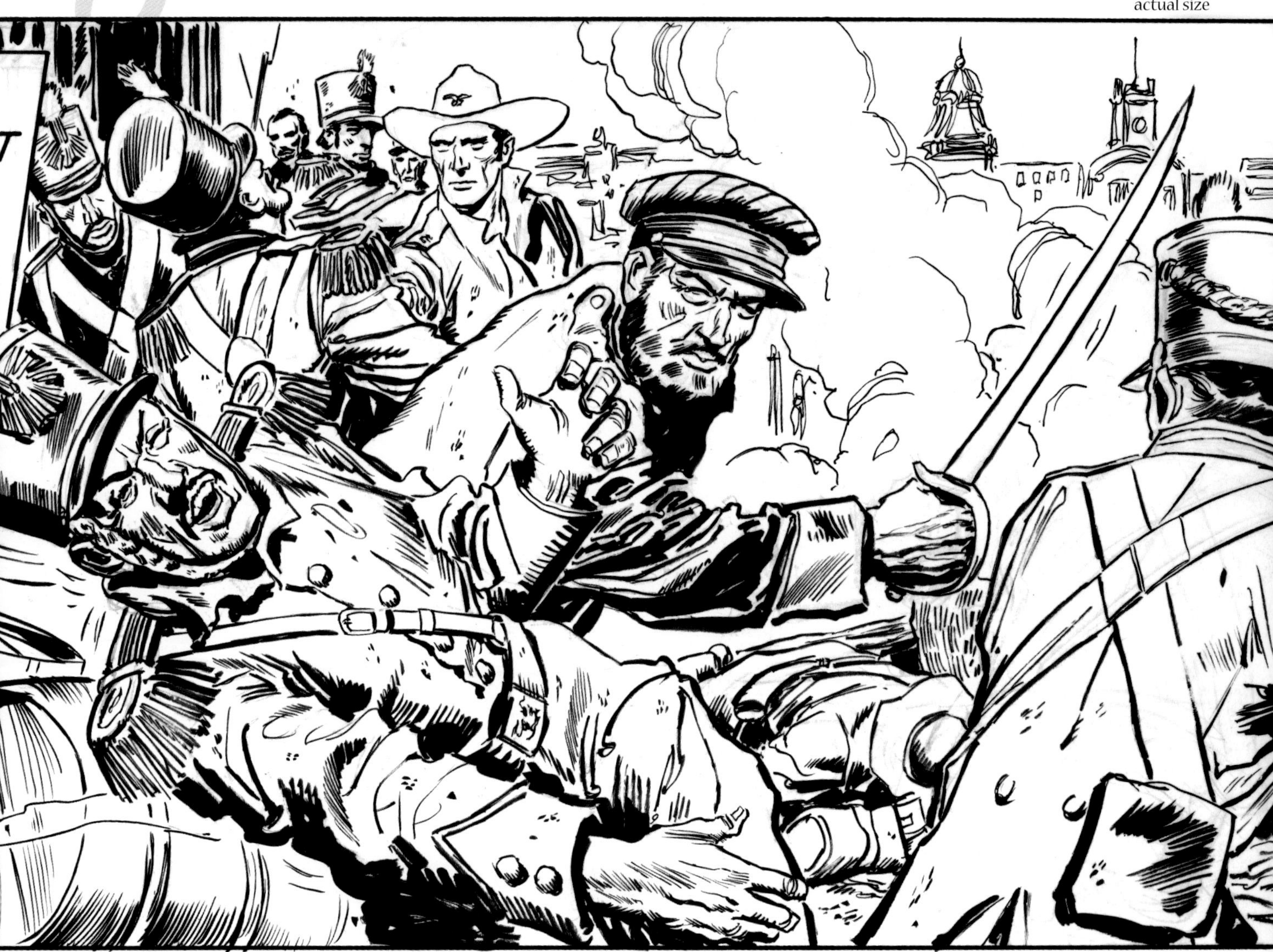

The Halls of Montezuma
Classics Illustrated Special — The World Around Us – Marines
Gilberton, July, 1959

My stint at Classics Illustrated was the most uncomfortable experience I had in the comics. Their need to control and to homogenize the work with simple outline drawings made me feel as if I were back inking Ken Battefield at Cinema Comics.

I was a professional with sixteen years of experience and that experience wasn't appreciated. I don't think it was even wanted.

It was a very distasteful and almost demeaning period for me and I don't really consider it to be part of my comic book work, but I had just been married about a year and I had a wife to support. For the first time I wasn't just responsible for myself. The paperback cover styles were changing in ways that made me look old-fashioned. Hardback book editors were after more graphic and design-oriented styles.

Classics was close by and it looked like the short pieces would be enough to cover my rent. But it was the least fun I ever had and I came close to hating it.

pulp magazines 1944 to 1958

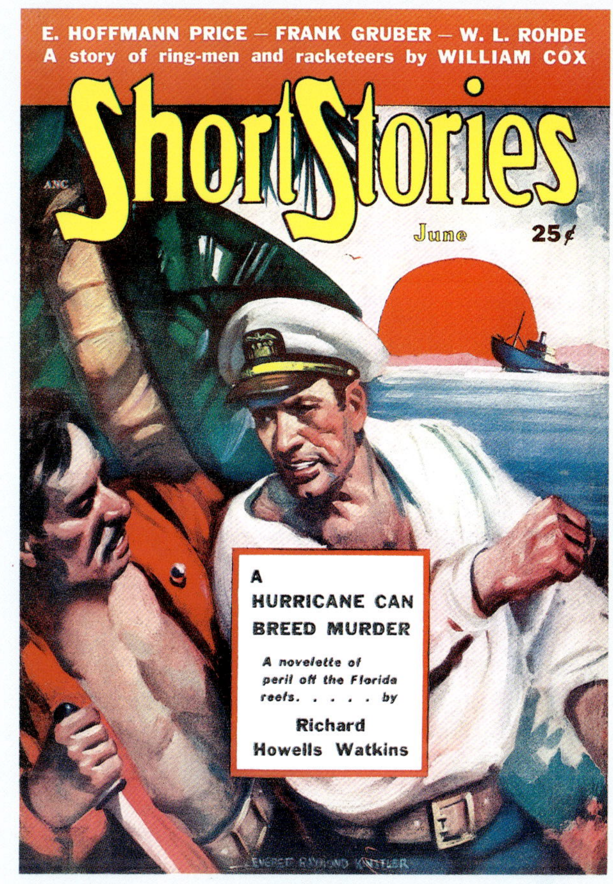

The pulps were a natural outlet and training ground.

The "Pulps" had always been an entry-level market for writers and illustrators. They paid low wages but gave creative types a place to hone their craft. Printed on cheap "pulp" newsprint with brash, colorful covers, they generally sold for ten or fifteen cents and were the literature of the masses.

Adventure, Western, Romance, Sports, Science Fiction, Aviation, Heroes, Weird, Romance, Spicy, Detective and Mystery were the major genres—with each having dozens of monthly titles. *The Shadow* came from the pulps. So did *Conan the Barbarian* and *Doc Savage*. Many of *Tarzan*'s adventures appeared there.

Some of the writers who made their reputations in pulps were Isaac Asimov, Edgar Rice Burroughs, Dashiel Hammett, Robert E. Howard, August Derleth, Ray Bradbury, H.P. Lovecraft, Tennessee Williams, Luke Short and Max Brand. Wages were just ¼ cent a word, but there was a market for all the words they could write.

In 1945, when Ray Kinstler went back to school and became a freelance illustrator, the pulps were a natural outlet and training ground. One of his first sales was to the prestigious Street & Smith Publications' ***The Shadow***.

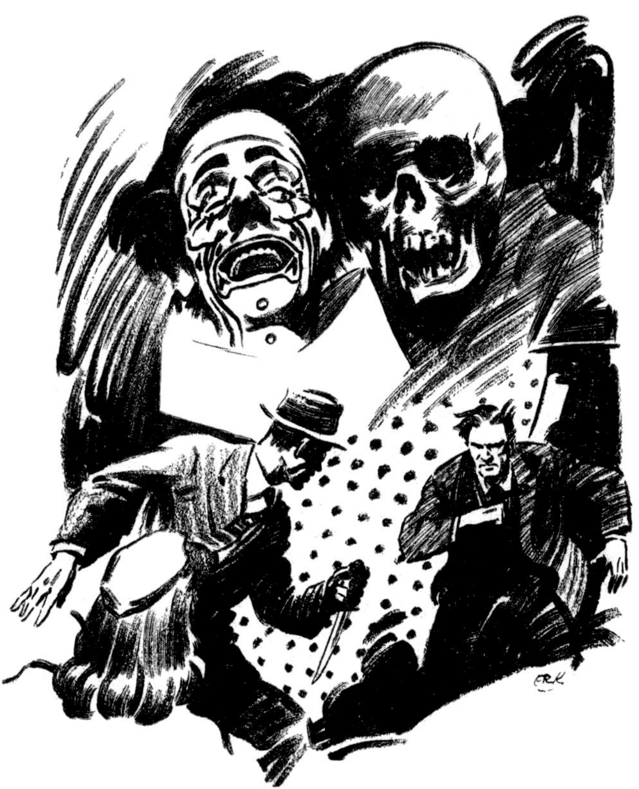

Laugh, Corpse Laugh
Detective Tales
November, 1945

By the time Kinstler got out of the Army in late 1946, there were more artists available than there were jobs. ***Collier's***, ***The Saturday Evening Post***, ***The American Magazine*** and other top drawer magazines were beginning their slow decline and their art directors were exploring alternatives to the classical romantic illustration art that captivated Kinstler.

The pulp magazines were facing the same downward spiral of the "slicks." But there was a place for Ray's pen and ink drawings on their pages and, eventually, some of his paintings on their covers.

Ray's stylistic influences here were Tom Lovell and Matt Clark, whose drybrush techniques were put to good use in this illustration for *Laugh, Corpse Laugh* from the November, 1945 issue of ***Detective Tales***.

Pulp work gradually replaced comic books for Ray from 1945 to 1947. They generally needed only a few drawings which he could do quickly in his spare time. This gave him time to paint and even allowed him to accept assignments during his year in the Army.

He was stationed at Fort Dix in New Jersey and he would zip up to New York during the week to deliver finished work and pick up new jobs.

Because he preferred getting his leave during "business hours," he was always able to trade his weekend passes advantageously with other G.I.s who were anxious to go to the city on weekends when family and friends were more available. Consequently, his art appeared regularly in the pulps during these years and would continue uninterrupted until 1958.

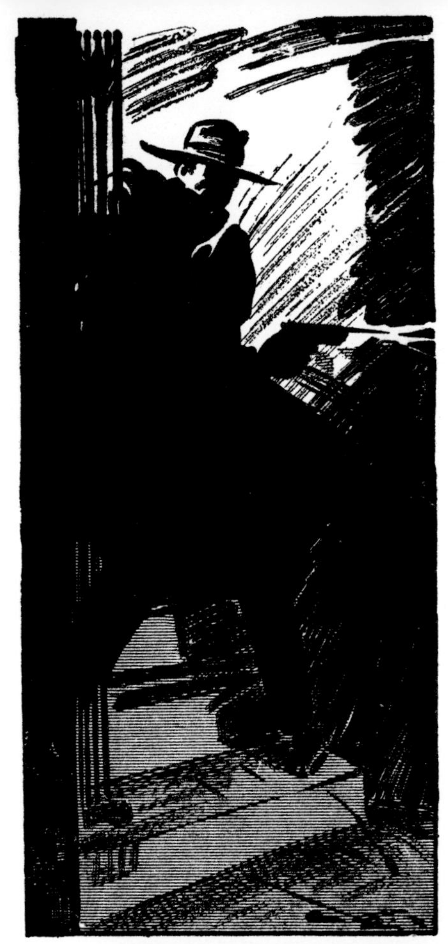

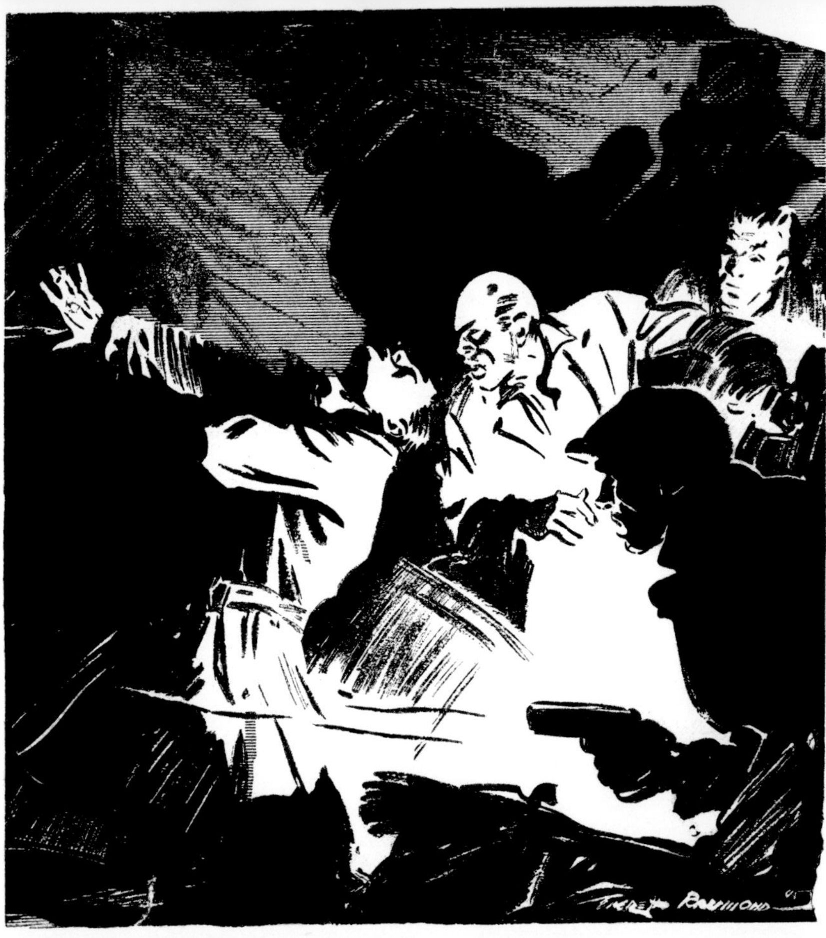

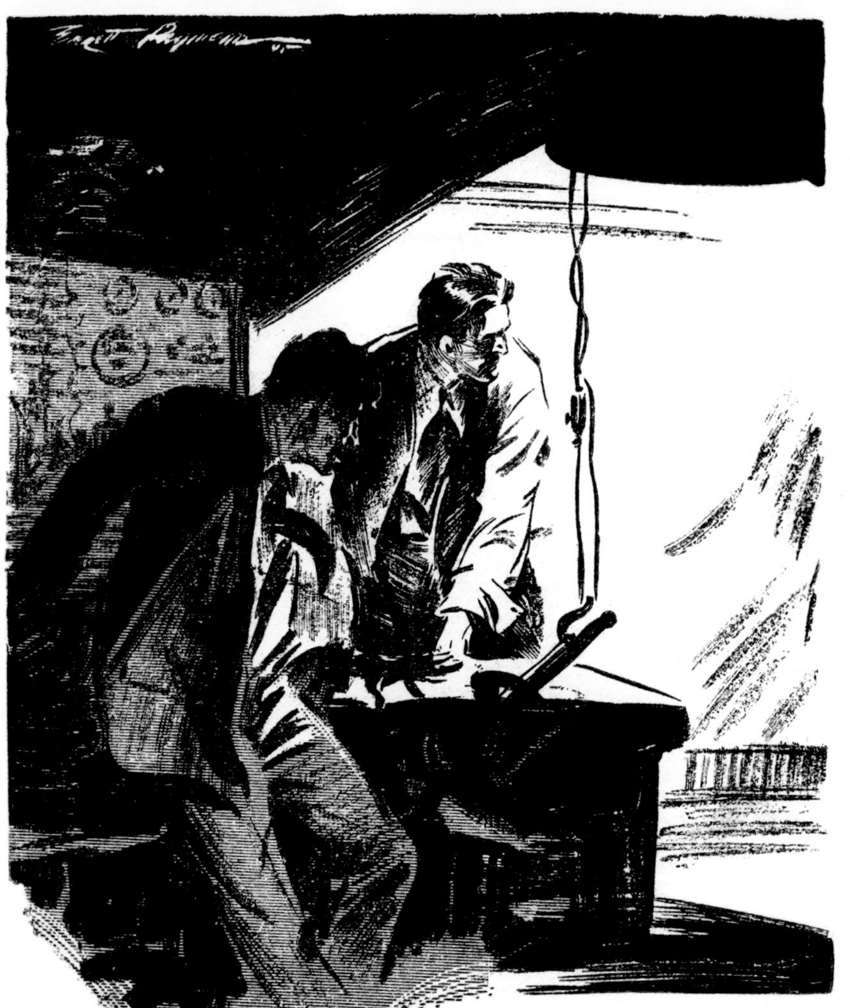

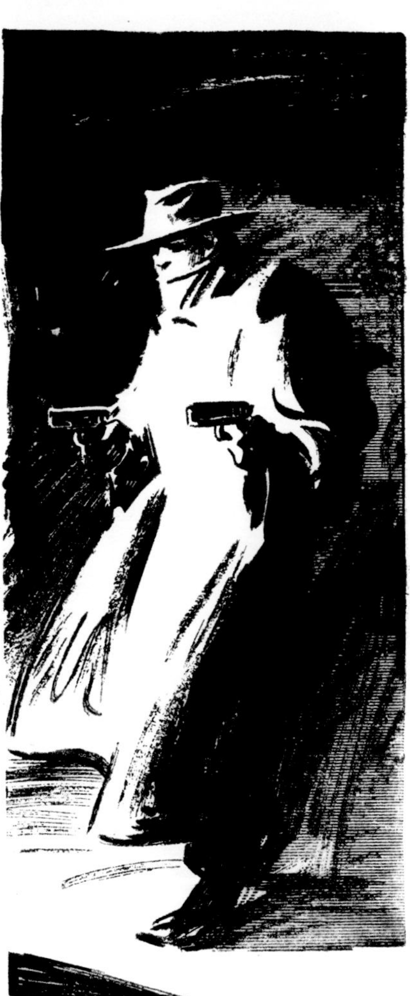

The White Skull
The Shadow
November, 1945

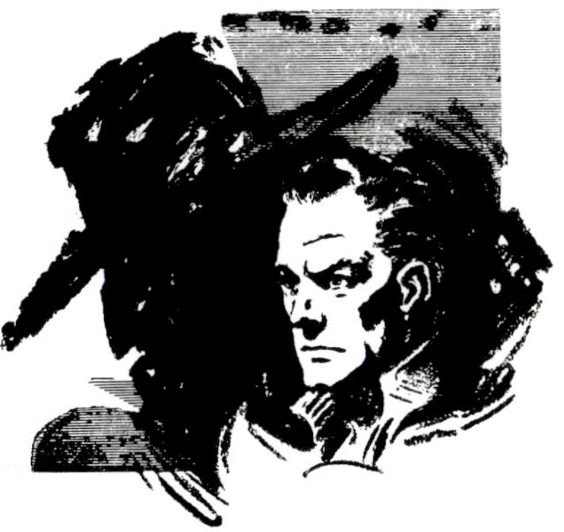

The publication information of some material reproduced here was taken from pencilled notations on Kinstler's original artwork. It is possible that story titles or issue numbers were changed between the commission of the drawing and its publication.

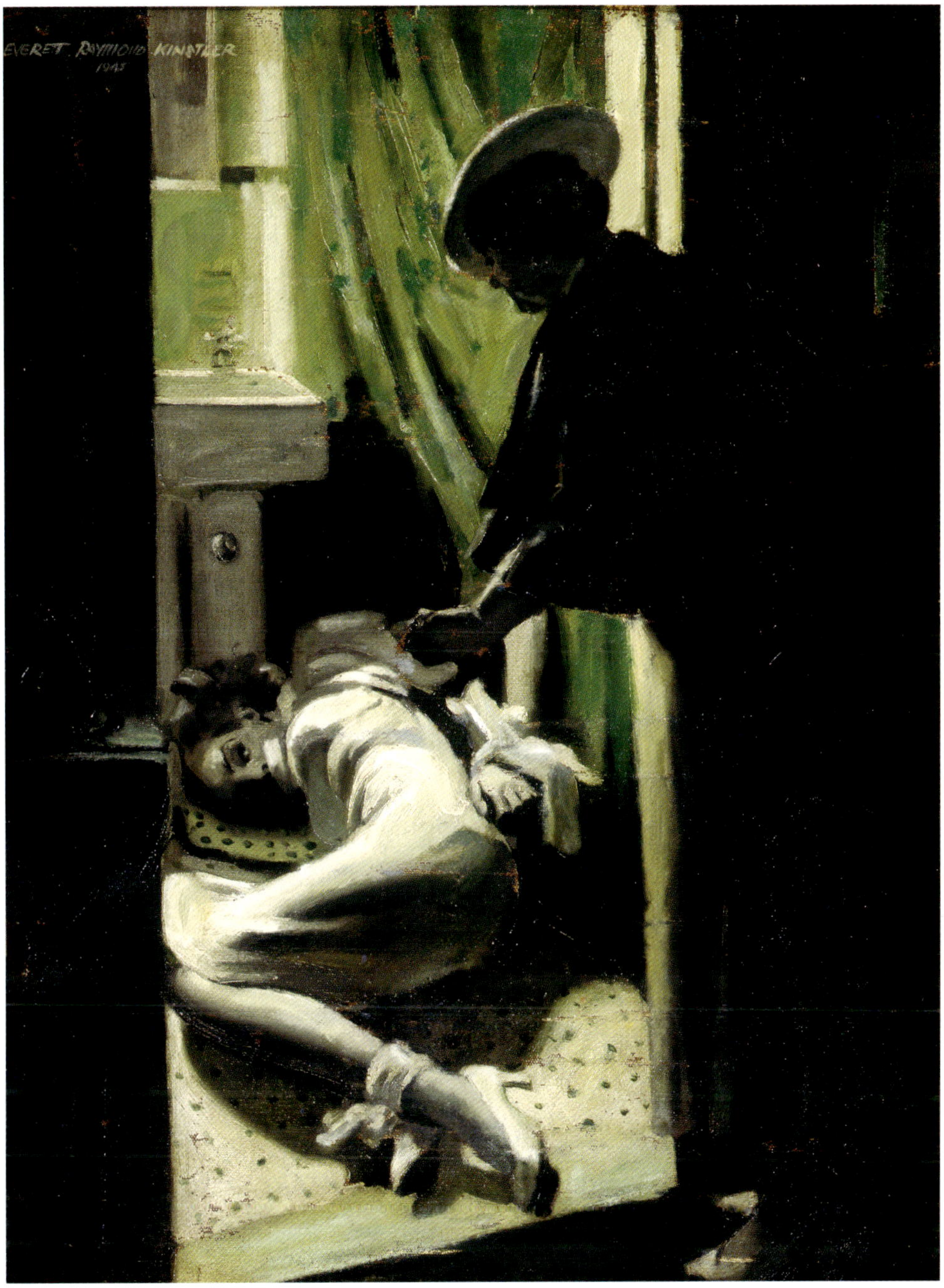

DuMond painting class work 1945 based on a John Falter magazine illustration

His pulp career featured early illustrations for Street & Smith's renowned ***The Shadow*** magazine on a 1945 story starring the title character. The drawings were influenced by the work of Tom Lovell, one of the many fine illustrators who drew *The Shadow*. Although Kinstler would also have drawings in the companion ***Doc Savage*** magazine, he was never called upon to render that character, nor did he ever work on *The Shadow* again. All of his Street & Smith work occurred just before or while he was in the Army.

Ray's painting exercises at The Art Students League doubled as portfolio pieces to show to art directors. It wasn't until 1949 or 1950 that his painting efforts paid off and he received some cover assignments for ***Short Stories Magazine***.

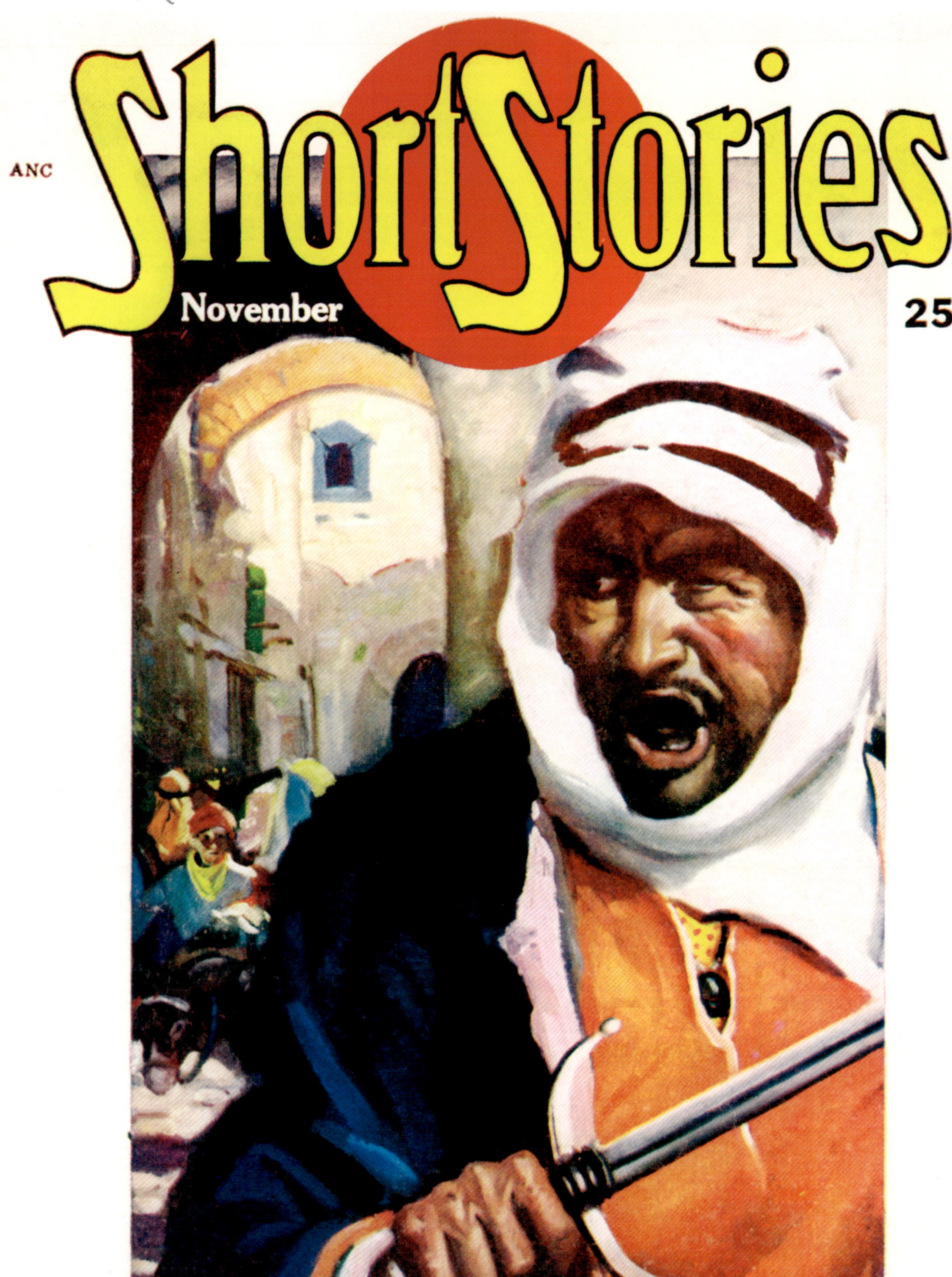

"A Deal with Allah"
E.
HOFFMANN PRICE

"The Lost Arrow"
ALLAN
VAUGHAN ELSTON

Short Stories

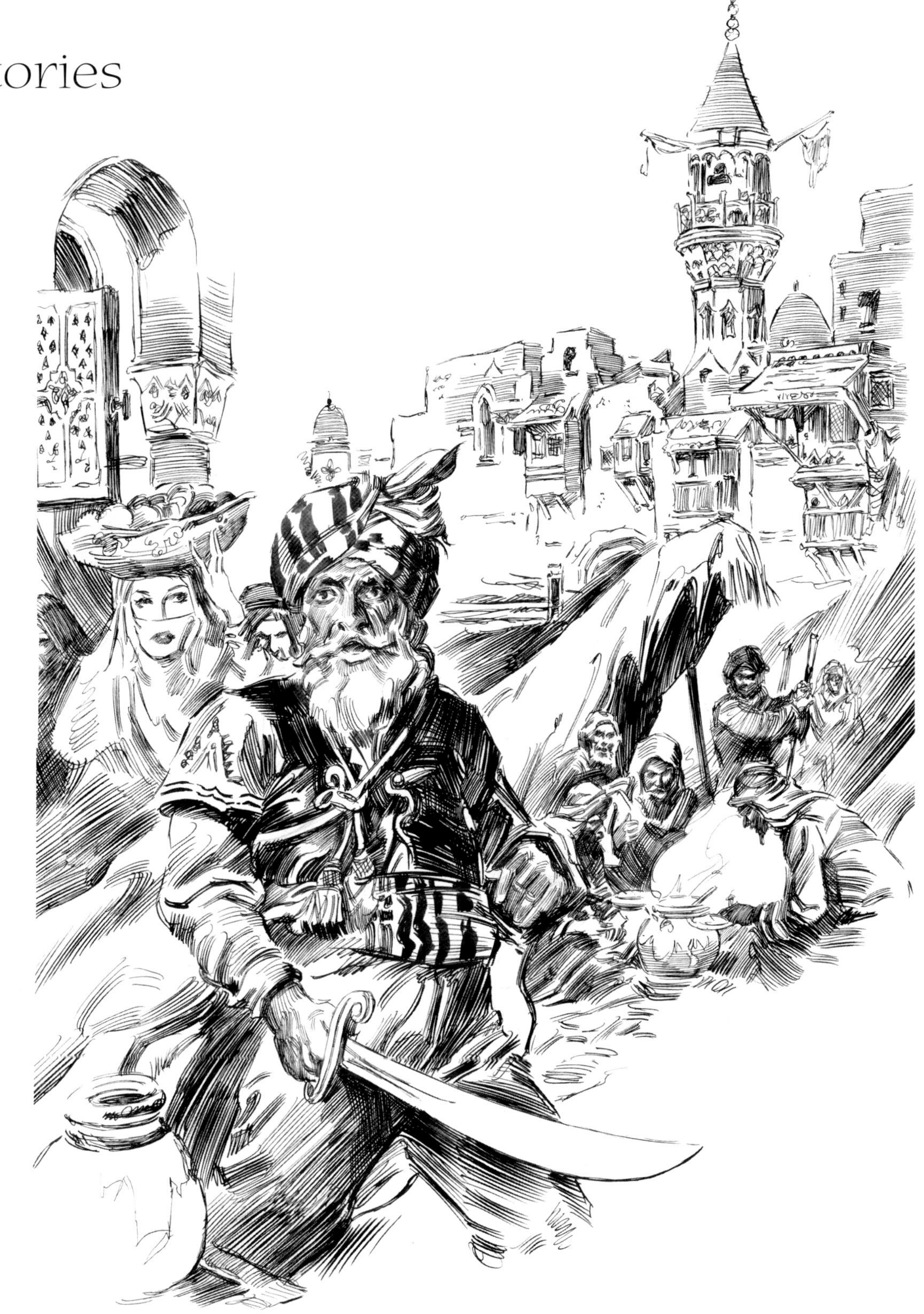

A Deal With Allah
Short Stories
November, 1950
original size: 11"x19"

***S**hort Stories* **was a long-lived pulp** magazine and a frequent outlet for Kinstler art from the mid-1940s to the late 1950s.

Here's an example of the different approaches taken for the cover painting versus an interior illustration for the same story. Such cover assignments at ***Short Stories*** were an indication of his rising artistic status in the pulp world.

Flexible nib pens were still Ray's tool of choice for the black and white drawings, but he wasn't above the occasional use of a brush, as can be seen here in the stripes on the turban and the sash.

ANC
Short Stories
July
"The Copper Chest"
WILLIAM CHAMBERLAIN
EVERETT RAYMOND KINSTLER
July, 1951

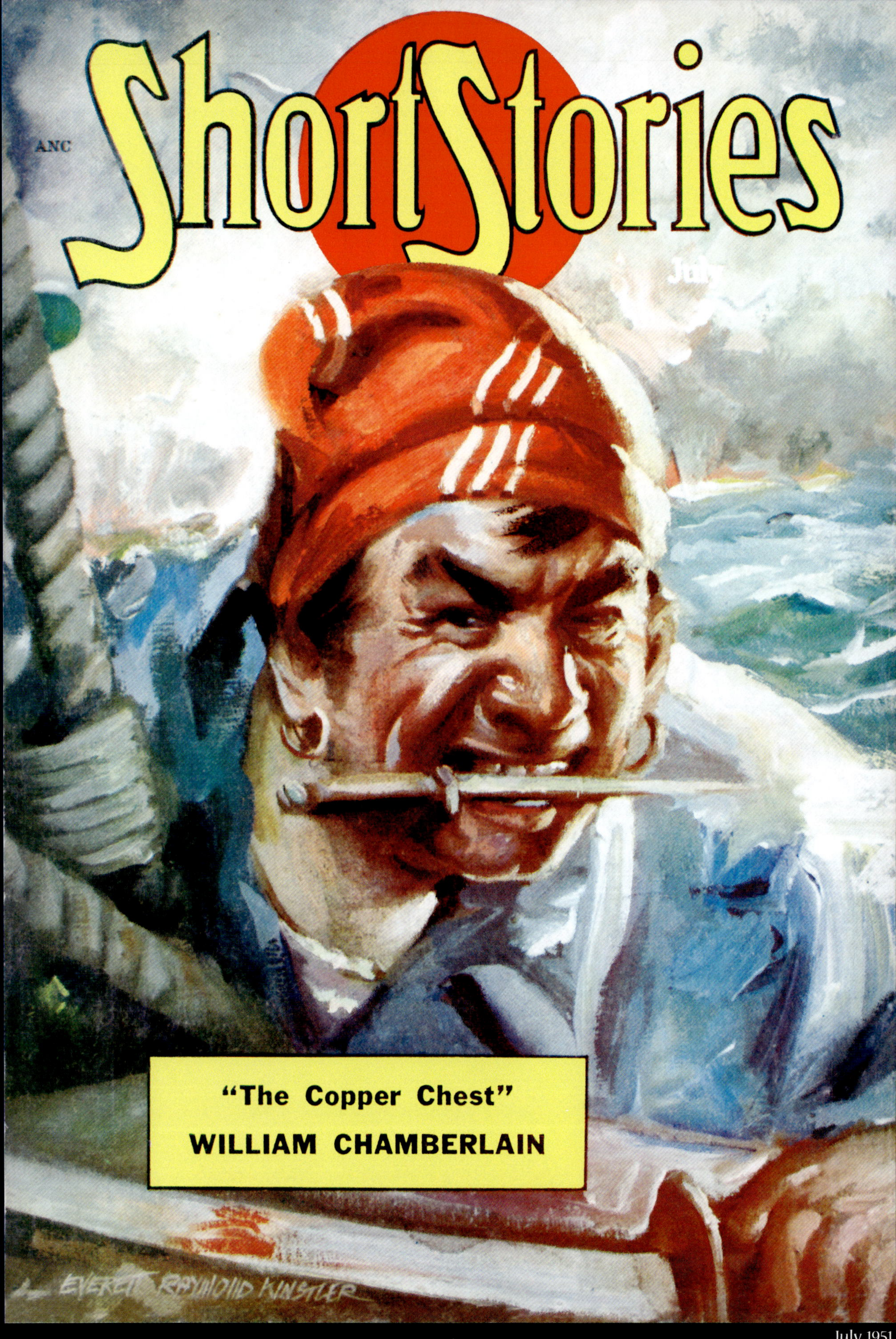

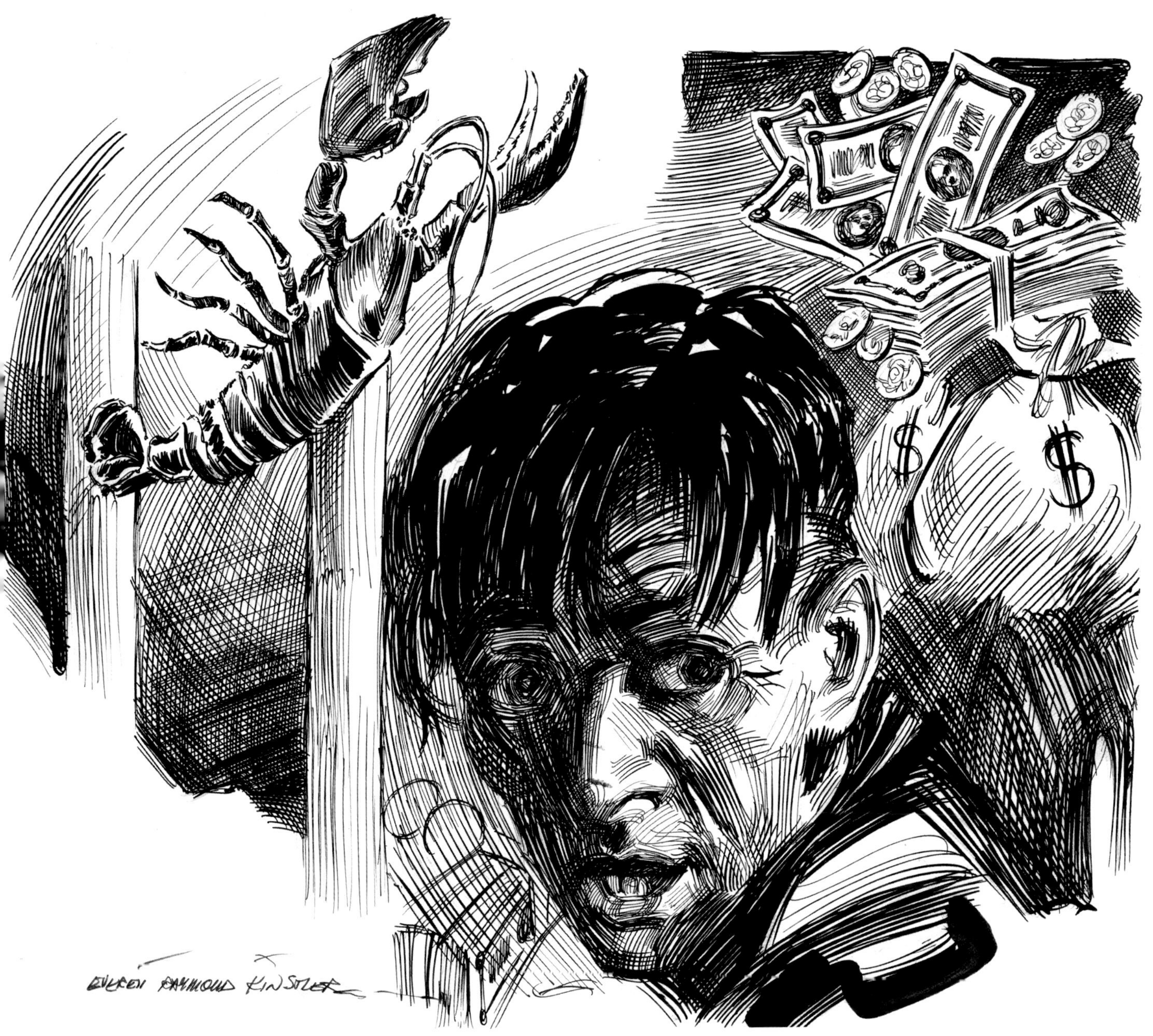

Ray's penchant for retaining the original drawings for his favorite assignments is a double-edged sword. On one hand, it is possible to reproduce them more accurately than they have ever been printed before. On the other hand, the publication information that may have been preserved had he retained tear sheet records has been irretrievably lost.

It's possible to decipher the art director's notations on some of the boards that Ray still has in his files. However, when they do appear, some of those notes are cryptic at best, and simply contradict the historic record at worst: e.g. magazine titles and dates don't jibe or the story title written on the drawing doesn't appear in the issue noted there.

Some drawings, like the one here and those following, that are undated and contain no markings in the margins, are placed in an approximation of their historic sequence based on stylistic traits and the artist's memory.

unknown source & date
probably ***Short Stories***
circa 1950
original size: 15"x13"

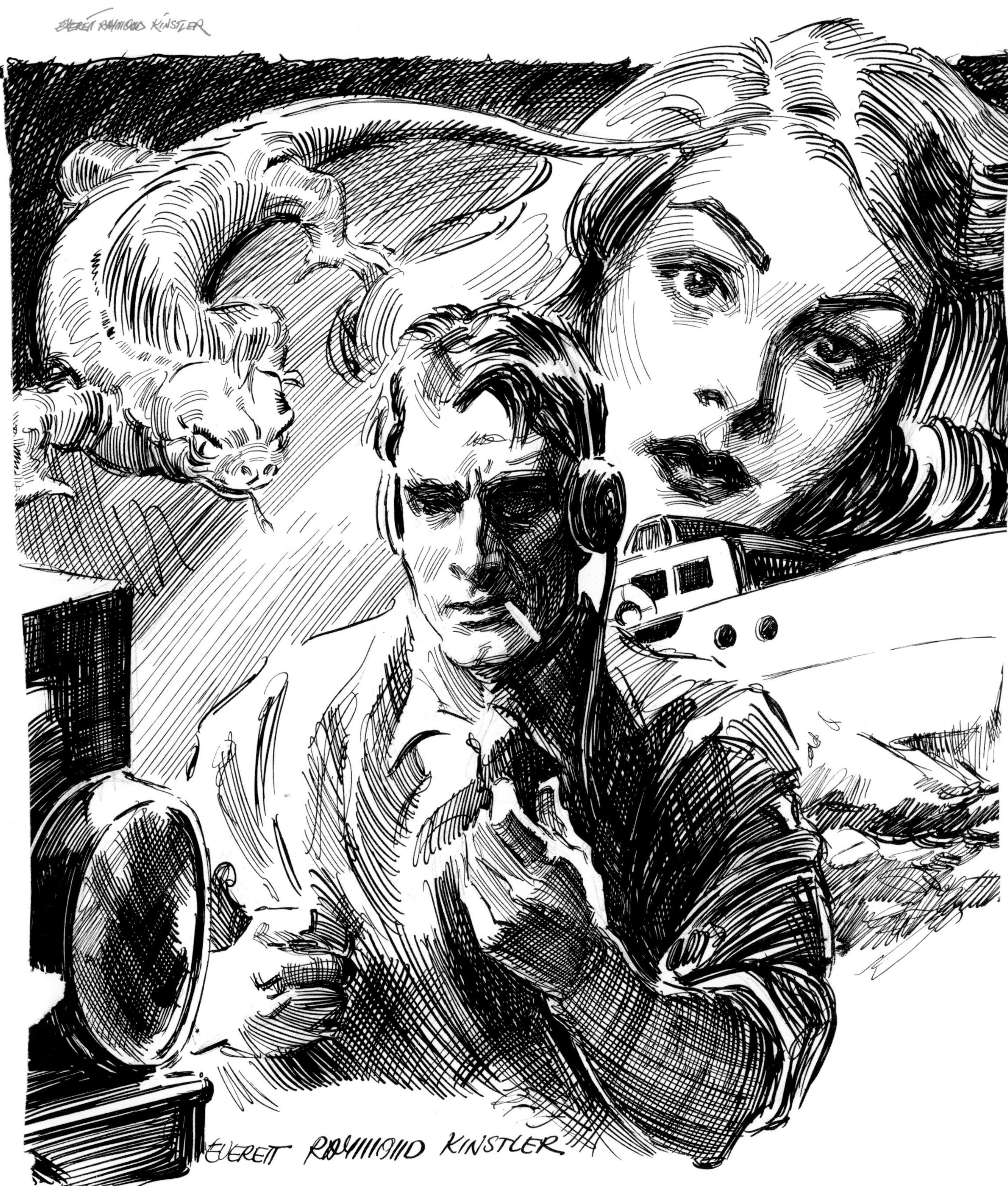

unknown source & date
probably ***Short Stories***
circa 1952
original size: 12½"x14"

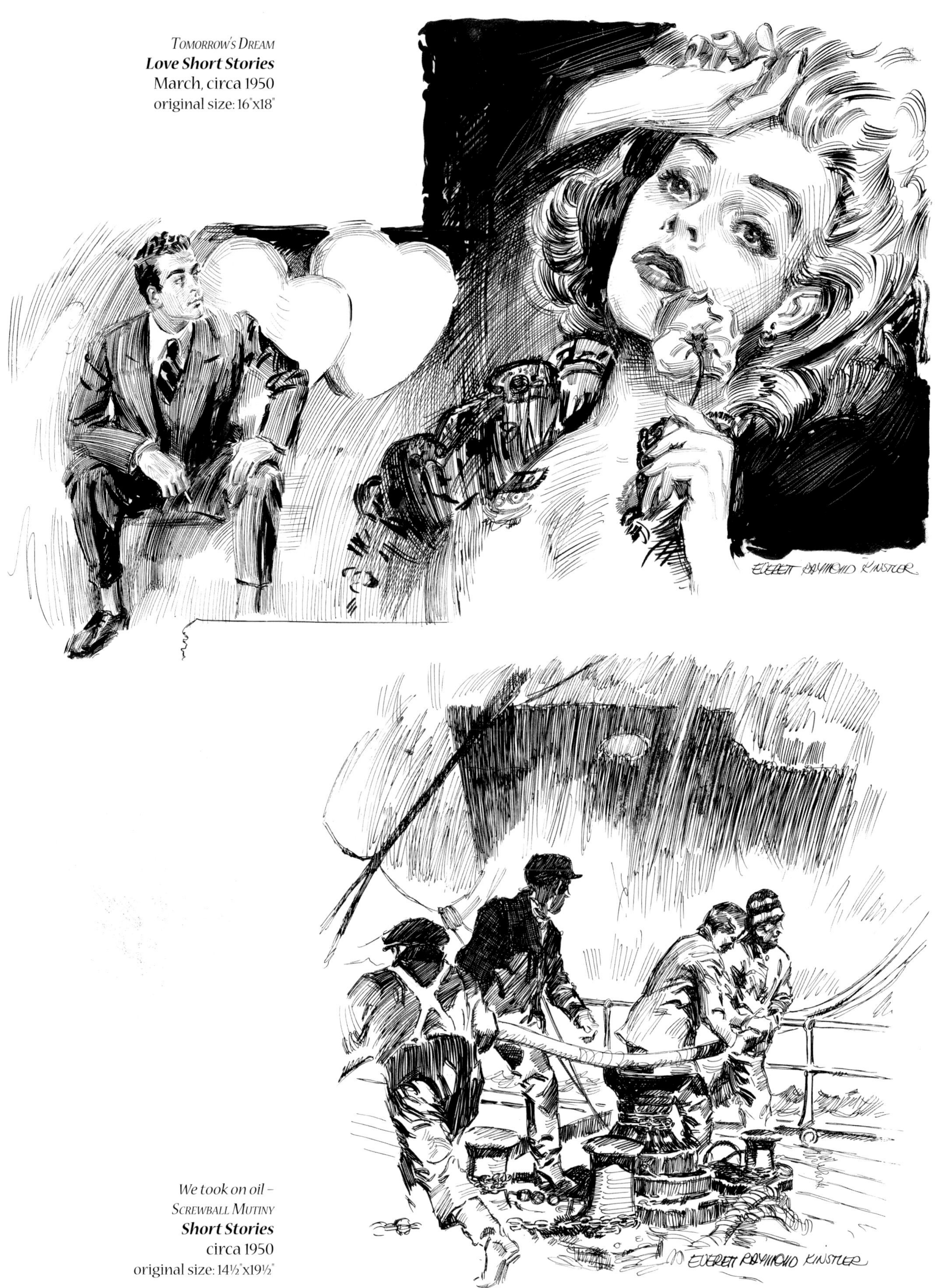

Tomorrow's Dream
Love Short Stories
March, circa 1950
original size: 16"x18"

We took on oil –
Screwball Mutiny
Short Stories
circa 1950
original size: 14½"x19½"

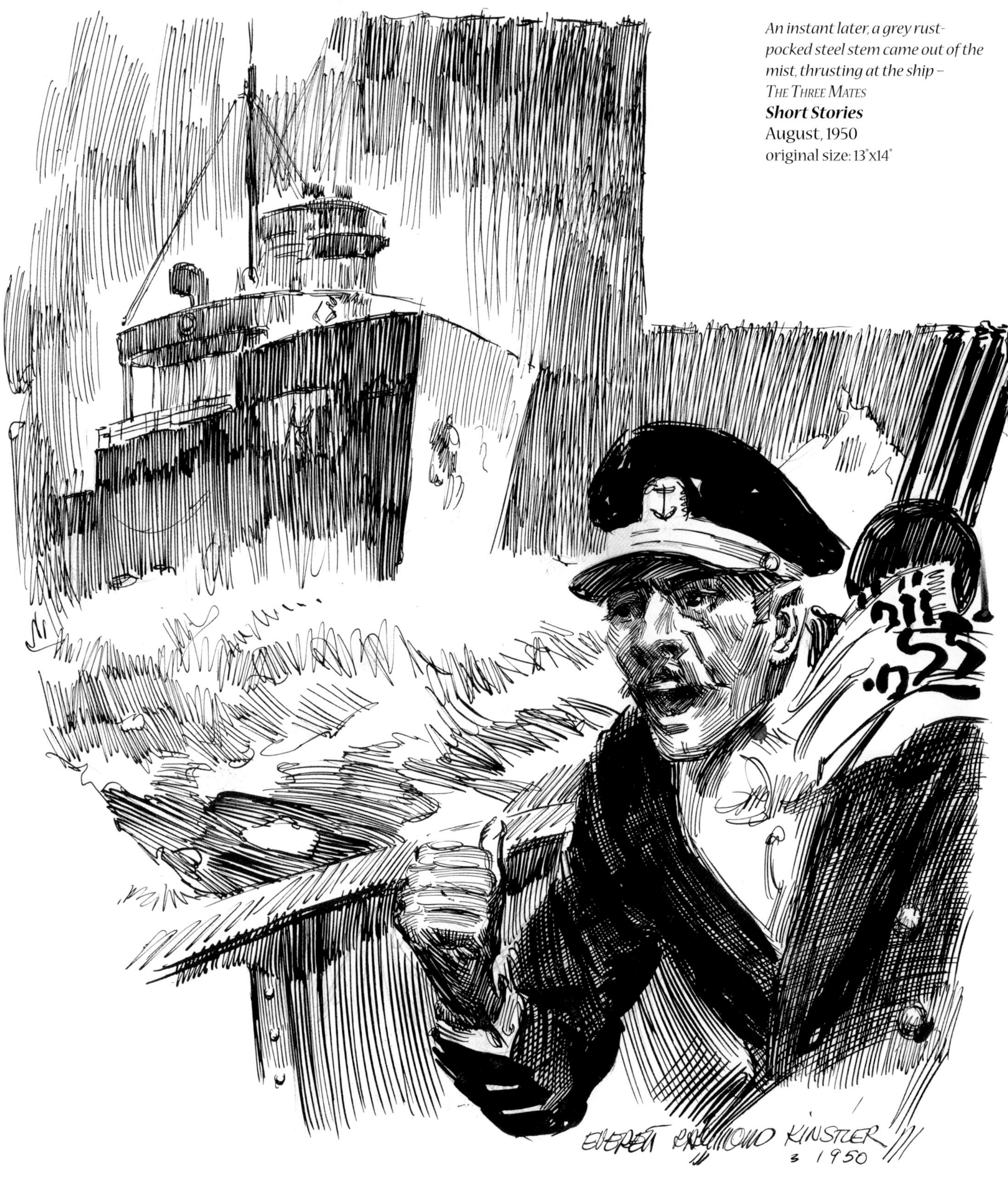

An instant later, a grey rust-pocked steel stem came out of the mist, thrusting at the ship –
THE THREE MATES
Short Stories
August, 1950
original size: 13"x14"

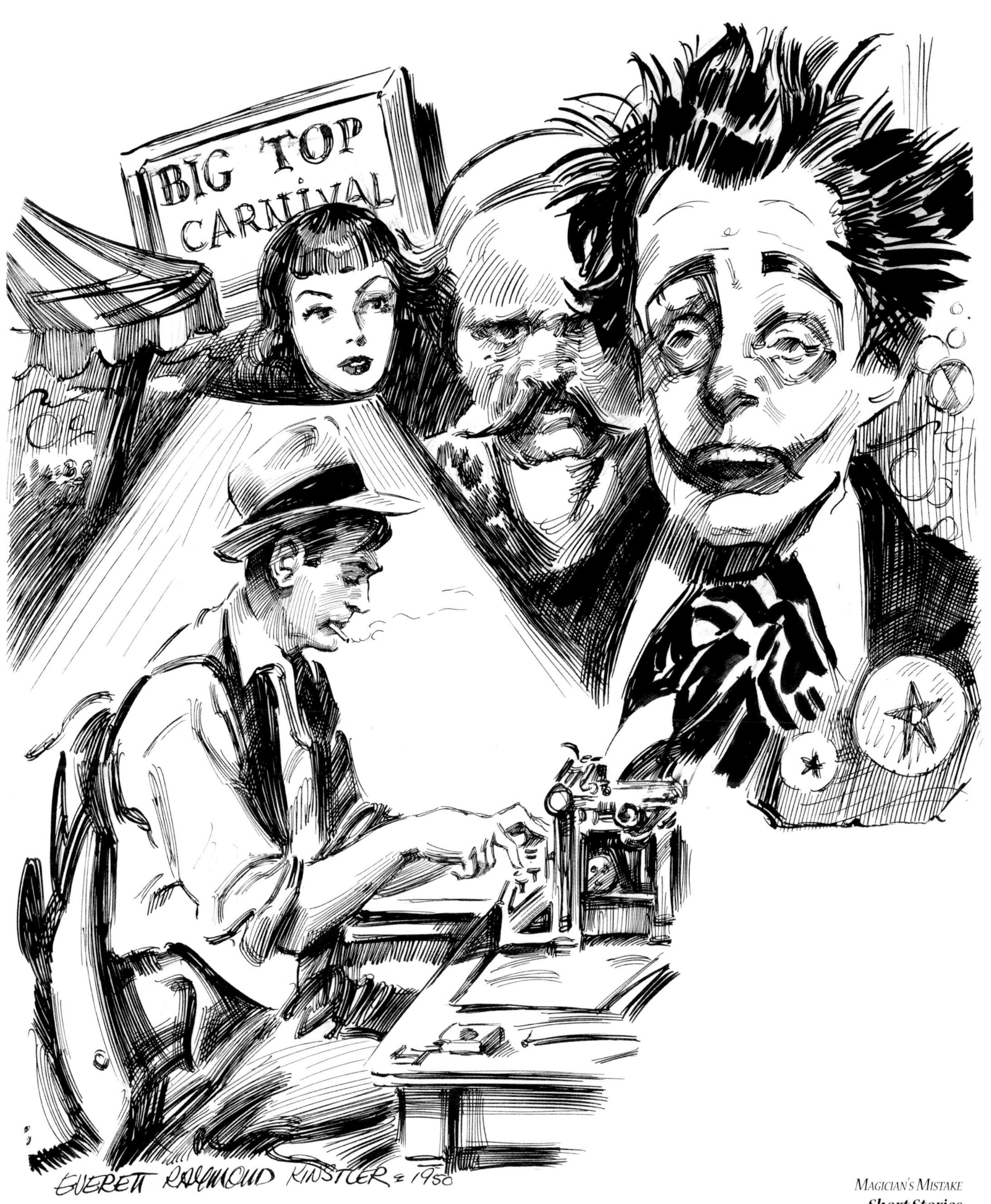

Magician's Mistake
Short Stories
August, 1950
original size: 15"x19"

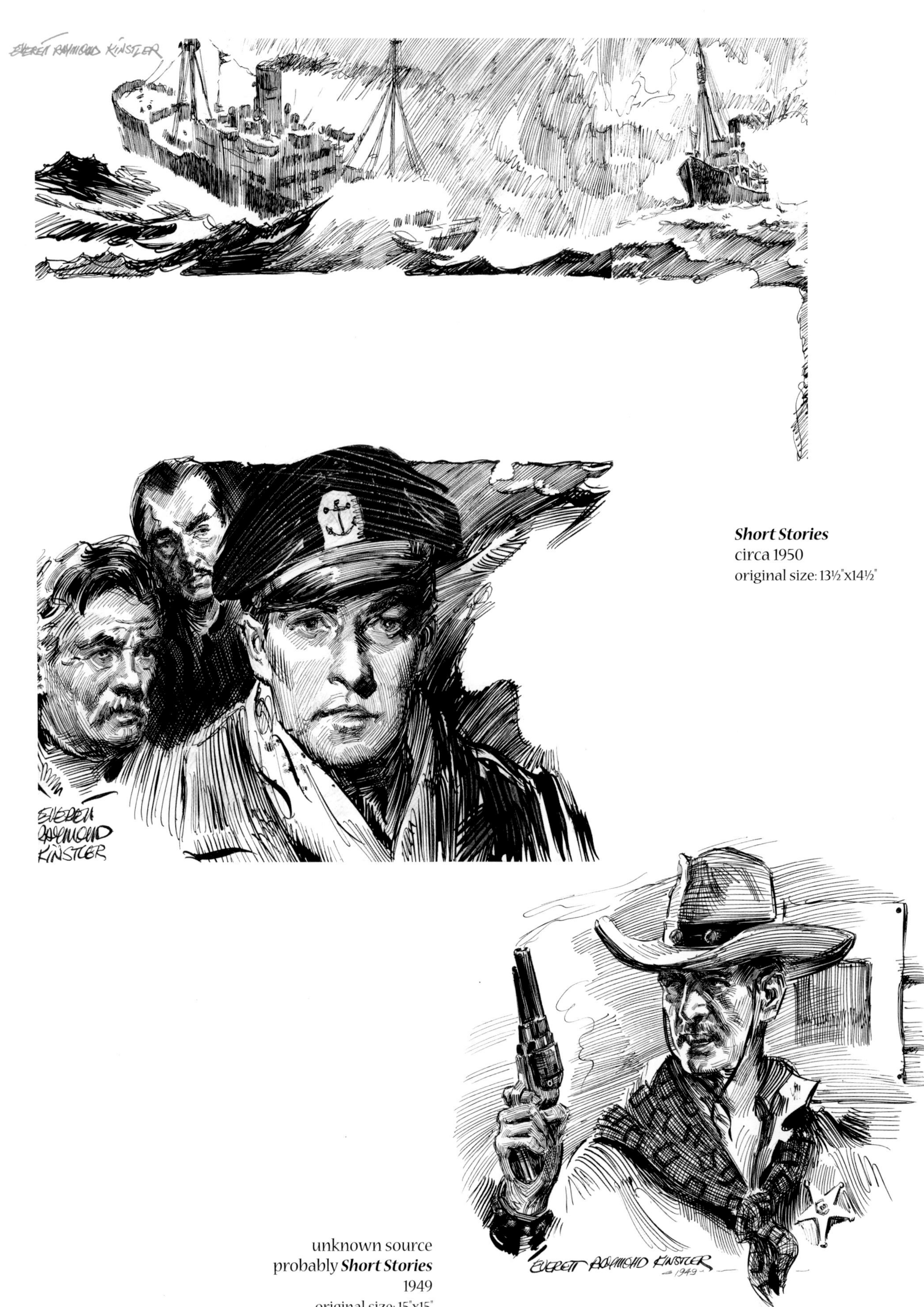

Short Stories
circa 1950
original size: 13½"x14½"

unknown source
probably ***Short Stories***
1949
original size: 15"x15"

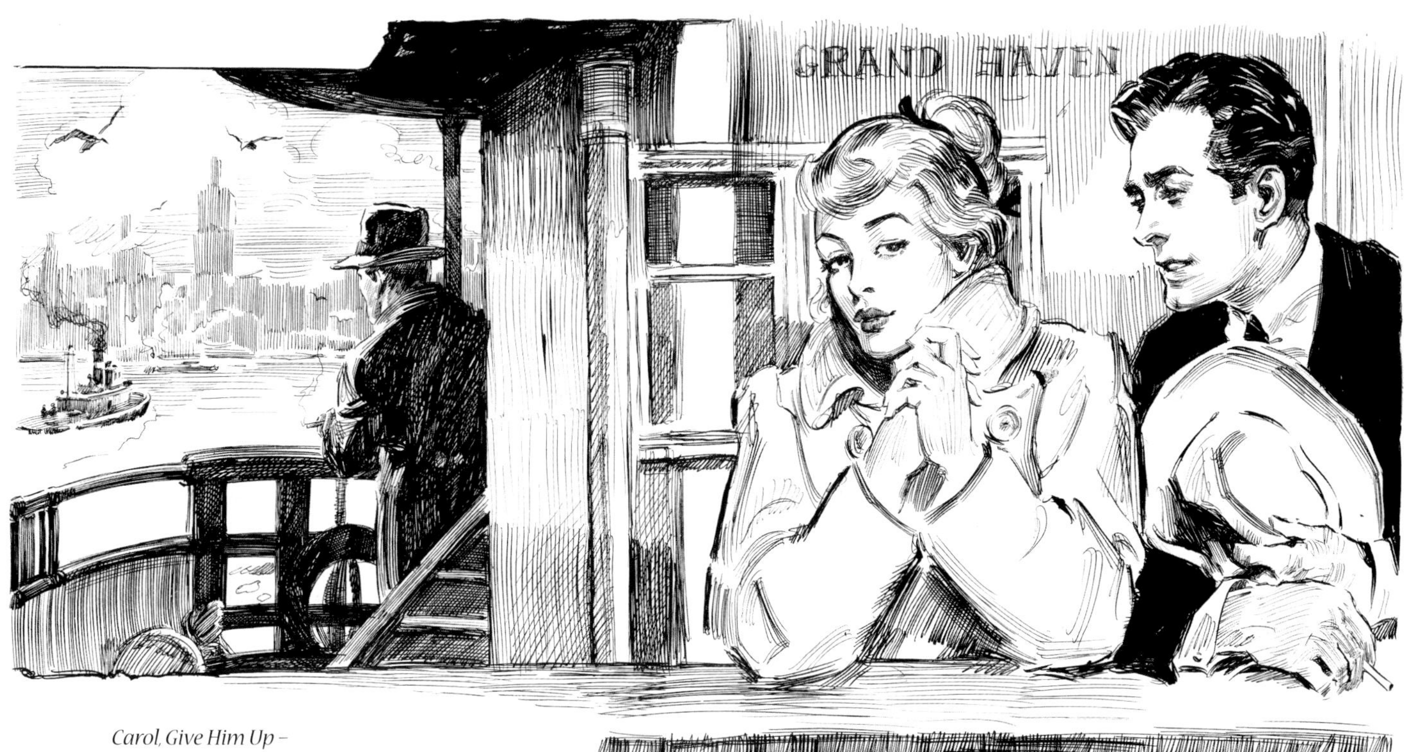

Carol, Give Him Up –
Extra Man
unknown source & date
circa 1949
original size: 30"x16"

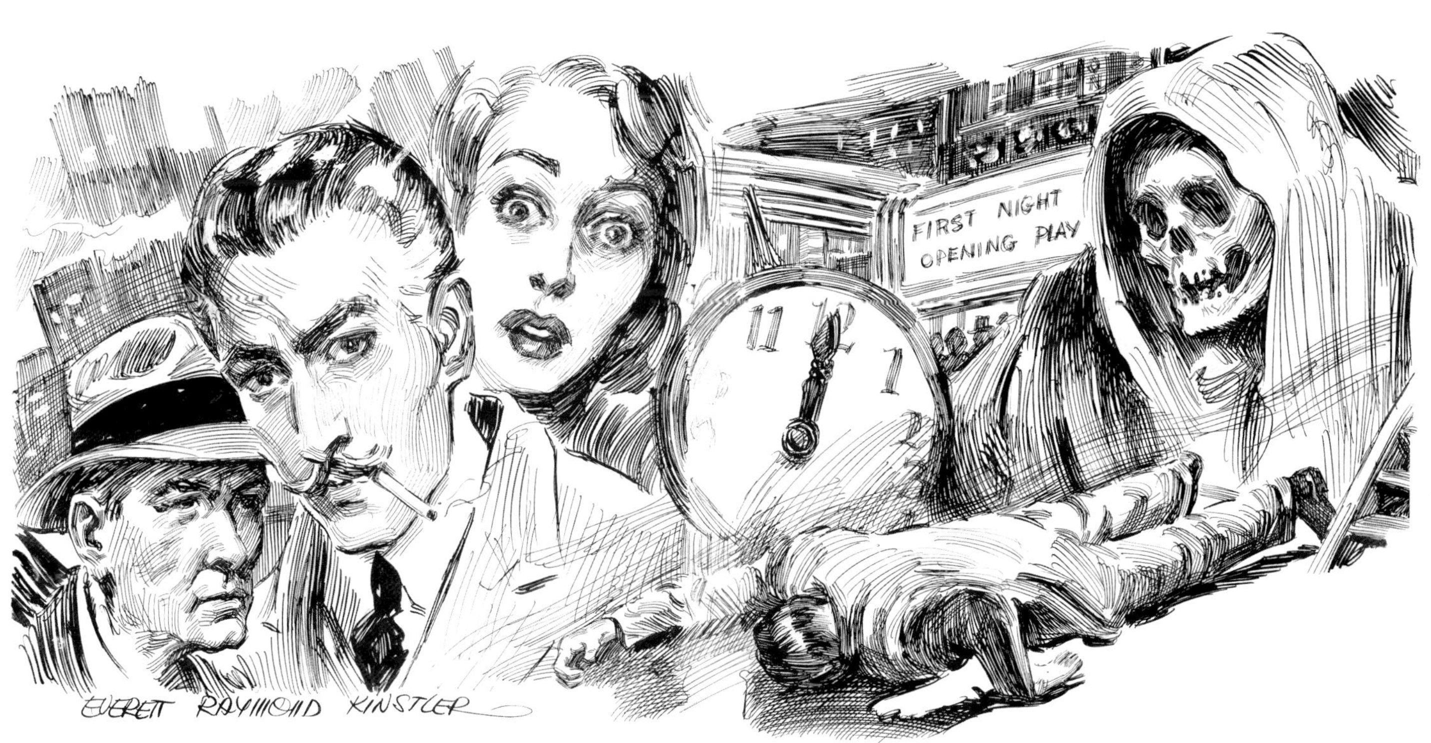

Betty discovered the body face down… A silver-haired gambler and a man who loved her determined to trap a killer!! –
Dead Men Do Tell Tales
Short Stories Magazine, circa 1950
original size: 29"x15½"

Technique

This one illustration provides a study in Kinstler's drawing techniques and shows how they combine in the published drawing to convey texture, depth, and focus.

Reproduction in the pulps was adequate at best, and most often limited strictly to black and white line art, as halftones tended to print too muddy and dark on the cheap paper. Some artists experimented with techniques that they hoped would convey gray tones within that simple black and white line reproduction method. These included textured boards, the use of dry-brush, and the time-consuming stipple techniques of artists like Virgil Finlay.

This undated and unsourced illustration on the facing page is reproduced here in line and at the size it appeared in the pulp magazine. Surrounding it are full-size details from the original drawing reproduced in tone to make evident all of the graphic techniques Kinstler used to achieve the various textures and to focus the viewer's eye within the drawing.

Kinstler's application of these methods appears so natural as to make them almost unnoticeable in the published illustration. By accomplishing this, he creates a drawing that communicates effectively on many levels and doesn't call attention to itself, yet still holds up under, and rewards, closer scrutiny.

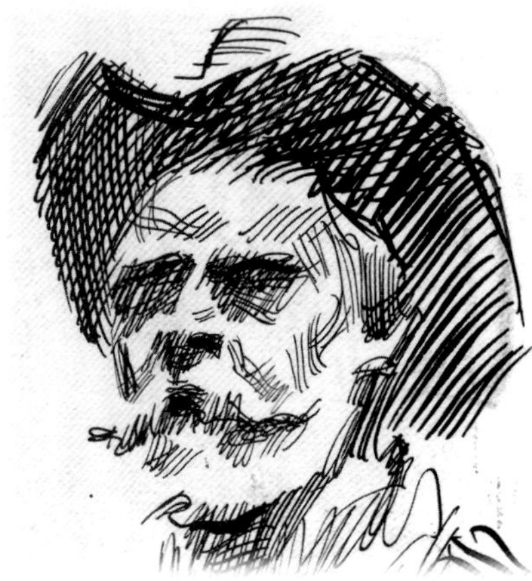

Fine line pen on the face, brush and pen on the hat.

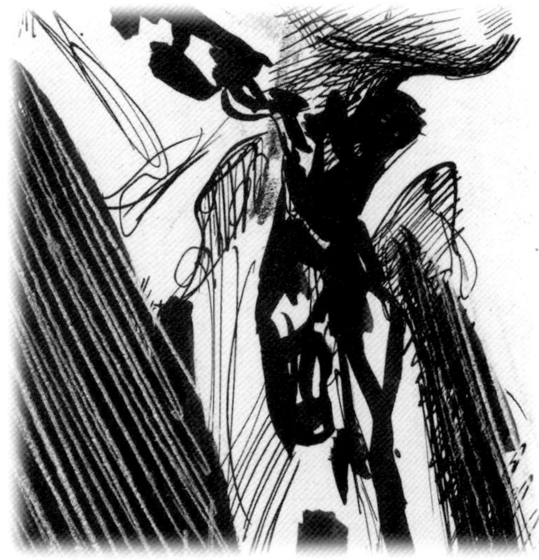

Fine line pen on the facial detail, brushwork on the bandana and vest—which is scratched to lighten the black. Note the near abstact approach to the neck area.

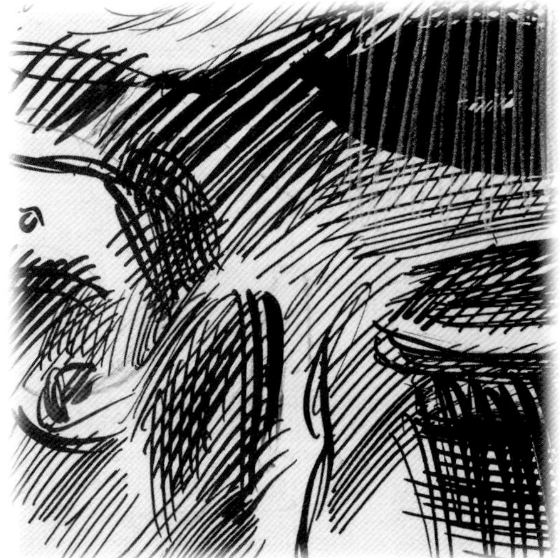

Shapes are indicated in pen while the shading and depth are rounded out with the brush. More details are implied than are actually there.

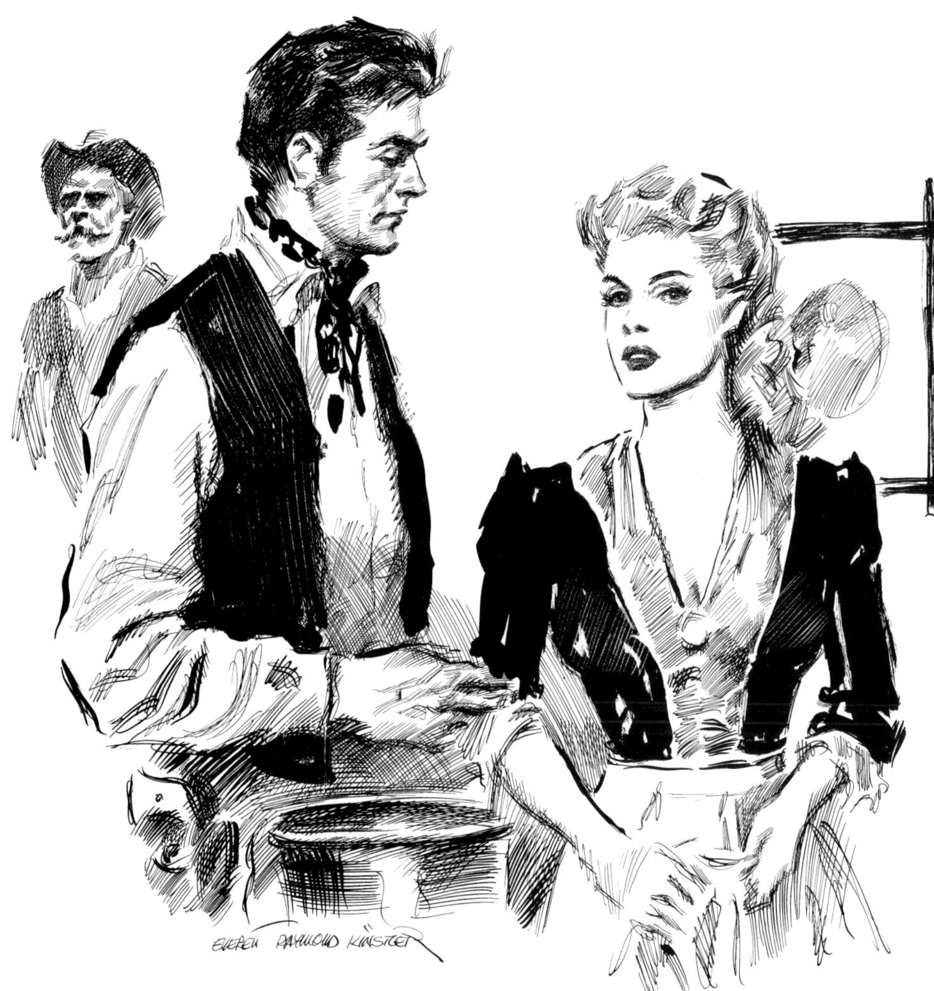

According to the art directors' notations on Ray's original drawings, the typical pulp illustration was reproduced at approximately five and one quarter inches wide, with two-page spreads at ten and one half inches in total width.

In general, he drew his artwork about three times the size it would be printed, despite knowing full-well that the detail he was creating would be lost in the reproduction process.

No shading was available in the printed image, so Ray had to make it appear as if there were.

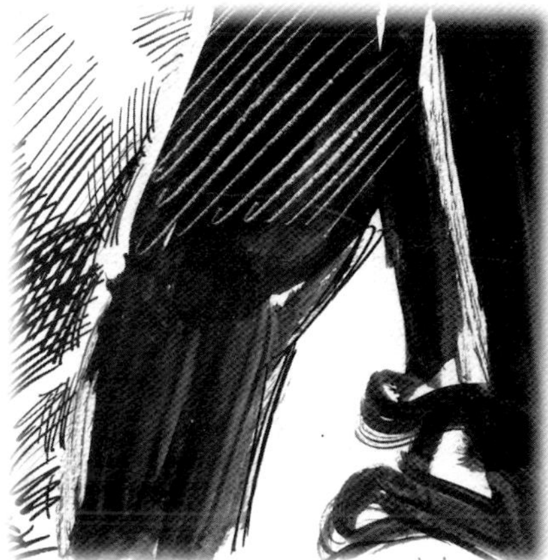

Pen crosshatching on bodice detail is contrasted with loose brush work on the sleeves and scratched highlights.

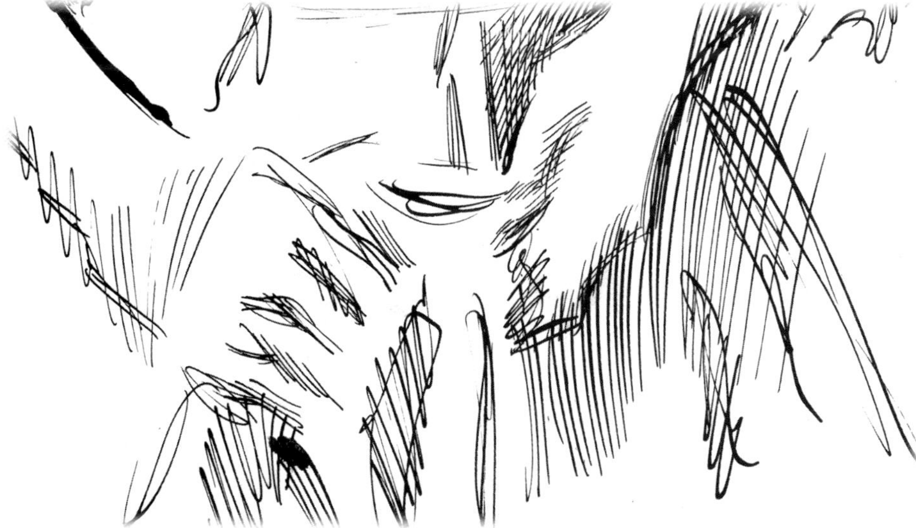

Foreground details at the edges of the composition are done in light pen lines so that the viewer's eye is drawn back into the darker focal areas at the center of the drawing.

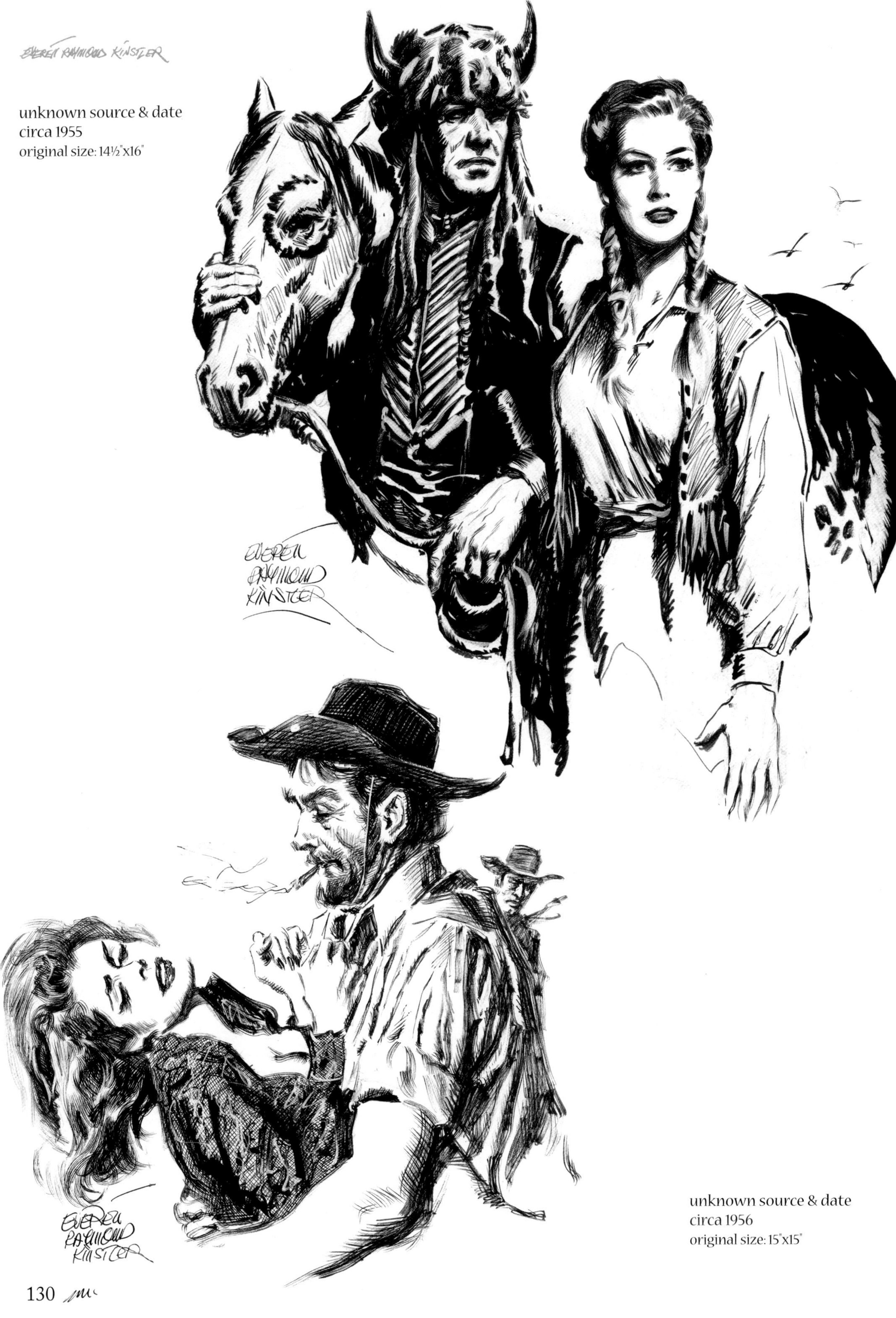

unknown source & date
circa 1955
original size: 14½"x16"

unknown source & date
circa 1956
original size: 15"x15"

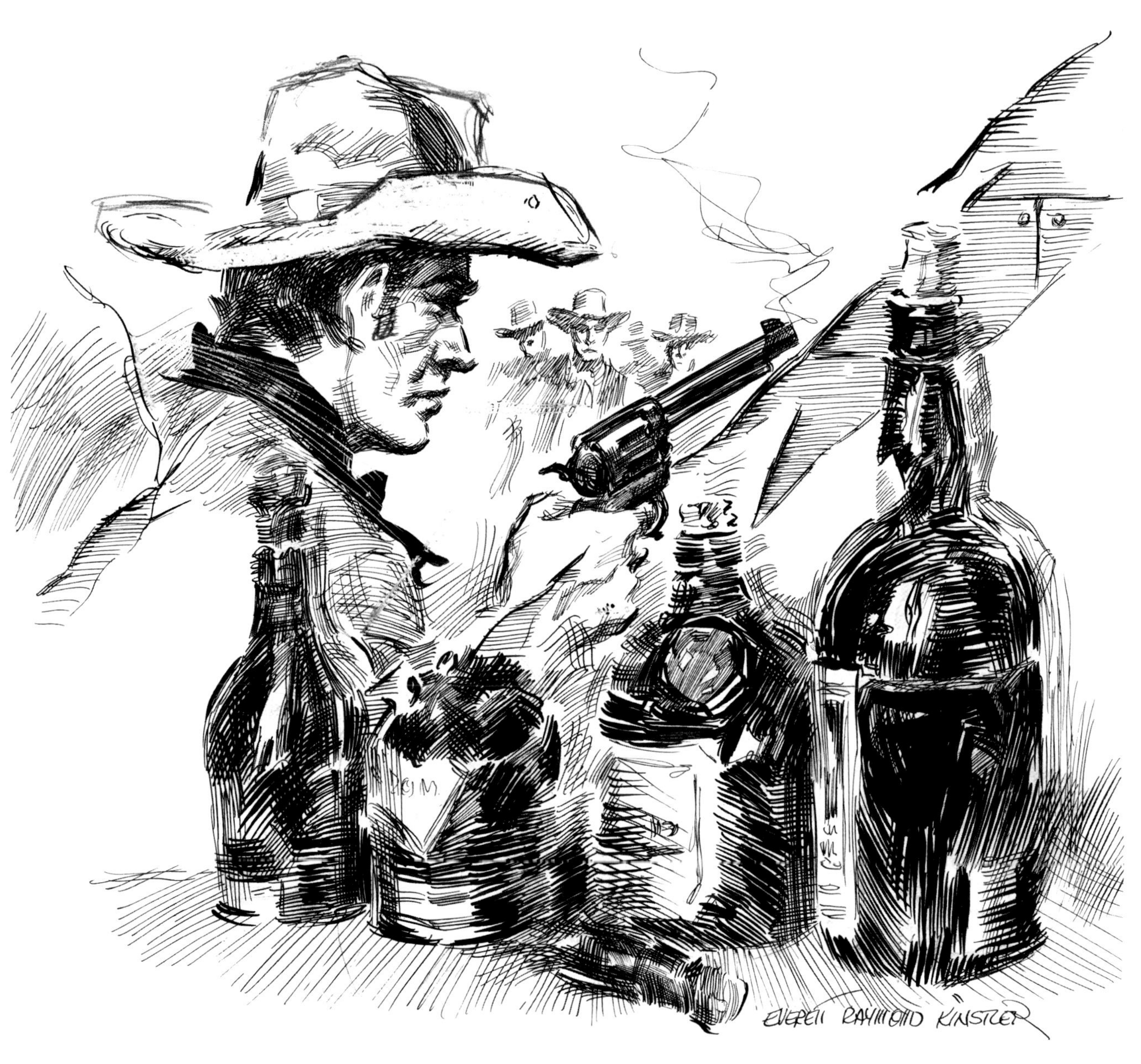

unknown source & date
circa 1952
original size: 15½"x15½"

Popular Publications

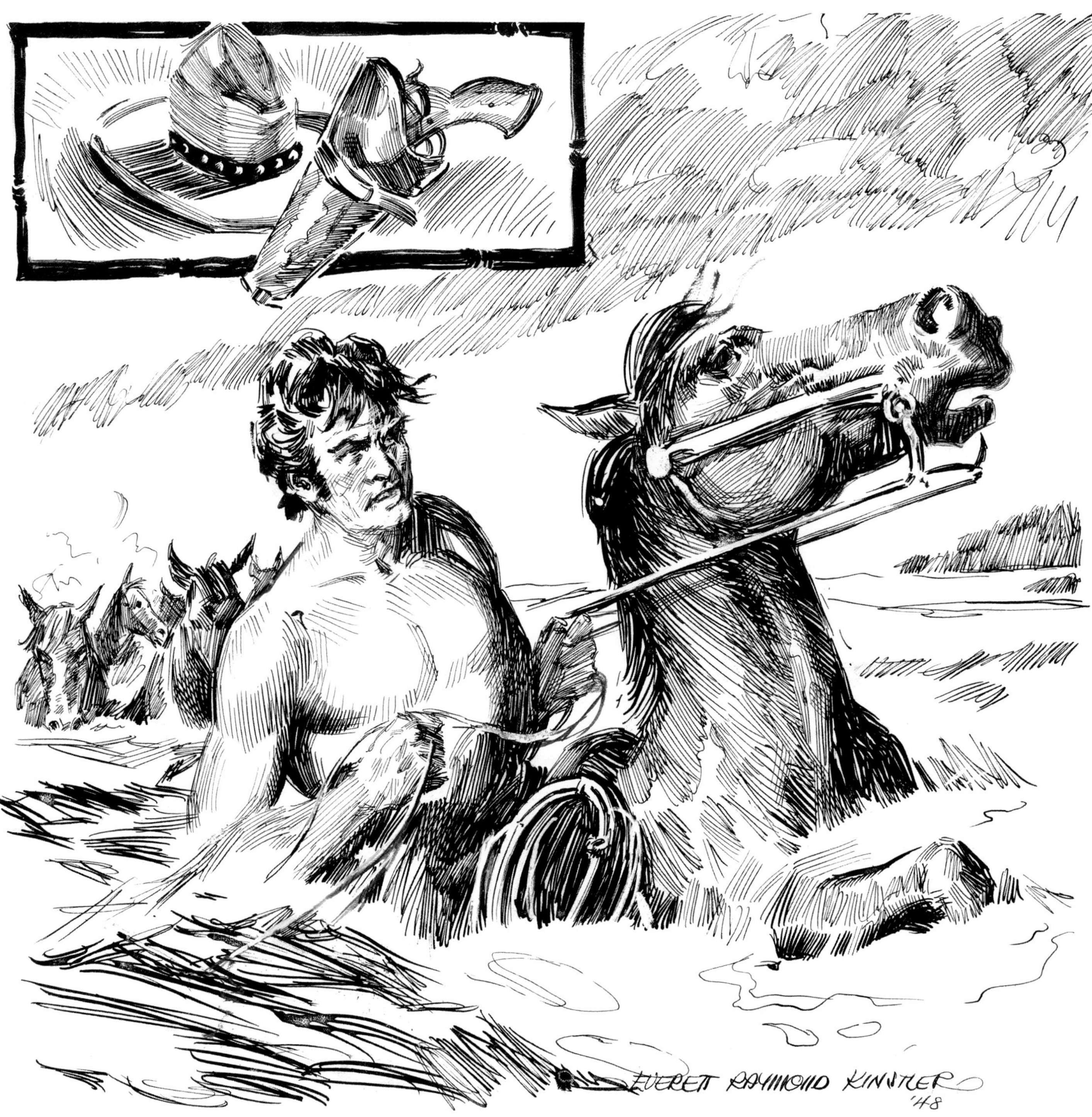

Colvin made it to midstream, the bay thrashing out amid the mass of horse-flesh surrounding him –
TRAIL BY TRAIL DRIVE
Dime Western #452
circa February, 1949
original size: 15"x14½"

Popular Publications was one of the most prolific of the publishers of pulp magazines and one of Kinstler's most consistent markets. Red Murphy was an editor for whom Ray enjoyed working and, as was often the case, Kinstler did his best work under those conditions. He was often allowed to create impressive two-page illustrations, for many of which Ray still retains the originals.

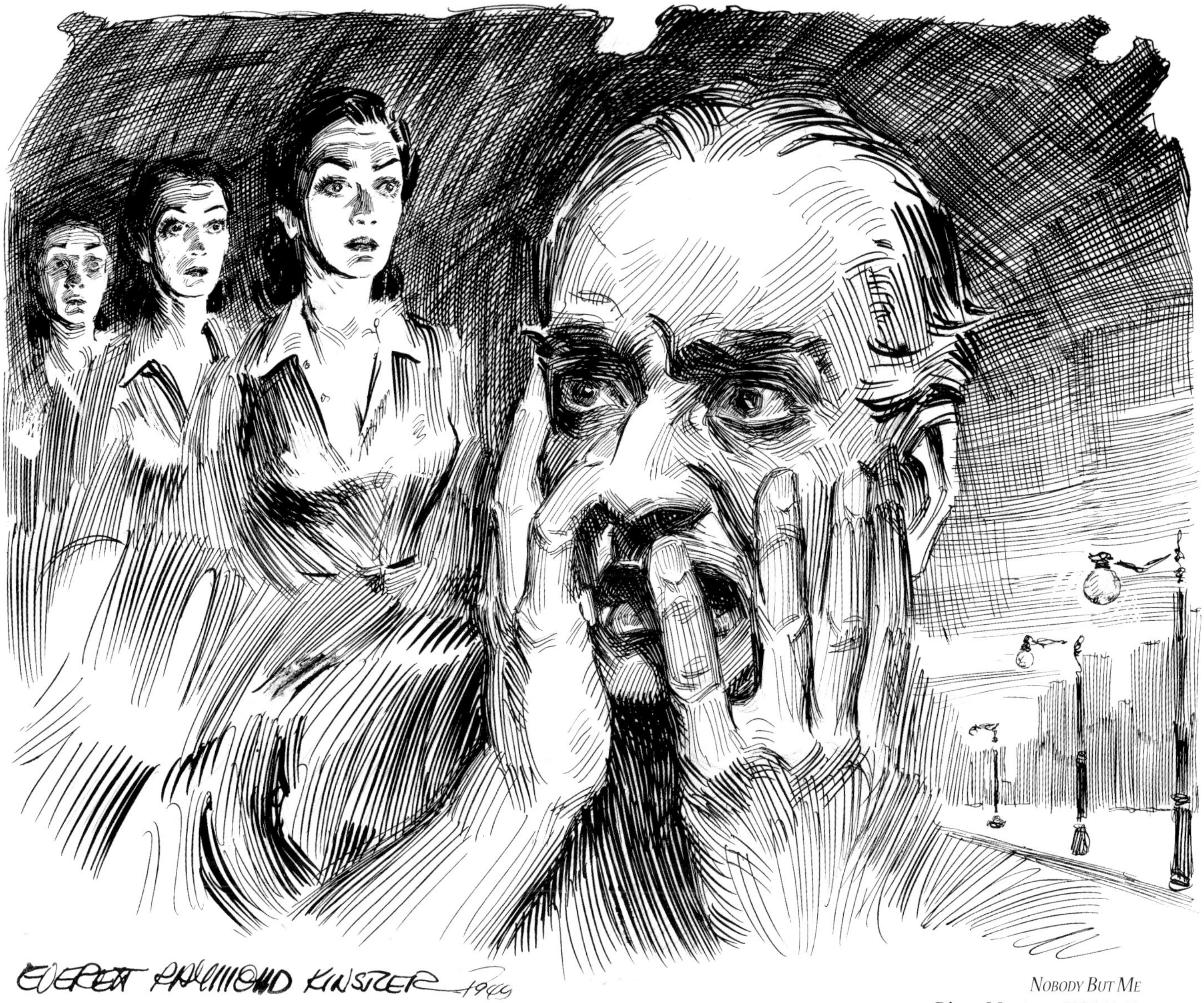

Nobody But Me
Dime Mystery #327, 1949
original size: 15"x13"

Ray's pen and ink extravaganzas were never shown in their best light in the pulps. Early on, as he moved away from the dry-brush techniques of influences like Matt Clark and concentrated solely on the pen, the detail of his art increased significantly. The pen offered flexibility coupled with control and the challenge of tone and texture built up only with line. These same seemingly contradictory aspects had enthralled Flagg, Gibson and other great pen artists of the past.

Fortunately for us, these pen illustrations were some that meant the most to him, so he tried to make certain that his drawings were returned to him after they were printed. We reproduce many of those original drawings here, shown for the first time with the high quality they deserve.

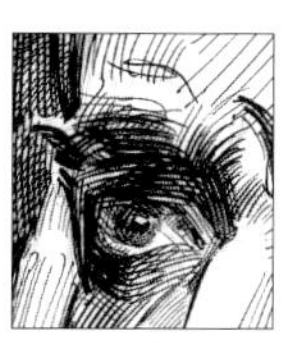
printed size

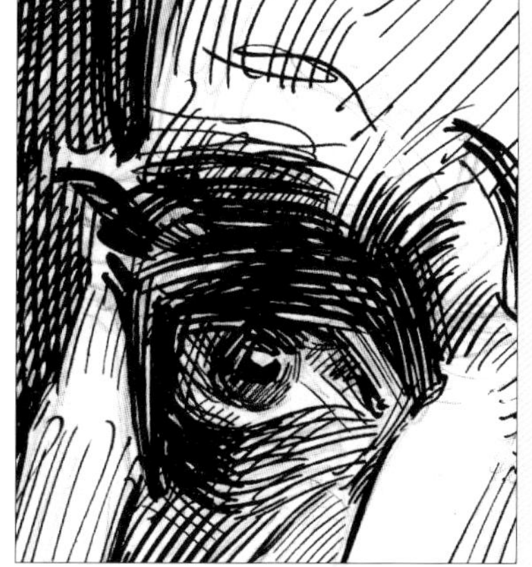
original size

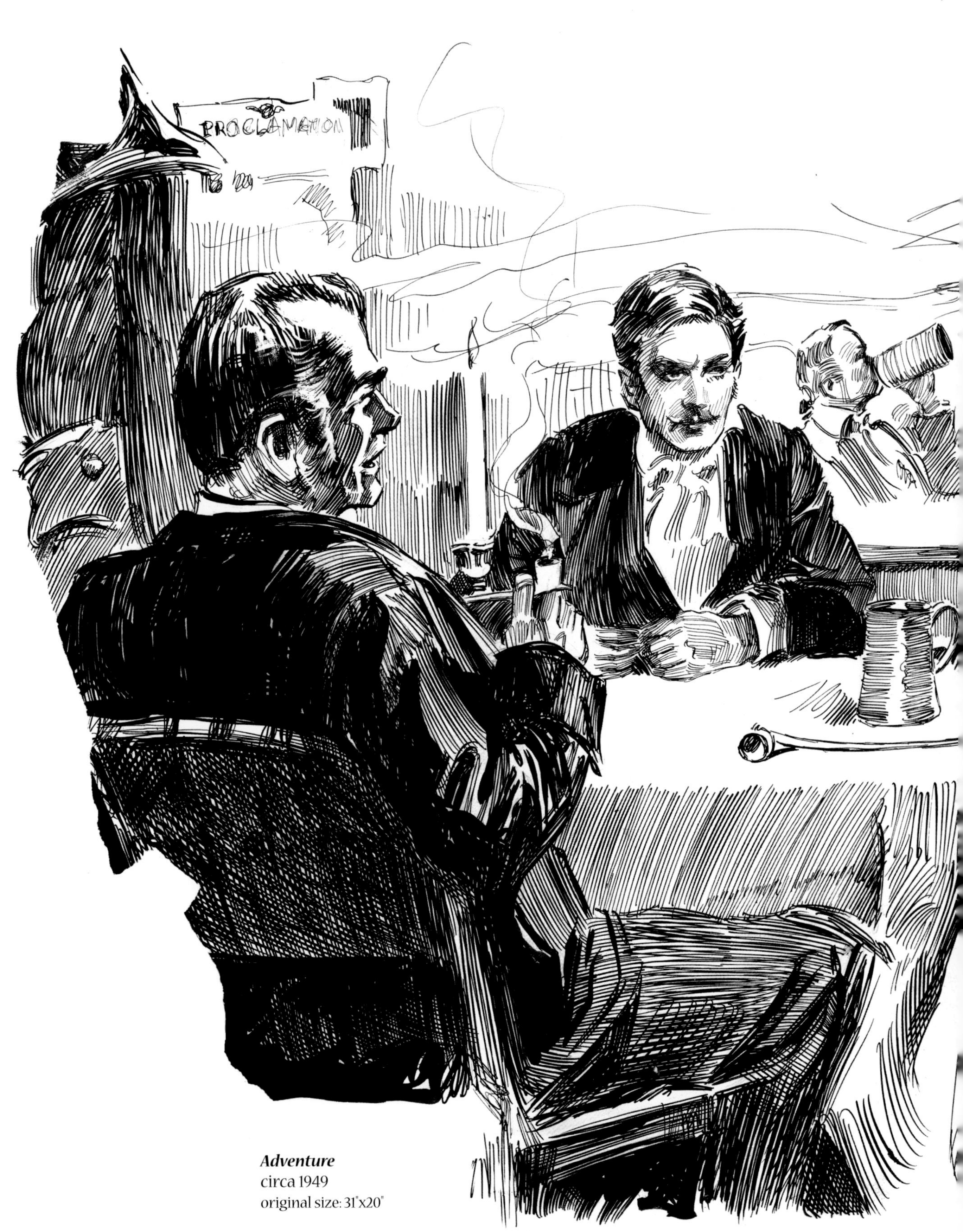

Adventure
circa 1949
original size: 31"x20"

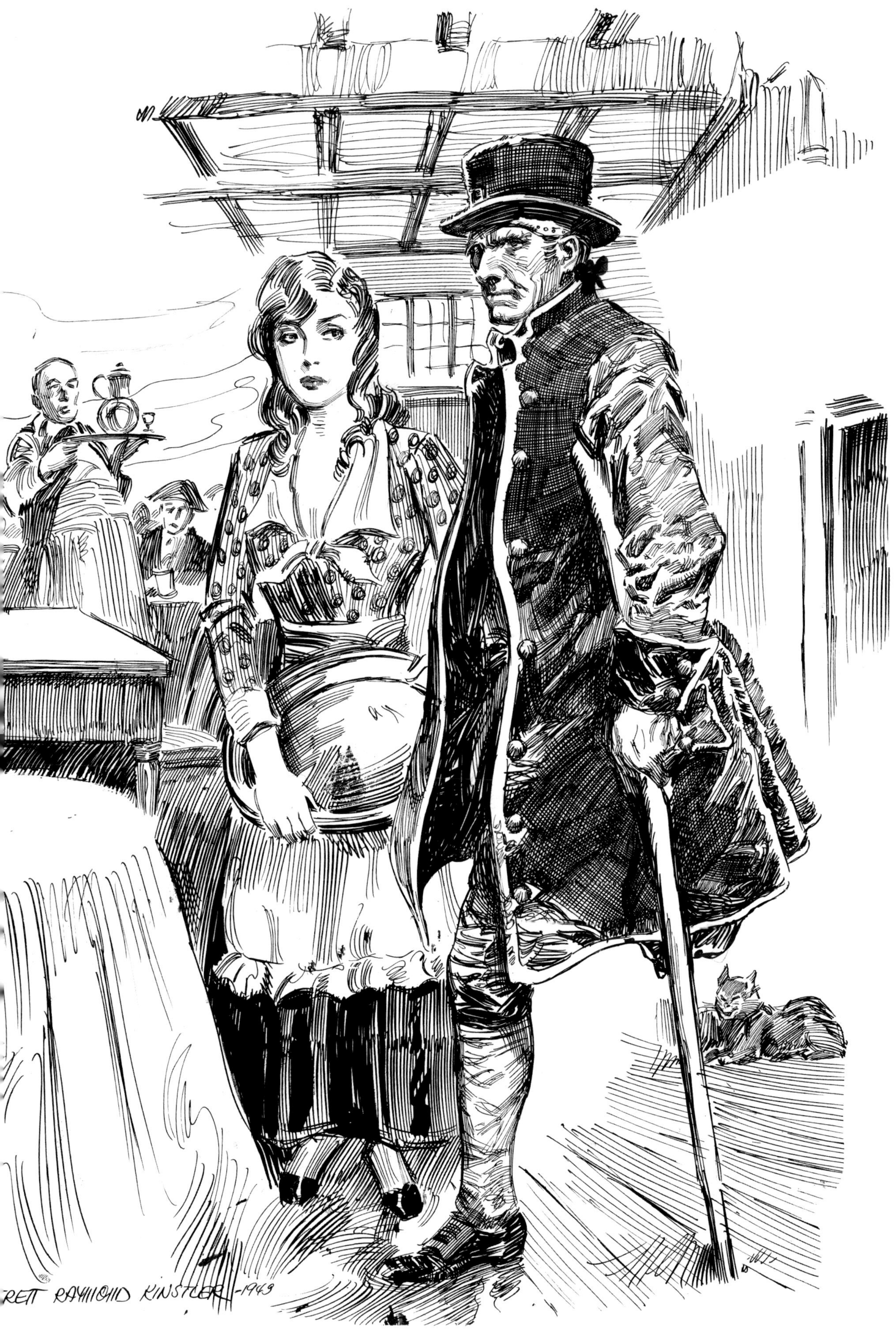
RETT RAYMOND KINSTLER -1949

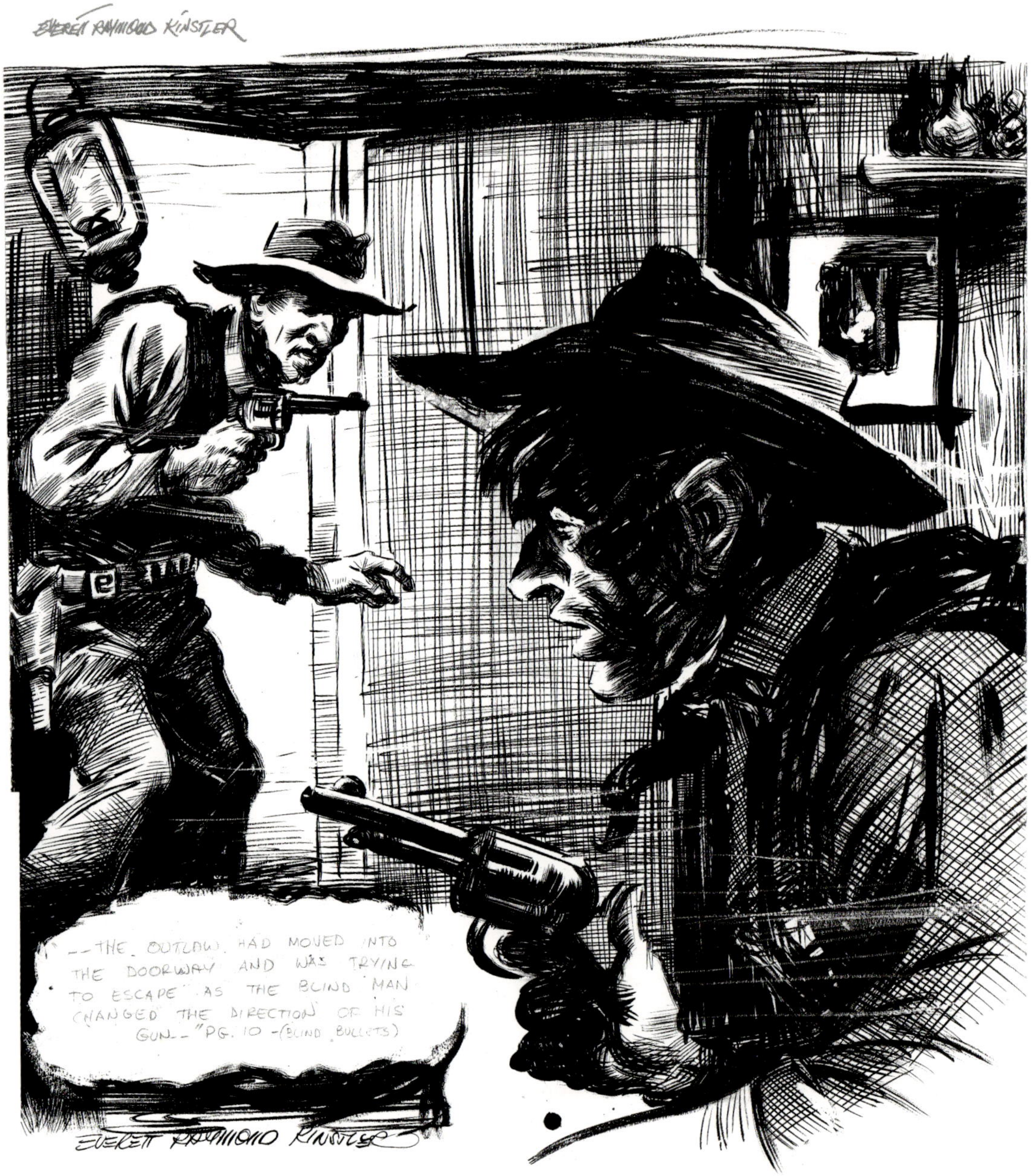

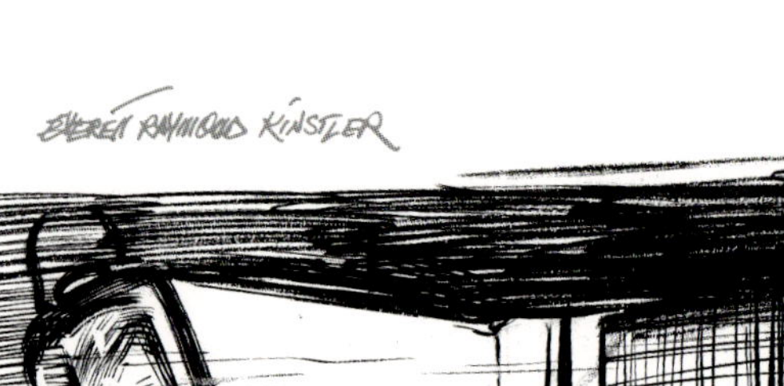

The outlaw had moved into the doorway and was trying to escape as the blind man changed the direction of his gun –
Blind Bullets
Fifteen Western Tales
November, 1948
original size: 15"x14½"

A Typical Pulp Assignment:
Popular Publications' editor Red Murphy knew what his readers wanted, and knew how to communicate that to his artists.

We don't have access to the actual illustration Ray completed for this assignment, but "Cowboys and Cleavage" seems to have been the order of the day.

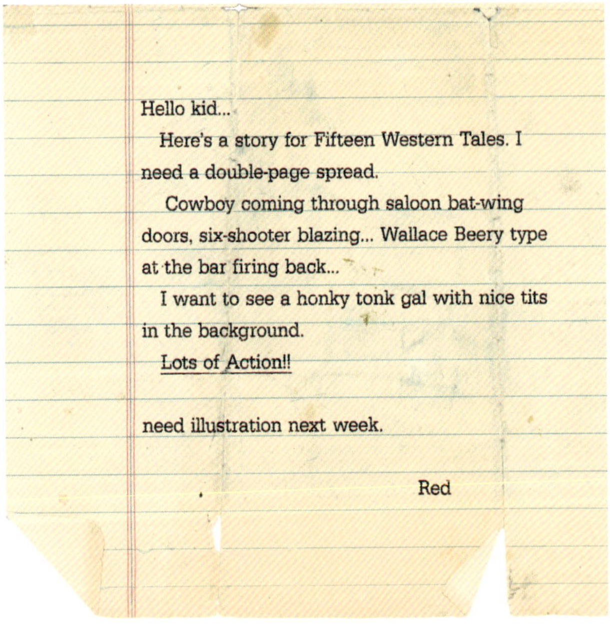

Hello kid...

Here's a story for Fifteen Western Tales. I need a double-page spread.

Cowboy coming through saloon bat-wing doors, six-shooter blazing... Wallace Beery type at the bar firing back...

I want to see a honky tonk gal with nice tits in the background.

Lots of Action!!

need illustration next week.

Red

25¢
FIFTEEN
MAY
A POPULAR PUBLICATION
WESTERN
15 STORIES
TALES
25 CENTS
GRANGER, GET YOUR GUN!
A TALE OF DEATH-BAITED TRAILS
by
WALLACE UMPHREY
THE LAST GRUBSTAKE
by MURRAY LEINSTER
PHILIP KETCHUM
•
ROD PATTERSON
MANY OTHERS!

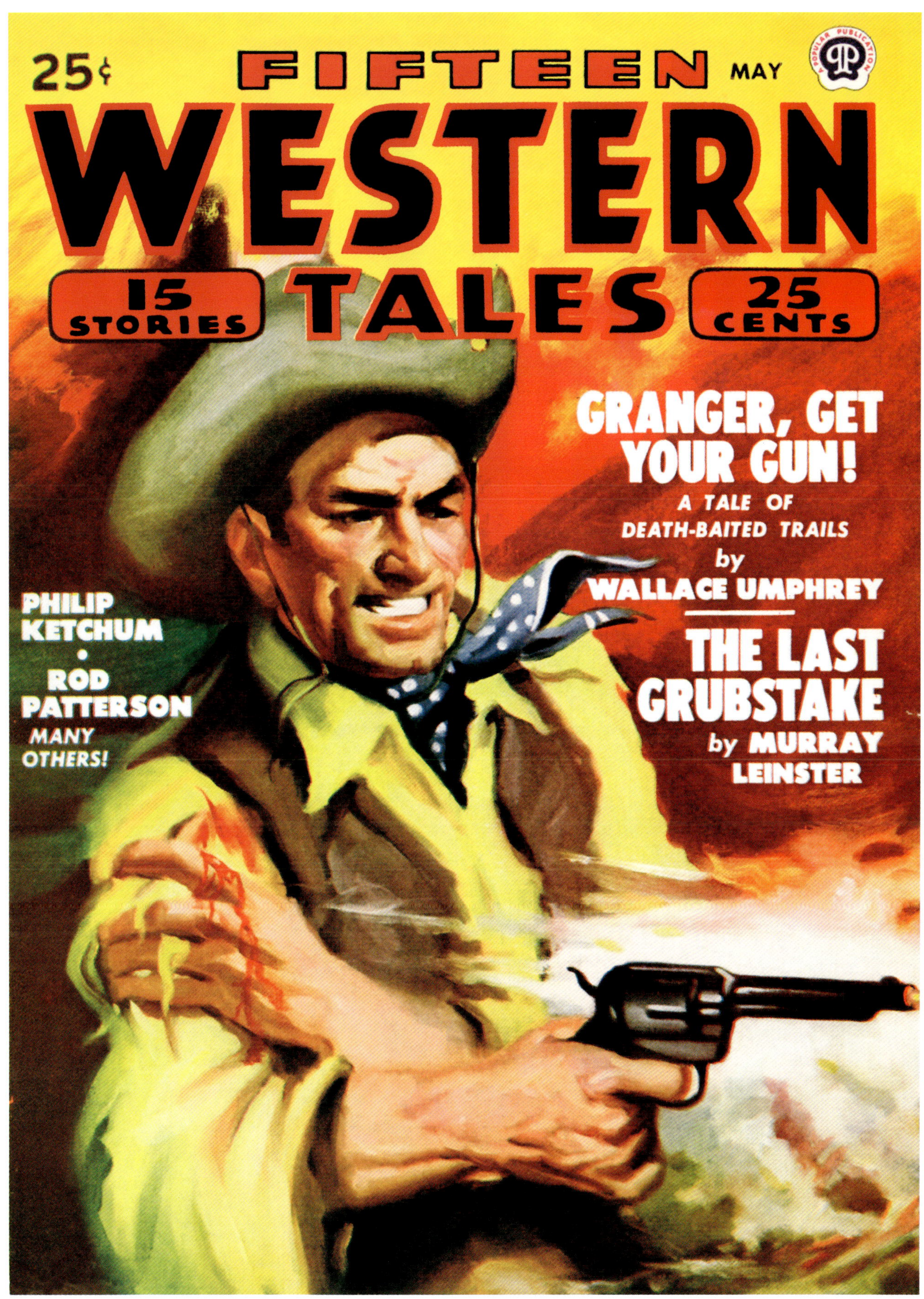

May, 1958

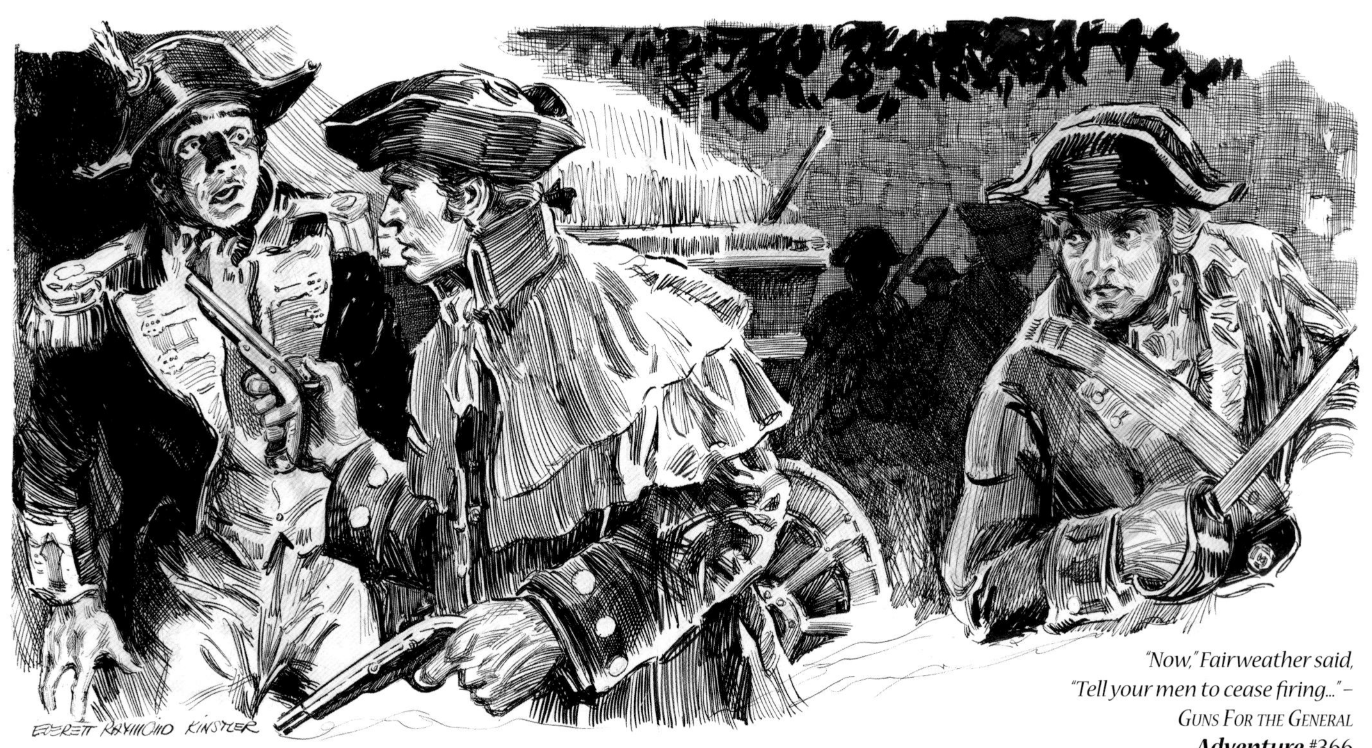

"Now," Fairweather said, "Tell your men to cease firing..." –
GUNS FOR THE GENERAL
Adventure #366
circa 1949.
original size: 29"x16"

CANNONADE
Adventure
circa 1950
original size: 29"x18"

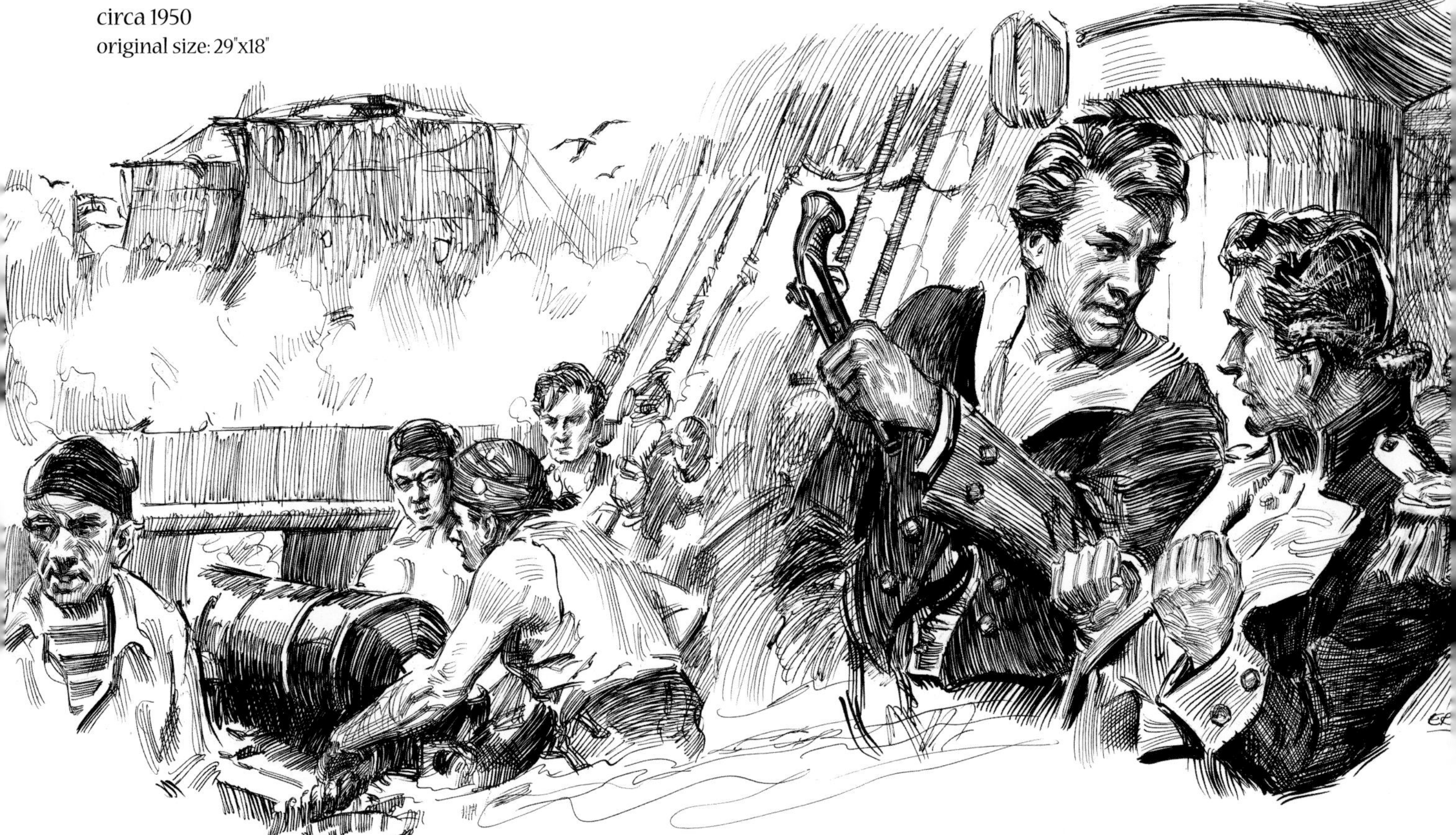

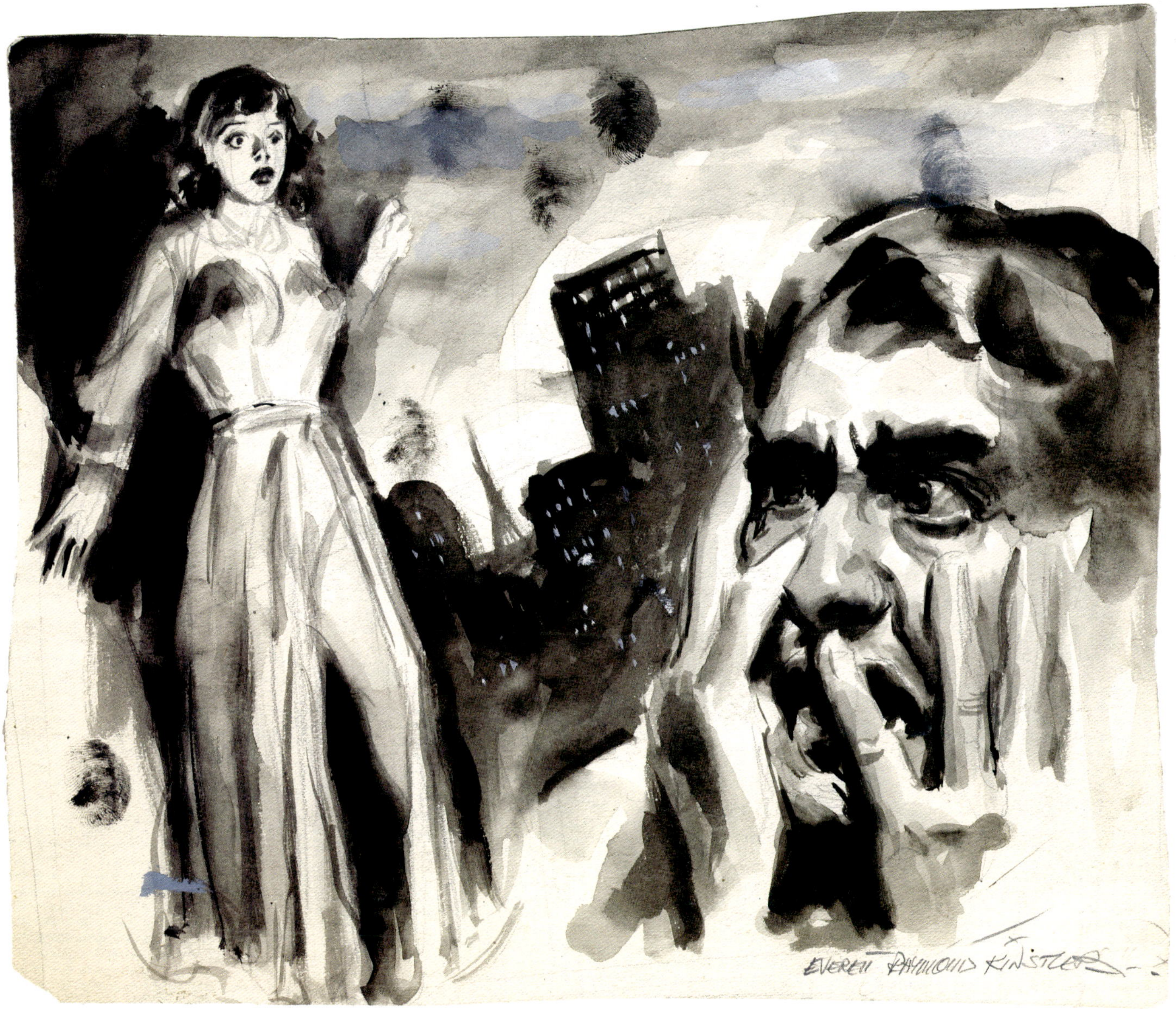

Night Fright – *wash study*
circa 1950
original size: 11½"x9½"

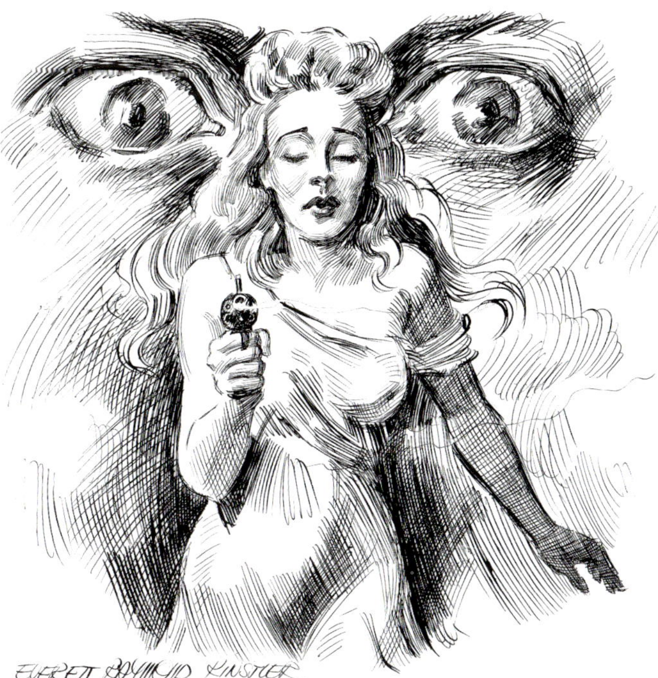

I remember she was wearing that thin nightgown. She handled the gun carefully. –
YOU'LL HAVE A FINE FUNERAL
Dime Mystery #282
circa 1949
original size: 14"x19½"

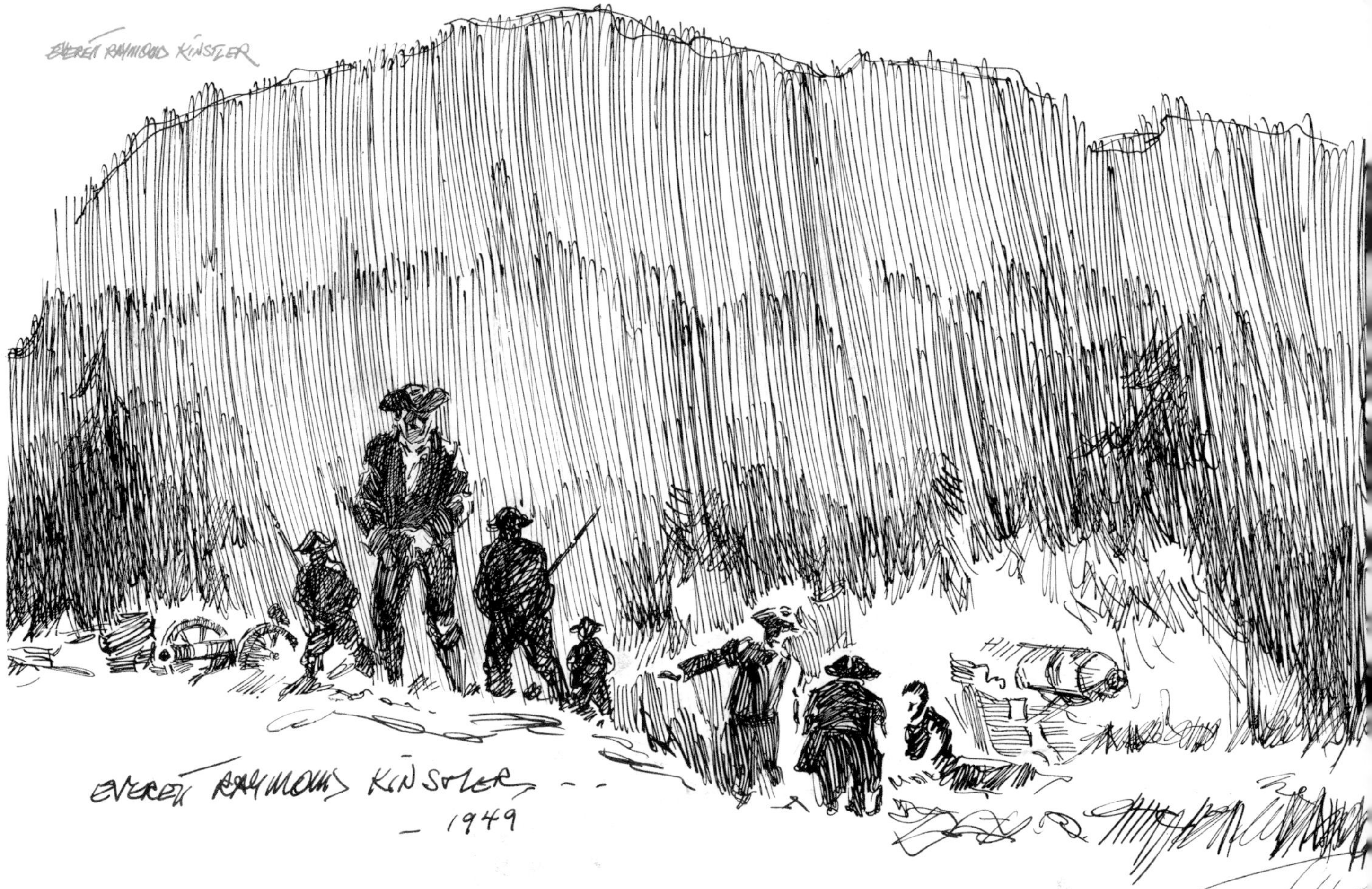

The artist in Ray Kinstler didn't much care how the finished illustration would be reproduced. Despite the fact that the final printed size of this drawing was only ten and one-half inches across two pages in the published pulp magazine, Ray drew it two and a half times larger.

This was typical of his working method—with as much weight given to the process as to the product. Never mind that the cheap printing and the cheaper paper of the pulps could never reproduce his line work, he used the opportunity to exercise his artistic muscles. The drawing had to be functional and professional, but the art director's satisfaction was secondary to his own.

He was twenty-two years old.

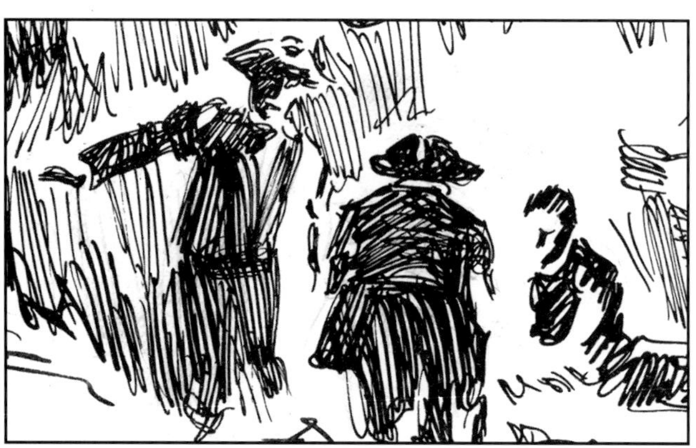

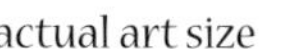

actual art size

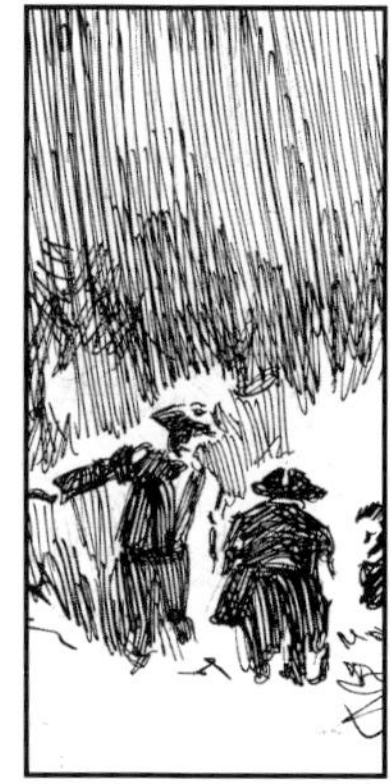

printed art size

The body on his shoulders, pursuit at his heels, Burr staggered thru the high snow!!! – LITTLE BURR
Adventure #470, 1949
original size: 28"x19"

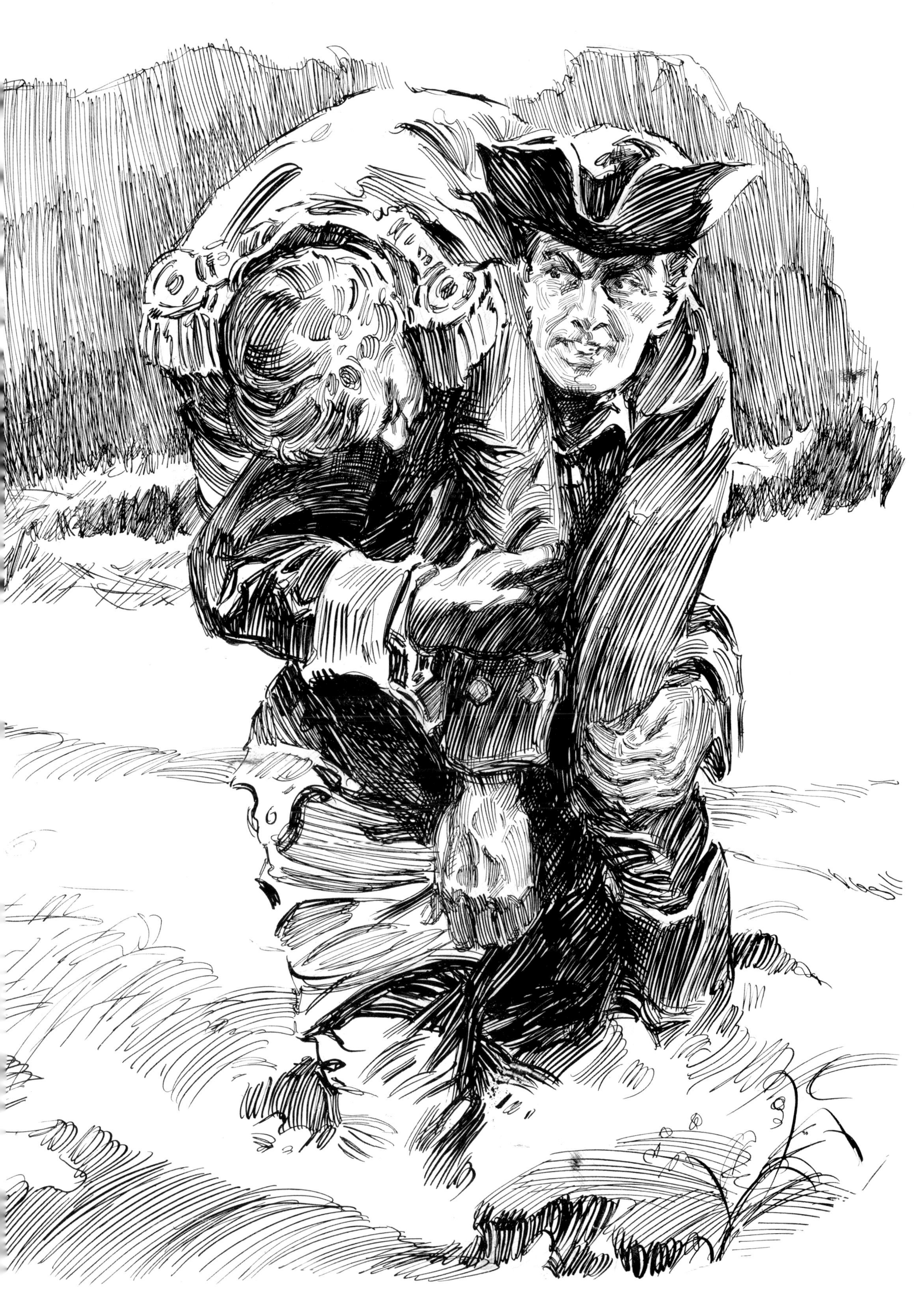

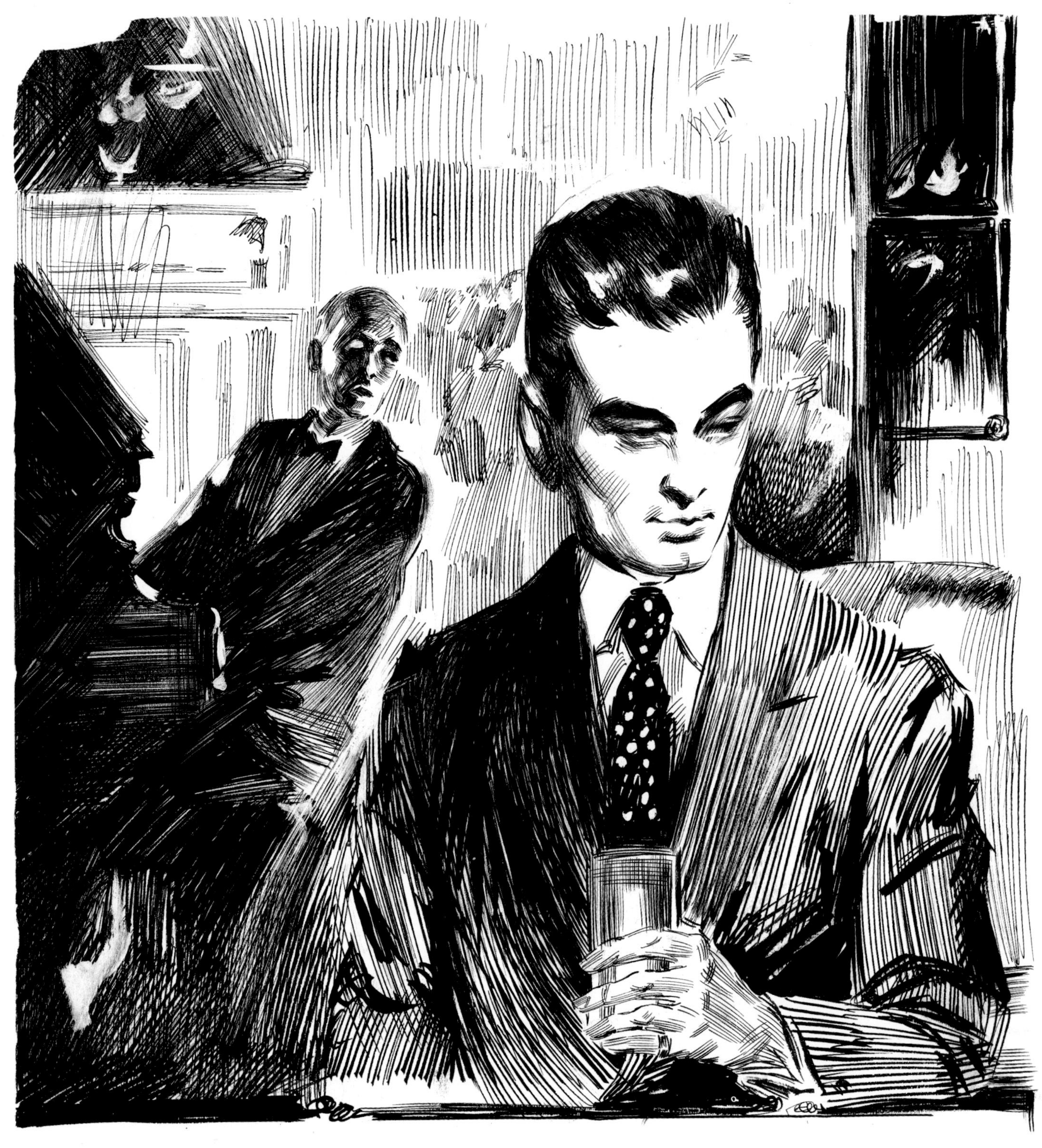

Kissed by Proxy
source unknown, 1948
original size: 26"x16"

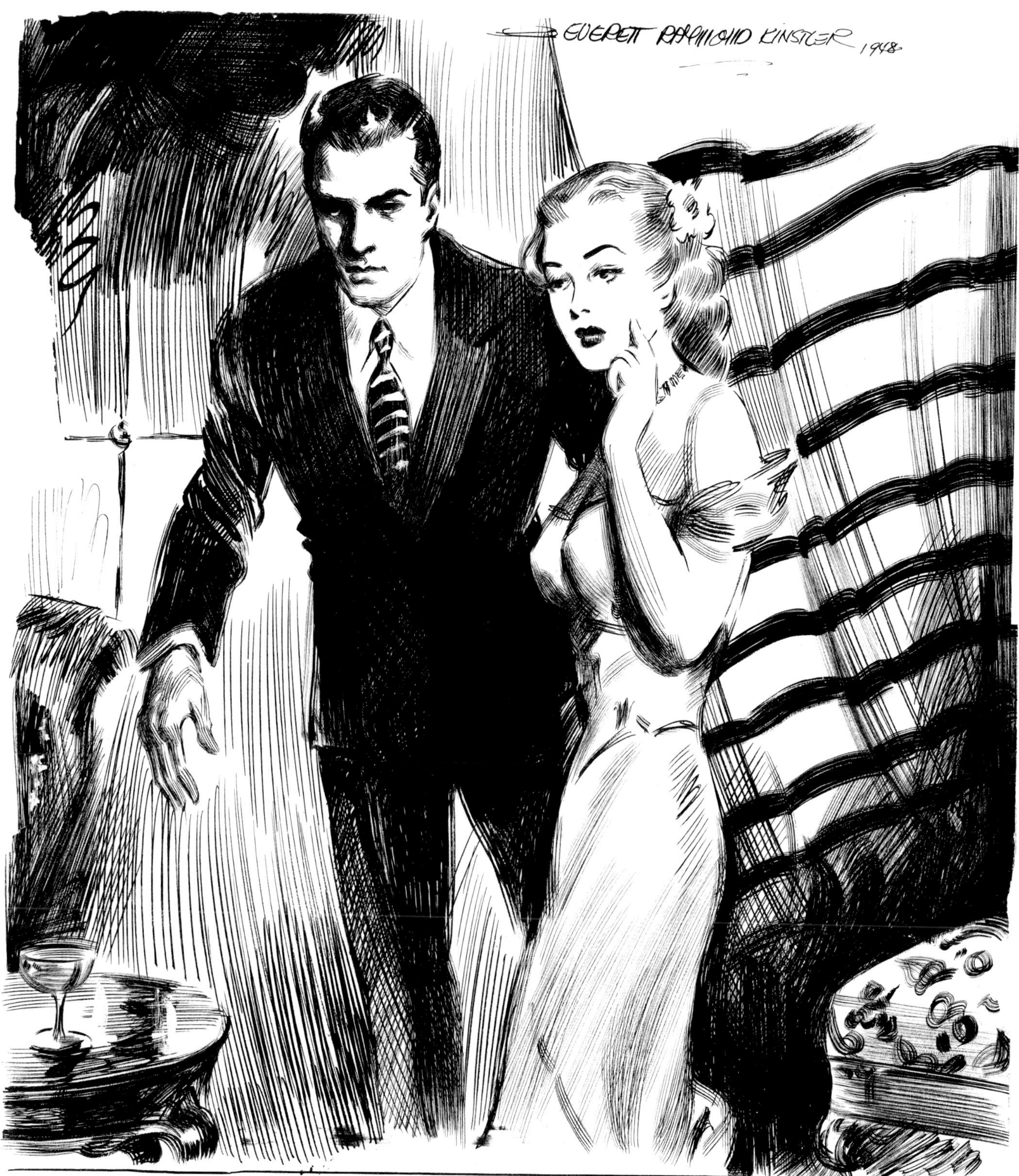

Space was usually left between two sections of a drawing to allow for the center margin of the magazine. It was a necessary artifice in artwork that spanned two published pages.

When he retrieved the originals after publication, Kinstler often filled in that space. However, this particular piece was done on two art boards and was therefore not made whole after publication.

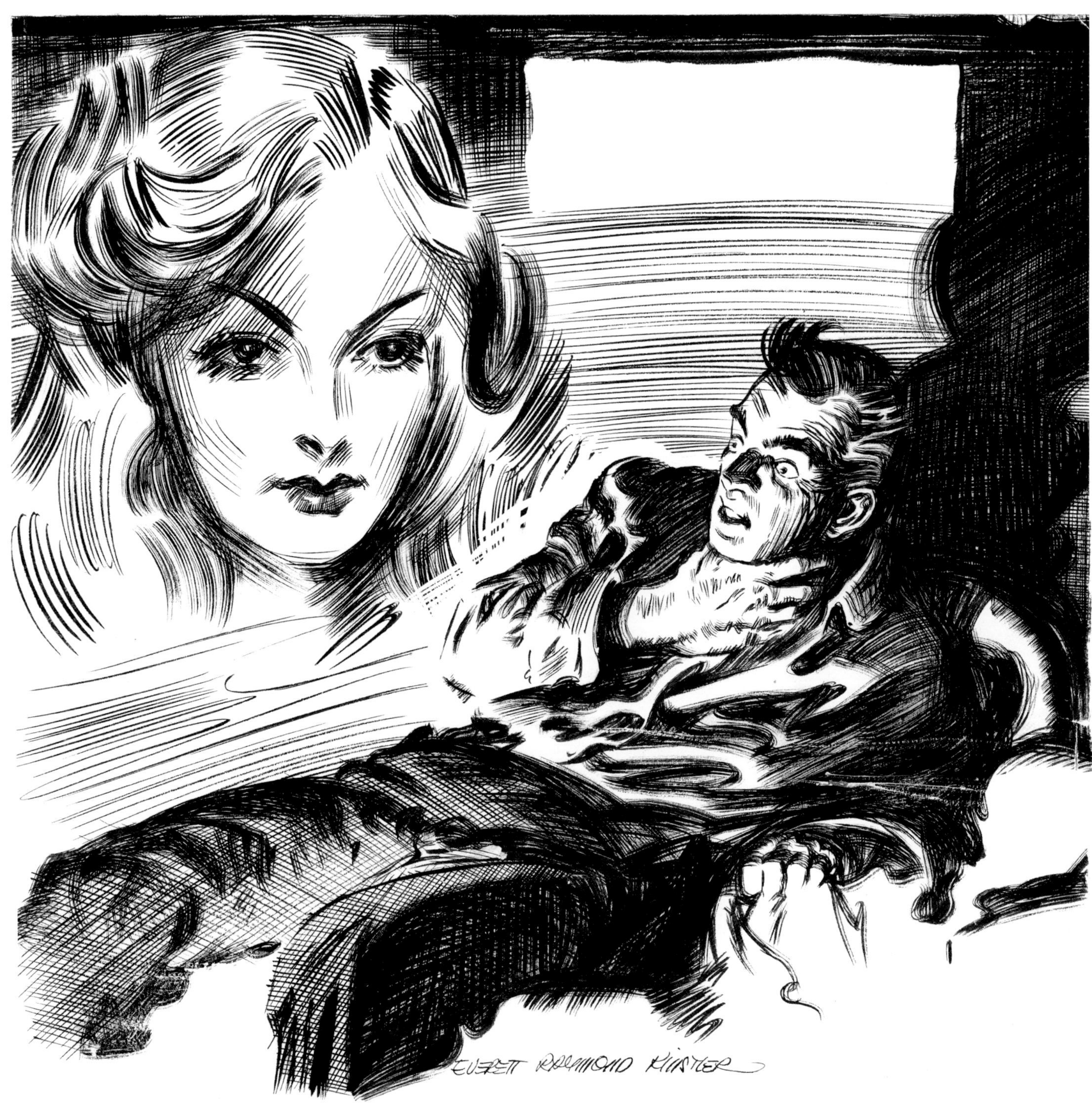

Dime Mystery #205
circa 1949
original size: 15"x14½"

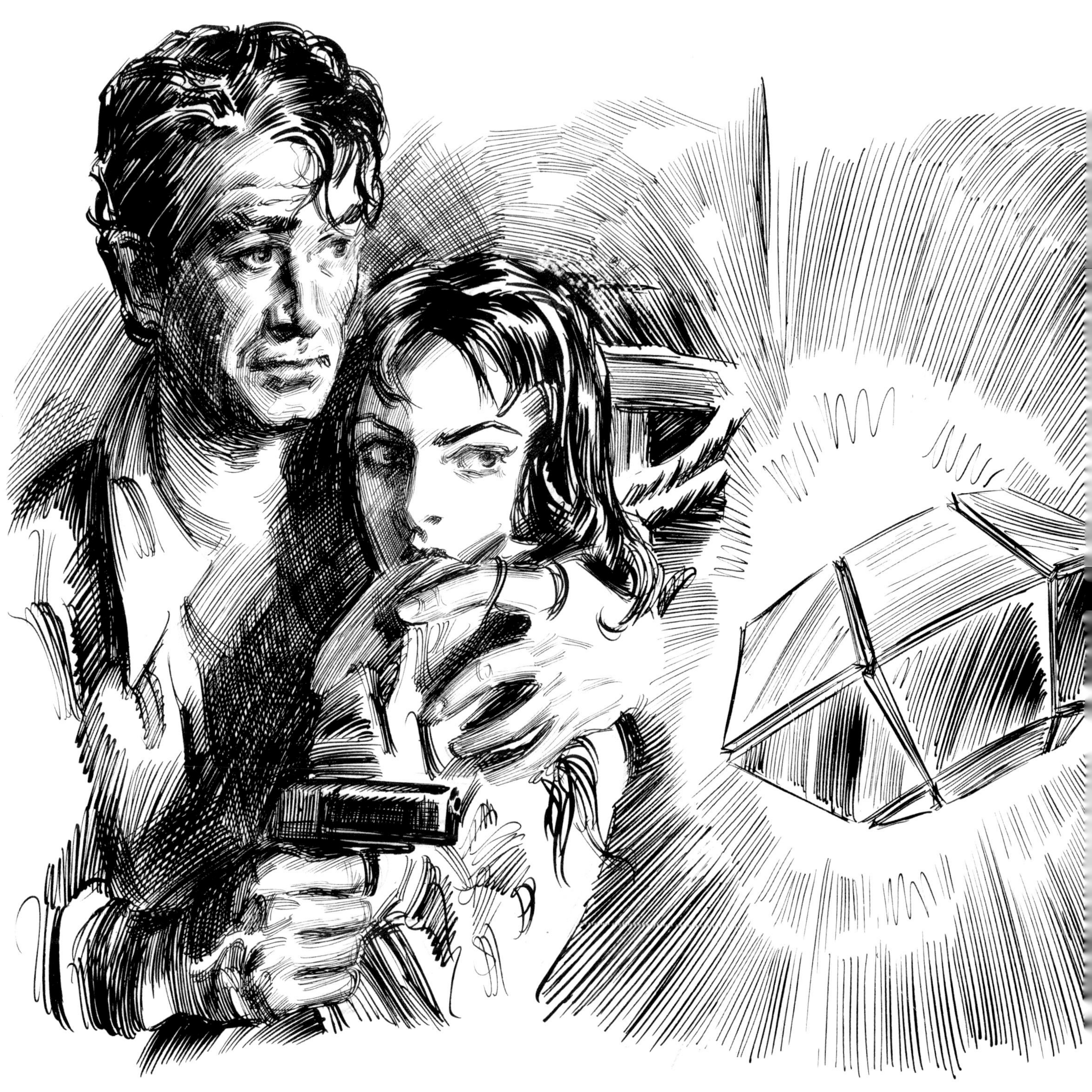

Diamond! Diamond!
unknown source & date
circa 1949
original size: 16"x15"

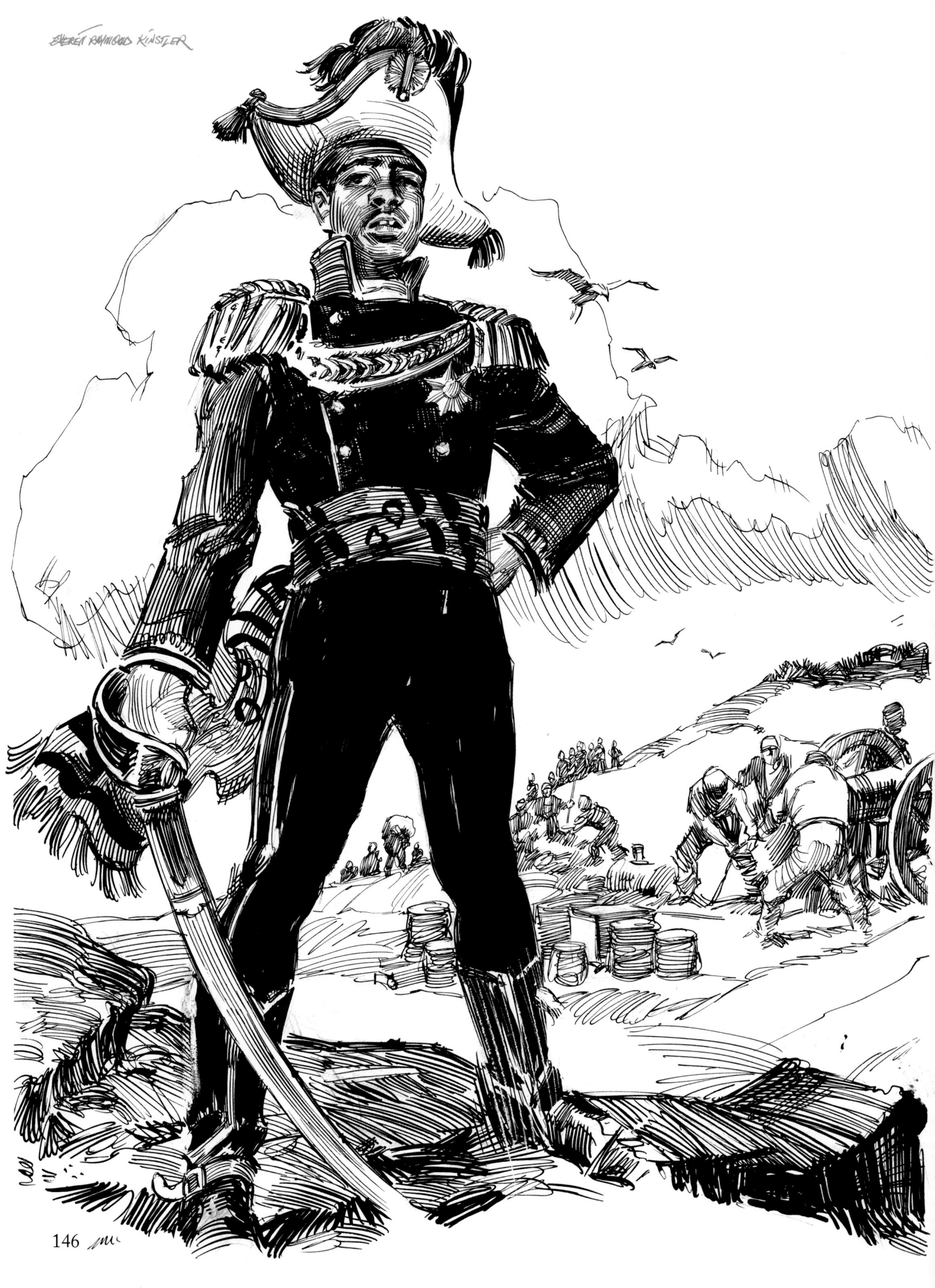
EVERETT RAYMOND KINSTLER

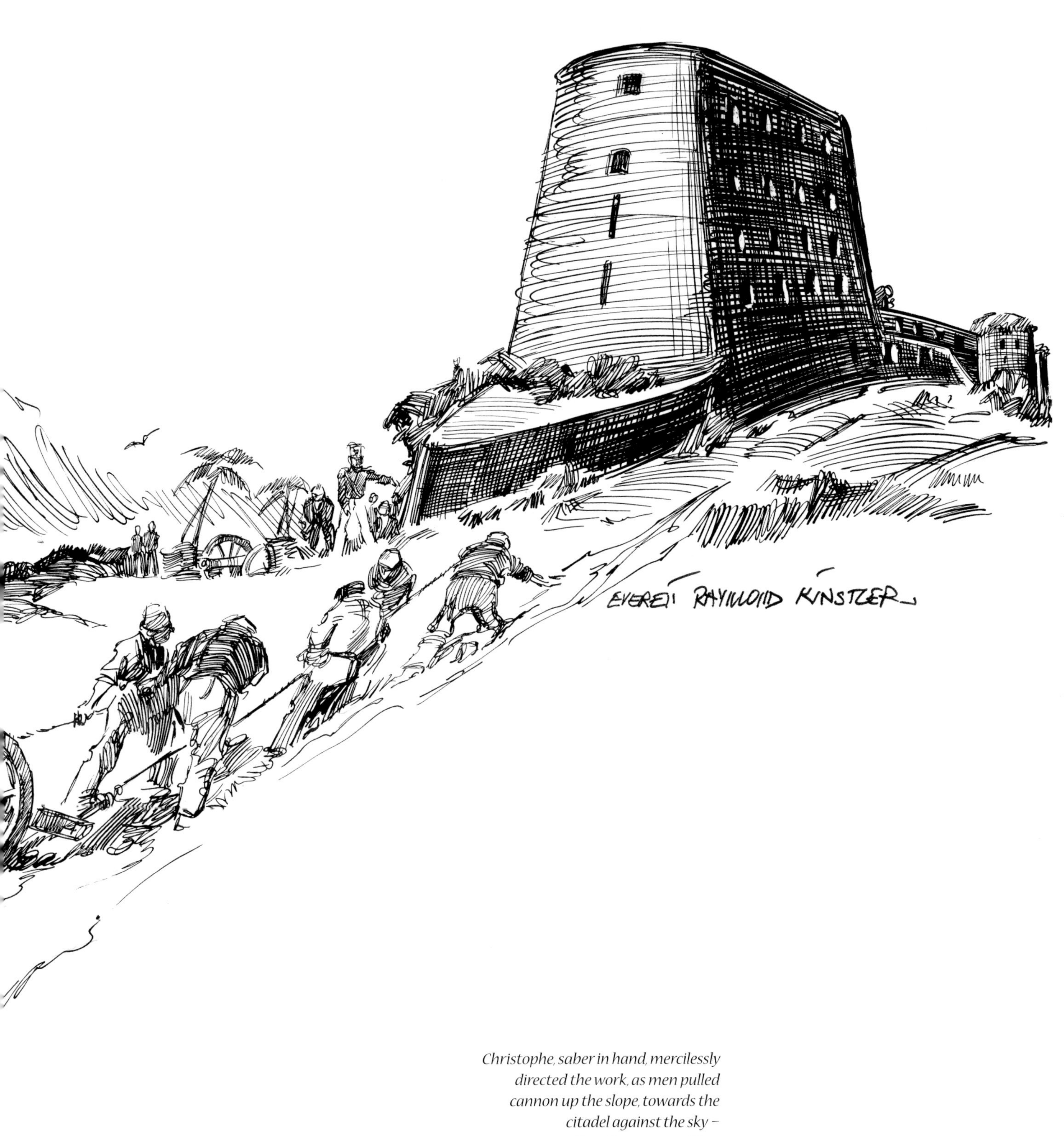

Christophe, saber in hand, mercilessly directed the work, as men pulled cannon up the slope, towards the citadel against the sky –
Henri Christophe of Haiti
Adventure circa 1950
original size: 29"x19"

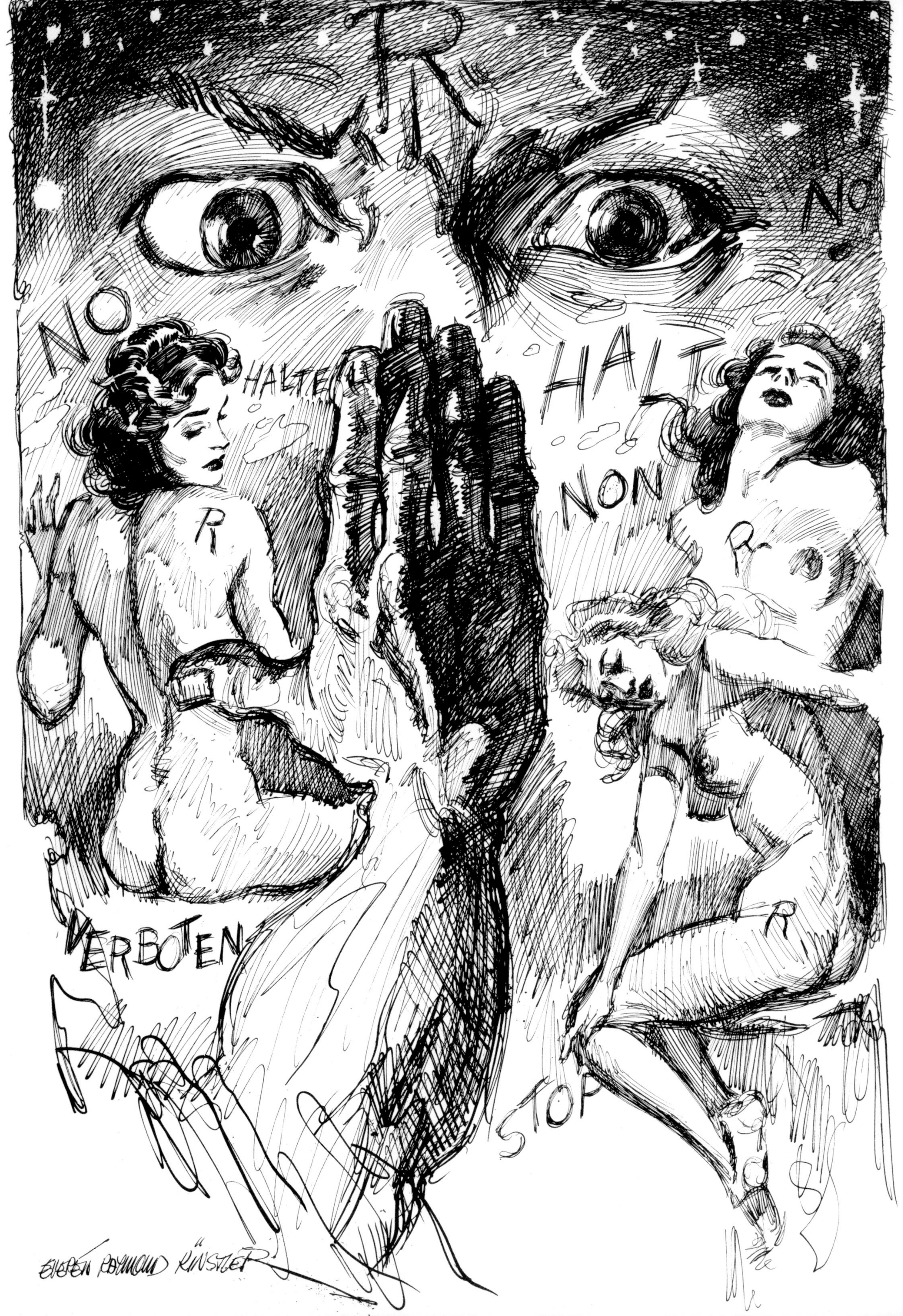
NO
NO
HALTE
HALT
NON
VERBOTEN
STOP

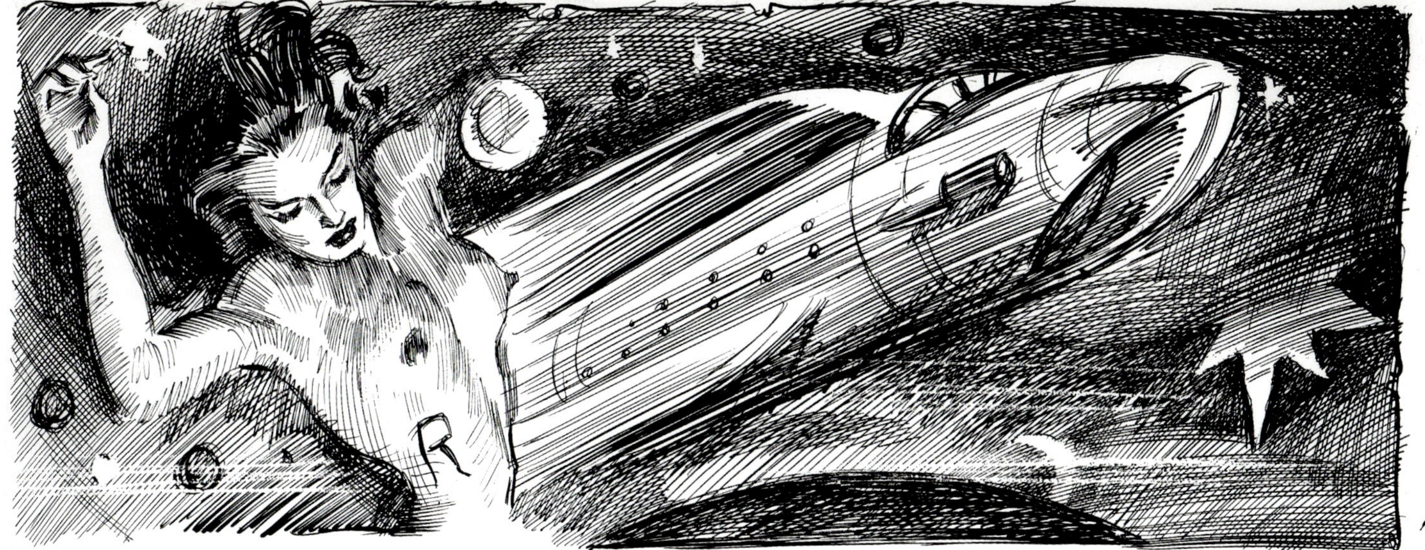

For Humans Only
Avon Science Fiction & Fantasy Reader #1
January, 1953

Avon

Kinstler was busy creating stunning pen and ink extravaganzas on the inside front covers of Avon comic books in 1952. These proved to editor Sol Cohen that he was capable of greater things than sequential storytelling, and a showcase was created to take advantage of his talent.

In the late 1940s and early 1950s, Avon had published two digest pulps: ***Avon Fantasy Reader*** and ***Avon Science Fiction Reader***. Both titles had the traditional pulpish paintings on the covers, but neither contained interior illustrations. However, when these two magazines were relaunched in January of 1953 under the combined title of ***Avon Science Fiction and Fantasy Reader***, the assistant editor was Kinstler's friend, Noah Gordon. The new title was quite heavily illustrated and most, and the most dynamic, of these illustrations were by Everett Raymond Kinstler.

Other artists were represented on the pages, but out of a combined twenty-two stories in both issues, seven were by Kinstler. (John Giunta was second with five.) Ray also rendered the logo for the "Book Review" section shown below, with a caricature of Noah Gordon shepherding books onto a rocket ship.

Fortunately, as with other works of which he was most proud, Ray retained most of the originals. They are printed here for the first time larger than the four and one-quarter inch width at which they were first presented.

It is unknown just how sophisticated the magazine might have become had it lasted more than two issues. Kinstler might have replaced Leo Manso as the cover artist and perhaps taken his pen work to the next level. As it was, these two digest-sized magazines have developed a mystique among aficionados like few others of that era.

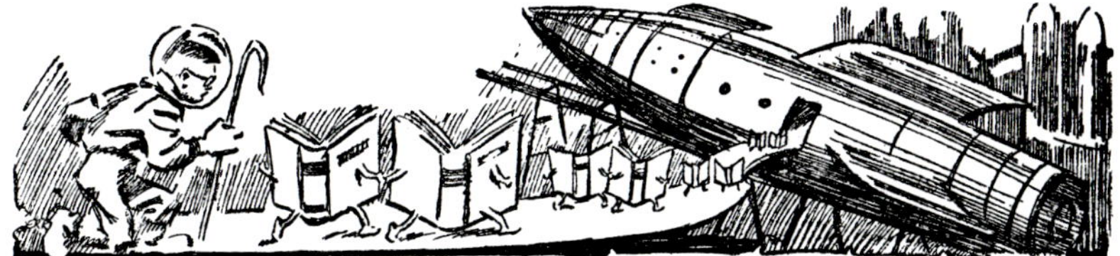

Cover paintings by Leo Manso.

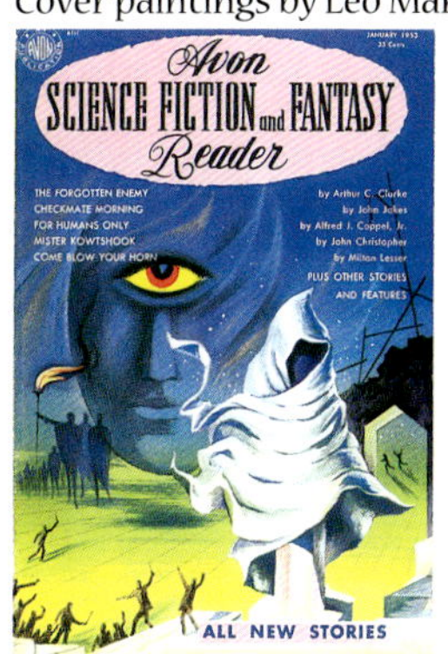

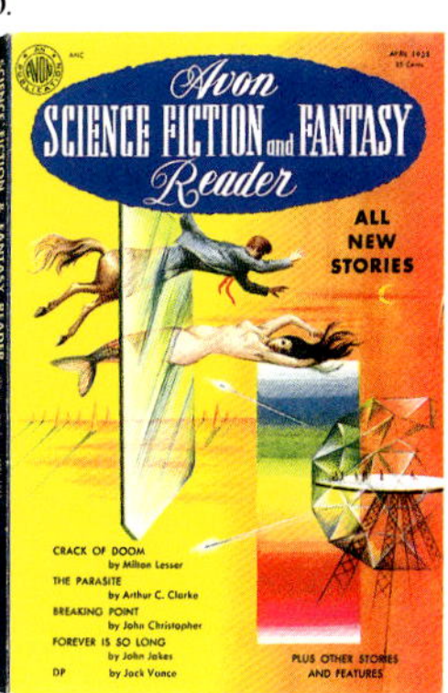

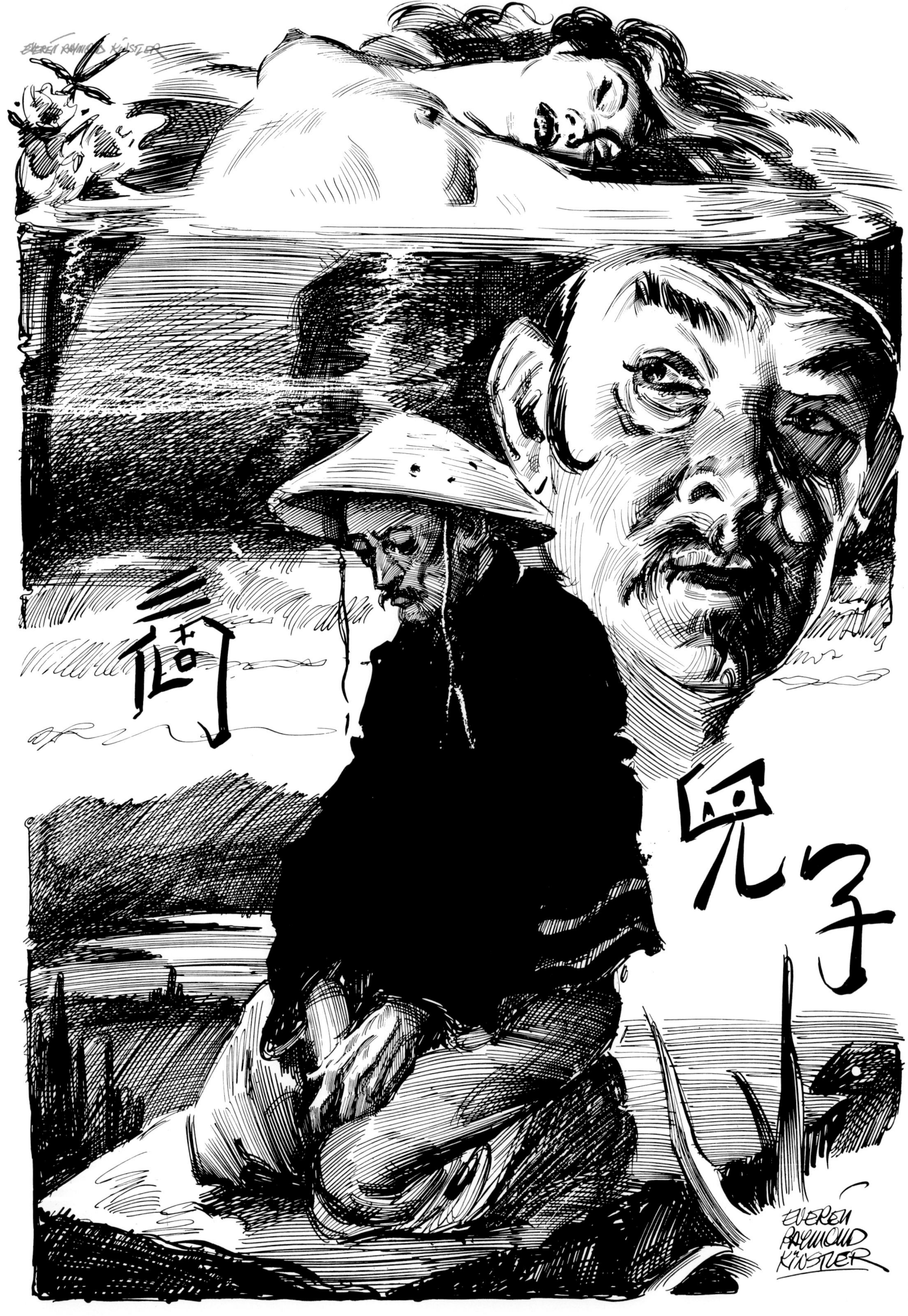
EVERETT RAYMOND KINSTLER

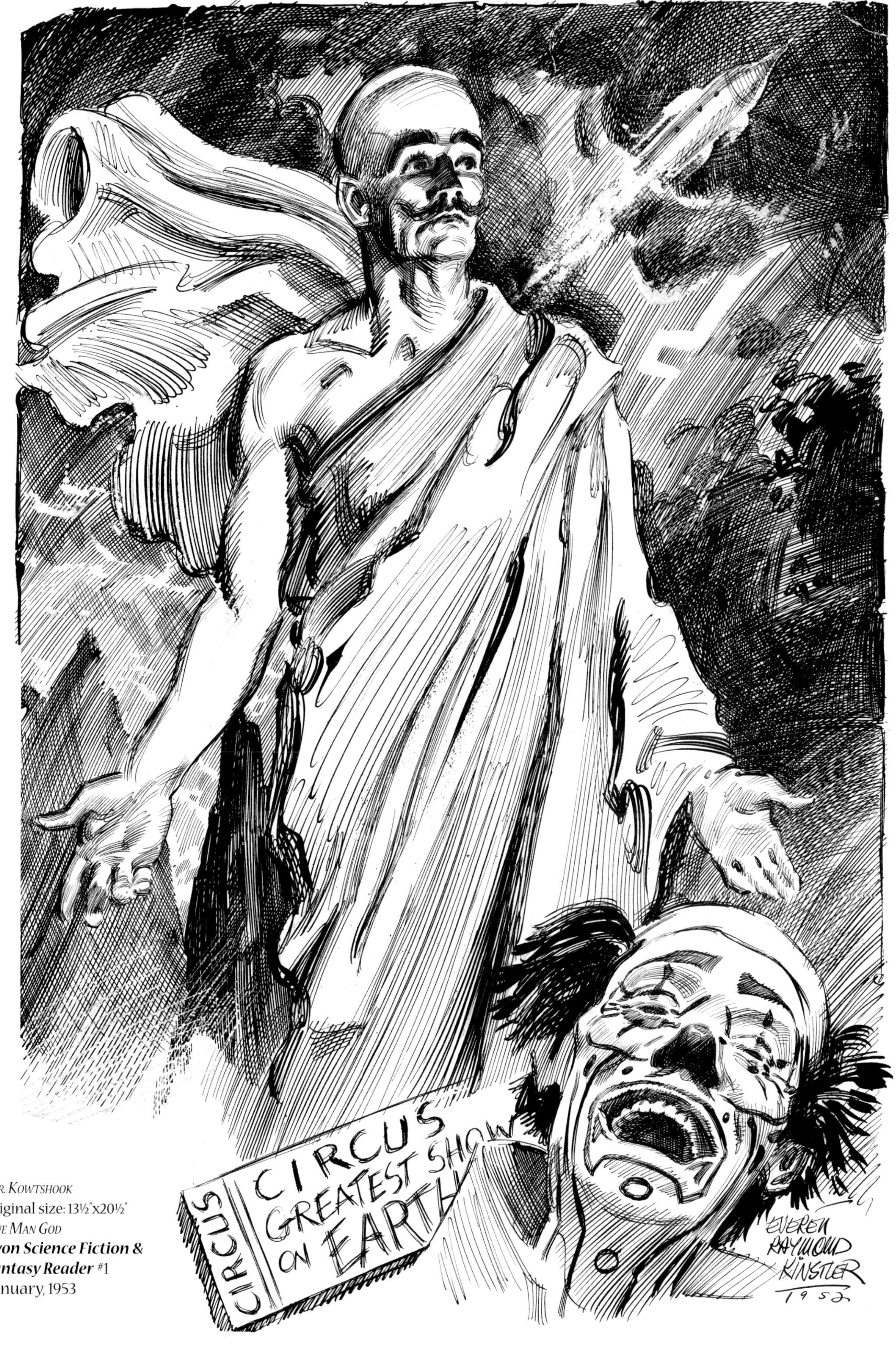

Mr. Kowtshook
original size: 13½"x20½"
One Man God
Avon Science Fiction & Fantasy Reader #1
January, 1953

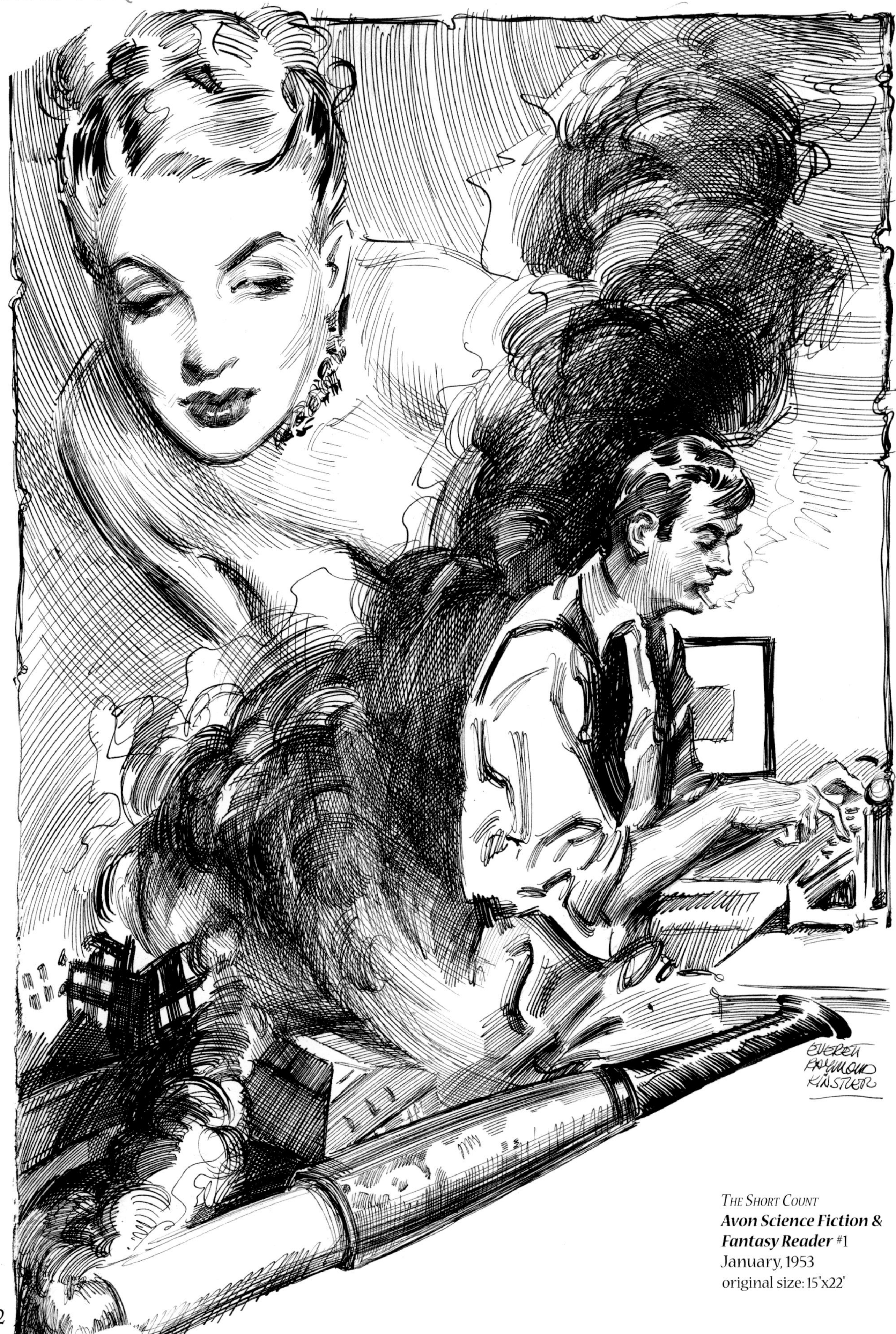

THE SHORT COUNT
Avon Science Fiction & Fantasy Reader #1
January, 1953
original size: 15"x22"

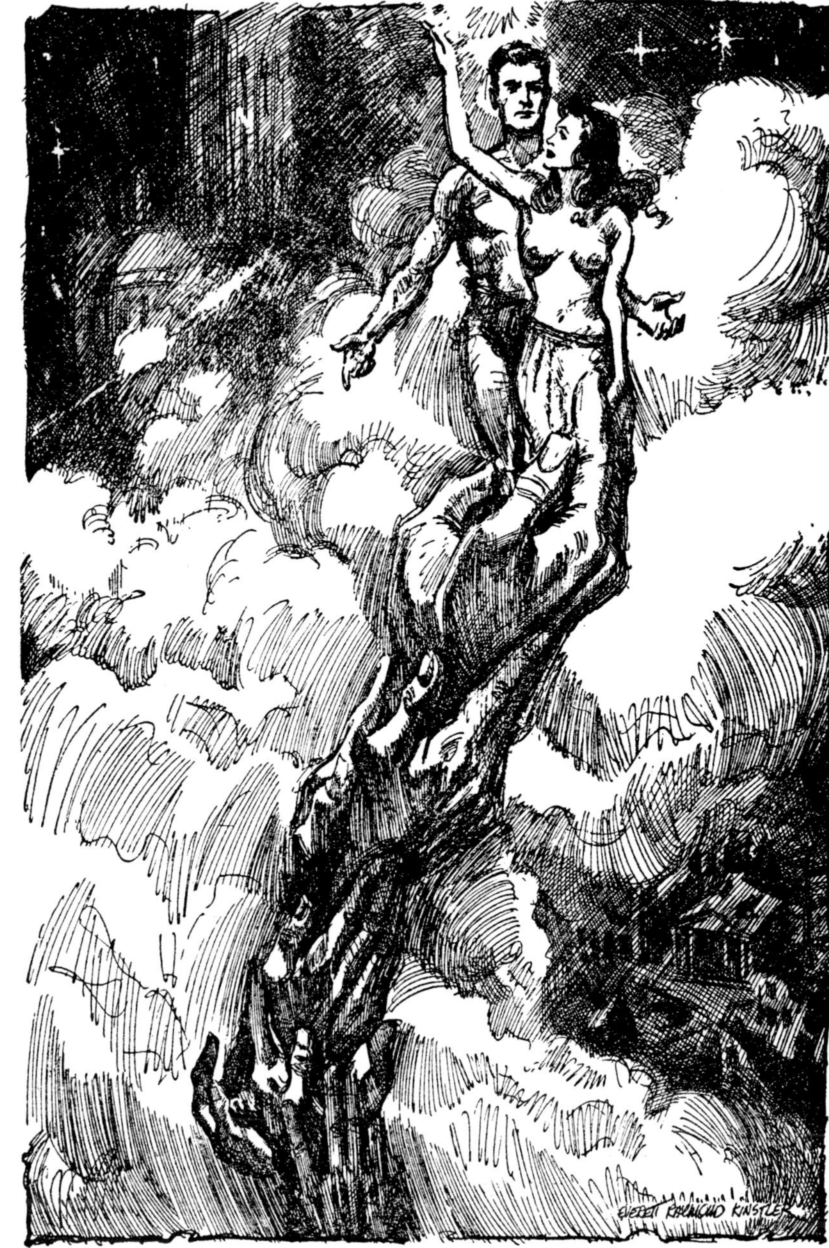

Forever Is So Long
Avon Science Fiction & Fantasy Reader #2
April, 1953

Both of the illustrations on this page are reproduced from a printed copy of the magazine. They are presented to complete the record of all of Kinstler's art for this classic science fiction magazine of the early 1950s.

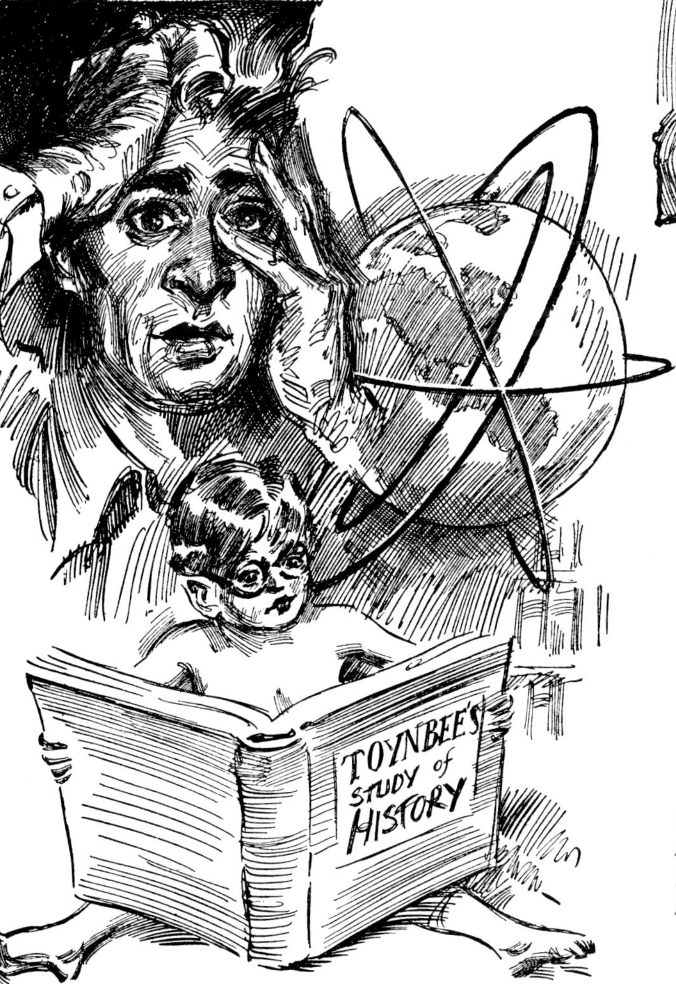

Crack of Doom
Avon Science Fiction & Fantasy Reader #2
April, 1953

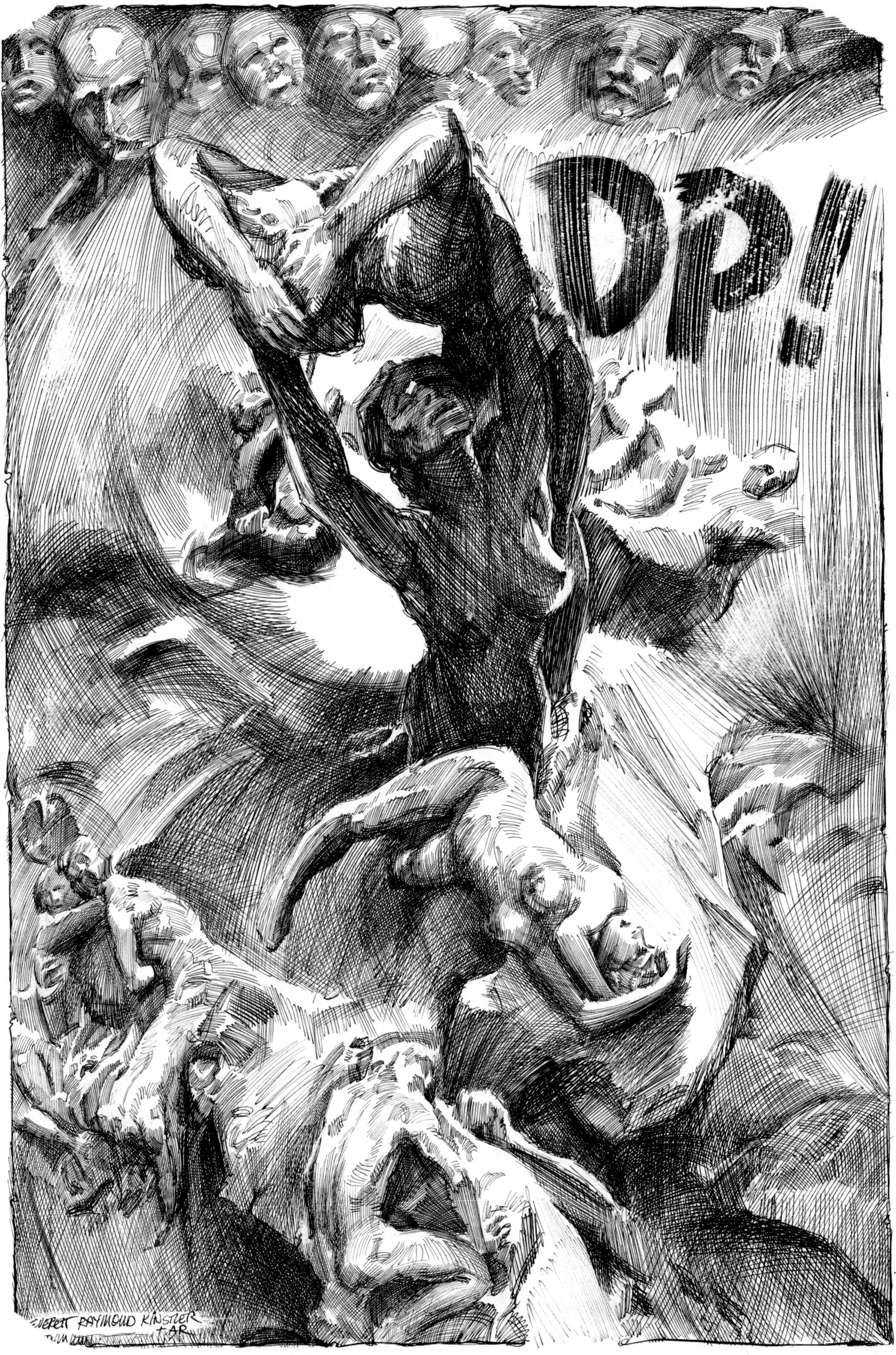
DP!!
EVERETT RAYMOND KINSTLER
+AR

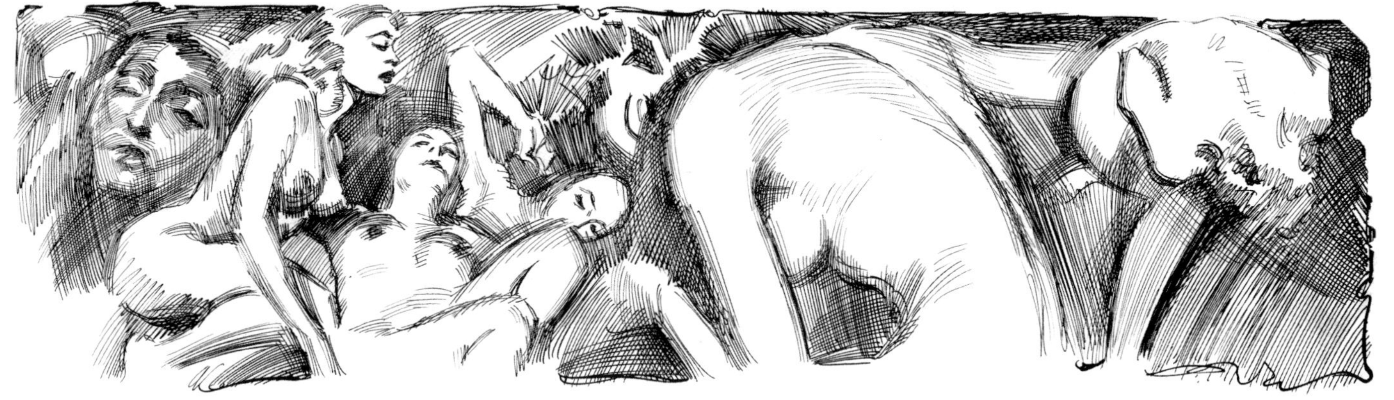

"DP" stands for "Displaced Persons"—a commonly used appellation after World War II when so many people had been relocated by the forces of war.

Jack Vance's 1953 story *"DP!"* appeared in the second (and final) issue of the ***Avon Science Fiction and Fantasy Reader.*** Both the Vance story, and the inspired Kinstler art which accompanied it, have resonated through the years with fans of both men.

More than fifty years after publication, many people who encountered the story in 1953 still remember the emotions it initially generated. Kinstler's art was a major factor in its impact. When author Harlan Ellison® learned of the present book, the first words out of his mouth were *"DP!"* Likewise with collector Philippe Angeli in France. Both immediately equated the story with the artist.

Originally printed just six and one-quarter inches high, the *"DP!"* art is finally getting a proper showing.

Ray's original drawings are twenty inches tall.

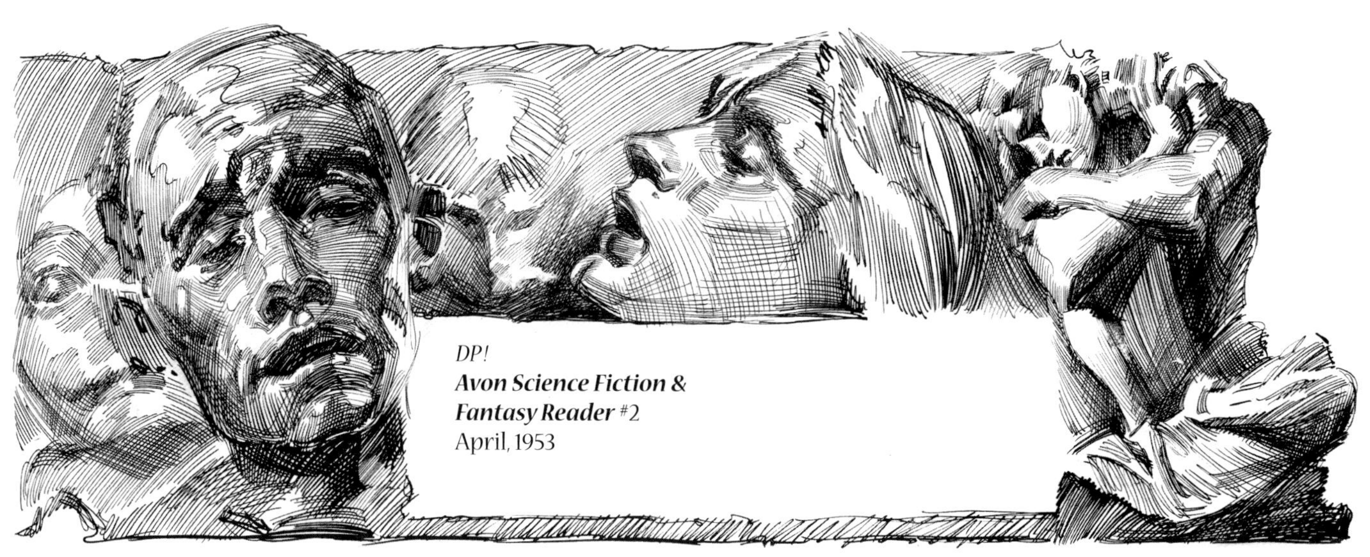

DP!
Avon Science Fiction & Fantasy Reader #2
April, 1953

ALL STORIES NEW...NO REPRINTS

RANCH ROMANCES

25c

SECOND MARCH NUMBER

A THRILLING PUBLICATION

25¢ RANCH ROMANCES 2nd MARCH 1957

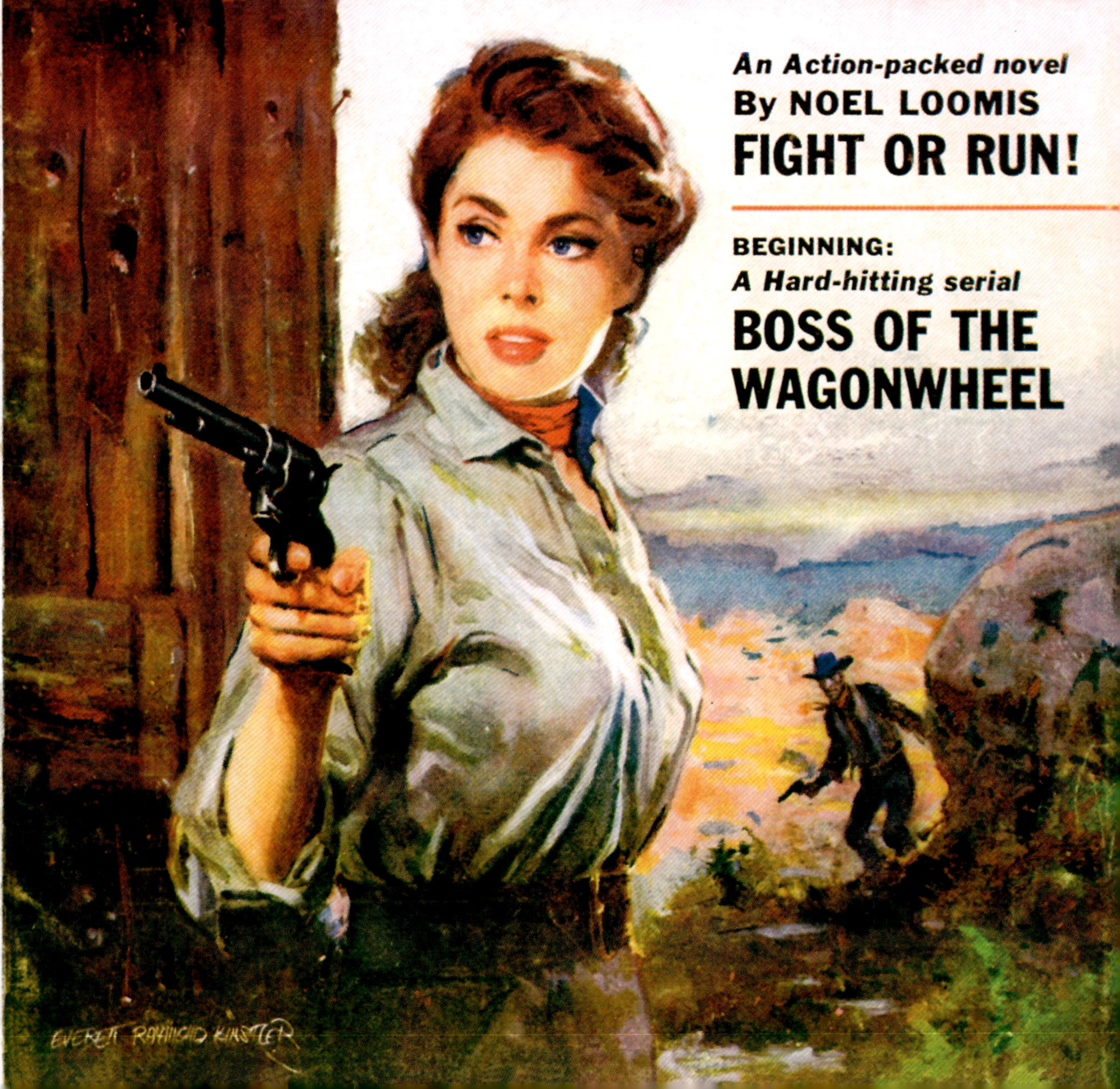

Ranch Romances

Ranch Romances* outlived most** of its more masculine competition. As the 1950s progressed, the only other survivors from the once-ubiquitous pulps were a few westerns and the science fiction titles that had converted to the smaller digest size. The adventure pulps had been replaced by the "Men's" magazines like ***True, ***Male*** and ***Man's Adventures***.

Originally published by William Clayton in 1924, ***Ranch Romances*** extended over 850 issues, finally riding off into the sunset in 1971. It was issued every two weeks through 1958, but less frequently thereafter.

Ned Pines purchased the title sometime around 1950. He added it to his stable of western romance pulps under his Popular Library imprint. It was probably the last of its genre.

The editor, Florence Hazard, was one of those people who inspired loyalty and extra effort in Kinstler, who stayed with the title until the schedule became less reliable.

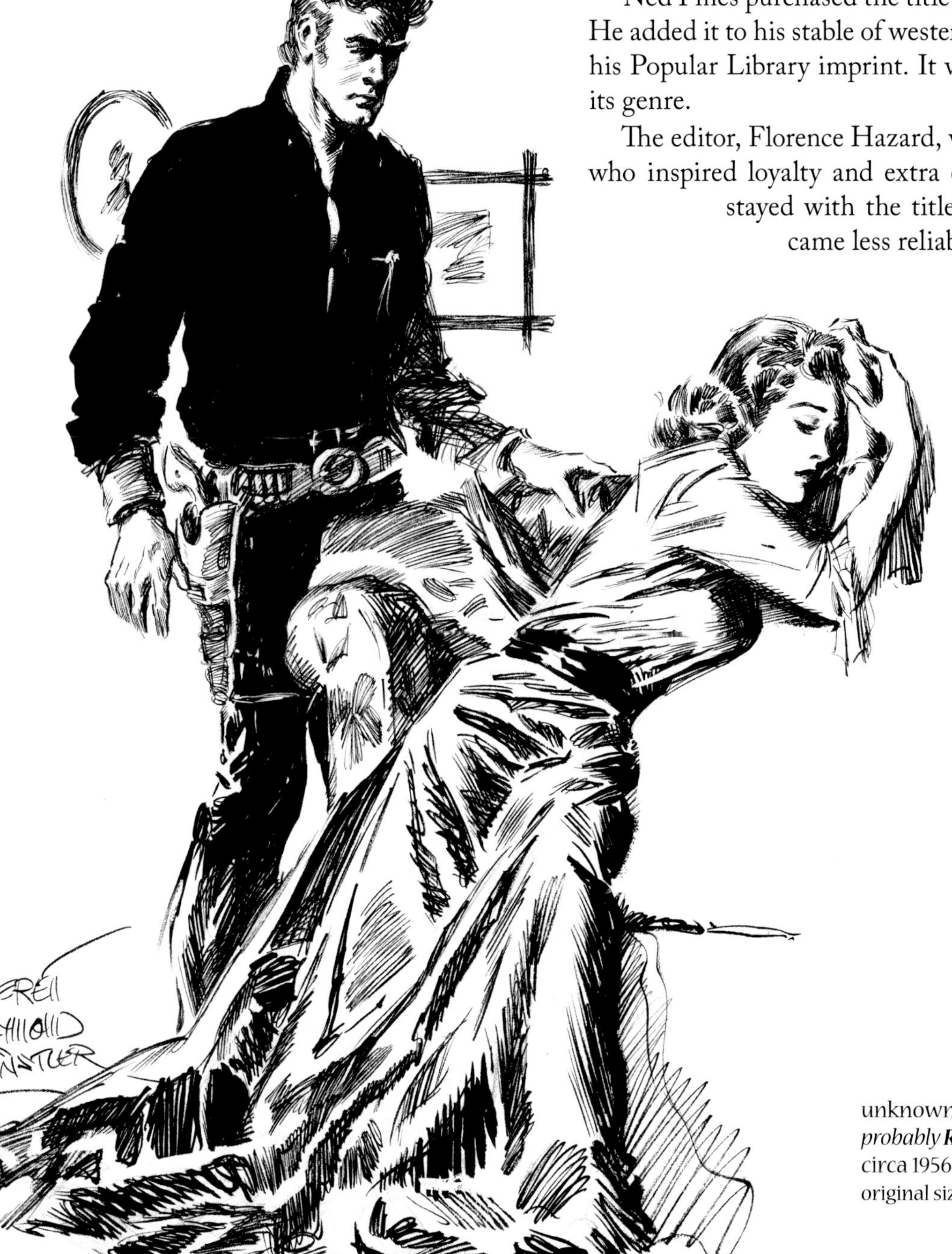

unknown source & date
probably ***Ranch Romances***
circa 1956
original size 12"x16"

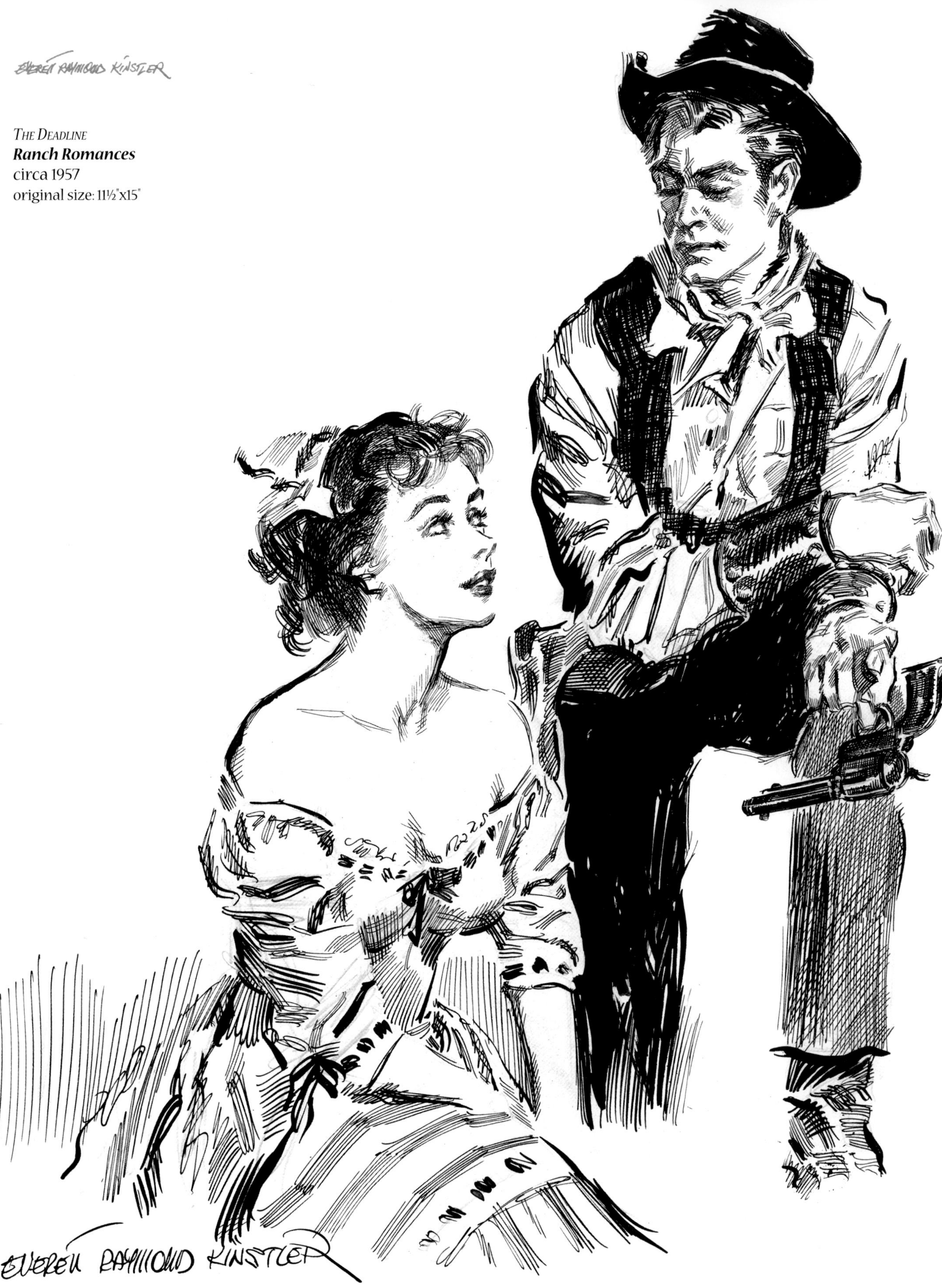

The Deadline
Ranch Romances
circa 1957
original size: 11½"x15"

Illustrations for western pulps were as varied as the stories they depicted. When the "romance" angle was added, the subject matter narrowed to variations on a theme: cowboy/girl.

At ***Ranch Romances***, Kinstler's compositional skills were put to the test. For ten years he depicted couples in an endless variety of situations and poses—often relying only on a simple prop or item of apparel to put across the "western" motif.

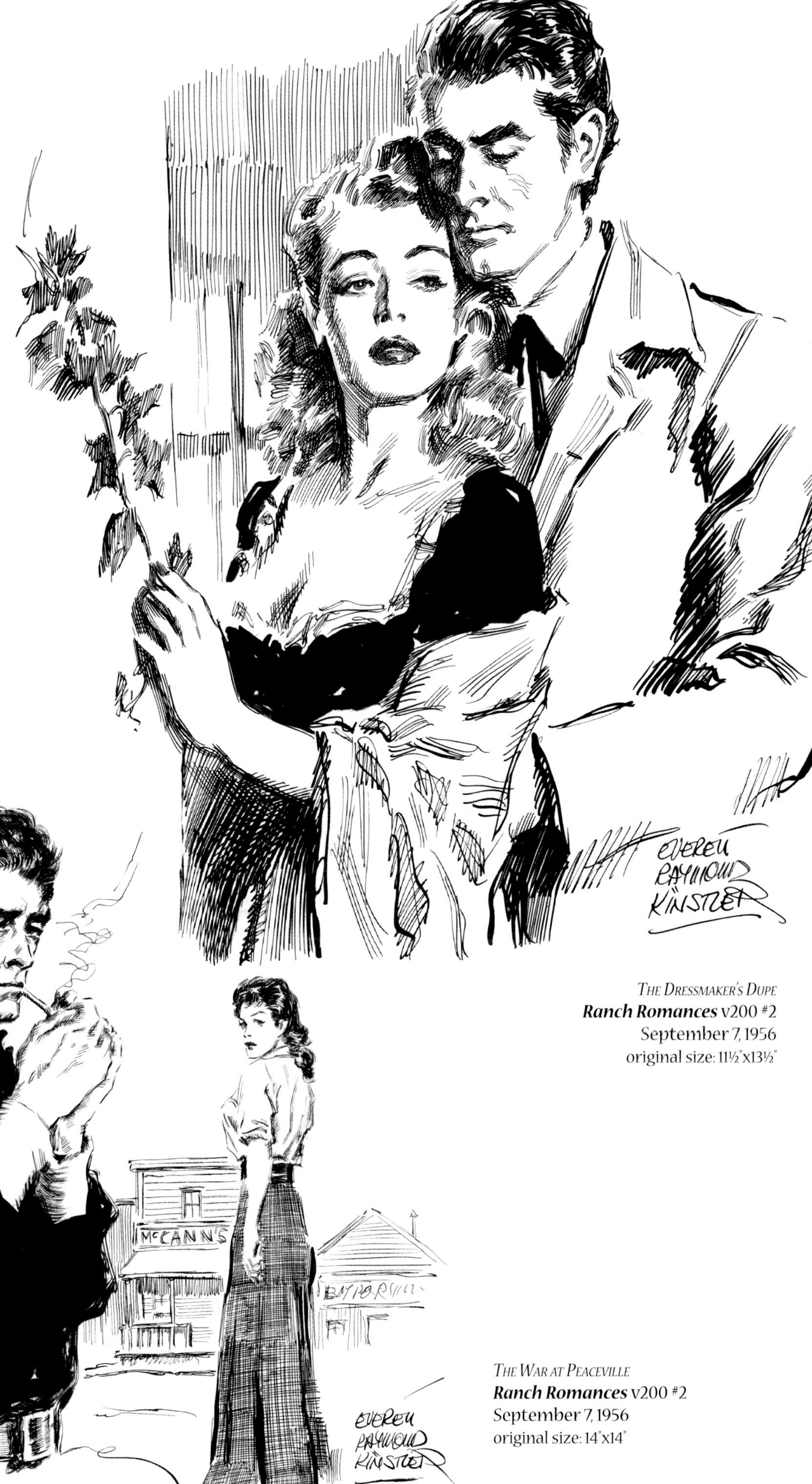

The Dressmaker's Dupe
Ranch Romances v200 #2
September 7, 1956
original size: 11½"x13½"

The War at Peaceville
Ranch Romances v200 #2
September 7, 1956
original size: 14"x14"

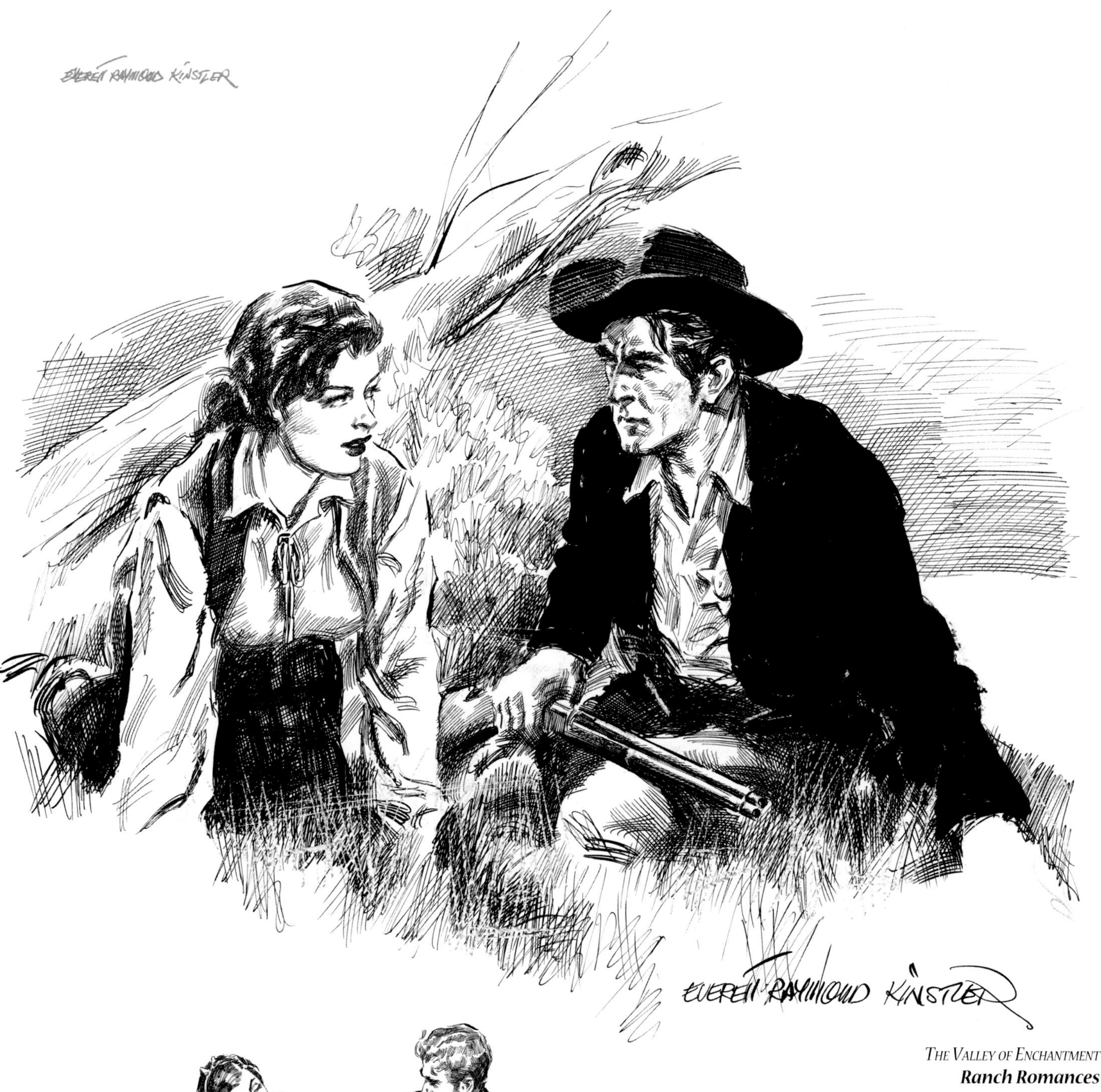

The Valley of Enchantment
Ranch Romances
circa 1958
original size: 14½"x14"

Kate murmured, "Dance with me," and he moved with her out on the floor. – *Night in Town*
Ranch Romances
circa 1957
original size: 14"x13½"

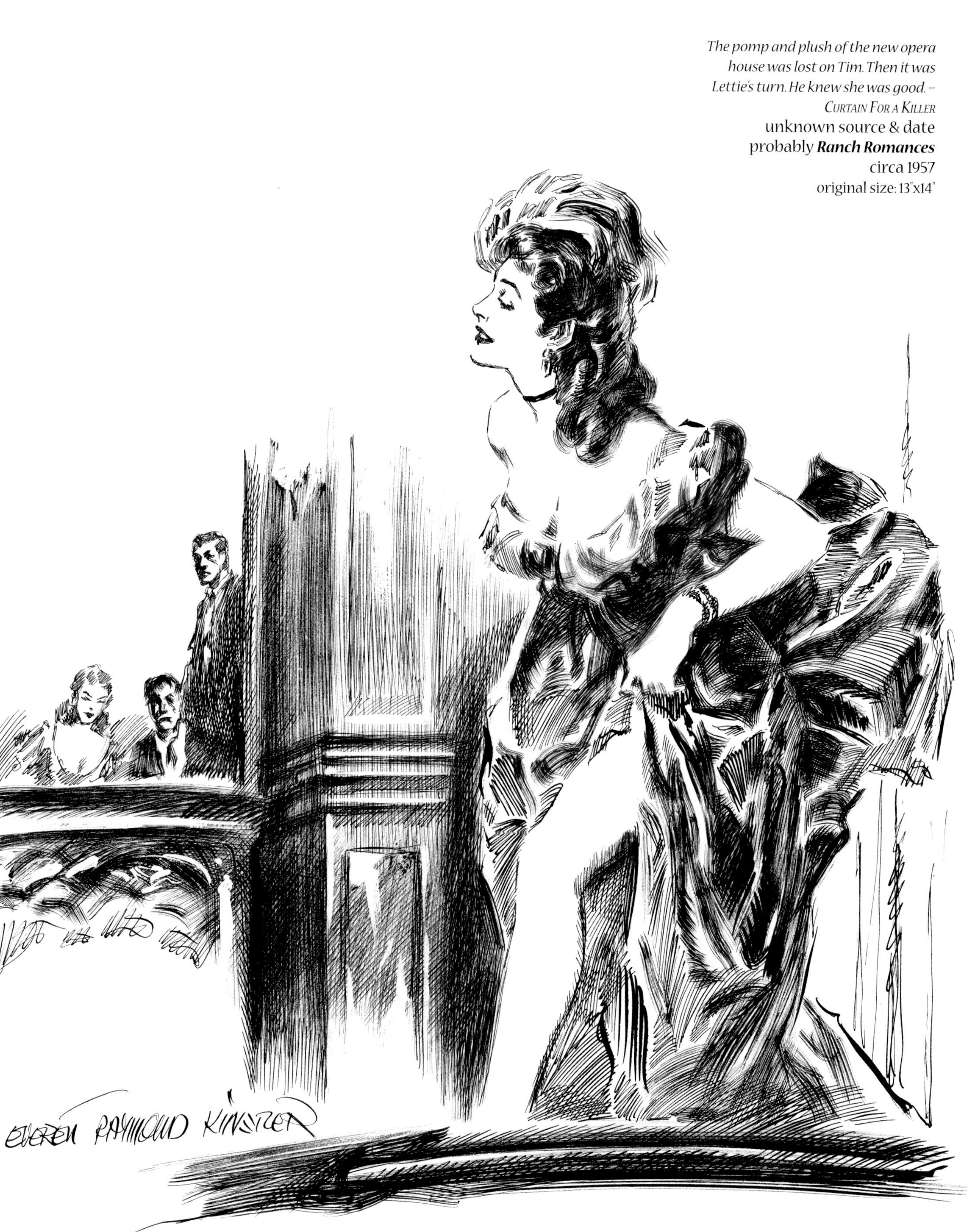

The pomp and plush of the new opera house was lost on Tim. Then it was Lettie's turn. He knew she was good. – *Curtain For a Killer*
unknown source & date
probably ***Ranch Romances***
circa 1957
original size: 13"x14"

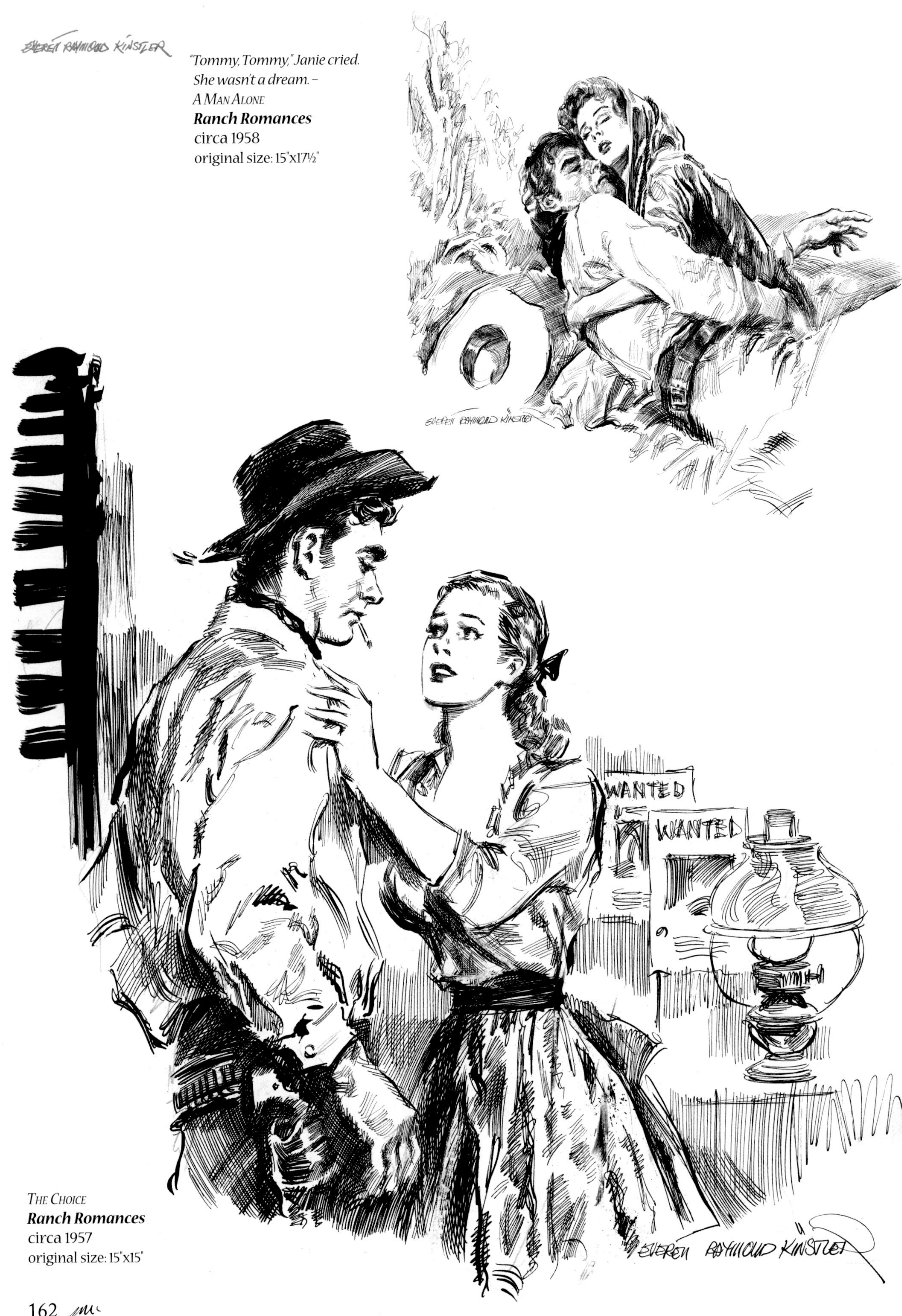

"Tommy, Tommy," Janie cried.
She wasn't a dream. –
A Man Alone
Ranch Romances
circa 1958
original size: 15"x17½"

The Choice
Ranch Romances
circa 1957
original size: 15"x15"

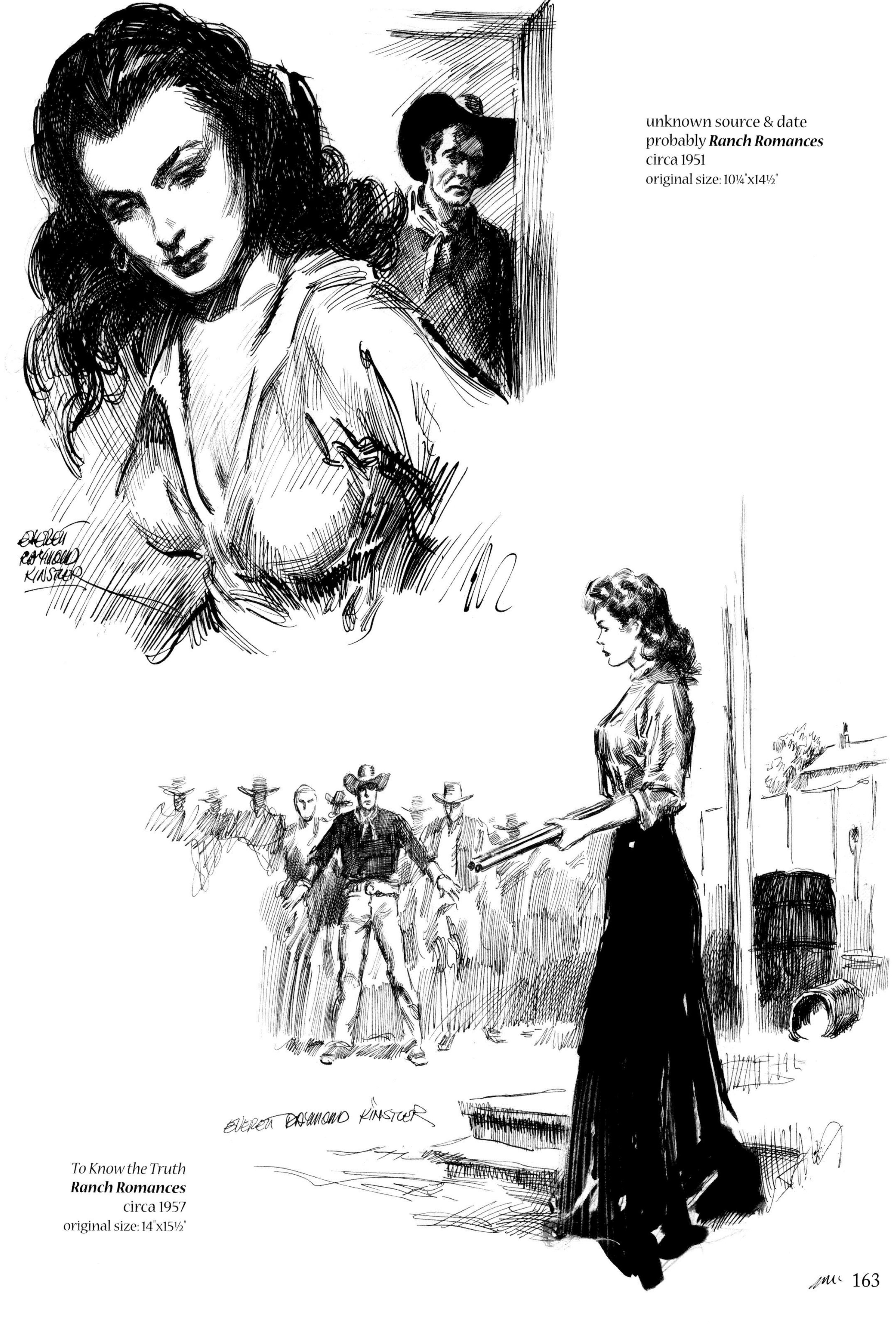

unknown source & date
probably ***Ranch Romances***
circa 1951
original size: 10¼"x14½"

To Know the Truth
Ranch Romances
circa 1957
original size: 14"x15½"

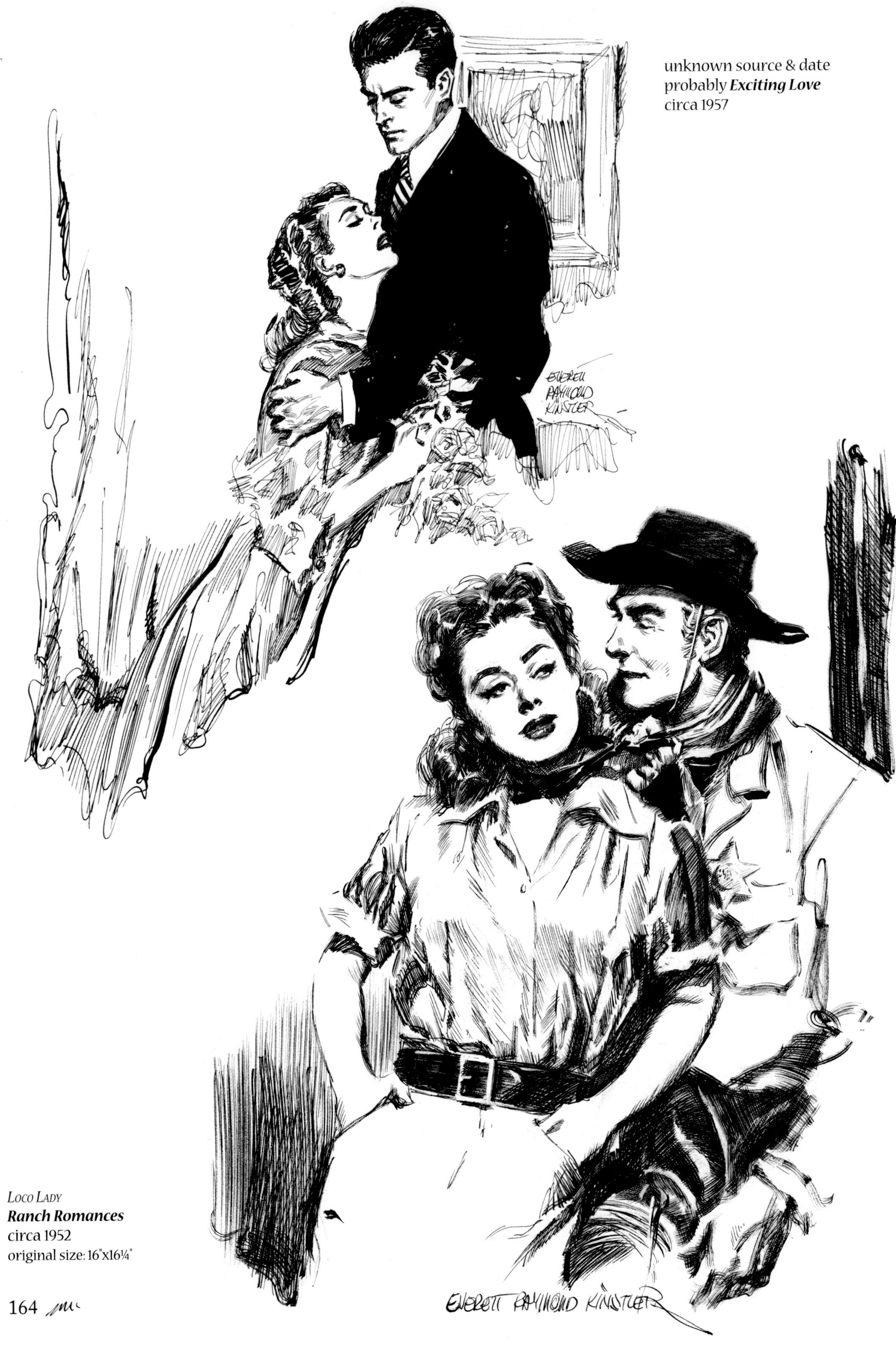

unknown source & date
probably ***Exciting Love***
circa 1957

Loco Lady
Ranch Romances
circa 1952
original size: 16"x16¼"

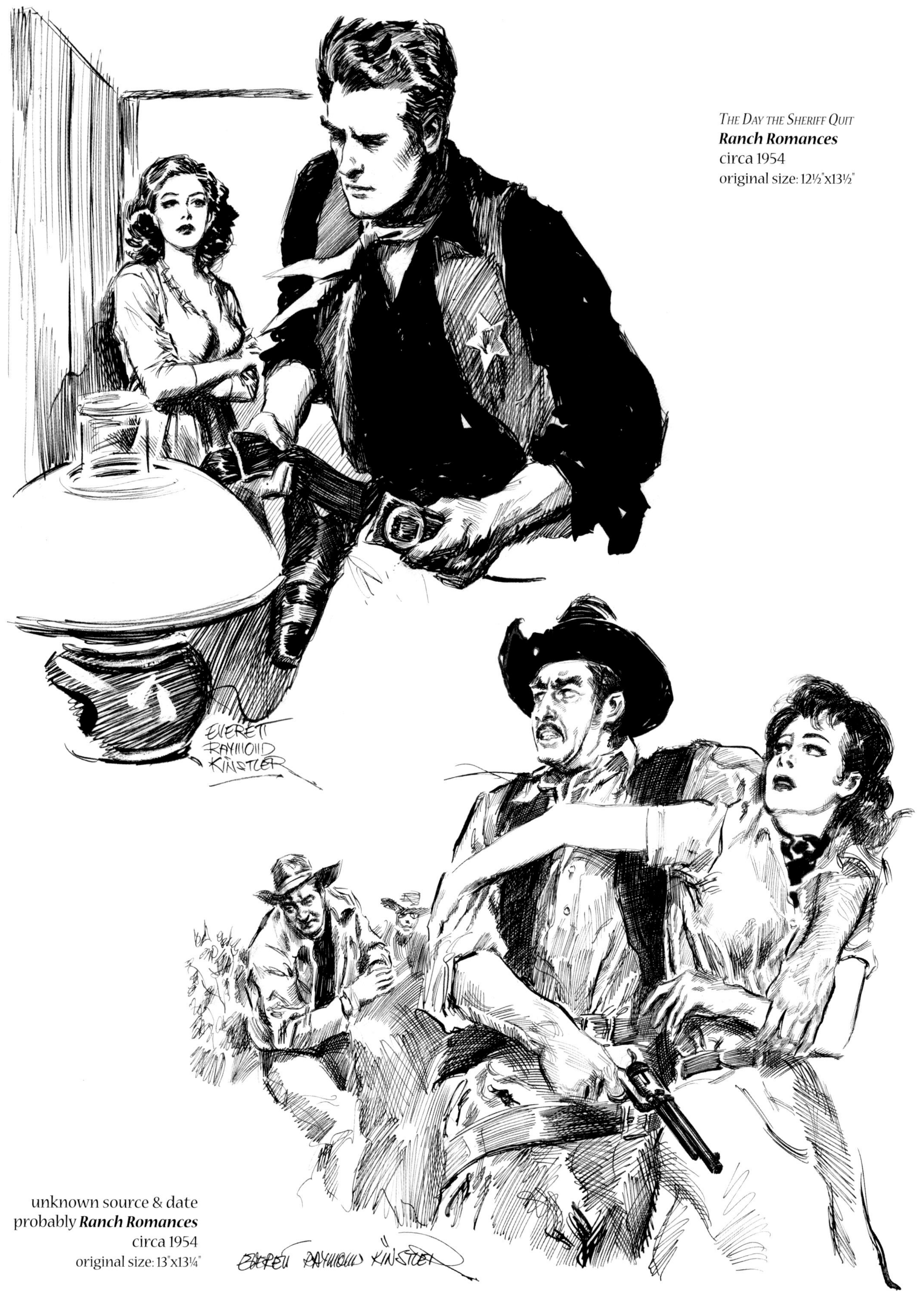

The Day the Sheriff Quit
Ranch Romances
circa 1954
original size: 12½"x13½"

unknown source & date
probably ***Ranch Romances***
circa 1954
original size: 13"x13¼"

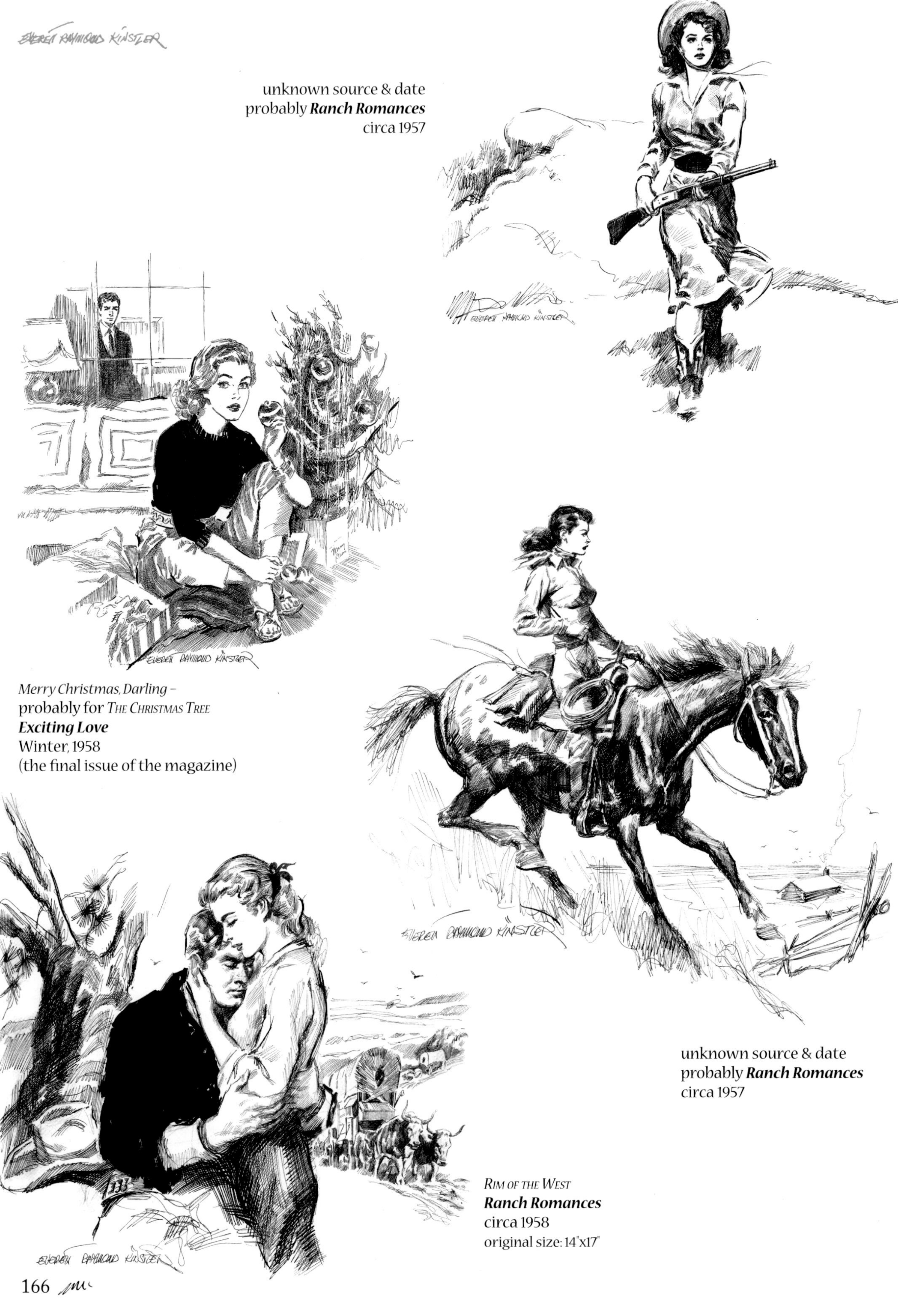

unknown source & date
probably ***Ranch Romances***
circa 1957

Merry Christmas, Darling –
probably for *The Christmas Tree*
Exciting Love
Winter, 1958
(the final issue of the magazine)

unknown source & date
probably ***Ranch Romances***
circa 1957

Rim of the West
Ranch Romances
circa 1958
original size: 14"x17"

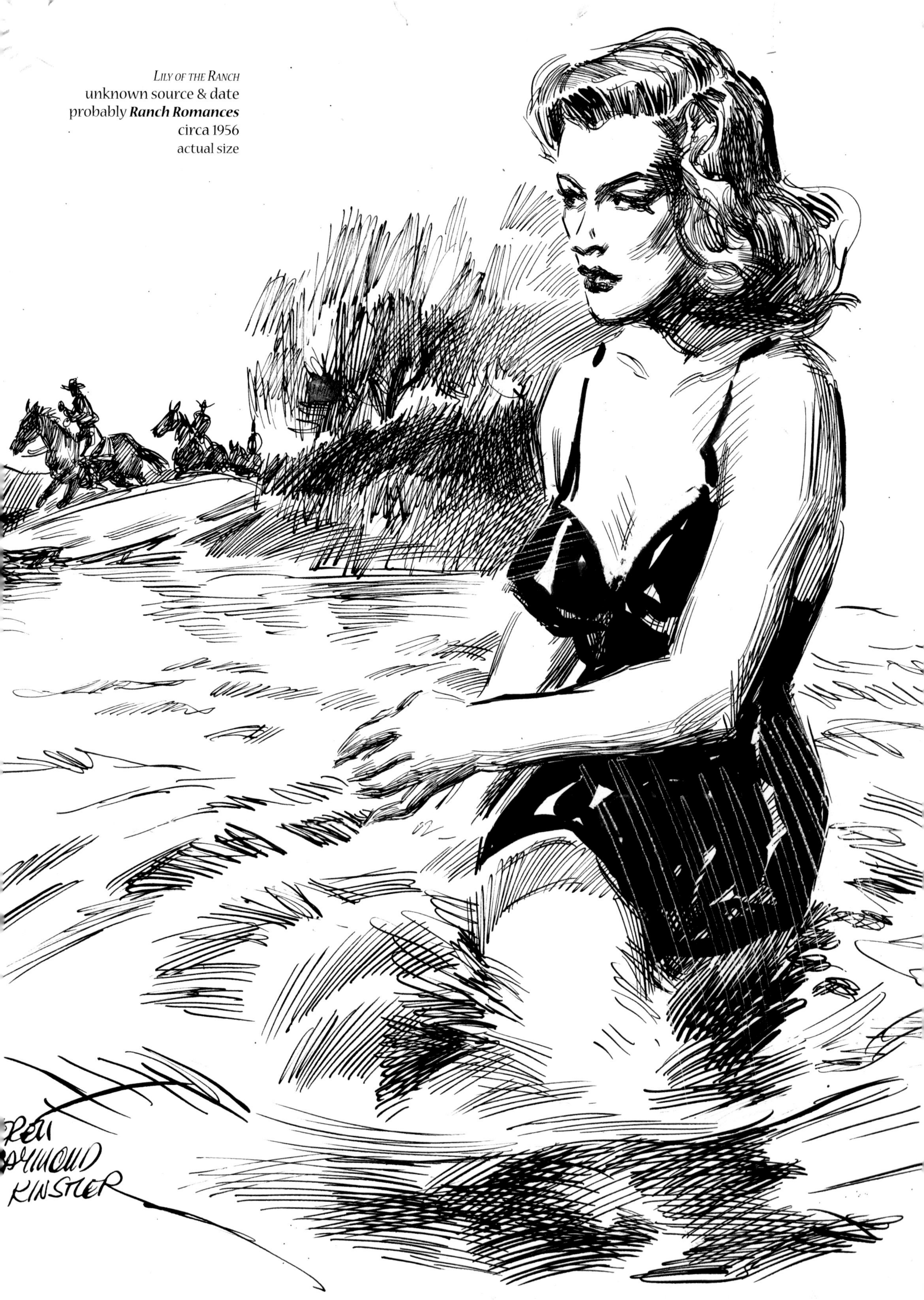

Lily of the Ranch
unknown source & date
probably ***Ranch Romances***
circa 1956
actual size

Cantankerous Woman
probably ***Ranch Romances***
circa 1955
original size: 15½"x15"

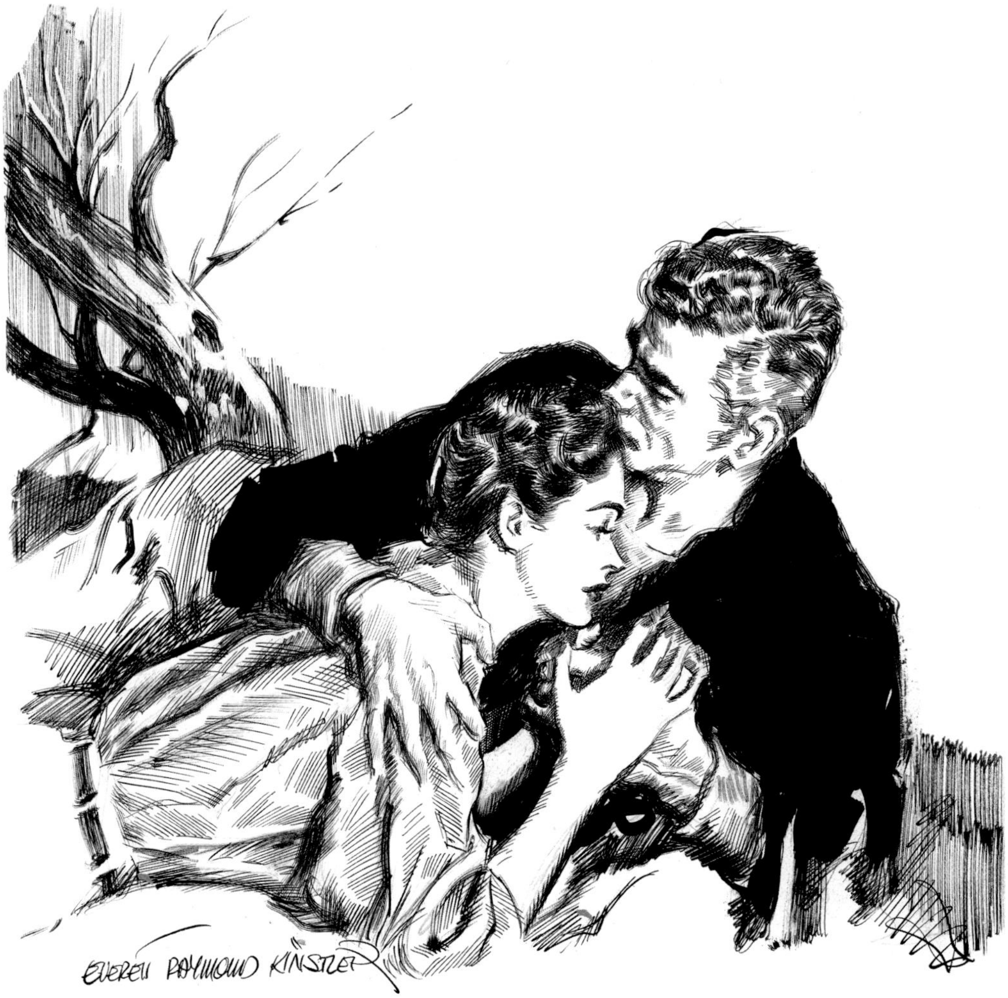

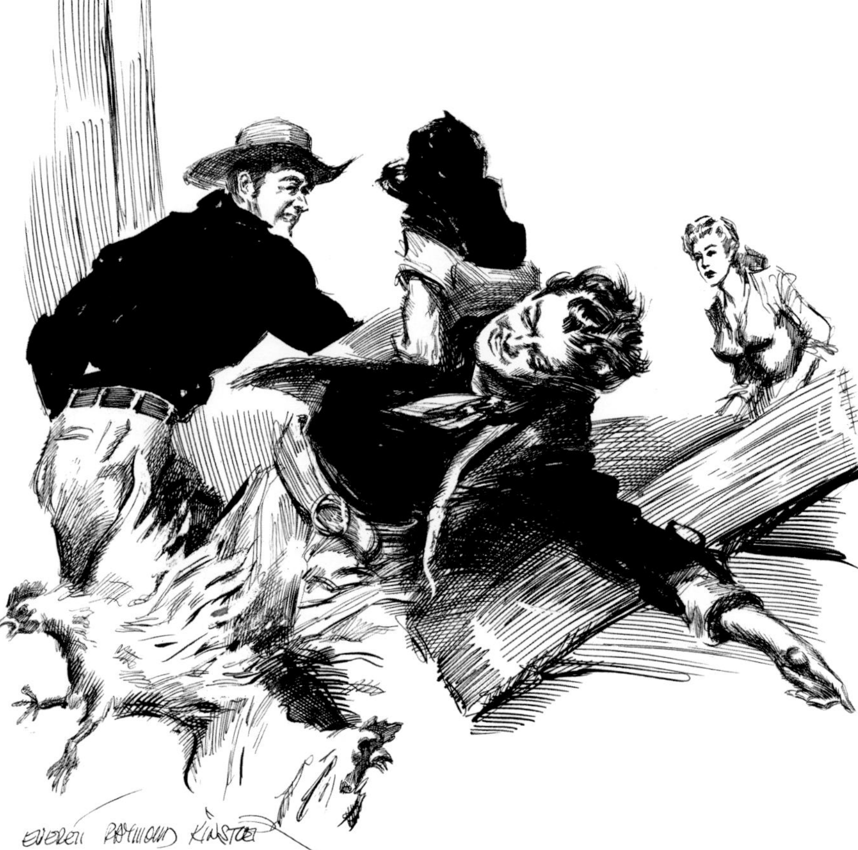

Showdown at Battle River
Ranch Romances
circa 1954
original size: 12½"x13½"

books
1954 TO 1962

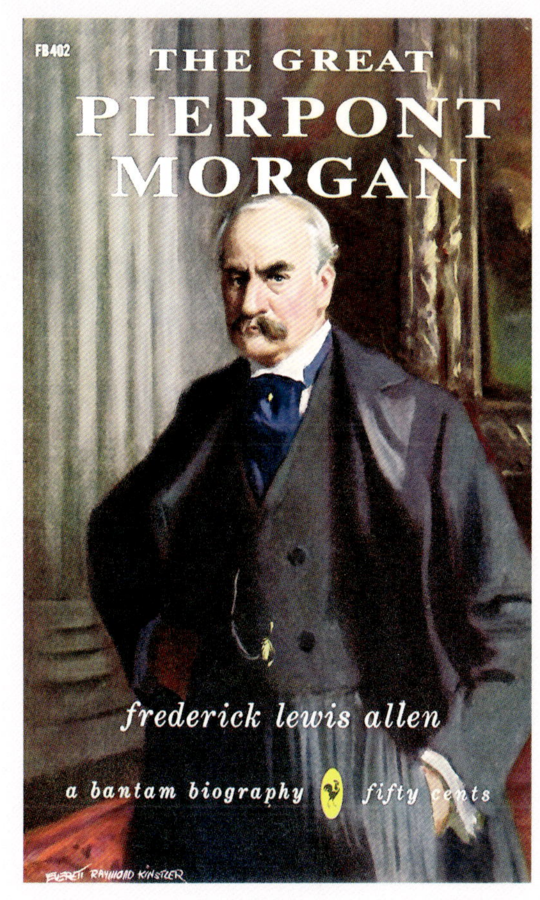

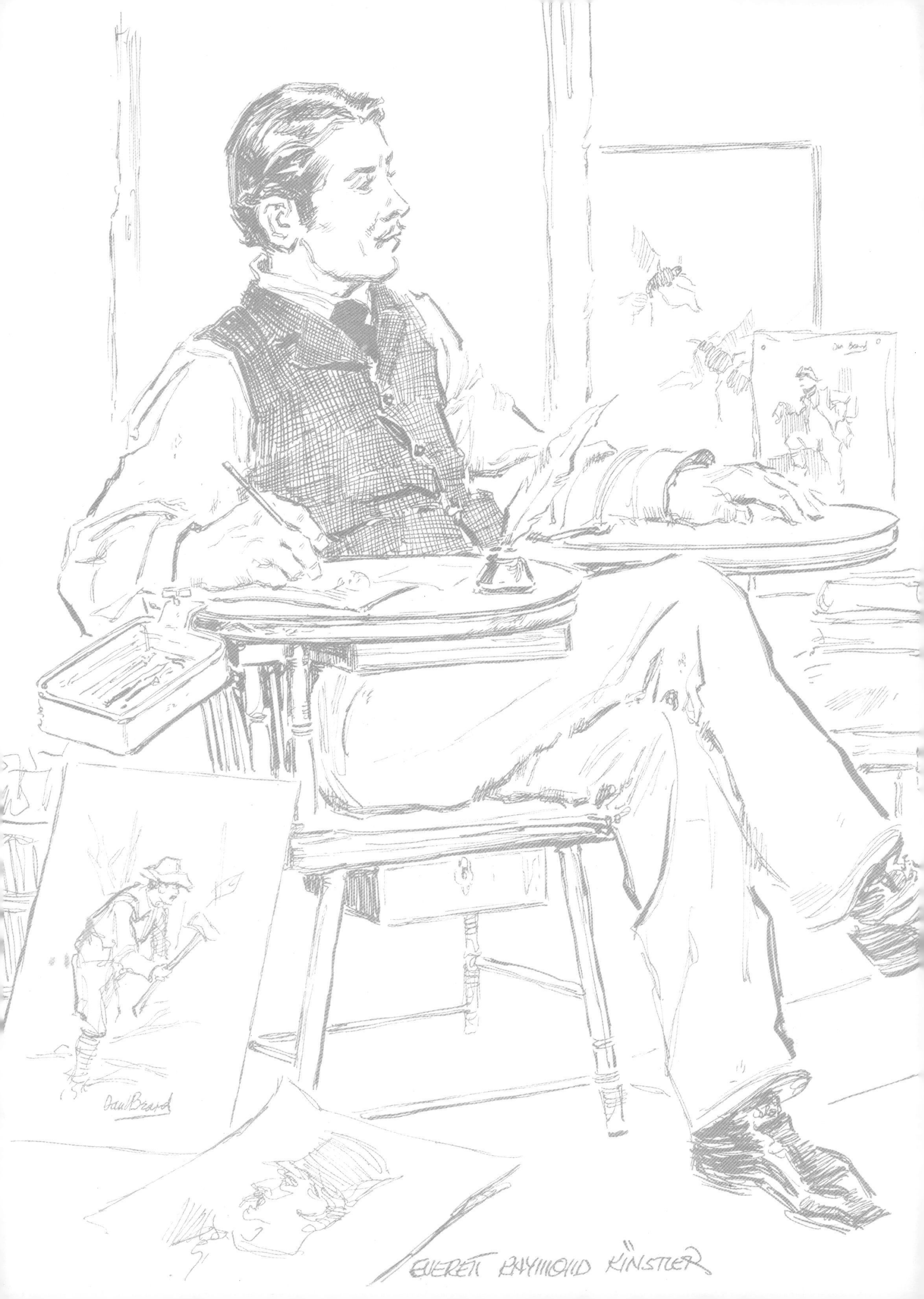
Dan Beard
Dan Beard
EVERETT RAYMOND KINSTLER

...sales were higher for those books with the most lurid covers.

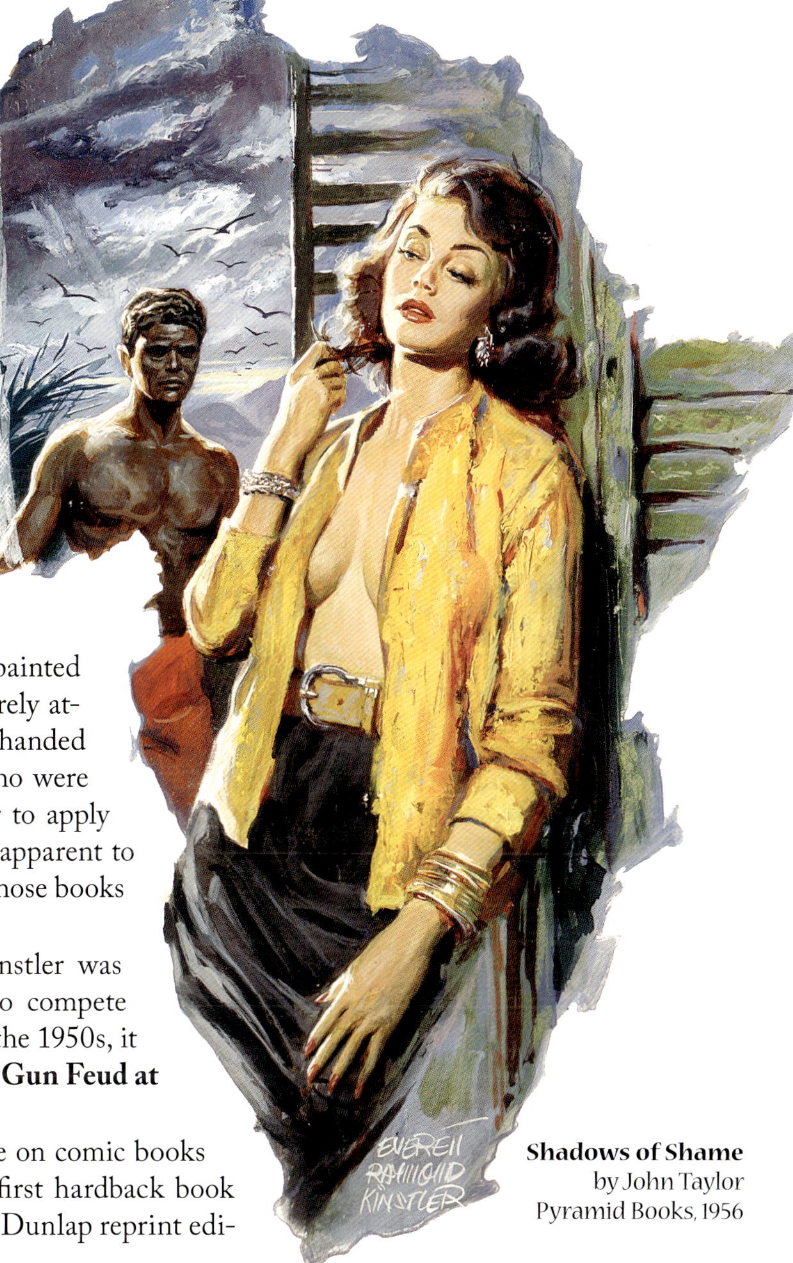

Shadows of Shame
by John Taylor
Pyramid Books, 1956

In the 1940s, the paperback book phenomenon exploded. The inexpensive format was originated in the U.S. by Pocket Books in 1939 and became a wartime wonder. Paperbacks were easy to carry, easy to store and, best of all, only twenty-five cents. They quickly replaced the "cheap edition" hardbacks that were published by such companies as A.L. Burt and Grosset and Dunlap and which sold for one dollar.

In lieu of dustwrappers, paperbacks sported painted covers. Unlike pulp covers, these remained securely attached, so the book could be read, reread and handed on to additional readers. Publishers of pulps, who were quick to embrace the new format, were quicker to apply pulpish sensibilities to these covers. It was soon apparent to the fledgling industry that sales were higher for those books with the most lurid covers.

Avon, the comic company with which Kinstler was most associated, was the first U.S. company to compete with Pocket Books in the paperback market. By the 1950s, it was a major force. Ray's first cover for Avon was **Gun Feud at Stampede Valley** in 1954.

Kinstler, whose first published paintings were on comic books and then on pulp covers, managed to land his first hardback book assignment for the dustwrapper of a Grosset and Dunlap reprint edition of Zane Grey's **Riders of the Purple Sage**.

As the paperback market shifted emphasis (it's tempting to say "matured" but that obviously had *yet* to happen), Kinstler sought work in the growing "young adult" book industry, painting and drawing covers for a cross-section of that market.

In some few instances, he was also commissioned to draw interior illustrations. His work can be found in the pages of such titles as **The Story of Dan Beard** and **Verdi** and appreciators of his pen and ink drawings would do well to seek these out.

His book work extended into 1963 in a few instances, but by then Everett Raymond Kinstler was primarily a painter of portraits.

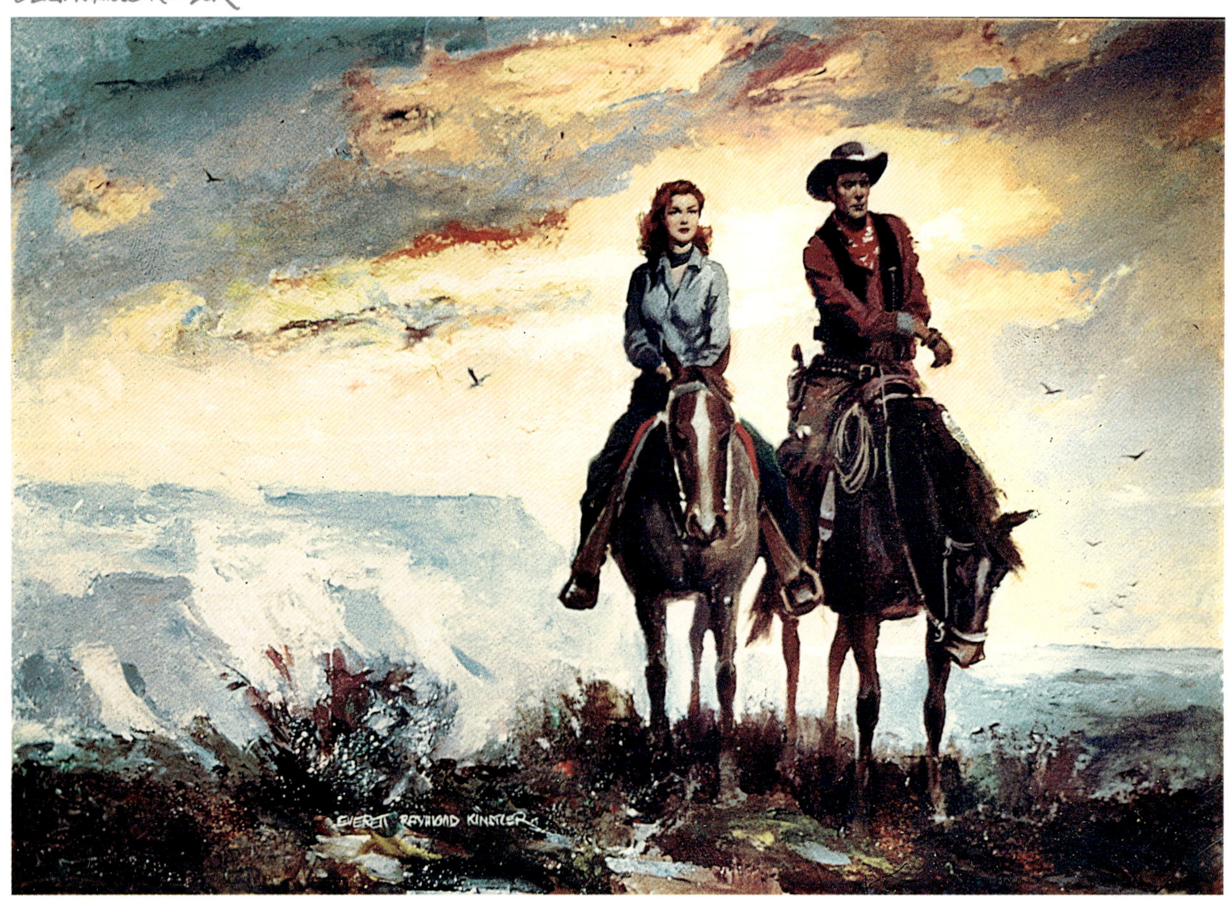

First dustwrapper painting
Riders of the Purple Sage
Grosset and Dunlap, circa 1954

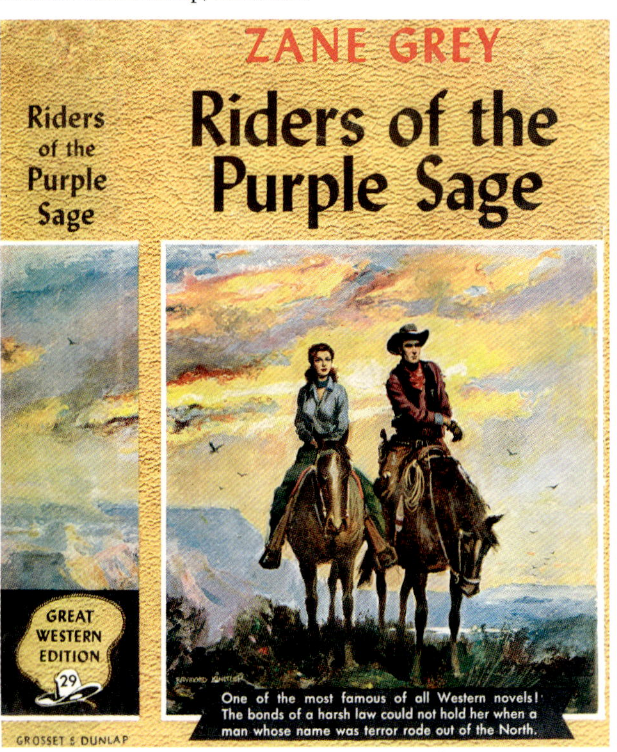

First paperback book cover
Avon Books, 1954

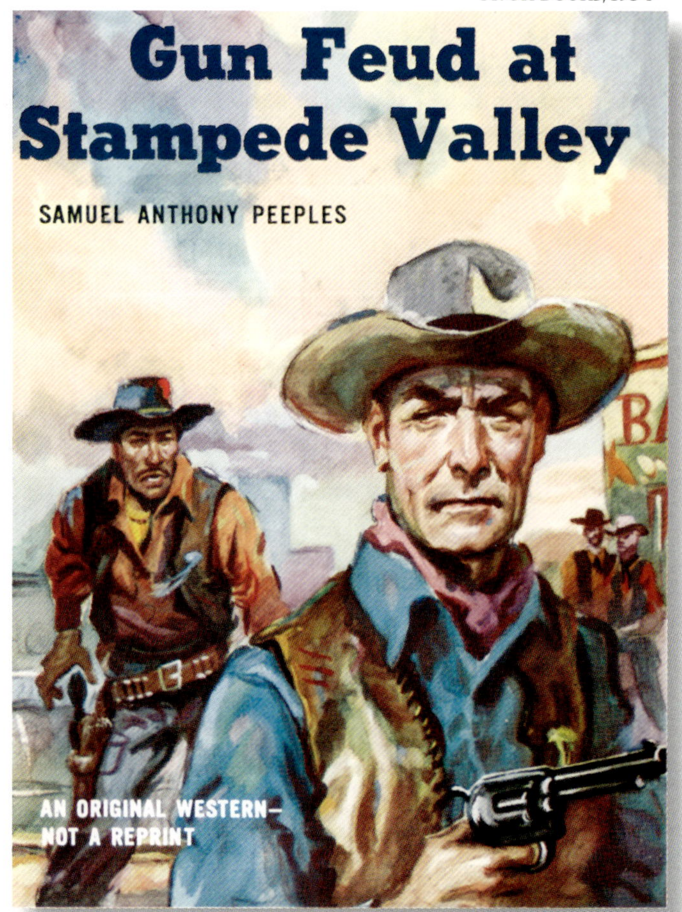

Avon

Kinstler painted covers for Avon paperbacks from 1954 to 1958. He broke into the market when the comic book industry was retrenching, reprinting and reducing the number of titles they published.

While he continued to draw covers for Sol Cohen's Avon comic book line, he gradually increased his newsstand presence by painting covers for Charlie Byrnes at Avon's paperback division.

Avon Books, 1955

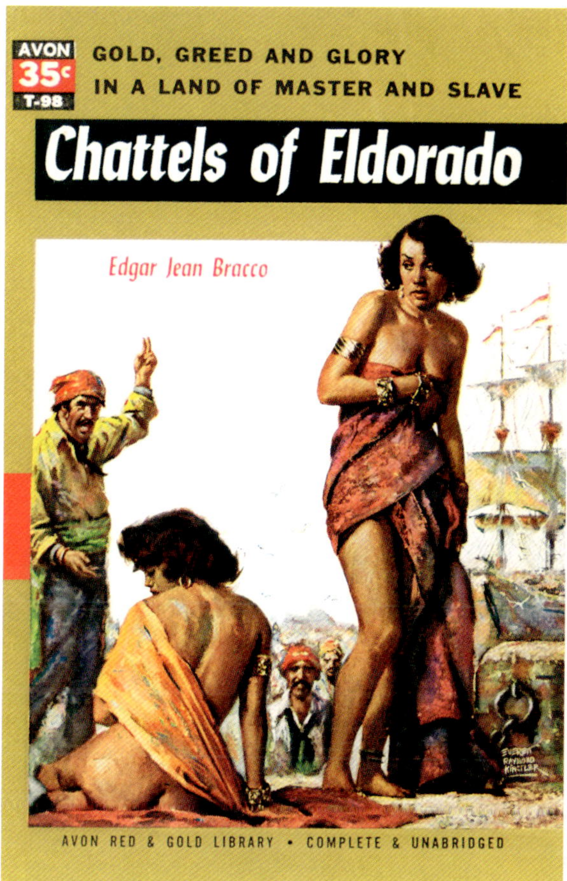

Avon Books, 1956

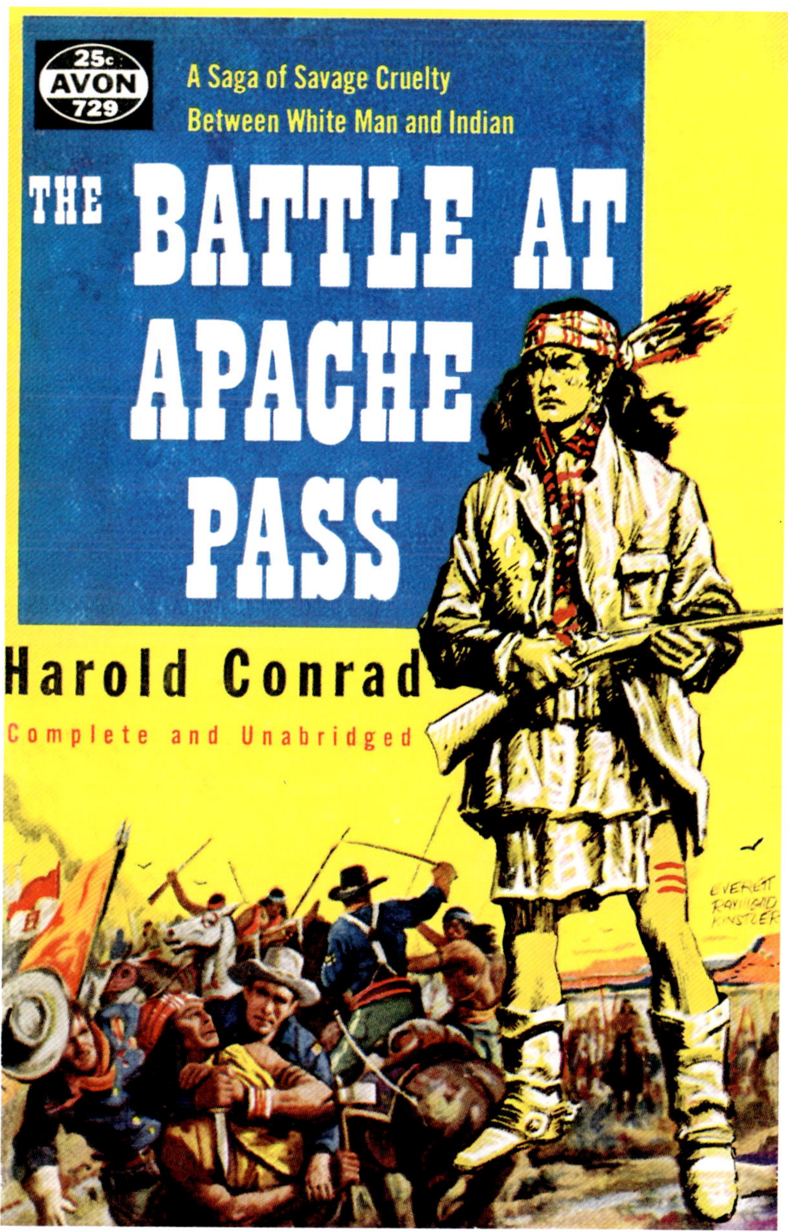

For this painted cover on Avon's **Gun Feud at Stampede Valley**, the art director insisted that I add the hand at the lower right with the gun.

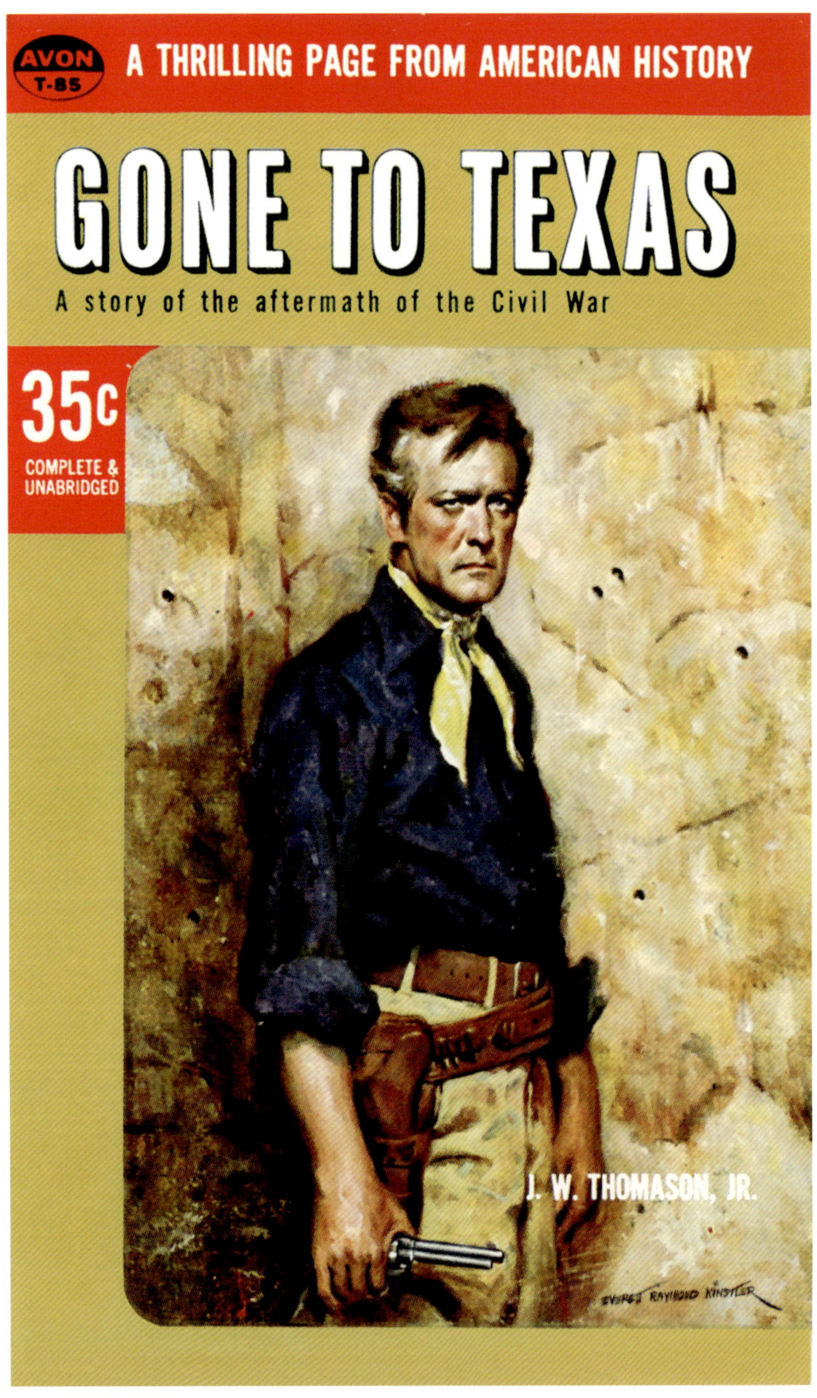

Avon Books, 1954

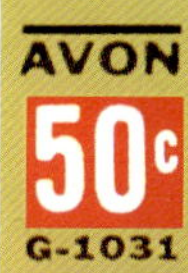

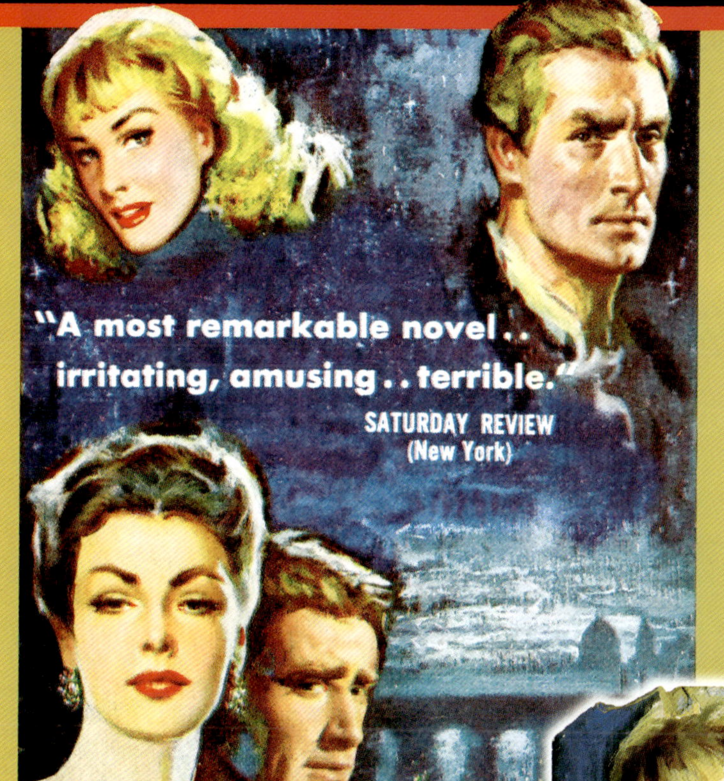

Avon Books, 1957

revised original

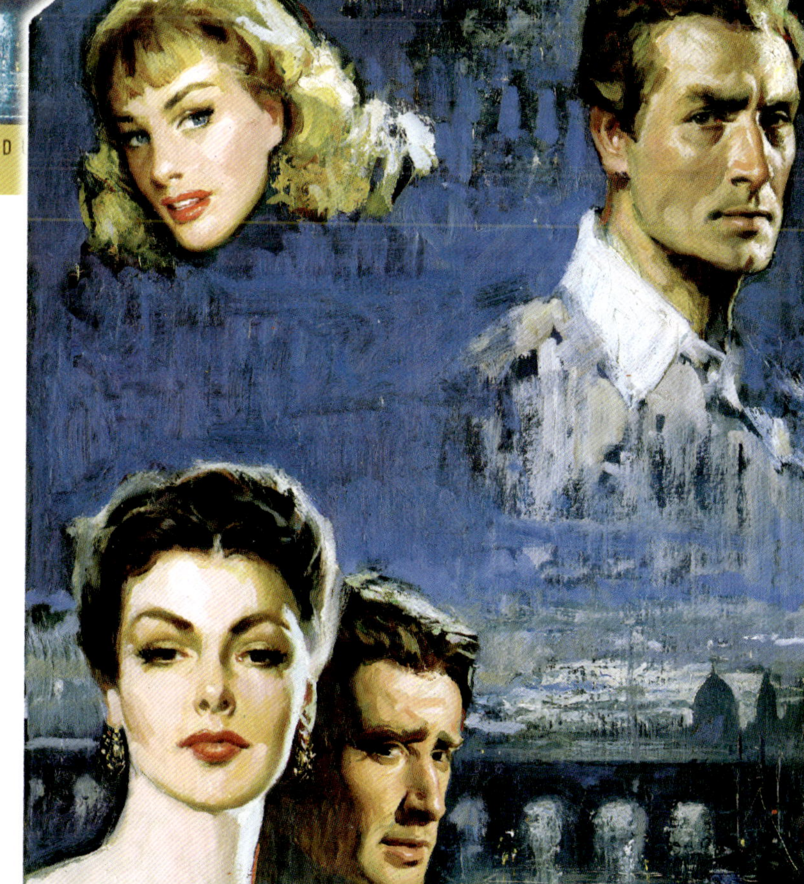

Avon Books, 1955

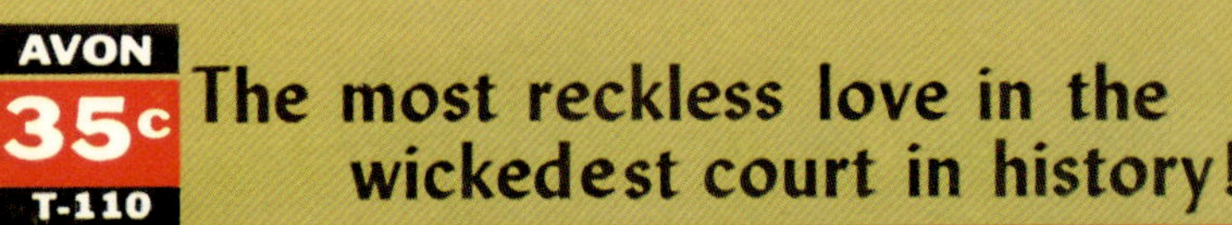

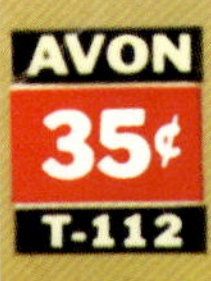

Avon Books, 1955

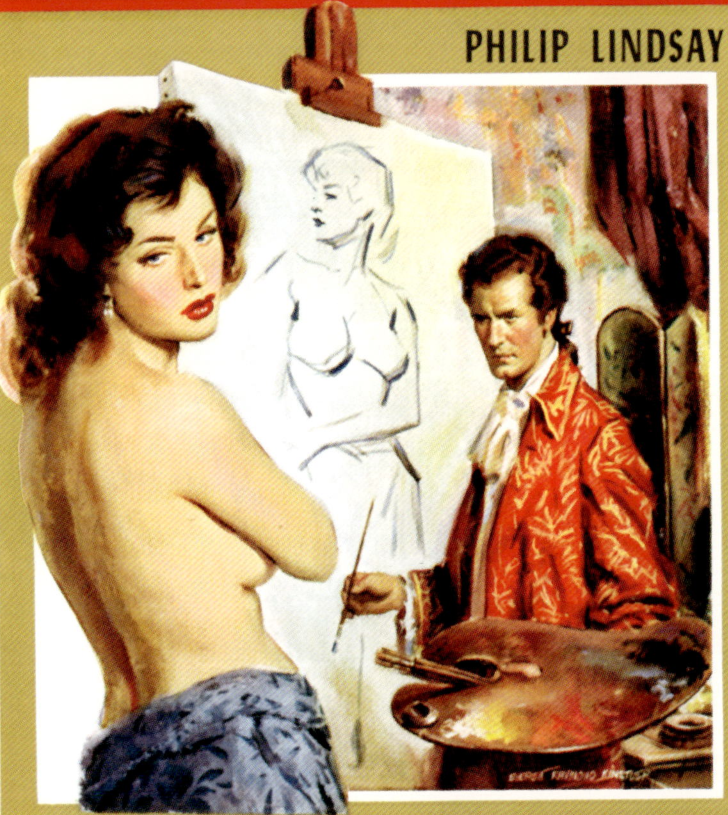

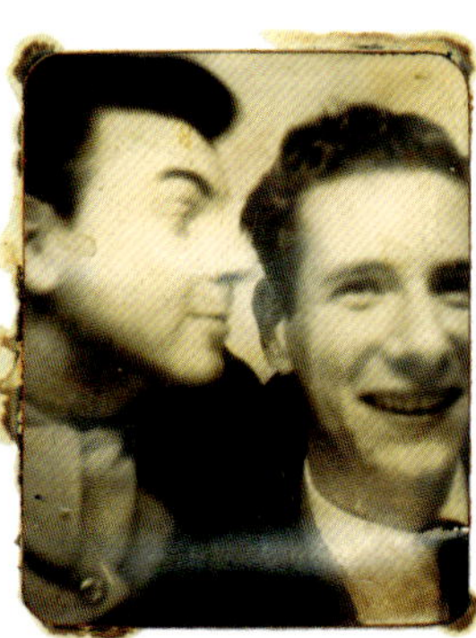

Ray and his boyhood chum Bob Brustein, who modeled for **Artist in Love** and **Royal Scandal**

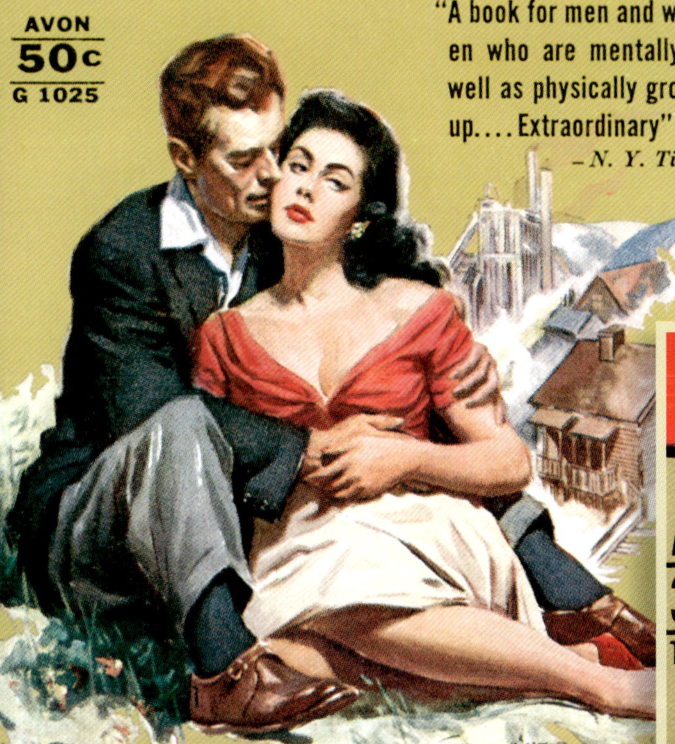

Avon Books, 1956

Avon Books, 1956

W. SOMERSET MAUGHAM
ASHENDEN or THE BRITISH AGENT
AVON
35c
T-119
The World's Greatest Novel of Spies and Espionage
AN AVON RED AND GOLD EDITION · COMPLETE AND UNABRIDGED

Avon Books, 1955

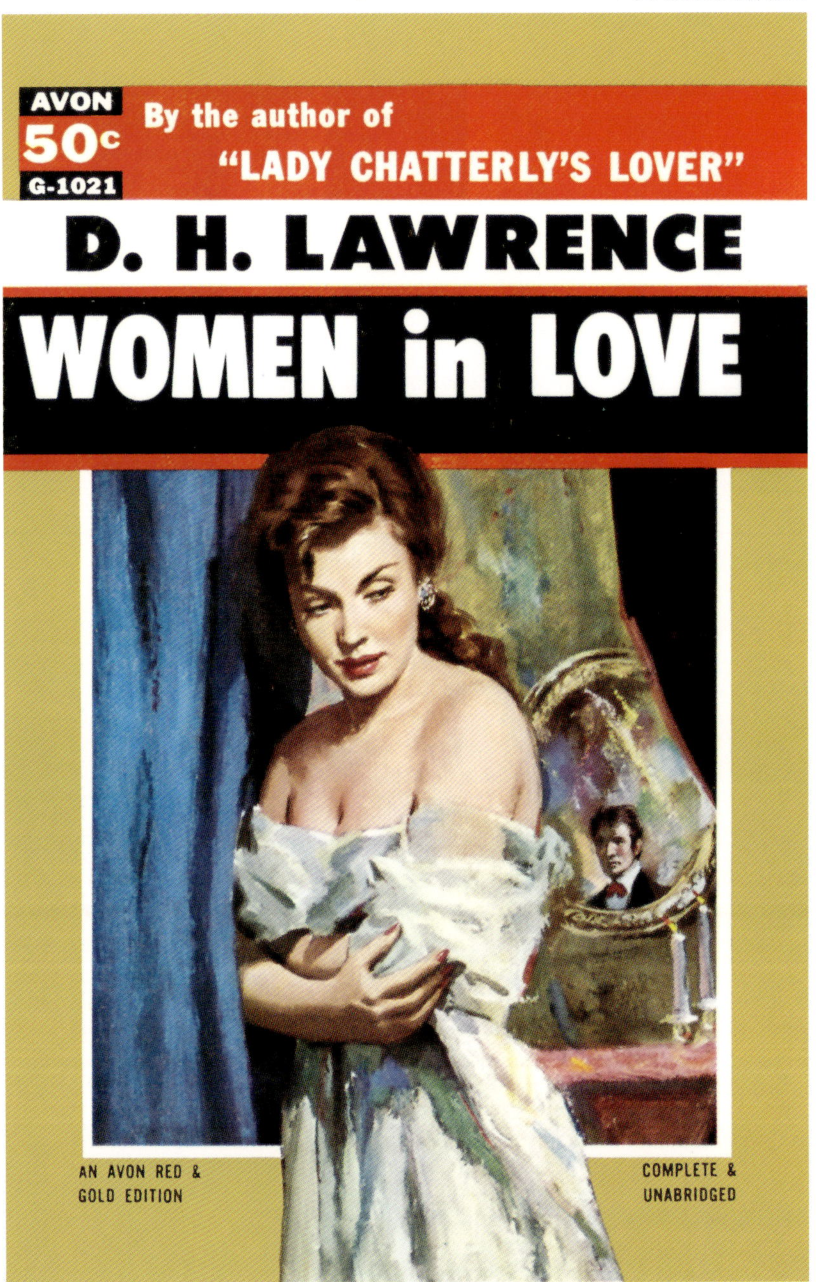

This was a rare occasion where the cleavage dipped a little too far for the Avon art director, Charlie Byrnes. When Ray got the artwork back for **Women in Love**, he restored the décolletage to his original version as seen at right.

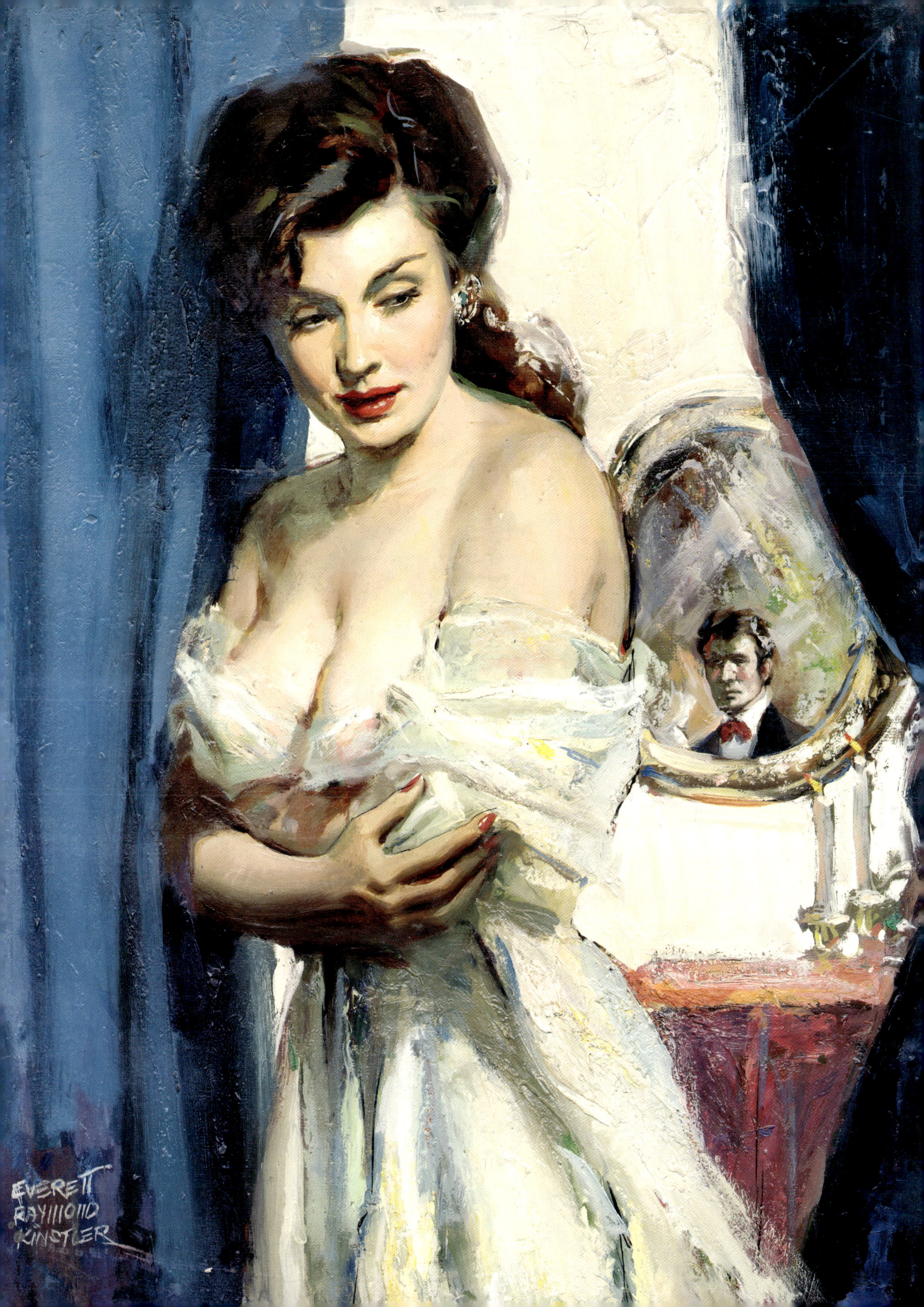
EVERETT
RAYMOND
KINSTLER

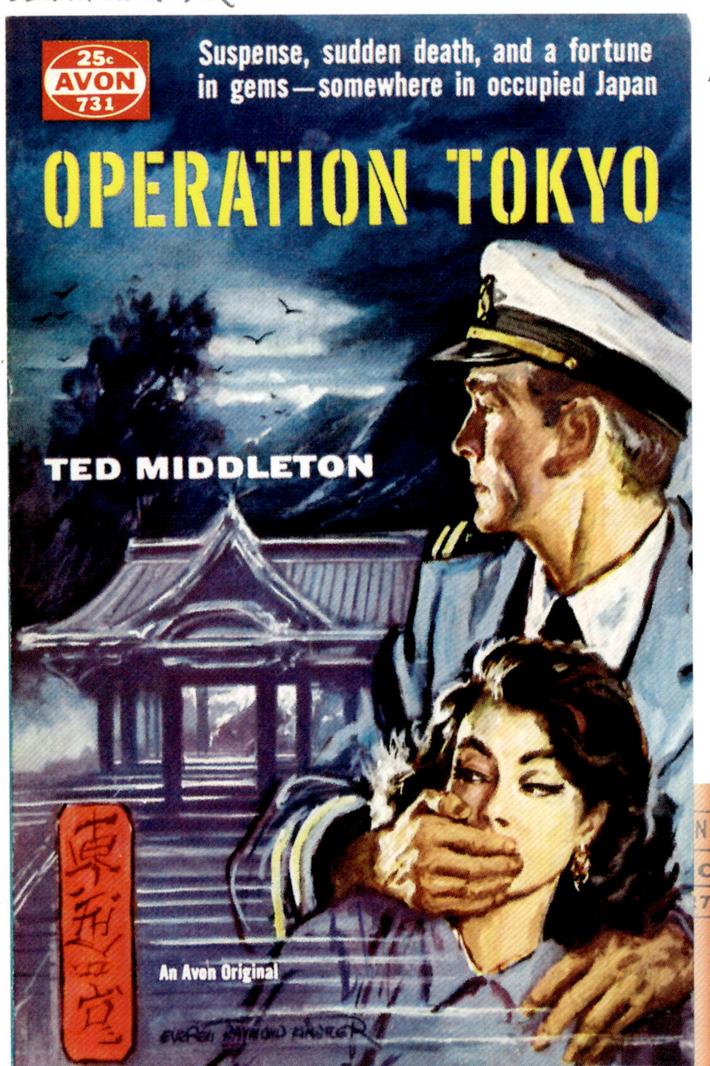

Avon Books, 1956

Avon Books, 1954

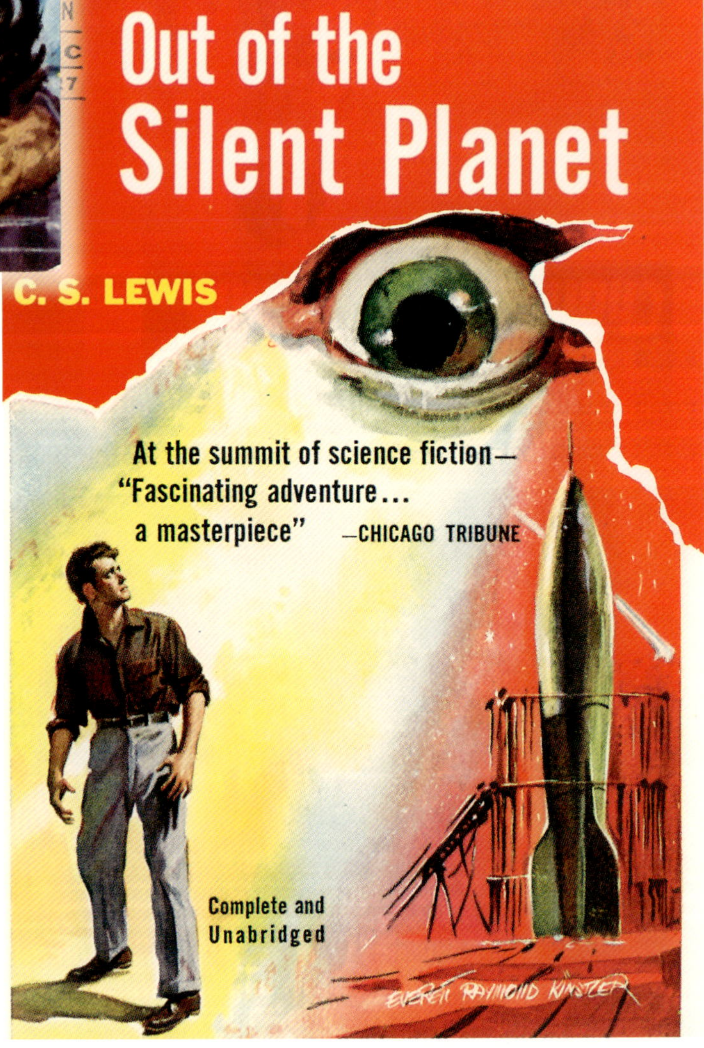

Noah Gordon was an assistant editor in Avon's periodicals division when Ray was given the cover assignment for **Out of the Silent Planet**.

Noah recalls: "He had me pose for the cover of **Out of the Silent Planet**, both shirtless and wearing a shirt. In those days I was a skinny kid and Everett buffed up my musculature nicely in the images; Brad Pitt never got into fighting shape so easily!

"It was clear to me even then that Ray was an artist who would be heard from in a major way. Now and then we would get together socially. I used to like to go to his studio at the National Arts Club if there was a problem with a script; we would drink his brandy and talk about everything."

Avon Books, 1956

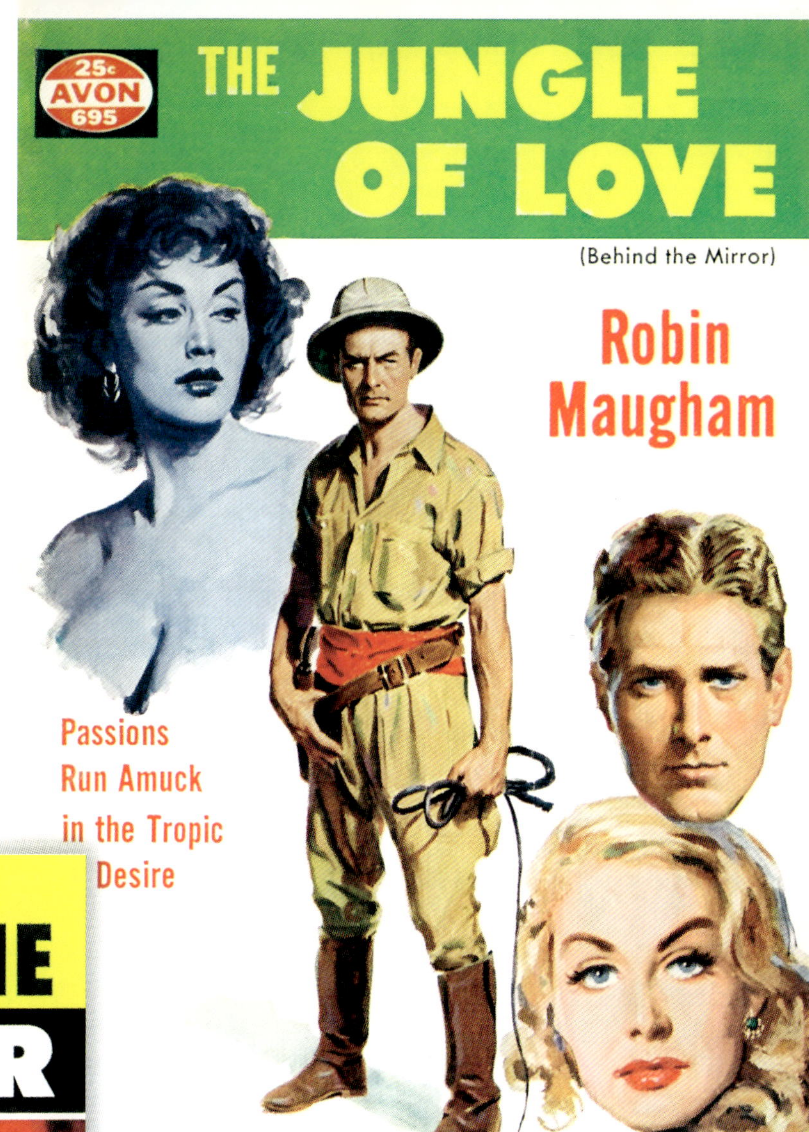

Avon Books, 1956

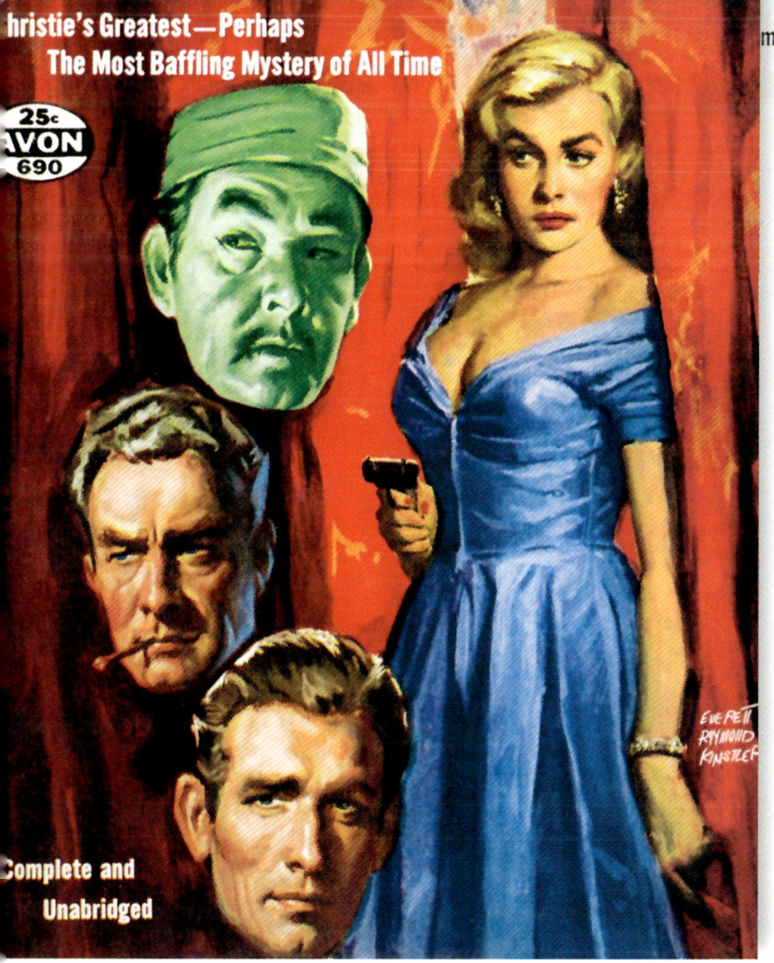

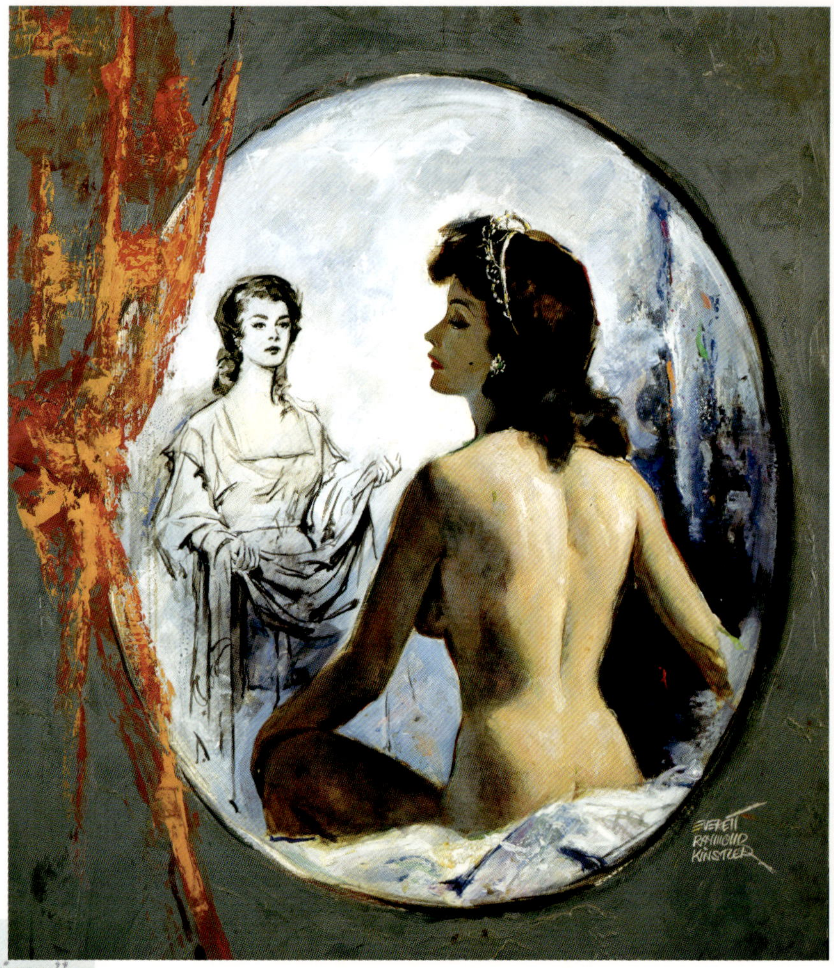

Avon Books, 1957

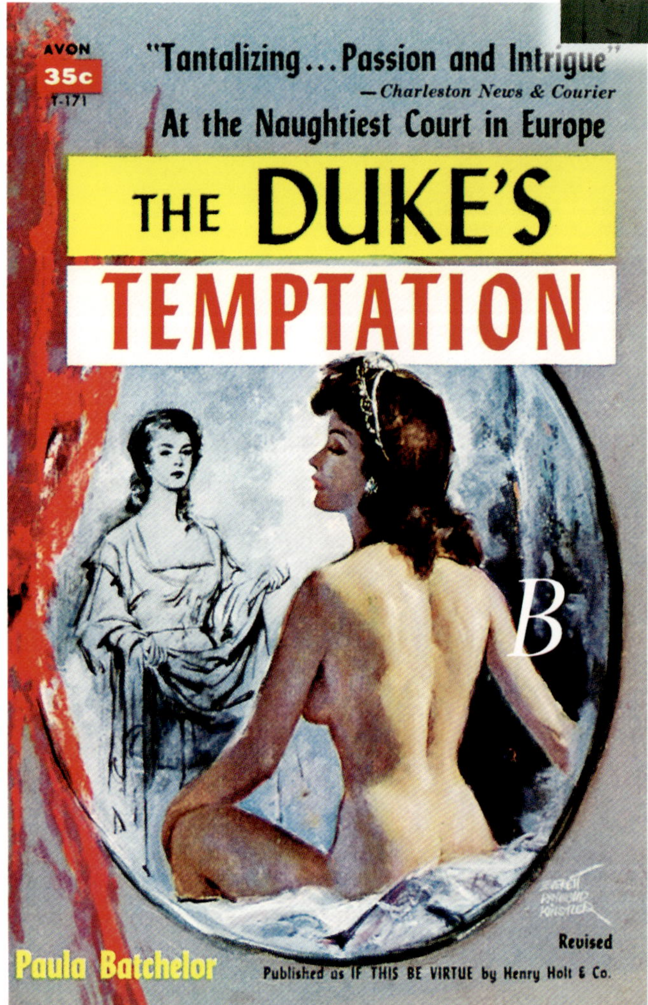

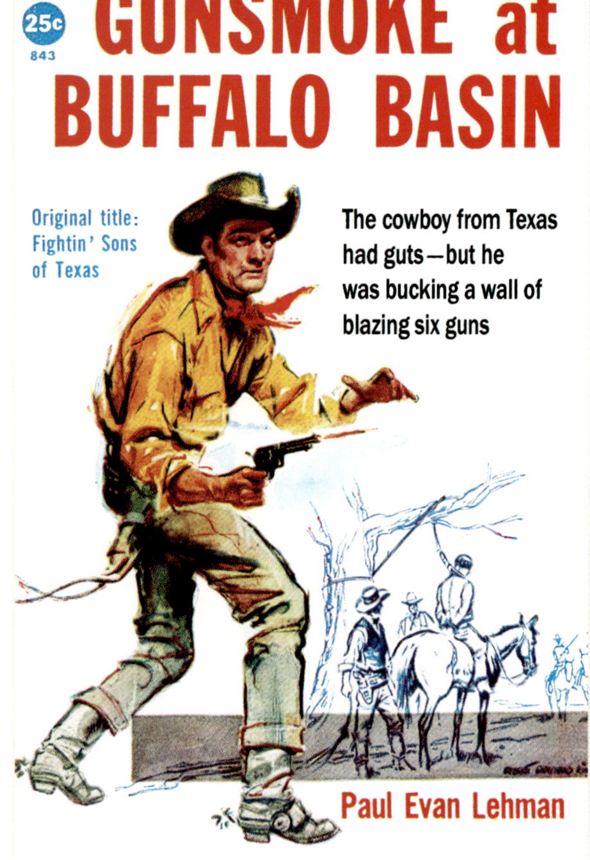

Avon Books, 1958

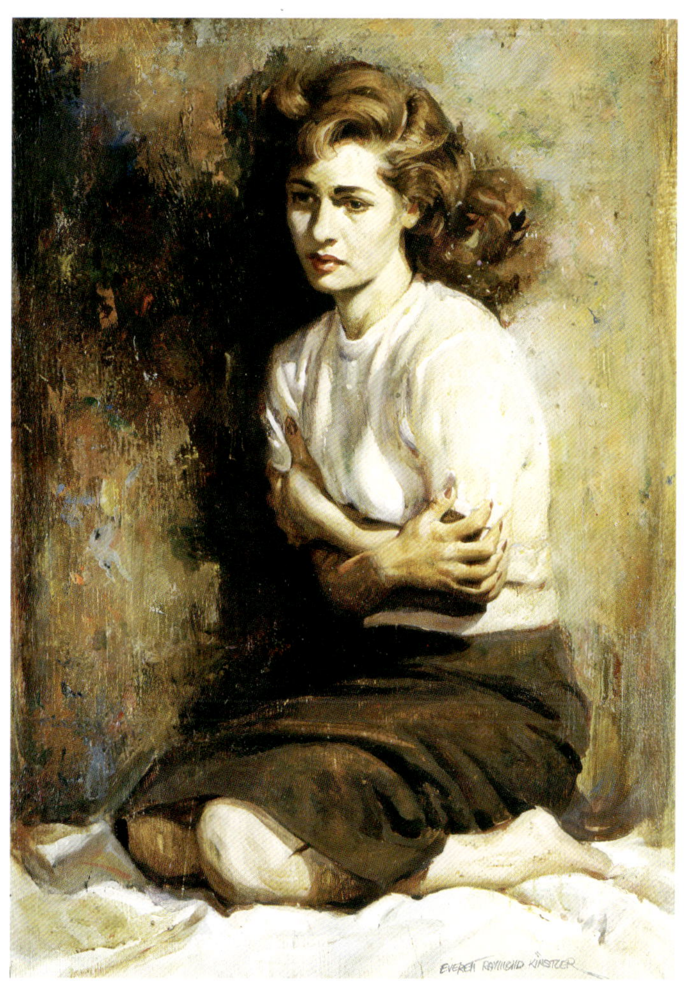

This was a sample cover for a Bantam Books art director. He gave me a black and white photograph and asked me to paint it. I think this led to his commissioning me to paint **The Great Pierpont Morgan** cover.

Bantam Books, 1956

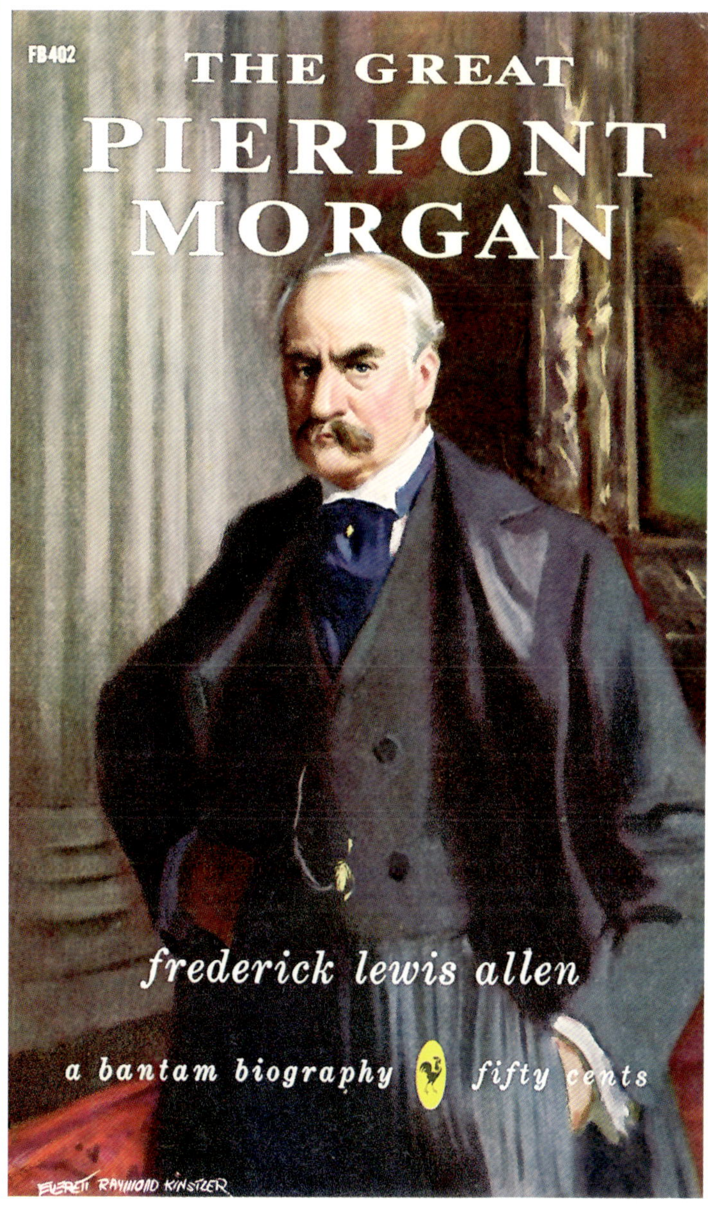

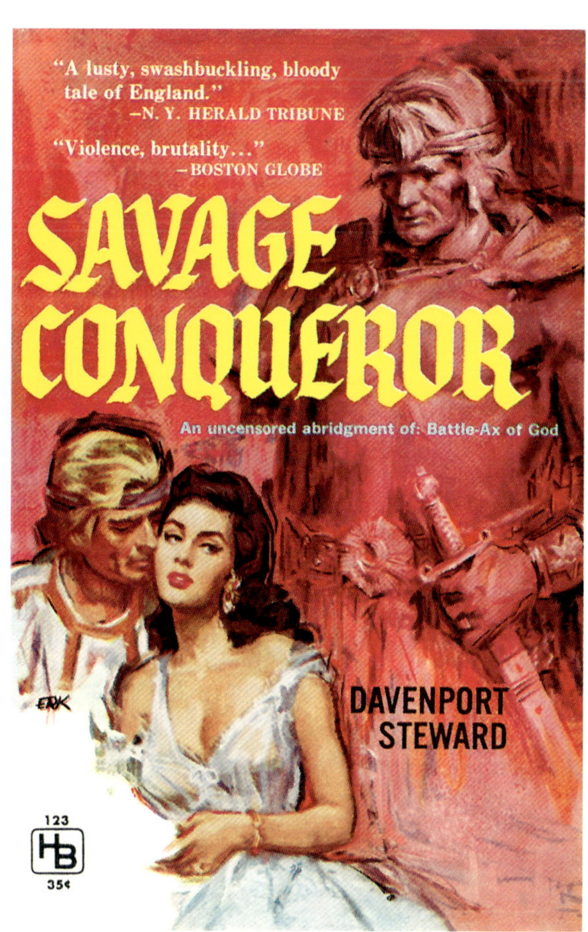

Hillman Books, 1959

Magazines, McCarthy, and more...

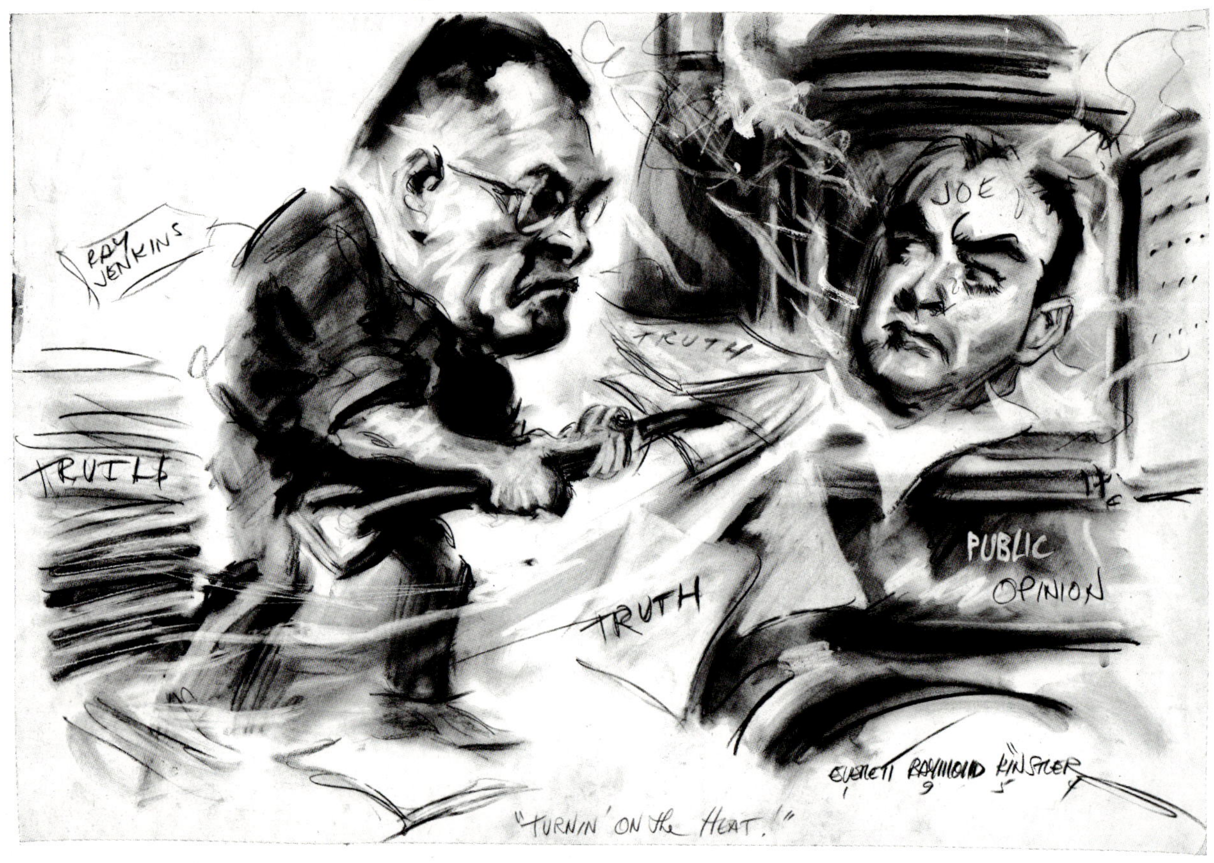

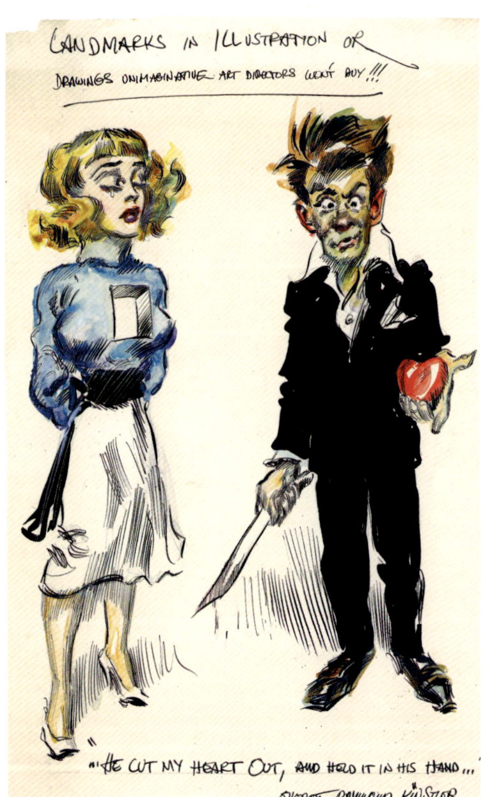

Like every other freelance illustrator, Kinstler looked for jobs in every available market. He explored all possibilities: from cartoons, both political and humorous, to the program covers of local theaters.

Often there would be one or two sales and then he would focus back upon the more familiar comic books or pulps. He did one ***Bluebook*** illustration, three illustrations for Martin Goodman's men's magazines, two LP sleeves for Columbia Records and though his files contain the atypical illustrations at left and above, there is no indication that they were sold or printed.

October, 1956

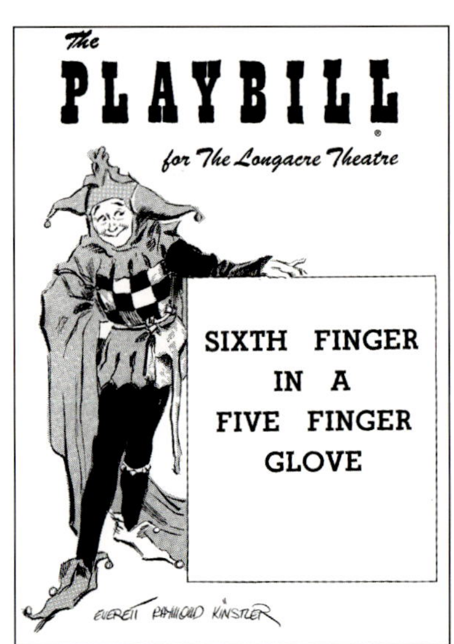

Although Ray only had this one tearsheet of his sole *Bluebook Magazine* illustration, he didn't hesitate to make his disappointment with the magazine's art director evident.

Kinstler's artwork had included an overlay for the traditional blue color they used for their illustrations, but the tones he had indicated for the face were eliminated. On this printed copy, Ray carefully brushed them back in, as the mismatched colors at right attest.

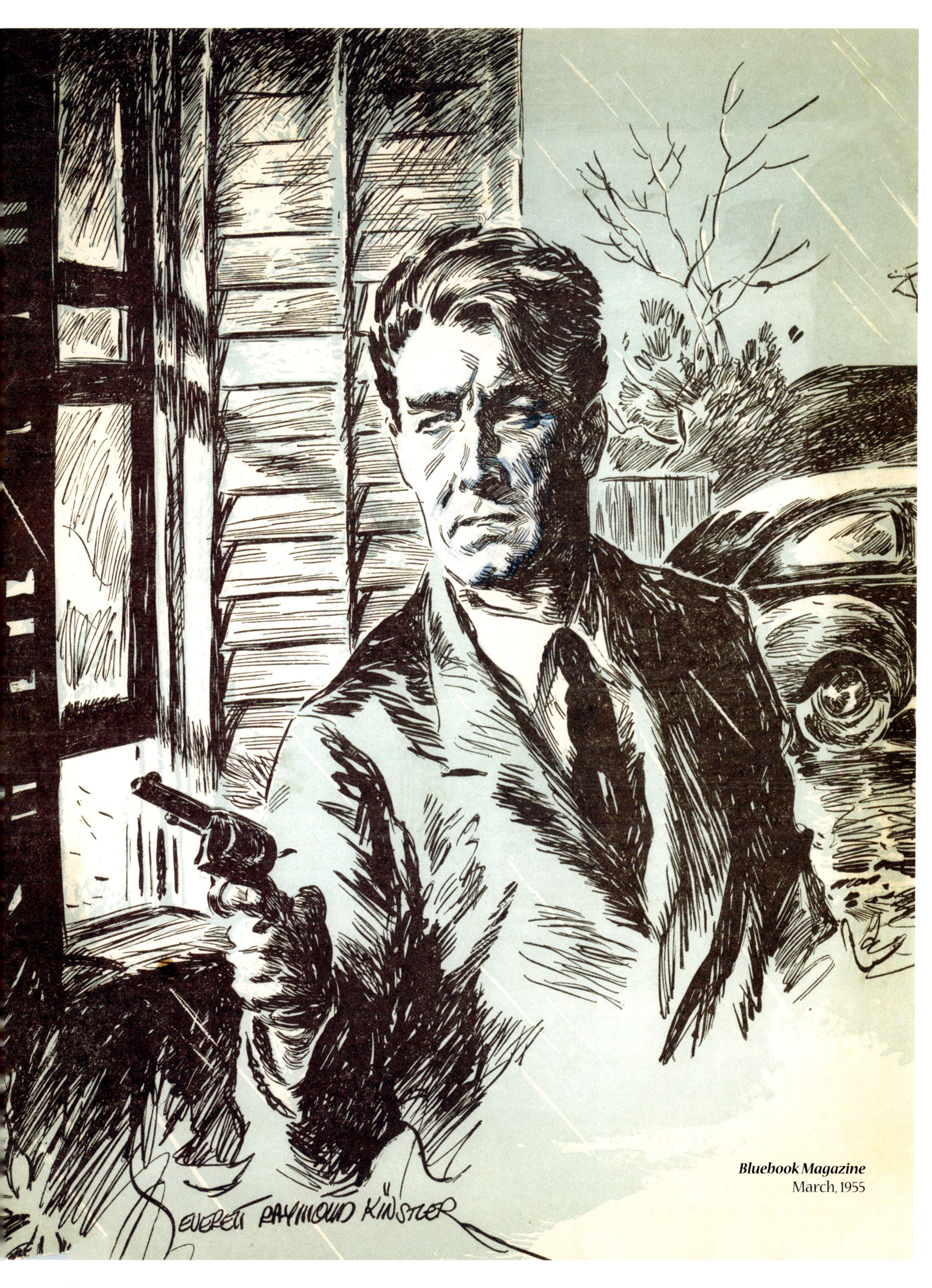

Bluebook Magazine
March, 1955

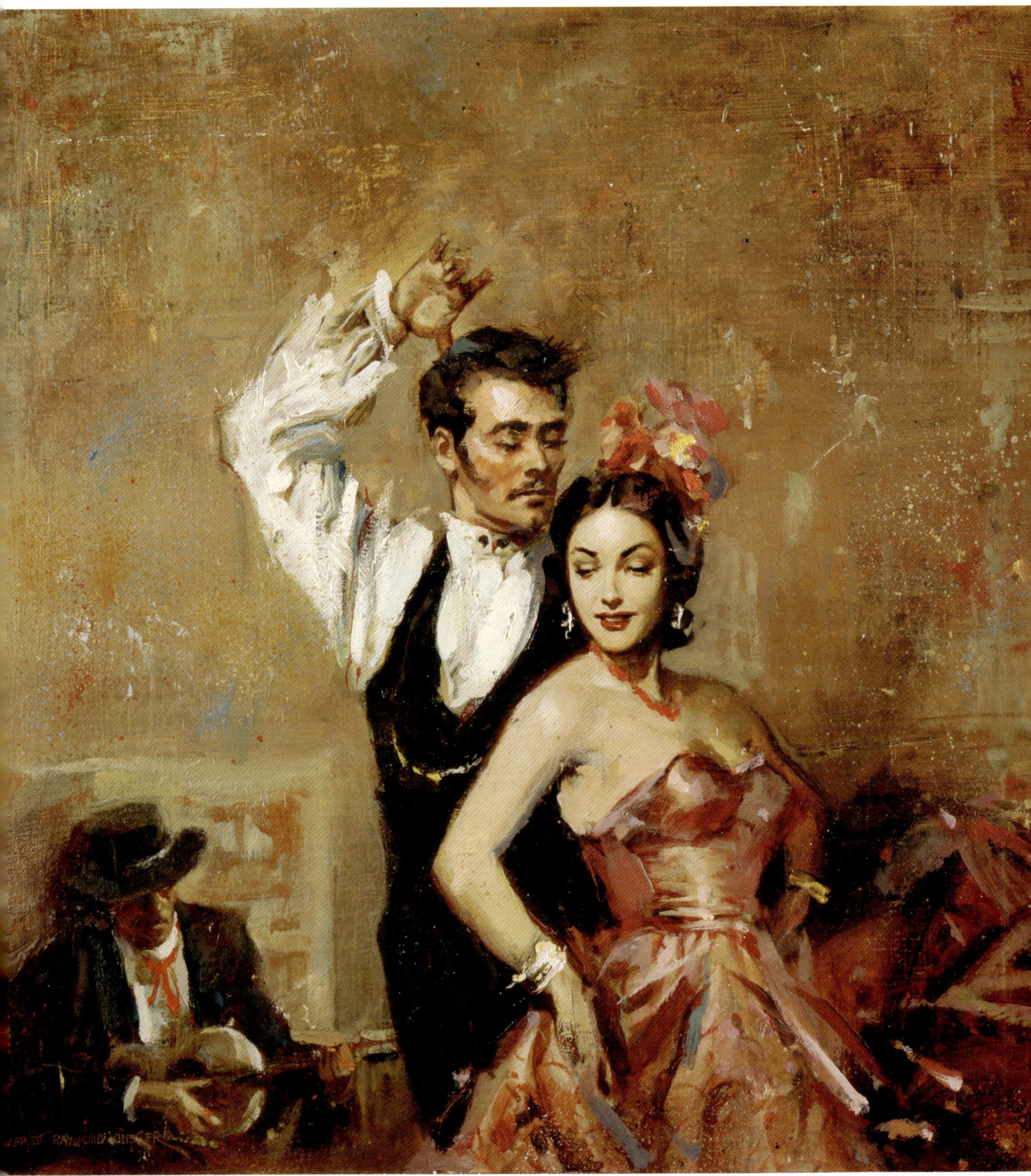

Bolero—la Valse - Ravel
The Philadelphia Orchestra: Eugene Ormandy, conductor
Columbia Records, 1954

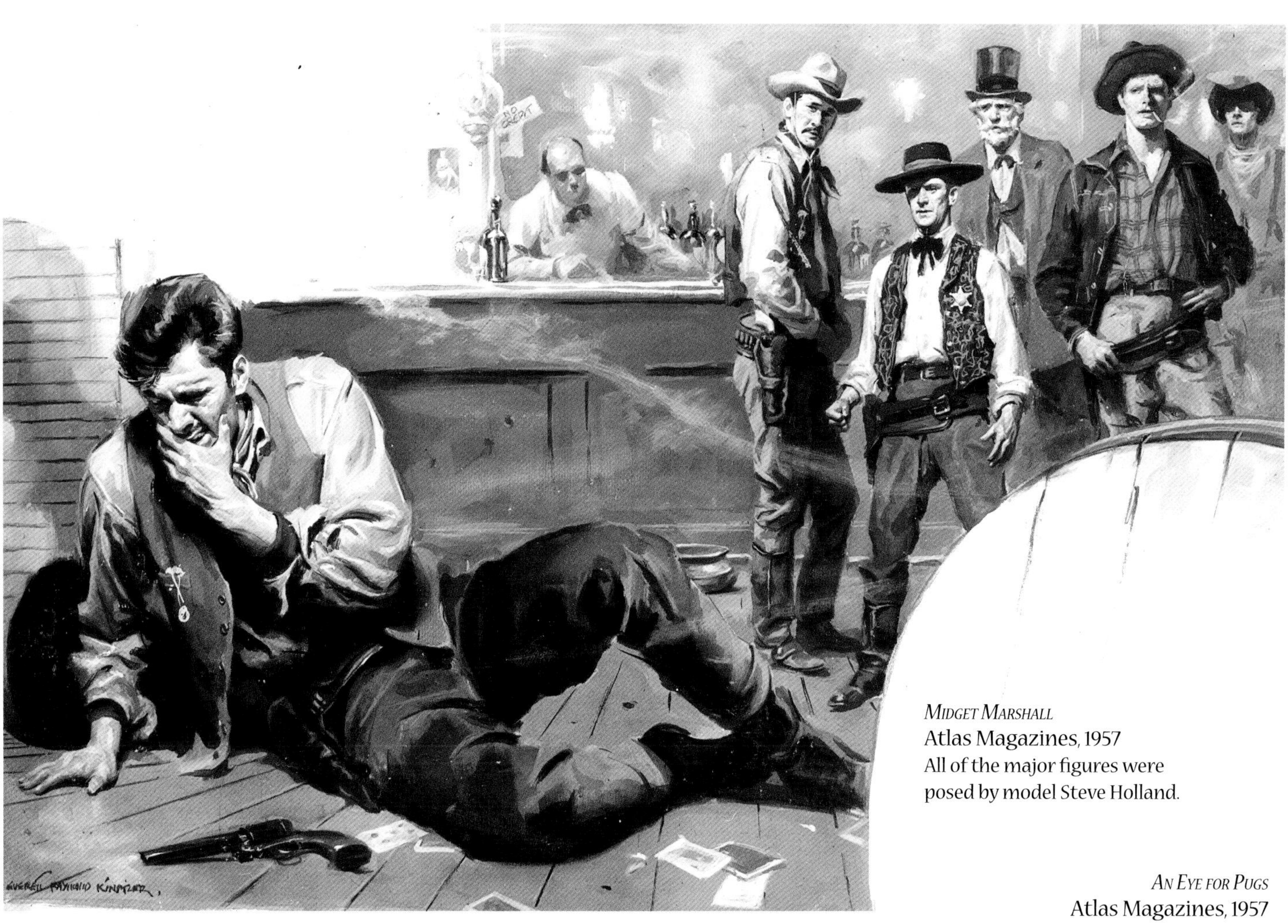

Midget Marshall
Atlas Magazines, 1957
All of the major figures were posed by model Steve Holland.

An Eye for Pugs
Atlas Magazines, 1957

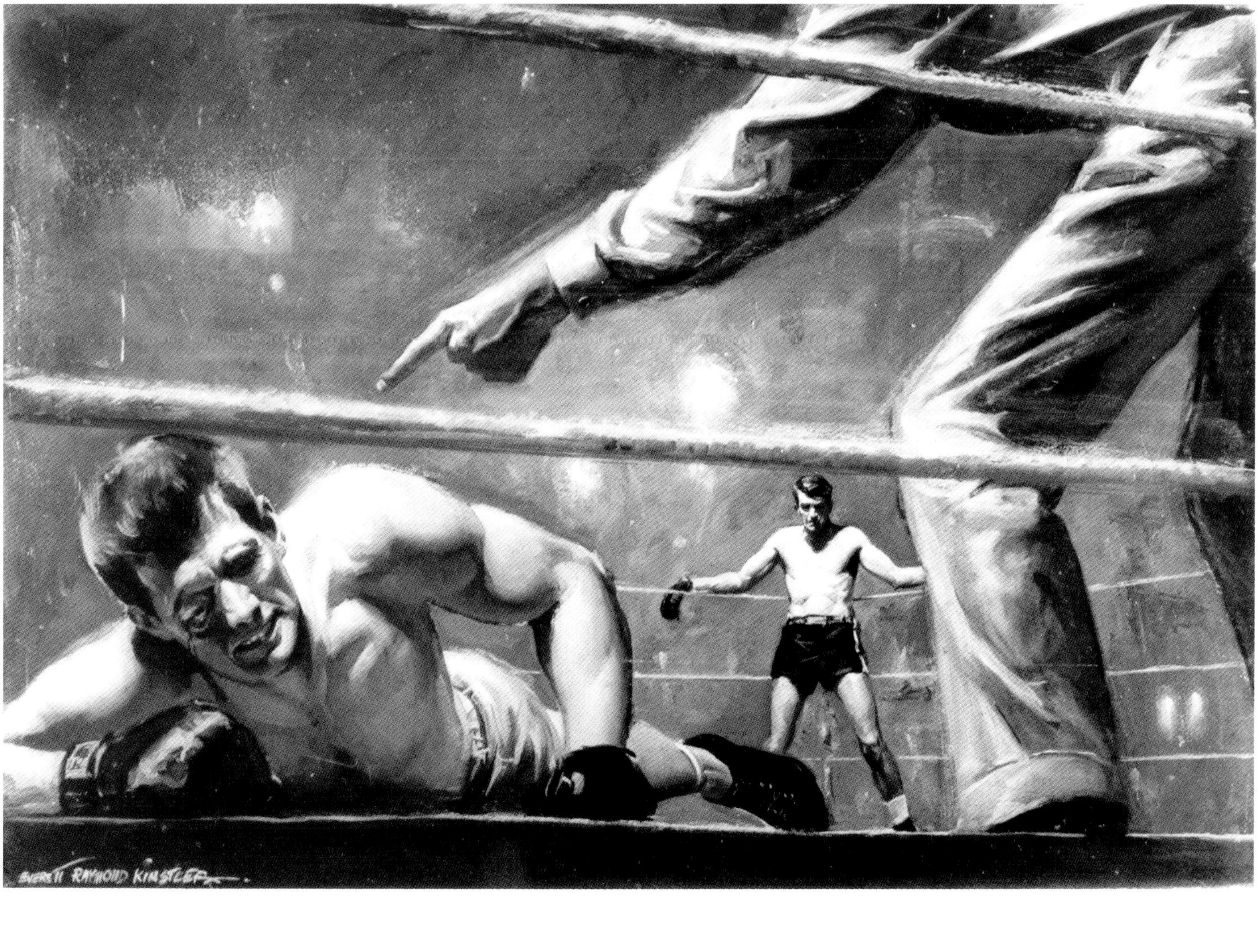

EVERETT RAYMOND KINSTLER

Thoughts in Paint

Ray's rough layout paintings were done quickly. Some were meant to indicate compositional ideas to an art director while others were done in hopes of securing a commission for a specific cover assignment.

Whatever the impetus for their creation, they remain some of his most intriguing work. The frontispiece to this book and the illustration on page 191 are samples of more elaborate versions of this type of art—intermediate steps between the thought and the final expression.

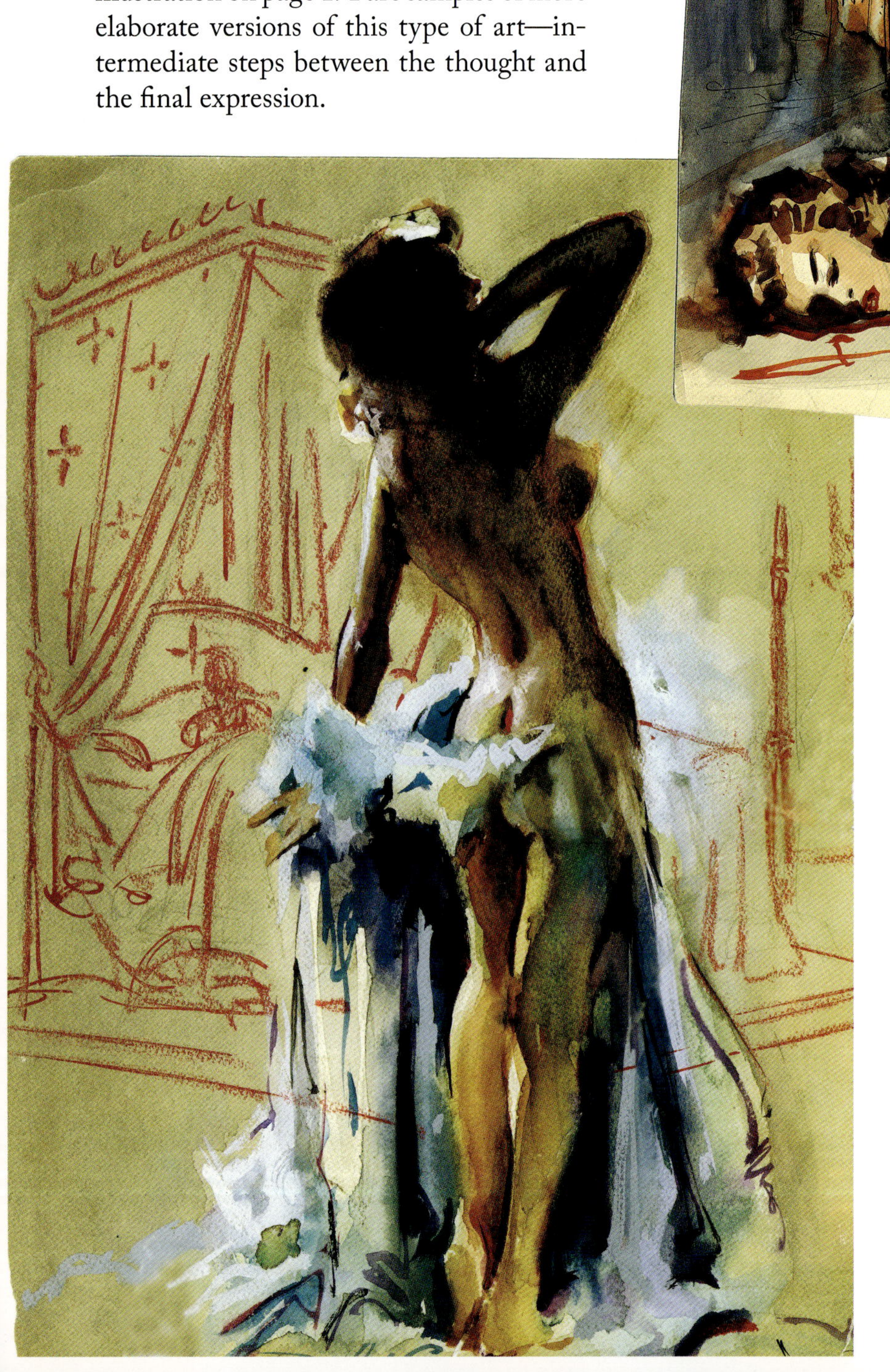

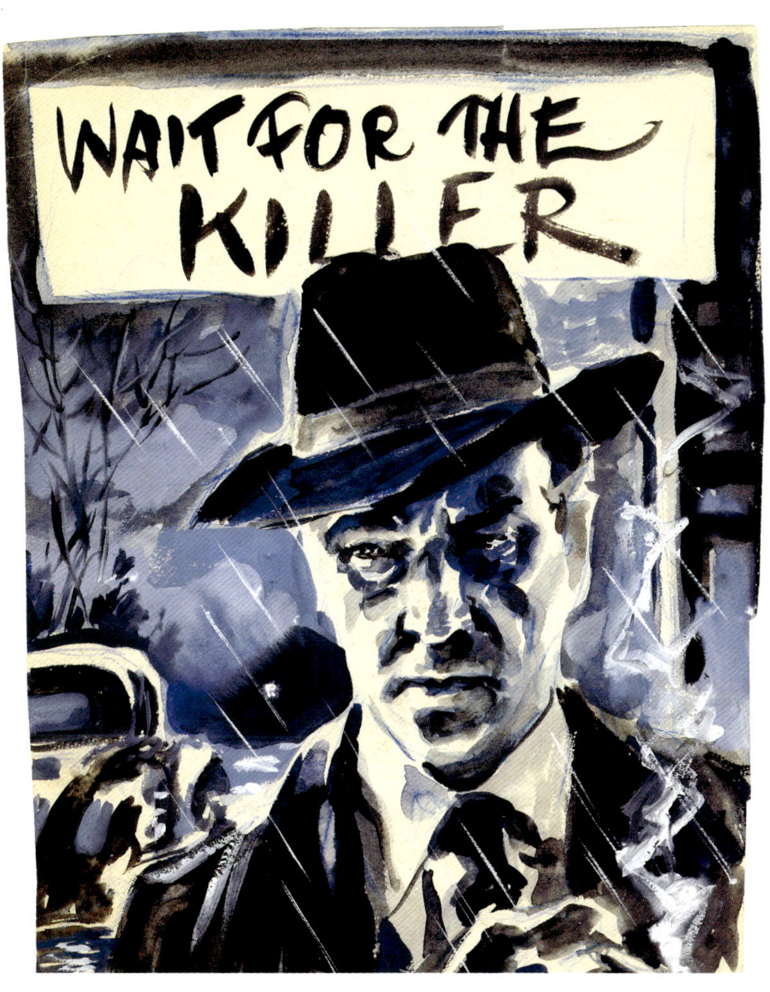
WAIT FOR THE
KILLER

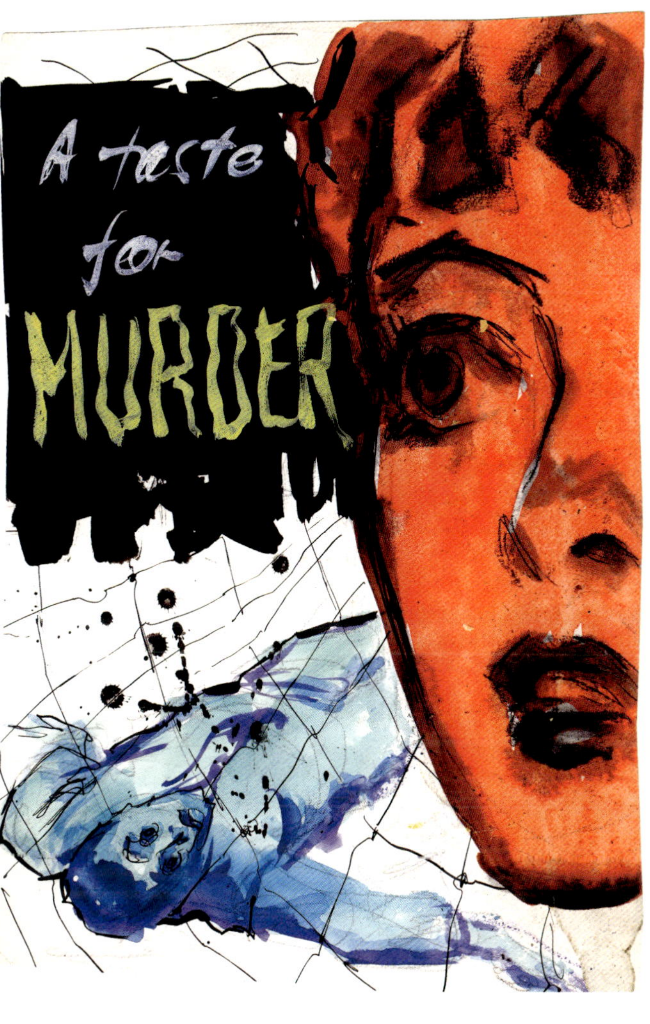
A taste
for
MURDER

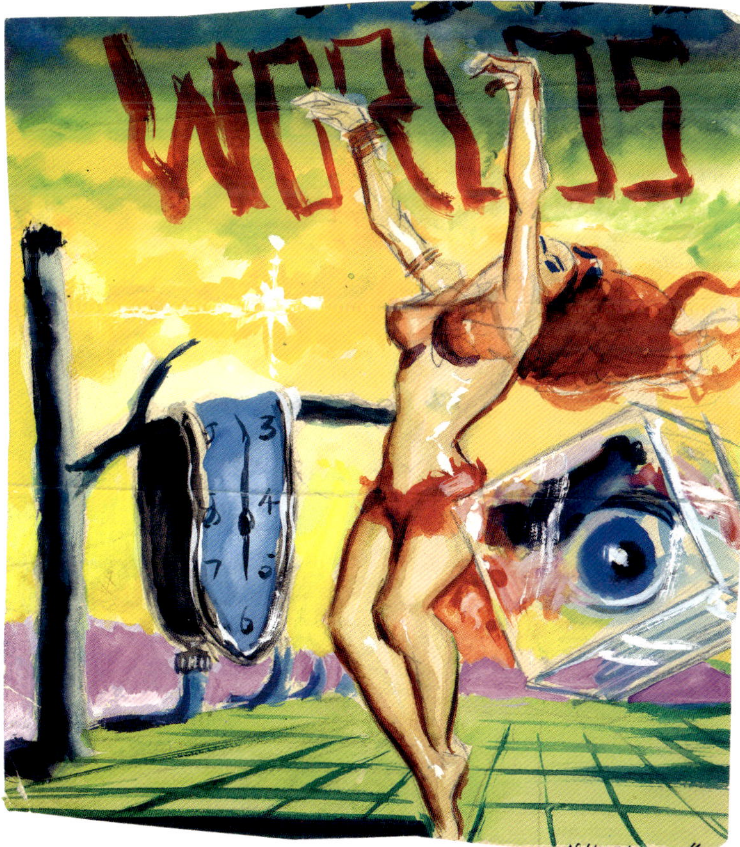
WORLDS

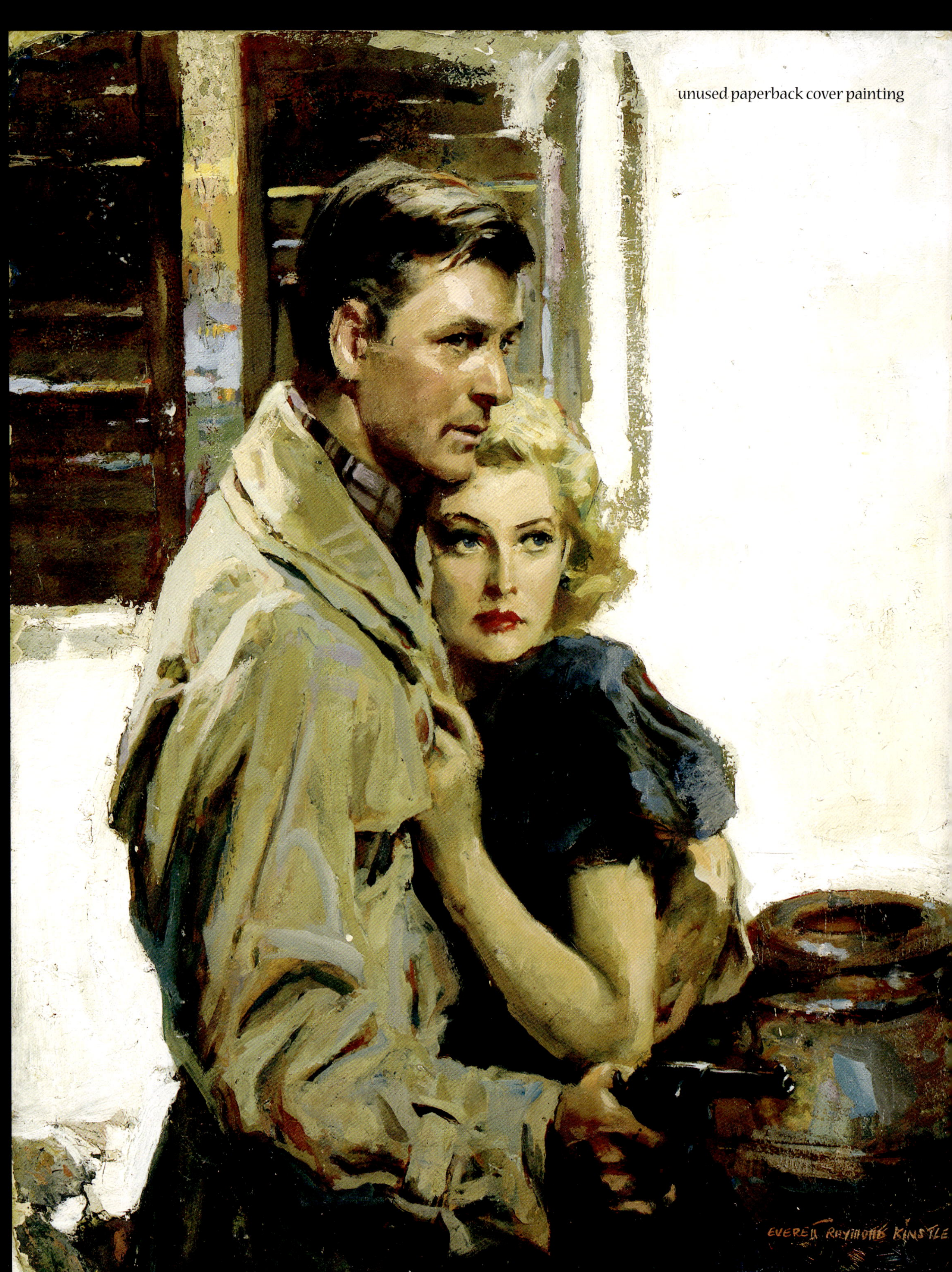

unused paperback cover painting

ugh

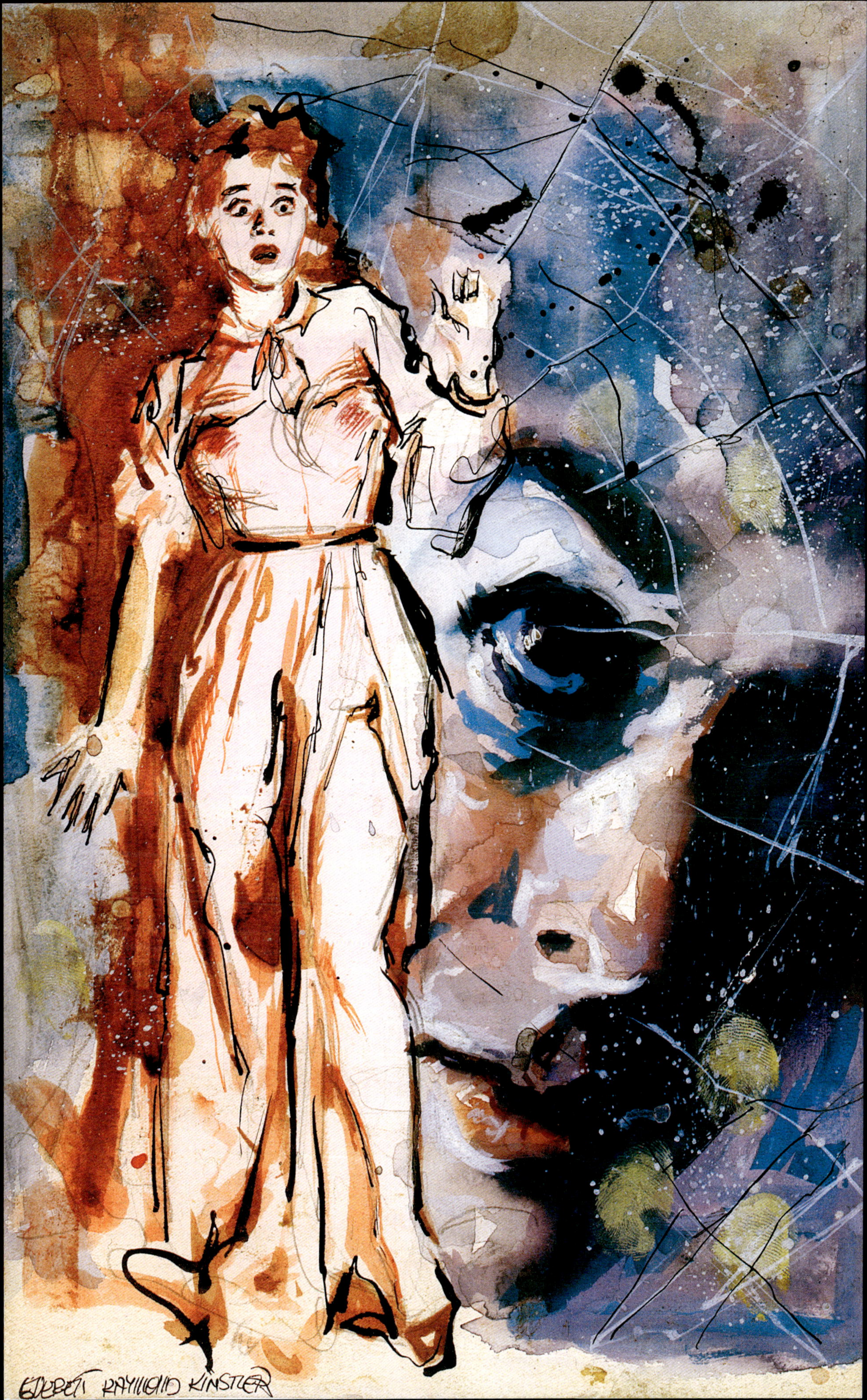

EVERETT RAYMOND KINSTLER

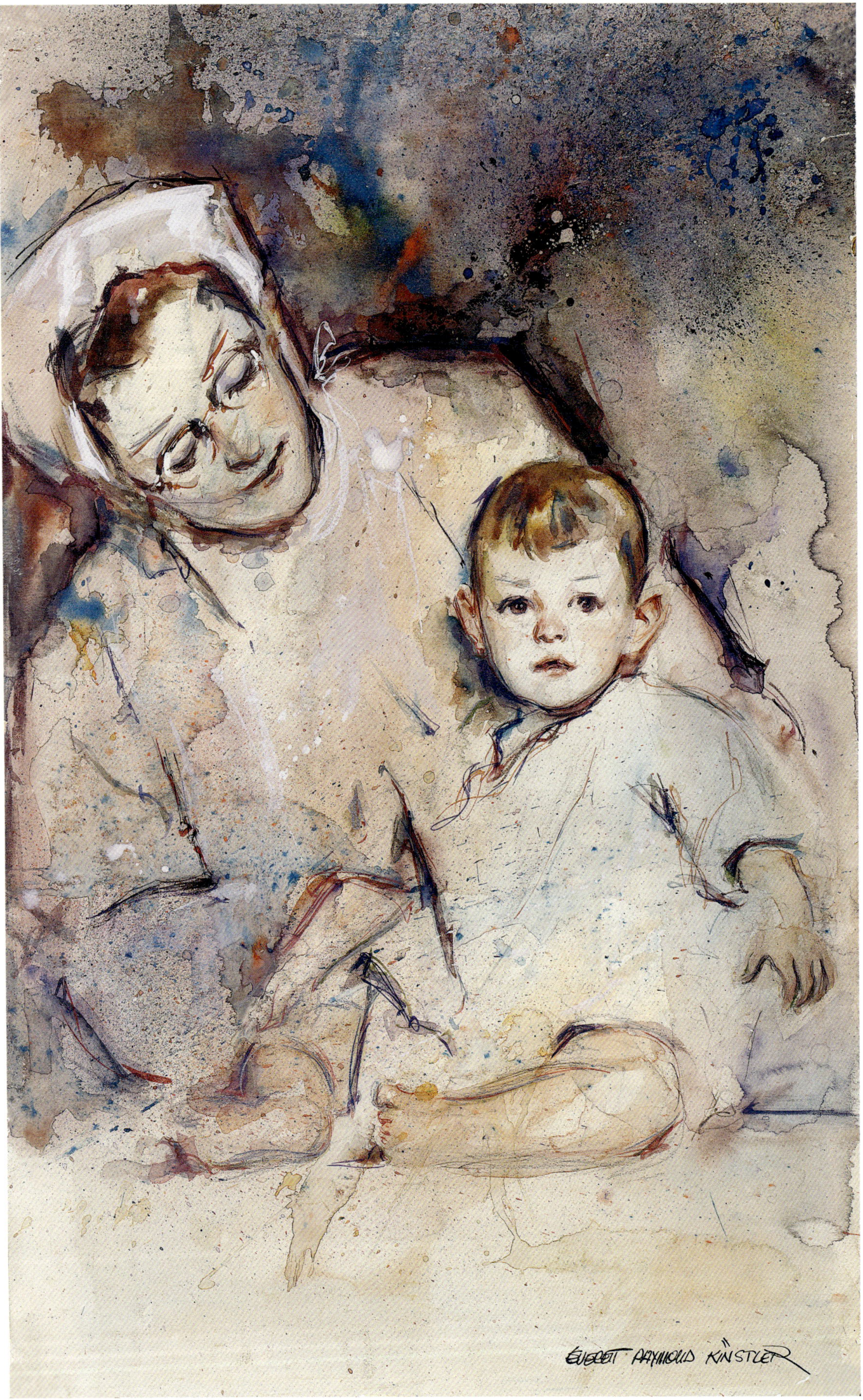

Hospital benefit poster

Grosset and Dunlap, 1958

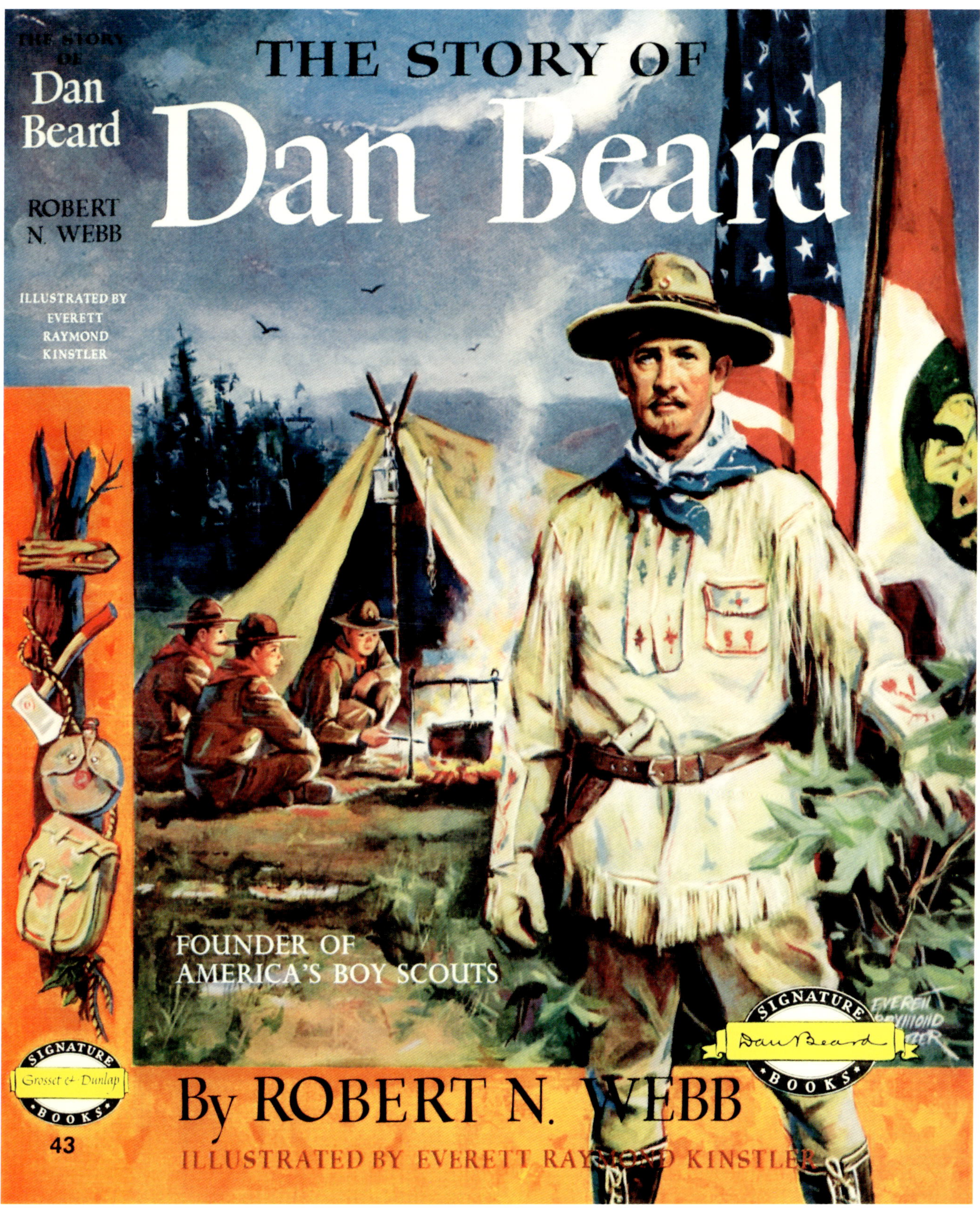

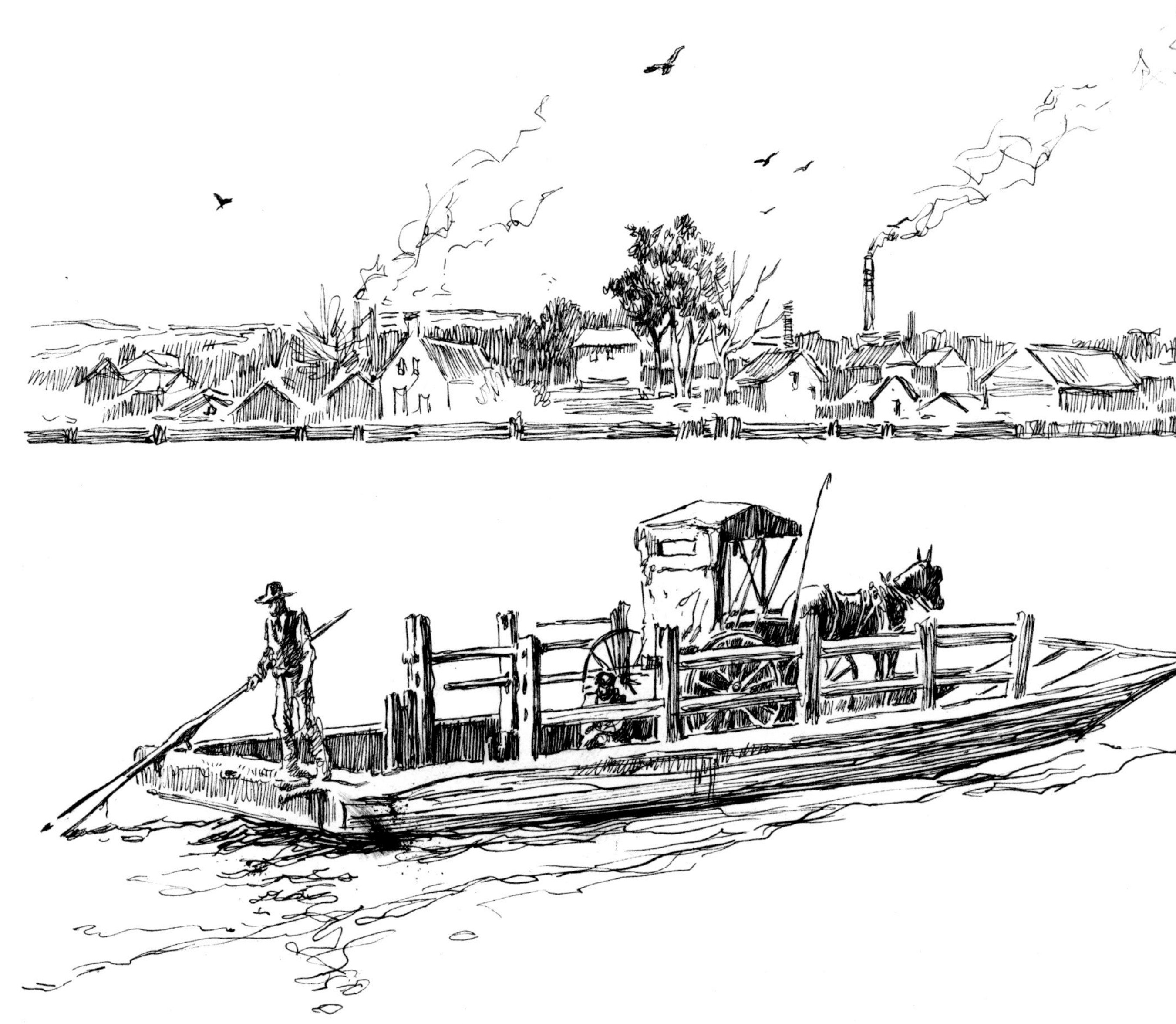

Immense pride and effort went into these illustrations for the biography of Dan Beard, a fellow illustrator. Kinstler researched the era extensively in order to bring the times to life in his art. Beard was the artist who created the two hundred drawings for the 1889 first edition of Mark Twain's **A Connecticut Yankee in King Arthur's Court**.

There was a connection here that Ray felt strongly and he did his best to be faithful to the man and his work. The illustration of Beard and Twain on pages 202–203 often provokes comment regarding the very unusual drawing chair/table that Beard is using, but it is historically accurate. Kinstler tracked down and drew the actual piece of furniture that Beard sat in while drawing those **Connecticut Yankee** illustrations.

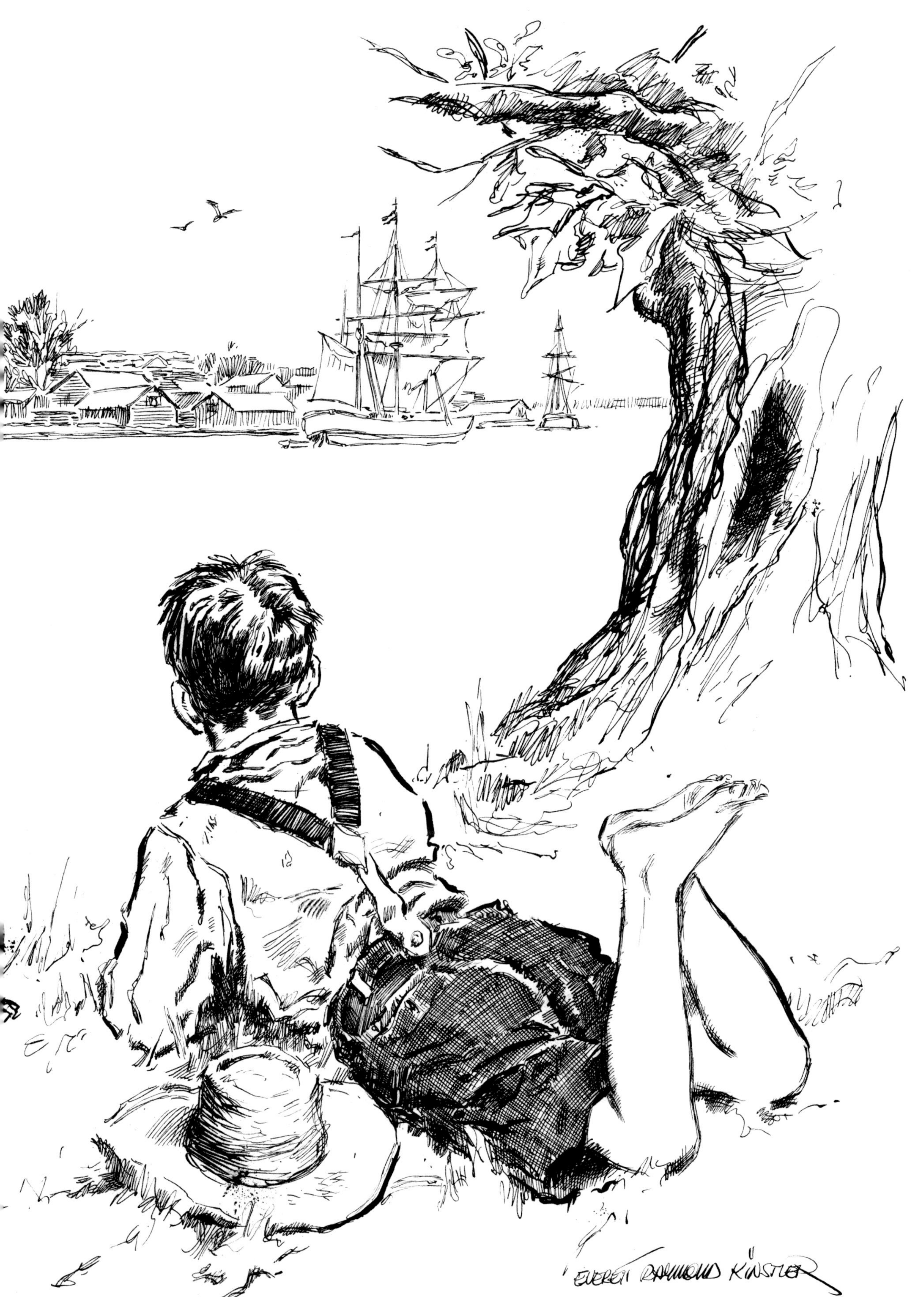
EVERETT RAYMOND KINSTLER

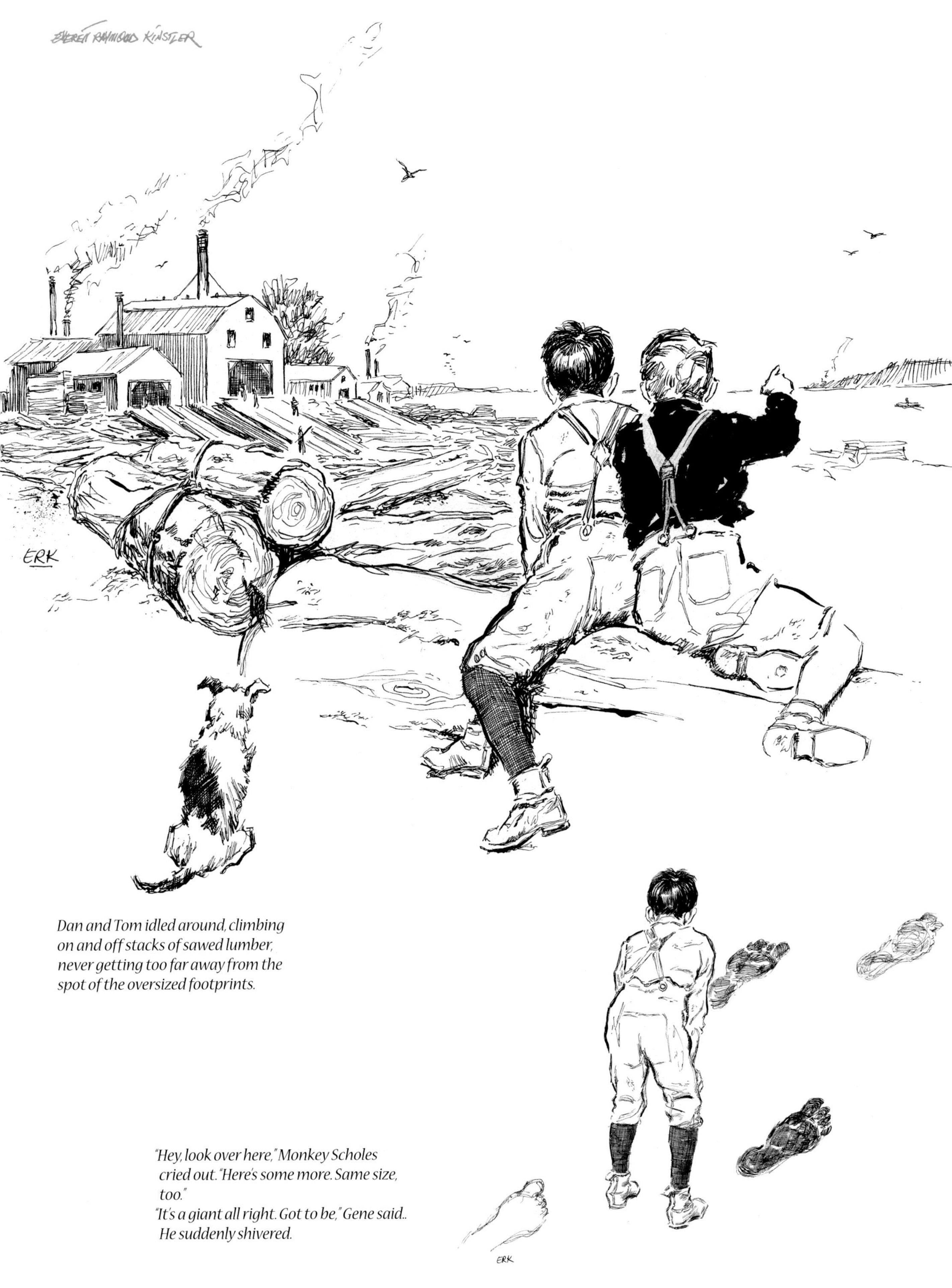

Dan and Tom idled around, climbing on and off stacks of sawed lumber, never getting too far away from the spot of the oversized footprints.

"Hey, look over here," Monkey Scholes cried out. "Here's some more. Same size, too."
"It's a giant all right. Got to be," Gene said.. He suddenly shivered.

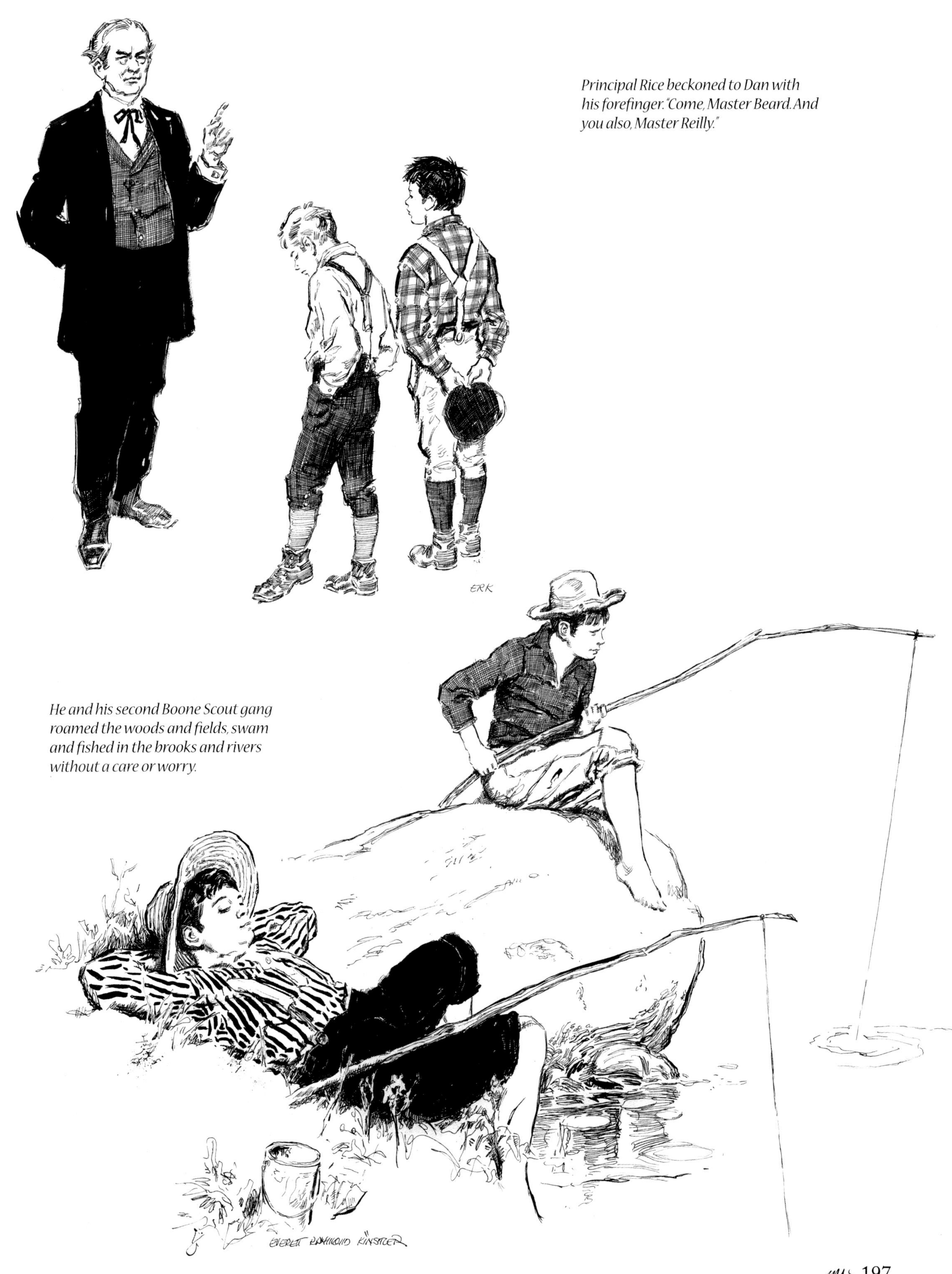

Principal Rice beckoned to Dan with his forefinger. "Come, Master Beard. And you also, Master Reilly."

He and his second Boone Scout gang roamed the woods and fields, swam and fished in the brooks and rivers without a care or worry.

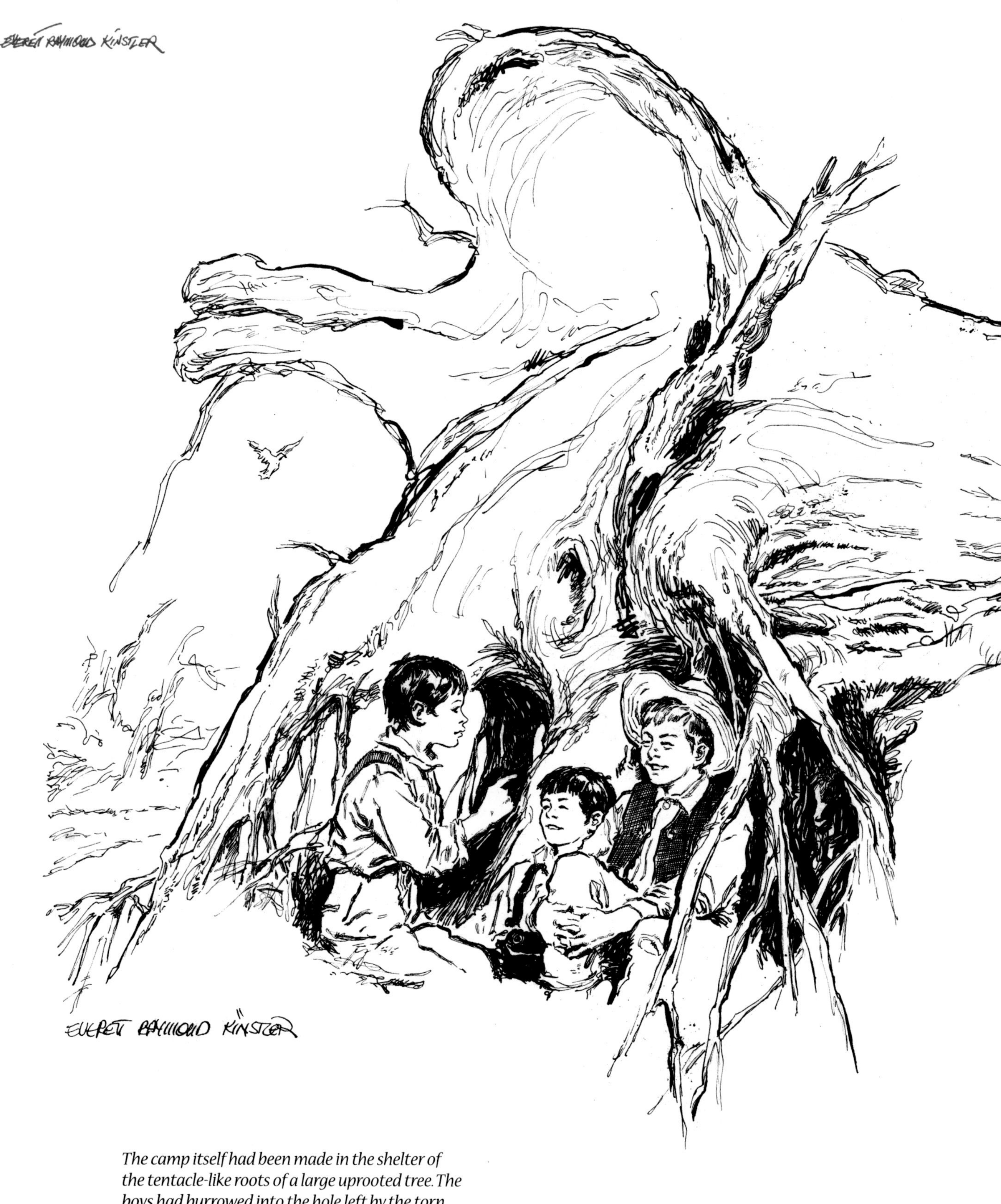

The camp itself had been made in the shelter of the tentacle-like roots of a large uprooted tree. The boys had burrowed into the hole left by the torn roots, and deepened it.

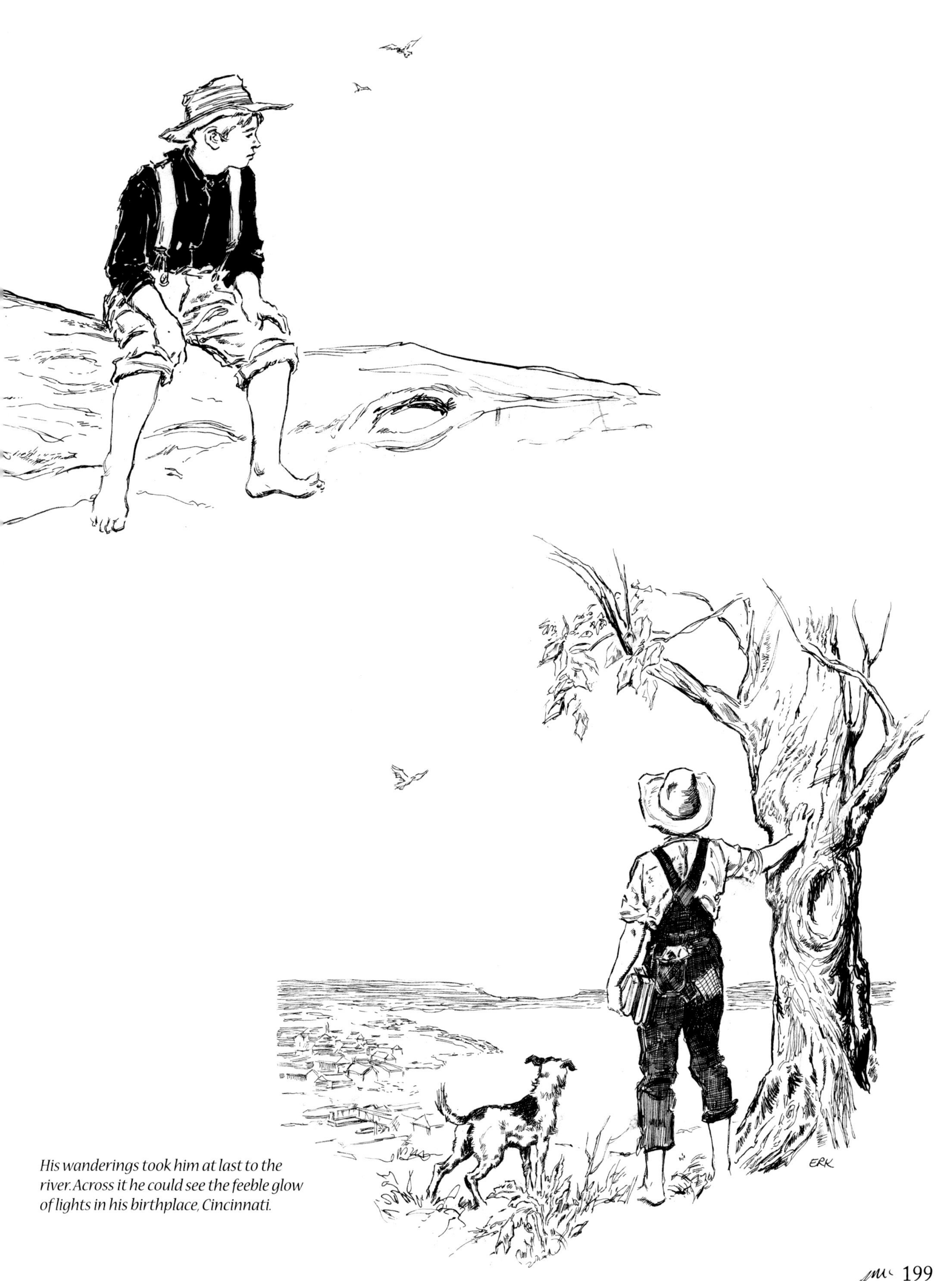

His wanderings took him at last to the river. Across it he could see the feeble glow of lights in his birthplace, Cincinnati.

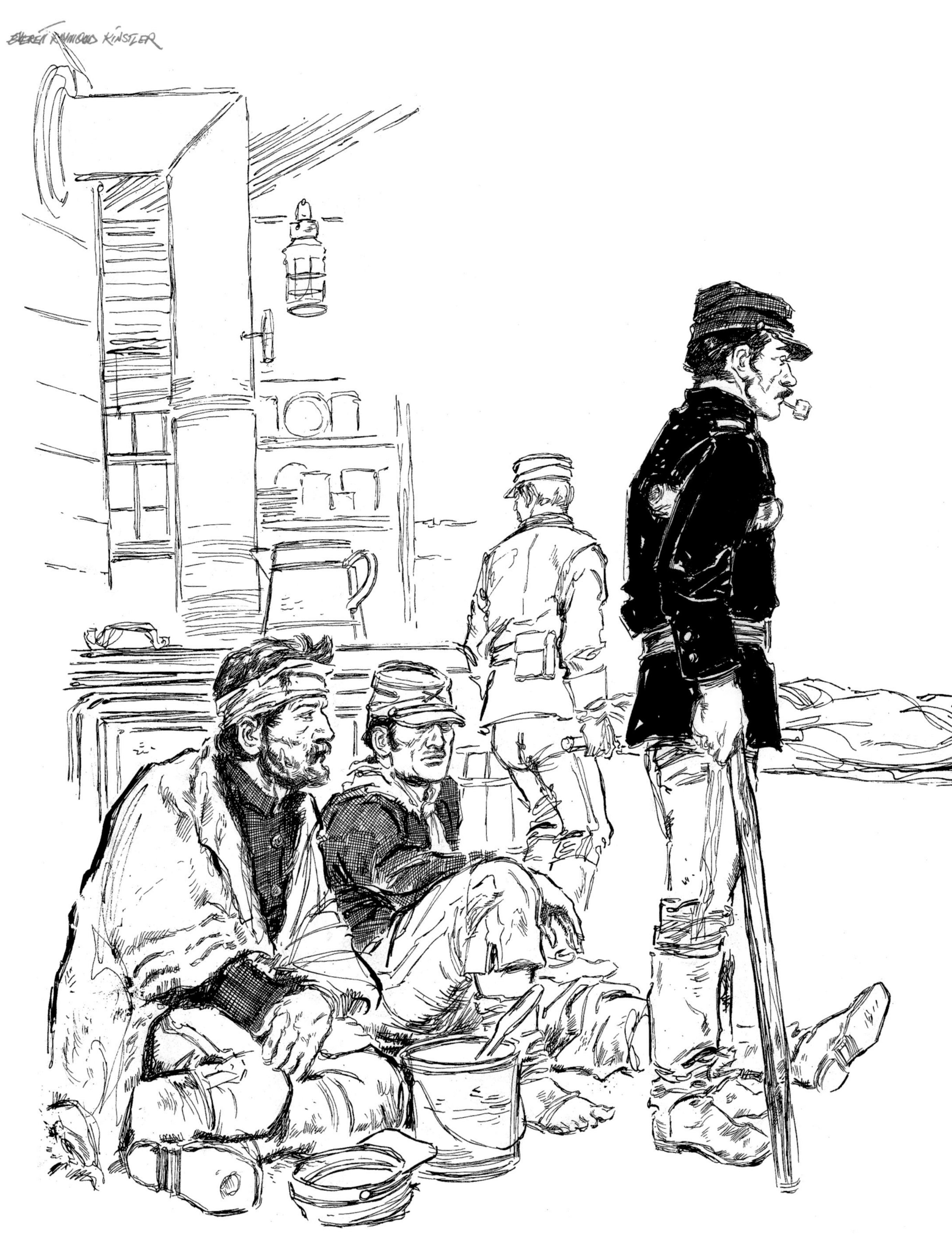

Sometimes, when he sat beside a wounded soldier, listening to him talk, he felt as though he were loafing on the job. But the men in the hospital were often lonely, unhappy and in pain. They needed someone to whom to tell their troubles.

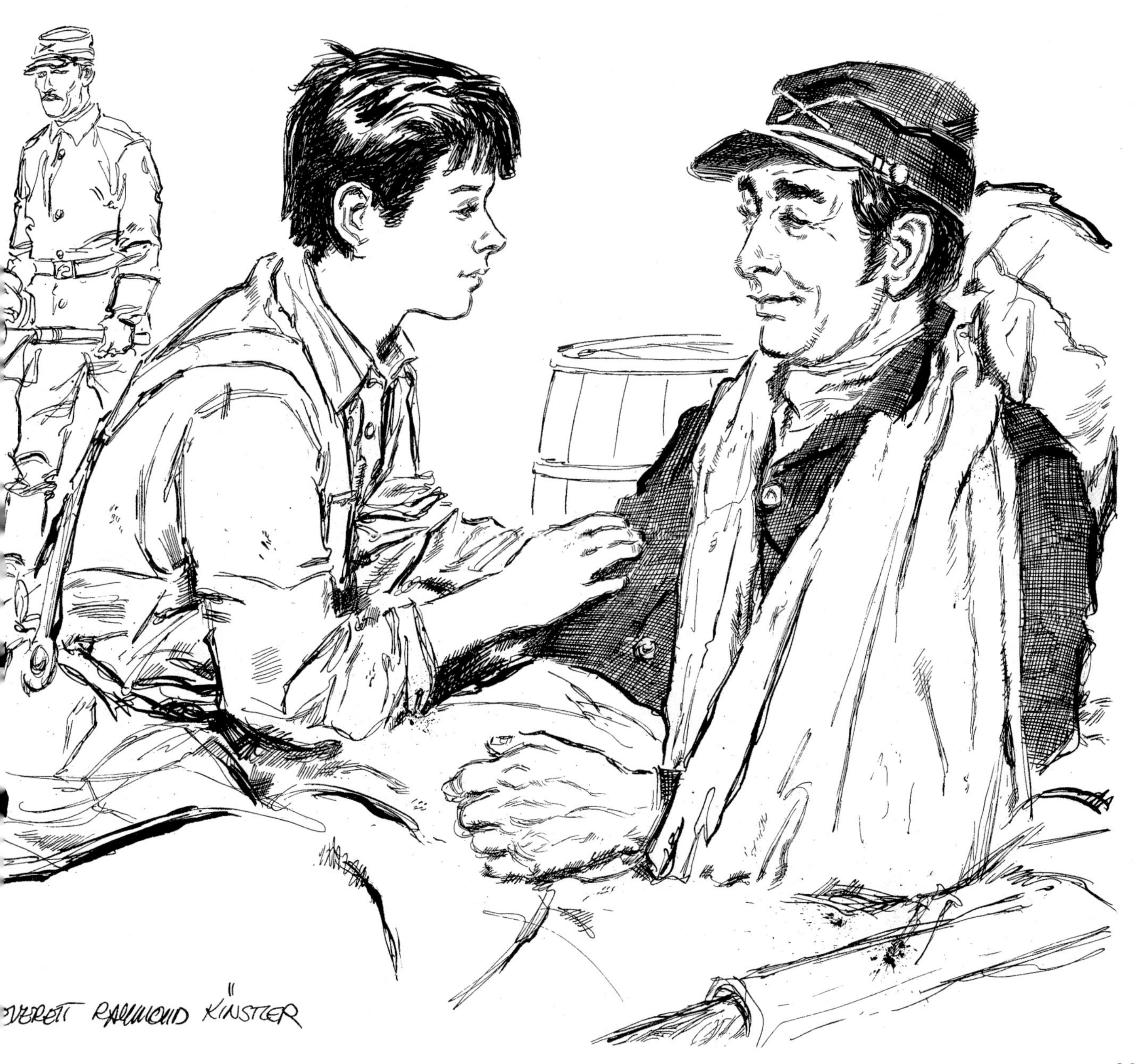

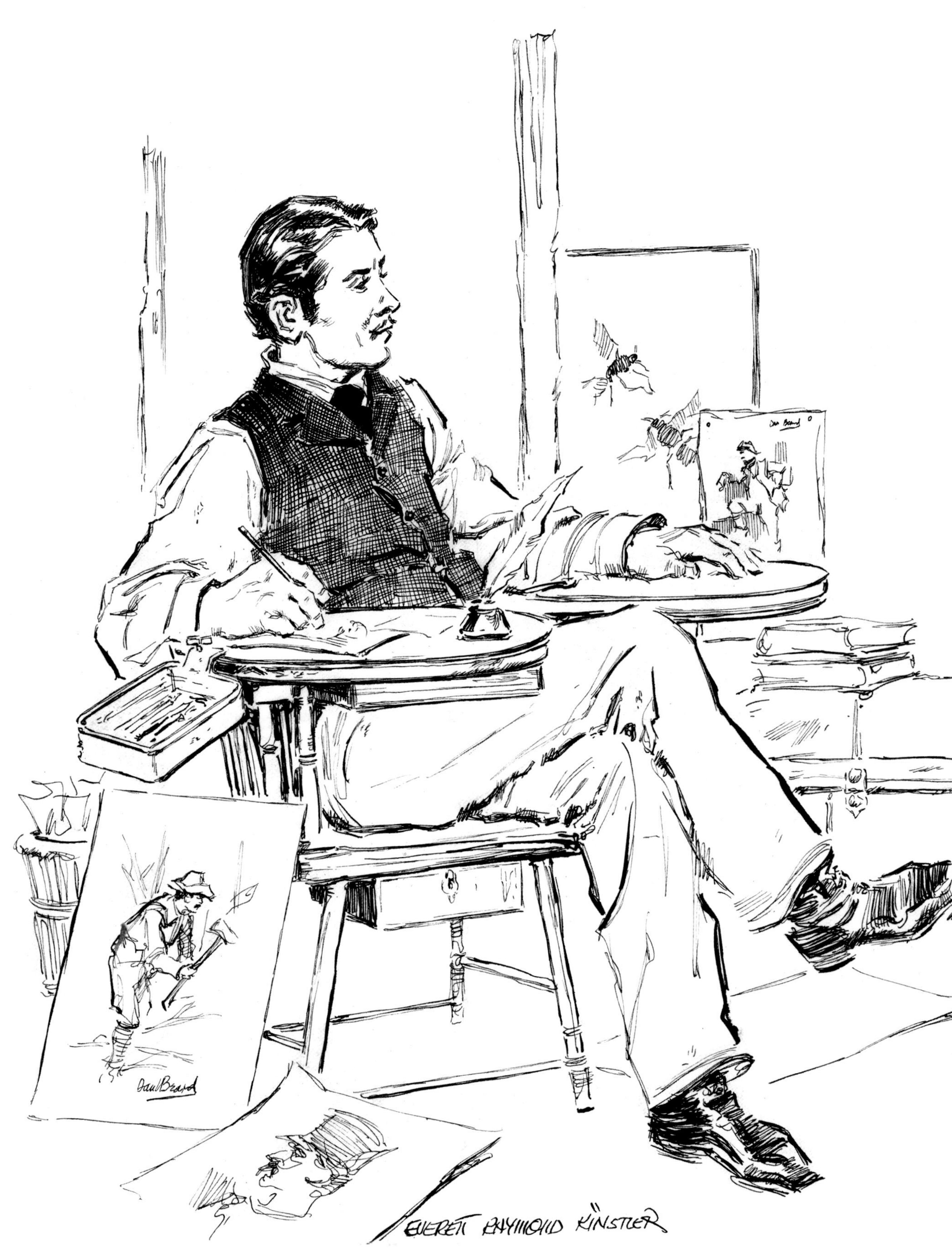
Dan Beard
Dan Beard
EVERETT RAYMOND KINSTLER

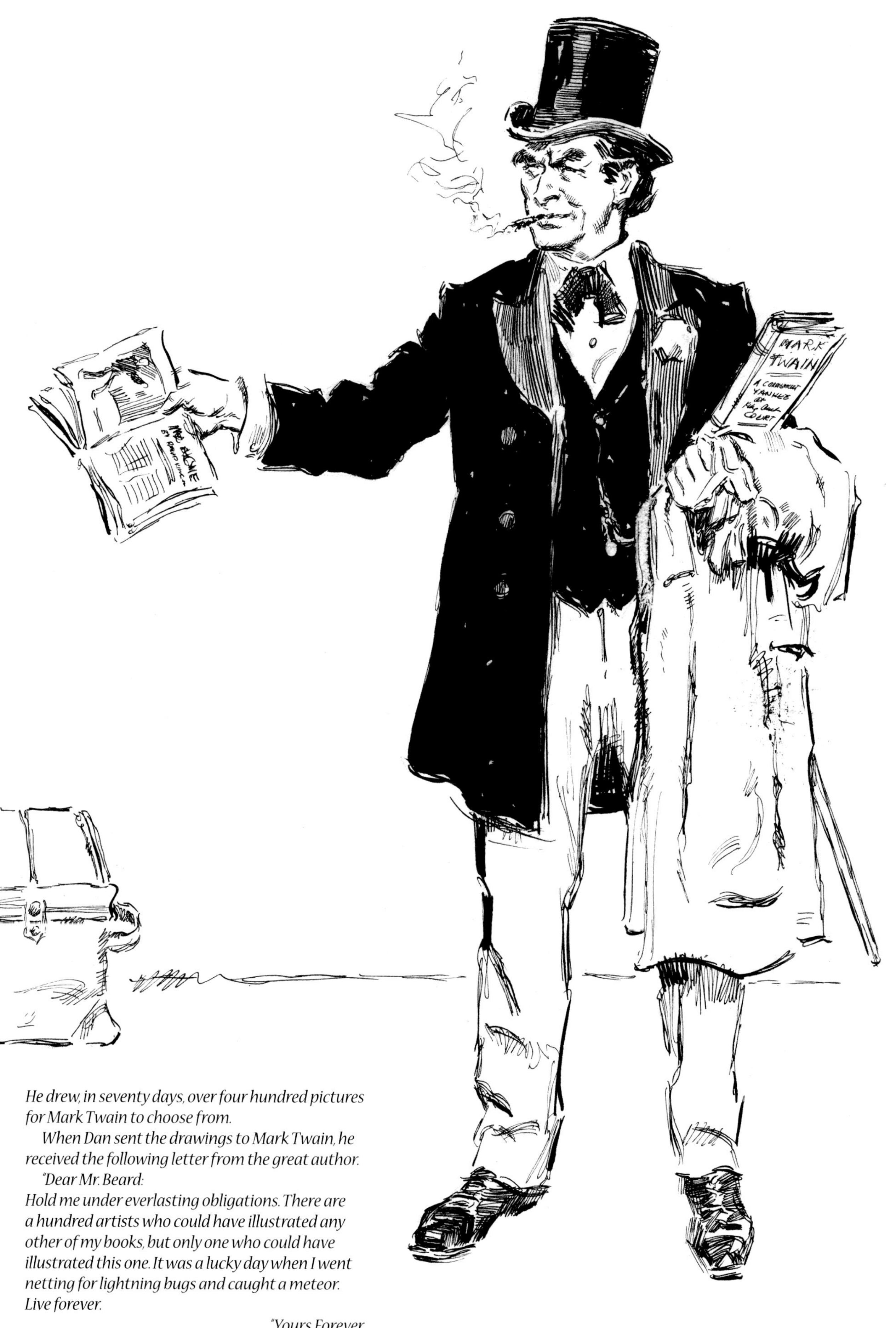

He drew, in seventy days, over four hundred pictures for Mark Twain to choose from.

When Dan sent the drawings to Mark Twain, he received the following letter from the great author.

"Dear Mr. Beard:
Hold me under everlasting obligations. There are a hundred artists who could have illustrated any other of my books, but only one who could have illustrated this one. It was a lucky day when I went netting for lightning bugs and caught a meteor. Live forever.

"Yours Forever,
"S. L. Clemens"

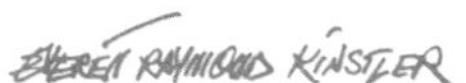

"There's one more person we'd like to have very much, Mr. President."
"Name him."
"You, sir."
President Roosevelt let out a roar of laughter and once again smote the table with his fists.

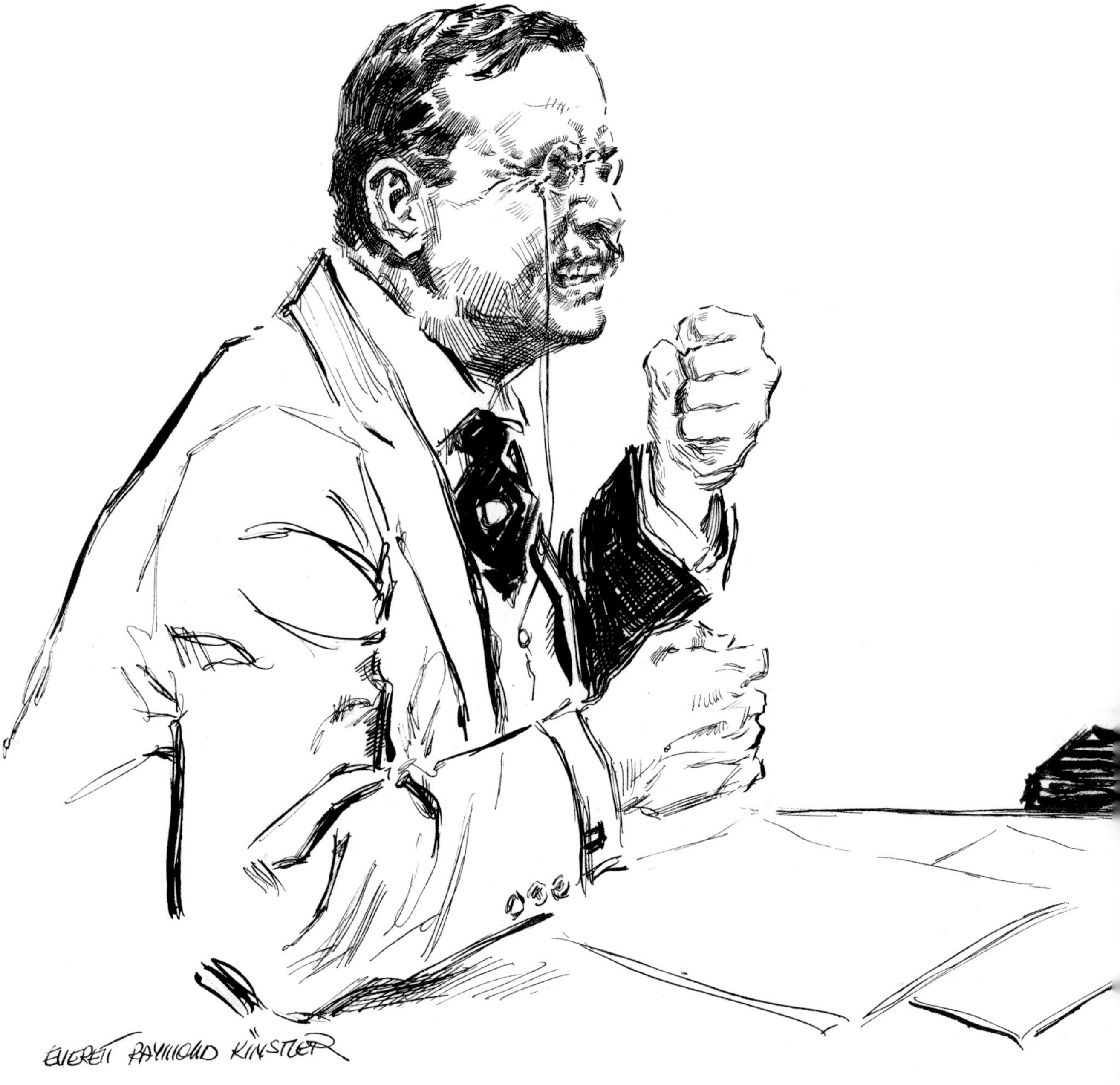

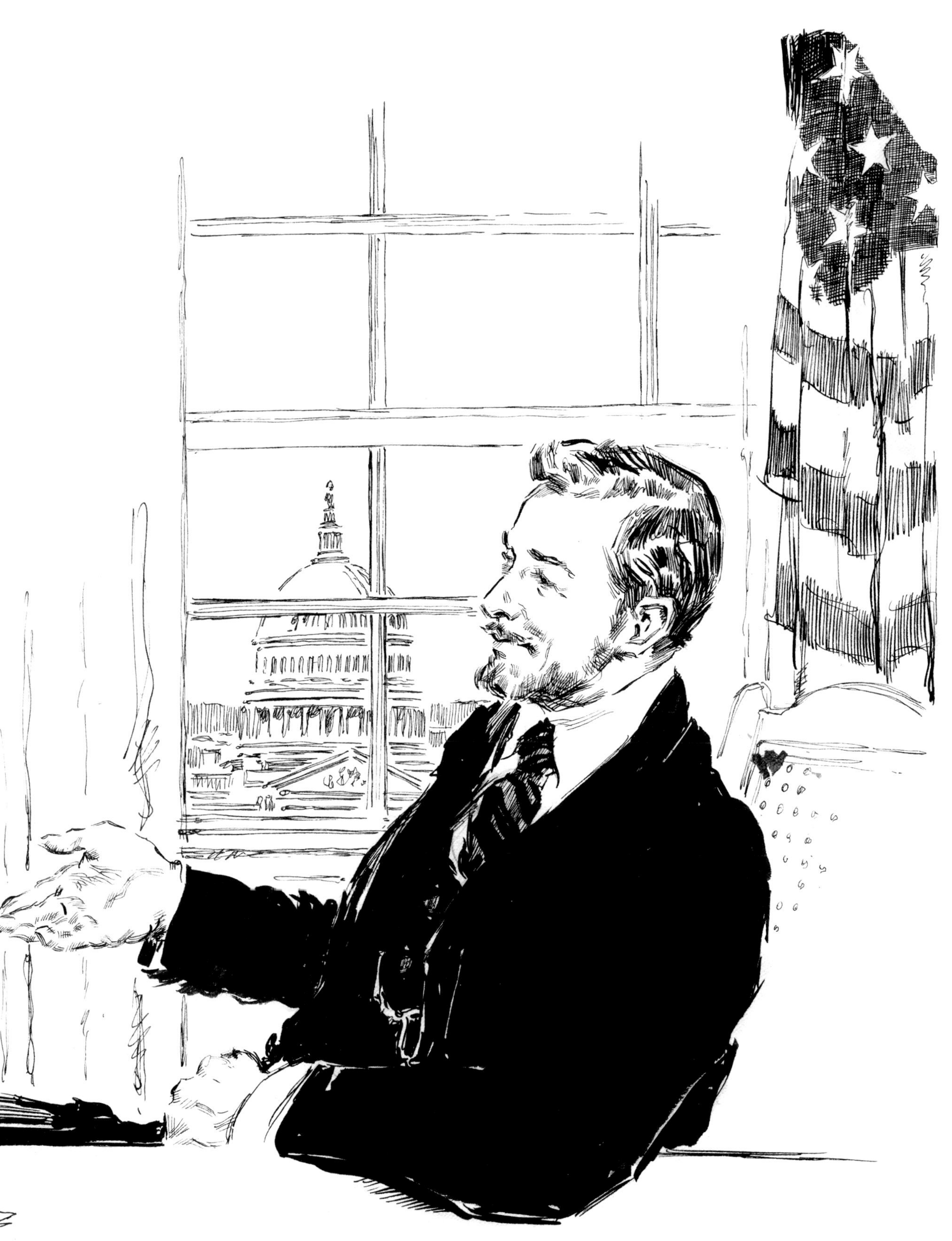

Young Adult Books
biography

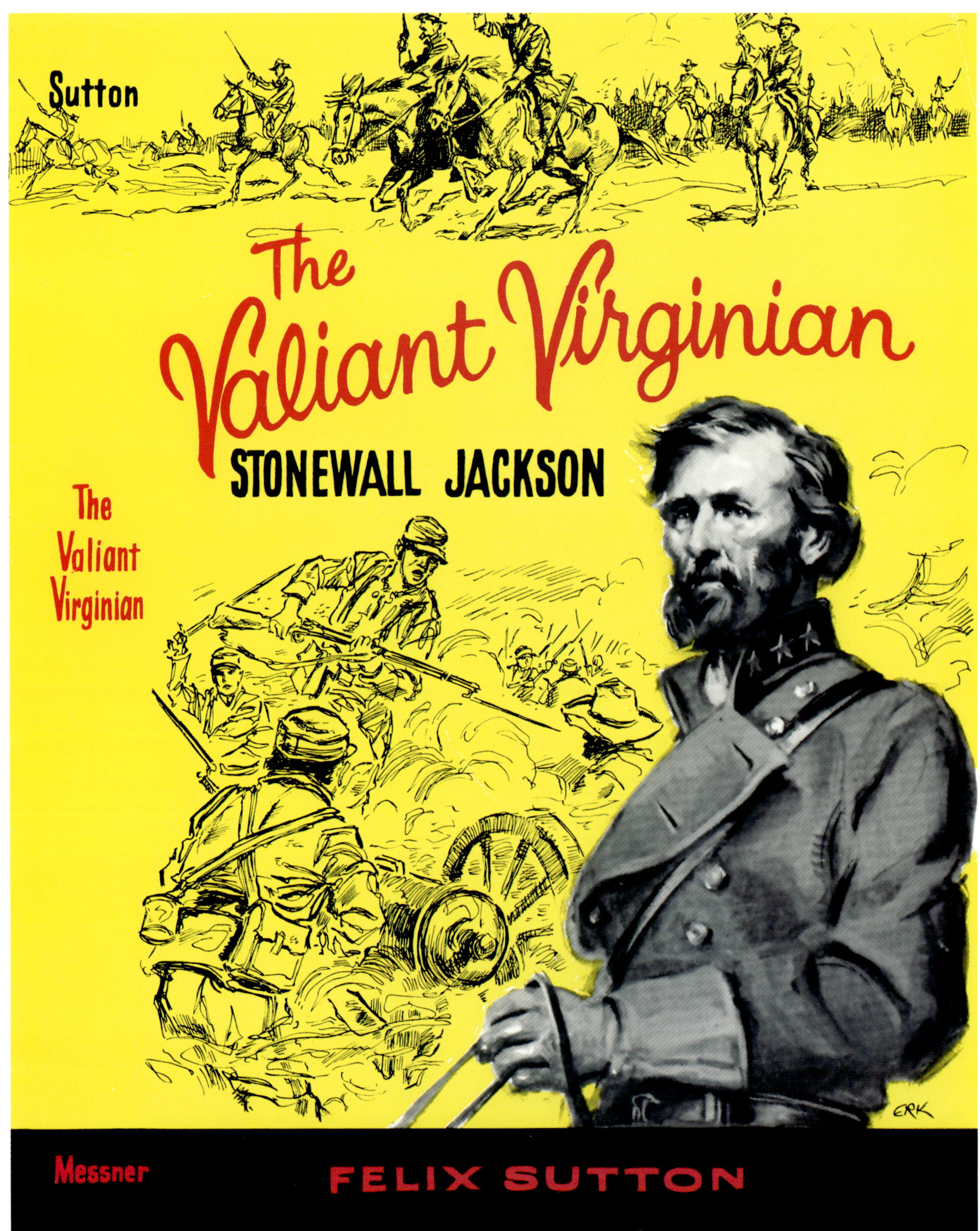

Julian Messner, 1961

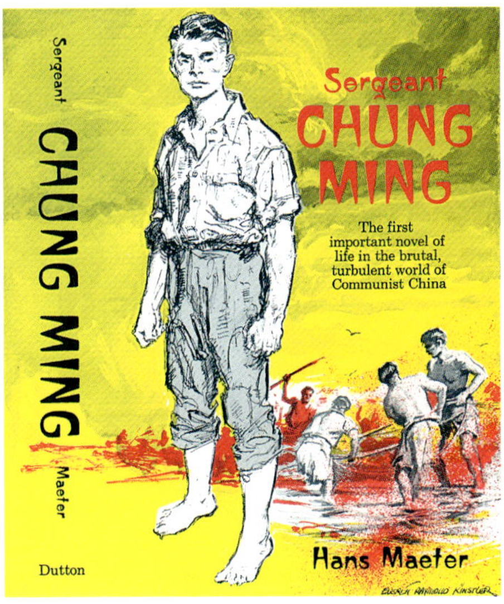

E.P. Dutton, 1961

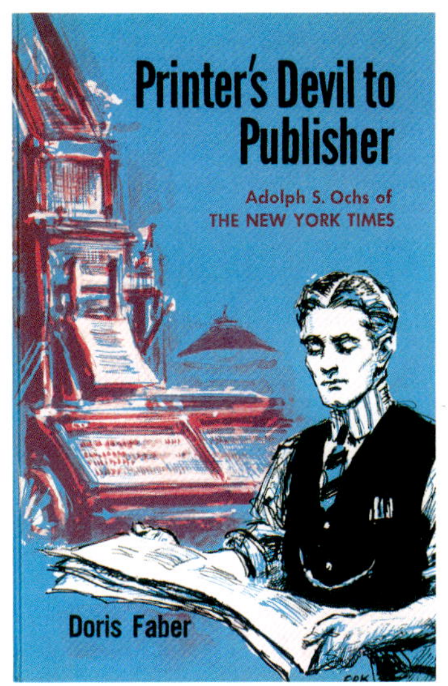

Julian Messner, 1963

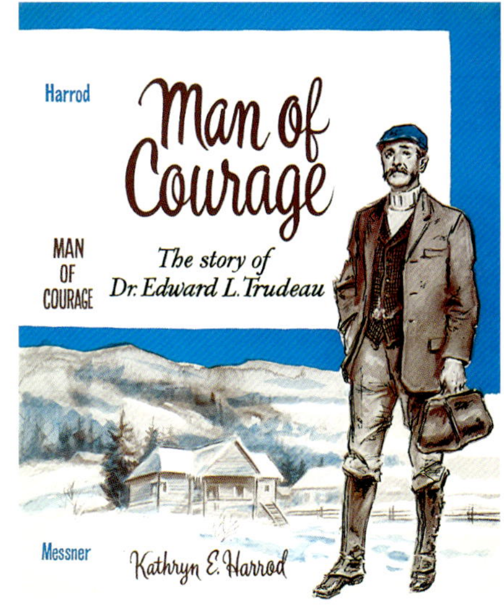

Julian Messner, 1959

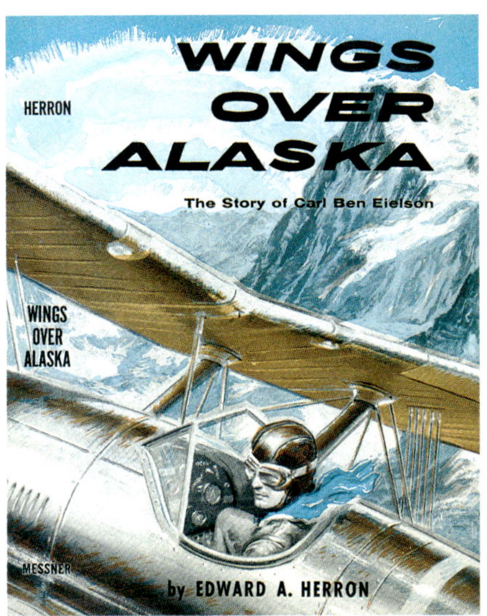

Julian Messner, 1959

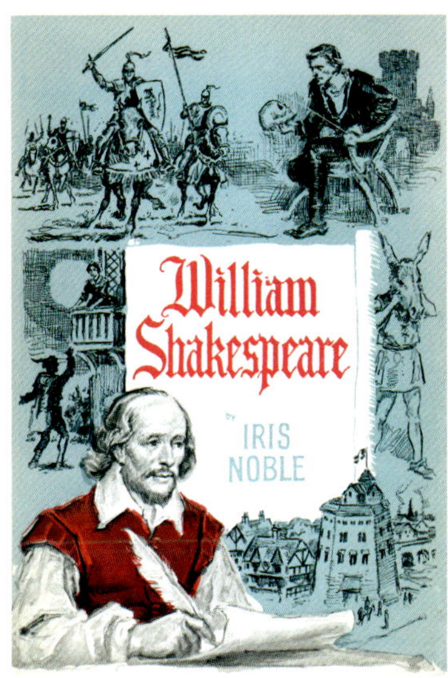

Julian Messner, 1961

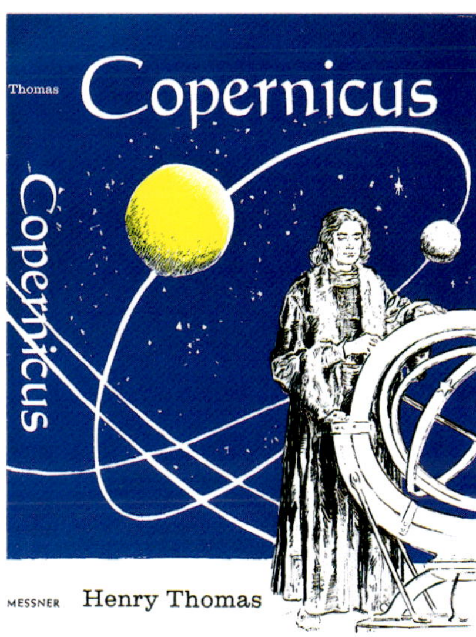

Julian Messner, 1960

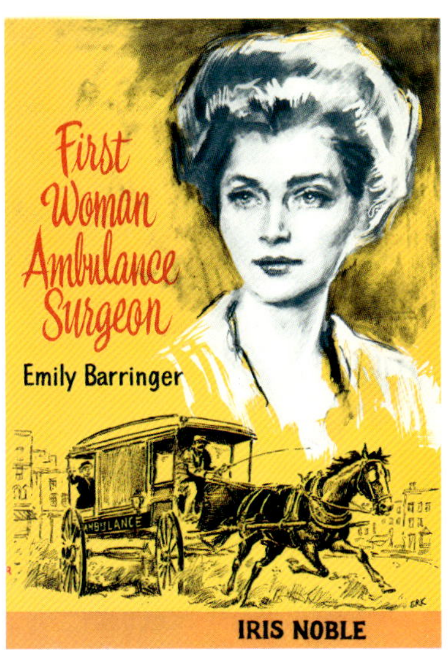

Julian Messner, 1962

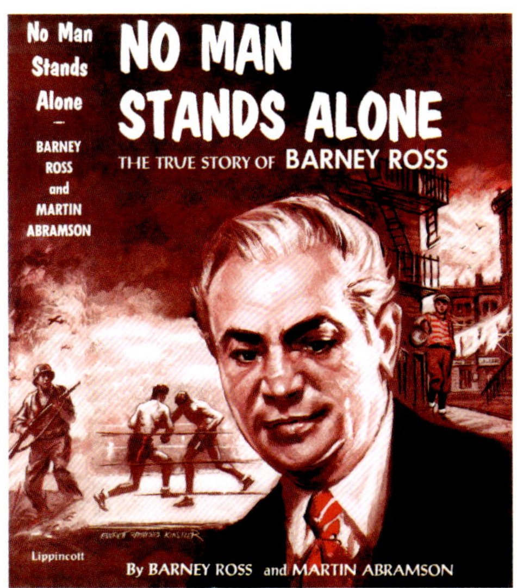

J.B. Lippincott, 1957

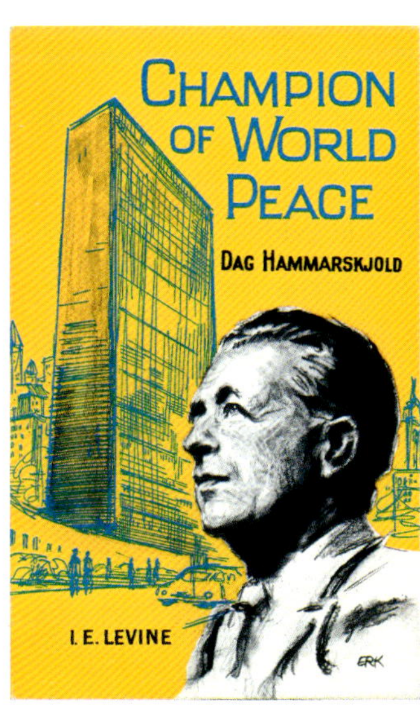

Julian Messner, 1962

Young Adult Books
romance

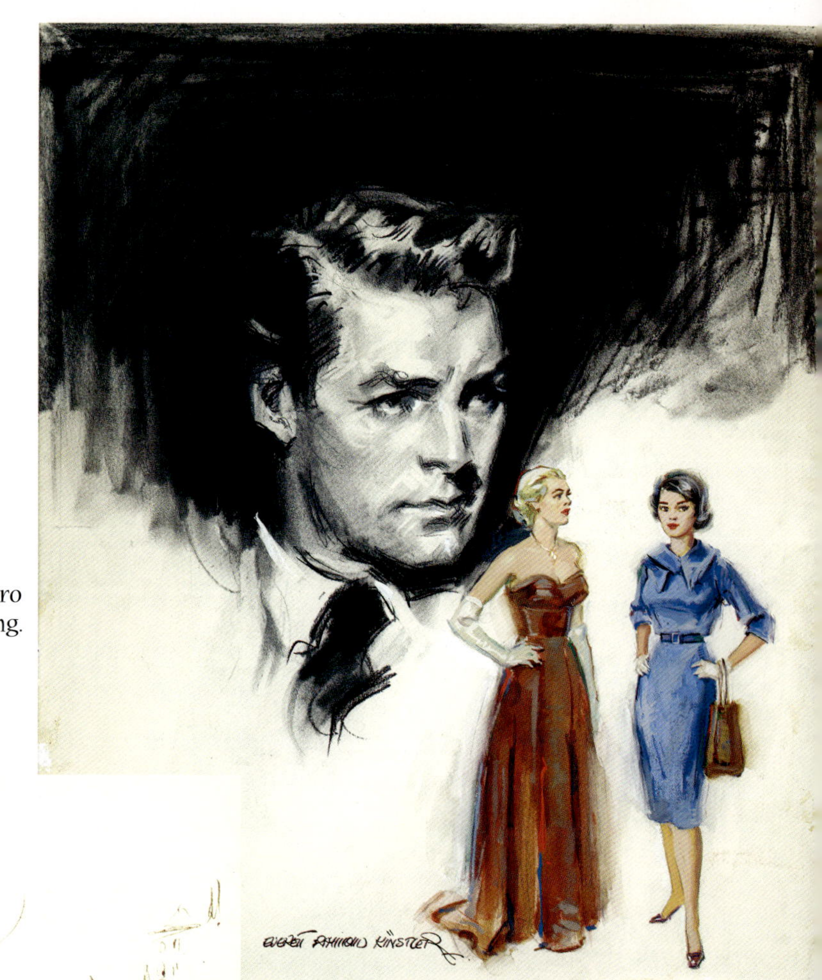

Cary Grant inspired the handsome hero in this unsourced cover painting.

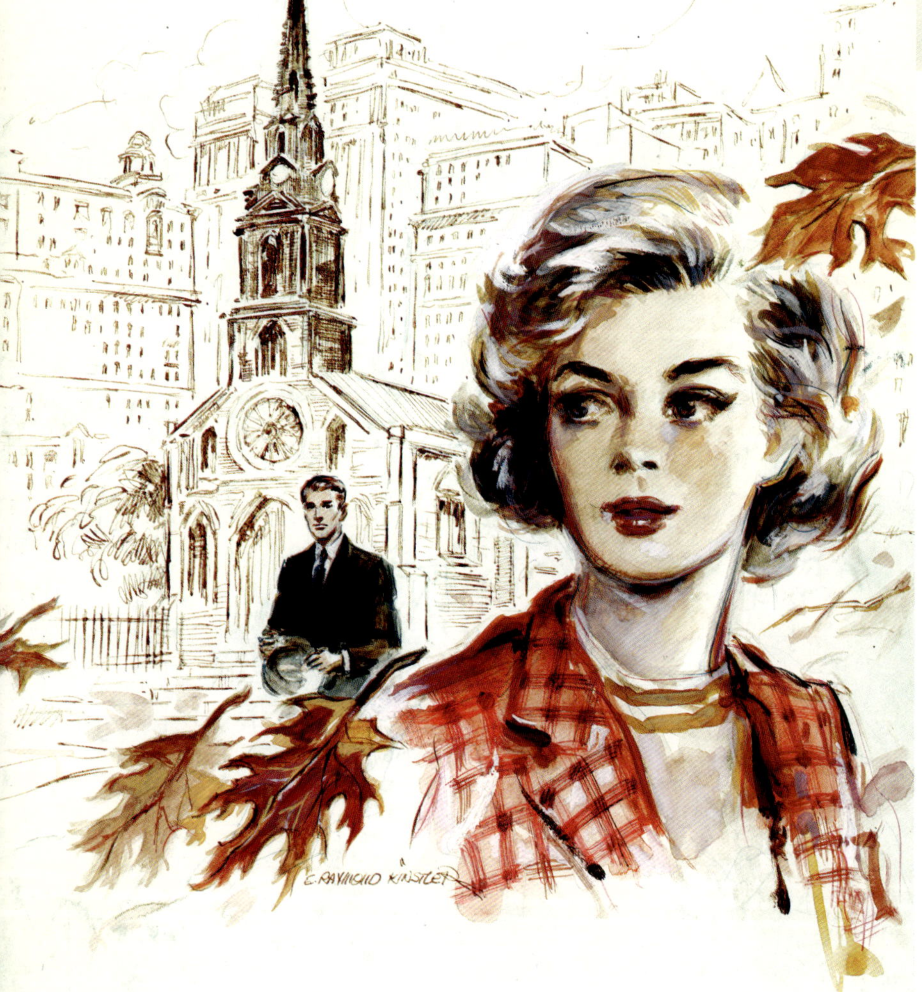

This tear sheet in Kinstler's file seems to be the only trace of this book to be found. There is no evidence that it was ever published.

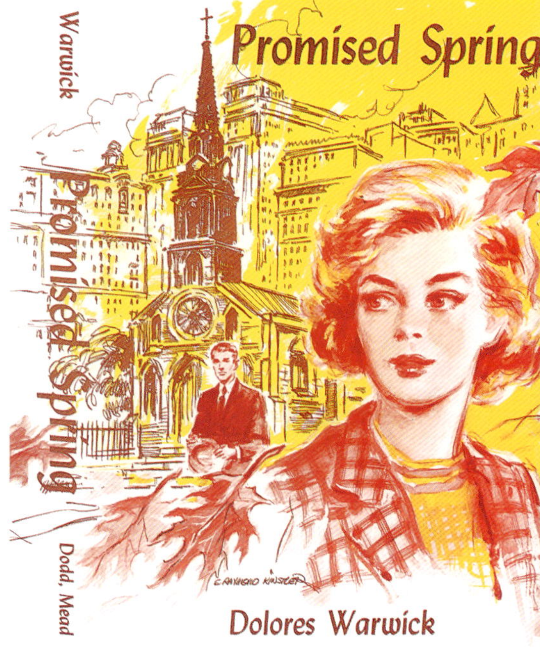

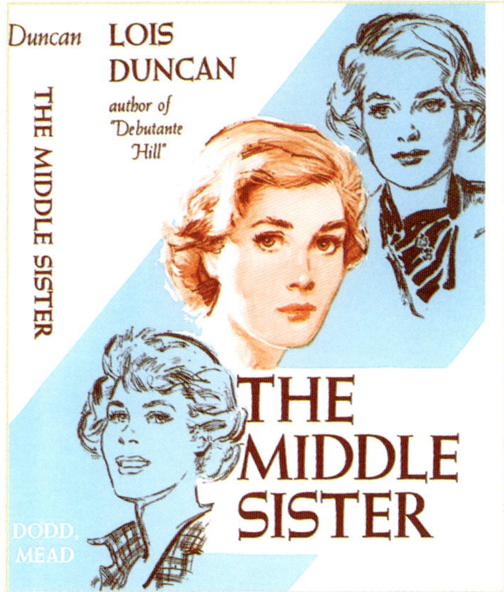

Dodd, Mead, 1960

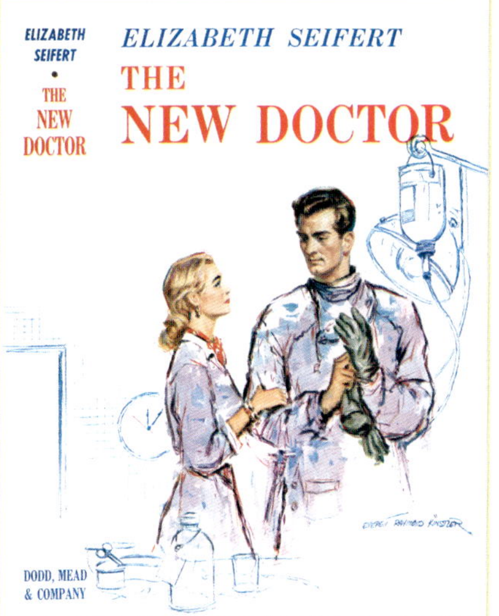

Dodd, Mead, 1958

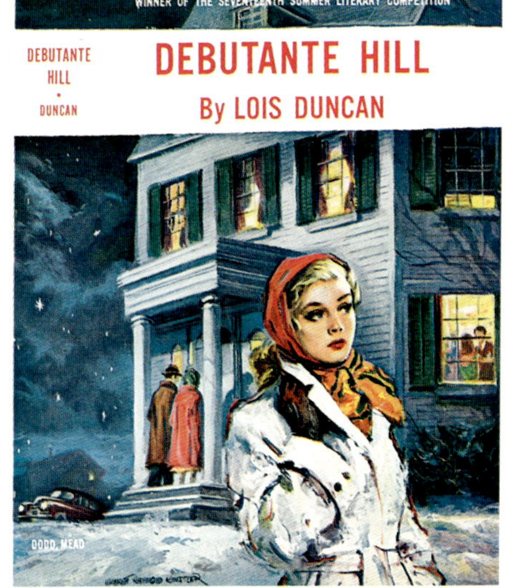

Dodd, Mead, 1958

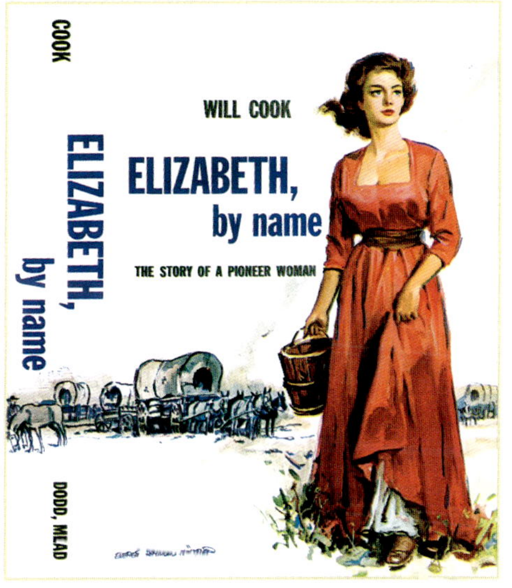

Dodd, Mead, 1958

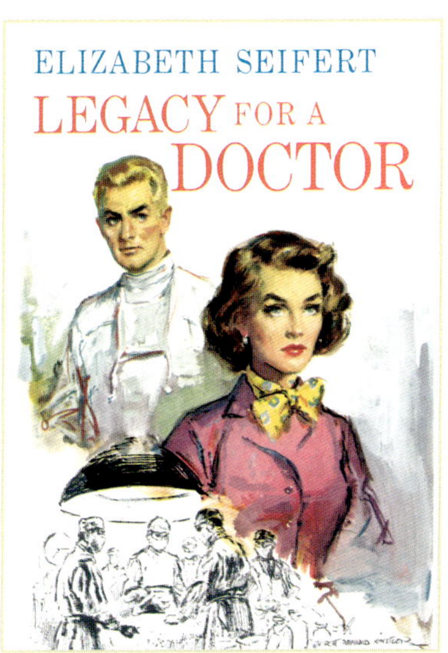

Dodd, Mead, 1963

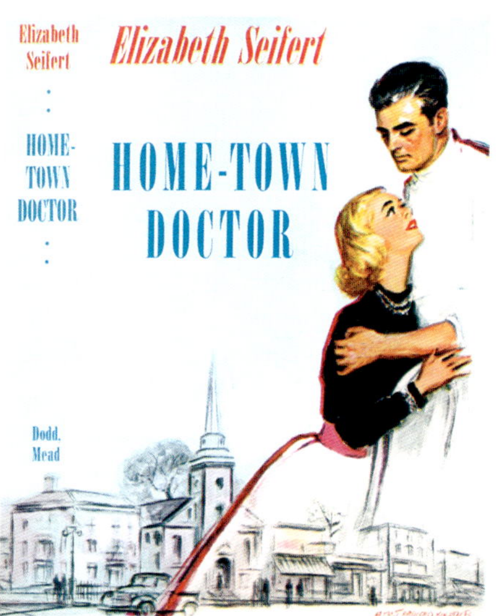

Dodd, Mead, 1959

By 1958, the first Baby Boomers were approaching puberty and a new market arose to help them through it. Scores of "coming of age" novels were written and published, directly aimed at this new generation of young women. Where prior generations had read Nancy Drew, The Bobbsey Twins or The Hardy Boys, these new young adults insisted that there be more emphasis on the "Adult" rather than the "Young."

Kinstler's approach to this market can be seen in almost every cover. Most of them feature a color painting, usually in oil, of a main character or couple, with a pen and ink background drawing. These were often mechanically enhanced with color by the publisher's production department. Ray's facility with faces kept the romantic pairs from looking too familiar and each of his heroines was a unique individual.

To some extent, he was still painting types, but more and more they were becoming portraits, albeit of imaginary people.

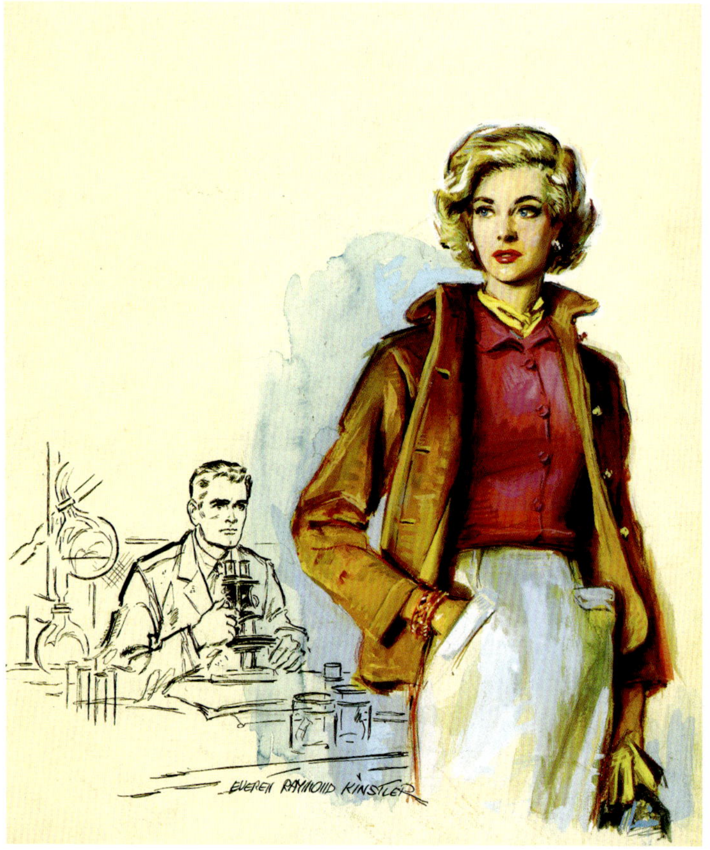

Dodd, Mead, 1959

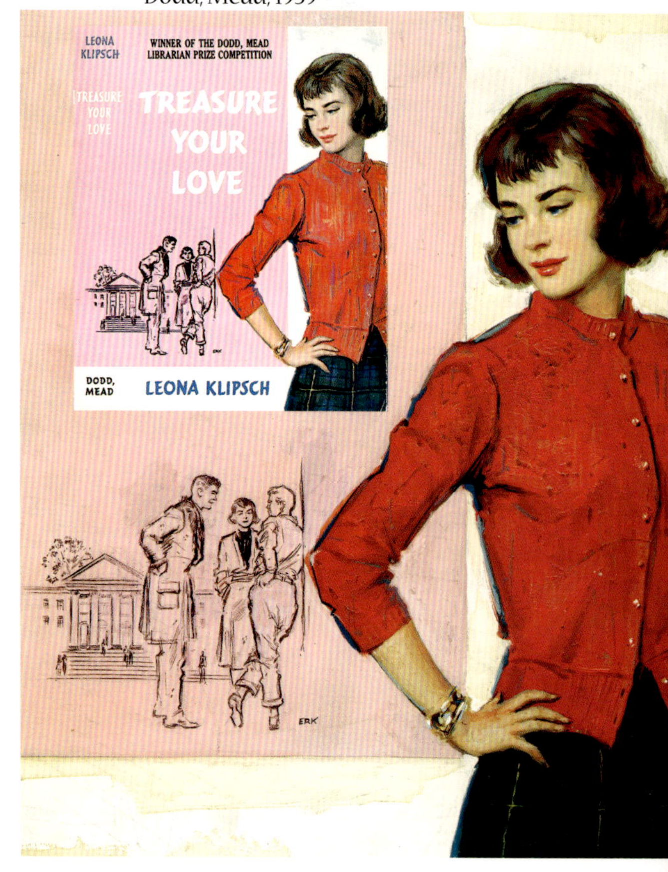

These four paintings were done for the Young Adult Book—Romance market in the late 1950s. All feature Kinstler's unique combination of portraiture and line art.

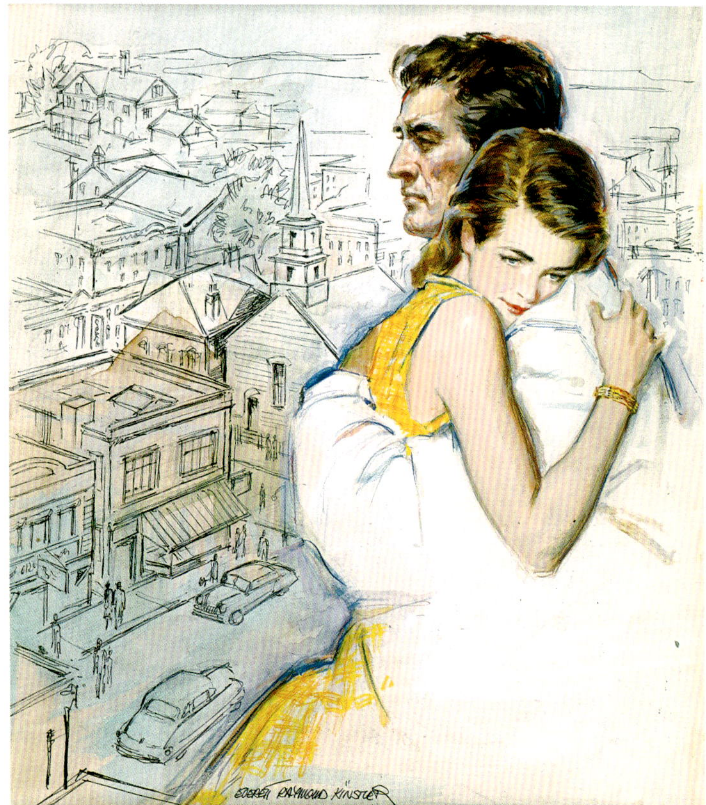

Dr. Jeremy's Wife by Elizabeth Seifert
Dodd, Mead, 1961

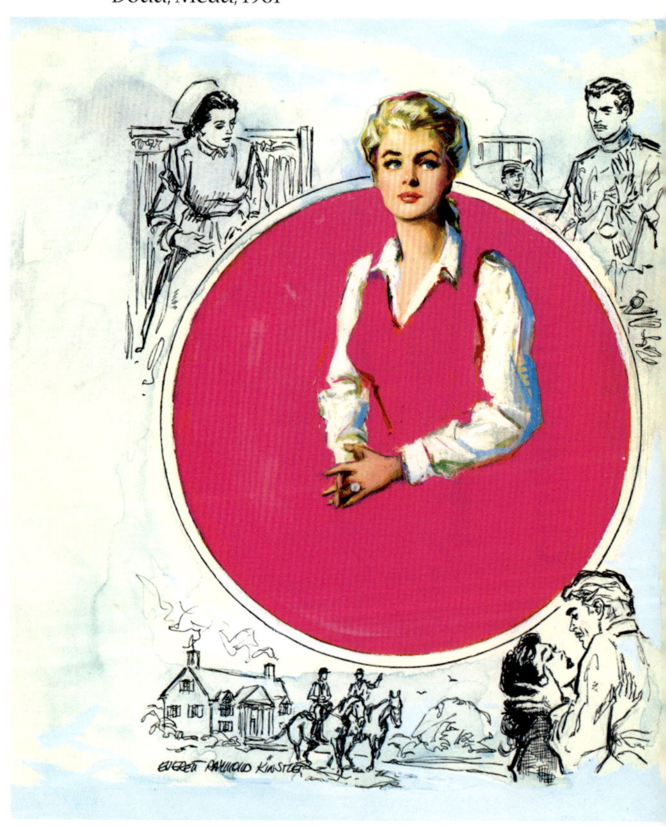

Young Adult Books
adventure

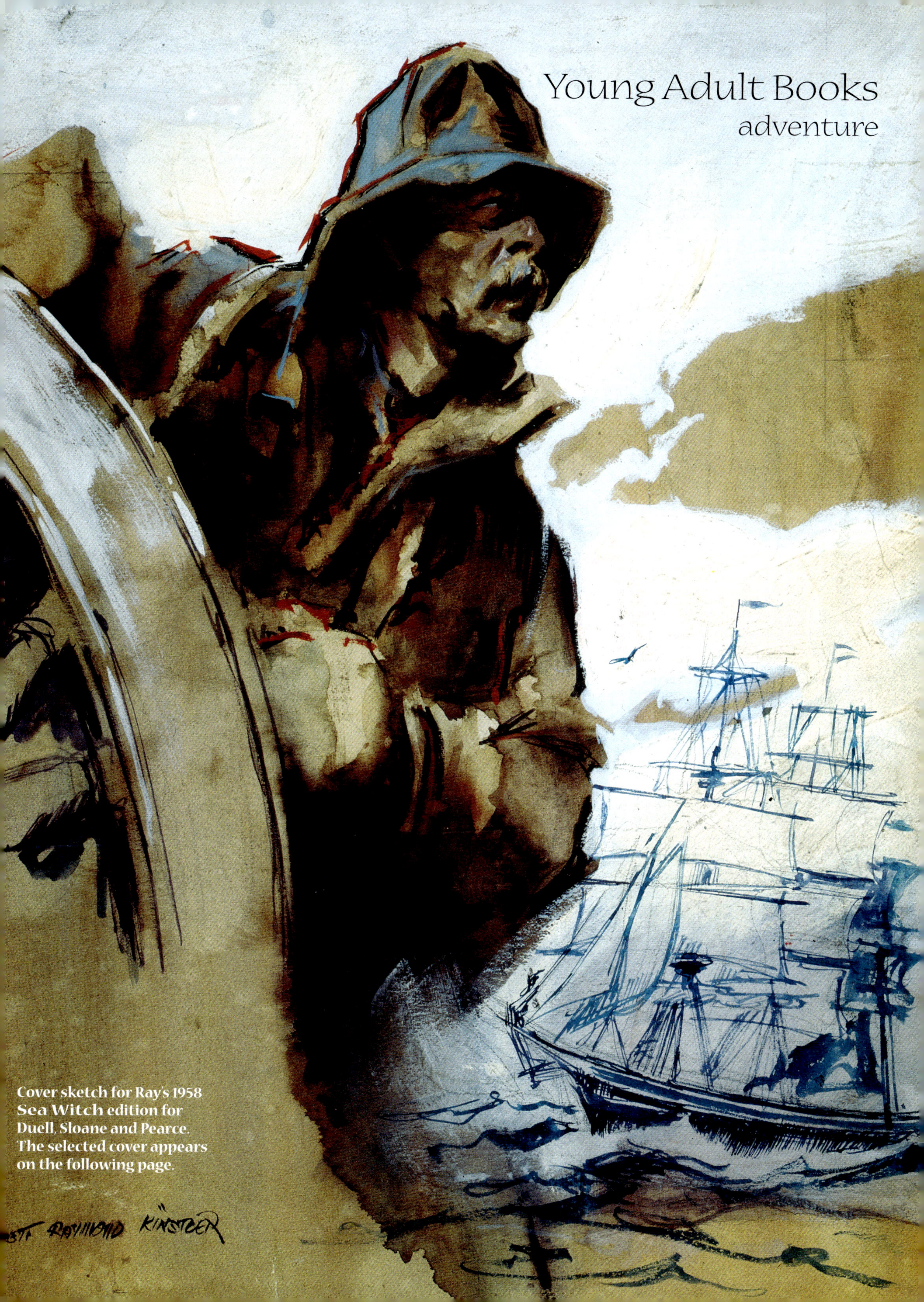

Cover sketch for Ray's 1958 **Sea Witch** edition for Duell, Sloane and Pearce. The selected cover appears on the following page.

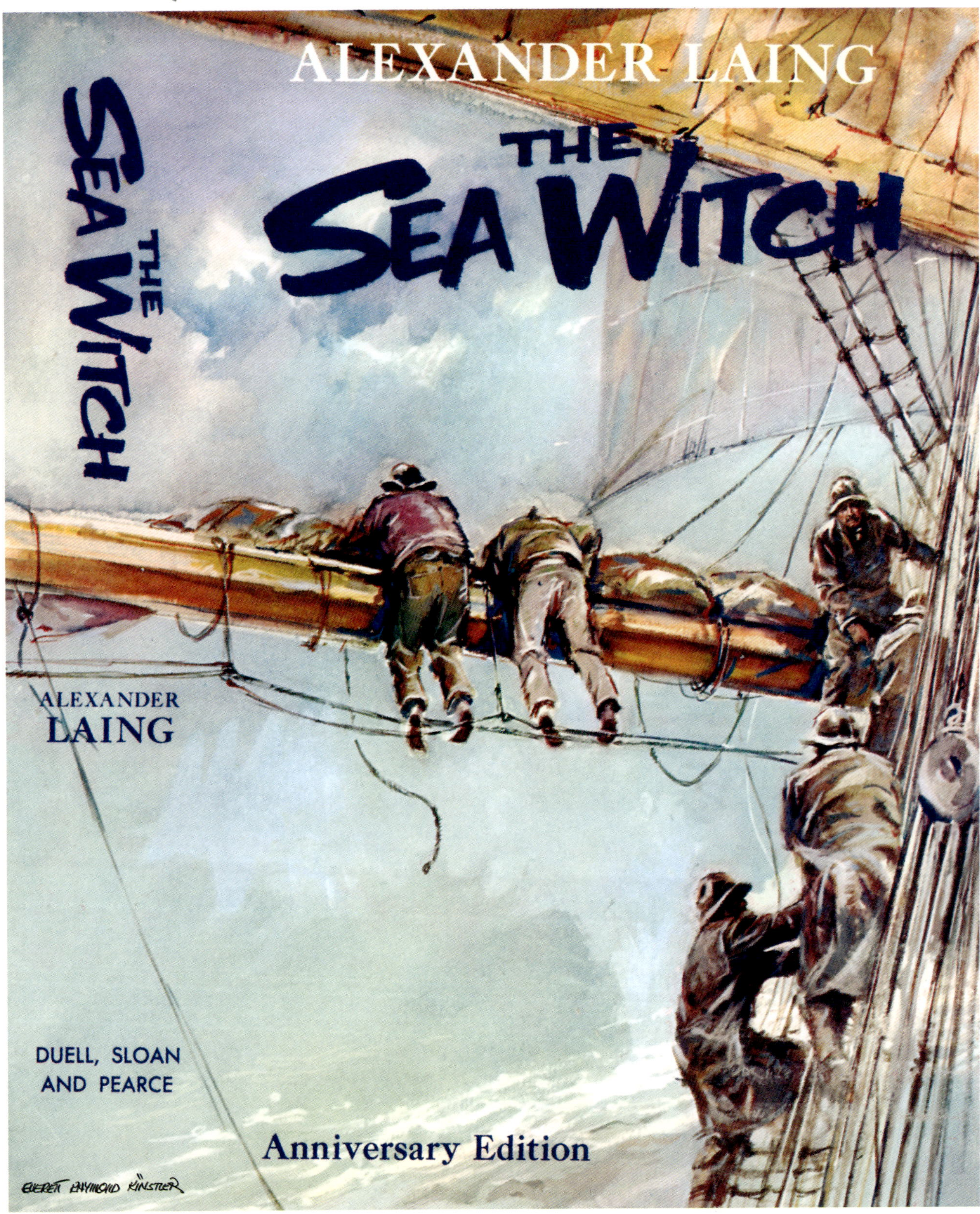

Duell, Sloan and Pearce, 1958

I met Gordon Grant, who illustrated the 1944 edition of this book, around 1950 in the offices of Popular Publications, where we were both doing pen and ink illustrations for ***Adventure Magazine***. Mr. Grant was doing pulp illustrations just to keep his hand in and getting the same rates as I was. He was like an old baseball player who likes to hit fungoes. He would pick up six illustrations and make a hundred dollars for an afternoon's work that he enjoyed. Gordon Grant was a great professional.

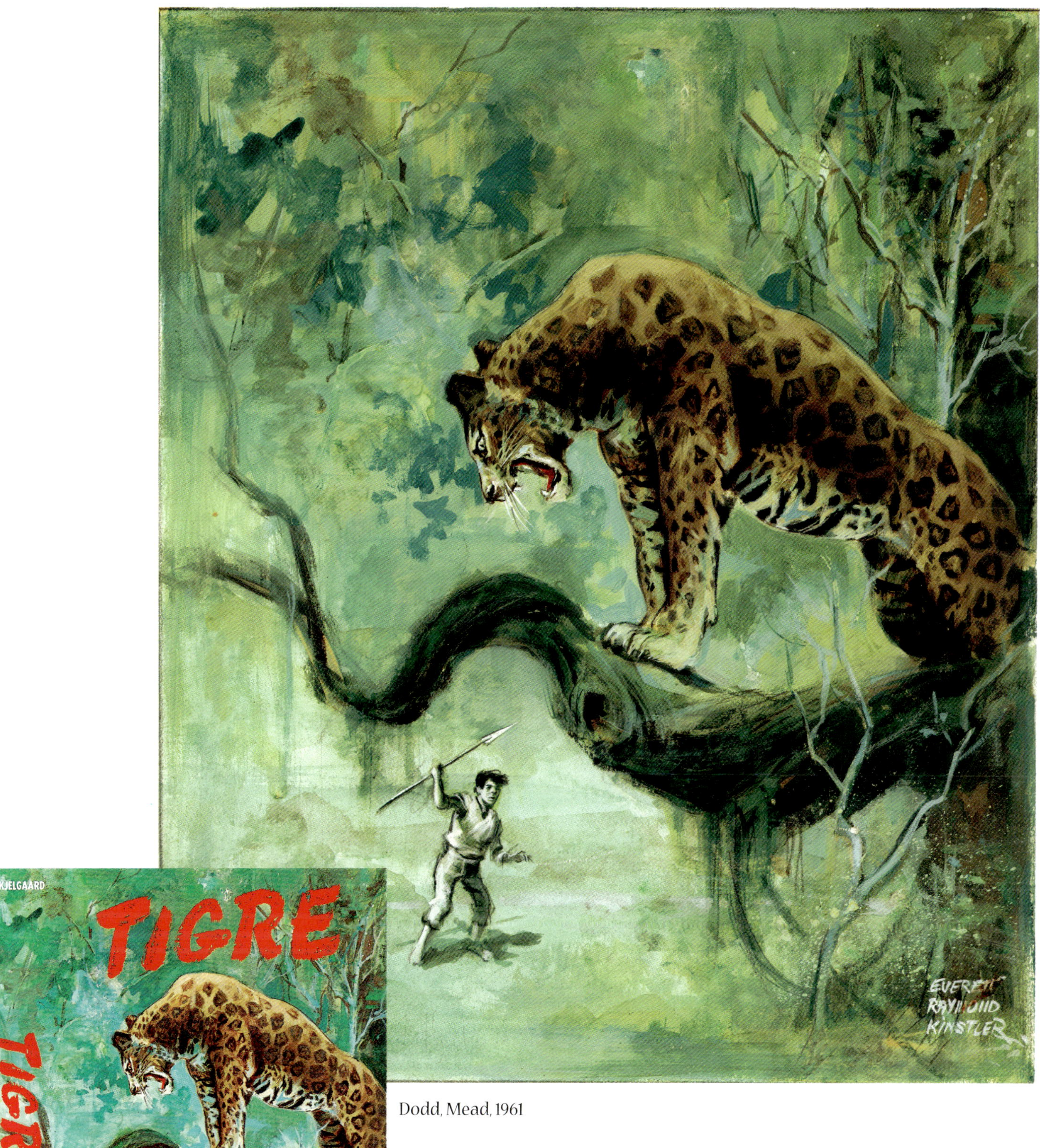

Dodd, Mead, 1961

The young men coming of age in the late Fifties would not settle for merely exploring caves with the Hardy Boys. Certainly there were new stories of young adventurers/detectives and updated Hardy Boys books, too. But there were just as many stories set in exotic locales where young men faced new and different dangers than those encountered in 1950s America.

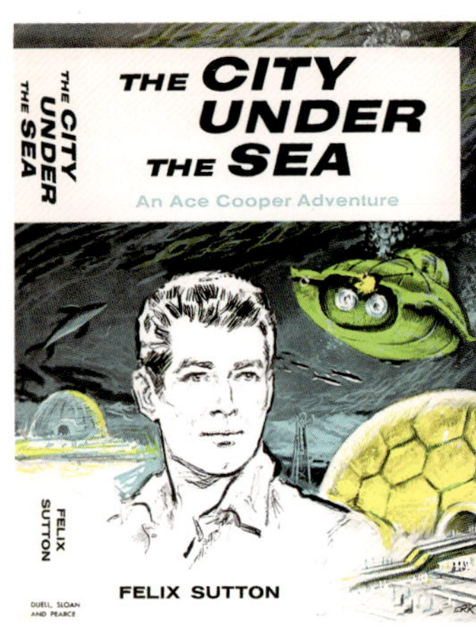

Duell, Sloan and Pearce, 1961

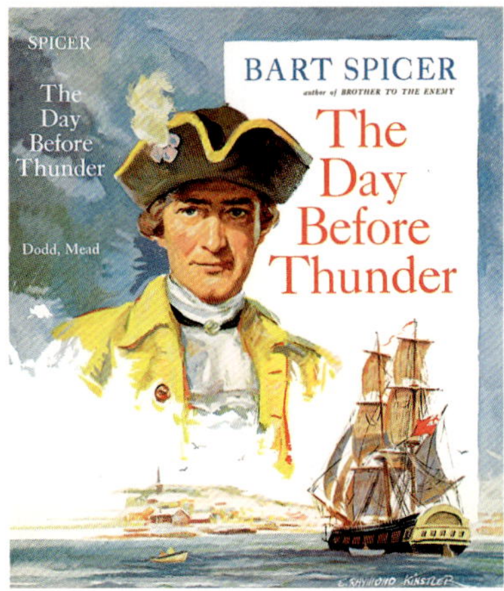

Dodd, Mead, 1960

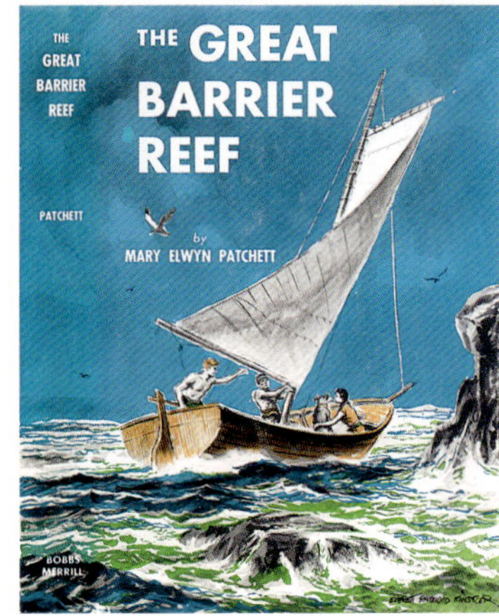

Bobbs-Merrill, 1958

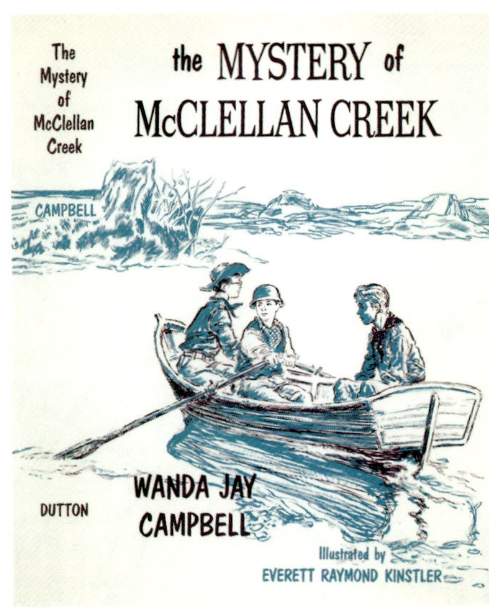

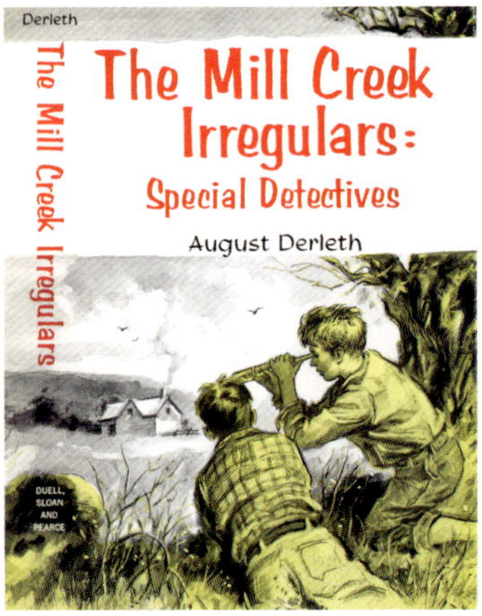

Duell, Sloan and Pearce, 1961

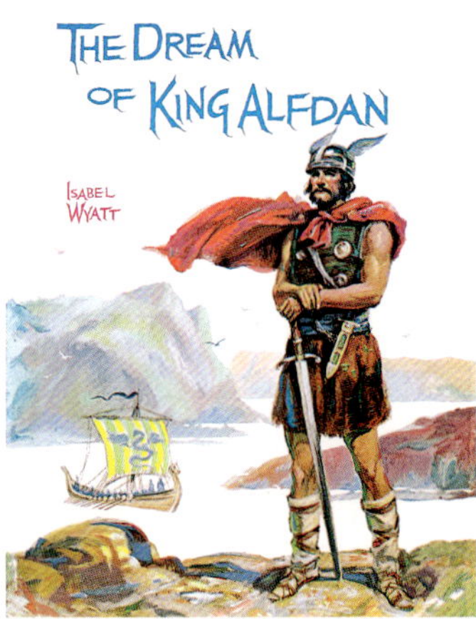

Follett, 1961

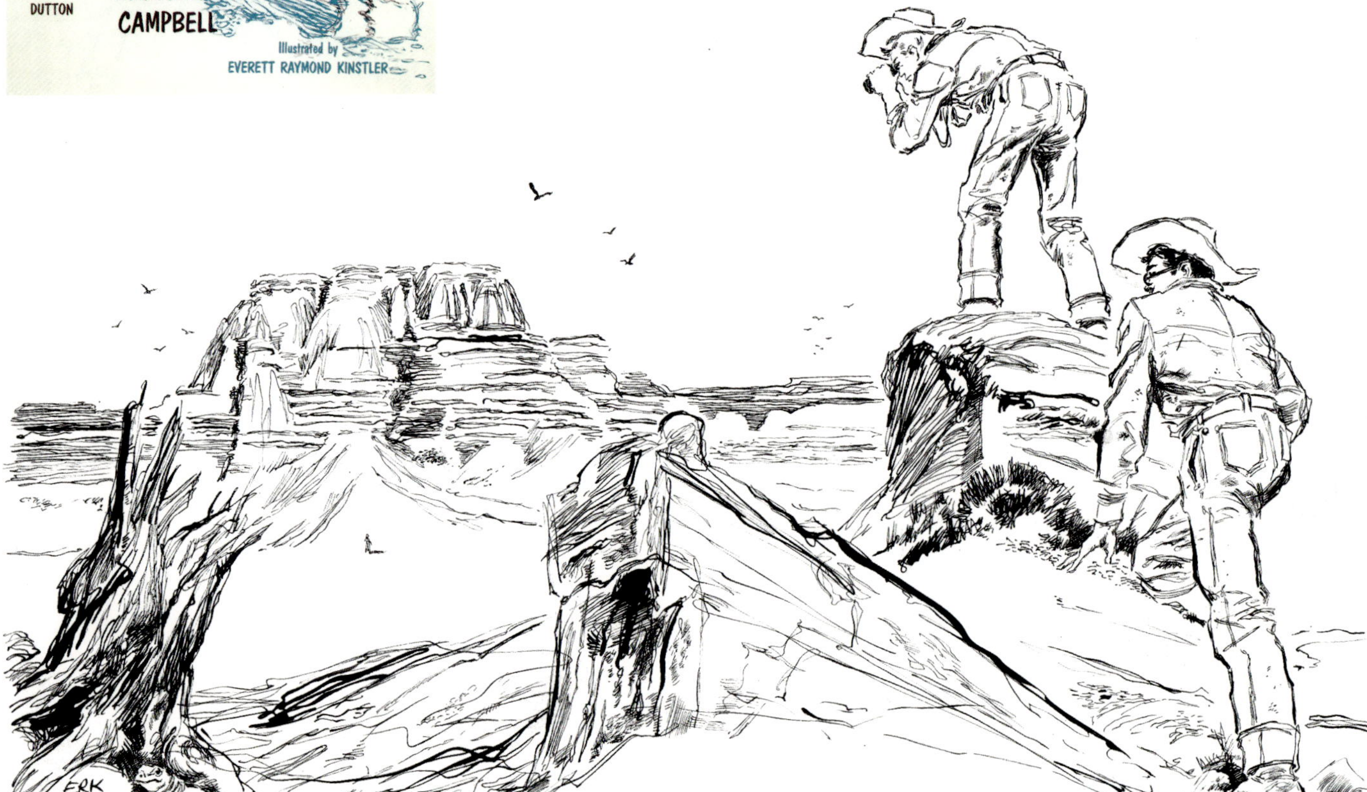

Mike saw the small moving figure and led the way to the high peak.
The Mystery of McClellan Creek
E.P. Dutton, 1958

Juvenile Fiction

Black Beauty was one of Kinstler's three book appearances dated 1963. The work for these was created in 1962. Only **Fury** seems to have been commissioned and finished in 1963. It was published in 1964, the final commercial illustration work he would do.

Grosset and Dunlap, 1964

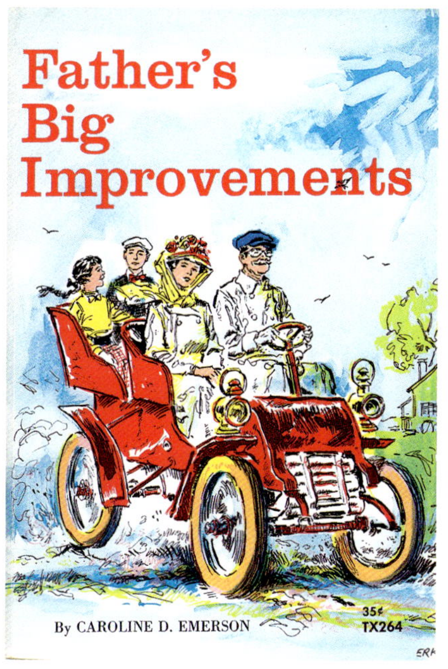

Scholastic, 1960

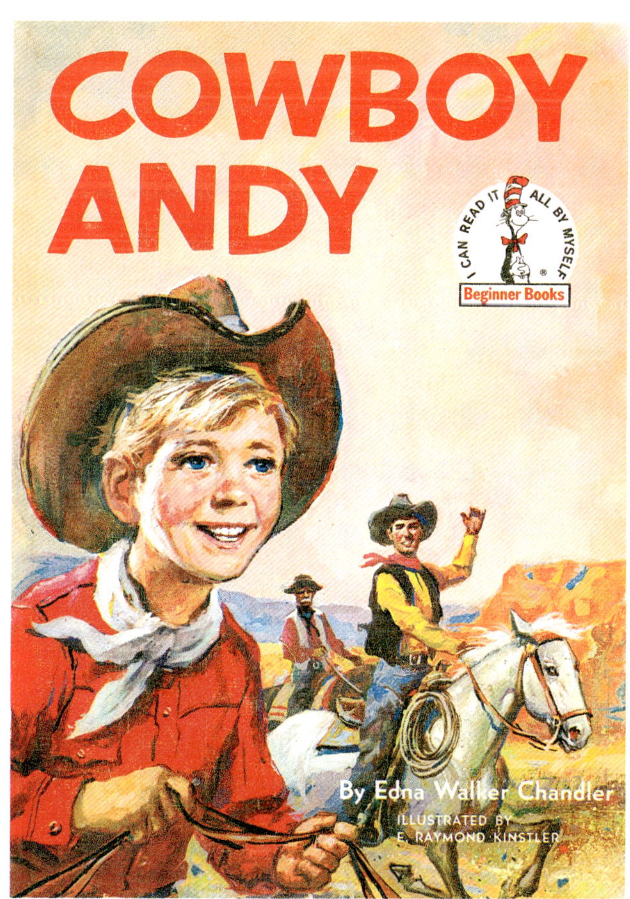

Random House, 1959

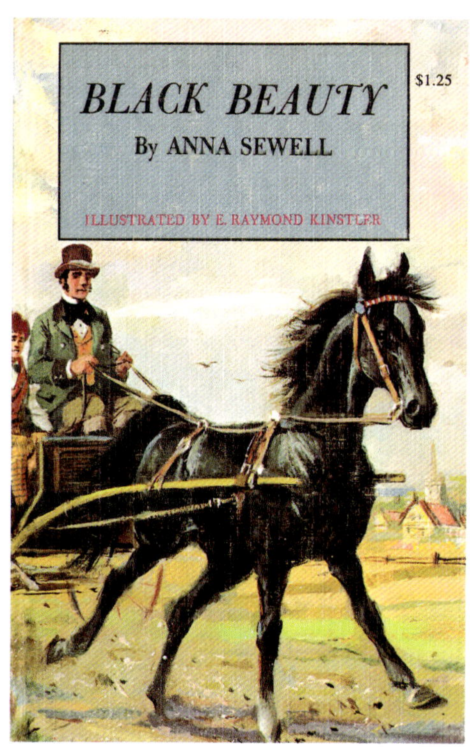

Grosset and Dunlap, 1963

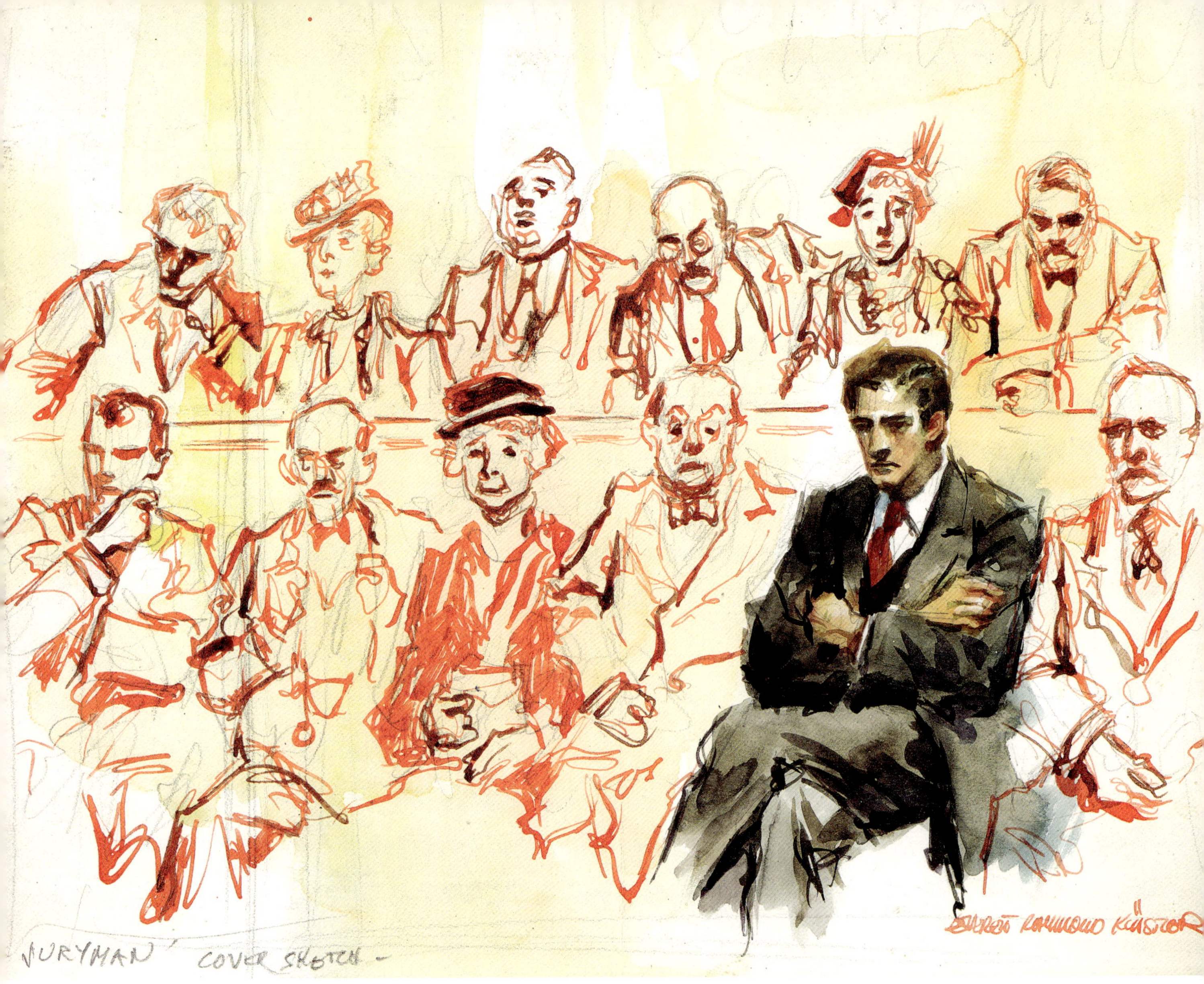

interesting. My thought would be to handle the 'Juryman' in full colour, more dramatically than here illustrated + the remaining jurors in a combination line, nailing down the character of each member.

Ray's involvement with the conceptualization of the book covers is evident in the note he wrote on the back side of the above sketch. This wasn't even his favorite design idea, yet he had a clear vision of just how powerfully it could work.

The art director at Houghton-Mifflin obviously agreed with him.

It's interesting to note this printed proof in Kinstler's file has the author's name misspelled. It's Donald "MacKenzie."

THE
Juryman
McKENZIE

THE Juryman
by DONALD McKENZIE

EVERETT RAYMOND KINSTLER

H.M.CO.

Houghton-Mifflin, 1958

Non-Fiction

As with Sol Cohen at Avon, Kinstler found a kindred spirit in art director John Blair at Dodd, Mead. For five years they worked together and produced over three dozen books, far more than he did for any other publisher.

He received his first assignment from Blair in June of 1957 and was still accepting assignments from him in late 1962. After that final Dodd, Mead commission, Ray only did two more books for Grosset and Dunlap—footnotes to a long and illustrious career in commercial art.

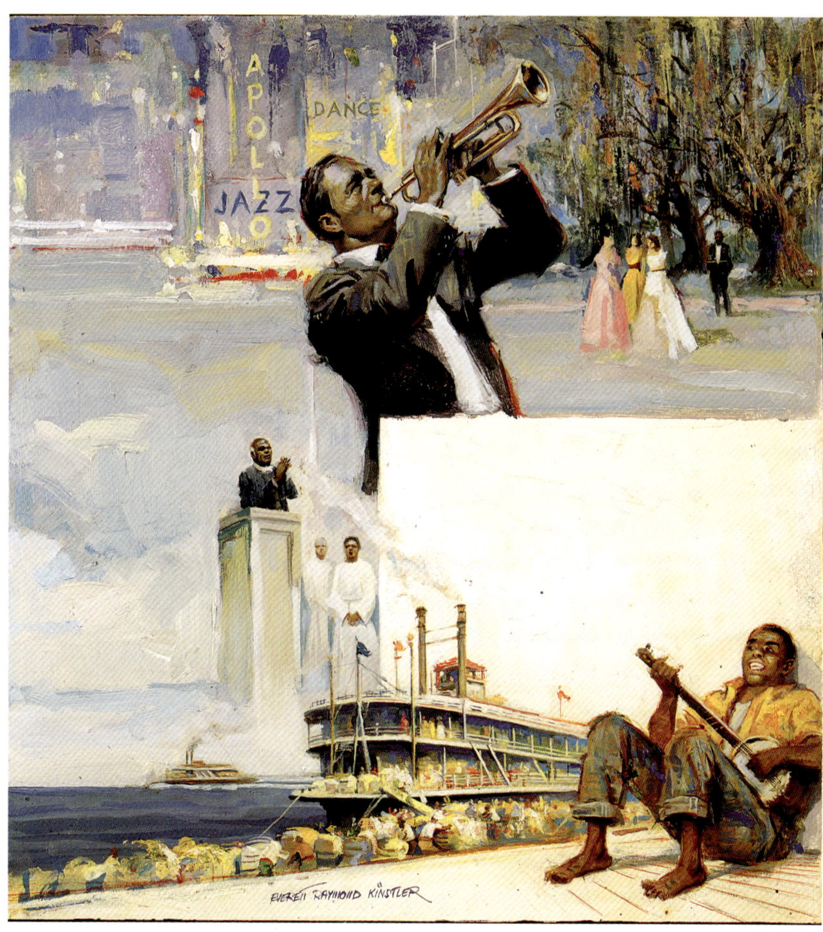

Dodd, Mead, 1958

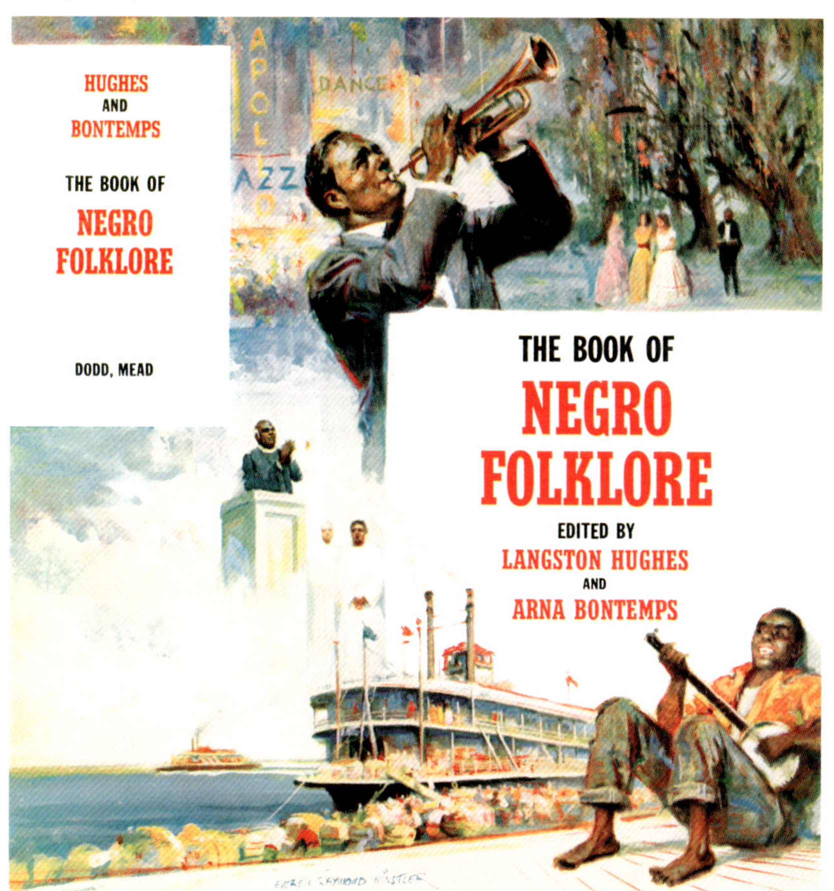

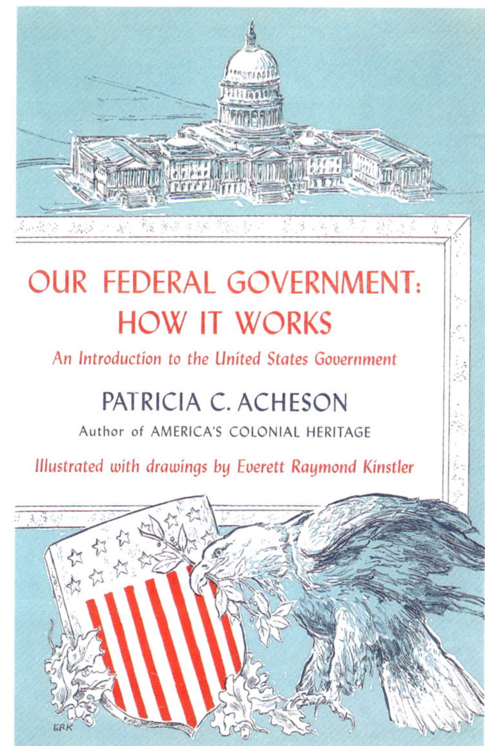

Dodd, Mead, 1958

Verdi

Kinstler's final book for Dodd, Mead and John Blair was George Martin's **Verdi: His Music, Life and Times**. It was published in 1963. Inexplicably, of the forty black and white drawings inside, only a very small "death mask" drawing—the final one in the book—depicted Verdi.

The masterful cover illustration was reproduced directly from one of the conceptual drawings Kinstler submitted to the publisher. Ray convinced them to simply use the sketch to keep the freshness of his design. It's a powerful and striking portrait and one of his favorite cover paintings.

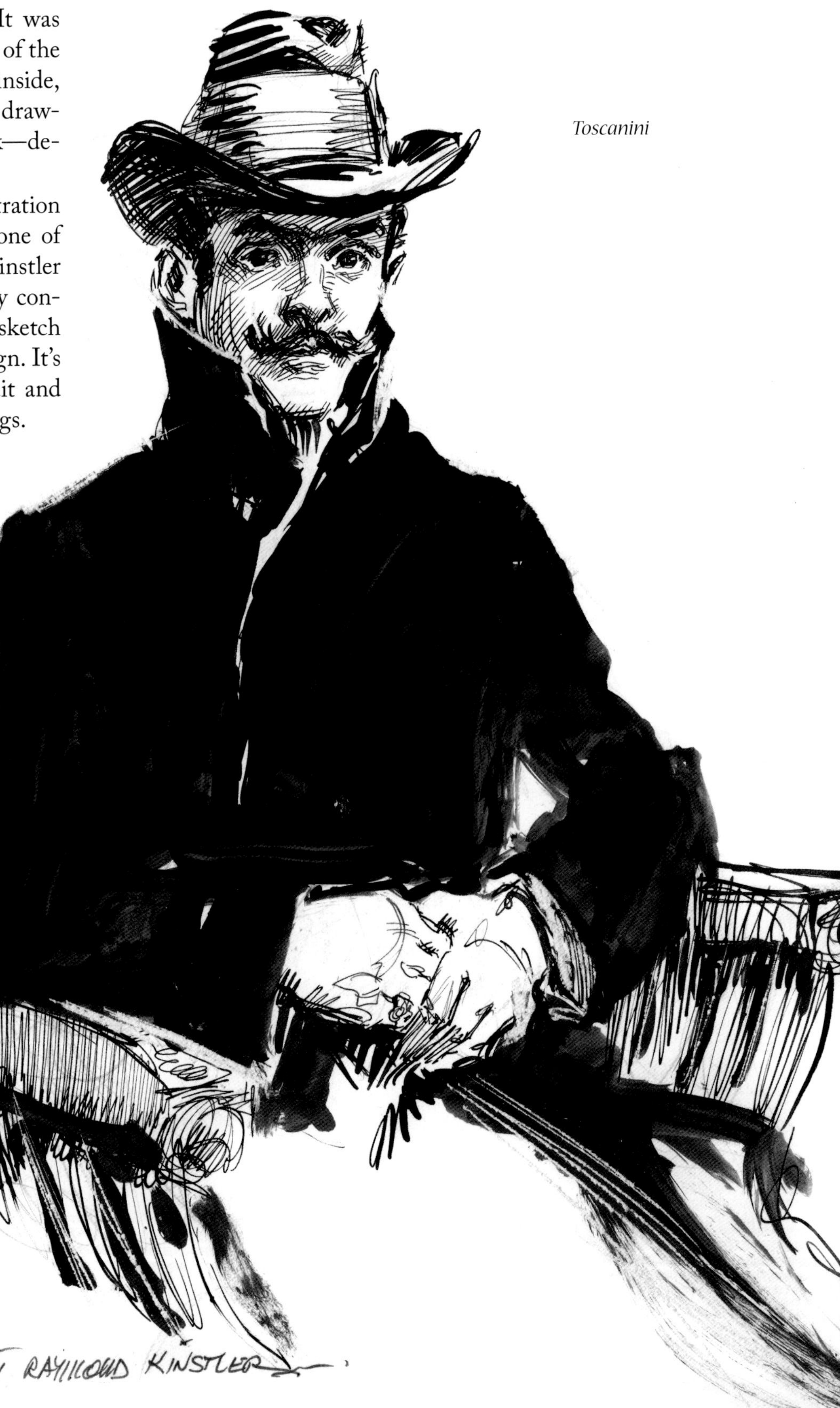

Toscanini

VERDI

HIS MUSIC, LIFE AND TIMES

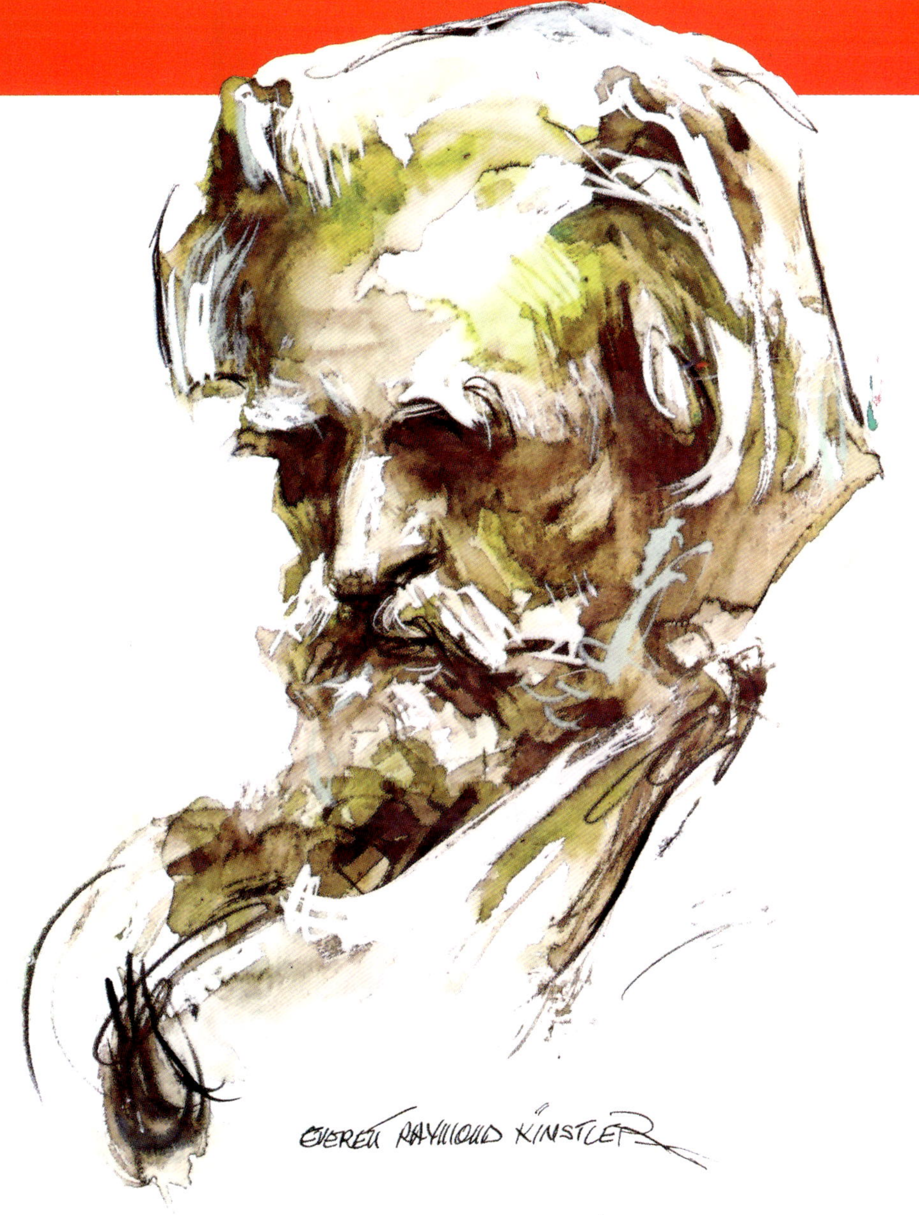

George Martin

Author of THE OPERA COMPANION

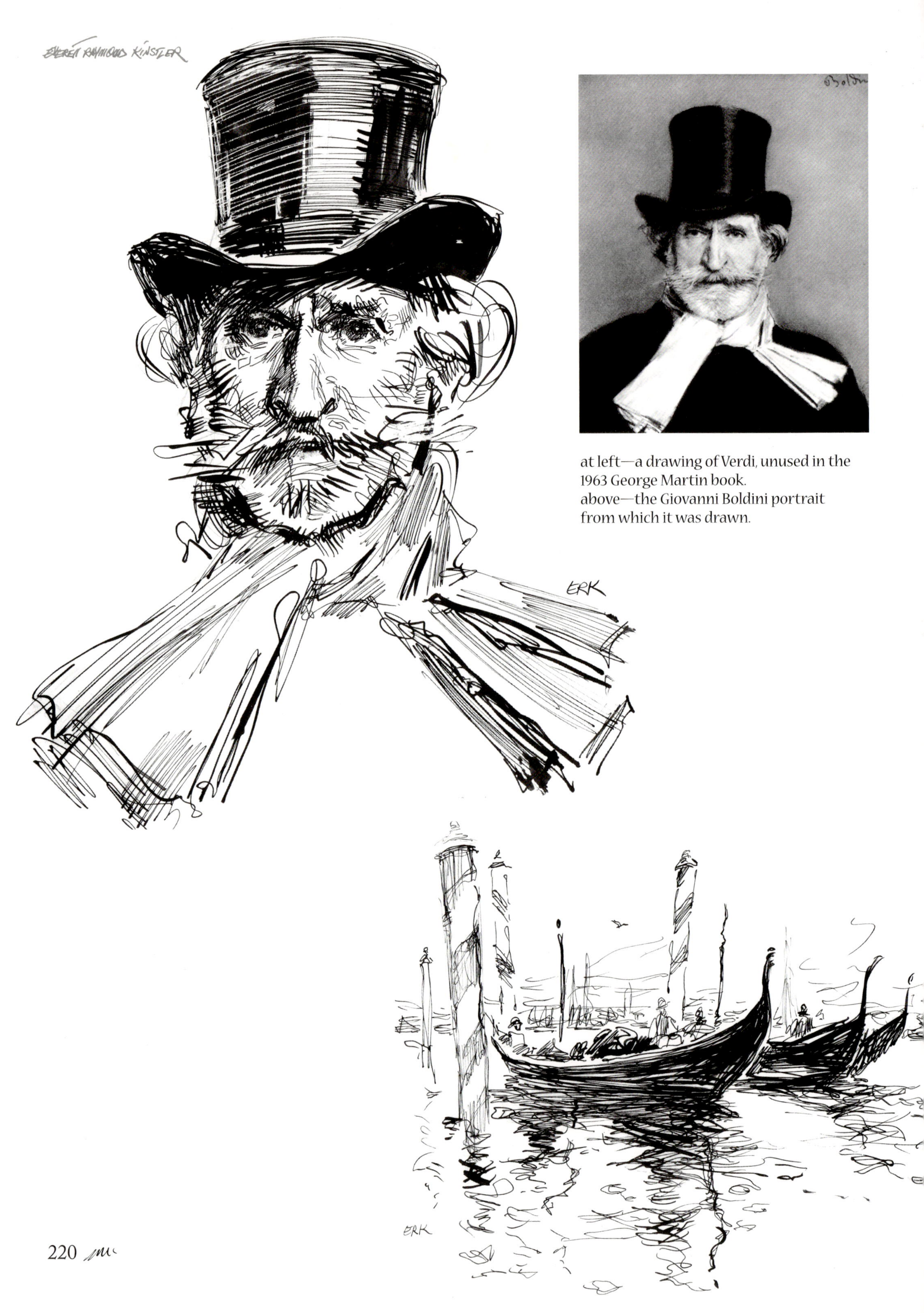

at left—a drawing of Verdi, unused in the 1963 George Martin book.
above—the Giovanni Boldini portrait from which it was drawn.

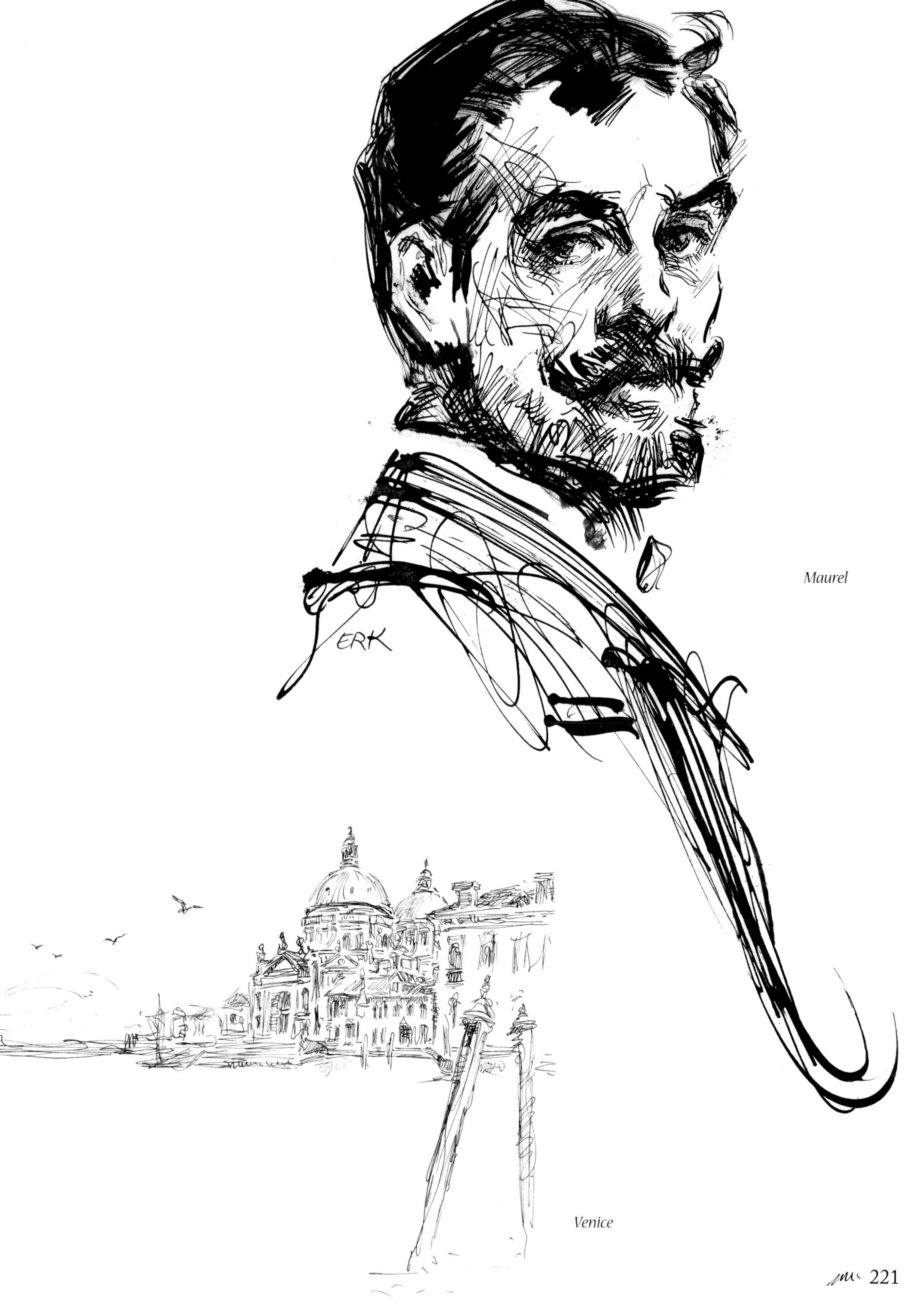

Maurel

Venice

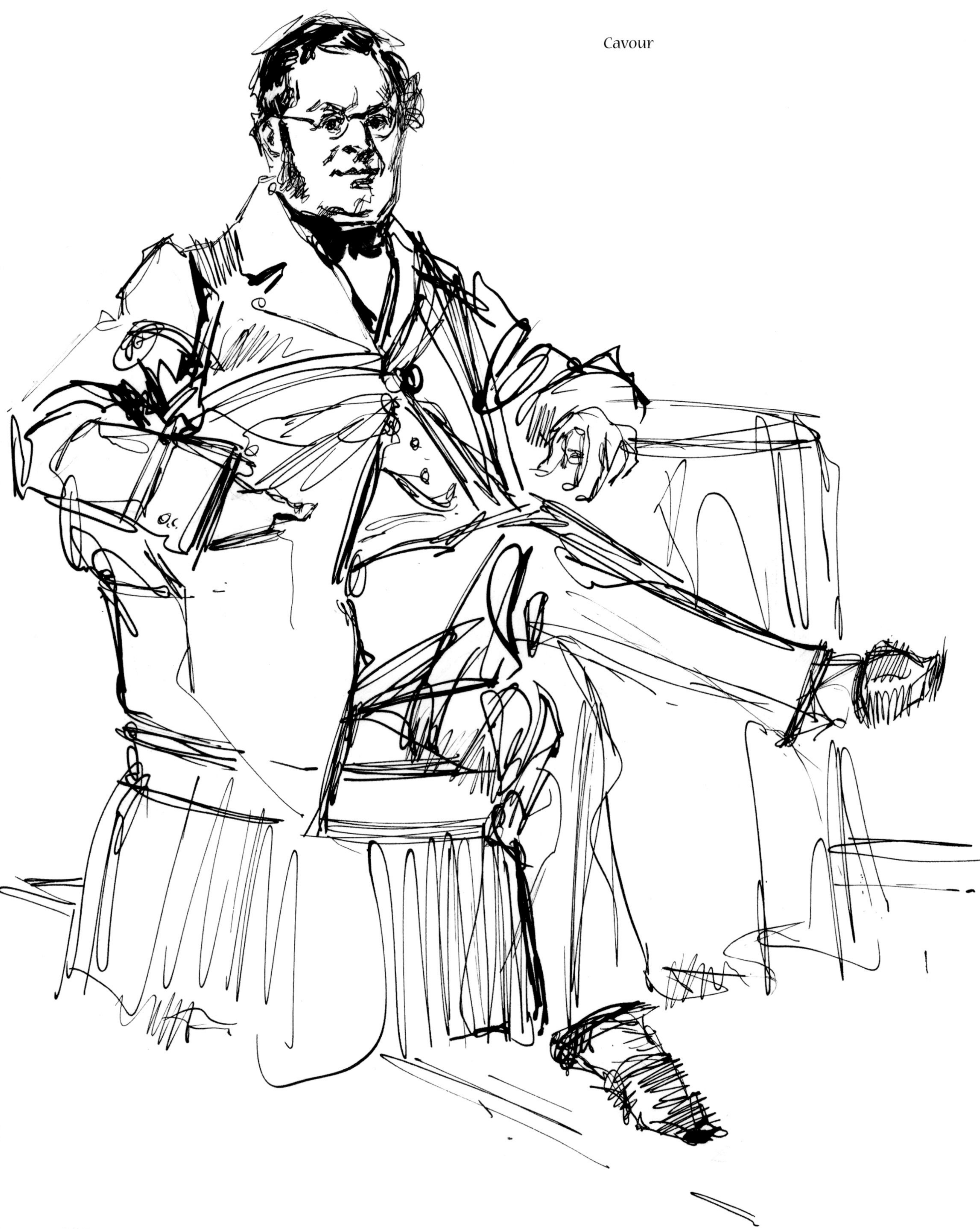

Cavour

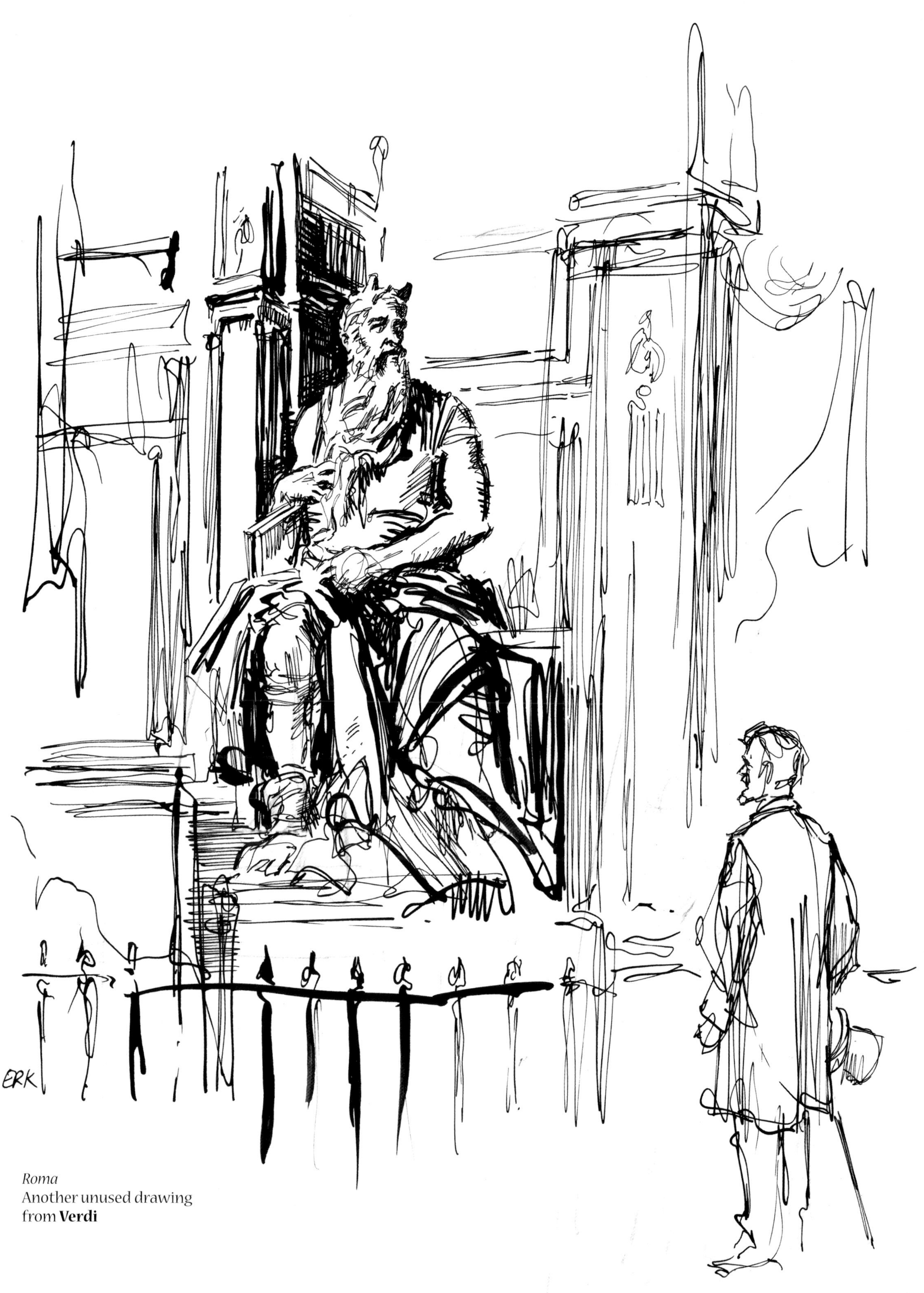

Roma
Another unused drawing
from **Verdi**

epilogue

Walter Kinstler

When Ray joined the Dutch Treat Club in 1964, one of the first things he did was ask Rube Goldberg about the cousin whom his mother claimed had worked for Mr. Goldberg. He told Ray that he'd never heard of a Walter Kinstler. When that reaction was relayed to Essie, she flatly stated "He doesn't know what he's talking about!"

I said, you mean Rube Goldberg doesn't know... "No," she said, "He used to work for Rube Goldberg."

Well, I was used to taking my mother's stories with a grain of salt, and considered this to be so seasoned, but somewhere around 1983 I received a call from Terry Brown, director of The Society of Illustrators. Terry told me that a woman had recently shown him some drawings from a trunk that her grandfather had purchased at an estate sale somewhere in the state of New York. Among the trunk's contents were drawings, sketches and newspaper clippings by an artist named Walter Kinstler.

"She approached us here at the Society," said Terry, "and wanted to know what we knew about him. I told her that we had never heard of him, but there is an Everett Raymond Kinstler who might know something. I'm calling to see if it is all right to give her your phone number?"

When the woman called me, I arranged to visit her and to view the material. She lived in a swank apartment on East 66th Street. She told me the story of how she came by the trunk and she showed me at least one hundred pen and ink portraits and caricatures of theatrical personalities, along with some drawings of some artists, like James Montgomery Flagg and Howard Chandler Christy. There were a lot of tear-sheets from ***The Brooklyn Eagle***, where he worked under the nom de plume, *The Inchworm*, writing a column on the theater and its personalities which he illustrated with his drawings and cartoons.

The work was all on one- or two-ply paper, cleanly outlined pen and ink, a bit similar to what Al Hirschfeld would later do. The art and the clippings were all from about 1923 and the woman told me that she didn't know what to do with them. I introduced her to Walt Reed at Illustration House and he helped her sell them, many to the National Portrait Gallery.

She gave several to The Players Club and offered me a couple of them for my help. Among those I chose was a self-portrait that I have hanging in my New York studio. When I told Essie about them, she said, "See, I told you." But I don't think she was right about Rube Goldberg.

So now a lot of people have heard of Walter Kinstler and my mother was at least partially vindicated!

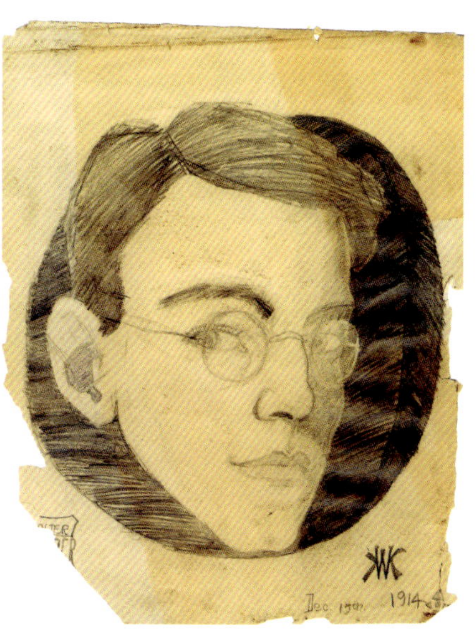

self-portrait
Walter Kinstler
December 13, 1914

Index

A

B

C

D

E

F

G

H

I

erratum

Just as we were going to press, evidence surfaced of Kinstler's earliest paperback effort. Three years before he painted his first cover for Avon Books, he drew five pen and ink illustrations for a 1951 Avon paperback edition of Lion Feuchtwanger's 1925 novel **Jew Süss** (which was also known as **Power** in earlier English language editions).

The plates are quite intricate and complex, as can be seen in the sample below. Ray rendered at least two of these plates in wash before executing them in ink. The "tonal study" on page twenty one and the first plate of the Limited Edition bonus plates are paintings that were created for that purpose.

As with any archeological exploration of the past, one is occasionally required to revise estimated dates. In this case we can now extend Kinstler's involvement in books back to 1951.

In 1952, Ray also contributed a line-drawing for the back cover of another Avon paperback, Leslie Charteris' **Saint's Getaway**.

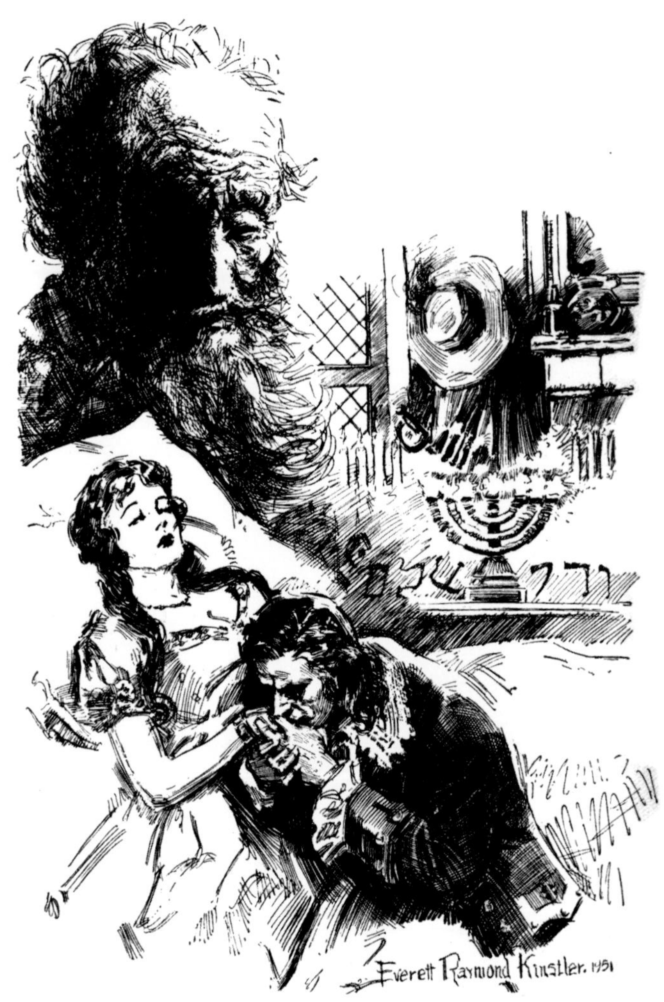